Angelika Epple, Walter Erhart, Johannes Grave (eds.)
Practices of Comparing

BiUP General

Angelika Epple, born 1966, is vice-rector for International Affairs and Diversity at Universität Bielefeld and teaches history with a focus on the history of the 19th and 20th century. Since January 2017, she has been the spokesperson of the Collaborative Research Center SFB 1288 "Practices of Comparing". She has broadly published on the history of globalization/s, theory of history, and historiography.

Walter Erhart, born 1959, teaches German literature at Universität Bielefeld. Since 2017, he has been vice-speaker of the Collaborative Research Center SFB 1288 "Practices of Comparing". His research focuses on German literature from the 18th to the 20th century and practices of comparing in world travel literature and in autobiographical writing.

Johannes Grave, born 1976, teaches art history at the Friedrich-Schiller-Universität Jena. Since 2017, he has been principal investigator in the Collaborative Research Center SFB 1288 "Practices of Comparing". His research focuses on theories of the image, the temporality of pictures and of their perception, practices of comparing, art around 1800, as well as Italian paintings of the early Renaissance.

Angelika Epple, Walter Erhart, Johannes Grave (eds.)
Practices of Comparing
Towards a New Understanding of a Fundamental Human Practice

[transcript]

This Volume has been prepared within the framework of the Collaborative Research Center SFB 1288 "Practices of Comparing. Ordering and changing the world", Bielefeld University, Germany, funded by the German Research Foundation (DFG).

Bibliographic information published by the Deutsche Nationalbibliothek

The Deutsche Nationalbibliothek lists this publication in the Deutsche Nationalbibliografie; detailed bibliographic data are available in the Internet at http://dnb.d-nb.de

This work is licensed under the Creative Commons Attribution-Non Commercial 4.0 (BY-NC) license, which means that the text may be may be remixed, build upon and be distributed, provided credit is given to the author, but may not be used for commercial purposes. For details go to: http://creativecommons.org/licenses/by-nc/4.0/
Permission to use the text for commercial purposes can be obtained by contacting rights@transcript-verlag.de
Creative Commons license terms for re-use do not apply to any content (such as graphs, figures, photos, excerpts, etc.) not original to the Open Access publication and further permission may be required from the rights holder. The obligation to research and clear permission lies solely with the party re-using the material.

© 2020 Bielefeld University Press. An Imprint of transcript Verlag

http://www.bielefeld-university-press.de

All rights reserved. No part of this book may be reprinted or reproduced or utilized in any form or by any electronic, mechanical, or other means, now known or hereafter invented, including photocopying and recording, or in any information storage or retrieval system, without permission in writing from the publisher.

Cover layout: Maria Arndt, Bielefeld
Proofread by Dipl. Psych. Jonathan Harrow
Printed by Majuskel Medienproduktion GmbH, Wetzlar
Print-ISBN 978-3-8376-5166-9
PDF-ISBN 978-3-8394-5166-3
https://doi.org/10.14361/9783839451663

Printed on permanent acid-free text paper.

Contents

Acknowledgements 7

Typologies and Forms

Practices of Comparing
A New Research Agenda Between Typological and Historical Approaches
Angelika Epple/Walter Erhart 11

Preliminary Typology of Comparative Utterances
A Tree and Some Binaries
Kirill Postoutenko 39

Incomparability
A Tentative Guide for the Perplexed
Hartmut von Sass 87

Odysseus, Blackbirds, and Rain Barrels
Literature as a Comparative Practice
Walter Erhart 111

Where Do Rankings Come From?
A Historical-Sociological Perspective on the History of Modern Rankings
Leopold Ringel/Tobias Werron 137

Histories

The Weight of Comparing in Medieval England
David Gary Shaw 173

The Shifting Grounds of Comparison in the French Renaissance
The Case of Louis Le Roy
Andrea Frisch 199

Comparison and East-West Encounter
The Seventeenth and the Eighteenth Centuries
Zhang Longxi 213

Japan as the Absolute 'Other'
Genealogy and Variations of a Topos
Emmanuel Lozerand 229

"Goût de Comparaison"
Practices of Comparative Viewing in Eighteenth-Century Connoisseurship
Joris Corin Heyder 257

Inventing White Beauty and Fighting Black Slavery
How Blumenbach, Humboldt, and Arango y Parreño Contributed to Cuban Race Comparisons in the Long Nineteenth Century
Angelika Epple 295

The Politicisation of Comparisons
The East-West Dispute over Military Force Comparisons in the Cold War
Thomas Müller 329

Genealogies of Modernism
Curatorial Practices of Comparing in the Exhibitions *Cubism and Abstract Art* and *documenta I*
Britta Hochkirchen 349

Comparing in the Digital Age
The Transformation of Practices
Anna Neubert/Silke Schwandt 377

Authors and Editors 401

Acknowledgements

The publication of this book has been made possible through the help of many people. It all started at a conference in October 2017 at Bielefeld University where we met up with numerous colleagues to discuss the basic idea that we should try to understand comparing as a central human practice. We owe our thanks to Vera Breitner, Rebecca Moltmann, and Sabrina Timmer for preparing and organizing the conference; Vera Breitner, Sandra Sensmeyer, Clara Bernhard, Sabrina Timmer, and her team for their help in the various stages of preparing the book; Jonathan Harrow for reviewing and revising the English translations; and Gero Wierichs and Kai Reinhardt for their support from the publishing house *transcript*.

Our thanks also go out to the conference's keynote speakers for their inspiring and thought-provoking perspectives on our topic. These were Ann Laura Stoler (whose contribution is not part of this volume) and Haun Saussy (who agreed to expand his talk to a book-length essay published by Bielefeld University Press: *Are We Comparing Yet? On Standards, Justice, and Incomparability*, 2019). We also thank Emmanuel Lozerand (who did not attend the conference) for contributing an exciting talk to this volume that he delivered in Bielefeld in 2019. We owe our particular thanks to all the contributors who made this book happen, and, last not least, to the numerous scholars and colleagues who—with great commitment—were and are involved in the Collaborative Research Center SFB 1288 *Practices of Comparing. Ordering and Changing the World*. It is thanks to the generous support of the German Research Foundation (DFG) that we have the opportunity to explore the questions set out here in much more detail and greater depth.

Bielefeld and Jena, April 2020
Angelika Epple, Walter Erhart, Johannes Grave

Typologies and Forms

Practices of Comparing
A New Research Agenda Between Typological and Historical Approaches

Angelika Epple/Walter Erhart

Comparisons—a ubiquitous tool of powerful thinking?
Introduction to a multidisciplinary field of manifold controversies[1]

"It's like comparing apples and oranges"—this is what one might well say when a comparison is deemed to be impossible. This fruit-based example for not being able to compare holds at least in the Anglo-American world; Germans prefer to state the same impossibility by comparing apples and pears (likewise supposed to be in vain). Speaking of comparison in general, the opposite also holds true: You can compare everything with everything—as another quite common saying goes. You definitely can compare apples with oranges. Being fruit, they share a commonality while differing in many other respects. They are truly comparable in terms of their size or shape; their weight, color, taste, health index, origin, and history, the ease of peeling them; their local and global distribution; their economic positions on markets; and their appearances in seventeenth-century paintings or world literature. The comparisons are endless, and the fate of apples, oranges, and pears—being both comparable and incomparable at the same time—might befall human beings as well: They become objects of comparisons and, what is more, they constantly compare themselves to each other. But in the end, more than often, they think of themselves as being truly incomparable.

There is more than one seeming paradox when it comes to comparisons. On the one hand, comparing is surrounded by warnings and prohibitions: You cannot compare this; you must not compare that. This therefore implies an important, even dangerous issue: It addresses and relates things that are different and have to

---

1   This book has been prepared within the framework of the Collaborative Research Center SFB 1288 "Practices of Comparing. Changing and Ordering the World", Bielefeld University, Germany, funded by the German Research Foundation (DFG). The introduction owes many suggestions to the lively discussions with colleagues, especially with the co-editor Johannes Grave.

be kept separate—be they objects, actions, values, or human beings. A statement in the form of "this cannot be compared" may be just a different version of saying that these things are not the same; but when it comes to love and hate, for example, or to war atrocities and genocides, the much contested statement might also build walls around "incomparable" entities and differences either treasured or abhorred. It marks comparison as an outreaching and overbearing mode of thinking that blurs borders and connects things that may not belong together (or should not be seen next to each other). Respectively, however, the prohibitions and warnings surrounding comparisons classify them as powerful tools of thinking: seeing things as being equal and different at the same time, putting formerly separated things together, or even distorting common ways of thinking.

On the other hand, when you can compare everything with everything, comparisons may lack specificity and contours. Then comparisons are always at hand and may, therefore, seem arbitrary or irrelevant. The omnipresence of comparisons makes them a quite trivial everyday phenomenon—and may turn the warnings and prohibitions into an equally trivial caveat, probably a mere rhetorical game. Everything can be compared with everything—so what?

These two sides of comparisons—their ubiquity and their power as a thinking tool—can be moved and indeed have been moved in different directions. On the one hand, comparing can be considered a ubiquitous activity that is easily at hand and—as a condition of mind—does not require any further investigation. People, while thinking, compare—no matter what. On the other hand, comparing is a socially defined practice that provokes both warnings or prohibitions, and further comparisons (i.e., the discerning, measuring, and judging of similarities and differences) may be an important and powerful tool for evaluating things, persons, and groups; for demonstrating relations of power; and—last not least—for arguing, convincing, and making decisions. You should always compare, but, at the same time, you should always be aware of things that cannot be compared. The more one thinks about it, the more complicated things become. Are these imperatives (compare and don't compare) just two sides of a complicated matter, a theoretical aporia, or a language game (in the sense of Ludwig Wittgenstein)? How could we better understand what comparisons as a condition of mind and comparing as a social practice define?

Since Aristotle, comparison has been part of rhetoric, a proper tool to demonstrate and persuade,[2] but also an ingredient of logical thinking through classifying and concluding, judging and measuring, as well as detecting and sorting out sameness and difference between all kinds of related (and seemingly unrelated) entities and matters. As a method of adequate thinking, comparison elevated itself to a

---

2   Cf. Aristotle, *Rhetoric*. Book III, Chap. 4 (1406–1407) and 11 (1412–1413). See also Quintilian, *Institutes of Oratory*, 1, 105, 353.

scientific method in the sciences, especially as a logically proven instrument of knowledge, judgment, and cognition. In his *Regulae ad directionem ingenii* (1628/29), René Descartes builds science and its methods on the foundation that "in all reasoning it is only by means of comparison that we attain an exact knowledge of the truth."[3] This advice was crystallized into a set of methods by gradually specializing academic disciplines in the eighteenth and nineteenth centuries that were formed and understood themselves as explicit comparative sciences in the fields of anatomy, religion, law, linguistics, philology, ethnography, and anthropology.[4]

As a self-evident cognitive tool and as a clear-cut method in scientific contexts, comparison gained attention as a quite basic activity of thinking as well as a propaedeutic instrument for doing scientific research. Psychology established social comparison research as an analysis of how people compare themselves to each other in social settings.[5] Cognitive sciences have started to examine those brain-based comparative perceptions that are processed when humans discern and select objects in general.[6] Theories and methodologies of specialized sciences have tried to reflect on their tools of comparison by shaping and refining the ways to identify and measure the similarities and differences between their scientific objects and fields.[7]

---

3   René Descartes, Rules for the Direction of the Mind, in: John Cottingham/Robert Stoothoff/Dugald Murdoch (eds.), *The Philosophical Writings of Descartes*, vol. I, Cambridge 1985, 57. The statement plays a famous role in the distinction between the "episteme," the age of resemblances, and the early modern age of representation in Michel Foucault, *The Order of Things: An Archaeology of the Human Sciences*, New York 1970, 51. For a later scientific validation of the general standpoint that thinking is comparing, see, for example, Max Schießl, Untersuchungen über die Ideenassociation und ihren Einfluß auf den Erkenntnisakt, in: *Zeitschrift für Philosophie und philosophische Kritik*, Neue Folge 61 (1872), 247–282, see 257.
4   See Guy Jucquois/Christophe Vielle (eds.), *Le comparatism dans les sciences de l'homme*, Brussels 2000; Peter Zima, *Vergleichende Wissenschaften*, Tübingen 2000; Michael Eggers, *Vergleichendes Erkennen. Zur Wissenschaftsgeschichte und zur Epistemologie des Vergleichs und zur Genealogie der Komparatistik*, Heidelberg 2016.
5   A now classic account is Leon Feistinger, A Theory of Social Comparison Processes, in: *Human Relations* 7 (1954), 117–140. See Jerry Suls/Ladd Wheeler (eds.), *Handbook of Social Comparison. Theory and Research*, New York 2000.
6   See, for example, Christian H. Poth, *Episodic visual cognition: Implications for object and short-term recognition*, URL: https://pub.uni-bielefeld.de/publication/2911816 [last accessed December 9, 2019].
7   Cf. Joachim Matthes, The Operation called "Vergleichen", in: Joachim Matthes (ed.), *Zwischen den Kulturen? Die Sozialwissenschaften vor dem Problem des Kulturvergleichs*, Göttingen 1992, 75-99; Hartmut Kaelble, *Der Historische Vergleich. Eine Einführung zum 19. und 20. Jahrhundert*, Frankfurt a.M./New York 1999; Ann Laura Stoler, Tense and Tender Ties: The Politics of Comparison in North American History and (Post)Colonial Studies, in: *The Journal of American History* 88 (3/2001), 829-865; Hans-Gerhard Haupt, Comparative History, in: *International Encyclopedia of the Social and Behavioral Sciences* 4, Amsterdam 2001, 2397–2403; Hans-Gerhard Haupt/Jürgen Kocka (eds.), *Comparative and Transnational History. Central Eu-

So far, comparisons have been discussed as a mental activity or as being involved in theories and methodologies. With a few exceptions that we shall come back to later on, comparisons *per se* were, for a long time, not even considered a problem. This is remarkable, because related antonyms such as incomparability, noncommensurability, or incommensurability have been disputed broadly and controversially in philosophy and the theory of science ever since Thomas Kuhn's intervention regarding the structure of scientific revolutions in the 1960s.[8] Apart from these discussions, comparisons as an object of investigation, their history, and their seeming paradoxes have not gained similar attention for a long time. This changed for the first time in recent years when scholars from different disciplines began to think critically about the simultaneity of the so-called "ages of discovery" and the emergence of comparative sciences in the eighteenth and nineteenth centuries. What has been called the onset of "Western modernity" not only relies on numerous encounters with non-European cultures and civilizations, but is also intertwined with comparisons or, in other words, with the power, the forces, the causes, the functions, and the effects of comparisons.[9] Scholars have begun to ask whether comparison as a scientific and cultural tool that flourished in Europe's imperial era might be a predominately Western and European preoccupation, even a kind of obsession that is closely tied to enlightened and colonial ways of understanding, exploring, and dominating the world.[10] Starting with the notion of progress and civilization as temporal measures of comparing who is ahead and who

---

ropean Approaches and New Perspectives, New York/Oxford 2009; Thomas Welskopp, Vergleichende Geschichte, in: *Europäische Geschichte Online*, URL: http://ieg-ego.eu/de/threads/theorien-und-methoden/vergleichende-geschichte [last accessed December 9, 2019]; Ann Christiane Solte-Gresser/Hans-Jürgen Lüsebrink/Manfred Schmeling (eds.), *Zwischen Transfer und Vergleich. Theorien und Methoden der Literatur- und Kulturbeziehungen aus deutsch-französischer Perspektive*, Stuttgart 2013; Annette Simonis/Linda Simonis (eds.), *Kulturen des Vergleichens*, Heidelberg 2016.

8 Cf. Thomas Kuhn, *The Structure of Scientific Revolutions*, Chicago 1962; Carl G. Hempel, *Grundzüge der Begriffsbildung in der empirischen Wissenschaft*, Düsseldorf 1974, 83–86; Ruth Chang, *Making Comparisons Count*, London/New York 2002; Paul Borghossian, *Fear of Knowledge: Against Relativism and Constructivism*, Oxford 2006; Martin Carrier, Incommensurability and Empirical Comparability: The Case of the Phlogiston Theory, in: Peter Gärdenfors/Jan Woleński/Katarzyna Kijania-Placek (eds), *In the Scope of Logic, Methodology and Philosophy of Science*, Dordrecht 2002, 551–564.

9 See Pheng Cheah, Grounds of Comparison, in: *Diacritics* 29 (1999), 3–18; Pheng Cheah, The Material World of Comparison, in: Rita Felski/Susan Stanford Friedman (eds.), *Comparison: Theories, Approaches, Uses*, Baltimore 2013, 168–190; Angelika Epple/Walter Erhart (eds.), *Die Welt beobachten. Praktiken des Vergleichens*, Frankfurt a. M./New York 2015; Willibald Steinmetz (ed.), *The Force of Comparison. A New Perspective on Modern European History and the Contemporary World*, New York/Oxford 2019.

10 Cf. Natalie Melas, *All the Difference in the World. Postcoloniality and the Ends of Comparison*, Stanford 2007; Walter Mignolo, On Comparison: Who is Comparing What and Why? In: Rita Fel-

is lagging behind,[11] the quantitative comparisons of populations and economic data went on to create a world society that is finally united and charted by comparison through numbers, statistics, and graphs.[12] Today, comparing is not just an all-pervasive global instrument. The practice of instant digital comparisons along with the proliferation of rankings, lists, and comparative evaluations is beginning to dominate—or even tyrannize—private and public lives in the digital age.[13] Whereas sociology points to an increase of comparative means as a side effect of or a stimulus for modernization processes—be it through the development of media and technology or the emergence of culture as a field of second-order observation and therefore comparison[14]—postcolonial critics have argued that comparing has always put and kept those persons, groups, and agents in power who actually decide what is worth comparing, whose perspective is adopted, and who, by starting to compare, set the standards and norms that are automatically involved in the act of comparing.[15] Does that indicate that comparative methodologies must be thrown overboard?

Before making a momentous decision, we should take a closer look at the terminology. A comparison might be described as a logical operation that puts into perspective two entities, the two *comparata*, in respect to a *tertium comparationis*. A comparison carried out by actors, in contrast, is a socially determined activity. Its distinctive feature is that actors assume comparability and then relate similarities and differences between two or more entities. The assumption of comparability seems to be a crucial point. Only if actors feel that apples and pears *are* comparable, they will carry out comparisons. In other words, you truly can compare everything with everything, but you can do so only, first, when you assume comparability;

---

ski/Susan Stanford Friedman (eds.), *Comparison: Theories, Approaches, Uses*, Baltimore 2013, 99–111.

[11] See the now classical work by Johannes Fabian, *Time and the Other*, New York 1983.

[12] Cf. Sally Engle Merry, Measuring the World. Indicators, Human Rights, and Global Governance, in: *Current Anthropology* 52 (2011), 83–95; Bettina Heintz/Tobias Werron, Wie ist Globalisierung möglich? Zur Entstehung globaler Vergleichshorizonte am Beispiel von Wissenschaft und Sport, in: *Kölner Zeitschrift für Soziologie und Sozialpsychologie* 63 (2011), 359–394; Bettina Heintz, Welterzeugung durch Zahlen. Modelle politischer Differenzierung in internationalen Statistiken 1948-2010, in: Cornelia Bohn/Arno Schubbach/Leon Wansleben (eds.), *Welterzeugung durch Bilder*, Stuttgart 2012, 7–39.

[13] Cf. Steffen Mau, *Das metrische Wir. Über die Quantifizierung des Sozialen*, Berlin 2017; Bettina Heintz, "Wir leben im Zeitalter der Vergleichung". Perspektiven einer Soziologie des Vergleichs, in: *Zeitschrift für Soziologie* 45 (2016), 305–323.

[14] Cf. Niklas Luhmann, Kultur als historischer Begriff, in: Niklas Luhmann, *Gesellschaftsstruktur und Semantik 4*, Frankfurt a. M. 1999, 31–54; Bettina Heintz, Numerische Differenz. Überlegungen zu einer Soziologie des (quantitativen) Vergleichs, in: *Zeitschrift für Soziologie* 39 (2010), 162–181.

[15] Rajagopalan Radhakrishnan, Why Compare?, in: *New Literary History* 40 (2009), 453–475.

and, second, when you find an adequate *tertium comparationis*. Both features depend heavily on the societal and historical context. Every comparison is made only with respect to a perspective from which the sorting out of differences and similarities makes sense. Comparing is based on that which the particular comparisons are aimed toward, the *tertium comparationis* that is set up or implicitly engaged within the whole process of comparing.[16] Apples, oranges, and pears might be compared, but this is done very differently by traders, sellers, or consumers who choose very different purposes and *tertia* for their comparative actions.

Reconsidering comparisons as practices of comparing— with a history of their own

Far exceeding a mere mental activity and a methodological instrument, we suggest that comparisons should be reconsidered as practices of comparing that have a history of their own with different actors, multifaceted deployments, and often unprecedented effects—all to be studied in their own right. Comparing is not an activity that could be analyzed as a logical operation that would start with the characteristics of the *comparata*. Comparing is shaped (though not determined) by societal practices. We understand practices as repeatable patterns of action that, at the same time, enable or even provoke comparisons and shape them. However, practices are not completely fixed or stable; they depend on being performed by actors. If an actor carries out comparisons, she or he actualizes a specific practice; and simply because of a time index, every repetition also shifts the practice slightly. If other actors take up the shift—willingly or not—practices might change. The self-evidence of the seemingly objective use of comparisons in everyday life, the media, the sciences, and the humanities has actually obscured the fact that comparing is not neutral or innocent, but is always interwoven with the interests and perspectives of the ones who compare and is related to the situations and contexts in which comparisons are made. How *tertia comparationis* are taken up implicitly for different purposes—how, for example, they may be altered or left behind while the objects of comparison stay the same—is in no way self-evident or objective. The postcolonial critique has convincingly questioned the historical uses of comparison as a quasineutral tool of Western hegemony and domination. It even went so far as to ask whether comparing itself could be a predominately Eurocentric instrument of thinking and judging that might be replaced by other means in order to renounce the normative implications of comparison: by juxtaposition while cut-

---

16   Cf. Andreas Mauz/Hartmut von Sass (eds.), *Hermeneutik des Vergleichs. Strukturen, Anwendungen und Grenzen komparativer Verfahren*, Würzburg 2011.

ting out judgment and evaluation,[17] by stopping at the mere acknowledgment of "comparability,"[18] and by emphasizing "lateral comparisons" in order to balance the "frontal comparisons" of "us" and "them" as practiced in much traditional as well as in postcolonial anthropology.[19] Postcolonial approaches, however, more often than not, have repeated the dichotomies of the "colonial powers" and the "colonial other" within their studies. This repetition has to do with the postcolonial interest in analyzing "othering," as Homi K. Bhabha would have it.[20] We would like to suggest a new research agenda that, instead of criticizing the methods and the construction of the Other through comparison, focuses on the very practices of comparing. The analysis of comparative practices makes it possible to gain a better understanding of both the doing of differences and the doing of similarities. It helps reveal the constructed relation between the two and puts the dynamics of comparing in the foreground. Sometimes actors do not mention, and sometimes they do not even realize, that comparing puts differences and similarities evenly in perspective. Comparing is a "relationing" activity that goes way beyond stating mere differences. As a consequence, "othering" might appear as an extreme form of comparing—a form that might point exclusively to differences in respect to a specific *tertium*, but that, nevertheless, relies primarily on the broad assumption of comparability.

We could summarize so far in two points:

1. With the postcolonial critique at the latest, it is the phenomena of comparing itself that comes into view. Instead of comparison as an instrument or tool, be it cognitive, socially or scientifically, instead of the substantive and the entity of "comparison," we rather should take the verb and thereby the action of "comparing" into account. Comparing as a social and historical practice is always bound up with actors and agencies that perform the comparisons and connect them with their purposes and possible outcomes—intended or not. At the end of the day, the question of who is comparing and why actors compare becomes more important than the objects that are actually compared. Instead of objects ever waiting for all possible kinds of comparisons, there are actors who actually start the comparing process while charging it with purposes and shifting *tertia comparationis*.

While doing comparisons, actors are never free from their normative background and the historical context in which comparisons are situated. As a prac-

---

17   Cf. Susan Stanford Friedman, Why not Compare?, in: Rita Felski/Susan Stanford Friedman (eds.), *Comparison: Theories, Approaches, Uses*, Baltimore 2013, 34–45.
18   Natalie Melas, Merely Comparative, in: *PMLA* 128 (2013), 652–659.
19   Matei Candea, Going Full Frontal: Two Modalities of Comparison in Social Anthropology, in: Renaud Gagné/Simon Goldhill/Geoffrey E.R. Lloyd (eds.), *Regimes of Comparatism. Frameworks of Comparison in History, Religion and Anthropology*, Leiden/Boston 2019, 343–371.
20   Homi Bhabha, *The Location of Culture*, New York 1994.

tice—according to the insights of practice theory[21]—comparing has to be reconsidered not as an individual singular action performed randomly and spontaneously across space and time (and correspondingly hard to grasp), but as part of a framework of comparative practices that have been established through repetition and routines, cultural habits, and historical patterns.[22] As such practices, comparative acts in history are no longer contingent and arbitrary, but are clustered and organized along collective cultural schemes and models according to different framings of actors, groups, classes, nations, or other historical conditions and circumstances.

This shift in perspective also sheds new light on what at first sight appeared to be contradictory or even the paradoxes of comparison: trivial mental activity versus powerful tool of thinking, arbitrariness versus importance, everyday practice versus historical change, or permanence of comparisons versus incomparability. If we analyze the practices of comparing instead, mental activities are no longer the exclusive objects of research. In addition, comparisons are no longer perceived as a neutral instrument that is always at hand with the same devices, but as a practice that changes its rules according to its use and context. As a consequence of the "practical turn" in comparison research, the permanence of comparing and the simultaneous statements of incomparability appear either as divergent tensions or conflicting positions of different actors or as different stages within the very process of comparing. An actor can first assume comparability and then assert incomparability or vice versa. Practices do not necessarily live up to logical operations. The shift in perspective also reacts to the postcolonial critique by slightly changing its point of attack. The analysis of practices of comparing overcomes the analysis of "othering" and thus opens the door for deeper insights into the subtle and not so subtle power relations in comparative situations. The one who claims comparability and detects or determines the perspective, the *tertium comparationis*, holds the power to confront and to evaluate the *comparata*, to keep them either fixed to established normative standards, or to open them up to hitherto unknown perspectives.

---

21 Cf. Theodore R. Schatzki, *Social Practices. A Wittgensteinian Approach to Human Activity and the Social*, Cambridge 1996; Andreas Reckwitz, Grundelemente einer Theorie sozialer Praktiken. Eine sozialtheoretische Perspektive, in: *Zeitschrift für Soziologie* 32 (2003), 282–301; Marian Füssel/Tim Neu, Doing Discourse. Diskursiver Wandel aus praxeologischer Perspektive, in: Achim Landwehr (ed.), *Diskursiver Wandel*, Wiesbaden 2010, 213–235.

22 Cf. Johannes Grave, Vergleichen als Praxis. Vorüberlegungen zu einer praxistheoretisch orientierten Untersuchung von Vergleichen, in: Angelika Epple/Walter Erhart (eds.), *Die Welt beobachten. Praktiken des Vergleichens*, Frankfurt a. M./New York 2015, 135–159; Johannes Grave, Comparative Practices and their Implications: The Case of Comparative Viewing, in: Willibald Steinmetz (ed.), *The Force of Comparison. A New Perspective on Modern European History and the Contemporary World*, New York/Oxford 2019, 53–79.

However, the act of comparing, by relating entities, objects, processes, living beings, or humans vis-à-vis a *tertium comparationis*, always challenges the *comparata* involved. To compare distant objects, for instance, always means decontextualizing each object and putting—recontextualizing—it in a new framework with a new *tertium comparationis*. What is more, comparing relies not only on the assumption of comparability but also on a *tertium comparationis* that has also been called the *tertium commune*. The latter expression makes it even clearer that comparing puts similarity and difference into perspective.

2. Comparing as a practice depends not only on the societal context but also on the historical situation. Whereas psychological and sociobiological investigations point to the everlasting pervasiveness of comparing as a quite stable resource of human cognition,[23] the historiographies of comparative sciences have not come to terms with the history of comparing as a social and historical practice whose means, perspectives, and performances may change according to different actors and to either *longues durées* or shorter time periods. "This is the age of comparison!"[24] Friedrich Nietzsche once was quick to diagnose the predicaments of his imperial and antiquarian nineteenth century. However, histories and transformations in the manners and magnitudes of comparisons are quite difficult to assess and to analyze. It is by no means certain and self-explanatory that comparisons writ large started with the "bourgeois" imperial age,[25] and it is equally doubtful whether comparisons have remained the same across time and space over the centuries.

A broadly discussed example might illustrate this: During the so-called "dispute of the New World," long-lasting traditions of comparing were picked up and reframed. The comparison of fruits (and other plants) played a major role when European scholars such as Georges-Louis Leclerc de Buffon or Cornelis de Pauw proved the American climate to have a degenerative effect for humans, animals, and plants alike by also reducing the variety of all living organisms. Comparisons did vary depending on the cultural background. However, the native Mexican Fray

---

23 See, for example, Bram P. Buunk/Thomas Mussweiler, New Directions in Social Comparison Research, in: *European Journal of Social Psychology* 31 (2001), 467–475. "In its broadest sense, the concept of social comparison—relating one's own features to those of others and vice versa—is an important, if not central, characteristic of human life. [...] the need to compare self with others is phylogenetically very old, biologically very powerful, and recognizable in many species." Transferring the concept and the practice of social comparison from humans to animals has recently led to skepticism: See Vanessa Schmitt et al., Do Monkeys Compare Themselves to Others?, in: *Animal Cognition* 19 (2016), 417–428.
24 Friedrich Nietzsche, *Human, all too human*, Cambridge 1996, 24.
25 For a different perspective see, for example, Anthony Grafton, Comparisons Compared: A Study in the Early Modern Roots of Cultural History, in: Renaud Gagné/Simon Goldhill/Geoffrey E. R. Lloyd (eds.), *Regimes of Comparatism. Frameworks of Comparison in History, Religion and Anthropology*, Leiden/Boston 2019, 18–48.

Francisco Javier Clavijero, for instance, did not hesitate to counter the argument with a different fruit-based comparison: "If America had no pomegranates, lemons &c. it has them now: but Europe never had, has nor can have, chirimoyas, aguacates, musas, chicozapotes, &c."[26] Behind the fruit comparisons, we easily detect that actually something else was being negotiated: the question which world region should be the standard, the norm against which others are to be compared. Who is meant to set the standards for evaluation; who is in the position to decide whether a comparison-based hierarchy is convincing; and who, on the other hand, is forced to react? Whatever the reaction looks like, it is difficult to escape comparisons once they are in the world. However big the differences in standpoints between Clavijero and de Pauw, both scholars were familiar with a long-lasting tradition of comparing the old and the new world. Already in 1609, Inca Garcilaso wrote about comparing America to Europe and the difficulty in countering the imposition of already introduced patterns of comparison. He tried in vain to get rid of comparisons between Europe and America by simply declaring: "every comparison is odious"[27] (as Gary Shaw shows in his contribution to this volume, the saying "comparisons are odious" goes back at least to John Fortescue in 1471 but spread rapidly and with little hindrance in the early modern period). As Garcilaso was claiming incomparability, he nevertheless continued with comparisons. However, long-lasting traditions of comparing Europe to America (tellingly, hardly ever vice versa) should not hide the specific differences and the significant changes in the respective practices. Not only the *comparata* and the *tertia* were changing but also the subjects and the goals, the complexity, and the contexts. Garcilaso around 1600 and de Pauw or Clavijero roughly 200 years later used comparisons very differently insofar as the former tried to render visible the given divine order whereas the latter insisted on proving the truth quite empirically by doing comparisons. For an evaluation of the outcome of comparisons with different *tertia*, de Pauw and Clavijero both needed a measure for weighing the importance of comparisons. What is to be more important: the size of the animals or the variety of species? For an evaluation, a ranking of comparisons so to say, they carried out comparisons of comparisons—a complex and

---

26 Francisco Javier Clavijero, *History of Mexico*, London 1787, 189. For the dispute of the new world, see: Ottmar Ette, Die 'Berliner Debatte' um die Neue Welt. Globalisierung aus der Perspektive der europäischen Aufklärung, in: Vicente Bernaschina/Kraft, Tobias/Kraume, Anne (eds.), *Globalisierung in Zeiten der Aufklärung. Texte und Kontexte zur 'Berliner Debatte' um die Neue Welt (17./18. Jh.)*. Frankfurt a. M. 2015, 27–55; Hans-Jürgen Lüsebrink, De l'usage de la comparaison dans les écrits des Jésuites sur les Amériques, in: Marc André Bernier/Clorinda Donato/Hans-Jürgen Lüsebrink (eds.), *Jesuit Accounts of the Colonial Americas. Intercultural Transfers, Intellectual Disputes, And Textualities*, Toronto 2014, 418–436.

27 Inca Garcilaso de la Vega, *Primera Parte de los Commentarios Reales*, Lisbon 1609, 56.

reflexive comparison. Without a given divine or natural order, actors themselves were forced to find arguments for searching and proving truth by comparing.[28]

The "dispute of the new world" is but one example illustrating historically differing practices of comparing. There can be no doubt that we need to know far more about it. How can we achieve more knowledge? We would like to put to discussion the combination of a typological endeavor and the investigation of the history of practices of comparing.

Making the new agenda feasible: Typology and the historicity of comparative practices

When postcolonial critique vigorously cast doubt on "Western" practices of comparing, the question of comparison—as a problem; as a way of thinking; and as a contested arena of cultural theory, intercultural perception, and history—arose anew. Despite all the historical vices and defaults of comparison, and even while vigorously facing its rhetorical and ideological bias, comparison is even more in need of a reevaluation that takes the ambivalent status of comparing fully into account.[29] A once colonial practice of comparing may give way to a new "ethics" of comparison based on the "inevitability" and the translation processes of comparison[30] as well as on the "self-relativizing and self-critical function" of a "comparative viewpoint."[31] The European history of comparing may be paralleled and viewed differently by looking at comparative examples and histories of comparison in other equally central parts of the world.[32] The scientific undertakings of comparative re-

---

28 See for the long-lasting tradition of comparing the new and the old world: Angelika Epple, *Comparing Europe and the Americas: The Dispute of the New World between the Sixteenth and Nineteenth Centuries*, in: Willibald Steinmetz (ed.), *The Force of Comparison*, New York 2019, 137–163.
29 Haun Saussy, *Are We Comparing Yet? On Standards, Justice, and Incomparability*, Bielefeld 2019.
30 Zhang Longxi, Crossroads, Distant Killing, and Translation: On the Ethics and Politics of Comparison, in: Rita Felski/Susan Stanford Friedman (eds.), *Comparison: Theories, Approaches, Uses*, Baltimore 2013, 46–63, see 59–60.
31 Xie Ming, What Does the Comparative to Theory?, in: *PMLA* 128 (2013), 676–682, see 680.
32 Cf. Marcel Detienne, *Comparing the Incomparable*, Stanford 2008; Xie Ming, *Conditions of Comparison: Reflections on Comparative Intercultural Inquiry*, London 2011; Zhang Longxi, Comparison and Correspondence: Revisiting an Old Idea for the Present Time, in: *Comparative Literature Studies* 53 (4/2016), 766–785.

ligious studies,[33] comparative literature,[34] and anthropology[35] currently seem to be transforming their practices in search for "comparatism as an *ethos*"[36] immediately after it became apparent that the grand theories of comparing "us" and "them"—which had taken center stage in the enlightened and colonial historiographies of religion, history, and anthropology—may have failed altogether. However, what would render such a comparative approach to the history of comparisons feasible? There is a sense of new beginnings in the air. Anil Bhatti and Dorothee Kimmich, for instance, instead of being satisfied with just postcolonial criticism, have recently argued for a new cultural theoretical paradigm that will rely on similarities instead of differences. Their hope to overcome difference-oriented comparisons by a strategic emphasis on similarity shares the moral commitment of postcolonialism.[37] However, we would like to make a slightly different suggestion by taking the full picture of comparing and its dynamic into account. For the time being, we would like to structure all kinds of questions concerning the ethics and the politics of comparison along with the variations, the enabling conditions, the history, and the effects of comparing according to two, partly overlapping bundles of questions that make up a rather typological approach on the one side, and a rather historical approach on the other.

The first bundle of questions deals with typological features and general challenges of comparing without pointing primarily to a temporal index. Given that comparisons are not an innocent tool in the service of objective insights, but a practice shaped by actors situated in a specific societal and historical context, this first bundle of questions points to issues that characterize all practices of com-

---

33   Cf. Guy G. Stroumsa, History of Religions: The Comparative Moment, in: Renaud Gagné/Simon Goldhill/Geoffrey E.R. Lloyd (eds.), *Regimes of Comparatism. Frameworks of Comparison in History, Religion and Anthropology*, Leiden/Boston 2019, 318–342.

34   Cf. Rey Chow, The Old/New Question of Comparison in Literary Studies: A Post-European Perspective, in: *English Literary History* 71 (2004), 289–311; David Ferris, Why Compare?, in: Ali Behdat/Dominic Thomas (eds.), *A Companion to Comparative Literature*, Malden/Oxford 2011, 28–45; David Porter, The Crisis of Comparison and the World Literature Debate, in: *Profession* 2011, 244–258; Jacob Edmond, No Discipline: An Introduction to "The Indiscipline of Comparison", in: *Comparative Literature Studies* 53 (2016), 647–659.

35   Cf. Richard Handler, The Uses of Incommensurability in Anthropology, in: Rita Felski/Susan Stanford Friedman (eds.), *Comparison: Theories, Approaches, Uses*, Baltimore 2013, 271–291; Matei Candea, *Comparison in Anthropology. The Impossible Method*, Cambridge 2018; Philippe Descola, Anthropological Comparatisms: Generalisations, Symmetrisation, Bifurcation, in: Renaud Gagné/Simon Goldhill/Geoffrey E.R. Lloyd (eds.), *Regimes of Comparatism. Frameworks of Comparison in History, Religion and Anthropology*, Leiden/Boston 2019, 402–417.

36   Stroumsa, History of Religions, 339.

37   Cf. Anil Bhatti/Dorothee Kimmich (eds.), *Similarity. A Paradigme for Culture Theory*, New Delhi 2018.

paring—no matter where and when they are carried out. This would also include reflections on the academic methodology of comparing.

During the last decade, scholars from different disciplines have been discussing the advantages and shortcomings of typologizing comparisons.[38] Most have not referred explicitly to practices of comparing but to comparisons as such.[39] However, their suggestions can also help to typologize the respective practices. When it comes to comparing other humans, groups, and societies, Geoffrey E. R. Lloyd has offered a typology of five "valences" of comparatism as a way of using comparisons.[40] First, "comparatism can be used to claim superiority for the views and practices of those who are doing the comparing."[41] Second, comparing, in turn, may be used to acknowledge the superiority of the other (or at least in certain respects). Third, instead of differences, the commonalities between the two *comparata* may be emphasized. The fourth possibility is to discern only differences, thus stressing incomparability. The fifth valence consists in taking radical difference not as a matter of ranking and judging or not just stopping at incomparability, but looking at comparisons "as a resource for learning something new."[42] Whereas Lloyd tries to put comparing in a typological order, sketching almost ideal types in the sense of Max Weber, Willibald Steinmetz has a similar but more historical typology in mind when he—proceeding from social comparison research—differentiates between comparisons along the two axes of "above/below" and "better/worse" while adding as a third possibility the emphasis on differences and incomparabilities ("just different").[43] In a way, this typology combines the two different bundles of questions that run through this volume, because it also carries a historical index: Whereas comparison as a social scale of "above and below" ranks is quite common in premodern times, better/worse comparisons situated within a competitive framework and incomparability as a sign of uniqueness attributed to persons and individuals are specific modern features of comparative actions.

However, even by establishing typologies of comparisons (and Kirill Postoutenko gives a first-off example of their linguistic possibilities in this volume), the tensions and ambivalences of comparing might not disappear and not even have been fully understood. It is important to note, though, that historical typologies do not

---

38 See, for instance, Hartmut von Sass, Vergleiche(n). Ein hermeneutischer Rund- und Sinkflug, in: Andreas Mautz/Hartmut von Sass (eds.), *Hermeneutik des Vergleichs*, Würzburg 2011, 25–48.
39 For some thoughts on how to integrate typologies of comparisons into research on practices of comparing, see Grave, Vergleichen als Praxis, 135–159.
40 Geoffrey E. R. Lloyd, *Analogical Investigations. Historical and Cross-Cultural Perspectives on Human Reasoning*, Cambridge 2015, 29–42.
41 Lloyd, *Analogical Investigations*, 30.
42 Lloyd, *Analogical Investigations*, 31.
43 Willibald Steinmetz, Above/below, better/worse, or simply different? Metamorphoses of Social Comparison, 1600–1900, in: Willibald Steinmetz (ed.), *The Force of Comparison, A New Perspective on Modern European History and the Contemporary World*, New York/Oxford 2019, 80–112.

necessarily conflict with the dynamic of comparative practices that—once constructed and performed—moves easily beyond typological confines. Comparing the self and the other in a colonial or postcolonial context, for example, can lead to stereotypes fixing judgments and established norms within a wide array of public and philosophical thinking. Comparing the self and the other can also—almost at the same time—open up horizons that restructure the whole field of comparative knowledge.[44]

The second bundle of questions has a temporal index—in different ways: It looks at practices of comparison built on inherited traditions and incorporated routines or patterns of comparisons thus pointing back to historical continuities. Comparing cultures, for instance, has been a constant focus of attention and a driving force of irritation and transformation from early modern time onward[45] (and Andrea Frisch gives another intriguing example in this volume), and it may well even be Greek ethnography that laid the groundwork for this kind of double-faced comparatism.[46] Comparative practices served to negotiate matters of religion, ethnicity, and law in early modern contact zones. They were also tools to fuel competition in a nationalist and capitalist age—from ethnic uprisings in global conflicts and colonial wars to economic competition or military rivalry and arms races between nation states and superpowers in the twentieth and twenty-first centuries.

Practices of comparing, however, do not just follow historical traditions and point to continuities; they also change over time. A thought-provoking suggestion by Renaud Gagné and his research group points to different "regimes of comparatism"[47] that have been established over time but that also may have changed

---

44   A perfect example may be the so-called ages of discovery with multiple encounters of traveling Europeans with non-European civilizations that—with their quite obvious but frequently neglected emphasis on comparison—have been studied in research on world travel literature: See Anthony Pagden, *European Encounters with the New World: From Renaissance to Romanticism*, New Haven 1993; Walter Erhart, Weltreisen, Weltwissen, Weltvergleich – Perspektiven der Forschung, in: *Internationales Archiv für Sozialgeschichte der deutschen Literatur* 42 (2017), 292–321; Christine Peters, Reisen und Vergleichen. Praktiken des Vergleichens in Alexander von Humboldts "Reise in die Äquinoktial-Gegenden des Neuen Kontinents" und Adam Johann von Krusensterns "Reise um die Welt", in: *Internationales Archiv für Sozialgeschichte der deutschen Literatur* 42 (2017), 441–465.

45   See Joan-Pau Rubiés, Comparing Cultures in the Early Modern World: Hierarchies, Genealogies and the Idea of European Modernity, in: Renaud Gagné/Simon Goldhill/Geoffrey E.R. Lloyd (eds.), *Regimes of Comparatism. Frameworks of Comparison in History, Religion and Anthropology*, Leiden/Boston 2019, 116–176.

46   Cf. Raimund Schulz, *Als Odysseus staunte. Die griechische Sicht des Fremden und das ethnographische Vergleichen von Homer bis Herodot*, Göttingen 2020.

47   See Renaud Gagné/Simon Goldhill/Geoffrey E.R. Lloyd (eds.), *Regimes of Comparatism. Frameworks of Comparison in History, Religion and Anthropology*, Leiden/Boston 2019.

slightly or even vanished completely. Most often though, these practices and practice formations, these patterns and regimes of comparing, combine continuities with either ruptures or transformations. This general observation opens the door for challenging questions. In the history of comparisons, what does exactly change: the techniques, the procedures, the topics, the *tertium* (or *tertia*) *comparationis*, the power constellations, or the societal circumstances? Why do comparative practices change and to what end? If we want to write a comprehensive history of comparing, we have to know far more about different historical comparative practices in different cultures or communities or in other kinds of groups that share specific practices. As the example of the scholarly comparisons of the old and the new world in the sixteenth and seventeenth centuries has clearly shown, there are, at first sight, many continuities in the history of comparing. However, a closer inspection reveals significant differences that might question or even displace the assumed continuity.

There is an even more complex question about comparative practices that accompanies temporality and addresses the problem and phenomenon of historical change itself: Do practices of comparing trigger historical change? This question is challenging, because the causes of historical change are always manifold. Contingency and nonhuman influences play a major role, and the effects of practices are difficult to prove. Nonetheless, recent research has found strong arguments in support of the assumption that comparing provokes change. This is most obvious in situations of conflict and competition. Discussions about the strength of a hostile army, for instance, are usually based on comparisons—be they comparisons of courage, bodily shape, strategy, or equipment and the power of weapons. Military experts derive instructions for action from these discussions, and these instructions are bound to bring change into the world. In competitive contexts, it is also immediately convincing that comparisons are carried out to legitimize or at least to ask for change. The proliferation of rankings and ratings are another case in point. But does the power of comparative practices also apply to broader historical changes?

Recent research at least supports the idea that the encounters, conflicts, and entanglements of different cultures and the evolution of a comparative scholarly methodology were just two sides of one coin: the making of so-called "Western" modernity. The question whether "Western" modernity is an outcome of specific practices of comparing seems to be a promising thesis. It combines the postcolonial criticism of comparative methodology with a historical finding: In eighteenth-century European academia, comparisons became the basis for methodology in many different disciplines such as anatomy, ethnology, literature, and the like. They also were crucial for coming to terms with new, sometimes challenging, or even confusing and irritating encounters with formerly little or unknown regions, cultures, geographies, people, plants, and animals—both within and outside of

Europe. With comparisons, scholars, adventurers, military experts, explorers, and travelers helped—willingly or not—to naturalize or hide hierarchies by introducing allegedly neutral norms and standards for evaluations. Through comparison, they ordered the world. The decisive point, however, goes beyond this: By ordering the world, the doing of comparison also helped to change the world. Not only the request for equal rights is based on comparisons, also the stress on inequality or unevenness cannot do without comparing. Both ask for change. In the nineteenth century colonial context, imperialism and conquest were legitimized (among others) through the comparison-based argument that people "without history" were in need of education by "people with history."[48] If the importance of comparisons as drivers of historical change applies for a specific time period in a specific part of a specific world region, would that mean that comparing is also an important practice for triggering change in world regions beyond Europe? What would that mean? There are many more questions to be asked about the relation between comparisons and historical change, some of which are taken up in contributions to this volume.

Contributions to this volume

We have sorted the two parts of this book according to the two bundles of questions. The first part includes four chapters that chart the field of comparative practices by taking typological, methodological, and theoretical approaches to comparative speech acts, incomparability, metaphors and poetry, and rankings as a way of comparing by numbers. The second part of the book includes nine contributions that deal with the historicity of comparison. Contributions range from the Middle Ages and the early modern period to the twentieth century and present times; they cover religion; historiography; East–West encounters between Europe, China, and Japan; art and aesthetics; race and slavery systems; politics; and the issue of comparing in the digital age.

The first part starts with preliminary linguistic, semantic, and philosophical reflections on comparison as an operation of thinking, arguing, and speaking. The endeavor to identify comparative utterances and speech acts in languages does not just provide the path to comparison's practices, it also lays the foundation for computer-based methods of detecting comparative phrases within languages and written texts that would enable research on their statistical occurrences and historical transformations. As Kirill Postoutenko shows in his contribution (*Preliminary Typology of Comparative Utterances: A Tree and Some Binaries*), a vast taxonomy of possible comparisons must be taken into account if we want to order and classify different

---

48 Fabian, *Time and the Other*.

types of comparative utterances. Such typologies—with their examples and highly specified classifications—give a first impression of the wide range of speech acts that are used and performed for comparative purposes. Their data may be taken into consideration each time the historical material of comparative practices has to be structured and scrutinized in written documents.

Whereas a linguistic and semantic archive of possible comparisons composed in this way may be inexhaustible, Hartmut von Sass undertakes the almost opposite move and looks at incomparability as a statement about entities—be they actions, objects, or human beings—that allegedly cannot be compared at all (*Incomparability. A Tentative Guide for the Perplexed*). Also starting with semantic, linguistic, and, this time, philosophical and logical-analytical observations, von Sass shows with great care that the assertion of incomparability—the very opposite of the common-sense statement that everything can be compared with everything—is hard to maintain in a strict logical or structural sense. If objects or statements could be said to be incomparable to each other, the realm and the range, even the very practices of comparison, might have been left and abandoned altogether. Whereas noncommensurability—putting objects together that have nothing in common—is a synonym for "incomparability" (but usually is just the starting point of comparisons to come), incommensurability is the outcome of bringing up so many similarities and differences between objects that an overall comparison is no longer possible.[49] Whereas statements about the principal incomparability of two or more things need to be specified or just remain problematic, a "performative incomparability"—according to Hartmut von Sass—is widely used to address the most important moral, personal, and political issues. What incomparability loses on the side of logical thinking, it clearly gains as a performative practice turning incomparability and incommensurability into a rhetoric and a discourse on shared and contested values among couples and groups, communities and societies.

The contributions of Kirill Postoutenko and Hartmut von Sass both point to the fact that characteristics and descriptions of the linguistic and philosophical structure, the very "nature" of comparison, are almost impossible to have as long as the performative uses of comparing are not taken into account. The paradoxes of comparison as a speech act and as a language game make sense or break down only when the practice and the actors of comparing gain full-blown attention. What is characterized as a problem of proper definition, as a loss or a circuit of never-ending efforts for clear-cut and all-encompassing definitions and typologies, turns into an important aspect for research on the historical, social, and cultural functions of comparative practices.

---

49 We owe this clarification to Martin Carrier. On "incommensurability" see Martin Carrier, Changing Laws and Shifting Concepts. On the Nature and Impact of Incommensurability, in: *Boston Studies in the Philosophy of Science* 216 (2001), 65–90.

From early on, ever since *comparatio* was coined a rhetorical device, metaphors and similes have gained attention as the smallest and maybe purest form of comparisons. These and other rhetorical and literary comparisons constantly move between the world as it is and the possibilities of creating a fictional or poetic world of its own. As Walter Erhart shows in his contribution (*Odysseus, Blackbirds, and Rain Barrels: Literature as a Comparative Practice*), the "semantic innovations" (Paul Ricœur) provided by literary comparisons disclose relations that have not been there before. Literature and poetry extend the range and the dynamics of comparing not only by doing comparisons on microlevels such as metaphors and similes, especially in poetry, but also by comparing literary figures and narratives throughout literary history and world literature.

Whereas metaphors, poetry, and fictional narratives create new worlds and worldviews by the world-disclosing activities of their comparative practices, statistics and rankings, quite on the opposite side, seem to register and actually narrow down the world as it is by displaying comparisons by numbers. However, although rankings and graphs seem to represent the peak of neutrality and objectivity, they, nevertheless, do not just collect facts and classify realities but construct their competitive fields while simultaneously just pretending to describe them. The examples in Tobias Werron's and Leopold Ringel's contribution—art, sports, and university rankings—quite tellingly demonstrate that rankings have a history of their own that is closely linked to the emergence of modernity and the rise of fast changing markets, publics, and technologies (*Where Do Rankings Come From? A Historical-Sociological Perspective on the History of Modern Rankings*). Their analyses of rankings quite explicitly dismantle the *illusio* of comparison's most foregrounded, in this case almost mathematically proven neutrality, while, at the same time, calling for a genealogy of the diverse historical forms of comparative practices. While opening up the competitive field of contemporary comparisons made easy by computers, the internet, algorithms, and artificial intelligence, *Where Do Rankings Come From?* reveals the agenda and the history of doing comparisons in general. By shaping and transforming the realities that comparisons pretend to just register and rearrange, practices of comparing make history in more than one sense: They are bound to specific historical media and technologies that transform comparative acts correspondingly, and they change the realities that they allegedly describe in a seemingly innocent comparative way.

The second part of the volume starts with a contribution by Gary Shaw that fills a whole unmarked chapter in the history of comparative practices (*The Weight of Comparing in Medieval England*). Until now, the history of comparisons and comparatisms has been traced back mostly to early modern and modern periods, thus implicitly falling back on the old notion of medieval times as a dark age that had seen neither the rise of individuality nor decisive encounters with non-European civilizations and the important cross-cultural comparisons they produce. Contrary to this hardly contested notion, Gary Shaw draws on a broad picture of the role of medieval comparisons—from everyday practices such as weighing, selling, and buying on agricultural markets to the increasing importance of money for facilitating comparative acts on a daily basis. Furthermore, he highlights comparing as an administrative tool that easily expands to and fosters economic and political matters including questions of rank and clothing that actually permeate medieval societies on a very general basis. It is by no means incidental that Francis Bacon stretches the range of comparisons to the religious realm or that the warning against comparison—the saying that "comparisons are odious"—appears almost simultaneously in poetry and law in the fifteenth century, thus emphasizing the dynamics that made comparing a routinized practice but also a site of political and moral as well as legal and religious conflicts and contestations. Moreover, Shaw makes an important methodological point: He asks how the historian is able to trace comparative practices, even when these practices are not addressed explicitly in his sources. By taking into consideration different social, economic, and cultural fields, Shaw demonstrates that it is indeed possible to reconstruct comparative practices without relying on explicit documents alone.

In France, almost at the same time, history is another site of these contestations in which the act of comparing—according to Andrea Frisch—triggers epochal "transformative effects" precisely by being continued, taken to its very limits, and loaded with implicit underlying ambivalences and contradictions (*The Shifting Grounds of Comparison in the French Renaissance: The Case of Louis Le Roy*). The work of Louis le Roy in the sixteenth century is a quite telling case in point. Comparing civilizations—overall France with ancient Greece and Rome—is challenged as much by a third term such as Islam as by following subcomparisons and juxtapositions. Instead of clear-cut traditional worldviews and rankings, a lack of common ground starts to unsettle old notions of differences and sameness, while slowly indicating losses of historiographical standards that open up history (and its writing) in unforeseen directions.

This may also apply to larger cross-cultural comparisons—as Zhang Longxi explores in his contribution on the comparisons between Europe and China (*Comparison and East-West Encounters: The Seventeenth and Eighteenth Centuries*). Starting with the Renaissance and Marco Polo's travels, these comparisons, right from the beginning, did not just provide a tool to compare civilizations on an almost equal level of civilization in terms of culture, refined manners, and taste—thus creating resemblances and comparables on a large scale. The portraits of China in the seventeenth and eighteenth centuries are also used to shift cultural difference from a reflection on one's own achievements to a medium of social critique addressing Europe itself.

Nonetheless, Asian countries and Far-Eastern civilizations remain a resource for imagining the other in numerous ways. As Emanuel Lozerand makes clear in his contribution on the European reports and fantasies on Japan from the fifteenth to the twentieth century (*Japan as the Absolute Other: Geneology and Variations of a Topos*), Japan has served as an image and a projection of alterity throughout the centuries. Yet, the content of this mirror image and the implied comparative negotiations vary at great length due to the different comparative methods applied. From time to time, for example, in the eighteenth century (paralleling the cases of China and Japan on this point), differences were reduced and similarities gained ground. Yet, as Lozerand shows in great detail, the observed facts and the content of the respective comparisons often remained in place while the perspectives and the interpretations, the *tertia comparationis*, were shifted and changed, invented, and left behind. Therefore, former opposites turned into resemblances under a new heading, and the mirror image of Japan as a topsy-turvy version of Europe—up until Claude Lévi-Strauss—does not reveal a rigid structure (or stereotype) at all, but a very mobile comparative strategy with numerous variations and quite different purposes.

The range and contestations of comparative practices over the centuries extend not only geographically but also according to the modes and objects of knowing, the *episteme*, and scientific practices in general. As Leopold Ringel and Tobias Werron already showed in their contribution, art has a long history of rankings, but also developed as a field of its own in the seventeenth and eighteenth century. Artworks are utilized as a realm of taste and common sense (*sensus communis*). The "*je ne sais quoi*" as a quite common formula of the undefinable evaluation of beauty and art works in the seventeenth century leads to the emergence of the philosophical subdiscipline of "aesthetics" as an analysis of the lower capacities of mind in Alexander Gottlieb Baumgarten's *Aesthetica* (1750/58). But such theoretical or philosophical discourses eclipsed important practices, particularly practices of comparison that were established by connoisseurs, amateurs, and collectors. In his contribution ('*Goût de Comparison*'. *Practices of Comparative Viewing in Eighteenth-Century Connoisseurship*), Joris C. Heyder points to an important trajectory in the history of art when comparing became the very essence of judging artworks long before the comparative sciences also took hold of the institutionalized academic efforts of art criticism. When Jean-Baptist Dubos claimed a "*goût de comparison*" as the core method of judging the value of art in 1719, he was referring to taste and connoisseurship that mark not only a community of art critics but also a practice in front of paintings that was being remodeled and refined as well as continued up to the nineteenth century. The communities of connoisseurs doing and establishing specific patterns of comparing art gave way to academic practices in the nineteenth and twentieth centuries that often denigrated those comparing judgments as amateurish but nevertheless depended on similar criteria for their own comparative judgments.

As in art history, studying comparative practices in seemingly well-known topics such as the construction of the Other, theories of race, and practices of slavery often challenges the established temporal, geographical, and theoretical scope of research. Angelika Epple in her contribution (*Inventing White Beauty, Fighting Black Slavery: Blumenbach's, Humboldt's, and Arango y Parreño's Share in Cuban Race Comparisons in the Long Nineteenth Century*) shows that the concept of race, however vague it used to be, has always been strongly combined with the discussion on slavery and "limpieza de sangre" (blood purity) ever since the sixteenth century. Around 1800, when Humboldt visited Cuba for the first time, race comparisons partly merged with new instruments of statistical population control. Humboldt's famous essay on Cuba became a seminal point of reference in Cuba and beyond—even in the US presidential election of 1856. The contribution traces how Humboldt was influenced not only by the Göttingen-based comparative anatomist, Johann von Blumenbach, but also by the Cuban slave owner, Arango y Parreño. Blumenbach, a committed abolitionist, tried to prove the equal roots of all races, and used this to derive equal rights for all humans. Arango y Parreño, in contrast, defended the Cuban way of slavery that—in his eyes—made Cuban slaves "the happiest in the world." The (comparative) question whether or not a better slavery existed undermined Humboldt's conviction that slavery was incomparable to other systems of violence. In addition, even though Humboldt mistrusted statistics, with his huge collection of data and supported by Arango y Parreño, he helped to establish the race comparisons by numbers that triggered conflicts in Cuba until the twentieth century.

The comparison of the "old" and "new" world, of race and matters of slavery and domination, as well as the temporalities of comparisons in terms of progress and development opens an arena in which different types of comparative situations come into play. Comparative practices are used widely either in situations of competition and conflict or in situations of negotiation, contact, and distinction. Comparative arguments in a site of conflict or negotiation can arise all of sudden, whereas comparative judgements might develop differently in situations in which they are reflected and contemplated retrospectively. The twentieth century as a much-disputed "age of extremes" might have seen a lot of comparative practices borne out of conflict and competition that were enhanced by capitalism and the market economy (as also outlined by the contribution of Leopold Ringel and Tobias Werron). As a specific case in point, Thomas Müller studies the politicization of comparisons in the realm of arms races and military competition between superpowers in the Cold War (*The Politicization of Comparisons: The East–West Dispute Over Military Force Comparisons in the Cold War*). As much as the politicization of comparisons of these comparisons depends on public disputes, the dynamic set forth by political actors could also alter the comparative framework, thus changing the whole situation and opening the way to either more conflict and competition or to a depoliticization of the whole debate.

Whereas the politicization of comparisons in the arenas of conflict and competition might be a dominant course in the twentieth century—often blurring the boundaries between politics, economics, and moral issues—the modern and contemporary system of art seems to have developed as a sphere of its own in terms of its markets, its values, its critics, and its public. Yet, as Britta Hochkirchen clearly demonstrates in her contribution (*Genealogies of Modernism: Curatorial Practices of Comparing in the Exhibitions "Cubism and Abstract Art" and "Documenta I"*), comparisons do not only have their place in the evaluative judgments of spectators and art critics (as already developed with the practices of connoisseurship studied in Joris C. Heyder's contribution). However, by means of spatial arrangements and displays, exhibitions and presentations in museums themselves enable, stimulate, and perform comparisons. Hence, Hochkirchen's examples from the middle of the 20th century show that museums and exhibitions create their own narratives of modernism. By suggesting temporalities via the differences and similarities of artworks that inevitably carry implicit temporal indices, curators and art critics displayed those kinds of comparative settings and storylines that implied the corresponding framework of modernist history. Therefore, their practices induced a term and phenomenon such as "modernity" or "modernism" going far beyond just art history. By taking this approach, the chapter explicitly draws attention to interrelations between comparative practices and concepts or experiences of time.

Studying comparative practices in detail offers a different view on history in general. Whereas many well-established comparisons seem to draw on either dichotomies or on results of long-lasting developments, a closer look reveals a surprising complexity of short-ranged transformations, renegotiations, and historical change. The dynamics of comparative practices sometimes allow the compared objects, the *comparata*, to stay in place while the framework, the perspectives, and the *tertium comparationis* change implicitly. Or, vice versa, an established framework organizing the comparisons slowly relates the differences and similarities of the *comparata* in unforeseen new and different ways, thus changing the whole picture. Therefore, the analysis of the shifting, recalibrating, and changing of comparative practices does not just deepen and strengthen the way a relational history might operate without falling back on the assumption of seemingly strong binaries, entities, or dichotomies. It also delivers an insight into how historical change is about to happen on the microlevel of everyday comparative practices and discourses that range from the basic forms of perception, judging, and knowing to the structuring of reality; and it does this by discerning cultural patterns of differences and similarities between human beings, religions, morals, societies, or civilizations.

The contemporary digitalization, at the latest, has brought to mind that media and technologies contribute heavily to the formation and transformation of comparative practices—be it through new media such as money exchange (in Gary Shaw's example of the Middle Ages) or the printing press; or through numbers, graphs, statistics, or algorithms. Technologies change the way comparing is conducted on a daily basis, and they change the way we reconstruct the past and do historical research. The final contribution in this volume by Anna Maria Neubert and Silke Schwandt (*Comparing in the Digital Age: About the Transformation of Practices*) presents an outlook on how contemporary and future comparative practices are being remodeled by digital devices. Again, comparing as a practice sets in motion an unpredictable dynamic that does not leave the *comparata* untouched and does not leave the frame of references in place. As much as digital analyses—as demonstrated by Neubert and Schwandt—will shed a new light and provide new research on the historical practices of comparing, this general "transformation" of relating and comparing objects of knowledge that is coming about through digitalization will also strongly influence our everyday practices of perceiving, learning, and knowing. Practices and patterns of comparing have shaped history in what were previously unknown ways; they will also go on to shape the future in many unpredictable ways as well.

References

ARISTOTLE, *Rhetoric*, Cambridge 2010.
BHABHA, Homi, *The Location of Culture*, New York 1994.
BHATTI, Anil/KIMMICH, Dorothee (eds.), *Similarity. A Paradigme for Culture Theory*, New Delhi 2018.
BORGHOSSIAN, Paul, *Fear of Knowledge: Against Relativism and Constructivism*, Oxford 2006.
BUUNK, Bram P./MUSSWEILER, Thomas, New Directions in Social Comparison Research, in: *European Journal of Social Psychology* 31 (2001), 467–475.
CANDEA, Matei, Going Full Frontal: Two Modalities of Comparison in Social Anthropology, in: Renaud Gagné/Simon Goldhill/Geoffrey E.R. Lloyd (eds.), *Regimes of Comparatism. Frameworks of Comparison in History, Religion and Anthropology*, Leiden/Boston 2019, 343–371.
CANDEA, Matei, *Comparison in Anthropology. The Impossible Method*, Cambridge 2018.
CARRIER, Martin, Incommensurability and Empirical Comparability: The Case of the Phlogiston Theory, in: Peter Gärdenfors/Jan Woleński/Katarzyna Kijania-Placek (eds.), *In the Scope of Logic, Methodology and Philosophy of Science*, Dordrecht 2002, 551–564.
CARRIER, Martin, Changing Laws and Shifting Concepts. On the Nature and Impact of Incommensurability, in: *Boston Studies in the Philosophy of Science* 216 (2001), 65-90.
CHANG, Ruth, *Making Comparisons Count*, London/New York 2002.
CHEAH, Pheng, The Material World of Comparison, in: Rita Felski/Susan Stanford Friedman (eds.), *Comparison: Theories, Approaches, Uses*, Baltimore 2013, 168–190.
CHEAH, Pheng, Grounds of Comparison, in: *Diacritics* 29 (1999), 3-18.

CHOW, Rey, The Old/New Question of Comparison in Literary Studies: A Post-European Perspective, in: *English Literary History* 71 (2004), 289–311.

CLAVIJERO, Francisco Javier, *History of Mexico*, London 1787.

DESCARTES, René, Rules for the Direction of the Mind, in: John Cottingham/Robert Stoothoff/Dugald Murdoch (eds.), *The Philosophical Writings of Descartes*, vol. I, Cambridge 1985.

DESCOLA, Philippe, Anthropological Comparatisms: Generalisations, Symmetrisation, Bifurcation, in: Renaud Gagné/Simon Goldhill/Geoffrey E.R. Lloyd (eds.), *Regimes of Comparatism. Frameworks of Comparison in History, Religion and Anthropology*, Leiden/Boston 2019, 402–417.

DETIENNE, Marcel, *Comparing the Incomparable*, Stanford 2008.

EDMOND, Jacob, No Discipline: An Introduction to "The Indiscipline of Comparison", in: *Comparative Literature Studies* 53 (2016), 647–659.

EGGERS, Michael, *Vergleichendes Erkennen. Zur Wissenschaftsgeschichte und zur Epistemologie des Vergleichs und zur Genealogie der Komparatistik*, Heidelberg 2016.

ENGLE MERRY, Sally, Measuring the World. Indicators, Human Rights, and Global Governance, in: *Current Anthropology* 52 (2011), 83–95.

EPPLE, Angelika, Comparing Europe and the Americas: The Dispute of the New World between the Sixteenth and Nineteenth Centuries, in: Willibald Steinmetz (ed.), *The Force of Comparison*, New York/Oxford 2019, 137–163.

EPPLE, Angelika/ERHART, Walter (eds.), *Die Welt beobachten. Praktiken des Vergleichens*, Frankfurt a. M./New York 2015.

ERHART, Walter, Weltreisen, Weltwissen, Weltvergleich – Perspektiven der Forschung, in: *Internationales Archiv für Sozialgeschichte der deutschen Literatur* 42 (2017), 292–321.

ETTE, Ottmar, Die 'Berliner Debatte' um die Neue Welt. Globalisierung aus der Perspektive der europäischen Aufklärung, in: Vicente Bernaschina/Tobias Kraft/Anne Kraume (eds.), *Globalisierung in Zeiten der Aufklärung. Texte und Kontexte zur 'Berliner Debatte' um die Neue Welt (17./18. Jh.)*, Frankfurt a.M. 2015, 27–55.

FABIAN, Johannes, *Time and the Other*, New York 1983.

FEISTINGER, Leon, A Theory of Social Comparison Processes, in: *Human Relations* 7 (1954), 117–140.

FERRIS, David, Why Compare?, in: Ali Behdat/Dominic Thomas (eds.), *A Companion to Comparative Literature*, Malden/Oxford 2011, 28–45.

FOUCAULT, Michel: *The Order of Things: An Archaeology of the Human Sciences*, New York 1970.

FRIEDMAN, Susan Stanford, Why not Compare?, in: Rita Felski/Susan Stanford Friedman (eds.), *Comparison: Theories, Approaches, Uses*, Baltimore 2013, 34–45.

FÜSSEL, Marian/NEU, Tim, Doing Discourse. Diskursiver Wandel aus praxeologischer Perspektive, in: Achim Landwehr (ed.), *Diskursiver Wandel*, Wiesbaden 2010, 213–235.

GAGNÉ, Renaud/GOLDHILL, Simon/LLOYD, Geoffrey E.R. (eds.), *Regimes of Comparatism. Frameworks of Comparison in History, Religion and Anthropology*, Leiden/Boston 2019.

GARCILASO DE LA VEGA, Inca, *Primera Parte de los Commentarios Reales*, Lisbon 1609.

GRAFTON, Anthony, Comparisons Compared: A Study in the Early Modern Roots of Cultural History, in: Renaud Gagné/Simon Goldhill/Geoffrey E. R. Lloyd (eds.), *Regimes of Comparatism. Frameworks of Comparison in History, Religion and Anthropology*, Leiden/Boston 2019, 18–48.

GRAVE, Johannes, Comparative Practices and their Implications: The Case of Comparative Viewing, in: Willibald Steinmetz (ed.), *The Force of Comparison. A New Perspective on Modern European History and the Contemporary World*, New York/Oxford 2019, 53–79.

GRAVE, Johannes, Vergleichen als Praxis. Vorüberlegungen zu einer praxistheoretisch orientierten Untersuchung von Vergleichen, in: Angelika Epple/Walter Erhart (eds.), *Die Welt beobachten. Praktiken des Vergleichens*, Frankfurt a. M./New York 2015, 135–159.

HANDLER, Richard, The Uses of Incommensurability in Anthropology, in: Rita Felski/Susan Stanford Friedman (eds.), *Comparison: Theories, Approaches, Uses*, Baltimore 2013, 271–291.

HAUPT, Hans-Gerhard, Comparative History, in: *International Encyclopedia of the Social and Behavioral Sciences* 4, Amsterdam 2001, 2397–2403.

HAUPT, Hans-Gerhard/KOCKA, Jürgen (eds.), *Comparative and Transnational History. Central European Approaches and New Perspectives*, New York/Oxford 2009.

HEINTZ, Bettina: "Wir leben im Zeitalter der Vergleichung". Perspektiven einer Soziologie des Vergleichs, in: *Zeitschrift für Soziologie* 45 (2016), 305–323.

HEINTZ, Bettina, Welterzeugung durch Zahlen. Modelle politischer Differenzierung in internationalen Statistiken 1948-2010, in: Cornelia Bohn/Arno Schubbach/Leon Wansleben (eds.), *Welterzeugung durch Bilder*, Stuttgart 2012, 7–39.

HEINTZ, Bettina, Numerische Differenz. Überlegungen zu einer Soziologie des (quantitativen) Vergleichs, in: *Zeitschrift für Soziologie* 39 (2010), 162–181.

HEINTZ, Bettina/WERRON, Tobias, Wie ist Globalisierung möglich? Zur Entstehung globaler Vergleichshorizonte am Beispiel von Wissenschaft und Sport, in: *Kölner Zeitschrift für Soziologie und Sozialpsychologie* 63 (2011), 359–394.

HEMPEL, Carl G., *Grundzüge der Begriffsbildung in der empirischen Wissenschaft*, Düsseldorf 1974.

JUCQUOIS, Guy/VIELLE, Christophe (eds.), *Le comparatism dans les sciences de l'homme*, Brussels 2000.

KAELBLE, Hartmut, *Der Historische Vergleich. Eine Einführung zum 19. und 20. Jahrhundert*, Frankfurt a.M./New York 1999.

KUHN, Thomas, *The Structure of Scientific Revolutions*, Chicago 1962.

LLOYD, Geoffrey E. R., *Analogical Investigations. Historical and Cross-Cultural Perspectives on Human Reasoning*, Cambridge 2015.

LUHMANN, Niklas, Kultur als historischer Begriff, in: Niklas Luhmann, *Gesellschaftsstruktur und Semantik 4*, Frankfurt a. M. 1999, 31–54.

LÜSEBRINK, Hans-Jürgen, De L'usage de la comparaison dans les écrits des Jésuites sur les Amériques, in: Marc André Bernier/Clorinda Donato/Hans-Jürgen Lüsebrink (eds.), *Jesuit Accounts of the Colonial Americas. Intercultural Transfers, Intellectual Disputes, And Textualities*, Toronto 2014, 418–436.

MATTHES, Joachim, The Operation called "Vergleichen", in: Joachim Matthes (ed.), *Zwischen den Kulturen? Die Sozialwissenschaften vor dem Problem des Kulturvergleichs*. Göttingen 1992, 75-99.

MAU, Steffen, *Das metrische Wir. Über die Quantifizierung des Sozialen*, Berlin 2017.

MAUZ, Andreas/SASS, Hartmut von (eds.), *Hermeneutik des Vergleichs. Strukturen, Anwendungen und Grenzen komparativer Verfahren*, Würzburg 2011.

MELAS, Natalie, Merely Comparative, in: *PMLA* 128 (2013), 652–659.

MELAS, Natalie, *All the Difference in the World. Postcoloniality and the Ends of Comparison*, Stanford 2007.

MIGNOLO, Walter, On Comparison: Who is Comparing What and Why? In: Rita Felski/Susan Stanford Friedman (eds.), *Comparison: Theories, Approaches, Uses*, Baltimore 2013, 99–111.

NIETZSCHE, Friedrich, *Human, all too human*, Cambridge 1996.

PAGDEN, Anthony, *European Encounters with the New World: From Renaissance to Romanticism*, New Haven 1993.

PETERS, Christine, Reisen und Vergleichen. Praktiken des Vergleichens in Alexander von Humboldts "Reise in die Äquinoktial-Gegenden des Neuen Kontinents" und Adam Johann von Krusensterns "Reise um die Welt", in: *Internationales Archiv für Sozialgeschichte der deutschen Literatur* 42 (2017), 441–465.

PORTER, David, The Crisis of Comparison and the World Literature Debate, in: *Profession* 2011, 244–258.

POTH, Christian H., *Episodic visual cognition: Implications for object and short-term recognition*, URL: https://pub.uni-bielefeld.de/publication/2911816 [last accessed December 9, 2019].

QUINTILIAN, *Institutes of Oratory*. 4 vols. Cambridge 1980.

RADHAKRISHNAN, Rajagopalan, Why Compare?, in: *New Literary History* 40 (2009), 453–475.

RECKWITZ, Andreas, Grundelemente einer Theorie sozialer Praktiken. Eine sozialtheoretische Perspektive, in: *Zeitschrift für Soziologie* 32 (2003), 282–301.

Rubiés, Joan-Pau, Comparing Cultures in the Early Modern World: Hierarchies, Genealogies and the Idea of European Modernity, in: Renaud Gagné/Simon Goldhill/Geoffrey E.R. Lloyd (eds.), *Regimes of Comparatism. Frameworks of Comparison in History, Religion and Anthropology*, Leiden/Boston 2019, 116–176.

Sass, Hartmut von, Vergleiche(n). Ein hermeneutischer Rund- und Sinkflug, in: Andreas Mautz/Hartmut von Sass (eds.), *Hermeneutik des Vergleichs*, Würzburg 2011, 25–48.

Saussy, Haun, *Are We Comparing Yet? On Standards, Justice, and Incomparability*, Bielefeld 2019.

Schatzki, Theodore R., *Social Practices. A Wittgensteinian Approach to Human Activity and the Social*, Cambridge 1996.

Schiessl, Max, Untersuchungen über die Ideenassociation und ihren Einfluß auf den Erkenntnisakt, in: *Zeitschrift für Philosophie und philosophische Kritik*, Neue Folge 61 (1872), 247–282.

Schmitt, Vanessa et al., Do Monkeys Compare Themselves to Others?, in: *Animal Cognition* 19 (2016), 417–428.

Schulz, Raimund, *Als Odysseus staunte. Die griechische Sicht des Fremden und das ethnographische Vergleichen von Homer bis Herodot*, Göttingen 2020.

Simonis, Annette/Simonis, Linda (eds.), *Kulturen des Vergleichens*, Heidelberg 2016.

Solte-Gresser, Ann Christiane/Lüsebrink, Hans-Jürgen/Schmeling, Manfred (eds.), *Zwischen Transfer und Vergleich. Theorien und Methoden der Literatur- und Kulturbeziehungen aus deutsch-französischer Perspektive*, Stuttgart 2013.

Steinmetz, Willibald (ed.), *The Force of Comparison. A New Perspective on Modern European History and the Contemporary World*, New York/Oxford 2019.

Steinmetz, Willibald, Above/below, better/worse, or simply different? Metamorphoses of Social Comparison, 1600–1900, in: Steinmetz, Willibald (ed.), *The Force of Comparison. A New Perspective on Modern European History and the Contemporary World*, New York/Oxford 2019, 80–112.

Stoler, Ann Laura, Tense and Tender Ties: The Politics of Comparison in North American History and (Post)Colonial Studies, in: *The Journal of American History* 88 (3/2001), 829–865.

Stroumsa, Guy G., History of Religions: The Comparative Moment, in: Renaud Gagné/Simon Goldhill/Geoffrey E.R. Lloyd (eds.), *Regimes of Comparatism. Frameworks of Comparison in History, Religion and Anthropology*, Leiden/Boston 2019, 318–342.

Suls, Jerry/Wheeler, Ladd (eds.), *Handbook of Social Comparison. Theory and Research*, New York 2000.

Welskopp, Thomas, Vergleichende Geschichte, in: *Europäische Geschichte Online*, URL: http://ieg-ego.eu/de/threads/theorien-und-methoden/vergleichende-geschichte, [last accessed December 9, 2019].

Xie, Ming, What Does the Comparative to Theory?, in: *PMLA* 128 (2013), 676–682.

XIE, Ming, *Conditions of Comparison: Reflections on Comparative Intercultural Inquiry*, London 2011.

ZHANG, Longxi, Comparison and Correspondence: Revisiting an Old Idea for the Present Time, in: *Comparative Literature Studies* 53 (4/2016), 766–785.

ZHANG, Longxi, Crossroads, Distant Killing, and Translation: On the Ethics and Politics of Comparison, in: Rita Felski/Susan Stanford Friedman (eds.), *Comparison: Theories, Approaches, Uses*, Baltimore 2013, 46–63.

ZIMA, Peter, *Vergleichende Wissenschaften*, Tübingen 2000.

Preliminary Typology of Comparative Utterances
A Tree and Some Binaries

Kirill Postoutenko

Abstract[1]

The paper presents the classification of comparative utterances and offsets its logical precision with a sample of typical inconsistencies informing comparisons in poems, political speeches, and religious pamphlets. Unlike formal languages used in logical, mathematical or mechanical communication, discourse- or image-based communication favors (or, at least, tolerates) fuzzy logic: as a result, some seemingly robust and basic differentiations (such as comparability vs. incomparability, or quantitative vs. qualitative differences) routinely cancel out or duplicate each other without jeopardizing narrative clarity. Rather than despairing at the sight of collapsing binary oppositions, the paper argues for careful conceptual and semantic analysis of bundling between various comparative expressions which may unearth regular correlations between text types and patterns of comparison. Along with the studies of comparative inventories as such, the assessment of formation, spread, and historical development of such recurrent patterns may be the contribution of conceptual history to the wider study of comparative practices.

I.

The importance of tracking comparative utterances down and putting them in order is manifold: On the one hand, the ubiquity of comparisons is readily admitted.[2]

---

1 Designed and conceived as part of a collaborative effort, this article benefited from criticism offered at various stages by Angelika Epple, Joris Heyder, and Thomas Müller.
2 Just a few examples: *"in omni ratiocinatione per comparationem tantùm veritatem præcise cognoscamus"* (Rene Descartes, Regulae ad directionem ingenii [1619], in: Rene Descartes, Œuvres, T. X, Paris 1908, 439); "The faculty of comparison is that which produces ideas, and is therefore the foundation of intellect, and all the intellectual powers of the human mind" (James B. Lord Monboddo, *Of the Origin and Progress of Language*, Vol.1, Edinburgh 1779, 68); *"Toutes les opérations de notre esprit sont des comparaisons. Ainsi, une idée générale ne peut être, d'une part, que le résultat des comparaisons que l'esprit a faites, de l'autre, que l'aperçu de celles qu'il doit faire"* (Henri Saint-Simon, *Science de l'homme, physiologie religieuse*, Paris 1813.—Henri Saint-

On the other, there is little understanding of how comparative operations in human minds are mapped onto codes routinely employed in communication. Even if this gap between mental and social facts is not going to be closed at once, one could at least attempt to look at comparisons from the standpoint of their realization in interactional practices.[3] The first step in this direction would be to go beyond single words or even word combinations and focus instead on utterances (understood here as elementary units of social interaction, usually expressed by means of verbal language).[4] Next, one could try to find out to what extent their internal organization of comparative discourse mimics the systemic construction of language. It stands to reason that privative opposition (a vs. $-a$) could be a convenient common denominator:[5] Whereas comparisons are commonly described as combinations of similarities and differences,[6] various subsystems of language (and, somewhat less convincingly, discourse, society, and culture) have been portrayed in the linguistics,

---

Simon, *Œuvres choisies*, Paris 1859, 212); and *"Denken heißt Vergleichen!"* (Walther Rathenau, *"Auf dem Fechtboden des Geistes – Aphorismen aus seinen Notizbüchern"* [1922], Wiesbaden 1953, 71). There is a growing body of literature on these and similar absolutizations of comparison: Peter Galison, Descartes's Comparisons: From the Invisible to the Visible, in: *Isis* 75 (2/1984), 311–326, see 323. Melvin Richter, Two Eighteenth-Century Senses of "Comparison" in Locke and Montesquieu, in: *Jahrbuch für Recht und Ethik* 8 (2000), 385-406, see 391, 405; Walter D. Mignolo, Who Is Comparing What and Why?, in: Rita Felski/Susan Stanford Friedman (eds.), *Comparison: Theories, Approaches, Uses*, Baltimore 2013, 99-119, see 99; Willibald Steinmetz, 'Vergleich'– eine begriffsgeschichtliche Skizze, in: Angelika Epple/Walter Erhart (eds.), *Die Welt beobachten. Praktiken des Vergleichens*, Frankfurt a. M./New York 2015, 91; Michael Eggers, *Vergleichendes Erkennen*, Heidelberg 2016, 35.

3   Cf. Bettina Heintz, Numerische Differenz. Überlegungen zu einer Soziologie des (quantitativen) Vergleichs, in: *Zeitschrift für Soziologie* 39 (3/2010), 162-181, see 163.

4   Cf. John R. Searle, *Speech Acts: An Essay in the Philosophy of Language*, Cambridge 1978, 16. Actually, there are sound reasons for going even further, including reception of comparative messages into the contents of comparative utterances and the treatment of minimal exchanges between sender and recipient as atoms of a comparative world (cf. Harvey B. Sarles, *Language and Human Nature*, Minneapolis 1985, 35). This could be truly indispensable for visual comparisons in which comparative intentions are shared more equally between communication participants than is the case in verbal texts (cf. Heintz, Numerische Differenz, 164; Johannes Grave, Vergleichen als Praxis. Vorüberlegungen zu einer praxistheoretisch orientierten Untersuchung von Vergleichen, in: Angelika Epple/Walter Erhart (eds.), *Die Welt beobachten. Praktiken des Vergleichens*, Frankfurt a. M./New York 2015, 135-159, see 146; Steinmetz, 'Vergleich', see 108–110). However, just one exception aside, this article confines itself to words not images, and taking up the speaker's/writer's position is probably an acceptable price for avoiding excessive intricacy.

5   See the convenient summary: Ryszard Zuber, Privative opposition as a semantic relation, in: *Journal of Pragmatics* 4 (5/1980), 413–424.

6   For the representative sample, see: Günther Schenk/Andrej Krause, Vergleich, in: Joachim Ritter/Karlfried Gründer/Gottfried Gabriel (eds.), *Historisches Wörterbuch der Philosophie* 11 (2001), 677.

philosophy, and anthropology of the last two centuries as huge bundles of distinctive features.[7] Even if comparisons cannot be broken down into privative oppositions as easily as, say, phonemes in language—and they probably cannot—they might still reveal some internal organization akin to the one of language, which, in turn, would simplify the study of their embeddedness in discourse.[8]

Before proceeding with the actual classification of comparative utterances, though, it might be worth sketching out the convergences and divergences informing distinctions within comparative and discursive practices.

Generally speaking, all communicative activities generate information by producing handfuls of minimal differences against the backdrops of innumerable similarities. Whereas in the theater, we watch a play about real life and find most of the things seen and heard eminently familiar; in speech production, we mostly try to choose the right words for the respective (inner and outer) situations. What we do *not* normally do is go over the likenesses and unlikenesses between life and theater while enjoying a play, or explore all possible alternatives to saying "hello!" to a friend. If we did not behave like machines in most of the situations calling for decisions, our brains would explode, and life would stop in its tracks.[9] But "most" is not "all", and occasionally we do step out of the flow and ponder upon the relations between theater and life[10] or associate words with minimal distinctive features.[11] The

---

7 Cf. Claude Lévi-Strauss, The Structural Study of Myth, in: *The Journal of American Folklore* 68 (270/1955), 428-444, see 443; Roman Jakobson, Verbal Communication, in: *Scientific American* 227 (3/1972), 72-81, see 76; Algirdas J. Greimas, *On Meaning. Selected Writings in Semiotic Theory*, Minneapolis 1987, 65; Edna Andrews, *Markedness Theory: The Union of Asymmetry and Semiosis in Language*, Durham 1990, 154; Edwin L. Batistella, *The Logic of Markedness*, New York 1996, 17.

8 Perhaps the analogy between phonetics and comparisons is even less misleading than it might seem: One of the founding fathers of structuralism admitted "multidimensional oppositions" into the club of phonetic distinctive feartures (cf. Nikolai S. Trubetskoy, *Grundzüge der Phonologie*, Prague 1939, 60). That is probably as close as we can get to comparisons in the realm of formal linguistic analysis (for some related ideas, see: Ruth Chang, *Making Comparisons Count*, London 2014, 25).

9 A case in point is everyday communication that simply cannot afford doubts about its semantics: "'I had a flat tire'.—'What do you mean, you had a flat tire?' She appeared momentarily stunned. Then she answered in a hostile way: 'What do you mean "What do you mean?" A flat tire is a flat tire. That is what I meant. Nothing special. What a crazy question!'" (Harold Garfinkel, *Studies in Ethnomethodology*, Englewood Cliffs 1967, 50).

10 "In ordinary life she tried to stifle a passion that she knew very well was ridiculous, a love that was unworthy of the woman she was, and she steeled herself to think as little as possible of the wretched boy who had wrought such havoc with her; but when she came to this scene she let herself go" (William Somerset Maugham, Theatre [1937], in: W. Somerset Maugham, *Selected Novels*, Vol. 1, Melbourne 1953, 145).

11 "In spoken English, the difference between a stop [in *p*] and a continuant consonant [in *f*], other things being equal, may change the meaning of the message" (Roman Jakobson, The Cardinal Dichotomy of Language, in: Ruth Nanda Anshen (ed.), *Language: An Inquiry into its Meaning and Function*, Port Washington, NZ 1971, 155-173, see 157). Jakobson makes use of the

only practical way to perform this associating and pondering upon is to produce comparative utterances—reflexive references to semantic oppositions within the social world. But why should they be "reflexive"? And what does "reflexivity" mean in this context? This probably calls for a more detailed explication of the variance between difference and comparison briefly outlined above.[12]

Each and every sign necessarily relates to its "own" visual, verbal, or tactile code in two different ways: First, it marks the difference between the meaningful order of the linguistic system and the noisy chaos of its environment. Whatever may be the meanings of the letter *i* in the English language, it stands first and foremost for human speech per se (as opposed to twittering or a waterfall's roar). Second, the same *i* signals dissimilarity within innumerable minimal pairs in English in which its presence (or absence) changes the meaning of words (e.g., big vs. bag, big vs. beg, big vs. bog, big vs. bug, bin vs. ban, bin vs. ben, bin vs. Ben, bin vs. bun, etc. etc.).[13] But, again, in order to talk, write, speak, or listen, none of these distinctive features must be invoked or even registered—normally, they just accompany communication without being noticed, let alone reflected upon. By means of being used, human language refers to itself as a functionally differentiated, intact, and relatively autonomous system fit for transmitting messages, as opposed to its disorderly, mute, and uncertain surroundings. In this self-referential activity of language, humans play a modest instrumental role, jointly upholding the semantic potential of verbal communication without giving it pause.

Things change, however, when the semantic differentials of language become the object of human reflection. Reflexivity presupposes agency, which, in the case of communication, means ability to arbitrarily select and combine distinctive features of language on the top of preexisting semantic differentials that are more or less obligatory for all competent language users. Nonreflective beings—such as thermometers—cannot but continually mirror environmental pressures in an externally predetermined way. In contrast, the subjects of reflection are capable of cherry-picking data about the environment and using them for various adaptative purposes.[14] *Homo sapiens*, for instance, can use a thermometer twice a day to scan

---

following passage that conveniently singles out the minmal pair of comparata but stops short of comparing them: "'Did you say pig, or fig?' said the Cat. 'I said pig,' replied Alice" (Lewis Caroll, *Alice's Adventures in Wonderland*, London 1866, 92).

12   The following two paragraphs are loosely related to the opposition between the "basal self-reference" of the communicative system and its "reflexivity" suggested by Niklas Luhmann (Niklas Luhmann, *Soziale Systeme: Grundriß einer allgemeinen Theorie*, Frankfurt a. M. 1987, 600–601).

13   Needless to say, the same kind of minimal pairs (for example, *"hot* versus *cold"*) exists in semantics (Matt Davies, *Advances in Stylistics: Oppositions and Ideology in News Discourse*, London 2014, 94).

14   For this distinction, see: Heinz von Foerster, *Wissen und Gewissen: Versuch einer Brücke*, Frankfurt a. M. 1993, 246.

and write down day and night temperatures all year round; significantly, she or he can also comment upon the device's aesthetic features as opposed to the other thermometers in the neighborhood. The last detail is quite important for understanding that human selections within verbal semantics are in no way limited by the respective language's established distinctive features. For example, when Ernst Jünger calls the vowels [a] and [o] high and sublime, [i] and [u] low and dark, and puts [e] in-between,[15] he is ignoring both the phonetics and the phonology of German. Indeed, Jünger's grouping reflects neither the vocal features of the sounds in question (roundness, openness, and depth of the sounds vary more within the groups than between them)[16] nor their ability to differentiate within minimal lexical pairs (see examples in the previous paragraph). However, the writer's indifference to the basic distinctive features of the sounds he is writing about does not make his remarks incomprehensible or even senseless: Quite on the contrary, Jünger furnishes us with unique information unavailable anywhere else. This is achieved in three more or less simultaneous steps:

1. Selecting a novel set of objects (*comparata*) picked out of the existing phonosemantic repertoire of German ([a] + [o]), [e], and ([i]
2. Producing a fresh bundle of distinctive features by relating those objects—positively or negatively—to the previously unapplied categories "height," "sublimity," and "likeness" (*tertia*)
3. Forcing these selections and combinations into a procrustean bed of verbal language (*utterance*)

At first glance, the comparative utterance thus defined looks like a motley collection of its creator's whims, and stands in stark contrast to the impersonal regularity of speech in general. To take this impression at face value, however, would be a grotesque exaggeration of the actual disparity between comparative and linguistic semantics. To be sure, the role of sender in the production of comparative utterances is highly important—particularly if we are talking about the verbal

---

15 "*Innerhalb dieser größeren Spannung drängt sich die allgemeine Beobachtung auf, daß das A und das O den hohen und erhabenen, das I und das U den tieferen und dunklen Dingen zugewandt sind, während das E eine Mittellage beizubehalten strebt. An eine Welt des A und O schließt sich eine andere des I und U, und es klingen hier nicht nur die Unterschiede zwischen Oben und Unten, Hoch und Tief, Flamme und Dunkelheit, sondern auch die zwischen Vater und Mutter an*" (Ernst Jünger, Lob der Vokale [1934], in: Ernst Jünger, *Sämtliche Werke* (Band 14, Essays VI), Stuttgart 2015, 28). Like many other authors writing about vowels, Jünger fails to differentiate them clearly from letters. However, the unmistakable reference to sound (*klingen*) allows, it seems, for the phonetic interpretation of his passage.
16 Cf. Thomas Becker, *Das Vokalsystem der deutschen Standardsprache*, Frankfurt a. M. 1998, 11–13.

and written language.[17] However, similar to all other human choices, selections in comparative practices are rarely made completely at random. On the one hand, the number of comparata and tertia is subject to the constraints imposed by human computational capacity.[18] On the other hand, the specific references to both things compared and grounds for comparison are conditioned multiply by various social factors (which are yet to be studied closely). All in all, both comparisons and language operate in a gray zone between rational and irrational,[19] and every taxonomy of comparative utterances (**II**) is likely to be seriously compromised by the limited consistency of verbal language, not to mention further irregularities provoked by intrusions of political, legal, and moral systems (**III**). Still, what may look like a disappointment for a classificator with structuralist leanings could hopefully serve as a roadmap (replete with detour signs) for the historical studies of comparative practices (**IV**).

II.

If we attempt to conceptualize comparative utterances as a bundle of distinctive features reminiscent of verbal language, their classification could look like this (Fig.1).

The heterogeneity—a tree and a list of binaries—is inevitable because some privative oppositions have a more limited scope than others: All comparative utterances must be either qualitative (**4.1**) or quantitative (**4.2**), but only some—namely, messages containing the division between relative (**1.1.2.2.1**) and absolute (**1.1.2.2.2**) grading comparisons—makes sense only within comparative sentences displaying or featuring gradability (**1.1.2.2**). As for the second part of the typology, it could be, in principle, formulated as a list of formally impeccable but clumsy-sounding privative oppositions (e.g., "**4.1** *Nonquantitative* comparisons vs. **4.2** Quantitative

---

17 Cf. Andreas Dorschel, Einwände gegen das Vergleichen, in: *Philosophisches Jahrbuch* 113 (1/2006), 178; Hartmut von Sass, Vergleiche(n). Ein hermeneutischer Rund- und Sinkflug, in: Andreas Mauz/Hartmut von Sass (eds.), *Hermeneutik des Vergleichs. Strukturen, Anwendungen und Grenzen komparativer Verfahren*, Würzburg 2011, 25-48, see 27; Angelika Epple/Walter Erhart, Die Welt beobachten. Praktiken des Vergleichens, in: Angelika Epple/Walter Erhart (eds.), *Die Welt beobachten. Praktiken des Vergleichens*, Frankfurt a. M./New York 2015, 7-31 see 18; Angelika Epple, Doing Comparisons – Ein praxeologischer Zugang zur Geschichte der Globalisierung/en, in: Angelika Epple/Walter Erhart (eds.), *Die Welt beobachten. Praktiken des Vergleichens*, Frankfurt a. M./New York 2015, 161-199, see 163.

18 See, for instance, Herbert A. Simon, A Behavioral Model of Rational Choice, in: *The Quarterly Journal of Economics* 69 (1/1955), 99-118, see 101.

19 See the characteristic admission from the bastions of generative grammar: Ray Jackendoff, *A User's Guide to Thought and Meaning*, Oxford 2012, 233–244.

comparisons"). Here, as elsewhere in the text, the pedantic precision is abandoned for the sake of readability.

Fig. 1

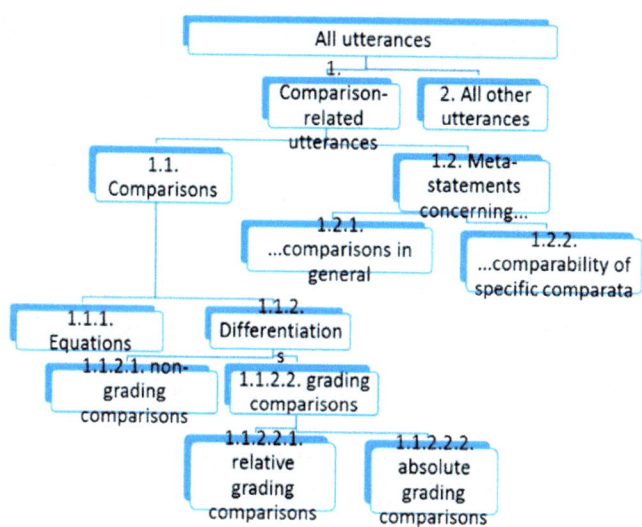

2.1 Narratives *vs.* **2.2** Sets
3.1 Evaluative comparisons *vs.* **3.2** Nonevaluative comparisons
4.1 Qualitative comparisons vs. **4.2** Quantitative comparisons
5.1 Comparisons with explicit *tertia comparationis* vs. **5.2** Comparisons without explicit *tertia comparationis*
6.1 Comparisons with all *comparata* present *vs.* **6.2** Comparisons with some *comparata* hidden
7.1 Self-comparisons *vs.* **7.2** Other-comparisons
8.1 Positive comparisons *vs.* **8.2** Negative comparisons
9.1 Nondiachronic comparisons *vs.* **9.2** Diachronic comparisons
10.1 Comparisons with x-*tium non datur* (finite sets) *vs.* **10.2** Comparisons without x-*tium non datur* (infinite sets).
11.1 Comparisons with exocentrically defined *comparata* vs. **11.2** Comparisons with egocentrically defined *comparata*
12.1 Reversible (symmetrical) *vs.* **12.2** Irreversible (asymmetrical) comparisons
13.1 Real comparisons *vs.* **13.2** Irreal comparisons
14.1 Auctorial *vs.* **14.2** Nonauctorial comparisons

1. Comparison-related utterances vs. 2. All other utterances

This privative opposition seems to be straightforward, almost perfunctory, but it does conceal some relatively fine distinctions invisible on the level of single lexemes. The first example should not raise any eyebrows:

(1). "The theoretical and practical problems of sustained strict comparison are enormous. Experienced comparatists, usually acutely aware of many of these difficulties, tend to skirt the pitfalls, make disclaimers, and lower their sights. Few comparatists compare, for they know the difficulties."[20]

The quotation features comparison professionals—specialists in comparative law ("comparatists") as well as their comparative practice ("compare")—so it comes as almost natural that this is a comparison-related utterance. The qualification "almost" refers to the unpopularity of comparisons described in the passage, but—even if this "few" comes perilously close to "nobody"—there is no denial that the passage somehow has to do with comparative practices (which may or may not take place).

Note, however, the counterexample:

(2). "Au cours de la première moitié du XXe siècle, les comparatistes évitent le mot comparaison."[21]

Here, too, we have two words related to comparisons, and one of them, as in the previous example, refers to scholars—this time, literary critics—dealing with comparisons. The second reference, however, has no discernible relation to the practices of comparing, describing lexical idiosyncrasies instead. True, common sense makes it likely that at least some comparatists mentioned in the passage could have engaged in some comparative activities as a part of their research, but the sentence neither confirms nor denies this supposition, focusing entirely on the word usage.

1.1 Comparisons vs. 1.2 Metastatements concerning comparisons

Having singled out the utterances having to do with comparison, it seems natural to tell the actual comparative utterances (X in relation n to Y is Z)[22] from the second-

---

20 William Twining, *The Great Juristic Bazaar: Jurists' Texts and Lawyers Stories*, London 2017, 182.
21 Daniel-Henri Pageaux, Littérature comparée et comparaisons, in: *Revue de Littérature comparée* 72 (3/1998), 285-307, see 289.
22 In this model of comparative utterance, I deliberately abstain from the misleading translation of verbal relational terms into logical symbols.

order statements *about* them ("*X in relation n to Y is Z*" *is a peculiar statement*). Logically, metastatements antecede their objects—first-order utterances.[23] However, cultural memory can turn this order backward. For example, the word combination "comparing apples and pears" is mostly known to the speakers of German as an allegory of ill-conceived appraisal. In the modern discursive field, it rarely descends from its homey metalevel and not infrequently climbs to the meta-metalevel, as in the following passage in which strongly suggesting the incomparability of both fruits is said to be "based upon a popular prejudice":

(1.2). "*Wer im Brustton der Überzeugung äußert, Äpfel und Birnen solle man nicht vergleichen, beruft sich auf ein verbreitetes Vorurteil.*"[24]

1.2.1 Metastatements concerning comparisons in general vs. 1.2.2 Metastatements concerning comparability of specific comparata in particular

Metastatements could be subdivided into references to comparison as a universal practice (*Comparisons are N*) and allusions to specific kinds or even cases of comparison (*The comparison [type of comparisons] X is N*). A good example of the first variety is a dictionary entry, which is normally supposed to provide a general overview of the notion in question. Wilhelm Krug's definition stands out as one of the very few second-order statements about comparisons that allow for the existence of more than two comparata:

(1.2.1). "*Comparation [...] ist Vergleichung, d. h. Gegeneinanderhaltung* **zweier oder mehrer Dinge**, *um sich ihrer Einerleiheit (Gleichheit, Parität) oder Verschiedenheit (Ungleichheit, Imparität) bewusst zu werden.*"[25]

In the second category, the variations of scope and modality are so enormous that each illustration would be more or less accidental. Bearing that in mind, it might make sense to use examples combining reference to various kinds and levels of comparisons in a single utterance: William James, for instance, constructs a comparison of metacomparisons: Grading simultaneous and successive comparisons in nearly every area of perception (from hearing to touch) on the scale between "easy"

---

23   Cf. Paul F. Strawson, *Introduction to Logical Theory* (Routledge Revivals [1952]), London 2012, 15.
24   Horst Wenzel, Initialen in der Manuskriptkultur und im digitalen Medium, in: Helga Lutz/Jan-Friedrich Missfelder/Tilo Renz (eds.), *Äpfel und Birnen. Illegitimes Vergleichen in den Kulturwissenschaften*, Bielefeld 2006, 41-56, see 175.
25   Wilhelm T. Krug, *Allgemeines Handwörterbuch der philosophischen Wissenschaften*, Band 1, A bis E, Leipzig 1832, 499. I am grateful to Olga Sabelfeld for sharing this quotation with me.

and "impossible," he goes on to compare data not only within, but also between perceptual categories:

> **(1.2.2)**. "It is easier to compare successive than simultaneous sounds, easier to compare two weights or two temperatures by testing one after the other with the same hand, than by using both hands and comparing both at once. [...] in the case of smell and taste it is well-nigh impossible to compare simultaneous impressions at all."[26]

1.1.1 Equations *vs.* 1.1.2 Differentiations[27]

In the sample of definitions of comparison presented in the note 1, both similarity and dissimilarity of comparata feature prominently. Hence, the breakdown of comparative utterances into equations and differentiations, stressing respectively likeness and unlikeness of comparata in relation to specific tertia, comes as no surprise. So, in John Locke's identification between the unity of consciousness and human identity, the differences are overshadowed by similarities:

> **(1.1.1)**. "As far as this consciousness can be extended backwards to any past action or thought, so far reaches the identity of that person; it is the same self now it was then."[28]

The otherwise polyvalent opposition between "now" and "then" is used here merely to set two comparata apart (i.e., to manufacture a set of discrete human states out of the continuous memory flow). For the sake of the argument made by Locke, it could be replaced by nearly any other two-word marker of *différance*. Inversely, in Claude d'Abbeville's account of his missionary travel to Brazil, the corresponding spatial difference "here" versus "there" is intensified by a triple reiteration of dissimilarity between the animal worlds of continental France and the isle of Maranhão:

> **(1.1.2)**. *"Nous ne voyons icy rien de toutes les especes d'animaux qu'ils ont là, comme aussi ils n'ont rien de semblable aux nostres, au moins qu'il ne soit de beaucoup differend."*[29]

1.1.2.1. Nongrading comparisons *vs.* 1.1.2.2. Grading comparisons[30]

The very concept of *tertium comparationis* seemingly calls for a scalar interpretation of differences between comparata: If there is a common ground *n* for comparing X

---

26   William James, *The Principles of Psychology* [1907], New York 2007, 495.
27   On this opposition in general, see: Willibald Steinmetz, 'Vergleich', 88–89.
28   John Locke, *An Essay Concerning Human Understanding* [1689], Vol.1, New York 1894, 449.
29   Claude d'Abbeville, *Histoire de la mission des pères Capucins en l'isle de Maragnan et terres circonvoisines*, Paris 1614, 208.
30   On this contradistinction, see: Willibald Steinmetz. 'Vergleich', 88.

and Y, both comparata should somehow be graded on the scale in which the value of n is expressed in some terms (numbers?) falling between 0 and ∞. However, not all tertia are gradable—one person can hardly be more vegan than another, and the language—under normal circumstances—cannot be "most" or "least English."[31] As with many other minimal pairs, the opposition between grading and nongrading comparisons could be rather indifferent to the content of comparison: In other words, the same situation could be described in one or another way with minimal semantic variation. The case in point is Voltaire's obsession with the so-called "Jewish self-alienation" depicted at various occasions as either the nongradable apartness:

(1.1.2.1). *"Les Juifs, par leur religion et leur politique, étaient séparés du reste du monde"*[32]

or the highest degree of self-imposed isolation:

(1.1.2.2). *"La nation juive est la plus singulière qui jamais ait été dans le monde."*[33]

1.1.2.2.1 Relative grading comparisons vs. 1.1.2.2.2 Absolute grading comparisons

Once the grounds of comparison allow for gradation, the choice between relative and absolute values of comparata is usually expressed by, respectively, comparative and superlative adjectives ("usually" does not mean "always"—see below **III**, 1.1.2.2.1/1.1.2.2.2). The first variety could be exemplified by one of the numerous excursions of the seventeenth-century French classicism to its Antique origins. In contrast to many of his contemporaries, though, François Blondel was not preoccupied with the cross-evaluation of the "new" and "old" classicism, but more interested in the internal hierarchy of the latter. In his opinion, Horace was beating Pindar on no less than nine counts (*"knowledge," "equality," "tenderness," "playfulness," "faultlessness," "nobility of thought," "precision," "purity of language,"* and, finally, *"cheerfulness"*):

(1.1.2.2.1). *"Mais pour Horace, il a bien plus d'étenduë de sçavoir et de connaissances que Pindare, plus d'égalité, plus de douceur & d'enjoüement & beaucoup moins de deffauts. Ses pensées ont aussi tres nobles, mais sa diction est bien plus correcte & plus épurée […], et souvent mesme beaucoup plus heureux."*[34]

---

31   Peter Klecha, *Bridging the Divide: Scalarity and Modality*, Chicago, IL 2014, 24.
32   Voltaire, [Review:] De Sacra Poesi Hebraeorum Praelectiones Academicae, Oxonii Habitae, a Roberto Lowth, A. M. Poeticae Publico Praelectore, etc. [1764], in: André Versaille (ed.), *Dictionnaire de la pensée de Voltaire par lui-même*, Paris 1994, 677.
33   Voltaire, Des Juifs [1756], in: André Versaille (ed.), *Dictionnaire de la pensée de Voltaire par lui-même*, Paris 1994, 688.
34   François Blondel, *Comparaison de Pindare et d'Horace*, Amsterdam 1686, 77.

In its turn, the absolute grading comparison features prominently in Alfred Tennyson's apologetic obituary to Arthur Wellesley, the famous longtime head of the British army:

(**1.1.2.2.2**). "Thine island loves thee well, thou famous man, // The greatest sailor since our world began".[35]

2.1 Narratives vs. 2.2 Sets

Verbal languages can produce differences and engender comparisons in ways unknown to other kinds of messaging systems, which probably has to do, among other things, with their directionality. Whatever makes it to the surface of language—tertia, comparata, and relations thereof—gets organized in narratives (the sequences of before–after relations between signs that are loosely modeled upon time asymmetry).[36] At various speeds and levels, information is being generated, and it is only natural that the logical reflexivity (*for every A, A = A*) is one of the first candidates for going down in the mighty stream of one-way semantic differentiations. In its classical form, the equation $A = A$ is a symmetrical tautology with no possibility of differentiation, let alone comparison.[37] But, of course, narrative asymmetries are bound to eclipse this time invariance—for example, supplying information that would create a gap between the first and the second *A* notwithstanding their homonymy. The case in point is the following passage from the *Divine Comedy*:

(**2.1**). "*Io cominciai: 'Voi siete il padre mio; // voi mi date a parlar tutta baldezza; // voi mi levate sì, ch'i' son più ch'io.*"[38]

The narrator's accolade to Cacciaguida is structured as an anaphoric series of sentences all beginning with the second-person personal pronoun *voi* ("*you are my father ...*/*you prompt me to speak with bold assurance*"). It is, however, in the last sentence that this list begins referring to a change ("*you raise me up*") that—together with the causal relation between the main and the subordinate clause—makes possible, if

---

35 Alfred Tennyson, Ode on the Death of the Duke of Wellington (1852), in: Alfred Tennyson, *Selected Poetry*, London 1995, 112.
36 For a general pespective, see, for instance: David K. Berlo, *The Process of Communication: An Introduction to Theory and Practice*, New York 1960, 25; Vilém Flusser, *Kommunikologie*, Frankfurt a. M. 1996, 38, 55–56; Kirill Postoutenko, From Asymmetries to Concepts, in: Kay Junge/Kirill Postoutenko (eds.), *Asymmetrical Concepts after Reinhart Koselleck: Historical Semantics and Beyond*, Bielefeld 2011, 197-251, see 199.
37 Cf. Martin Heidegger, *Identität und Differenz*, Pfüllingen 1957, 5.
38 Dante, *Paradiso* [1321], Indianapolis, IN 2017, 154.

not necessary, the difference and comparison between the earlier ("smaller") and later ("bigger") self ("*I am more than I*").[39]

However, many narratives tend to offset their sequential and directional properties by gravitating toward sets (messages with semantics that are invariant to the ordering of their elements).[40] In the example below, this includes asyndetic coordination between individual sentences and the multiple repetitions of the *tertium* ("*law*") in their same (final) position:

> **(2.2)**. "*Die Heiden hatten ein ungeschriebenes, die Juden ein geschriebenes Gesetz, die Christen ein Exempel, ein Vorbild, ein sichtbares, persönlich lebendiges Gesetz, ein Fleisch gewordenes, ein menschliches Gesetz.*"[41]

To be sure, these symmetrical tendencies do a fine job of selecting clearly commensurable *comparata*: The utterance even includes one privative opposition expressed by the presence/absence of the negative prefix *un-* ("*written*"/"*unwritten law*"). Still, the internal cohesion of the sentence hangs by a thread: In the absence of explicit references to comparison, it is held together by some minor syntactic features such as omission of similar verbs in the coordinated sentences. In sets, the sender's comparative autonomy is at its lowest: No other kind of comparative utterances stands so close to rankings, lists, pendants, and other interaction-based comparisons (see also note 3 above).[42]

---

39   A slightly more intricate case of dissociation between two homonyms preceding their comparison is the example from August Strindberg's drama with the telling title *Crimes and Crimes* (1899) discussed below in 7.2.
40   Cf. Bernard Bolzano, *Einleitung zur Größenlehre und erste Begriffe der allgemeinen Größenlehre* [1841], Stuttgart 1975, 152.
41   Ludwig Feuerbach, *Das Wesen des Christentums* [1849], Stuttgart 1994, 226.
42   The problem is dealt with in the following article: Susan Stanford Friedman, Why Not Compare?, in: *PMLA* 126 (3/2011), 753-762, see 758. Of course, the situation changes dramatically in favor of a full-blown, solid comparison when the set is complemented by a special comparative sentence. This is the case of a summary demolition of monotheism undertaken by Holbach that begins like a *différance* with some genealogical undertones, and ends as equation: "*La Religion d'Égypte servit évidemment de base à la Religion de Moyse, qui en bannit le culte des idoles; Moyse ne fut qu'un Egyptien schismatique. Le Christianisme n'est qu'un Judaïsme réformé. Le Mahométisme est composé du Judaisme, du Christianisme & de l'ancienne Religion d'Arabie. [...] Toutes les religions, anciennes et modernes, se sont mutuellement empruntées leurs abstraites rêveries et leurs ridicules pratiques*" (Jean Meslier [Paul Henri Thiry, baron d'Holbach], *Le bon-sens; ou, Idées naturelles opposées aux Idées surnaturelles*, Londres/Amsterdam 1772, 292).

3.1 Evaluative comparisons vs. 3.2 Nonevaluative comparisons[43]

A handful of old and influential traditions treat all practices of comparison as evaluations, tacitly smuggling in grading comparisons (1.1.2.2) as the middle ground. For example, the institution of ranking strives to reduce all aesthetic, intellectual, and economic diversity to a single scale grading relative goodness of objects compared.[44] In a similar vein, reflexive comparisons in which one of the comparata is identifiable with the sender of the comparative message are routinely nailed to the one-dimensional scalarity assessing humanness or propriety, with the maximal value placed as close as possible to the messenger.[45] For Arthur de Gobineau, one of the founders of modern xenophobia, speaking about races was indeed impossible without an absolute grading comparison (1.1.2.2.2) placing his own ethnic group at the top of any racial ladder. In the nineteenth century, European anti-Semitism switched from religion to economics without hile retaining much of its rhetorical ammunition.[46] Under such circumstances, Gobineau's choice of *tertium* ("*beauty*") was more or less random:

---

43   For the discussion of this opposition, see: Heintz, Numerische Differenz, 165; Mauz/Sass, Vergleiche verstehen , 13–14; Willibald Steinmetz, 'Vergleich', 88–89 ; Grave, Vergleichen als Praxis, 144.

44   Cf. Carlos Spoerhase, Das Maß der Potsdamer Garde, Die ästhetische Vorgeschichte des Rankings in der europäischen Literatur- und Kunstkritik des 18. Jahrhunderts, in: *Jahrbuch der Deutschen Schillergesellschaft* 58 (2014), 90–126; Willibald Steinmetz, Above/below, better/worse, or simply different? Metamorphoses of Social Comparisons, 1600–1900, in: Steinmetz, Willibald (ed.), *The Force of Comparison. A New Perspective on Modern European History and the Contemporary World*, New York/Oxford 2019, 80–112; Tobias Werron/Leopold Ringel, Rankings in a comparative perspective, (manuscript, 2015); Bettina Heintz, "Wir leben im Zeitalter der Vergleichung." Perspektiven einer Soziologie des Vergleichs, in: *Zeitschrift für Soziologie* 45 (5/2016), 305-323, see 307, 311; Elena Esposito, What's Observed in a Rating? Rankings as Orientation in the Face of Uncertainty, (manuscript, 2016); Robert Eberhardt, Bilderpaare und Pendanthängung. Praxeologische Überlegungen zum Ordnungssinn, (manuscript, 2019).

45   For a general overview of this tradition, comdemned first by Rousseau in *Émile, ou de l'éducation* (1762) and later by Nietzsche in *Menschliches, Allzumenschliches* (1879) but still influential, see: Joachim Matthes, The Operation Called 'Vergleichen', in: Joachim Matthes, *Zwischen den Kulturen? Die Sozialwissenschaften vor dem Problem des Kulturvergleichs*, Göttingen 1992, 75-100, see 75; William J. T. Mitchell, Why Comparisons are Odious, in: *World Literature Today* 70 (2/1996), 321-324, see 32; Pheng Cheah, The Material World of Comparison, in: *New Literary History* 40 (3/2009), 523-545, see 524; Willibald Steinmetz, Above/below.

46   Cf. Kirill Postoutenko, Wandering as Circulation: Dostoevsky and Marx on the "Jewish Question", in: Gideon Reuveni/Sarah Wobick-Segev (eds.), *The Economy in Jewish History: New Perspectives on the Interrelationship between Ethnicity and Economic Life*, New York/Oxford 2010, 43–61.

(3.1). *"Je n'hésite pas à reconnaître la race blanche pour supérieure en beauté à toutes les autres."*[47]

But, of course, it is perfectly possible to compare differently colored people—and many other phenomena—without either grading or evaluating them. The following example is no less common for the modern urban anthropology as Gobineau's racist outbursts were for late nineteenth-century France:

(3.2). "A high percentage of whites reside in the suburbs, whereas African Americans and other minorities, especially the less affluent, mainly occupy urban areas left behind by white flight."[48]

Those on the lookout for biases would probably frown upon lumping together diverse "minorities," but, in fact, neither Whiteness nor affluency have any firm association with any values—positive or negative—in this passage.

4.1 Qualitative comparisons vs. 4.2 Quantitative comparisons[49]

Along with the streamlining of evaluation by means of grading, briefly discussed a couple of paragraphs above, the use of numbers for comparing quantities is a standard, if equally controversial, way of reducing comparative complexity. The pros and contras of both abstractions are perhaps best illustrated by juxtaposing quantitative and qualitative comparisons between the same comparata:

(4.1). *Entre tous ces Cantons [...], Bale a la plus belle ville, le sejour & le rendez-vous de plusieurs sçavans.*[50]

(4.2). *Basel zählt, ohnerachtet sie die größte Stadt der Schweiz ist, nur 15000 Einwohner; also noch nicht halb so viel, wie Brünn.*[51]

Calling Basel—in a slightly circuitous way—the most beautiful city in Switzerland, Pierre Du Val is no doubt aware of the highly subjective nature of his comparison. Sensing that his personal opinion may not be enough to sway the readers' minds, the French geographer seems to deploy a thinly veiled *argumentum ad verecundiam*, citing the residence of "many scholars" in Basel as possible proof of his high opinion of the city. In contrast, the objectivity of the measure used in the second statement is clearly beyond doubt: Even if one—in theory—agrees with Christian C. Andre's calculation, nobody would ask *why* the city with 15,000 inhabitants is bigger than the one with a population of 14,999 or less. However, sensing

---

47 Arthur de Gobineau, *Essai sur l'inégalité des races humaines*, Paris 1853, 256.
48 Charles M. Lamb, *Housing Segregation in Suburban America since 1960*, Cambridge 2005, 2.
49 On this difference, see: Grave, Vergleichen als Praxis, 144.
50 Pierre Du Val, *La géographie universelle*, Band 2, Lyon, 1688, 482.
51 Christian C. Andre, *Hesperus, oder Belehrung und Unterhaltung für die Bewohner des österreichischen Staats*, Brünn, 1810, 281.

that an absolute grading quantitative comparison (**1.1.2.2.2 + 4.2**) is too abstract for his fellow Austro-Hungarians (what does it *feel* like a city of 15,000?), Andre literally drives his argument home—comparing remote Basel with his hometown Brno. This second comparative utterance is actually a pair of intertwined relative grading comparisons: Whereas its quantitative part (**1.1.2.2.1 + 4.2**) gives a rough approximation of Basel's population in relation to the Moravian capital (**less than a half*), the second, qualitative part (**1.1.2.2.1 + 4.1**), conveys the author's personal evaluation of this difference (*"the biggest city of Switzerland [...]is not even a half as big as Brno"*). In the examples shown, the complementary semantics of comparative utterances countervails their precision and intelligibility; however, as one could see below (**III, 4.1/4.2**), the interweaving of quantitative and qualitative comparisons can also cause incoherence and confusion—deliberate or not.

5.1 Comparisons with explicit tertia *comparationis* vs. 5.2 Comparisons without explicit *tertia comparationis*[52]

Including *tertium comparationis* into the body of comparative utterance is an option, not an obligation. One could easily expect many explicit *tertia* in contexts possessing the stringent requirement of clarity (such as science or law). But this is also possible in politics, if the real or fake precision can contribute to the speaker's aura of knowledgeable authority. In a thoroughly calculated radio speech on national defense given a year after the outbreak of World War 2, the president Franklin D. Roosevelt offers a characteristic sequence of two almost identical (and closely linked) comparisons:

> (**5.1, 5.2**). "The navy is far stronger today than at any peace-time period in the whole long history of the nation. In hitting power and efficiency, I would even make the assertion that it is stronger today than it was during the World War [I]."[53]

Here, as in the case above (**II, 4.2**), combining two diametrically opposed distinctive features within a single comparative utterance creates synergy that goes beyond individual persuasive potentials of the same comparisons standing alone. Understandably, the first sentence lacks details: No experienced politician would barrage his nonspecialist audiences with numerous technical parameters of the past and present American naval fleets in a short radio appearance. Instead, the unspecific positive evaluation of the defense capabilities is probably aimed at conveying to the worried nation a sense of watertight security around the United States. Still, for the more inquisitive part of the audience, which may be looking for an expert

---

52   On this minimal pair, see: Mauz/Sass, *Hermeneutik des Vergleichs*, 13–14.
53   Franklin D. Roosevelt, Fireside Chat 15 (On National Defense [1940]), in: Franklin D. Roosevelt, *FDR's Fireside Chats*, Norman, OK 1992, 156.

rather than a savior at the helm of the state, a couple of *tertia* ("*hitting power and efficiency*") are displayed to make essentially the same statement *look* like an indisputable quantitative comparison. Because no exact figures are given, and a cautious subjective qualification ("I would even make the assertion") is added to the claim, the objective validity of the second comparison is not much higher than that of the first one. Still, together, the two parts of the comparative utterance make a desired impression of a broad and yet factual statement confirming the safety of the United States in the approaching war.

6.1 Comparisons with all *comparata* present *vs.* 6.2 Comparisons with some *comparata* hidden[54]

As shown in the previous paragraph, the flexibility of comparisons allows for omission of *tertia* from the comparative discourse without jeopardizing their meanings (and sometimes even boosting their pragmatic efficiency). In a similar vein, there is no requirement for all *comparata* to be present in the text of a comparative utterance in order for a comparison to be valid. Juxtaposing comparisons with all (**6.1**) and some (**6.2**) *comparata* present, one can see how this variation makes it possible to achieve both semantic diversification and precision within relatively constrained semantic areas. Five years past his exploratory trip to Russia, Marquis Astolphe de Custine, a French conservative essayist and travel writer, produced a damning indictment of Russian society and politics:

> (**6.1**). "*Le servage se légalisait en Russie quand on l'abolissait dans le reste de l'Europe*".[55]
> (**6.2**). "*S'il n'y a pas de justice en Russie, vous voyez qu'il y a des habitudes plus fortes que la loi suprême*".[56]

In the first sentence, lamenting the reluctance of tsars to press ahead with the abolition of serfdom, de Custine skillfully balances on the verge of redundancy to highlight the legal gap between the two *comparata*. Indeed, if "*Russia*" and "*the rest of Europe*" constitute a privative opposition, as they do, the utterance "*serfdom was abolished in the rest of Europe*" means, by default, that in Russia, at the same time, it remained in force. Still, despite little evidence to back his claim, de Custine insists on an even sharper distinction between the "*legalization*" and **de-legalization* ("*abolition*") of serfdom, choosing a contrary opposition instead of a contradictory one. It seems at least likely that for the sake of de Custine's argument, the presence of both *comparata* in the comparative utterance is not essential; however, supported by noticeable syntactical, grammatical, and even phonetic parallelism (the verbs

---

54   On this distinction, see: Mauz/Sass, *Hermeneutik des Vergleichs*, 13–14.
55   Astolphe de Custine, *La Russie en 1839*, Bruxelles 1844, 109.
56   Custine, *La Russie*, 162.

légalisait and *abolissait* have the same stress pattern of – – – /), the hypercorrect contradistinction does make for good prose.

Alternatively, the second example of comparative utterance from de Custine's travel diary, also devoted to Russia's difficult relations with moral and legal norms, is (at least) one *comparatum* short. Uttered by a disgruntled Russian, the saying *"there is no justice in Russia"* could well be understood outside of the comparative context; but in the mouth of a skeptical foreigner, it is likely to have comparative semantics. But "likely" is not "certain," and de Custine seems to reduce this ambiguity by adding the second—this time relative grading—comparison (**1.1.2.2.2 + 6.2**): Russia is said to be governed by "customs stronger than the supreme law." The author of *Russia in 1839* neither defines the areas over which this *suprema lex* holds sway nor spells out what kind of traditions trump it in the Russian empire. However, both the general historical and the local narrative contexts—for instance, the abundance of statements such as (**II, 6.1**) in de Custine's text—tell us where the diarist's heart lies and where the counterpole to Russia's lack of justice is located. To sum up, both complete and partial presence of *comparata* in comparative utterances can provide templates for specialization of their semantics, although the choices between reinforcement and attenuation of differences are more context- than form-specific.

7.1 Self-Comparisons *vs.* 7.2 Other-Comparisons

The opposition *self/other* is commonly used in European discourse for reflexive messages telling their sender (*self*) from her or his environment (which could be anything from the message's recipient to a piece of inanimate nature). But there is also a tradition of using the term "*self*" (or, rather –*self*) to refer to the different states of the same object separated by time and/or space; and it is this meaning that will be used for the minimal pair below.[57] Although such gaps seem to correlate with differences (from the temporal "evolution" to the spatial "variety"), they could also suggest similarity despite detachment, and this contrastive semantics looks tailormade for praising—or cursing—permanence against the odds (see also **III, 3.1/3.2**). For instance, Joaquin Ruiz de Morales comes up with an anaphoric series of equations (**1.1.1 + 7.1**) between "Spain then" and "Spain now" in order to describe—and decry—the immutability of the Spanish political landscape: Clearly, he is fed up with the perpetual choices between the bad and the worse, the underdevelopment of citizenship, the unpopularity of the liberal cause, and the blind faith in the crown:

---

57   See the survey of both traditions: Kirill Postoutenko, Social Identity as a Complementarity of Performance and Proposition, in: Edmundo Balsemão Pires/Burkhard Nonnenmacher/Stefan Buttner-von Stulpnagel (eds.), *Bezüge des Selbst. Selbstreferentielle Prozesse in philosophischen Perspektiven*, Coimbra 2010, 271–298.

(7.1). *"España se encontraba entonces, como se encuentra ahora, en la anómala situacion de no poder estirpar lo malo, sin esponerse de unu manera cierta á un mal mayor. En España ahora como entonces, los ciudadanos no constituían la gran masa de la nacion, sino que estaban circunscriptos al límite numérico de un partido, del partido liberal; y decimos que ni entonces ni ahora eran ciudadanos todos los españoles [...] Y en España entonces como ahora habia una gran mayoría realista, para la cual no hay mas que el rey, y siempre el rey."*[58]

In its turn, other-comparisons deal with any sets of comparata except references to the same object in different situations. This sounds like an extremely broad definition, and, indeed, the bulk of comparative utterances employ not self- but other-comparisons. However, the unmarkedness of the latter does not disqualify them from the same interplay between differences and similarities that one could observe in (7.1). For instance, the superficial sameness of homonyms can conceal their essential difference:

(7.2). *"ADOLPHE (liksom för sig sjelf). Det fins brott som icke upptas i lagboken, och de äro de värsta, ty dem måste vi straffa sjelfva, och ingen domare är så sträng som vi."*[59]

As in (6.2), the second comparatum is missing, but is easily restored through the provocative title (*Crimes and Crimes*) and the undoing of negation (**crimes ~~un~~mentioned in the Criminal Code* vs. *"crimes unmentioned in the Criminal Code"*). The semantic opposition is then reinforced by means of an absolute grading comparison: the judges—who are the perpetrators themselves—are the harshest one could imagine (1.1.2.2.2). With such a forceful support, the opposition between comparata, invisible at first, looks like a deep abyss (see also III, 1.1.2.2.1/1.1.2.2.2).

8.1 Positive comparisons *vs.* 8.2 Negative comparisons

The centrality of negativity for comparative practices stems from the fact that it can by itself produce seamless sets of distinctive features. Thus, the pair *affirmation/negation* has noticeable affinity with the structure of privative opposition in which the presence of a certain distinctive feature is opposed to its absence (see

---

[58] Joaquin Ruiz de Morales, *Historia de la milicia nacional: desde su creación hasta nuestros días*, Madrid 1856, 180.
[59] August Strindberg, *Brott och brott*, Stockholm 1899, 263. The quote is eerily reminiscent of the aforecited example from *Divine Comedy* (II, 2.1) in which the relative grading comparison (1.1.2.2.1) differentiates between comparata despite their formal indistinguishability (both are first-person personal pronouns referring to the same person). However, in Dante's poem, one deals with a self-comparison (7.1); whereas Strindberg, on the contrary, emphasizes the essential difference of the *comparata*.

multiple examples in **I**). At first sight, this resemblance turns negation into a difference-making machine capable of greatly simplifying comparative practices: In fact, it is much easier to compare *white* and *nonwhite* than, say, *white* and *red* right away. Alas, negation has no special place in natural language: unless one is inclined to go one level up and negate the whole statement—which, in most contexts, would make for an awkward sentence (*I deny that this wine is white*)—the relation between negation and differentiation of *comparata* is all but straightforward.[60] Still, it appears possible to detect a special role of negation in comparative utterances—which is underspecification: Unless one deals with externally defined binaries such as chess colors, "white" normally means "white" and "nonwhite" stands for "anything but white" (where "anything" could fluctuate between 2 in wines and ∞ in paints). Indeed, when applied to single words within a sentence, negation may well produce an approximate equation (**1.1.1**) instead of an expected full-blown differentiation (**1.1.2**):

(**8.2**). "ἄρα τηλικοίδε γέροντες ἄνδρες πρὸς ἀλλήλους σπουδῇ διαλεγόμενοι ἐλάθομεν ἡμᾶς αὐτοὺς παίδων οὐδὲν διαφέροντες." (*Plato Crit. 49 a–b*)

Mildly scolding Crito (and himself) for being "no different from children in serious discussions," Socrates stops short of stating direct equivalence between the two ages: Unlike in mathematics, double negation in natural language does not yield affirmation: "no different" is not the same as "similar."[61]

As for the positive comparisons, being more semantically determined in specific comparative utterances, they are also less determined as an analytical category: In effect, all comparative utterances without negation should be classified as manifestations of positive comparisons. Another equation—a simile—turning the popular identification between "savages" and "children" upside down, is chosen as a typical example:

---

60 "That negation applies to sentences is true only for artificial languages [...]. In natural languages, negation applies to expressions other than sentences, namely words and non-sentential phrases." (Jaakko Hintikka, Negation in Logic and Natural Reasoning, in: *Linguistics and Philosophy* 25 (5–6/2002), 585-600, see 590—591; cf. Paul A. Chilton, Negation as Maximal Distance in Discourse Space Theory, in: *Groupe de Recherches Anglo-Américaines de Tours* 1 (2006), 351–378; Ernesto Napoli, Negation, in: *Grazer Philosophische Studien* 72 (2006), 233-252, see 233). For a general interdisciplinary perspective, see: Kirill Postoutenko, Der Antichrist und seine Widersacher, in: Kay Junge et al. (eds.), *Kippfiguren. Ambivalenz in Bewegung*, Weilerswist 2013, 143–152.

61 As Stoics did not fail to notice, "Socrates is just" entails, but is not entailed by, "Socrates is not unjust" (see: Laurence Horn, *A Natural History of Negation*, Chicago, IL 1989, 22; Michael Israel, The Pragmatics of Polarity, in: Laurence Horn/Gregory Ward (eds.), *Handbook of Pragmatics*, New York 2004, 701-723, see 711).

(8.1). *"Wendet man ein, es sei nur darum, weil Kinder wie Wilde einander ähnlich sehen und ähnlich reden und handeln, und man also an fremden nur die Echos der eignen Liebe habe."*⁶²

9.1 Nondiachronic comparisons *vs.* 9.2 Diachronic comparisons

With this pair of distinctive features, we have another classical privative opposition with vastly unequal level of semantic certainty on both ends. The marked part of the binary (**9.2.**) subsumes all "before–after" comparisons regardless of their location in the past, present, and future. Conversely, its unmarked counterpart (**9.1**) includes an even wider and much more mixed assortment of comparative utterances disregarding relations of their comparata to all kinds of time markers. This sounds like a covert reference to synchronicity, but, in fact, it is perfectly possible to compare things with obviously different time spans and orientations without paying attention to them.⁶³ The case in point is another simile

> (**9.1**). "It is a beauteous evening, calm and free, // The holy time is quiet as a Nun // Breathless with adoration."⁶⁴

Few would consider "the holy time"—one single end of the day—analogous (let alone identical) with the lifetime of a holy sister, but this incommensurability has no bearing upon the meaning of comparative utterance: Clearly, the alleged quietness of comparata is perceived as their summary feature, unrelated to any specific date(s) or duration(s).

---

62   Jean Paul, Die Elternliebe gegen Kinder. Eine einfache Erzählung [1810], in: Jean Paul [Richter], *Werke* (Band 2, Teil 3), München 1978, 217. Unlike metaphors in which "dangerous" (in Aristotle's words) equations are packaged as subject–predicate constructions (*X is Y*), similes operate with discernible sets (usually pairs) of comparata separated, if not created, by a preposition "like" (*X is like Y*)—cf. Aristotle, Rh. 3.4; Willibald Steinmetz. 'Vergleich', 88–89, 91). The typical absence of an explicit *tertium* encourages similes to stray far away from the paths of everyday language, which explains their popularity in poetry (cf. Mitchell, Why Comparisons are Odious, 322; Stefano Agosti, Remarques sur la figure de la comparaison dans la poésie baudelairienne, in: Dagmar Wieser/Patrick Labarthe (eds.), *Mémoire et oubli dans le lyrisme européen: hommage à John E. Jackson*, Paris 2008, 57; Bertrand Marschal, De quelques comparaisons baudelairiennes, in: Max Milner (ed.), *Baudelaire toujours: hommage à Claude Pichois*, Paris 2007, 189-201, see 189; Stefan Willer, The problem of theorizing comparisons (in science and literature), in: *Neohelicon* 41 (2/2014), 371–380; Adam Gargani, Similes as Poetic Comparisons, in: *Lingua* 175–176 (2016), 54–68.
63   This is one of the reasons for rejecting the term "synchronic" that is widely used in other typologies,see: Grave, Vergleichen als Praxis, 144; Sass, Vergleiche(n), 34.
64   William Wordsworth, "It is a beauteous evening, calm and free..." [1802], in: William Wordsworth, *Poetical Works*, London 1896, 332.

Alternatively, the temporal gaps are often exposed and laid bare in diachronic comparisons, although this explicitness may well conceal the indeterminacy concerning comparata and even tertia, as in the following passage:

(9.2). "Ah, Dickens! You admired him, **then**! That is where we **moderns** agree with you."[65]

It seems natural to associate diachronic comparisons with self-comparisons (7.1), because relating A at the time $t°$ to B at the time $t° ^{±n}$ appears to lack common ground. This association holds ground even if the readerships compared clearly differ from one another, because relations can also function as comparata.[66] In this respect, the relations between Dickens and his readers in the capitalist past (referred to as "then") and in the communist future (disguised in the utopian novel as the narrator's present) are indeed quite similar.[67] It is probably not too far-fetched to see the role of such equations in utopian/dystopian narratives as conveying the sense of continuity between unbridgeable gaps in social experience.[68] However, in less extravagant genres. They could merely suggest the internal coherence of the development of genres and other discursive subsystems.[69]

10.1 Comparisons with *tertium, quartum, quintum,* [...] etc., *non datur* (finite sets) *vs.* 10.2 Comparisons without *tertium, quartum, quintum,* [...] etc., *non datur* (infinite sets)

All comparisons, regardless of their type and medium, operate with two distinctly different kinds of comparata sets: Whereas in the first case, the selection of comparata is attributed to the environment and is commonly seen as "objective," that is, beyond anyone's control (**10.1**); in the second, the things compared are seen as more

---

65 Edward Bellamy, *Looking Backward from 2000 to 1887* [1887], Boston 2012, 73.
66 Cf. Grave, Vergleichen als Praxis, 144. The tradition goes at least as far back as Aristotle (cf. Ursula Coope, *Time for Aristotle: Physics IV. 10–14*, Oxford 2005, 116).
67 Cf. Niklas Luhmann, Weltzeit und Systemgeschichte. Über Beziehungen zwischen Zeithorizonten und sozialen Strukturen gesellschaftlicher Systeme, in: Peter Ch. Ludz (ed.), *Soziologie und Sozialgeschichte*, Opladen 1973, 81–115, see 91.
68 "Jede Zukunftsutopie muß zeitliche Kontinuitäten unterstellen, gleich ob sie offen thematisiert werden oder nicht" (Reinhart Koselleck, Zeitschichten, Frankfurt a. M. 2000, 135–136).
69 The case in point ist the functional equivalence of successive stanzaic structures in German verse expressed through equation of relations verse/meaning "then" (in classicism) and "now" (in Baroque): "*Eine lyrische Strophe, die, wie der Alexandriner uns jetzt lang dünket, galt damals für eine schöne poetische Periode*" (Johann Gottfried von Herder, Früchte sogenannt – goldenen Zeiten des achtzehnten Jahrhunderts [1803], in: Johann Gottfried von Herder, *Sämtliche Werke*, Bände 9–10, Stuttgart 1862, 296).

or less freely chosen by the sender of the comparative message (**10.2**).⁷⁰ The first case can be illustrated by the habitual sets of binary oppositions pieced together in the attempt at worldly wisdom:

> (**10.1**). "What lies behind us and what lies before us are tiny matters compared to what lies within us. And when we bring what is within us out into the world, miracles happen."⁷¹

The pairs *before/behind* and *within/out in the world*, interlinked in the sentence in the X-like fashion, are commonly perceived as finite sets of comparata in verbal languages along with other orientational markers such as *here/there*, *life/death*, or *Asia/Africa/North America/South America/Antarctica/Europe/Australia*. Naturally, poetry and scholarship occasionally challenge and even change the contents of sets: For example, the planet Pluto was added to the list of planets in 1930, only to be removed from it in 2006.⁷² However, it is highly uncommon to change the set status between finite and infinite, although, as one could see below (note 72), the poetic discourse can be an exception.

Alternatively, some sets of comparata are perceived as dependent on the circumstances of their uses:

> (**10.2**). "*Dagegen hat die nordische Sage* **den Zusammenhang erhalten**, *während die deutschen Lieder, deren Daseyn und Inhalt andere Zeugnisse außer Zweifel setzen, gleichfalls* **verloren** *sind.*"⁷³

Of course, the choice of comparata here is also far from being accidental. Since Grimm had taken it upon himself to track down and contextualize the roots of German literary tradition, the disappearance of German folk poetry was cunningly contrasted with the preservation of the linguistically close Nordic tradition. Still, the history of oral poetic traditions is replete with lacunae, and the folklorist could have made his point just as easily by mentioning the lost texts of Archaic Greek or Early Arabic poetry. So, although the genre and topic do constrain the selection of comparata, this limitation is largely self-imposed following the choices made by the author of the comparative utterance.⁷⁴

---

70   This division has a long philosophical prehistory going back to the ancient wrangling about the status of relation (cf. Eelcko Ypma, La relation est-elle un être réel ou seulement un être de raison, d'après Jacques de Viterbe, in: Jean Jolivet/Zenon Kałuża/Alain de Libera (eds.), *Lectionum varietates: Hommage à Paul Vignaux*, Paris 1991, 155–162).
71   Cf. Henry S. Haskins, *Meditations in Wall Street*, New York 1940, 121.
72   Cf. David A. Weintraub, *Is Pluto a Planet? A Historical Journey through the Solar System*, Princeton 2007, 121–128.
73   Wilhelm Grimm, *Deutsche Heldensage* [1829], Berlin 1867, 2.
74   The opposition (10.1)/(10.2) gets compromised when the comparata and the tertium send conflicting signals to the reader about the semantics of comparative utterance. The case in point is the famous poem Vowels by Arthur Rimbaud: *A noir, E blanc, I rouge, U vert, O bleu*:

11.1 Comparisons with exocentrically defined *comparata* vs. 11.2 Comparisons with egocentrically defined *comparata*

The difference between "subjective" (speaker-based) selections of comparata and their "intersubjective" (environment-based) preselections concerns not only the configuration of comparative sets (as in (**10.1/10.2**) but also the wording of comparata: Whereas some references to the things compared can make sense only in relation to the speaker's position (*"you"/"the person next to me"/"stranger,"* etc.), others would be more or less invariant to it (*"mister X"/"the person at the podium"/"the teacher at school X"*). The difference could best be illustrated by relatively independent parts of the same sentence devoted to the cross-evaluation of American and European cities:

> (**11.1**). "I could see very much in New York, which contrasted favorably with what I had seen in Paris and London; (**11.2**) but, in one thing, that of cleanliness, I was sorry to notice that she fell far behind those old foreign cities."[75]

The first comparative utterance (**11.1**) contains an extremely vague relative grading comparison (**1.1.2.2.1**) without explicit *tertia comparationis* (**5.2**)—virtually all we can say is that, on many instances, the travel writer had a higher opinion of New York than Paris and London. Aside from a minor side remark hinting at Thompson's extensive sightseeing at all three locations, there is no information about the reasons for putting one city ahead of two others: To accept the positive evaluation (**3.1**) of New York on some unspecified counts, one has to trust the narrator's personal predisposition. For all that, the references to comparata are made in a thoroughly impersonal fashion, so that the utterance could be attributed to a travel writer from Paris, London, or any other place on earth.

---

voyelles, //Je dirai quelque jour vos naissances latentes: //A, noir corset velu des mouches éclatantes //Qui bombinent autour des puanteurs cruelles, //Golfes d'ombre; E, candeurs des vapeurs et des tentes, //Lances des glaciers fiers, rois blancs, frissons d'ombelles; //I, pourpres, sang craché, rire des lèvres belles //Dans la colère ou les ivresses pénitentes; //U, cycles, vibrements divins des mers virides, //Paix des pâtis semés d'animaux, paix des rides //Que l'alchimie imprime aux grands fronts studieux; //O, suprême Clairon plein des strideurs étranges, //Silences traversés des [Mondes et des Anges]: //—O l'Oméga, rayon violet de [Ses] Yeux! (Arthur Rimbaud, Voyelles [1871], in: Arthur Rimbaud, Œuvres, Paris 1983, 110.) The first line suggests, in fact, a sort of *"sextium non datur"*—the five colored letters stand for the full set of French vowels and are referred to as such. However, the main body of the poem challenges this tertium: The alleged vowels turn into random colors (black, white, red, green, and blue), iconic signs (V as a wave), and sounds (O as a trumpet). At the end, this murky hodgepodge of diverse comparata puts the original finiteness of the set of "vowels" (?) into question.

75 Zadock Thompson, *Journal of a Trip to London, Paris, and the Great Exhibition, in 1851*, Burlington 1852, 133.

As for the second half of the long sentence (**11.2**), it differs from the former one on many, if not most, counts. Most importantly, two of the three cities compared in the first half are named here in a way revealing the speaker's own position: By referring to Paris and London—but not New York—as "old foreign cities," the author discloses his belonging to the United States. This formal departure from the referential evenhandedness is amplified by the author's "sorrow" at the sight of New York lagging behind Paris and London. However, this emotional engagement is counterbalanced somewhat by the explicit reference to the *tertium comparationis* (**5.1**)—the "cleanliness" of the two cities in question: Thompson's patriotism could not be shared by Parisians or Londoners, but the common ground for comparisons provides experiential terrain for alternative evaluations. Taken together, both parts of the sentence neatly balance considerable personal engagement with relative impartiality.[76]

12.1 Reversible (symmetrical) *vs.* 12.2 Irreversible (asymmetrical) comparisons

The case made above (**II, 2.1/2.2**) for the asymmetry of narration in general (and comparative utterances in particular) has been tested briefly on the simplest possible symbolic expression of invariance to time (the logical reflexivity): In Dante's poem, the equation $A = A$ changed—literally—into $A > A$ because both the syntax and the lexicon of the line in question implied changes in its semantics; and, moreover, expressed the resulting difference by means of a relative grading comparison ("*I am more than I*") linking two first-person personal pronouns to one another (**2.1**). Expectedly, the logical symmetry (if $x = y$, then $y = x$), too, cannot always withstand the directionality of narration: In logic, $X = Y$ means the same as $Y = X$, but "*John is*

---

[76] Naturally, most of the comparisons with egocentrically defined comparata are not nearly as fair. Throughout the millennia, the prevailing tradition in cross-cultural comparisons was to egocentrically define the disjoint "other" as a manifestation of cultural, communicative, and moral inferiority under the motto "*L'enfer, c'est les autres*" (Jean-Paul Sartre, Huis clos, in: Jean Paul Sartre, *Théâtre I*, Paris 1947, 182).The case in point is the term "barbarians" summarily applied to disjoint groups whose only common feature was not belonging to the dominant sociopolitical discourse (cf. Reinhart Koselleck, *Vergangene Zukunft. Zur Semantik geschichtlicher Zeiten*, Frankfurt a. M. 1979, 211–259; João Feres Jr., Building a Typology of Forms of Misrecognition: Beyond the Republican-Hegelian Paradigm, in: *Contemporary Political Theory* 5 (2006), 259–277; Kirill Postoutenko, Asymmetrical Concepts and Political Asymmetries: A Comparative Glance at 20th Centuries Democracies and Totalitarianisms from a Discursive Standpoint, in: Kay Junge/Kirill Postoutenko (eds.), *Asymmetrical Concepts after Reinhart Koselleck: Historical Semantics and Beyond*, Bielefeld 2011, 81–114; Peter Strohschneider, Fremde in der Vormoderne. Über Negierbarkeitsverluste und Unbekanntheitsgewinne, in: Anja Becker (ed.), *Alterität als Leitkonzept für historisches Interpretieren* (Reihe: Deutsche Literatur, Bd. 8), Berlin 2012, 387–416.

my father" has a markedly different meaning from "*My father is John.*"[77] So it comes as no surprise that the schism between logic and narration within the semantics of verbal language becomes one of the distinctive features in the typology of comparative utterances. In such a conflict, many comparisons would side with logic, displaying a significant degree of symmetry. Consider the following sentence:

> **(12.1)**. "Amidst the enthusiasm, chivalry, or fanaticism of the other states of Europe, Venice stands, from first to last, like a masked statue; her coldness impenetrable, her exertion only aroused by the touch of a secret spring".[78]

The stark opposition between a single (former) city state and *all* "other states of Europe" could scarcely be seen as balanced, but, in terms of relations between comparata and their properties, it is quite reversible: Instead of saying that the comparata A and B have, respectively, attributes (X, Y, Z) and (M, N), one could state that A does not have M and N and B does not have X, Y, and Z. Indeed, it is possible to say that, while Venice lacks "enthusiasm, chivalry, or fanaticism," its counterimage has no "impenetrable coldness" and does not look like a "masked statue". To be sure, the elegance of Ruskin's style would be gone, but otherwise the comparison would be intact and mean pretty much the same. The sentence is reversible: It can move between positive (**8.1**) and negative (**8.2**) comparative utterances without losing much of its meaning.

This is not the case, however, with the following sentence:

> (12.2). "*Amsterdam est la Venise de Nord*".[79]

If we take this privative opposition at a face value, the two comparata—Amsterdam and Venice—share everything but location: the Dutch capital is in the north of Europe, and the capital city of the province Veneto, indeed, is to its south. But this description would be excessive, because, some exceptions aside, the latitudinal division of the globe has just two values—"above" and "below" the equator. The pair north/south is apparently employed here in this very sense—as a binary opposition, and a contrary one at that, with both positions marked. Under such circumstances, just one geographical reference, as in Cousin's text, is enough to figure out the other. What is "*not in the north*" is not just "*anywhere but in the north*"—it is "*in the south*"; the same, of course, is true for "*not in the south*"—it is nowhere else but "*in the north.*" This symmetry apparently allows one to turn around the comparative

---

77   Cf. Otto Jespersen, *The Philosophy of Grammar*, Woking/London 1963, 153.
78   John Ruskin, *The Stones of Venice*, London 1851, 6.
79   Victor Cousin, *De l'instruction publique en Allemagne*, Paris 1841, 253. The modifier "of the north" plays a crucial role here in assigning Cousin's saying to similes (comparisons), because it excludes the possibility of Amsterdam and Venice being the same thing (see Aristotle's distinction between "bow [is] a lyre" (a metaphor) and "bow [is] a lyre without strings" (a simile/comparison)—Aristotle Rh. 3.11.

utterance in the same way as the previous one: *Venice is the Amsterdam of the north must have the same meaning as "Amsterdam is the Venice of the north."[80] One tries, and . . . oops, it does not work: Wikipedia lists no less than 39 "Venices of the north," but not a single "Amsterdam of the south."[81] So the relation between comparata is asymmetrical indeed, and it is subject to further discussion whether the position of comparata in the sentence or their intrinsic meanings—if those factors can be separated at all—contribute to this violation of logic in a highly popular comparative utterance.

13.1 Real vs. 13.2 Irreal comparisons

Similar to the difference between the relative (**1.1.2.2.1**) and the absolute (**1.1.2.2.2**) grading comparisons, the opposition between real and irreal comparisons is linked closely to the choice between indicative (**13.1**) and other (subjunctive, conditional, imperative, interrogative) grammatical moods. For comparative utterances, the difference is relevant insofar as it may affect the distance between the comparata—in much the same way as literary fantasy (see note 59), dreams, wishes, or terrors expressed by means of ordinary language place less constraints upon the choices of comparata or tertia than observations of reality (whatever is taken for it).

Thus, the popular comparison between adults and children, already discussed above (see **8.1/8.2**), has a markedly different dynamics in indicative and irreal moods. Similar to Jean Paul and Plato, Lucretius portrays likeness across ages as a tangible part of everyday experience:

(13.1). "*nam vel uti pueri trepidant atque omnia caecis // in tenebris metuunt, sic nos in luce timemus // inter dum, nihilo quae sunt metuenda magis quam // quae pueri in tenebris pavitant finguntque futura.*"[82]

Paradoxically, this equation is amplified by an appended privative opposition of "darkness" (which scares children) and "light" (which fails to dispel the adults'

---

80   There is a more formal logical argument for reversibility based on the syntax of the comparative utterance. It consists of the subject *x* ("*Amsterdam*") and the predicate *y* ("*Venice*") with the modifier *z* ("*of the north*"). Syntax is not math, so we do not know if the modifier adds to or subtracts from the meaning of the predicate—but it does not matter. In the first case (the modifier *adds* to the meaning of the predicate), we have an equation x = y + z; in the second (the modifier *subtracts* from the meaning of the predicate), the respective formula is x = y − z. In the first case, "*Amsterdam is the Venice of North*" is $x = y + z$, and *Venice is the Amsterdam of North* is $y = x − z$. In the second case, "*Amsterdam is the Venice of North*" is $x = y − z$, and *Venice is the Amsterdam of North* is $y = x + z$. This, apparently, would work for all numbers—but not for words in a comparative utterance!

81   https://en.wikipedia.org/wiki/Venice_of_the_North [last accessed April 9, 2020].

82   Lucretius, *De rerum natura* (II, 55–58).

fears). Not only are the adults likened to children (because they, too, can be afraid); they are also shown to be more childish than children themselves (because while youngsters get scared at night, the grown-ups cannot get rid of their horrors in broad daylight).

In contrast, the very same equation between children and adults, put in one of the irreal moods in the Gospel, feels like a much bigger distance:

> **(13.2)**. "Unless you change and become like little children, you will never enter the kingdom of heaven".[83]

Besides the double negation, which substantially decreases the determinacy of the message (see **8.2**. above), the miraculous character of the expected effect of the equation widens, together with the adjective "little," the gap between children and adults that seemed to be so small in Plato and Lucretius.[84]

14.1 Auctorial comparisons *vs.* 14.2 Nonauctorial comparisons

Similar to the previous distinction, the difference between the authors' and their characters' comparative utterances expresses the contrast between "real-life" comparisons embedded in common wisdom with all the restrictions this puts on the selection of comparata and tertia, and fictional comparisons that are partially free from such limitations. The gaps between auctorial and nonauctorial comparisons could perhaps be evaluated best when the same comparisons appear in fictional and nonfictional contexts. Thus, when Leibniz insists on the fact that, thanks to Divine grace, humans live in the best possible world, this absolute grading of comparisons feels like a sound replica in a philosophical debate of his time and a natural offspring of his thinking:

> **(14.1)** "*Il y a une infinité de Mondes possibles, dont il faut que Dieu ait choisi le meilleur.*"[85]

However, when his satirical shadow—a pathological optimist Pangloss—extends the same property to the house and wife of his patron, which are also deemed "the best possible" of their kind, the improbability and pragmatic servility of the derivative comparisons invalidates the soundness of the main one:

---

83 Matthew 18.3.
84 In the saying, the tentative character of the relation between cause and effect has been routinely disregarded, so the words attributed by the Apostle Matthew to Jesus had been commonly treated as the imperative "be like children" ("*Будьте, как дети*'—*сказал спаситель.*"—Иван С. Тургенев, Путешествие по святым местам русским [1836], in: Иван С. Тургенев, *Сочинения*, Т. 1. М. 1978, 173).
85 Gottfried W. Leibniz, Essais sur la bonté de Dieu, la liberté de l'homme et l'origine du mal [1710], in: Gottfried W. Leibniz, *Œuvres*. Paris 1846, 115.

(14.2). *"Pangloss enseignait la métaphysico-théologo-cosmolonigologie. Il prouvait admirablement qu'il n'y a point d'effet sans cause, et que, dans ce meilleur des mondes possibles, le château de monseigneur le baron était le plus beau des châteaux et madame la meilleure des baronnes possibles.*[86]

* * *

It is hard to say how much the typology presented above accounts for the variety of meanings that comparative utterances might acquire in social interactions. What could be stated with certainty, though, is that it takes little notice of complications caused by the malfunctioning of certain distinctive features. Linguistics calls this the failure to distinguish "neutralization." In the normal case, the privative phonological opposition *"voiced"* versus *"voiceless"* is solely responsible for the semantic differentiations between *"time"* and *"dime," "tangle"* and *"dangle," "tee"* and *"D,"* and so forth, because it makes the only difference that between the consonants [t] and [d]. However, in a situation in which these consonants are paired and squeezed between two vowels (e.g., *"ladder"* vs. *"latter"*), the opposition does not work—what one says and hears is neither [t] nor [d], but something in-between. As a result, the recipient of the message containing any of these words has no direct way to find out whether its sender meant *"ladder"* or *"latter,"* and has to rely on the context in order to make the semantic distinction.[87] Expectedly, the notion of neutralization was developed within phonology as the most advanced part of structural linguistics, but the phenomenon is pervasive in other domains of human language,[88] and any theory of language ignoring it would be a wildly utopian enterprise. The same is ostensibly true for comparisons, and therefore it makes sense to cast a cursory glance at some neutralizations of distinctive features within comparative utterances: In both cases, it is the specific combination of adjacent distinctive features that results in nondifferentiation.

III.

1.1 Comparisons *vs.* 1.2 Metastatements concerning comparisons

The fragility of the distinction between comparative utterances and metautterances referring to them is predetermined by the fact that human beings cannot but use

---

86 Voltaire, *Candide* [1759], Paris 2012, 1.
87 Josef Vachek, *Selected Writings in English and General Linguistics*, The Hague 1976, 53.
88 Cf. Petr Sgall, *Jazyk, mluvení, psaní*, Praha 2011, 161–166; Daniel Silverman, *Neutralization*, Cambridge 2012, 1–12.

one and the same natural language for the first- and second-order statements: [89] Unless one strays away from habitual interaction into the realms of logic and mathematics, there is no code difference whatsoever between the statements "*Moscow is bigger than Bielefeld*" and "'*Moscow is bigger than Bielefeld*' *is a comparative utterance.*" As a result of this mixture, the separation between comparisons (**1.1**) and metastatements concerning comparisons (**1.2**) is enforced only in its universal variant (**1.2.1**). Indeed, the statements addressing the value or probability of comparative practices *in toto* (see note 1) can do without comparisons at all, although many of them are merely preludes to the more specific judgments and evaluations regarding specific comparative practices and specific circumstances (see below, **III, 1.2.1/1.2.2**). However, metastatements concerning comparability of specific comparata in particular (**1.2.2**) typically include one or several comparisons (**1.1**, for exceptions, see note 108). Even if the subordinated comparative utterance—the object of the metastatement—is represented on the surface of language by merely a pair of comparata—as quoted in **II, 1.2**—every competent reader would get the impression that it is the difference, not similarity, of apples and pears that stands in the way of their comparison.[90] Inversely, when George Sand describes sociopolitical circumstances before the French revolutions of 1789 and 1848 as being theoretically "comparable" to one another (**1.2.2 + 8.1. + 13.2**), the long list of common features including a critical attitude to the present ("real") and dream of the future ("ideal") society, as well as the freedom of press, strongly suggests the likeness of both time periods (**1.1.1 + 13.1**):

> "C'était en 1845, époque où la critique de la société réelle et le rêve d'une société idéale atteignirent dans la presse un degré de liberté de développement comparable à celui du XVIIIe siècle."[91]

Evidently, some metastatements regarding comparability of specific comparata can also be read as first-order comparative utterances; and at times, it is fairly easy to find out how comparata are related to one another, even if this relation has not been spelled out explicitly.[92] Of course, the associations of comparability with equation (**1.2.2 + 8.1 = 1.1.1**) and noncomparability with differentiation (**1.2.2 + 8.2 = 1.1.2**)

---

[89] See a survey of the studies on this topic, John A. Lucy, Reflexive language and the human disciplines, in: John A. Lucy/Lucy A. Lucy (eds.), *Reflexive Language: Reported Speech and Metapragmatics*, Cambridge 1993, 9–13.
[90] **II, 1.2** is actually a meta-metastatement seeking to quash this verdict, but, for our purposes, the second metalevel can be safely ignored.
[91] George Sand, *Le Péché de Monsieur Antoine* [1845], Paris 1864, 1.
[92] The famous Oxford Dictionaries second George Sand's interpretation, offering as definitions of the word "comparable" two references to similarity—"able to be likened to another; similar" and "of equivalent quality; worthy of comparison" <https://en.oxforddictionaries.com/definition/comparable>.

are far from being accidental. Traditionally, comparisons are associated far more strongly with similarity than difference: Alone the fact that most of the available dictionary entries on "comparison" in various languages literally put "similarity" before "difference" (**II, 1.2.1** is a typical case) attests to the unmistakable preference given to equations over differentiations within comparative semantics.[93] It is likely that such associations—especially the first, positive, one—facilitate extracting comparative meanings from metacomparative sentences.

1.2.1 Metastatements concerning comparisons in general vs.
1.2.2 Metastatements concerning comparability of specific *comparata* in particular

As has been stated in the previous paragraphs, the metastatements concerning comparisons in general can be unspecific: Referring to all comparisons in the world as a *type* of activity is enough, insofar as an average recipient of such a comparative message knows what the word "comparison" means.[94] In a world bent on efficiency of information transmission, one universal metastatement "*all comparisons are good*" (**1.2.1**) would turn evaluation of any specific comparata or classes thereof on the scale "*good*"/"*bad*" into a waste of time. However, in discussions of social practices, it is common, if not essential, to see how general principles function under specific circumstances, and this functioning leaves ample room for deductive reasoning moving from (**1.2.1**) to (**1.2.2**). Whenever this movement occurs outside of well-trodden paths of logical reasoning, it often stalls or gets stuck in between, thereby complicating the relation between premises and conclusions and sometimes obliterating their difference.

---

[93] Cf. Schenk/Krause, Vergleich, 676; Stefan Willer, Die Allgemeinheit des Vergleichs. Ein komparatistisches Problem und seine Entstehung um 1800, in: Michael Eggers (ed.), *Von Ähnlichkeiten und Unterschieden. Vergleich, Analogie und Klassifikation in Wissenschaft und Literatur*, Heidelberg 2011, 155; Mauz/Sass, Hermeneutik des Vergleichs, 10–11. The correspondences between comparison and similarity pop up at nearly every level of comparative activities—from terms (*similitudo*) to social practices (the consensus-building procedure known in German as "Vergleichung," see: Marsh H. McCall, *Ancient Rhetorical Theories of Simile and Comparison*, Cambridge 1969, IX; Steinmetz, 'Vergleich', 84, 106). Overalll, cross-evaluation of obviously different things is discouraged: Whereas Latin poetry contains standard apologies for comparing "big" things with "small" ones (Vergil, *Georgica*, IV, 170–178; Vergil, *Bucolica*, I, 19-25; Ovid, *Tristia* I, 3.25, 6.28), European political writers of the eighteenth and nineteenth centuries obsessively warn against juxtaposing "top" and "bottom" of the social ladder (cf. Steinmetz, 'Vergleich', 112; Steinmetz, Above/below). For the things that are even more disparate—such as God and humankind—the outright prohibition of comparisons was put in place (see below, **III, 8.2**).

[94] Cf. Bertrand Russell, Mathematical Logic as Based on the Theory of Types, in: *American Journal of Mathematics*, 30 (3/1908), 222-262, see 236.

In the history of comparative discourse, deduction often presents itself as a slightly duplicitous *totum pro parte*. A general—usually pejorative—evaluation of comparisons (**1.2.1**) loudly fronts for hidden specific metastatements (**1.2.2**), feeding the suspicion that the narrator's only goal is to borrow some authority for an otherwise petty claim. In this way, the two opposed kinds of metastatements melt together: Whereas the universal metastatements lose their generality, their particular counterparts tacitly uphold some mid-level generalization without bringing it to the narrative surface.

The case in point is the popular saying "All comparisons are odious," easily found on the pages of proverbial wisdom manuals in many languages.[95] Instead of ending all discussion of comparative practices, this general metastatement often introduces pointed bans on particularly explosive *comparata* (e.g., female beauty). So, in Fernando de Rojas' macabre comedy *Celestina* (1499), the prostitute Elicia refuses to share a table with a servant named Sempronio, because the latter has just showered the young Melibea with compliments. Sempronio, in turn, reminds furious Elicia that he has never looked at Elicia and Melibea from the comparative standpoint, and it was her, not him, who was "guilty" of "having compared":

> ELIC[IA]. [...]? Hauía yo de comer con esse maluado, que en mi cara me ha porfiado que es más gentil su andrajo de Melibea, que yo?
>
> SEMP[RONIO]. Calla, mi vida, que tú la comparaste. Toda comparación es odiosa: tú tienes la culpa y no yo.[96]

The same pseudological following from the general maxima ("*toda comparación es odiosa*") to its only relevant specific application—refraining from comparing mistresses of various *hidalgos*—is a recurrent topic in another milestone of pre-modern Spanish fiction.[97] And the gap between premises and conclusions appears to be even more glaring in John Fortescue's *Commendation of the Laws of England* (1499), in which the success of a comparative enterprise proving—surprise!—the supremacy of English laws is crowned by the phrase ("*comparaciones odiosas esse*") put in the mouths of both the auctorial narrator and his conversation partner (modeled upon Prince Edward, the only son of exiled Henry VI).[98] All in all, the chief purpose of deliberate paralogical mixing between general and specific metacomparative statements appears to be a case of isolating and ring fencing some unspoken incom-

---

95 Cf. Pedro Vallés, *Libro de refranes y sentencias* [1549], Madrid 2003, 66; Gonzalo Correas, *Vocabulario de refranes y frases proverbiales* [1627], Madrid 2000, 336; Giacomo du Bois de Gomicourt, *Sentenze, e proverbij italiani cavati da diversi famosi autori antichi, e moderni [...]*, Lyon 1683, 153.
96 Fernando de Rojas, *La Celestina, ó, Comedia de Calisto y Melibea* [1499], Barcelona 1841, 176. See also: Mauz/Sass, Vergleiche verstehen, 1.
97 Cf. Miguel de Cervantes Saavedra, *Don Quijote de la Mancha* [1615], Madrid 1999, 350, 386.
98 Cf. John Fortescue, *De laudibus legum Angliae* [1499], Cincinnati, OH 1874, 225–238.

parables—be they the object of romantic love or a subject of imperial rule (see in more detail below **III, 8.1/8.2**).[99]

1.1.1 Equations *vs.* 1.1.2 Differentiations

Above, it has been shown how the directionality of discourse, reflecting time asymmetry, produced the difference between "left" and "right" of the written line, or "before and after" of the spoken line. Indeed, the same signifier ("I"), referring to the same signified (the narrator), can have different meanings in the subject and the predicate parts of the statement, because the production of speech is accompanied by a steady influx of information that alters the overall semantics of the utterance while it is being produced **(II, 2.1)**. Mapped onto the lexical level of the sentence, this change (namely, the alleged spiritual growth of the narrator's identity), cancels out logical reflexivity, turning the standard equation (*$I = I$*, **1.1.1.**) into a relative grading comparison ("*I am more than I*," **1.1.2 + 1.1.2.2.1**): The latter statement sounds like an odd paradox until one tries it out on *any* saying involving comparata separated only by the time of their reference (see, e.g., below: **III, 3.1/3.2**).

If initial sameness of comparata can be turned into contrast in the process of message production, the neutralization of their difference appears equally possible: In any case, the *coincidentia oppositorum* has been one of the cornerstones of philosophical dialectics,[100] and many empirical observations of likeness and unlikeness of certain objects leave matters unsettled. Thus, departing from the a priori assumed difference in the feeling capacity between flora and fauna, Buffon inverts the habitual scheme of deductive reasoning, conditionally accepting the difference first, contesting its universality later, and refusing to make any judgment on the matter at the end:

> "*Une différence plus essentielle pourroit se tirer de la faculté de sentir, qu'on ne peut guère refuser aux animaux, et don't il semble que les végétaux soient privés. [...] Cette différence entre les animaux et les végétaux non-seule ment n'est pas générale, mais même n'est pas bien décidée.*"[101]

---

99   To be sure, there are exceptions: A handful of authors take the notion of "odious comparisons" seriously. See: Steinmetz, 'Vergleich', 114–115 (on the entry "Comparison" in the *Dictionary of the [French] Academy* (1694)); William Hazlitt, *Table Talk. Essays on Men and Manners* [1821], London 1903, 141.
100 The most basic expression of this tradition is Heraclitus' insistence on "being" and "nonbeing" at the same time: εἶμέν τε καὶ οὐκ εἶμεν (Heraclitus, *Alleg. Hom.* 24).
101 Georges-Louis Leclerc (Comte de Buffon), *Œuvres completes. Tome VIII. Histore des animaux* [1749], Paris 1833, 7. On Buffon's comparisons, see: Thierry Hoquet, Logique de la comparaison et physique de la génération chez Buffon, in: *La Découverte* 39 (1/2007), 595–612.

In a single, albeit extensive, comparative utterance, the relation between the comparata "animals and "plants" is presented in three ways: (1) a possible difference (**1.1.2 + 13.2**); (2) a mixture of difference and indifference (some animals and plants are similar in their ability to feel [**1.1.1**] and others are not [**1.1.2**]); and, finally, (3) no relation at all (**2**). Proceeding from surety to uncertainty, Buffon's statement has a negative informational value in relation to his subject. However, the zoologist's unvarnished report of his squabbling with the thorny subject more than makes up for this loss.

1.1.2.2.1 Relative grading comparisons vs. 1.1.2.2.2 Absolute grading comparisons

Superficially, the boundary between relative and absolute grading comparisons should be watertight, because the opposition seems to be directly and effortlessly translatable into the grammatical distinction between comparative (*better*) and superlative (*best*) adjectives. However, a second glance at the passage from Strindberg's *Crimes and Crimes* (see above, **II, 7.2**) documents the fairly easy neutralization of both oppositions at once. In the quote, as we remember, Adolphe clearly compares two kinds of crimes, and deems one category (moral wrongdoings) to be worse than the other (criminal transgressions). Notwithstanding the relativity of comparison, he uses for the first category the superlative adjective *"värsta,"* conflating a relative grading comparison (**moral wrongdoings are worse than criminal transgressions* [**1.1.2.2.1**]) with an absolute one (**nothing is worse than moral wrongdoings* [**1.1.2.2.2**]). Understandably, such conflations are particularly plentiful in finite sets consisting of two elements (**1.1.2.2 + 10.1**) in which it is impossible to drive a wedge between "*X is better/worse/... than N*" and "*X is the best/worst/... in the set (X, N)*."

3.1 Evaluative comparisons vs. 3.2 Nonevaluative comparisons

Unlike the previous binary, the privative opposition between evaluative and nonevaluative comparisons has a very diverse semantics. Accordingly, it can be expressed in a myriad of ways that sometimes have no discernible references to any values at all. Not infrequently, the diachronic nongrading self-comparisons (**1.1.2.1 + 3.2 + 7.1 + 9.2**) are cast in the idiomatic forms referring indirectly to progress or decay occurring within a certain entity (**3.1**). This is the case in Anthony Trollope's novel *Linda Tressel* (1868) in which "Herr Molk," the burgomaster of Nuremberg, is shown at pains to arrange the protagonist's marriage with the respectable Peter Steinmarc. In pursuit of this goal, he addresses Linda's aunt with the following words:

"The city is not what it used to be, Madame Staubach, but still Peter does his work very well".[102]

The semantics of the first part of the sentence swings back and forth between the disinterested contrasting of Nuremberg now to Nuremberg then (**3.1**), and the suggestion of the city's decline in the meantime (**3.2**). To tilt the utterance's meaning toward the latter possibility, the narrator inserts the coordinating conjunction "but" between the report on the city's changing fortunes, and the overt praise of Linda's prospective husband. In this situation, as in many similar ones, the neutralization of distinction (evaluative and nonevaluative comparisons within comparative utterance [**3.1/3.2**]) has been overcome by its context (the adjacent noncomparative evaluation of the external object named Peter Steinmarc).[103]

4.1 Qualitative comparisons vs. 4.2 Quantitative comparisons

Right from the outset, the handy and seemingly unchallengeable opposition between qualitative and quantitative comparisons is compromised by the latter's latent semantic inconsistency.[104] Although numbers are both precise references to sets ("*he has two children*") and approximate references to quantities ("*he is two meters high*"), the difference between the two has no direct linguistic expression: Typically, the exactness of counting is attributed automatically to measurement. Consequently, nearly every time a number appears in a comparative utterance, it is believed to stand for the incontrovertibly specific and intersubjectively verifiable relation between comparata. Alas, this is an illusion, and many numbers express highly subjective relations between immeasurable comparata. Charles Péguy's comparative utterance could illustrate the point:

---

102 Anthony Trollope, *Linda Tressel* [1868], Frankfurt a. M. 2018, 88.
103 A somewhat similar strategy of mixing up evaluative and nonevaluative comparative utterances could also be implemented in nondiachronical settings. It involves the tacit distancing of similar—and equated to one another—comparata (**1.1.1 + 3.1 + 7.1**) from observer: "*Die Linken sind doch alle gleich*" (Máriam Martínez-Bascuñán. Die Linken sind doch alle gleich.—Zeit Online (10.2.2017) https://www.zeit.de/politik/ausland/2017-02/podemos-spanien-linke-partei-pablo-iglesias-streit. Again, the sentence can be read both as a neutral equation of various left-wing movements from within (**1.1.1 + 3.2**) and as their critical differentiation from without (**1.1.2 + 3.1**).
104 "Between two and three, there is a jump, In the case of quantity, there is no such jump; and because jump is missing in the world of quantity, it is impossible for any quantity to be exact. You can have exactly three tomatoes, You can never have exactly three gallons of water. Always quantity is approximate" (Gregory Bateson, *Man and Nature. A necessary unity*, Glasgow 1980, 72; see also: Alfred Brunswig, *Das Vergleichen und die Relationserkenntnis*, Leipzig 1910; 16–17; Chang, *Making Comparisons Count*, 26–27).

"Nous entrons ici [...] dans un domaine inconnu, dans un domaine étranger qui est le domaine de la joie. Cent fois moins connu, cent fois plus étranger, cent fois moins"nous" que les royaumes de la douleur. Cent fois plus profond, je crois et cent fois plus fécond."[105]

Even before one attempts to check the distance between *"joy"* and *"suffering"* in the passage, a brief look at the comparata selected and the internal organization of the passage casts grave doubts on the quantitative character of the comparison. To begin with, both notions compared constitute a binary set with the fairly strong and largely predefined qualitative valuations (**2.2 + 3.1 + 4.1**): It would be fairly uncommon to see suffering as anything but "good" and joy as anything but "bad." Someone may argue that this is possible, and that the decision to assign a positive and a negative value to the respective poles of the opposition is based on thoroughly measuring and comparing their parameters that are, according to Péguy, "familiarity," "usness," "foreignness," "profundity," and "fertility." But even if this fanciful argument were accepted and the gap between joy and suffering lent itself to measurement, it would be wildly improbable for the variations of *all* their subcomparata to conform either to the ratio of 100:1 or to the ratio 1:100 as they do in the text.[106] In all probability, the reason for putting one and the same number in the same syntactic frame with two opposed valuations (*"100 times more/less [than] X"*) has nothing to do with quantification and a lot to do with literary and rhetorical properties. The growing rhythmic and phonetic regularity of the passage, culminating in the rhyme of two comparata (*"profond"/"fécond"*) shows that numbers in the *Note* serve exclusively as a rhetorical embellishment of the qualitative valuation, adding to it some faux quantitative flair.[107]

---

105 Charles Péguy, Note conjointe sur M. Descartes et la philosophie cartésienne [1914], in: Charles Péguy, Œuvres completes, T. IX, Paris 1924, 329.

106 Truth to be told, the numerical equality appears credible in antonyms and synonyms: "One hundred times less known" is roughly the same as "one hundred times more foreign" and "one hundred times less 'us'". However, this equation is valid with any number, as long as it is repeated in all parts, and also without any numbers. So it turns out that the value "100" in this contest does not mean anything, and can be removed or substituted at will without causing any noticeable change to the comparisons involved.

107 The dissolution of quantitative in qualitative comparisons can also take place whenever the strategic manipulation of multiple hidden tertia (5.2) discourages attention to comparability: The text on Viktor Koretsky's poster comparing Soviet and American schools (1950) informs the reader that in the USSR "the construction of city and village schools will increase approximately by 70 % compared to the previous five years", whereas in the U S, "1 % of the budget is devoted to the public education and 74 % of the budget are military expenses", "the illiterate population of USA amounts to 10 million", and "around one-third of the school age children do not study". It is easy to see that there is no common denominator for the figures describing the Soviet and American educational situation: For instance, the viewer never learns about the size of the Soviet military budget or the dynamics of school construction in the US, which would have enabled direct quantitative comparisons. The contrast between a pioneer smil-

8.1 Positive comparisons vs. 8.2 Negative comparisons

It has been shown above that the remarkable contrast between the perfect logical form of negation, ideally suitable for the mass production of privative oppositions, and its restlessness within natural language results in multiple inconsistencies and asymmetries within negative comparisons (**II, 8.2**). But perhaps the weakest point of linguistic negativity is its curious inability to draw the line between the negative and the negated statement:[108] It is impossible to withhold a statement "x" from "-x," "I deny that x," "anti-x," and any other thinkable negative statements. For this reason, negative comparisons (**8.1**) nearly always contain positive comparisons (**8.2**), and the difference between one and another appears neutralized, to some degree, in each and every negative comparative utterance.[109]

Needless to say, this habitual neutralization exercises a profound influence on the form and functions of (non)comparisons. Arguably the most productive social use of negative comparisons is the tacit transformation of nonevaluative incomparability into absolute and relative grading comparisons: "Incomparable" just means "very, very different." In the first case (**1.2.2. + 8.2. = 1.1.2.2.2**), the rejection of comparability between absolute manifestations of Good (e.g., God and its properties) or Evil (e.g., Shoah) automatically places them on the very top (or bottom) of every comparative ladder.[110] In the second (**1.2.2. + 8.2. = 1.1.2.2.1**), instead of focusing on

---

ing at the bright upper part of the poster, and a stooping American teenager on the picture's dark bottom leaves no doubt as to which school system is seen as the better one. However, the abundant statistics fail to take part in the comparison: Again, their role is to wrap the highly biased qualitative comparisons in the cloak of objectivity (I am grateful to Joris C. Heyder for generously sharing with me his insightful interpretation of the poster).

108 "*Negation ist keine Vernichtung, sondern ein Modus der Erhaltung von Sinn. Negation ist daher für gewisse Absichten zu positiv. Dann kann nur gehandelt werden*" (Niklas Luhmann, Über die Funktion der Negation in sinnkonstituierenden Systemen, in: Harald Weinrich (ed.), *Positionen der Negativität. (Poetik und Hermeneutik, vol. X)*, München 1975, 201-218, see 201.

109 "Negation is just as much Affirmation as Negation" (Herbert Marcuse, *Reason and Revolution*, Boston, MA 1960, 122); "Information introduced via negation is often retained rather than suppressed" (Rachel Giora et al., Negation as positivity in disguise, in: Herbert L. Colston/Albert Katz (eds.), *Figurative Language Comprehension: Social and Cultural Influences*, Hillsdale 2005, 233-258, 117). Specifically on incomparability statements, see: Niklas Luhmann, *Liebe als Passion. Zur Kodierung der Intimität*, Frankfurt a. M. 1982, 154.

110 The "incomparability" of God and its properties, common in monotheist canonic texts (The Quran 112.4, Isaiah 46: 09) and much beyond (e.g., Martin Luther, Auslegung uber das fünffte Buch Mose/Deuteronomium genant/Verdeudscht Anno 1525, in: *Der Achte Teil der Bücher des Ehrwirdigen Herrn D. Martini Lutheri*, Wittenberg 1556, 164; Søren Kierkegaard, Kjerlighedens Gjerninger, in: Søren Kierkegaard, *Samlede vaerker*, Band 9, Kjøbenhavn 1847, 177), provides a template for the similar superlativeness of a sovereign, master, lover, or romantic friend (see above **III, 1.2.1/1.2.2**). On the "incomparability" of the opposite side (Shoah), see: Andreas Mauz/Hartmut von Sass, Vergleiche verstehen. Einleitende Vorwegnahmen, in: An-

the extreme position of a single comparatum, the emphasis is put on the massive disparity between the phenomena compared. For example, Hitler's refusal to compare the "new Germany" with "Germany of the past" means, in effect, the propagation of considerable social and economic changes valued positively and attributed to the power grab of his party (NSDAP):

> „Dieses neue Deutschland kann daher nicht in Vergleich gebracht werden mit dem Deutschland der Vergangenheit."[111]

13.1 Real vs. 13.2 Irreal comparisons

The neutralization of the real and the possible in comparative utterances has a somewhat more intricate semantics than the conflations of other distinctive features discussed above. On the one hand, it may follow the logic of the previous examples (see above, **III, 1.2./1.2** and **8.1/8.2**): Often, the statement that some specific comparisons are admissible or even desirable contains a first-order comparative utterance suggesting equality of the comparata (**1.2.2. + 13.2. = 1.1.1**). This is the device deployed many times in Charles Perrault's juxtaposition of arts and sciences in Antiquity and in his own time:

> "Je voy les Anciens sans plier les genoux, // Ils sont grands, il est vray, mais hommes comme nous; // Et l'on peut comparer sans craindre d'estre injuste, // Le Siecle de LOUIS au beau Siecle d'Auguste."[112]

---

dreas Mauz/Hartmut von Sass (eds.), *Hermeneutik des Vergleichs. Strukturen, Anwendungen und Grenzen komparativer Verfahren*, Würzburg, 2011, 15; François Noudelmann, La Traite, la Shoah... sur les usages d'une comparaison, in : *Littérature* 174 (2/2014), 104–113, see 104.

111 Adolf Hitler, *Rede vor dem Reichstag am 21. Mai 1935*, Berlin 1935, 9. Again, even if the negative metastatement concerning comparability of specific objects has neutralizing potential, one should not treat this high probability as certainty. Particularly in scholarly discourse in which exaggerations are untypical, specific incomparability (**1.2.1 + 8.2**) can simply mean differentiation (**1.1.2**): "The duration of dreams bears no comparison to that of the events and circumstances which they picture" (William S. Savory, *On Dreaming and Somnambulism, in Relation to the Functions of Certain Nerve-Centres*, London 1864, see 207). Last but not least, there is always a small chance that the explicit negation of comparability is just what it is with no hidden comparisons lurking in the background. This usually occurs when the complexity of comparata prevents rigorous comparisons in the first place, as is the case with "state" and "religion" in Jakob Burkhardt's ambitious account of world history: "*Unmöglich ist es zu vergleichen, welcher Prozeß der größere gewesen: die Entstehung des Staates oder die einer Religion*" (Jakob Burkhardt, *Weltgeschichtliche Betrachtungen* [1905], in: Jakob Burkhardt, *Kritische Studienausgabe*, vol. 10, München 2000, 379).

112 Charles Perrault, *Parallèle des anciens et des modernes en ce qui regarde les arts et les sciences* [1687], München 1964, 10.

Even if the grammar of comparative utterance ("*one could compare*") suggests its irreality, the actuality of comparison is proved beyond doubt by adjacent sentences. The equality between the comparata is first suggested by the positional (interactive) symmetry of the speakers eschewing bodily hierarchies: Perrault looks at "the Ancients" "without bending his knees." Furthermore, this parity is reinforced by a simile ("*they are [...] like us*") and consolidated by the grammatical parallelism between "*the century of Louis [XIV]*" and "*the century of Augustus*." At the same time, Perrault's choice of conditional mood can also follow the practice of "mitigation": In most cultures, it is common to reduce the directness of indicative judgments in order to avert direct confrontation in case of disagreement.[113] As said before (see note 3), the standard—indicative—mood of comparative messages in verbal language "*X is better than Y*" concentrates all the comparing authority in the sender's hands: Every other result of cross-evaluation between *X* and *Y* would invariably take the shape of a *counter*statement challenging the validity of the original comparison (**I doubt/do not think/disagree . . . that X is better than Y*). Alternatively, the irreal mood comparison (**X might be better than Y *Isn't X better than Y?/. . .*) allows for less confrontational expressions of alternative opinions such as answering questions, specifying probability, and so forth. So, at the end, it is likely that Charles Perrault's controversial equation was styled as an irreal one to avoid confrontation, in case the controversial equation of the "Old" with the "New" were not to his interlocutor's liking.

IV.

As long as comparisons are seen as an actual social practice (rather than as an abstract set of rhetorical devices), their typological studies would take time, and the quality of the resulting classification would move only slowly toward the rigorous standards set by linguistic phonology. The attempt to describe the whole semantics of natural languages in terms of distinctive features called "componential analysis" could have provided, in principle, some guidance, but in its present form, this linguistic methodology appears to be both grotesquely complex and unsuitable for our purposes.[114] With these pitfalls in mind, the current typology has focused on

---

113 Cf. Penelope Brown/Stephen C. Levinson, *Politeness*, Cambridge 1978, 40, 87, 116, 145, 156–157, 172–173, 226; Bruce Fraser, *Conversational mitigation*, in: Journal of Pragmatics 4 (1980), 341–350; Geoffrey Leach, *Principles of Pragmatics*, Harlow 1983, 108; Claudia Caffi, On mitigation, in: Journal of Pragmatics 31 (1999), 881–909; Lotfi Abouda, Deux types d'imparfait atténuatif, in: Langue française 142 (2/2004), 58-74, see 58; Dominique Willems/Claire Blanche-Benveniste, A constructional corpus-based approach of 'weak' verbs in French, in: Hans C. Boas/Francisco Gonzálvez-García (eds.), *Romance perspectives on construction grammar*, Amsterdam 2014, 113–138.
114 Cf. John Lyons, *Linguistic Semantics: An Introduction*, London 1995, 114–115.

the most basic sets of distinctive features, presenting them first as ideal types (free from internal contradictions and external influences [II]) and then as real practices (generating their information in specific sociohistorical environments [III]). In the best-case scenario, the descriptions of distinctive features in the typology should have been unambiguous enough to enable automatic (computer-based) fishing for comparisons.

Geared primarily toward the practical use in sociocommunicative analyses of historical practices, the description above does not aim at sweeping generalizations. Nonetheless, a brief summary of some of the main findings is probably in order:

1. Comparisons—at least those expressed by means of verbal communication—have regular semantics that, similar to natural language, can be broken down into single bits of information by means of privative (*a* vs. non-*a*) oppositions. However, the overlap between the distinctive features of linguistic and comparative systems is not that big. Even when the meaning of the comparative distinction is roughly similar to the grammatical one (*relative vs. absolute grading comparisons ≈ comparative vs. superlative degree*), the means of expression could be very different.

2. Although the comparative system often amalgamates some logical (*"negation/affirmation," "first-/second-order statements"*) and mathematical (*"finite sets"/"infinite sets"*) distinctions, in communicative practice, it regularly overrides them: For instance, the absence of fully abstract, specialized "second-order" terms in language leads to the neutralizations between statements and metastatements within comparative utterances. Another example is the directionality of discourse that turns equations into differentiations.

3. Comparative utterances play a significant role in forming, upholding, and sustaining the basics of social order, supporting hierarchies (taboos on comparing "highest" and "lowest" values with all other comparata), and enabling cooperation (prevention of conflicts in case of alternative cross-evaluations by means of mitigation). Between these two extremes of societal regulation, multitudes of clichés ensure both the stability and flexibility of various socially meaningful mid-level comparative scales.

References

ABOUDA, Lotfi, Deux types d'imparfait atténuatif, in: *Langue française* 142 (2/2004), 58-74.

AGOSTI, Stefano, Remarques sur la figure de la comparaison dans la poésie baudelairienne, in: Dagmar Wieser/Patrick Labarthe (eds.), *Mémoire et oubli dans le lyrisme européen: hommage à John E. Jackson*, Paris 2008, 57.

ANDRE, Christian C., *Hesperus, oder Belehrung und Unterhaltung für die Bewohner des österreichischen Staats*, Brünn, 1810.

ANDREWS, Edna, *Markedness Theory: The Union of Asymmetry and Semiosis in Language*, Durham 1990.

ARISTOTLE, Rh. 3.4.

BATESON, Gregory, *Man and Nature. A necessary unity*, Glasgow 1980.

BATISTELLA, Edwin L., *The Logic of Markedness*, New York 1996.

BECKER, Thomas, *Das Vokalsystem der deutschen Standardsprache*, Frankfurt a. M. 1998.

BELLAMY, Edward, *Looking Backward from 2000 to 1887* [1887], Boston 2012.

BERLO, David K., *The Process of Communication: An Introduction to Theory and Practice*, New York 1960.

BLONDEL, François, *Comparaison de Pindare et d'Horace*, Amsterdam 1686.

BOLZANO, Bernard, *Einleitung zur Größenlehre und erste Begriffe der allgemeinen Größenlehre* [1841], Stuttgart 1975.

BROWN, Penelope/LEVINSON, Stephen C., *Politeness*, Cambridge 1978.

BRUNSWIG, Alfred, *Das Vergleichen und die Relationserkenntnis*, Leipzig 1910.

BURKHARDT, Jakob, Weltgeschichtliche Betrachtungen [1905], in: Jakob Burkhardt, *Kritische Studienausgabe*, Vol. 10, München 2000.

BURNETT, James (Lord Monboddo), *Of the Origin and Progress of Language*, Vol.1, Edinburgh 1779.

CAFFI, Claudia, On mitigation, in: *Journal of Pragmatics* 31 (1999), 881–909.

CAROLL, Lewis, *Alice's Adventures in Wonderland*, London 1866.

CERVANTES SAAVEDRA, Miguel de, *Don Quijote de la Mancha* [1615], Madrid 1999.

CHANG, Ruth, *Making Comparisons Count*, London 2014.

CHEAH, Pheng, The Material World of Comparison, in: *New Literary History* 40 (3/2009), 523-545.

CHILTON, Paul A., Negation as Maximal Distance in Discourse Space Theory, in: *Groupe de Recherches Anglo-Américaines de Tours* 1 (2006), 351–378.

COOPE, Ursula, *Time for Aristotle: Physics IV. 10–14*, Oxford 2005.

COUSIN, Victor, *De l'instruction publique en Allemagne*, Paris 1841.

CUSTINE, Astolphe de, *La Russie en 1839*, Bruxelles 1844.

D'ABBEVILLE, Claude, *Histoire de la mission des pères Capucins en l'isle de Maragnan et terres circonvoisines*, Paris 1614.

DANTE, *Paradiso* [1321], Indianapolis, IN 2017.

DAVIES, Matt, *Advances in Stylistics: Oppositions and Ideology in News Discourse*, London 2014.

DESCARTES, Rene, Regulae ad directionem ingenii [1619], in: Rene Descartes, Œuvres, T. X, Paris 1908, 439.

DORSCHEL, Andreas, Einwände gegen das Vergleichen, in: *Philosophisches Jahrbuch* 113 (1/2006), 177-185.

DU BOIS DE GOMICOURT, Giacomo, *Sentenze, e proverbij italiani cavati da diversi famosi autori antichi, e moderni [...]*, Lyon 1683.

DU VAL, Pierre, *La géographie universelle*, Band 2, Lyon, 1688.

EBERHARDT, Robert, Bilderpaare und Pendanthängung. Praxeologische Überlegungen zum Ordnungssinn, (manuscript, 2019).

EGGERS, Michael, *Vergleichendes Erkennen*, Heidelberg 2016.

EPPLE, Angelika, Doing Comparisons – Ein praxeologischer Zugang zur Geschichte der Globalisierung/en, in: Angelika Epple/Walter Erhart (eds.), *Die Welt beobachten. Praktiken des Vergleichens*, Frankfurt a. M./New York 2015, 161-199.

EPPLE, Angelika/ERHART, Walter, Die Welt beobachten. Praktiken des Vergleichens, in: Angelika Epple/Walter Erhart (eds.), *Die Welt beobachten. Praktiken des Vergleichens*, Frankfurt a. M./New York 2015, 7-31.

ESPOSITO, Elena, What's Observed in a Rating? Rankings as Orientation in the Face of Uncertainty, (manuscript, 2016).

FERES JR., João, Building a Typology of Forms of Misrecognition: Beyond the Republican-Hegelian Paradigm, in: *Contemporary Political Theory* 5 (2006), 259–277.

FEUERBACH, Ludwig, *Das Wesen des Christentums* [1849], Stuttgart 1994.

FLUSSER, Vilém, *Kommunikologie*, Frankfurt a. M. 1996.

FOERSTER, Heinz von, *Wissen und Gewissen: Versuch einer Brücke*, Frankfurt a. M. 1993.

FORTESCUE, John, *De laudibus legum Angliae* [1499], Cincinnati, OH 1874.

FRASER, Bruce, Conversational mitigation, in: *Journal of Pragmatics* 4 (1980), 341–350.

FRIEDMAN, Susan Stanford, Why Not Compare?, in: *PMLA* 126 (3/2011), 753-762.

GALISON, Peter, Descartes's Comparisons: From the Invisible to the Visible, in: *Isis* 75 (2/1984), 311-326.

GARFINKEL, Harold, *Studies in Ethnomethodology*, Englewood Cliffs 1967

GARGANI, Adam, Similes as Poetic Comparisons, in: *Lingua* 175–176 (2016), 54–68.

GIORA, Rachel et al., Negation as positivity in disguise, in: Herbert L. Colston/Albert Katz (eds.), *Figurative Language Comprehension: Social and Cultural Influences*, Hillsdale 2004, 233-258.

GOBINEAU, Arthur de, *Essai sur l'inégalité des races humaines*, Paris 1853.

GRAVE, Johannes, Vergleichen als Praxis. Vorüberlegungen zu einer praxistheoretisch orientierten Untersuchung von Vergleichen, in: Angelika Epple/Walter Erhart (eds.), *Die Welt beobachten. Praktiken des Vergleichens*, Frankfurt a. M./New York 2015, 135-159.

GREIMAS, Algirdas J., *On Meaning. Selected Writings in Semiotic Theory*, Minneapolis 1987.

Grimm, Wilhelm, *Deutsche Heldensage* [1829], Berlin 1867.
Haskins, Henry S., *Meditations in Wall Street*, New York 1940.
Hazlitt, William, *Table Talk. Essays on Men and Manners* [1821], London 1903.
Heidegger, Martin, *Identität und Differenz*, Pfüllingen 1957.
Heintz, Bettina, "Wir leben im Zeitalter der Vergleichung." Perspektiven einer Soziologie des Vergleichs, in: *Zeitschrift für Soziologie* 45 (5/2016), 305-323.
Heintz, Bettina, Numerische Differenz. Überlegungen zu einer Soziologie des (quantitativen) Vergleichs, in: *Zeitschrift für Soziologie* 39 (3/2010), 162-181.
Heracleitus, *Alleg. Hom.* 24.
Herder, Johann Gottfried von, Früchte sogenannt – goldenen Zeiten des achtzehnten Jahrhunderts [1803], in: Johann Gottfried von Herder, *Sämtliche Werke*, Bände 9–10, Stuttgart 1862.
Hintikka, Jaakko, Negation in Logic and Natural Reasoning, in: *Linguistics and Philosophy* 25 (5–6/2002), 585-600.
Hitler, Adolf, *Rede vor dem Reichstag am 21. Mai 1935*, Berlin 1935.
Hoquet, Thierry, Logique de la comparaison et physique de la génération chez Buffon, in: *La Découverte* 39 (1/2007), 595–612.
Horn, Laurence, *A Natural History of Negation*, Chicago 1989.
Isaiah 46: 09.
Israel, Michael, The Pragmatics of Polarity, in: Laurence Horn/Gregory Ward (eds.), *Handbook of Pragmatics*, New York 2004, 701-723.
Jackendoff, Ray, *A User's Guide to Thought and Meaning*, Oxford 2012.
Jakobson, Roman, Verbal Communication, in: *Scientific American* 227 (1972), 72-81.
Jakobson, Roman, The Cardinal Dichotomy of Language, in: Ruth Nanda Anshen (ed.), *Language: An Inquiry into its Meaning and Function*, Port Washington, NZ 1971, 155-173.
James, William, *The Principles of Psychology* [1907], New York 2007.
Jean Paul, Die Elternliebe gegen Kinder. Eine einfache Erzählung [1810], in: Jean Paul [Richter], *Werke* (Band 2, Teil 3), München 1978, 217.
Jespersen, Otto, *The Philosophy of Grammar*, Woking/London 1963.
Jünger, Ernst, Lob der Vokale [1934], in: Ernst Jünger, *Sämtliche Werke* (Band 14, Essays VI), Stuttgart 2015, 28.
Kierkegaard, Søren, Kjerlighedens Gjerninger, in: Søren Kierkegaard, *Samlede vaerker*, Band 9, Kjøbenhavn 1847.
Klecha, Peter, *Bridging the Divide: Scalarity and Modality*, Chicago 2014.
Koselleck, Reinhart, *Zeitschichten*, Frankfurt a. M. 2000.
Koselleck, Reinhart, *Vergangene Zukunft. Zur Semantik geschichtlicher Zeiten*, Frankfurt a. M. 1979.
Krug, Wilhelm T., *Allgemeines Handwörterbuch der philosophischen Wissenschaften*, Band 1, A bis E, Leipzig 1832, 499.

LAMB, Charles M., *Housing Segregation in Suburban America since 1960*, Cambridge 2005.
LEACH, Geoffrey, *Principles of Pragmatics*, Harlow 1983.
LECLERC, Georges-Louis (Comte de Buffon), *Œuvres completes. Tome VIII. Histore des animaux* [1749], Paris 1833.
LEIBNIZ, Gottfried W., Essais sur la bonté de dieu, la liberté de l'homme et l'origine du mal [1710], in: Gottfried W. Leibniz, *Œuvres*. Paris 1846, 110-371.
LÉVI-STRAUSS, Claude, The Structural Study of Myth, in: *The Journal of American Folklore* 68 (270/1955), 428-444.
LOCKE, John, *An Essay Concerning Human Understanding* [1689], Vol.1, New York 1894.
LUCRETIUS CARUS, Titus, *De rerum natura* (II, 55–58).
LUCY, John A., Reflexive language and the human disciplines, in: John A. Lucy/Lucy A. Lucy (eds.), *Reflexive Language: Reported Speech and Metapragmatics*, Cambridge 1993, 9–13.
LUHMANN, Niklas, *Soziale Systeme: Grundriß einer allgemeinen Theorie*, Frankfurt a. M. 1987.
LUHMANN, Niklas, *Liebe als Passion. Zur Kodierung der Intimität*, Frankfurt 1982.
LUHMANN, Niklas, Über die Funktion der Negation in sinnkonstituierenden Systemen, in: Harald Weinrich (ed.), *Positionen der Negativität. (Poetik und Hermeneutik, vol. X)*, München 1975, 201-208.
LUHMANN, Niklas, Weltzeit und Systemgeschichte. Über Beziehungen zwischen Zeithorizonten und sozialen Strukturen gesellschaftlicher Systeme, in: Peter Ch. Ludz (ed.), *Soziologie und Sozialgeschichte*, Opladen 1972, 81-115.
LUTHER, Martin, Auslegung uber das fünffte Buch Mose/Deuteronomium genant/Verdeudscht Anno 1525, in: *Der Achte Teil der Bücher des Ehrwirdigen Herrn D. Martini Lutheri*, Wittenberg 1556.
LYONS, John, *Linguistic Semantics: An Introduction*, London 1995.
MARCUSE, Herbert, *Reason and Revolution*, Boston 1960.
MARSCHAL, Bertrand, De quelques comparaisons baudelairiennes, in: Max Milner (ed.), *Baudelaire toujours: homage à Claude Pichois*, Paris 2007, 189-201.
MATTHES, Joachim, The Operation Called 'Vergleichen', in: Joachim Matthes, *Zwischen den Kulturen? Die Sozialwissenschaften vor dem Problem des Kulturvergleichs*, Göttingen 1992, 75-100.
MATTHEW 18.3.
MAUGHAM, William Somerset, Theatre [1937], in: William Somerset Maugham, *Selected Novels*, Vol. 1, Melbourne 1953, 145.
MAUZ, Andreas/SASS, Hartmut von, Vergleiche verstehen. Einleitende Vorwegnahmen..., in: Andreas Mauz/Hartmut von Sass (eds.), *Hermeneutik des Vergleichs. Strukturen, Anwendungen und Grenzen komparativer Verfahren*, Würzburg, 2011, 15.
MCCALL, Marsh H., *Ancient Rhetorical Theories of Simile and Comparison*, Cambridge 1969.

MESLIER, Jean [Paul Henri Thiry, baron d'Holbach], *Le bon-sens; ou, Idées naturelles opposées aux Idées surnaturelles*, Londres/Amsterdam 1772.

MIGNOLO, Walter D., Who Is Comparing What and Why?, in: Rita Felski/Susan Stanford Friedman (eds.), *Comparison: Theories, Approaches, Uses*, Baltimore 2013, 99-119.

MITCHELL, William J. T., Why Comparisons are Odious, in: *World Literature Today* 70 (2/1996), 321-324.

NAPOLI, Ernesto, Negation, in: *Grazer Philosophische Studien* 72 (2006), 233-252.

NOUDELMANN, François, La Traite, la Shoah... sur les usages d'une comparaison, in: *Littérature* 174 (2/2014), 104-113.

OVID, *Tristia*.

PAGEAUX, Daniel-Henri, Littérature comparée et comparaisons, in: *Revue de Littérature comparée* 72 (3/1998), 285-307.

PÉGUY, Charles, Note conjointe sur M. Descartes et la philosophie cartésienne [1914], in: Charles Péguy, *Œuvres completes*, T. IX, Paris 1924, 329.

PERRAULT, Charles, *Parallèle des anciens et des modernes en ce qui regarde les arts et les sciences* [1687], München 1964.

POSTOUTENKO, Kirill, Der Antichrist und seine Widersacher, in: Kay Junge et al. (eds.), *Kippfiguren. Ambivalenz in Bewegung*, Weilerswist 2013, 143–152.

POSTOUTENKO, Kirill, Asymmetrical Concepts and Political Asymmetries: A Comparative Glance at 20th Centuries Democracies and Totalitarianisms from a Discursive Standpoint, in: Kay Junge/Kirill Postoutenko (eds.), *Asymmetrical Concepts after Reinhart Koselleck: Historical Semantics and Beyond*, Bielefeld 2011, 81–114.

POSTOUTENKO, Kirill, From Asymmetries to Concepts, in: Kay Junge/Kirill Postoutenko (eds.), *Asymmetrical Concepts after Reinhart Koselleck: Historical Semantics and Beyond*, Bielefeld 2011, 197-251.

POSTOUTENKO, Kirill, Social Identity as a Complementarity of Performance and Proposition, in: Edmundo Balsemão Pires/Burkhard Nonnenmacher/Stefan Buttner-von Stulpnagel (eds.), *Bezüge des Selbst. Selbstreferentielle Prozesse in philosophischen Perspektiven*, Coimbra 2010, 271–298.

POSTOUTENKO, Kirill, Wandering as Circulation: Dostoevsky and Marx on the "Jewish Question", in: Gideon Reuveni/Sarah Wobick-Segev (eds.), *The Economy in Jewish History: New Perspectives on the Interrelationship between Ethnicity and Economic Life*, New York/Oxford 2010, 43–61.

RATHENAU, Walther, *Auf dem Fechtboden des Geistes – Aphorismen aus seinen Notizbüchern*" [1922], Wiesbaden 1953.

RICHTER, Melvin, Two Eighteenth-Century Senses of "Comparison" in Locke and Montesquieu, in: *Jahrbuch für Recht und Ethik* 8 (2000), 385-406.

RIMBAUD, Arthur, Voyelles [1871], in: Arthur Rimbaud, *Œuvres*, Paris 1983, 110.

ROJAS, Fernando de, *La Celestina, ó, Comedia de Calisto y Melibea* [1499], Barcelona 1841.
ROOSEVELT, Franklin D., Fireside Chat 15 (On National Defense [1940]), in: Franklin D. Roosevelt, *FDR's Fireside Chats*, Norman 1992.
RUIZ DE MORALES, Joaquin, *Historia de la milicia nacional: desde su creación hasta nuestros días*, Madrid 1856.
RUSKIN, John, *The Stones of Venice*, London 1851.
RUSSELL, Bertrand, Mathematical Logic as Based on the Theory of Types, in: *American Journal of Mathematics*, 30 (3/1908), 222-262.
SAINT-SIMON, Henri, *Œuvres choisies*, Paris 1859.
SAINT-SIMON, Henri, *Science de l'homme, physiologie religieuse*, Paris 1813.
SAND, George, *Le Péché de Monsieur Antoine* [1845], Paris 1864.
SARLES, Harvey B., *Language and Human Nature*, Minneapolis 1985.
SARTRE, Jean-Paul, Huis clos, in: Jean Paul Sartre, *Théâtre I*, Paris 1947, 182.
SASS, Hartmut von, Vergleiche(n). Ein hermeneutischer Rund- und Sinkflug, in: Andreas Mauz/Hartmut von Sass (eds.), *Hermeneutik des Vergleichs. Strukturen, Anwendungen und Grenzen komparativer Verfahren*, Würzburg, 2011, 25-48.
SAVORY, William S., *On Dreaming and Somnambulism, in Relation to the Functions of Certain Nerve-Centres*, London 1864.
SCHENK, Günther/KRAUSE, Andrej, Vergleich, in: Joachim Ritter/Karlfried Gründer/Gottfried Gabriel (eds.), *Historisches Wörterbuch der Philosophie* 11 (2001), 677.
SEARLE, John R., *Speech Acts: An Essay in the Philosophy of Language*, Cambridge 1978.
SGALL, Petr, *Jazyk, mluvení, psaní*, Praha 2011.
SILVERMAN, Daniel, *Neutralization*, Cambridge 2012.
SIMON, Herbert A., A Behavioral Model of Rational Choice, in: *The Quarterly Journal of Economics* 69 (1/1955), 99-118.
SPOERHASE, Carlos, Das Maß der Potsdamer Garde, Die ästhetische Vorgeschichte des Rankings in der europäischen Literatur- und Kunstkritik des 18. Jahrhunderts, in: *Jahrbuch der Deutschen Schillergesellschaft* 58 (2014), 90-126.
STEINMETZ, Willibald, Above/below, better/worse, or simply different? Metamorphoses of Social Comparisons, 1600-1900, in: Steinmetz, Willibald (ed.), *The Force of Comparison. A New Perspective on Modern European History and the Contemporary World*, New York/Oxford 2019, 80-112.
STEINMETZ, Willibald, 'Vergleich' - eine begriffsgeschichtliche Skizze, in: Angelika Epple/Walter Erhart (eds.), *Die Welt beobachten. Praktiken des Vergleichens*, Frankfurt a. M./New York 2015.
STRAWSON, Paul F., *Introduction to Logical Theory* (Routledge Revivals [1952]), London 2012.
STRINDBERG, August, *Brott och brott*, Stockholm 1899.

STROHSCHNEIDER, Peter, Fremde in der Vormoderne. Über Negierbarkeitsverluste und Unbekanntheitsgewinne, in: Anja Becker (ed.), *Alterität als Leitkonzept für historisches Interpretieren* (Reihe: Deutsche Literatur, Bd. 8), Berlin 2012, 387–416.

TENNYSON, Alfred, Ode on the Death of the Duke of Wellington (1852), in: Alfred Tennyson, *Selected Poetry*, London 1995, 112.

THE QURAN 112.4.

THOMPSON, Zadock, *Journal of a Trip to London, Paris, and the Great Exhibition, in 1851*, Burlington 1852.

TROLLOPE, Anthony, *Linda Tressel* [1868], Frankfurt a. M. 2018.

TRUBETSKOY, Nikolai S., *Grundzüge der Phonologie*, Prague 1939.

TWINING, William, *The Great Juristic Bazaar: Jurists' Texts and Lawyers Stories*, London 2017.

VACHEK, Josef, *Selected Writings in English and General Linguistics*, The Hague 1976.

VALLÉS, Pedro, *Libro de refranes y sentencias* [1549], Madrid 2003.

VERGIL, *Bucolica*.

VERGIL, *Georgica*.

VOLTAIRE, *Candide* [1759], Paris 2012.

VOLTAIRE, [Review:] De Sacra Poesi Hebraeorum Praelectiones Academicae, Oxonii Habitae, a Roberto Lowth, A. M. Poeticae Publico Praelectore, etc., [1764], in: André Versaille (ed.), *Dictionnaire de la pensée de Voltaire par lui-même*, Paris 1994, 677.

VOLTAIRE, Des Juifs [1756], in: André Versaille (ed.), *Dictionnaire de la pensée de Voltaire par lui-même*, Paris 1994, 688.

WEINTRAUB, David A., *Is Pluto a Planet? A Historical Journey through the Solar System*, Princeton 2007.

WENZEL, Horst, Initialen in der Manuskriptkultur und im digitalen Medium, in: Helga Lutz/Jan-Friedrich Missfelder/Tilo Renz (eds.), *Äpfel und Birnen. Illegitimes Vergleichen in den Kulturwissenschaften*, Bielefeld 2006, 41-56.

WERRON, Tobias/RINGEL, Leopold, Rankings in a comparative perspective, (manuscript, 2015).

WIESER, Dagmar/LABARTHE, Patrick (eds.), *Mémoire et oubli dans le lyrisme européen: hommage à John E. Jackson*, Paris 2008.

WILLEMS, Dominique/BLANCHE-BENVENISTE, Claire, A constructional corpus-based approach of 'weak' verbs in French, in: Hans C. Boas/Francisco Gonzálvez-García (eds.), *Romance perspectives on construction grammar*, Amsterdam 2014, 113–138.

WILLER, Stefan, The problem of theorizing comparisons (in science and literature), in: *Neohelicon* 41 (2014), 371-380.

WILLER, Stefan, Die Allgemeinheit des Vergleichs. Ein komparatistisches Problem und seine Entstehung um 1800, in: Michael Eggers (ed.), *Von Ähnlichkeiten und*

Unterschieden. Vergleich, Analogie und Klassifikation in Wissenschaft und Literartur, Heidelberg 2011, 143-165.

WORDSWORTH, William, "It is a beauteous evening, calm and free..." [1802], in: William Wordsworth, *Poetical Works*, London 1896, 332.

YPMA, Eelcko, La relation est-elle un être réel ou seulement un être de raison, d'après Jacques de Viterbe, in: Jean Jolivet/Zenon Kałuża/Alain de Libera/Charles Pietri (eds.), *Lectionum varietates: Hommage à Paul Vignaux*, Paris 1991, 155–162.

ZUBER, Ryszard, Privative opposition as a semantic relation, in: *Journal of Pragmatics* 4 (5/1980), 413–424.

ТУРГЕНЕВ, Иван С., Путешествие по святым местам русским [1836], in: Иван С. Тургенев, Сочинения, Т. 1. М. 1978, 173.

Incomparability
A Tentative Guide for the Perplexed

Hartmut von Sass

Abstract

The idea of incomparability has been an attractive one – and remains largely obscure. This paper aims at structuring the recent debate through distinguishing between different accounts, mostly defending the possibility of incomparability. Arguments for incomparability are critically scrutinized and a possibility for attacking them is presented by relying on the parity account. Lastly, what is coined as structural incomparability will be refuted in order to create a conceptual space for its evaluative (normative or moral) counterpart.

To begin with: Reporting from the margins of comparison

You can furnish an entire library with books solely dedicated to *metaphors*; you need a good part of that library for sheltering your volumes on *analogies*; and it still takes a couple of high shelves to store the exegetical and philosophical literature on *parables*. And what about comparing? A mini-board might already be more than you need. It is an interesting but hardly self-evident circumstance that tropes have traditionally gained a significant attention by rhetorics, in theories of argumentation as well as in semantics; and despite comparisons being the most prominent figure of speech given their permanent usage in our everyday dealings—who lives, compares –, they are academically still lingering in the shade. Hence, this striking misbalance between factual prominence and intellectual ignorance is telling. But what exactly does it tell us? That comparisons and the practice of comparing—as an exception to the rule among the tropes—are just trivial?

As a matter of fact, it is not easy to find contributions to the topic in question coming from theoretical or moral philosophy. And to do this from a philosophical angle might already be based on an assumption that is highly disputed: namely, that it is fruitful or makes at least sense to speak of comparisons without the immediate reference to a practical and scientific context. In other words: one might have to subscribe to the claim that there is (something like) a more general *hermeneutics* of comparison that lies in front of the divergent fields in which concrete comparisons are applied. If one repudiates this possibility of a general account applicable or being relevant to all these different areas of application while maintaining the academic interest in the practice of comparing, one could refer to the *disciplinary* work on comparisons and comparing. There are several comparatively oriented subjects—some of them have the term even in their name—and here we do find methodological reflections on what they are actually doing, yet always tied to a specific field: literature, law, religion, etc.[1] Hence, we are facing a simple and binary alternative: a general comparative structure actualized within different areas (top-down) or a variety of comparisons bound to particular areas (bottom-up)—*a* comparison or *practices* of comparing? This is, admittedly, an unhappy alternative, but for heuristic purposes I will go here with the former option.

This is not to say that the philosophical work on comparisons that actually exists would not be bound to more focussed issues. There are, as far as I can see, especially two specific debates in which comparisons and also the problem of incomparability play a significant role: the clash of *conflicting values* and the incommensurability of *rival scientific theories*.[2] The one issue belongs to the debate on value and virtue theories challenged by inner-personal or, more importantly, social and cultural plurality. The fear is here that without being able to compare values, a rational choice between moral or existential options is up in the air; comparability of divergent values is, then, considered to be part of moral rationality. The counter-position called *comparativism* meeting that fear defends this all-encompassing possibility of comparatively weighing values.[3] The other issue, the rivalry of scientific theories, is linked to the problem of incommensurability—a classical chapter within the philosophy of science since Fleck, Kuhn and Paul Feyerabend.[4] Here, the general view is, that theories are embedded in paradigms; and these paradigms are supposed to be diachronically or synchronically separated in such a way that there are no translations of one paradigm into another one possible. Since there is no meta-

---

1   Very instructive accounts are given by Charles C. Ragin, *The Comparative Method. Moving Beyond Qualitative and Quantitative Strategies*, Berkeley/Los Angeles/London 1987; and Charles Tilly, *Big Structures. Large Processes. Huge Comparisons*, New York 1985.

2   See Thomas S. Kuhn, Commensurability, Comparability, Communicability, in: *Proceedings of the Biennial Meeting of the Philosophy of Science Association*, Volume Two, Symposia and Invited Papers (1982), 669–688.

3   Cf. Ruth Chang, *Making Comparisons Count*, London/New York 2002, 43; see also Donald Regan, Value, Comparability, and Choice, in: Ruth Chang (ed.), *Incommensurability, Incomparability, and Practical Reason*, Cambridge/London 1997, 129–150.

4   For Ludwik Fleck see his *Entstehung und Entwicklung einer wissenschaftlichen Tatsache. Einführung in die Lehre vom Denkstil und Denkkollektiv*, ed. by Lothar Schäfer/Thomas Schnelle, 10th ed., Frankfurt a.M. 2015, 82 and 145; on Kuhn and Feyerabend see Eric Oberheim/Paul Hoyningen-Huene, The Incommensurability of Scientific Theories, in: Edward N. Zalta (ed.), *The Stanford Encyclopedia of Philosophy* (2016), URL: https://plato.stanford.edu/archives/win2016/entries/incommensurability/ [last accessed April 9, 2020].

paradigm either, incommensurability entails not only intranslatability, but also incomparability.

Now, while these debates, in particular the first one, did not amount to a general account on comparisons, they may help us to come nearer to that goal. For this purpose, I have to give a short reminder concerning the structure of comparisons that enables us, in further steps, to see more clearly where precisely the problem of incomparability might arise—and where and why not.

The structure of comparison: a short reminder

The structure of comparison is, at first glance, very simple. Different items (*relata*) are compared in relation to one respect (*tertium comparationis*). Since there is not and cannot be a comparison *simpliciter* the comparative regard is a necessary element of every act of comparing items. I suggest to call the items the *material* part while the *tertium* serves as the *formal* aspect of the comparison. However, this analysis is insufficient, since both, the material and the formal elements of the comparison, have a *context* that is essential for the comparison not only to be meaningful but also to be possible in the first place. This implies that the items do not exist in a void but within a concrete arrangement. Imagine, a friend of yours has birthday, and you have two ideas for a present or gift. Suppose now that it turns out (and you get to know) that your friend has already present B. Comparing A and B without that particular context might have led to a very different decision than the one you will actually make now, namely chosing A. One could also say that the connection between A and its context C_A (and the same goes for the contextualized B and C_B) entertain an 'internal' relation; C_A is then only analytically separatable from A but nevertheless intrinsically connected to it as long as the comparison between A and B should have any relevance.

Now, I, however, claimed more; namely that the comparison between A and B is not only meaningless (and not reliable) without taking the contexts C_A and C_B into account, but not possible either. Why that stronger claim? Since one cannot switch off the context. Assuming that your friend had not been given the gift B is itself part of an implicit context that was—here wrongly—presupposed, but that is, nevertheless, open to be made explicit. Hence, there are no As and Bs without Cs_A and Cs_B. These contexts may be tacit, but that does not mean that they are not there, at least latently.

There are not only the contexts of the material parts of the comparison to be considered. The formal aspect, the *tertium comparationis*, has also its specific context, call it C_T. Let us, again, refer to an example: it is an already established complain—typical within and for the discourse on comparisons—that one cannot compare apples with pears. What causes this reservation is simply the presupposition that A and B have to entertain a certain degree of resemblance (*similitudo*). Apples and pears connected to each other by comparison would, then, not meet that condition. This claim is, obviously, confused.

What is, however, not wrong-headed is the call for a specific similarity, but the question is of how to understand this call correctly. One might say, the similarity between A and B is not an *ontological* one (the actual semblance between apples and pears), but rather a *constructed* one—by way of already having or now chosing the formal respect (*tertium*) in virtue of which one delivers the relevant comparison.

Now, this constructive regard creates, in a way, the kind of resemblance needed for comparing even apples and pears. And that creation is based on the context of the comparative regard (C_T). For example, you want to bake a pie, and the question is which fruits are better fitting the taste the pie should have. According to that regard, one might prefer pears over apples. By C_T the fruits turned to be similar enough, while determinating as well as contextualizing the regard enabling the comparison in question. Here again, enabling is to be read not only in the sense of securing the meaning and significance of comparing A and B, but to make that comparative act possible.

To complicate things a bit more, one should also take into account that both kinds of contexts—of the material items (A, B, ...) and of the formal regard (T)—are not independent of each other. Refer again to our birthday present example: take T to be the criterion of newness and surprise—not the worst choice when speaking of the anniversary gift for your friend. The context of having a friend's birthday as an institution informs the significance and sense of T; to put simpler: usually, a birthday present should be surprising; that is the context T which establishes the criterion of newness. Hence, if you know that your friend has already present B, you will chose A. Change the example a bit now: imagine your friend possessed a loved watch and desperately forgot and lost it somewhere. Given that background, you decide to buy a new one of the same kind. Now, you will chose A, since the context of the items has changed so that the criterion T, newness and surprise, is met in a different way.

To sum up: a comparison (between two items; more are, obviously, possible) is a relation of, at least, five elements of three kinds:

- *material*: the items A and B;
- *formal*: the comparative regard T;
- *contextual*: the interacting contexts of the items (C_A, C_B) as well as the context of the particular regard (C_T).

At the outset, I have claimed that it is fruitful, but also possible to give a general account of comparisons without necessarily starting from a particular comparative usage or having a specific discipline in mind—but to apply the general formula to these contexts of potential application. Accordingly, this claim implies now that this account just given is relevant for the particular act of comparing, in everyday life as well as in disciplinary work, that it applies to different kinds of comparisons distinguishable by a typology,[5] and that it is independent of the status of comparing items, i.e. independent of the old philosophical question of whether the act to compare is just a *logical structure* or even a *mental operation* of the human mind, as authors like John Locke have it.[6]

Incomparability. A first spot

A lover might say that her loved one is unique—remember Sinéad O'Connor singing in the 1990 Prince cover "Nothing Compares to You"; or recall the constant warning not to relativize the Holocaust precisely by comparing it to other instances of mass murder and destruction; or take the late Karl Barth who took Mozart to be the incomparable, "Der Unvergleichliche".[7] "Incomparability" is, hence, a part of our ordinary language, a usual language-game we play, one might say. However, it would be exaggerated to claim, incomparability represented a major topic in theoretical or moral philosophy. To my knowledge, and as indicated, there are only two more concrete issues in which comparative moves and their limits play a significant role, the incommensurability of different theories and the plurality of divergent values. I will leave the first problem aside since it would entail questions whose answers would lead us astray given our topic; and instead, I would like to concentrate on comparing (moral) values—putting the stress on 'comparing' and not on 'values'—or on comparing non-evaluative things.

The significance of the debate might appear to be clear in a straightforward sense: It is hold by many authors that different values confront us with situations of partly severe choices; if we go with their incomparability, one might fear, then chosing rationally between alternatives is turned to be a hopeless endeavor. The counterpart to this position is called *comparativism* meaning "the view that a comparison of the alternatives with respect to an appropriate covering value 'determines' a choice as justified, where this relation of determination is to be filled out

---

5   For the typology see Hartmut von Sass, Vergleiche(n). Ein hermeneutischer Rund- und Sinkflug, in: Andreas Mauz/Hartmut von Sass (eds.), *Hermeneutik des Vergleichs. Strukturen, Anwendungen und Grenzen komparativer Verfahren* (Interpretation interdisziplinär 8), Würzburg 2011, 25-48, see 39.
6   Cf. Henrik Birus, Das Vergleichen als Grundoperation der Hermeneutik, in: Henk de Berg/Matthias Prangel (eds.), *Interpretation 2000: Positionen und Kontroversen* (Festschrift Horst Steinmetz), Heidelberg 1999, 95-117, see 97.
7   Cf. Peter Paul Sänger (ed.), *Der Unvergleichliche – Karl Barth über Wolfgang Amadeus Mozart*, Berlin 1983.

in due course"[8]. Hence, the more space we relinquish to incomparability the less rational choices can be justified. The lack of being able to compare A and B is, some say, tantamount to the threat of irrationality.[9]

Generally speaking, comparability means (or, according to the standard view, is defined as) the relating of A to B by either 'better than', 'worse than' or 'equally good' in terms of a particular regard. What we, hence, need for items to be comparable is, 1) a *positive* value relation (saying what is—and not only, what is not—the case between A and B) as well as 2) a *tertium comparationis* (since there is no comparison between A and B *simpliciter*, but only in regard to a certain respect) (see, again, section 1).[10]

It follows that incomparability—like comparability (at least) a three-place-relation—presupposes also a comparative respect while lacking a positive value relation (not necessarily a negative one). Or in definitive terms: "two items are incomparable with respect to a covering value if, for every positive value relation relativized to that covering value, it is not true that it holds between them."[11]

There are three general reactions to this view of having potential incomparability: the *epistemicist* tells us that there is no real incomparability which is, instead, only an apparent one based on ignorance or insufficient information;[12] the *incomparabilitist* defends the view that there are cases in which no positive value relation holds—and, thus, we have actually to deal with incomparability;[13] and finally, there are the *indeterminists* stating that alleged incomparability is nothing but the (semantic) vagueness of the predicates 'better than', 'worse than' and 'equally good'.[14] All three positions subscribe to the trichotomy thesis, i.e. to the claim that 'better than', 'worse than' and 'equally good' exhaust the conceptual space for comparability. This view has been contested (see section 7.3.).

---

8 Chang, *Making Comparisons Count*, 43.
9 Cf. Ruth Chang, Introduction, in: Ruth Chang (ed.), *Incommensurability, Incomparability, and Practical Reason*, Cambridge/London 1997, 1-34, see 23; for a different account criticizing the implicit rationalism in comparativism cf. Joseph Raz, *The Morality of Freedom*, Oxford 1986, 126-27.
10 Obviously, there are further logical relations possible, such as 'not worse than...' or 'at least as good as ...'—but, as the standard view has it, these are derivative relations reducible to the three basic ones.
11 Chang, Introduction, 6; see also Chang, *Making Comparisons Count*, 9; in italics in the original text.
12 Cf. Regan, Value, Comparability, and Choice, 130, 136, 144.
13 Cf. Raz, *The Morality of Freedom*.
14 Cf. John Broome, Incommensurable Values, in: Roger Crisp/Brad Hooker (eds.), *Well-Being and Morality: Essays of Honour of James Griffin*, Oxford 2001, 21-38.

On the conceptual neighborhood

There are some specific features that comparability possesses. Such as *categoriality, complementarity, reflexibility, transitivity*: if A is comparable (with B) this is either true or false and not a matter of degree or grades; A is either comparable to B or not, *tertium non datur*;[15] While A might be comparable to something else, it is not to itself (it is not better or worse than itself, but it is not equally good either); and finally, if A is comparable with B, and B is with C, A is also with C. Now, when we refer to *in*comparability nothing changes in terms of categoriality, complementarity and reflexibility. A bit different is the case of transitivity: it does, one might argue, not follow that if A is incomparable with B, and B is with C, that A is also incomparable with C. Take an example: if you cannot decide what to prefer, an orange or an apple, and if you cannot decide between an apple and a banana, it does not follow that you do not know what to do confronted with the admittingly trivial choice between an orange and a banana.[16]

Incomparability is, often enough, confounded with incommensurability as a covering term for relative, but different concepts; and it is helpful to save theses differences.[17] One might denote options as *incompatible* (and not incomparable) if the choice in favor of the one option is only possible at the cost of the alternative—you can't have it both ways.[18] Different items, values for instance, are incommensurable, according to another account, if they cannot be reduced to one superior value (think of 'happiness' in Mill and Bentham); this is the problem of *plurality* or *diversity*. Then, there is a phenomenon called *trumping*, i.e. a case in which the duty not to perform x outweights the benefitting from x; so, for example, one's obligation not to lie trumps the utility to do so in a given situation (now you see, that this kind of trumping has absolutely nothing to do with the nincompoop in the White House right now). Again another case is what is called *nonsubstitutability* meaning when the loss in one value cannot be compensated by the gain of (or in) another one; this applies particularly to values that are taken to be 'sacred' and per definitionem not replaceable.[19] Finally, there is *incommensurability in a narrower sense* meaning that items are incommensurable if there is no cardinal scale according to which both could be measured. This version has, again, two other subversions:

---

15   It does not follow, however, that, if A is comparable to B, non-A would be incomparable to B.
16   Please note, that in the example I transformed the imcomparability talk into talking about decision and choice.
17   See also James Griffin, Incommensurability: What's the Problem?, in: Ruth Chang (ed.), *Incommensurability, Incomparability, and Practical Reason*, Cambridge/London 1997, 35-51, see 38.
18   Cf. for these distinctions Ruth Chang, Incommensurability (and Incomparability), in: Hugh LaFollette (ed.), The International Encyclopedia of Ethics, Oxford 2013, 2591-2604.
19   Cf. Hans Joas, *The Sacredness of the Person: A New Genealogy of Human Rights*, Washington D.C. 2012.

either it is meant that the scales we have are insufficient to deliver a ranking or one accepts the items to be "unrankable"[20].

Performative and structural incomparability

How to compare a Mercedes 230 SEL with the description of how to use your TV-remote control? How to compare the imagination that you are the striker scoring at the final game of the soccer world cup with the moral conviction that it is necessary to help refugees coming from areas suffering from famine and war? How to compare the beauty of Bielefeld with the force of a deductively successful argument? One might find that these instances articulate complete nonsense. The standard answer might be: "Well, these items are *so different* that comparing them is undermined from the outset." But the problem is whether we are rather dealing with meaningless comparisons being open for the possibility to eventually find a regard under which a comparison is fruitful or whether comparing these items truly lead us to an impossibility of being compared. It is a debated issue if there are actually cases of that absolute and not only rhetorical incomparability or whether the *comparativistic* view is true according to which everything could, structurally speaking, be compared to anything else.

I hold, however, the quest for incomparability to be only partly a structural problem. If this is so, then one might refer to the dimensions of comparisons insofar as *structural incomparability* must be based on the relation between the material (items to be related to each other), formal (*tertia*) and contextual aspects of comparisons—I will come back to this in a minute. Nevertheless, not every version of incomparability is a structural one. Contrary to that first form we have to deal—and one might add, very often—with what we could call *performative incomparability*. Then, we have cases in which a comparison is indeed possible, and that very possiblity is actually the problem—with the consequence to commit oneself, morally or intimately, *not* to compare.

The distinction between performative (comparing is possible but suspended) and structural incomparability (comparing is impossible) is not self-evident. The first version is often dismissed as mere equivocation to restrict the term 'incomparability' to the second version.[21] I won't follow that suggestion because the performative and rhetorically accompanied suspension of structurally possible comparisons is a highly important institution, in morals and public life as well as in intimate contexts. I will briefly concentrate on cases in which the suspension to compare is *morally* loaden.

---

20 Griffin, Incommensurability: What's the Problem?, 37.
21 Cf. Chang, *Making Comparisons Count*, ch. 4.

By comparing items one creates a cluster on which one's orientation is based. Hence, a comparison is meaning- and successful insofar as it satisfies the practical need for a concrete orientation.[22] The call for suspending a structurally possible comparison could, therefore, be considered as a critique of creating a disputable cluster or a wrongheaded orientation. When, back in 1986, the German historian Ernst Nolte related the Holocaust to the Gulags in the Soviet Union insinuating that the first had been the reaction to the second the vast majority of replicas expressed a severe critique of Nolte's historiographic orientation based on a comparative attitude that was regarded to be morally indefensible. Either one assumed that comparing the Holocaust with other horrendous events undermined its singular character; or one did not assail the comparative mode itself, but referred critically to the devastating results of this instrumentalized comparison, as Jürgen Habermas had it.

What comes to the fore here is the dimension of an *ethics of comparison*. This is particularly significant for the limits of comparing different items, a demarcation that is not easy to define. One way to do this is to refer to our "reactive attitudes"[23] towards those stiking to debatable comparative orientations: "attitudes of discomfort, embarrassment, chock, outrage, or horror that is displayed when such calculation or commensuration is engaged in by others", as the English philosopher Steven Lukes holds.[24] Therefore, the performative incomparability is a reaction to the predicament that the comparison is actually possible and yet, for many, morally untenable. Put technically: performative incomparability implies structural comparability.

Constitutive incomparabilty

A case that, one might say, lies between structural and performative (or normative) incomparability is a version that is often labelled as constitutive. This idea goes back to what Charles Taylor and Joseph Raz refer to as "constitutive goods", goods that constitute our life.[25] What turns these goods to be so specific including being

---

22   Cf. Stefan Berg, Vergleichsweise orientiert. Eine orientierungstheoretische Betrachtung des Vergleichens, in: Andreas Mauz/Hartmut von Sass (eds.), *Hermeneutik des Vergleichs. Strukturen, Anwendungen und Grenzen komparativer Verfahren*, Würzburg 2011, 277-303, see 282.
23   Peter F. Strawson, Freedom and Resentment, in: *Proceedings of the British Academy* 48 (1/1962), 1-25.
24   Steven Lukes, Comparing the Incomparable: Trade-offs and Sacrifices, in: Ruth Chang (ed.), *Incommensurability, Incomparability, and Practical Reason*, Cambridge/New York 1997, 184-195, see 189.
25   See Charles Taylor, Leading a Life, in: Ruth Chang (ed.), *Incommensurability, Incomparability, and Practical Reason*, Cambridge, MA/London 1997, 170-183, see 173.

incomparable is, according to Raz, the following feature: "The view that two options cannot be compared is viewed as an obstacle to trade-offs."[26] As example serves often a couple wanting desperately to have a child. No money on earth would be an adequate replacement for that desire. They, Raz claims, would not only not compare both options, but would explicitly repudiate this comparison:

> "For many, having children does not have a money price because exchanging them for money, whether buying or selling, is inconsistent with a proper appreciation of the value of parenthood." (ibid., 348)

The incomparability in cases like parenthood versus money instead (or more classically: money versus friendship) is not based on the breakdown of the three predicates 'better than', 'worse than' and 'equally good', but the refusal to compare in the first place as an expression of the deep appreciation for the value in question. What makes this case to be located at the threshold between structural and performative incomparability is the ambivalent status of that refusal. This means that either one takes this appreciative act to be a 'noncognitive' attitude allowing for a structurally possible comparison that is refuted or one considers that refusal as an (conceptual) entailment of that very value.

Raz wants to say the second but, actually, the way in which he presents his case rather elicits connotations going into the first direction. He sees in this refusal the "symbolic significance" of the parenthood or friendship (349), that belongs to this value itself. For him, then, there is no real distinction between this judgment of incomparability and the case of incomparability itself. He states:

> "My claim regarding incommensurablity is that belief in incommensurability is itself a qualification for having certain relations. [...] Certain judgments about the non-comparability of certain options and certain attitudes to the exchangeability of options are constitutive of relations with friends, spouses, parents, etc." (351 and 352)

The constitutive character is this incomparability implies, for Raz, also that only those refuting to compare friendship with money are able to be real friends or to have real friends.[27] Someone saying that money is more valuable than friendship is neither confused nor is claiming something wrong, but is just incapable of true friendship (cf. 352-53).

The idea of constitutive incomparability has met severe criticism. One might argue that since incomparability between A and B is a symmetrical relation while

---

26 Raz, The Morality of Freedom, 346.
27 This is a similar and similarly debatable claim as the one by Aristotle who holds that one can only be a friend if one is friends with oneself; see Julia Annas, Plato and Aristotle on Friendship and Altruism, in: Mind 86 (344/1977), 532-554.

the relation between friendship and money is not, something must be wrong in Raz' analyses.[28] Furthermore, one has to take the concrete context into account: Assume someone has already more than 'enough' friends but is struggling financially. Would that person be incapable of friendship preferring money over an additional friendship under the particular conditions of having a vivid social life with an empty wallet? And is the expression to value friendship more, in a categorial sense, than money not itself a comparison? Perhaps, what Raz (and others) call constitutive and symbolic concerning this kind of incomparability is not structural, but a deepening of our understanding of instances of performative incomparability.

Locating incomparability I: On what it is *not*

There are further demarcations to be made in order to locate more precisely where we find cases of incomparability. First of all, in- and *noncomparability* are not the same. Two items are noncomparable if the formal requirements necessary for there to be a claim of comparability or incomparability are not fully met. For instance, one of these conditions is that there is a *tertium comparationis*, a regard according to which different items can be related to each other comparatively. If there is no such regard we are dealing with a formal failure, but not with incomparability. Apart from this formal understanding of noncomparability there is also a substantial one: here we do not have a lacking element to turn the comparison possible, but—in having all elements required together—the items to be compared to each other are belonging to different classes or categories (cf. again, section 1).

Take again our examples from above: how to compare a Mercedes 230 SEL with the description for using a TV-remote control? How to compare the notion that you are a successful striker with the moral conviction that it is necessary to help refugees? How to compare the beauty of Bielefeld with the power of a deductively successful argument? One might come up with a covering value, but it is hard to imagine a context in which these comparisons make any sense. Hence, in the one sense of noncomparability, the formal and rather trivial one, an element necessary for the comparison is lacking. In the substantial case, formally everything is in right order besides the problem that the comparatives cannot be related within a comparison that deserves its name. This last, slightly vage phrase indicates already the problem connected to substantial noncomparability: it is a fine line between meaningful comparisons and noncomparability based on lacking a common category.[29] However, that begs the question to the problem of categoriality: what does

---

28 Cf. Chang, Incommensurability (and Incomparability), 2601; she speaks, instead, of "emphatic comparability".
29 Cf. Chang, *Making Comparisons Count*, 9.

it exactly mean to belong to a shared category? A Mercedes and a remote control, a position and a conviction, beauty and an argument. What about comparing the "incomparable" Mozart with Michelangelo—do they belong to a common category, artists, or not, as a musician and a sculptor? Or David Bowie versus Bryan Ferry? While formal noncomparability is easy to detect, the substantial sibbling is not.

A second candidate of incomparability is *incommensurability*; it is a false candidate. While there are authors using both concepts interchangeably,[30] the field of their relevance is highly different. It is the established usage to speak of incommensurable scientific theories (itself a debatable idea)[31] while reserving the term incomparability to plural values and their potential clash.[32] A stronger argument for differentiation is the fruitful restriction of 'incommensurability' to instances where a scale is lacking and, hence, a precise measurement impossible. However, scalarity is not a necessary condition for comparability which means that incommensurability (in the sense just proposed) is compatible with comparability. It is still possible to ordinally compare items beyond scale, think of valuing friendship more than money.

A third case is *vagueness*. According to John Broome all instances of incomparability are based on the vagueness (of predicates). Take, for example, the term 'bald': when is someone bald or not? Obviously, there are cases in which applying that term to someone is a borderline case. Now, it is clear that even in vague cases a comparison might be easily possible. In those where the problem really arises one might say, as done by Ruth Chang,[33] that predicates such as 'bald' could be applied to a case or not—stipulation is possible and helpful here; whereas 'incomparable' is, per se, not a vague predicate: something is comparable or not—see above, *tertium non datur*. Therefore, a straightforward identification of incomparability with vagueness is not without problems (see below, section 7.5.).

---

30   See Raz, *The Morality of Freedom*, 322.
31   A case against the compartmentalisation by the incommensurability theory in Fleck and, more prominently, in Kuhn raises, for instance, Michael Hampe, *Die Lehren der Philosophie. Eine Kritik*, Berlin 2014, 199-201.
32   However, often enough both terms were, nevertheless, intertwined; see Oberheim/Hoyningen-Huene, The Incommensurability of Scientific Theories, 2: "By calling two fundamental theories incommensurable, Feyerabend meant that they were conceptually incompatible: The main concepts of one could neither be defined on the basis of the primitive descriptive terms of the other, nor related to them via a correct empirical statement.".
33   Cf. Ruth Chang, Parity. An Intuitive Case, in: *Ratio* 29 (4/2016), 395-411, see 396; Ruth Chang, The Possibility of Parity, in: *Ethics* 112 (4/2002), 659-688, see 682.

Locating incomparability II: On what it actually might be

If one has a clear measurement, a scale, to relate A to B, one does not have to deal with incomparability. It is obvious that the attendence at Trump's inaugural lecture was far lower than Obama's in 2013. Thus, incomparability, it is safe to say, belongs to the realm beyond (clear) measurement. However, it does not follow that everything that lacks a scale entails incomparability. Think, again, of friendship versus 1000 Dollars; for the vast majority it is perfectly clear what is 'better' (more valuable, more satisfying, etc.). All what we can infer from this might be that cases of comparative breakdown should be explained in terms of a certain kind of indeterminacy. Which kind? In the following passage I would like to distinguish four—alledged—sources of incomparability—plus an argument, to be refuted, that negates or mitigates the existence of incomparability:

Trichotomy and its failure (Joseph Raz)
Repudiating to compare (Derek Parfit*)
Parity—instead of incomparability? (Ruth Chang)
Indeterminacy of the covering value (John Broome)
Indeterminacy of (the meaning of) comparatives (John Broome)

Let's go!

1. Trichotomy and its failure

The moral philosopher Joseph Raz has presented what one might call the standard view of incomparability. This view is based in the trichotomy assumption meaning that there are (see above) three comparative predicates exhausting together the logical space of describing a comparison between A and B: better, worse, and equally good. Incomparability is, then, the breakdown of applying better, worse, and equally good to the relation between A and B. Is liberty or security preferable? Here, Raz claims, we have not only to deal with the sense of comparison and its limits, but also with the truth of that very relationship.[34]

Now, one could imagine to improve A a bit compared to B. The claim implied by their being incomparable is that this slight improvement cannot trigger comparability between A and B either. So, if one takes again liberty and security while 'improving' the latter by giving everyone in the 'secure(d)' world 1000 Dollars on top, nothing has changed. Liberty and security remain in the mode of being incomparable, since the improvement suggestion elicits the notion that the countable element of money might introduce the scalability of the whole comparison—but it doesn't.

---

34 Cf. Raz, *The Morality of Freedom*, 322-23.

Raz also underlines the difference between incomparability and equality. A judgment, Raz holds, concerning the relative value of *A* and *B* is impossible in the case of them being incomparable—whereas equality is precisely such a judgment. There is another difference, the case of transitivity: If *A* and *B* are equal, and if *B* and *C* are equal too, it follows that *A* and *C* are equal as well. However, if *A* and *B* are incomparable and *B* and *C* are too, it does not follow that one could not compare *A* and *C* (325). A similar response goes also for what has been coined as 'rough equality' meaning that *A* and *B* are in that relation when there difference is very small in such a way that all other options that are better (or worse) than *A* are also better (or worse) than *B* (330). In the case of rough equality one is, Raz adds, entitled to be indifferent concerning a preference between *A* and *B*. However, incomparability does not mean indifference and is not based on it either; it is rather the lack of sufficient reasons to go in one direction or the other.

Raz thinks that both elements just sketched—non-transitivity and non-improvement—constitute together a test (not a definition) for incomparability (335). That means: if *A* and *B* are incomparable, and an option *C* is better than *A* but not better than *B*, and if an improvement of *A* (or *B*) does not turn *A* (or *B*) better than *B* (or *A*) both, *A* and *B* are 'truly' incomparable.

This account has caused some protest since, for some, it is not clear whether trichotomy really exhausts the logical space of positive value relations. Especially Ruth Chang has suggested that some (or all?) cases that run under, in Raz, the heading of incomparability are, in reality, cases of 'parity' and, thus, of being comparable (see 7.3.).

2. Repudiating to compare

In part IV of his seminal *Reasons and Persons* Derek Parfit invites us to contemplate different and increasingly complicated scenarios of future states. The criteria are, for a good part, the amount of people who will populate the planet, the quality of their lives—combined with discussing what it means to speak of a life worth living (as a minimal standard of living) plus more specific conditions varying possible outcomes, for instance a higher standard of living for the next 100 years at the cost of a lower standard for the generations then to come—as part of 'future ethics'—or the promise of health while accepting a crucial sacrifice such as a nearer death or having a minority of people living under poor conditions while all others having a good life—as part of 'populations ethics'.[35]

Parfit starts off by introducing the picture you can see in figure 1 (on 385).

First of all, Parfit is not so much concerned with reflecting on comparisons (that's why I added a (*) to his name above; an exception is what he calls 'rough equality' and 'rough or partial comparability', cf. 357 i.a.). However, he *is* comparing

---

35 Cf. Derek Parfit, *Reasons and Persons*, Oxford 1984, 384–390.

Fig. 1

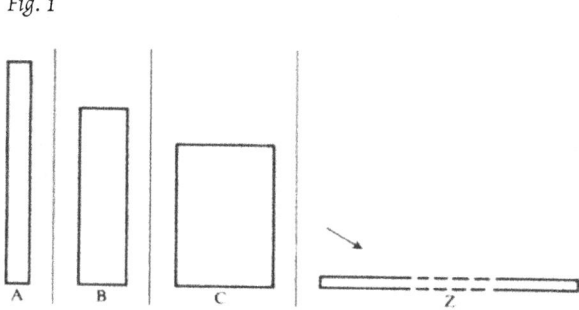

all the time scenarios like A, B, C, ... , Z—while the height of the columns signifies the quality of life and their width represents the amount of people living according to a specific scenario. Hence, in A people enjoy an extremely high standard of living whereas the population is rather small; its amount is doubled in B in having a population with a slightly lower standard.

If one conceptualizes both parameters—quality and quantity of life—and if one presupposes, as utilitarians may have it, that qualitative judgments are eventually reducible to a scalable measurement, one is, henceforth, entitled to compare future states of affairs: B is better than A, C is better than B, ... Now, the scope of Parfit's argument is the paradox that is waiting for us if we continue like this up the scenario Z: here, we have an enormous amount of people living a life hardly worth living. That is, obviously, a "repugnant conclusion" (387).

It is astonishing that Parfit invests so much effort in elaborating on scenarios like the sketched one (and its far more complex sibblings) without paying heed to the question of the comparability of their outcomes or, more to the point, of our willing- and readiness to compare here in the first place. Hence, what might justify this reservation on our part? To begin with, there are two trivial while far-reaching assumptions that make these scenarios keep going, namely that quality of life is somehow measurable and that, even if it were, we can measure that quality of life on the same scale as the one we may use for the amount of people. Both assumptions are either plainly false or have first to be defended.

Putting these deliberations aside for a moment, one might ask why one could hesitate to compare here. I don't think it is enough to refer again to the standard account by Raz and others saying that the comparative predicates 'better than', 'worse than' and 'equally good' remain out of business here since we do compare A and Z to refute the latter. But why not A and B or C? One answer is that we are dealing here with what Raz called 'constitutive incomparability', i.e. it is, then, an intrinsic element of A, B, C ... not to be compared in the case of really valuing A, B, C. His own example is, as seen above, money versus friendship—but there, we can compare in giving (usually) the privilege to friendship. However, what to do confronted by A, B, and C ... is not that clear.³⁶ Another way of explaining the difficulty at hand is to refer to the complex situation consisting of the mixture of quantitative and qualitative elements as well as divergent values that may come into the picture in evaluating the scenarios in question. By values (in a broad sense), I have in mind problems such as whether the notion to benefit a person by causing his/her existence, as Parfit holds (see 394 i.a.), has any sense. The way we answer that question influences our willingness to compare A and B (amounting to prefer B).

I stop here for a moment. For sure, there is more to be said concerning the phenomenology of these cases and our hesitation against a straightforward meeting these problems. However, one lesson that can be learnt from this here could be the direction in which we should go: the problems of comparability may be based on different kinds of indeterminacies effecting the elements constituting the comparison, i.e. the relata as well as the covering value by which these relata are set into a relation. We will come back to this in section 7.4. and 7.5.

3. Parity—Instead of incomparability?

A good deal of the debate concerning incomparability is, however, not dedicated to this notion itself, but to refuting the trichotomy thesis. Hence, it would be wrong to claim that comparing A and B means that one of them is better or both are equally good—since there is, it is argued, a forth logical relation possible that is called by the main proponent of this move, Ruth Chang, 'being on a par' or 'parity'.³⁷ This has obvious implications for the scope of incomparability, but it is not clear what exactly is meant to be achieved if the idea of parity could be established in the first place: sometimes it seems to entail the stronger claim according to which there is no room anymore for incomparability (of different values) by explaining these instances away in referring to parity;³⁸ sometimes, however, Chang is not attempting to replace incomparability but to reduce its scope, by correcting false characterisations of cases as allegedly being incomparable in describing these cases as being on a par.³⁹

But what exactly is parity? Chang uses a particular kind of arrangement to substantialize this somehow vague or surprising notion by attacking the trichotomy thesis and the standard view based on it. I quote the relevant passage at some length:

---

36 See also Lukes, Comparing the Incomparable, 184-195, 188 and 195.
37 Esp. in her influential paper "The Possibility of Parity", and one might take that to be the starting point of trying to establish further logical relations beyond the classical trichotomy plus parity.
38 Cf. Chang, *Making Comparisons Count*, xix.
39 Cf. Chang, The Possibility of Parity, 662.

"[T]ake an arbitrary pair (X, Y) of evaluatively diverse items. For at least some (X, Y) we can create a continuum of X-items by successively adding or subtracting dollars (or pleasurable tingles, etc.) from X. If we add enough dollars, we get an X-item, X+, that is better than Y, and if we subtract enough dollars, we get an X-item, X-, that is worse than Y. Now according to our abstract intuition, adding a dollar, pleasurable tingle, and so forth cannot make a difference to whether one item is better or worse than another item evaluatively very different from it. Therefore, there must be some X-item, X*, in the continuum between X- and X+ that is neither better nor worse than Y. But what relation holds between X* and Y? Suppose one of the trichotomy always holds. Then since X* is neither better nor worse than Y, it and Y must be equally good. According to our intuition that a dollar can't make a difference, however, this is impossible. For if we add fifty cents to X*, we get an item that is better than Y; if we take away fifty cents from X*, we get an item that is worse than Y. And the difference between X* fifty cents, which is better than Y, and X* fifty cents, which is worse than Y, is a dollar. Thus X* and Y cannot be equally good. Therefore, we must reject the assumption that one of the trichotomy always holds; X* is not better than Y, not worse than it, and the two are not equally good."[40]

The less abstract, but structurally parallel version of the argument uses the comparison between Mozart and Michelangelo in terms of creativity. What follows is the attempt to create a *reductio*: suppose the trichotomy holds and both Ms are incomparable, i.e. neither is better than the other and they are not equal either. Now, imagine, there is a guy called Talentlessi, a very bad sculptor. Obviously, he is far worse than Mozart in terms of creativity. Now, imagine that we successively improve Talentlessi to T+, T++, ... and so on—in the end, we will have, again, Michelangelo. However, the standard view entails also, what is called the "small improvement argument" according to which, as we have seen in section 2., a tinily improved element in A—given that A and B are taken to be incomparable—does not turn A better than B.[41] Hence, if Talentlessi is worse than Michelangelo and Mozart (and comparable with them), and if the small improvements (T+, T++, ...) cannot make a crucial difference meaning not to be able to trigger incomparability, Talentlessi+++++++..... is Michelangelo and he is not comparable with Mozart without being better or worse or equal. In other words, insofar as Mozart is comparable with Talentlessi, he is comparable with Talentlessi+, since the difference between T and T+ is just a small one, and such a difference cannot cause incomparability between different items when we had before comparability. If Mozart is comparable with T+, then applying the principle anew, it follows that he is comparable

---

40 Cf. Chang, The Possibility of Parity, 672.
41 Cf. Raz, *The Morality of Freedom*, 328.

with T++, and so on. Comparability with Mozart is secured through the reapplication of small differences, and hence we are lead to the conclusion that Mozart is, finally, comparable with Michelangelo. However, Mozart is not more or less creative than Michelangelo, and nor are both equally creative. Yet it seems that they are nevertheless comparable; thus, there is a forth relation between them.

Chang thinks that those rejecting parity are committing the same mistake as potential dichotomists only allowing for being better or worse than; a trichotomist has, then, to show that there is indeed a third relation, being equal; and a parallel discussion, Chang holds, we have between the standard view and defenders of parity.[42] Nevertheless, there is enough veil surrounding the notion of parity to maintain doubtful. First, one might try to explain what is captured by 'parity' in sticking to more common observations, such as indeterminacy and vagueness of the relation and relata in question.[43] Second, both arguments, the abstract and the Mozart/Michelangelo-form, seem to be based just on a sorites-argument—undermining the transitivity of comparability through small improvements.[44] And third, one might come back to the unclarity mentioned at the beginning of discussing parity, namely the ambivalance of adding a forth relation to comparability and the stronger claim that parity substitutes all cases of incomparability between values.[45] However, we in fact need a notion to express our comparing items under, let's say, *fuzzy* circumstances, i.e. that these items are different in kind while, nevertheless, being compared. In the case considered, we, one might say, actually do compare Mozart and Michelangelo. Holding that it is hard to privilege one of them in terms of creativity *is* itself a comparative result.

4. Indeterminacy of the covering value

According to Raz there are two types of incomparability going back to the following versions: number one is the position Raz himself was concerned with, namely meaning by 'being incomparable' that, as we have seen, all three traditional comparative predicates fail; number two is the alternative that John Broome, in criticizing Raz, was focussed on saying that it is neither true nor false that the traditional

---

42 Cf. Ruth Chang, Parity, Imprecise Comparability, and the Repugnant Conclusion, in: *Theoria* 82 (2016), 182-215, see 193.
43 For this option see Joshua Gert, Value and Parity, in: *Ethics* 114 (3/2004), 492-510; a counterdefence of parity is to be found here: Mozaffar Qizilbash, The Mere Addition Paradox, Parity and Vagueness, in: *Philosophy and Phenomenological Research* 75 (1/2007), 129-151.
44 Chang has tried to dispel the sorites appearance, but not in a convincing manner; see her The Possibility of Parity, 673 and 680; cf. also Erik Carlson, Parity Demystified, in: *Theoria* 76 (2010), 119-128.
45 For a general critique of (the possibility of) parity see Ryan Wasserman, Indeterminacy, Ignorance and the Possibility of Parity, in: *Philosophical Perspectives* 18 'Ethics' (2004), 391-403.

predicates apply. This second version puts the stress on the indeterminacy that is based on different candidates causing the vague character in question.[46]

This vagueness concerns either the covering value of the comparison or the elements that are compared in regard to that value. Let's begin with the first problem and take the example of baldness.[47] This predicate belongs to the non-gradable ones, denoting properties that do not possess certain degrees. Hence, we are often dealing here with borderline cases in, again, two forms: whether a person A falls under the extension of 'baldness' and whether it is possible to decide whether A or B is balder. Ghandi and Churchhill serve here as the prominent example. Who is balder? First of all, that might be a case of trivial vagueness that is accompanied by further circumstances typical for indeterminacy: tolerance meaning here that you could add or substract hairs from Churchhill without solving the question of who is balder; but also the sorites-danger we have encountered already that it leads to a paradox in applying that move too often.[48] Since Gandhi and Churchhill belong in terms of their hair to a particular range of applying the vague predicate 'being bald', it is, as Broome holds,[49] true that it is neither true nor false to state that one of them is balder than the other or that they are equally hairy.

To deepen that case a bit it might be helpful to recognize some differences in our predicates here. First, it is obvious that, for incomparability, we need predicates denoting non-countable elements; second, amoung these vague predicates (such as 'tall'), some have sharp comparatives (such as 'taller' contrary to 'bald' and 'balder than');[50] third, one might analyse a predicate by referring to its properties on which that predicate *supervenes*: for instance, one could hold that baldness is analysable by the amount of hairs, their distribution, their thickness. Now, these sub-features do not suffer from nonquantifiability, because amount and thickness are measurable, and the distribution is determined insofar one stipulates a particular cluster. However, measurement on the sub-level (amount of hair, distribution, thickness) does not bring about a measurement on the supervening level (baldness). And that move of having sub-layers is repeatable, of course.

Therefore, one might say that it is indeterminable whether Gandhi or Churchhill is balder. And this truly frustrating result might go back to two sources involved here: that being bald(er) is in this case a borderline application challenging a precise comparative result including equality; and that we have, on the sub-lever, a

---

46 Hence, I do not distinguish further between 'indeterminacy' and 'vagueness'.
47 See also Cristian Constantinescu, Vague Comparisons, in: *Ratio* 29 (4/2016), 357-377, see 359.
48 If one hair does not make the difference, and if you repeat the substraction, you end up with the contradictive result that a completely bald guy has fine hair.
49 See John Broome, Is incommensurability vagueness?, in: Ruth Chang (ed.), *Incommensurability, incomparability, and practical reasoning*, Cambridge/London 1997, 67-89.
50 Cf. again Constantinescu, Vague Comparisons, 365.

multidimensionality of different regards that entail precise comparatives while it still is not determinate how exactly to combine them.

Thus, the indeterminacy of the covering value challenging incomparability amounts to sub-cases: indeterminacy caused by the vague applicability of the predicate and the indeterminacy caused by the different regards of comparing *A* and *B* without knowing how to come to a comparative result between *A* and *B* in terms of a supervening regard. However, in both cases we can and we do compare, often enough by stipulation, by making the regard more concrete, by defining the relation between the sub-level and the covering value. If it is, then, still difficult to say who's balder—Gandhi or Churchhill—we might hold that they are, in this respect, fuzzily equal.

5. Indeterminacy of (the meaning of) comparatives

Apart from the indeterminacy of the comparative regard there is also indeterminacy possible—and widespread—concerning the items to be compared. Here, again, we have to distinguish two forms, one having to do with the application of a predicate, another one with its meaning, hence, a practical and a semantic version.

A somewhat weird but illustrative example for the first form is given in the following scenario:

> "Suppose Aye measures 180 cm with the mole and 179.5 cm without it. Exactly how tall is Aye? This may be vague—the sentence 'Aye is exactly 180 cm tall' seems indeterminate. But the vagueness at play is not predicate vagueness: expressions of the form 'exactly x cm tall' are paradigmatic examples of sharp predicates. Rather, the vagueness seems to reside in the name."[51]

So, the predicate ‚tall' might itself be vague while its comparative form 'taller than' is not at all. Nevertheless, comparability is only possible by stipulation to solve the indeterminacy here. But speaking of incomparability in these rather simple cases might resemble a stipulative act as well.

A bit more sophisticated is the semantic form. Take, for instance, the predicate 'virtuous' and compare two people in this regard. Obviously, 'virtuous' is a vague predicate, and—contrary to 'tall' and 'taller thwitan'—'being more virtuous' retains that vagueness. What precisely is meant here? Consider the following scenario: we attempt to determine whether *A* or *B* is more virtuous. There are different dimensions that are relevant to our comparing *A* and *B*; think of the classical list of virtues such as justice, prudence, modesty, truthfullness, but also love and hope. Now, what about the cardinal virtue that is missing in this list: faith. Even among theologians it is highly debated whether we should include *fides* here, not to speak of the com-

---

51   Cf. Constantinescu, Vague Comparisons, 363.

munity beyond dogmatic circles. Now, how to pursue with our comparing *A* and *B* in terms of their virtuousness?

One answer might be, again the reference to stipulation: if *A* is a true believer and if we include faith to the list, *A* is more virtuous—if all other things are same—than *B*; if we don't include faith as a virtue *A* and *B* are equally good. In total, *A* might be seen virtuously at least as good as *B*.

However, there are still two problematic aspects. First, it is assumed here that all this is a matter of plain addition without implicitly allowing for a *holistic* version of being virtuous, meaning that the virtues may inform each other possitively of negatively. Hence, enjoying an additional virtue (such as faith) does not automatically mean to be 'more' virtuous. Second, assume that we speak only of intellectual or epistemic virtues such as wisdom, understanding, creativity, or curiosity, among many others.[52] So, here again, it is impossible to put them on a scale and it is equally difficult, then, to come up with a all-encompassing result. Both problems could, of course, appear in a combined fashion.

Could we speak of incomparability here? We do not have to.[53] Not being able to state who is more virtuous is, again, itself a comparative result without having a scale. And it is not really clear what it should *mean* that *A* and *B* are not comparable given that we have a tertium and that *A* and *B* fall under the extension of that respect. What I want to suggest here is that incomparability—in a structural sense—is an empty concept denoting something incomprehensible.

Near the end

I distinguished two forms of incomparability, a performative (or normative) and a structural one. Performative incomparability presupposes the structural version: here, we can compare, but are asked or even morally forced to suspend the structurally possible comparison. I do think that performative incomparability is indeed an important institution within our private life as well as in the social and political discourse. Things are different with structural incomparability I focussed on here, i.e. the structurally impossible act of comparing items. I have tried to argue that *either* theses alledged cases of incomparability are, correctly conceived, cases of *non*comparability *or* they fall under the category of being *fuzzily equal*, an equality without scalability, but within the realm of comparability. This either/or leads to the suggestion that there is no such thing as structural incomparability.

---

52   Some even think of comparability to be a virtue; see Jonathan Culler, Comparability, in: *World Literature Today* 69 (2/1995), 268-270, see 270.
53   See also Ronald de Sousa, The Good and the True, in: *Mind* 83 (1974), 534-551, see 545.

References

ANNAS, Julia, Plato and Aristotle on Friendship and Altruism, in: *Mind* 86 (344/1977), 532-554.
BERG, Stefan, Vergleichsweise orientiert. Eine orientierungstheoretische Betrachtung des Vergleichens, in: Andreas Mauz/Hartmut von Sass (eds.), *Hermeneutik des Vergleichs. Strukturen, Anwendungen und Grenzen komparativer Verfahren*, Würzburg 2011, 277-303.
BIRUS, Henrik, Das Vergleichen als Grundoperation der Hermeneutik, in: Henk de Berg/Matthias Prangel (eds.), *Interpretation 2000: Positionen und Kontroversen* (Festschrift Horst Steinmetz), Heidelberg 1999, 95-117.
BROOME, John, Incommensurable Values, in: Roger Crisp/Brad Hooker (eds.), *Well-Being and Morality: Essays of Honour of James Griffin*, Oxford 2001, 21-38.
CARLSON, Erik, Parity Demystified, in: *Theoria* 76 (2010), 119-128.
CHANG, Ruth, Parity. An Intuitive Case, in: *Ratio* 29 (4/2016), 395-411.
CHANG, Ruth, Parity, Imprecise Comparability, and the Repugnant Conclusion, in: *Theoria* 82 (2016), 182-215.
CHANG, Ruth, Incommensurability (and Incomparability), in: Hugh LaFollette (ed.), *The International Encyclopedia of Ethics*, Oxford 2013, 2591-2604.
CHANG, Ruth, *Making Comparisons Count*, London/New York 2002.
CHANG, Ruth, The Possibility of Parity, in: *Ethics* 112 (4/2002), 659-688.
CHANG, Ruth, Introduction, in: Ruth Chang (ed.), *Incommensurability, Incomparability, and Practical Reason*, Cambridge/London 1997, 1-34.
CONSTANTINESCU, Cristian, Vague Comparisons, in: *Ratio* 29 (4/2016), 357-377.
CULLER, Jonathan, Comparability, in: *World Literature Today* 69 (2/1995), 268-270.
DE SOUSA, Ronald, The Good and the True, in: *Mind* 83 (1974), 534-551.
FLECK, Ludwik, *Entstehung und Entwicklung einer wissenschaftlichen Tatsache. Einführung in die Lehre vom Denkstil und Denkkollektiv*, ed. by Lothar Schäfer/Thomas Schnelle, 10th ed., Frankfurt a. M. 2015.
GERT, Joshua, Value and Parity, in: *Ethics* 114 (3/2004), 492-510.
GRIFFIN, James, Incommensurability: What's the Problem?, in: Ruth Chang (ed.), *Incommensurability, Incomparability, and Practical Reason*, Cambridge/London 1997, 35-51.
HAMPE, Michael, *Die Lehren der Philosophie. Eine Kritik*, Berlin 2014.
JOAS, Hans, *The Sacredness of the Person: A New Genealogy of Human Rights*, Washington D.C. 2012.
KUHN, Thomas S., Commensurability, Comparability, Communicability, in: *Proceedings of the Biennial Meeting of the Philosophy of Science Association*, Volume Two, Symposia and Invited Papers (1982), 669-688.

LUKES, Steven, Comparing the Incomparable: Trade-offs and Sacrifices, in: Ruth Chang (ed.), *Incommensurability, Incomparability, and Practical Reason*, Cambridge/London 1997, 184-195.

OBERHEIM, Eric/HOYNINGEN-HUENE, Paul, The Incommensurability of Scientific Theories, in: Edward N. Zalta (ed.), *The Stanford Encyclopedia of Philosophy* (2016), URL: https://plato.stanford.edu/archives/win2016/entries/incommensurability/ [last accessed April 9, 2020].

PARFIT, Derek, *Reasons and Persons*, Oxford 1984, 384-390.

QIZILBASH, Mozaffar, The Mere Addition Paradox, Parity and Vagueness, in: *Philosophy and Phenomenological Research* 75 (1/2007), 129-151.

RAGIN, Charles C., *The Comparative Method. Moving Beyond Qualitative and Quantitative Strategies*, Berkeley/Los Angeles/London 1987.

RAZ, Joseph, *The Morality of Freedom*, Oxford 1986.

REGAN, Donald, Value, Comparability, and Choice, in: Ruth Chang (ed.), *Incommensurability, Incomparability, and Practical Reason*, Cambridge/London 1997, 129-150.

SÄNGER, Peter Paul (ed.), *Der Unvergleichliche – Karl Barth über Wolfgang Amadeus Mozart*, Berlin 1983.

SASS, Hartmut von, Vergleiche(n). Ein hermeneutischer Rund- und Sinkflug, in: Andreas Mauz/Hartmut von Sass (eds.), *Hermeneutik des Vergleichs. Strukturen, Anwendungen und Grenzen komparativer Verfahren* (Interpretation interdisziplinär 8), Würzburg 2011, 25-48.

STRAWSON, Peter F., Freedom and Resentment, in: *Proceedings of the British Academy* 48 (1/1962), 1-25.

TAYLOR, Charles, Leading a Life, in: Ruth Chang (ed.), *Incommensurability, Incomparability, and Practical Reason*, Cambridge, MA/London 1997, 170-183.

TILLY, Charles, *Big Structures. Large Processes. Huge Comparisons*, New York 1985.

WASSERMAN, Ryan, Indeterminacy, Ignorance and the Possibility of Parity, in: *Philosophical Perspectives* 18 'Ethics' (2004), 391-403.

Odysseus, Blackbirds, and Rain Barrels
Literature as a Comparative Practice

Walter Erhart

Abstract
Instead of asking the well-known question, if and how literary works can be compared with each other, the paper asks if literature and poetry themselves can be seen as comparative practices. Starting with Paul Ricœur's assumption about the 'semantic innovation' through narrative and metaphor, the paper explores literary practices of comparing through two case studies: the reception of the literary figure of Odysseus in world literature and the function of metaphors in modernist poetry. While the comparing of literary figures as re-deployed and re-contextualized in succeeding literary adaptations can be analyzed as a key to the dynamics of world literature in general, metaphors and similes constitute the power of poetry to disclose relations that have not been there before.

The first part of the paper studies comparative techniques in Homer's "Odyssey" and the transformations of its hero, and its narrative from Vergil and Dante up to Adorno and Horkheimer's "Dialectic of the Enlightenment" (and Stanley Kubrick's "2001—A Space Odyssey"). The second part looks at the American modernist poet Wallace Stevens ("Thirteen Ways to Look at a Blackbird") and his famous poem's echo in the work of the German author Jan Wagner ("Regentonnenvariationen"). While Stevens' metaphors demonstrate the performative power of language by obliterating a tertium compatationis, Wagner's metaphors and similes melt the semantics of nature and culture in order to create an unprecedented post-materialist world-view of the 21st century.

The case of literary studies: For and against comparisons

In literary studies, comparisons are everywhere. Even the title of this chapter may stimulate the reader's imagination and draw scholars into a well-trained comparative habit: What is the *tertium commune* of these three terms: Odysseus, blackbirds, and rain barrels? There are obvious differences: between a human being, animals, and things. But there are also commonalities that link some of these items together: nature as signified by "blackbirds" and "rain," culture and human agency as indicated by the hero Odysseus, and the preservation of water in rain barrels. Or do the terms all appear in the *Odyssey*? Birds do; rain barrels, probably not.

An example such as this resonates with a famous article by Stanley Fish, "How to recognize a poem when you see one," in which Fish describes the following situation: A bunch of students, well-trained in interpreting religious poems of the seventeenth century, enter a classroom in which the notes from a previous class are written on the blackboard—in this case, the names of authors of linguistic textbooks one below the other: "Jacobs-Rosenbaum," "Levin," "Thorne," "Hayes," and "Ohman." Stanley Fish, the teacher, turned this into a philological experiment by telling his poetry students that the words on the blackboard were a religious poem and the students should start to interpret it. What the students actually did was to find meanings through comparisons. The term "Rosenbaum" [rose tree], for example, indicates a metaphorical "reference" to the Virgin Mary ("often characterized as a rose without thorns") and can be compared to the equally addressed "crown of thornes." The double name Jakob-Rosenbaum might be part of an allegory referring to Jacob's ladder and is followed by a comparison between "ladder" and "tree" (in which the "fruit" signifies the product of Mary's womb—that is, Jesus). The term "Ohman," through phonetic, semantic, and contextual similarities, triggers comparisons with the terms "omen" (as prophesy), "Oh man" (as a kind of title theme), or "amen" (as the poem's "proper conclusion"). The Hebrew names "Jacobs," "Rosenbaum," and "Levin," finally, can be held against the Christian names of "Thorne" and "Hayes," thus starting analogies and comparisons between the Old and New Testament.[1]

What Stanley Fish was trying to demonstrate, of course, was that we should not look for hidden meanings in poems, but that we create meanings and poems by ourselves—after all, that is what reader-response theory wanted to tell us.[2] Creating meaning in poetry seems to be all about comparison. Instead of training and testing our comparative habits, however, the three items in my title indicate the parts of a chapter aiming to tackle a rather general problem: Comparisons may be everywhere in literary studies, but is literature a comparative practice itself?

American comparative literature scholars have recently questioned "comparison" as a practice of literary studies.[3] Comparing is not a neutral business: By comparing works of literature, there is always a notion of measuring, judging, and evaluating involved: a *tertium comparationis* that has already structured the field of

---

[1] Cf. Stanley Fish, *Is There a Text in This Class? The Authority of Interpretive Communities*, Cambridge/London 1980, 322–337, see 324–325.
[2] For an early example within the Anglo-American context, see Jane P. Tompkins (ed.), *Reader-Response Criticism. From Formalism to Post-Structuralism*, Baltimore/London 1980.
[3] Cf. Rita Felski/Susan Stanford Friedman (eds.), *Comparison: Theories, Approaches, Uses*, Baltimore 2013

comparison; a "centrism"[4] that assembles the *comparata* as related objects seen from a dominant point of view. The comparing of cultures starts as a specific Western and European enterprise.[5] The term and the idea of "world literature" still holds true to the assumption that literary works can be measured and compared from a dominant point of view—wherever this may come from.[6] We should be aware of our prejudices while comparing, because there has always been a power structure deciding who is able to compare, who is interested in keeping the incommensurable "other" within the confines of a presupposed horizon of comparison, and who determines the norms of comparative judgments.[7]

In the meantime, however, some have questioned this rather one-sided notion of comparison by seeing comparing as an ambivalent practice that could just as well head off in the opposite direction. Comparisons are inevitable and set off a search for similarities and differences without knowing where this leads to.[8] The practice of comparing—like using metaphors—sets the compared objects in motion, thus transforming the objects by constantly challenging and changing the *tertium commune*. Therefore, you can just as well describe comparing as a way of "decentering" because it relates objects in a quite different and often unexpected way: It may as well be "a questioning of certainties and a suspension of security."[9] By putting common perceptions and our own world in unforeseen relations; that is, by looking at familiar settings from the outside, comparisons alter the perspectives when it comes to seeing ourselves and the "other" (an issue on which cultural and global comparisons, in the wake of the eighteenth century, have always performed their most centralizing and imperializing power). If performed differently, comparisons not only produce knowledge, they also challenge the way we see ourselves:

---

4   Rajagopalan Rhadakrishnan: Why Compare? In: Rita Felski/Susan Stanford Friedman (eds.), *Comparison: Theories, Approaches, Uses*, Baltimore 2013, 15–33, see 20.

5   Cf. Walter D. Mignolo, Who is Comparing What and Why?, in: Rita Felski/Susan Stanford Friedman (eds.), *Comparison: Theories, Approaches, Uses*, Baltimore 2013, 99–119.

6   Cf. Emily Apter, *Against World Literature. On the Politics of Untranslatability*, London 2013; Rajagopalan Rhadakrishnan, World Literature, by Any Other Name?, in: *PMLA* 131 (2016), 1396–1404; Walter Erhart, Weltliterarische Vergleichspraxis—am Beispiel des Odysseus, in: Dieter Lamping (ed.), *Vergleichende Weltliteraturen, DFG-Symposion 2018*, Stuttgart 2019, 137-155.

7   Cf. Sheldon Pollock, Comparison Without Hegemony, in: Hans Joas/Barbro Klein (eds.), *The Benefit of Broad Horizons. Intellectual and Institutional Preconditions for a Global Social Science*, Leiden/Boston 2010, 185–204; Zhang Longxi*, Comparison and Correspondence: Revisiting an Old Idea for the Present, in: *Comparative Literature Studies* 53 (2016), 767–781.

8   Cf. Susan Stanford Friedman, Why not compare?, in: Rita Felski/Susan Stanford Friedman (eds.), *Comparison: Theories, Approaches, Uses*, Baltimore 2013, 34–45; Haun Saussy, *Are We Comparing Yet? On Standards, Justice, and Incomparability*, Bielefeld 2019.

9   César Domínguez/Haun Saussy/Darío Villanueva, *Introducing Comparative Literature. New Trends and Applications*, London/New York 2015, xvi.

"Comparisons, to be educative, need to happen in a site that belongs to no one. Comparisons should not be the vehicles of a latent calculus that has predetermined who, within the comparative continuum, is more developed than whom. Rather, they should function as precarious and exciting experiments where every normative 'Self' is willing to be rendered vulnerable by the gaze of the 'Other' within the coordinates of a level playing field."[10]

The quite controversial assessment of comparison and comparative literature—the critique of comparison as a philological, cultural, and political measurement on the one hand; the call for decentering, relativizing, and provincializing the "western" perspectives via comparisons on the other—have all left the problem unresolved. As a practice of scholars and cultural critics, it might be up to a mere choice, a political conviction, or the confines of a historical paradigm to decide which strategies or options of comparing were picked up or should be picked up. By comparing while studying literature, it is supposedly we who choose the method and the strategy. The obvious two-sidedness of comparing, though, could also lead to a consideration whether and how these ambivalences and tensions are part of the practice of comparing itself.

Any comparison as a method of literary studies can be traced back to a well-known everyday reading practice. As readers, we constantly compare different heroes and different actions, different fictions and different reading experiences. Moreover, reading itself might be conceptualized as a "transfer" whereby readers always compare the fictional figures and actions with their own: a "constant analogizing" that enables the reader "to rewrite and extend the narrative of his own identity."[11]

The literature lays it out for us—and we, as readers, start to compare not only heroes and objects within the text but fictions with previous fictions, with our own reading and our own experiences. That is why comparative literature studies are so powerful and so self-evident: They double and deepen the practices of the readers who immediately start to compare when they start to read.

As readers and scholars, we partake and we invest in the practice of comparing, but we seldom ask whether literature itself is a comparative practice.[12] Comparing has been—at least since the eighteenth century—the declared self-evident basis of the sciences and the humanities alike[13], and it is up to a critical history of the hu-

---

10 Rhadakrishnan, Why Compare?, 32.
11 Winfried Fluck, Reading for Recognition, in: *New Literary History* 44 (2013), 45–67, see 59.
12 Cf. Ralf Schneider, Comparison, Analogy, and Knowledge in Literature: Some Basic Considerations and the Case of Early Modern English Texts, in: Christoph Haase/Anne Schröder (eds.): *Analogy, Copy, and Representation. Interdisciplinary Perspectives*, Bielefeld 2018, 139–156.
13 Cf. Michael Eggers, *Vergleichendes Erkennen. Zur Wissenschaftsgeschichte und zur Epistemologie des Vergleichs und zur Genealogie der Komparatistik*, Heidelberg 2016.

manities within the realm of *Science Studies* to study when and how literary scholars have used comparisons as scientific tools; what suppositions, interests, and consequences were at stake while scholars chose and abandoned their strategies and practices of comparing.

The recent discussions and negotiations of comparison in the field of comparative literature, however, limited their scope almost exclusively to comparison as a method and as an all-embracing tool of the humanities instead of taking different and often changing historical practices into account. However, if historians and literary scholars turn their attention away from comparison as a method to comparative practices, from comparison to comparing, they suspend their own habitual procedures by turning their eyes to the actors who compared, the situations in which comparing took place, and the interests and strategies that were involved.[14] Comparison may have its own history in the field of comparative history and comparative literature, but it has hardly ever been studied as a historical practice in itself. If our purpose is to study what actors did when they compared, we immediately face serious—and quite familiar—problems in literary studies. If not the scholars themselves, who is comparing in literature: the author, the narrator, the hero, or the reader? Literary communication partakes in ordinary language and everyday communication, but usually there is no author being held responsible for her or his words and actions. Narrators compare, literary figures sometimes compare—but does literature itself compare? I want to suggest that we at least try to approach this question by taking up Rita Felski's recent proposal to treat literature—with the help of Bruno Latour—as an agency, to treat literary works as actors who communicate and act across time and space.[15] How does literature do this? What does literature do when it compares?

From early on, since Aristotle at least, literary critics have trusted in the comparative power of the arts. When Aristotle, in the famous ninth chapter of his *Poetics*, declares that poetry and the *epos* are more philosophical than history because what is at stake in the *mimesis* of literature is the "general" instead of the "particular,"[16] comparison lies close at hand. The "general" that a literary hero embodies and that can be observed in his actions—Achilles' anger for example—is a kind of *tertium commune* that enables readers to measure and judge particular and contingent traits, patterns, and practices of human beings.

Within quite another historical context rooted in analytical philosophy and *Gestaltpsychologie*, I. A. Richards connected his *Principles of Literary Criticism* in the

---

14   Cf. Angelika Epple/Walter Erhart (eds.), *Die Welt beobachten. Praktiken des Vergleichens*, Frankfurt a. M./New York 2015.

15   Cf. Rita Felski, Latour und Literary Studies, in: *PMLA* 130 (2015), 737–742.; Rita Felski, Comparison and Translation. A Perspective from Actor-Network-Theory, in: *Comparative Literature Studies* 53 (2016), 747–765.

16   Aristotle, *Poetics*, 1451b.

1920s with the belief that literature and the arts—as a "storehouse of recorded values"—contain an internal mechanism to open up our capacities for experiencing and recognizing values via comparing: "For without the assistance of the arts we could compare very few of our experiences, and without such comparison we could hardly hope to agree as to which are to be preferred."[17] Quite explicitly, for Richards, the act of comparing is not rendered to the readers but to literature itself, to the works and the poets, a "body of evidence" and a "vehicle of communication" that contains and guides the comparisons.[18]

Paul Ricœur has considered literature's function as a capacity for "semantic innovation," a new perception and description of reality altogether: "the power of the metaphorical utterance to redescribe a reality inaccessible to direct description."[19] Ricœur identifies two literary forms of semantic innovation: fabula, narrative and mimesis on the one side, metaphor and metaphorical invention on the other. I want to argue that in both cases, comparison plays a crucial role; that comparing is, indeed, responsible for the semantic innovation that takes place in and through literature. In what follows, I shall try to give a short outline of different comparative practices that literature may be able to perform—from inner-textual comparisons to the circulation of literary forms, figures, and themes. Following Ricœur's distinction, I focus on comparing as a feature of narratives in the first part (Odysseus), then move on to the question of metaphors (such as "birds") by discussing poems by Wallace Stevens ("Thirteen Ways of Looking at a Blackbird") and Jan Wagner ("Regentonnenvariationen").

Suffering and success: Comparing Odysseus

In narrative mimesis, comparative acts are supposedly organized around actions and heroes, and for specific reasons, I would like to turn to the archetype of a hero, to Ulysses. As Odysseus, as Ulysses, in many languages and national literatures, he became a literary figure for centuries through both time and space. Comparison—I would say—plays a crucial role in answering a question that Hans Blumenberg once asked in his work on the continuity of mythic constellations: What makes Odysseus "a figure of mythical quality"?[20] Where Blumenberg spoke of the "significance" ("*Bedeutsamkeit*") of mythical themes and figures as a proof for their lasting existence through adaptations and variations, Haun Saussy recently described the comparative practice of world literature as an "atlas of migrating themes"[21] that—similar to

---

17 I. A. Richards, *Principles of Literary Criticism*, New York 1925, 32.
18 Richards, *Principles*, 32.
19 Paul Ricœur, *Time and Narrative*. 3 vols., vol. I, Chicago 1990, XI.
20 [My translation]. Hans Blumenberg, *Arbeit am Mythos*, Frankfurt a. M. 1984, 86.
21 Domínguez/Saussy/Villanueva, *Introducing Comparative Literature*, 66.

Ricœur's metaphorical power—invent and redescribe ways of being in the world: "They could be proofs-of-concept in the exploration of new ways of being human [...] useful precedents for reiteration—a formula that would apply as well to the poetic forms transiting across borders of language and costum."[22]

The *Odyssey* offers a variety of comparisons right from the start, as early as in the first canto, when Zeus responds to Athene: "How for all this could I forget godlike Odysseus, the man who is beyond all other mortal men in power of mind, and beyond all others has offered sacrifices to the immortal gods who hold the wide heaven?" (I, 65–68).[23]

The "godlike Odysseus" is the common translation of *"theioio"* (θείοιο). Being compared to the gods in this way is a quite common Homeric expression forming a whole set of *epitheta*: *theioio* (θείοιο), *dios* (δῖος), *theoeidés* (θεοειδής), and *theo enalichios* (θεῷ ἐναλίγκιος). These reappearing expressions are so-called formulaic compositions; the epithet "god-like" (δῖος) in the *Odyssey*—as has been observed (and counted)—is attributed to thirty-two different heroes.[24] These formulas are not specific to this particular epos, but deeply embedded in its overall cultural context: the relation of humans to gods.

The god-like character of Greek heroes is an inner-textual comparison. What the speech of Zeus also compares, within the literary work itself, is Odysseus as the wisest man, "beyond all other mortal men in power of mind," with the most sacrifices, the most obligations in dealing with the gods. In this respect, he is compared to all other heroes and figures who have sacrificed (that is the similarity) but not as much as Odysseus (that is the difference). Sacrifices point to the circumstances of the hero's sufferings that, later on in the *Odyssey*, are repeated over and over again. Take the words of Menelaos in the fourth canto: "because no man among the Achaians labored harder or took more on himself than Odysseus" (IV, 106).

Odysseus is beyond others but, at the same time, through comparing, a common ground, a *tertium comparationis*, is involved in which heroes might be similar but also different. "Power of mind" and "sufferings" as well as the dependency on gods documented by sacrifices are *tertia comparationis* that produce and enable comparisons between heroes (and readers).

Within the *Odyssey*, the point of comparison is coined by the epithets that lay at the source of the "mythical quality" of the Odysseus figure: the god-like endurer (*polytlas dios*, πολύτλας δῖος); the much-wandering, much-turned, wily, and crafty hero (*polytropos*, πολύτροπος); the skilled, ingenious Odysseus (*polymetis*,

---

22 Domínguez/Saussy/Villanueva, *Introducing Comparative Literature*, 66.
23 The translation of the *Odyssey* is by Martin Hammond in: Homer, *The Odyssey. Translated by Martin Hammond. With an Introduction by Jasper Griffin*, London et al. 2000.
24 Matthew Clark, Formulas, metre and type-scenes, in: Robert Fowler (ed.), *The Cambridge Companion to Homer*, Cambridge 2004, 117–138, see 128.

πολύμητις); and the talented and experienced sailor (*polymechanos*, πολυμήχανος). The hero Odysseus became a literary figure beyond the *Odyssey* through these attributes and qualities. He becomes a figure of suffering and of ingenuity by being compared to all other heroes, and he is transferred from the *Odyssey* to other texts and historical contexts now putting forward comparisons between the "old" and the "new" Odysseus.

Variations of themes and figures in world literature constitute a practice of comparing not by mere transfer or "adaptability"[25] of famous literary characters, but by a comparative action that puts the traditional figure in relation to the newly invented figure through an established *tertium comparationis* that sorts out similarities and differences. Virgil's *The Aeneid* starts with a hero who is thrown across land and sea by a god's rage—a much-turned man who suffers and endures like Odysseus, the over-all *exemplum* that is clearly implied in the opening of the Roman epos: "*multum ille et terris iactatus et alto / vi superum, saevae memorem Iunonis obi ram*" (I, 3f.).

There are obvious similarities with the Greek hero—and an important difference mentioned right at the beginning: Odysseus, in the end, comes home, whereas Aeneas founds a city. And the comparison goes even further by establishing the translation of myths to the Roman epos: Odysseus is turned into the "horrible Ulysses" [*dirus Ulixes*] (II, 261, 762) and (in the rhetoric of a Rutulian Latin prince) into the master of deceptive speech, "*fandi fictor Ulixes*" (IX, 602) who is held up against the straightforward virtuous founder of the Roman capital and Roman empire. While Aeneas' narrative and his travels are closely linked—as similar as the Roman epos itself—to the *Odyssey*, Ulysses, here, is different according to a newly established (or foregrounded) *tertium comparationis* based on warfare and related Roman virtues.

My case in point here is that the variations of figures and characters in world literature, their mythical qualities, are triggered by the dynamics of comparative practices. The *Odyssey* becomes a pre-text when its actions and characters, already borne out by comparative practices, appear in a new context, a post-text or—according to Genette's terminology—in a "hypertext"[26] in which similarities and differences are worked out through a common framework, be it the theme of suffering or ingenuity or the narrative structure that the two texts have in common: sufferings with a happy ending, man fighting against natural powers, culture conquering the "other," homecoming.

In Dante's *Inferno* in the *Divina Commedia*, Odysseus does not come home and does not found a city but—in the famous scene of the twenty-sixth canto—encour-

---

25 William B. Stanford, *The Ulysses Theme. A Study in the Adaptability of a Traditional Hero*, Oxford 1968.
26 Gerard Genette, *Palimpseste. Die Literatur auf zweiter Stufe*, Frankfurt a. M. 1993, 9–18.

ages his companions to sail outside of civilization to the open West and faraway lands where they are shipwrecked and swallowed by the sea. Sufferings lead to different narratives but what is at stake here, again, is the comparison of Dante's Ulysses to his ancient counterpart. Sufferings, ingenuity, the cunning art of lying and doing fraudulent tricks, endurance, or navigating power are common grounds for the variations of the literary figure Odysseus. They are turned into narratives, though, in which new meanings, new circumstances, new contexts are ascribed to the hero's suffering, his ingenuity, and his homecoming. With Dante, for example, Ulysses is suffering as a result of his ingenuity (and his burning restlessness: "*l'ardore*"),[27] he is a sinner punished for his *superbia* but he is also offering a new experience of exploring the world. Up until today, Dante's Ulysses is a much-disputed ambivalent counter-hero: a Christian *exemplum* of deadly pride and a self-portrait of the author who is travelling through hell and paradise.[28]

Adaptations of literary figures display the main dynamics of comparative practices: They decontextualize one element, one *comparatum* (here: the figure of Odysseus), and start to recontextualize it in a new environment, a new fictional setting that redescribes the themes of the *Odyssey*. Adaptations, allusions, and citations are not restricted to fiction, of course; but they reveal one of the powers of literary narratives: redescribing our experience through comparative practices. Fables, fictions, and narratives, for Paul Ricœur, are "privileged means whereby we reconfigure our confused, unformed and at the limit mute experience."[29]

Comparative practices: Experiencing modernity with Odysseus

The *tertia comparationis* that connect the traveling and migration of literary figures and themes are not fixed; they rather establish mobile points of reference that become loaded with new meanings and experiences. In the twentieth century, the narratives of the *Odyssey* and the figure of Odysseus gain their significance out of a *tertium commune* that gives meaning to wanderings, exiles, and homecomings.[30]

---

27 [...] *né dolcezza di figlio, né la pieta /del vecchio padre, né 'l debito amore /lo qual dovea Penelopè far lieta, /vincer potero dentro a me l'ardore /ch'i ebbi a divenir del mondo esperto / [...] /Noi ci allegrammo, e tosto tornò in pianto* XXVI, 94–98, 136.

28 Cf. Karl-Heinz Stierle, *Das große Meer des Sinns. Hermenautische Erkundungen in Dantes "Commedia"*, München 2007.

29 Ricœur, *Time and Narrative*, XI.

30 See the various contributions of Manfred Karnick, Formen der Fremdheit und Wandlungen der Odysseus-Rezeption in der frühen deutschen Nachkriegsliteratur, in: Eijiro Iwasaki (ed.), *Begegnung mit dem Fremden. Achter Internationaler Germanisten-Kongreß*, vol. 9, München 1991, 422–432; Volker Riedel, Metamorphosen des Odysseus-Bildes, in: *Deutschunterricht* 51 (1998), 394–406; Gunter E. Grimm, Irrfahrt als Motiv im Werk deutscher Exilautoren (1933–1950), in: Walter Erhart/Sigrid Nieberle (eds.), *Odysseen 2001. Fahrten—Passagen—Wanderun-*

Redescribing reality in this way also implies a social significance and sociological meaning of literature, because these comparisons—an odyssey, an Odysseus in a new textual environment—also point to hitherto unseen, even unfelt experiences of the social world: of conflicts, contradictions, inconsistencies, constraints, injustices, and pathologies. Therefore, to give one significant famous example, Max Horkheimer and Theodor W. Adorno, in their *Dialectic of Enlightenment* (1947), do not use the figure of Odysseus for the purpose of illustration as a simple example of a capitalist and bourgeois type of character—a method that could easily be criticized (and has been criticized) as a crude neglect of historicity. With the *Odyssey* as the main narrative, an "allegory"[31] (as Horkheimer and Adorno themselves call it), *The Dialectic of Enlightenment* recontextualizes a literary form to convey a new description of contemporary society.

Actually, Horkheimer's and Adorno's narrative puts the figure of Odysseus into new historical contexts by a series of comparative transactions. The hero moves through infinite but clearly geographical space; as a "trembling shipwrecked" he nevertheless anticipates "the work of the compass" (p. 53). He triumphs over mythical powers by behaving "like an actor" changing his roles and performances; he thinks in "equivalent terms" (p. 56) like a modern business-man; and his strategies already contain the "scheme of modern mathematics" and the philosophical tricks of "formalism" (p. 68). He already is—like Robinson Crusoe—a "homo oeconomicus" (p. 69), and he betrays the gods of nature "like the civilized traveler once has done" with the "natives" trading "glass beads for ivory" (p. 55). Odysseus—in the episode with the Sirens—is like a "landlord who lets others work for him" (p. 40); he is chained and passive while listening to the sirens, motionless "like, in later times, the concertgoers" (p. 40).

The rhetoric of comparison constantly moves the figure of Odysseus into contexts of modernity—from the age of discoveries to modern landlords, from robinsonades to businessmen and analytic philosophers, from early imperialism to bourgeois concert halls. Horkheimer and Adorno call the *Odyssey* a "founding text of European civilization" (p. 52), not because everything that is in capitalism and in the "dialectic of enlightenment" is already to be found in Homer, but because the ancient epos provides a formula for unforeseen adaptations and continuities made

---

gen, München 2003, 102–118; Günter Häntzschel, Odysseus in der deutschen Literatur vor und nach 1945, in: Walter Erhart/Sigrid Nieberle (eds.), *Odysseen 2001. Fahrten—Passagen—Wanderungen*, München 2003, 119-131; Bernd Seidensticker, Aufbruch zu neuen Ufern. Transformationen der Odysseusgestalt in der literarischen Moderne, in: Bernd Seidensticker/Martin Vöhler (eds.), *Urgeschichten der Moderne. Die Antike im 20. Jahrhundert*, Stuttgart/Weimar 2001, 249–270.

31   Max Horkheimer/Theodor W. Adorno, *Dialektik der Aufklärung. Philosophische Fragmente*, [1947], Frankfurt a. M. 2002, 41 [in the following, page numbers are given within the text with my translations].

out of comparisons. To equate Odysseus and modern man, ancient Greek and capitalism, would be a crude sociological statement or a false historiographic argument; what makes the *Dialectic of Enlightenment* a literary text, though, is the transposition of Odysseus into a new narrative containing different scenes of civilization while embodying ethnographic encounters, economics, science, and art. Every one of these images tells a different story, not the Odyssey again or an illustrated Marxist world history, but new ways of experiencing modernity—"suffering" and "ingenuity" retold.

The double aspect of the *Odyssey* as a suffering and a successful homecoming, as a figuration of "suffering that leads to success"[32] (Hans Blumenberg), marks the ambiguity of the history of civilization. As a hero who finally triumphs over mythical and natural powers but also—because of this—suffers and has to make sacrifices, he is easily adapted to Critical Theory's dark tales about instrumental reason. When Homer und Odysseus describe the home of the cyclops as self-contained, without work, without law, there is, in this comparative view of the epos and modernity's history, a "guilty plea" on behalf of "civilization" (p. 72). Odysseus's skills and smartness lead to rationality and power, but they also produce isolation (for the homo oeconomicus as well as for the art connoisseur); his wanderings are legible as an experience of suffering, endurance, and loss put forth precisely by the domination of nature and rationality. Odysseus, after all, may be the *exemplum* of a hero prone to adaptations, renewals, and these kinds of comparative practices because, in Homer as well as in European literature, he inhabits a threshold between an old mythical and a new, self-reflexive, and restless figure: "simultaneously ancient and modern" already in classical times, "an ideal observation point from which to measure the similarities and differences between the 'alterity' of the past and the 'modernity' of the present."[33]

Like numerous other literary adaptations of the *Odyssey*, Adorno's and Horkheimer's redescriptions of modernity do not possess theoretical value or historical truth in themselves but, as Axel Honneth has claimed, are literary comparisons that serve to defamiliarize the everyday world, to distance the self-evidence of our social practices, and to make us aware of something we have not registered before.[34] Horkheimer and Adorno read the *Odyssey* as an allegory, a *metaphora continua* in rhetorical terms: They create a series of metaphors and comparisons (with the particle "like") to put modernity's experience in a new light, to let it be experienced in another way.

---

32 [My translation]. Blumenberg, *Arbeit am Mythos*, 87.
33 Piero Boitani, *The Shadows of Ulysses. Figures of a Myth*, Oxford 1994, 2.
34 Cf. Axel Honneth, Über die Möglichkeit einer erschließenden Kritik. Die "Dialektik der Aufklärung" im Horizont gegenwärtiger Debatten über Sozialkritik, in: Axel Honneth, *Das Andere der Gerechtigkeit. Aufsätze zur praktischen Philosophie*, Frankfurt a. M. 2000, 70–87.

Comparing humankind's travels: *2001—A Space Odyssey*

Following Ricœur again, we can call "metaphors" specific "local" events, whereas narratives provide "regional' context"[35]—both being part of comparative practices that aim to alter the familiar ways of seeing and redescribing our realities. Whereas *The Dialectic of Enlightenment* constructs a narrative out of "local" metaphors and comparisons, thus performing the comparative practice of world literature's migrating forms, metaphors themselves establish a *tertium comparationis* that is open for "regional" narrative space.

One of the most famous metaphors in film history also draws its energy from the *Odyssey*: in Stanley Kubrick's *2001—A Space Odyssey* (1968). The film's opening scenes titled "Dawn of Mankind" finish on the image of an animal bone that is discovered by an ape as a powerful weapon with which to kill other animals. In one of the most spectacular cuts in film history, the bone thrown into the air turns into a spaceship by its sheer form and movement, turning, twisting, and floating through the sky. The bone and the spacecraft form two similar objects at the beginning and the end of an Odyssey writ large in which several departures—the hominids, humans leaving Earth for outer space, the self-reflexive computer's artificial intelligence transcending humanity—mark the Odyssey's new plot. After the juxtaposition of bone and spacecraft, and a little later on when, for the first time, human beings appear inside the spacecraft, a third comparable object comes into sight: the floating weightless pen of Captain Dr. Floyd, a new Odysseus of course, who is floating in outer space on a new mission.

In a quite mechanical theory of metaphor, we would look for one *tertium comparationis* that unites bone, spacecraft, and pen: be it the shape, the form, or the floating of these objects. However, we also are drawn immediately into the dynamics of a comparative practice that is worked out by the metaphors and by the film's narrative alike. The series and variations of three *comparata*—bone, spaceship, pen—form a complex net of possible narratives by metonymic and metaphorical operations. While bone and spacecraft may easily be compared with the help of one *tertium* (a tool, a weapon, a phallus), the bone, the pen, and the spacecraft also form a story: three stages of world history (prehistory, humankind, posthuman); three cultures (based on weapon, literacy, technology); three anthropological and technological extensions of the human body; and three technical objects moving away from the human body, gaining a life of their own, and floating through space

---

[35] Paul Ricœur, Die Metapher und das Hauptproblem der Hermeneutik [1972], in: Anselm Haverkamp (ed.), *Theorie der Metapher*, Darmstadt 1996, 356–375, see 373.

by being freed from gravity and human control.[36] You can see the different *tertia comparationis*—world history, machines, and floating—move and change according to the context and the narrative that the film itself provides.

Apart from an often fruitless discussion over whether metaphors are comparisons with abbreviations or missing links or maybe no comparisons at all,[37] comparing is the key element and an essential dynamic operation in the practice and rhetoric of metaphors, tropes, and similes alike. Comparative practices, therefore, might be reintroduced in literary theory as one of the basic elements of literature. Metaphors are a central feature of ordinary language use and of conceptual thinking.[38] What turns literature, the aesthetic use and the poetic variations of metaphorical thinking, into a specific and productive practice is not just new metaphors, but—as we have seen with the bone, the pen, and the spacecraft—the possibility of moving the metaphor into new sets of relationships constructed by fictional contexts.

With the spaceship, human civilization not only moves into foreign uncontrollable territories but has lost its control: It is no longer guided by human agency and power but by the artificial intelligence of the computer HAL. The new Odysseus and the new *Odyssey* in Kubrick's film use their metaphors—and the comparative practice—to invert Homer's and Adorno's narrative. The "old" hero as an agent of civilization is surpassed and defeated by posthuman technology; the navigating hero who once triumphed over space becomes a rather passive object of the final space trip that dissolves time and narrative into mythical space again.[39] The course of human civilization as a *tertium comparationis* of Homer's, Adorno's, and Kubrick's *Odyssey* is finally directed to an unforeseen future in which times and epochs collapse and history's teleological course is put to rest and turned into a cyclical repetition (with an evolving, circling, and floating embryo as its very last sign).

There is an appearance of a transcendent power, however, that virtually takes over humankind's agency. The bone and the spaceship in the initial scenes of Kubrick's film are also metaphorically related to the black monolith that, first in the ape scenes of the Stone Age, appears out of space and seems to govern the course of humankind by moving it to a next step. Its appearance first triggers the "dawn of mankind" with the apes gathering around it, and, in the final scene,

---

36 "Gravity" as a central theme of the film is emphasized in: Jay P. Telotte, The Gravity of 2001: A Space Odyssey, in: Robert Phillip Kolker (ed.), *Stanley Kubrick's 2001: A Space Odyssey. New Essays*, Oxford 2006, 43–53.
37 Cf. Schneider, Comparison, 142–143.
38 Cf. George Lakoff/Mark Johnson, *Metaphors We Live By*, Chicago 1980.
39 Cf. Hans-Thies Lehmann, Die Raumfabrik—Mythos im Kino und Kinomythos, in: Karl Heinz Bohrer (ed.), *Mythos und Moderne. Begriff und Bild einer Rekonstruktion*, Frankfurt a. M. 1983, 572–609, see 594.

the psychedelic trip of the spaceship ends in an eighteenth-century-like luxurious chamber in which the dying old astronaut, again, reaches out his hand to the black monolith. Compared to Homer's *Odyssey*, the monolith could be seen as a variation of Athena guiding and protecting the human heroes, whereas the all-mighty (one-eyed) computer HAL signifies the cyclops. The astronaut David Bowman disconnects ("blinds") the computer, thus using his human "ingenuity" to triumph not over natural but over posthuman (artificial) power.[40]

The reappearing monolith as well as the spaceship moving through sky and universe represent powerful superhuman artifacts and formal equivalents to the Homeric gods appearing and disappearing in the sky. After her first appearance on earth, Athena, in Homer's *Odyssey*, flies away "like a bird" (I, 320), marking a well-known metaphorical context in the Greek epos: connecting the gods with the power of nature. Since then, the bird, of course, is part of a metaphorical context that links "birds" and "flying" to the semantics of freedom, from the godlike power moving across the sky to the iconographic imagery of science fiction and Kubrick's *Space Odyssey*. Metaphors, however, are never limited to a fixed *tertium comparationis*; the range of metaphorical comparisons may be endless in relation to the context in which the comparative sign may be placed.

How to look at birds and rain barrels: Poetry's comparative practice

One of the most famous poems of Modern American poetry is Wallace Stevens' "Thirteen ways to look at a blackbird" (written around 1917).[41] It is also famous and well-studied because it is a poem about the fact that "every perception is a metaphor."[42] The blackbird, as a sign, enfolds its metaphorical power exactly as a poetic device to never stand still and therefore links its "freedom" to the world-disclosing gesture of poetry itself.

"Among twenty snowy mountains, / The only moving thing / Was the eye of a blackbird." (p. 92). The opening chapter of thirteen stanzas marks a difference: There are two objects, the mountains and the blackbird's eye; one standing still, one moving. But what is more, the "moving eye" also figures as the poetic freedom to move the word and the sign, the perception and the imagination of a "blackbird" into entirely different directions and contexts: "The mind seeks meaning through

---

40 Cf. David W. Cole, Homer's Odyssey and Clarke's/Kubrick's 2001: A Space Odyssey, in: *Notes on Contemporary Literature* 31 (2001), 5–6. A rather forced allegorical reading of Kubrick's *2001* in the light of Homer's *Odyssey* is presented by Leonhard F. Wheat, *2001: A Triple Allegory*, Lanham 2000, 41–62.

41 Wallace Stevens, *The Collected Poems*, New York 1990, 92–95. (In the following, the page numbers of the poem's citations are given within the text).

42 Robert Rehder, *The Poetry of Wallace Stevens*, Basingstoke/London 1988, 59.

discovery of resemblance, through metaphor, and each subsequent stanza offers a metaphoric context against which the moving eye can find meaning."[43] "Thirteen Ways of Looking at a Blackbird" is not about viewpoints but about thirteen metaphorical and comparative transformations, "a series of examples of how the imagination works."[44] The second stanza uses another comparative context but also performs several movements of comparing. "I was of three minds, / Like a tree / In which there are three blackbirds." (p. 92). The comparison, here (with the copula "like"), is between the "I" and the "tree," but it moves on to an equation of the "three minds" and the "three blackbirds" pointing to the plurality of the mind and the imagination. The stanza also marks another comparison on a phonetic basis with the rhyming assonance of the "three" and the "tree" already binding together the images phonetically and linguistically.

As often in poetry, *tertia comparationis* are hard to find—but they are everywhere. They are evoked and performed as a fluid convergence and a range of possibilities that are created, continued, and acted out by the reader's mind. The *tertium commune* of the lyrical speaker with the three minds and the tree ("like a tree") is quite difficult to discern as being a clear case of a "bold" or "audacious" metaphor in Harald Weinrich's sense: with wide semantic distances and conceptual gaps.[45] When—in Stevens' case—the "three minds" and the "three blackbirds" are juxtaposed poetically ("I was of three minds, / Like a tree / In which there are three blackbirds"), the "tree" becomes the *tertium* (as does the number "three") fusing a sign and an image ("three blackbirds") with a mental state ("three minds") but leaving the semantic distance as wide open as possible.

Almost every stanza of the poem tells us that seeing, perceiving, and recognizing are a comparative practice. In the thirteen sections, minipoems like Japanese haikus, perception is moving with the verbal sign of the "blackbird." Like a bird rising, it is put next to a *comparatum* (be it mountains, the mind, a river, language, man and woman) where it creates its own poetic space out of similarities and differences mixed up in imaginary landscapes or pure imaginative powers of language and mind. "Thirteen Ways of Looking at a Blackbird" forms variations of—sometimes explicit—comparative acts: "I do not know which to prefer, / The beauty of inflections / Or the beauty of innuendoes, / The blackbird whistling / Or just after." (p. 93). There is no end to these comparisons because—as in this case—a *tertium comparationis* is clearly missing. At the same time, like many other poems of Wallace Stevens, the whole poem marks poetry as a practice that opens up comparative space by words and by imagination.

---

43 Herbert J. Stern, *Wallace Stevens' Art of Uncertainty*, Ann Arbor 1966, 130.
44 Ronald Sukenik, *Wallace Stevens. Musing the Obscure*, New York 1967, 72.
45 Harald Weinrich, Semantik der kühnen Metapher, in: Anselm Haverkamp (ed.), *Theorie der Metapher*, Darmstadt 1996, 316–339.

The works of Wallace Stevens strive to portray a world in which religion and analogy as ways of transcending the material and human world via metaphysical and cosmological resemblances are substituted by poetic descriptions of the world as it is and of the way things simply are.[46] This is the reason why Stevens' poems often refer to sights, sounds, and objects while the lyrical speaker uses the verb "to be" as in "it was," "I was," "it is."[47] "The eye's plain version" (p. 465), for example, is the starting point of the late poem "An Ordinary Evening In New Haven" followed by the endeavor to get hold of a poetic experience based solely on things and their corresponding words: "The poem of pure reality, untouched / By trope or deviation, straight to the word, / Straight to the transfixing object, to the object / At the exactest point at which it is itself, / Transfixing by being purely what it is" (p. 471).

The desire to be "exact" does not exclude similes and metaphors. On the contrary. It is the metaphor (or the simile) in Stevens' poetry that often turns into a statement about things (how they supposedly really are); at the same time, it reveals the world's hidden materiality or points to metonymic extensions of signs and objects: "The blackbird whirled in the autumn winds. / It was a small part of the pantomime." (p. 93). The simple sight and picture (a blackbird whirling in the autumn winds) exercises its metaphoric power in the eye of the beholder who sees and interprets it as a "part" of something else, a "pantomime" as an unfolding of nature's spectacle.

Therefore, in Stevens' poetry, things, perceptions, and imaginations are intertwined in a process in which language unfolds its comparative power by establishing similarities between opposed independent elements, by exercising poetry's power to convey and to produce meaning at the same time. On the one hand, language and words identify and signify the world; on the other hand, they constantly move away from the signified order of things by pointing to language-related similarities of signifiers (often working with the "likeness" of similes).[48] The "creation of resemblance by the imagination"[49] is a synonym for metaphor, Stevens concludes in his late essay "Three Academic Pieces" (1951), a human activity and a human desire that are performed in their purest form in poetry: "The study of the activity of resemblance is an approach to the understanding of poetry. Poetry is a satisfying of the desire for resemblance. [...] Its singularity is that in the act of satisfying

---

46 Cf. Matthew Mutter, Wallace Stevens, Analogy and Tautology: The Problem of a Secular Poetics, in: *English Literary History* 78 (2011), 741–768.
47 Cf. Beverly Maeder, Stevens and linguistic structure, in: John N. Serio (ed.), *The Cambridge Companion to Wallace Stevens*, Cambridge 2007, 161.
48 Cf. Jacqueline Vaught Brogan, *Stevens and Simile. A Theory of Language*, Princeton 1986.
49 Wallace Stevens, Three Academic Pieces: I, in: Marie Borroff (ed.): *Wallace Stevens. A Collection of Critical Essays*, Englewood Cliffs 1963, 24–29, see 24.

the desire for resemblance it touches the sense of reality, it enhances the sense of reality, heightens it, intensifies it."[50]

"Thirteen Ways of Looking at a Blackbird" is an early poem about the impossibility of looking at objects straightforwardly and about the impossibility of fixing and grasping their identity and their meaning. On the other hand, this poetry opens up the richness of creating meaning by simply putting words and perceptions together. Stevens' poetry wants to portray the world made out of things as they are, but exactly by looking and observing, the lyrical activity turns into a comparative process with words, things, and meanings; it turns into a cubist-like collage that assembles juxtapositions and combinations, thus creating unforeseen differences and similarities.[51] The poem about looking at a blackbird, therefore, puts literature's affinity to a comparative practice to the test: As a *comparatum*, the blackbird unfolds images and a variety of surprising and never-ending ('thirteen')[52] *comparata*, whereas the *tertium comparationis* is almost hidden or "moving" away like the blackbird itself.

Jan Wagner, the 2015 winner of one of Germany's most prestigious literary awards, the *Georg-Büchner-Preis*, has taken up Stevens' variations about the blackbird in the title poem of his volume *Regentonnenvariationen* (2014).[53] It's about looking at a rain barrel, in fourteen stanzas—actually thirteen, because the first stanza starts the whole process going:"Ich hob den Deckel / Und blickte ins riesige / Auge der Amsel" (p. 76).

Opening the lid of a rain barrel leads to a metaphor, the "giant eye of the blackbird": poetry awakened by Stevens' pre-text.[54] First, it is the sheer form that triggers the metaphorical comparison: The rim and the surface of a rain barrel are similar to a blackbird's eye. The metaphor, though, is just the starting point to let the rain barrel move into different metaphorical contexts marking—this time—thirteen new and different ways of looking at a rain barrel. "Regentonnenvariationen" is a poem about variations and, through variations and comparisons, a poem about poetry's affinity to comparative practices. The word "Regentonnenvariationen" is a phonetic variation in itself—the *"Tonnen"* and the *"variaTIONEN,"* and, with each variation, the rain barrel—like the blackbird in Stevens' poem—turns into something else.

---

50 Stevens, Three Academic Pieces, 27.
51 Cf. Daniel R. Schwarz, *Narrative and Representation in the Poetry of Wallace Stevens*, New York 1993, 38–57 ("'Thirteen Ways of Looking at a Blackbird': Stevens's Cubist Narrative").
52 "Thirteen has long been the favorite number for anyone wishing to represent uncontainability and irreducible plurality." Bart Eeckhout, Stevens and philosophy, in: John N. Serio (ed.), *The Cambridge Companion to Wallace Stevens*, Cambridge 2007, 103–117, see 114.
53 Jan Wagner, *Regentonnenvariationen*, München/Berlin 2014, 76–78 (in the following, page numbers are given within the text).
54 See Wagner's homage to Stevens in: Jan Wagner, *Die Sandale des Propheten. Beiläufige Prosa*, Berlin 2011, 113–122 („*Seidenkleider aus Würmern. Über Wallace Stevens*").

In the second stanza, the rain barrel is compared (again with the copula "like") to a "Zen master": *"unterm pflaumenbaum / hinterm haus – gelassen, kühl / wie ein zenmeister."* (p. 76). There are two *tertia comparationis* (*"gelassen"* and *"kühl"*, "serenely" and "cool") that are respectively produced by the reversal of the metaphor's elements (the "barrel" and the "Zen master"), changing the source domain (or 'vehicle') and the target domain (or 'tenor'). The metaphorical ground of comparison between the rain barrel and the Zen master is shifting with the concomitant metaphors: the imaginary of the water on the one hand ("cool"), the Zen master's attitude on the other ("serenely"). In the third stanza, the rain barrel turns into an oven ("a sort of oven") in its "negative" form, one that "does not smoke" and—instead of burning and using up wood—"swallowed the clouds": *"eine art ofen / im negativ; qualmte nicht, / schluckte die wolken."* (p. 76).

There are all kinds of comparative acts in this poem: similes (*"als stiege durch sie die Unterwelt herauf"*), comparative likenesses (*"wie ein zenmeister", "alt wie der garten, / duftend wie ein waldsee"*), metaphors and personifications (*"bleib, sprach das Dunkel"*), and allegories (the barrel is giggling, beaten up but not divulging: "gluckste nur kurz auf, / trat man zornig dagegen, / aber gab nichts preis"). The characteristics of the rain barrel blend objects and things with states of mind providing strong metaphoric meanings (when, for example, the barrel is calm and immersed in summer while angrily brimming over in an autumn storm): *"einen sommer lang / ganz versunken, dann / bei sturm, / schäumte sie über."* (p. 77).

'Fourteen ways to look at a rain barrel' moves the object in all kinds of directions again, though this time not randomly as in Stevens' case. Instead, Jan Wagner's poem also forms a narrative out of "local" metaphors. The rain barrel changes with the seasons: "self-absorbed in summer," "overfull" in autumn, and, in winter, after moments of "brooding" (*"ein grübeln, grübeln"*), the inspiration comes in the form of ice giving the barrel, once again, a twist of Zen master's wisdom: *"die erleuchtung als scheibe von eis."*

The rain barrel, while being similar to landscapes, human emotions, teachings of a Zen master, to cultural- symbolic forms like "pumping" organ pipes, underworlds ("ein barrel styx") and mental activities, comes alive as a human being, and as an agency: It is swallowing clouds, it is discreet but talking, it is calm and it moves.

"Thirteen Ways of Looking at a Blackbird" by Wallace Stevens and the corresponding *"Regentonnenvariationen"* by Jan Wagner highlight poetry's power to transform the world by metaphoric acts and "semantic innovation" (Paul Ricœur). At the heart of these poetic transformations lies a comparative practice—through similes, juxtapositions, comparisons, and metaphors—that moves the object in directions and contexts where the borders between reality, perceptions, and imaginations as well as between nature and humans are constantly blurred. While both poems look at one object from many perspectives to make it signify other things, the purpose and function of the poems, however, and the *tertia comparationis* of their comparisons, are quite different.

Wallace Stevens' poem is using the sign and the metaphor of the blackbird to point to the randomness and the language-based conceptual frames of perception. In doing this, in moving signs and imagination beyond recognition and beyond a *tertium comparationis*, Stevens' early poetry—at the beginning of the twentieth century—articulates the epistemological skepticism of his age. Poetry itself tries to give an answer to the on-going metaphysical needs in a secular time: by creating worldviews that appear unexpectedly within rearranged settings of poetic forms; by forming the connectedness of sounds, visions, and things within imaginary landscapes. Instead of allegorizing the blackbird (what scholars have done), instead of decoding it as a symbol (for "death," or "poetry," or "life"), the poem's blackbird evades a common ground, and the transforming of meaning, the metaphors and comparisons, do not lead to a fixed or unified *tertium* that binds the "ways of looking" together.

Jan Wagner opens up a world of the twenty-first century by remodeling our experiences with nature. The comparative practice of his *"Regentonnenvariationen"* transforms a natural object into a living thing. The rain barrel, as a *compositum*, connects nature ("rain") and culture ("barrel"); it links nature's power to human needs while, at the same time, it opens up a third space in which humans and natural things form entities and alliances. The poem therefore points to an ecology of attention and awareness. The rain barrel, seen from this perspective, is disclosed as a thing and a cultural form in which human and nature's attentiveness work and fit together—nature being part of the human world; the human, in turn, being embedded in the natural and the material world. The poem's capacity to "materialize" human worldliness and to animate things lies in the resemblances and the *tertia comparationis* that are played out in every stanza.

The barrel in the sixth stanza, for example, is compared to an organ because the "organ pipe" and a "downspout" are similar in form. Moreover, though, the rain barrel becomes a silver pump organ because the "weather" is "pumped through" like the sounds of music (and the "falling" and "pumping" action is made sensible and audible by the enjambement): *"silberne orgel- / pfeife, fallrohr: dort hindurch / pumpte das wetter."* (p. 77). Nature and culture become virtually indistinguishable by creating a third ground of comparison in which they meet through similarity of forms or actions. By the different ways of looking at the rain barrel, the stanzas of the poem transform human agency and material things into a web of references and networks that, not by chance, perform the style and rhetoric of contemporary theories that question the anthropology of the moderns, the separation of humans from their material word.[55] Reframing adaptations and variations in literary narratives, poetry and metaphors as powerful comparative practices opens the way to address literature's function as a world-disclosing activity. Literature, while doing comparisons, gives existence to a context, a "tertium" that has not been there before. At the same time, this creation reflects back on our real-life experiences, rearranging the ways of seeing and experiencing the world as we know it.

How to do things with words and poems—Odysseus' last journey

The poetry of Wallace Stevens deals with metaphors even in the titles of some of his major poems. "The Motive for Metaphor" traces the origin of metaphoric thinking back to a world that never reveals itself completely: "The obscure moon lighting an obscure world / Of things that would never be quite expressed, / Where you yourself were never quite yourself" (p. 288). Freed from gods and transcending powers, the world as it is is always connecting objects through the power of words and the activities of perception. Metaphoric thinking, therefore, is contained in doing things with words; they create resemblances with words and imaginations that were not there before.

In one of his late poems, "Not Ideas About The Thing But The Thing Itself," the scene opens with a sound that originates in nature as well as in the cognitive and imaginative inner-side of humankind: "At the earliest ending of winter, / In March, a scrawny cry from outside / Seemed like a sound in his mind." (p. 534). Only after echoing in the mind is this "scrawny cry" labeled and truly "heard" as a "bird's cry" and later compared to a "chorister" and being (in a metonymic as well as a metaphoric move) "part of the colossal sun, / Surrounded by its choral rings." (p. 534). That "cry" made up by nature and the mind's imagination finally, in the very last verse, is compared (again with the copula "like") with what poetry is disclosing after all: "Still far away. It was like / A new knowledge of reality." (p. 534).

By wanting to get rid of a religious and cosmic analogical thinking, Stevens' poems discover—more and more—the comparative power of words and language to form relations, similarities, and metaphors. Therefore, almost mysteriously, they connect things and unknown words, human attitudes, and feelings. Pure objects, sounds, perceptions, images, and imaginations—like the blackbird that was looked upon in the early poem—never rest but become involved in ever more comparative transactions of newly found similarities and differences. The "fisherman"—in the poem "Thinking Of A Relation Between The Images Of Metaphors"—is "all / One

---

55 See Philippe Descola, *Jenseits von Natur und Kultur*, Berlin 2011; Bruno Latour, *Existenzweisen. Eine Anthropologie der Modernen*, Berlin 2014.

ear" and "all / One eye" when he hears and sees the "wood-doves," but reality is multifolded because things get at least doubled in the eye of observer: "The fisherman is all / One eye, in which the dove resembles a dove." (p. 356). The resemblance of objects in relation to their words may be deceptive as well as illuminating, because things stay the same as they are ("In that one eye the dove / Might spring to sight and yet remain a dove."), but the image and the object, through seeing and hearing, might immediately change, become different, or something else within the spectator's inner life: "The fisherman might be the single man / In whose breast, the dove, alighting, would grow still." (p. 357).

Like Jan Wagner today, the late Wallace Stevens uses poetic language to represent the world and imagination in its entanglement. His poems circle around objects and landscapes while constantly using comparisons—metaphors, similes, juxtapositions, blending nature and culture—to test and sharpen perceptions, yet, at the same time, to transform the world through metaphoric acts and semantic innovations. In Stevens' last years, he discovers the figure of Odysseus as an explorer of the unknown that has not been signified yet, as a man who transforms himself beyond recognition: "Is it Ulysses that approaches from the east, / The interminable adventurer?" (p. 520) ("The World as Meditation").

In a poem titled "Prologues to What Is Possible" (1954), Wallace Stevens has added another comparative space for the reception and adaptation of the figure of Odysseus who is clearly alluded to in the poem: "being alone in a boat at sea" with his "rowers" (p. 516) and his "oarsmen" (p. 517), "he that stood up in the boat leaning and looking before him" (p. 515). The poem obviously hinges on Dante's vision of the audacious, restless and exiled sailor navigating even farer into remote territories as another version of the *polytropos* (already well-represented by Alfred Tennyson's and Gabriele d'Annunzio's Ulysses[56]) exercising modernity's quest into the unknown: "He belonged to the far-foreign departure of his vessel and was part of it, / Part of the speculum of fire on its prow." (p. 516). In Stevens' poem, however, the new Odysseus moves into a completely new ground of comparison and takes on a *comparatum* that transforms the Odyssey into an adventure and exploration of language. "As he traveled alone, like a man lured on by a syllable without any meaning, / A syllable of which he felt, with an appointed sureness, / That it contained the meaning into which he wanted to enter, / A meaning which, as he entered it, would shatter the boat" (p. 516).

Steven Wallace, here, draws on the episode of the sirens, the pure sound of the "syllables" that promises meaning that never really is captured or brought together with the linguistic signifier of pure words. The poetic and most intrusive form of this cleavage, again, is the metaphor, a comparative process in which meaning

---

56 Cf. Boitani, *The Shadows of Ulysses*, 97–106, 130–134.

is created by something—a *tertium*—that is not there in the single syllables and signifiers.

"The metaphor stirred his fear" (p. 516) is the opening of the second part of the poem in which the unseen, undiscovered meaning takes on the form of Odysseus' final destination (that never comes close to a homecoming this time). Moreover, the hero himself is looking for his own meaning, his own self that is transformed while being "removed from any shore, from any man or woman, and needing none"; he moves into the unknown of things and of himself: "The object with which he was compared / Was beyond his recognizing. By this he knew that likeness of him extended / Only a little way, and not beyond, unless between himself / And things beyond resemblance there was this and that intended to be recognized" (p. 516).

The quest of this new Ulysses, painful again ("fear"), and born out of ingenuity again, focuses on "comparing" and "recognizing" this time, on language and the self as modes of constantly changing, unconceivable forms. The transforming power of the Odyssey—as a trip to the unknown feature of the world (and the self)—serves as a simile of metaphors and similes, as a constant proof that "recognizing" and "likeness" form the exchange between humans, language, and the "things." Stevens' poem adds a new comparative space to the *Odyssey* by an epistemological journey to the lands of metaphorical and comparative thinking: The "fear" of losing ground matches up with "a free universe out of nothingness" and "unexpected magnitudes" that are present in the poem's final verses: "A flick which added to what was real and its vocabulary, / The way some first thing coming into Northern trees / Adds to them the whole vocabulary of the South, / The way the earliest single light in the evening sky, in spring, / Creates a fresh universe out of nothingness by adding itself, / The way a look or a touch reveals its unexpected magnitudes." (p. 517).

"Prologues to What Is Possible" takes sailing and traveling as models and metaphors by reframing the *Odyssey* as humankind's parable for the transformative power of language and literature. By putting the comparative power of world literature's narrative and the poetic innovation of poems and metaphors into one place and one poem, these "prologues" transform an origin of literature, the Greek epos, the adventure ride and fairy tale of the *Odyssey*, into the starting point of what is "possible" in language and poetry, a promising prologue to all the poetic comparisons that are still to come.

References

APTER, Emily, *Against World Literature. On the Politics of Untranslatability*, London 2013.
ARISTOTLE, *Poetics*, Cambridge 2005.
BLUMENBERG, Hans, *Arbeit am Mythos*, Frankfurt a. M. 1984.

BOITANI, Piero, *The Shadows of Ulysses. Figures of a Myth*, Oxford 1994.
BROGAN, Jacqueline Vaught, *Stevens and Simile. A Theory of Language*, Princeton 1986.
CLARK, Matthew, Formulas, metre and type-scenes, in: Robert Fowler (ed.), *The Cambridge Companion to Homer*, Cambridge 2004, 117–138.
COLE, David W., Homer's Odyssey and Clarke's/Kubrick's 2001: A Space Odyssey, in: *Notes on Contemporary Literature* 31 (2001), 5–6.
DANTE, Alighieri: *La Commedia/Die Göttliche Komödie*. Italienisch/Deutsch. 3 vols. Stuttgart 2010.
DESCOLA, Philippe, *Jenseits von Natur und Kultur*, Berlin 2011.
DOMÍNGUEZ, César/SAUSSY, Haun/VILLANUEVA, Darío, *Introducing Comparative Literature. New Trends and Applications*, London/New York 2015.
EECKHOUT, Bart, Stevens and philosophy, in: John N. Serio (ed.), *The Cambridge Companion to Wallace Stevens*, Cambridge 2007, 103–117.
EGGERS, Michael, *Vergleichendes Erkennen. Zur Wissenschaftsgeschichte und zur Epistemologie des Vergleichs und zur Genealogie der Komparatistik*, Heidelberg 2016.
EPPLE, Angelika/ERHART, Walter (eds.), *Die Welt beobachten. Praktiken des Vergleichens*, Frankfurt a. M./New York 2015.
ERHART, Walter, Weltliterarische Vergleichspraxis—am Beispiel des Odysseus, in: Dieter Lamping (ed.), *Vergleichende Weltliteraturen, DFG-Symposion 2018*, Stuttgart 2019, 137-155.
FELSKI, Rita, Comparison and Translation. A Perspective from Actor-Network-Theory, in: *Comparative Literature Studies* 53 (2016), 747–765.
FELSKI, Rita, Latour und Literary Studies, in: *PMLA* 130 (2015), 737–742.
FELSKI, Rita/FRIEDMAN, Susan Stanford (eds.), *Comparison: Theories, Approaches, Uses*, Baltimore 2013.
FISH, Stanley, *Is There a Text in This Class? The Authority of Interpretive Communities*, Cambridge/London 1980.
FLUCK, Winfried, Reading for Recognition, in: *New Literary History* 44 (2013), 45–67.
FRIEDMAN, Susan Stanford, Why not compare?, in: Rita Felski/Susan Stanford Friedman (eds.), *Comparison: Theories, Approaches, Uses*, Baltimore 2013, 34–45.
GENETTE, Gerard, *Palimpseste. Die Literatur auf zweiter Stufe*, Frankfurt a. M. 1993.
GRIMM, Gunter E., Irrfahrt als Motiv im Werk deutscher Exilautoren (1933-1950), in: Walter Erhart/Sigrid Nieberle (eds.), *Odyseen 2001. Fahrten—Passagen—Wanderungen*, München 2003, 102–118.
HÄNTZSCHEL, Günter, Odysseus in der deutschen Literatur vor und nach 1945, in: Walter Erhart/Sigrid Nieberle (eds.), *Odyseen 2001. Fahrten—Passagen—Wanderungen*, München 2003, 119-131.
HOMER, *The Odyssey*. Translated by Martin Hammond. With an Introduction by Jasper Griffin, London et al. 2000.
HONNETH, Axel, Über die Möglichkeit einer erschließenden Kritik. Die "Dialektik der Aufklärung" im Horizont gegenwärtiger Debatten über Sozialkritik, in:

Axel Honneth, *Das Andere der Gerechtigkeit. Aufsätze zur praktischen Philosophie*, Frankfurt a. M. 2000, 70–87.

HORKHEIMER, Max/ADORNO, Theodor W., *Dialektik der Aufklärung. Philosophische Fragmente*, [1947], Frankfurt a. M. 2002.

KARNICK, Manfred, Formen der Fremdheit und Wandlungen der Odysseus-Rezeption in der frühen deutschen Nachkriegsliteratur, in: Eijiro Iwasaki (ed.), *Begegnung mit dem Fremden. Achter Internationaler Germanisten-Kongreß*, vol. 9., München 1991, 422–432.

LAKOFF, George/JOHNSON, Mark, *Metaphors We Live By*, Chicago 1980.

LATOUR, Bruno, *Existenzweisen. Eine Anthropologie der Modernen*, Berlin 2014.

LEHMANN, Hans-Thies, Die Raumfabrik—Mythos im Kino und Kinomythos, in: Karl Heinz Bohrer (ed.), *Mythos und Moderne. Begriff und Bild einer Rekonstruktion*, Frankfurt a. M. 1983, 572–609.

MAEDER, Beverly, Stevens and linguistic structure, in: John N. Serio (ed.), *The Cambridge Companion to Wallace Stevens*, Cambridge 2007, 161.

MIGNOLO, Walter D., Who is Comparing What and Why?, in: Rita Felski/Susan Stanford Friedman (eds.), *Comparison: Theories, Approaches, Uses*, Baltimore 2013, 99–119.

MUTTER, Matthew, Wallace Stevens, Analogy and Tautology: The Problem of a Secular Poetics, in: *English Literary History* 78 (2011), 741–768.

POLLOCK, Sheldon, Comparison Without Hegemony, in: Hans Joas/Barbro Klein (eds.), *The Benefit of Broad Horizons. Intellectual and Institutional Preconditions for a Global Social Science*, Leiden/Boston 2010, 185–204.

REHDER, Robert, *The Poetry of Wallace Stevens*, Basingstoke/London 1988.

RHADAKRISHNAN, Rajagopalan, World Literature, by Any Other Name?, in: *PMLA* 131 (2016), 1396–1404.

RHADAKRISHNAN, Rajagopalan, Why Compare?, in: Rita Felski/Susan Stanford Friedman (eds.), *Comparison: Theories, Approaches, Uses*, Baltimore 2013, 15–33.

RICHARDS, I. A., *Principles of Literary Criticism*, New York 1925.

RICŒUR, Paul, Die Metapher und das Hauptproblem der Hermeneutik [1972], in: Anselm Haverkamp (ed.), *Theorie der Metapher*, Darmstadt 1996, 356–375.

RICŒUR, Paul, *Time and Narrative*. 3 vols., vol. I, Chicago 1990.

RIEDEL, Volker, Metamorphosen des Odysseus-Bildes, in: *Deutschunterricht* 51 (1998), 394–406.

SAUSSY, Haun, *Are We Comparing Yet? On Standards, Justice, and Incomparability*, Bielefeld 2019.

SCHNEIDER, Ralf, Comparison, Analogy, and Knowledge in Literature: Some Basic Considerations and the Case of Early Modern English Texts, in: Christoph Haase/Anne Schröder (eds.): *Analogy, Copy, and Representation. Interdisciplinary Perspectives*, Bielefeld 2018, 139–156.

SCHWARZ, Daniel R., *Narrative and Representation in the Poetry of Wallace Stevens*, New York 1993.

SEIDENSTICKER, Bernd, Aufbruch zu neuen Ufern. Transformationen der Odysseusgestalt in der literarischen Moderne, in: Bernd Seidensticker/Martin Vöhler (eds.), *Urgeschichten der Moderne. Die Antike im 20. Jahrhundert*, Stuttgart/Weimar 2001, 249–270.

STANFORD, William B., *The Ulysses Theme. A Study in the Adaptability of a Traditional Hero*, Oxford 1968.

STERN, Herbert J., *Wallace Stevens' Art of Uncertainty*, Ann Arbor 1966.

STEVENS, Wallace, *The Collected Poems*, New York 1990.

STEVENS, Wallace, Three Academic Pieces: I, in: Marie Borroff (ed.): *Wallace Stevens. A Collection of Critical Essays*, Englewood Cliffs 1963, 24–29.

STIERLE, Karl-Heinz, *Das große Meer des Sinns. Hermenautische Erkundungen in Dantes "Commedia"*, München 2007.

SUKENIK, Ronald, *Wallace Stevens. Musing the Obscure*, New York 1967.

TELOTTE, Jay P., The Gravity of 2001: A Space Odyssey, in: Robert Phillip Kolker (ed.), *Stanley Kubrick's 2001: A Space Odyssey. New Essays*, Oxford 2006, 43–53.

TOMPKINS, Jane P. (ed.), *Reader-Response Criticism. From Formalism to Post-Structuralism*, Baltimore/London 1980.

VERGILIUS MARO, Publius: *Aeneis. Lateinisch/Deutsch*. Stuttgart 1994.

WAGNER, Jan, *Regentonnenvariationen*, München/Berlin 2014.

WAGNER, Jan, *Die Sandale des Propheten. Beiläufige Prosa*, Berlin 2011.

WEINRICH, Harald, Semantik der kühnen Metapher, in: Anselm Haverkamp (ed.), *Theorie der Metapher*, Darmstadt 1996, 316–339.

WHEAT, Leonhard F., *2001: A Triple Allegory*, Lanham 2000.

ZHANG, Longxi, Comparison and Correspondence: Revisiting an Old Idea for the Present, in: *Comparative Literature Studies* 53 (2016), 767–781.

Where Do Rankings Come From?
A Historical-Sociological Perspective on the History of Modern Rankings

Leopold Ringel/Tobias Werron

Abstract

Extant research tends to perceive rankings as a relatively new phenomenon. This chapter argues that rankings have a long history that we need to study if we want to explain the recent rise and the specific roles that they play in different societal fields. We start by defining rankings as modern practices of comparison that, by comparing performances quantitatively and publicly on a continual basis, contribute to the social construction of competitive fields. We particularly highlight what we call the performative dimension of modern rankings—that is, the fact that they visualize the results of comparisons and publish them on a regular basis. We use this concept as a heuristic tool to develop a sociological perspective on the historical trajectories of rankings in three fields: the arts, competitive sports, and science/universities. Our findings suggest that (1) the institutionalization of rankings can be traced back to a largely Anglo-American context in the mid-to-late nineteenth century when modern notions of performance, competition, and publicity/transparency created a favorable environment for their production and proliferation. They also indicate that (2) variation between the fields can be attributed to the degree to which these notions guide communication within these fields and to the different ways in which rankings have been institutionalized. This has led to a seamless integration in the case of sports and to constant debate and controversy in the other two fields.

Introduction: Mapping the field of ranking research

Every year, Transparency International's Corruption Perception Index compares the success of countries in their fight against corruption; every year, global university rankings compare the best universities worldwide; week per week, the ATP or WTA world rankings compare the best tennis players based on a continually updated scoring system; Trip Advisor, by constantly keeping track of guest reviews, creates "popularity indices" that advise us on the best hotels and restaurants whenever and wherever we want; and the PiPa Ranking provides "pigeon connoisseurs" with up-to-date information on the best racing pigeons everywhere around the world. As these examples demonstrate, rankings have become an inseparable part of modern life. Whether universities, athletes, artists, hospitals, businesses, hotels, restaurants, nation states, or racing pigeons, rankings measure and publicly compare the products and performances of all kinds of actors on a continual basis. The omnipresence of rankings has not failed to attract the attention of social scientists. These studies, however, tend to focus on the kind of rankings that have proliferated since the 1980s. They can be divided roughly into studies on (1) the production, (2) the effects, and (3) the discursive reception and institutionalization of rankings.

(1) Studies on the *production of rankings* emphasize social processes such as the editing of data in order to regulate an organizational field,[1] the legitimization of rankings,[2] the public construction of competition[3] and the intricacies of visualizing comparisons[4]. Such studies tend to focus on the sociomateriality of rankings and describe them as performative "devices" that not only observe but also generate fields, markets, or reputation. Yet others criticize rankings on methodological grounds, thus suggesting the need to improve indicators and the underlying calculative operations.[5] (2) Scholars studying the *effects of rankings* have found that organizations adapt their structures and routines to the measured criteria.[6] Poorly ranked organizations strive to improve their status,[7] whereas those at the top try to maintain theirs, which becomes all the more important considering that reputation tends to be sticky.[8] This is particularly the case in higher education where, accord-

---

[1] Cf. Afshin Mehrpouya/Rita Samiolo, Performance Measurement in Global Governance: Ranking and the Politics of Variability, in: *Accounting, organizations and society* 55 (2016), 12-31.

[2] Cf. Garry R. Barron, The Berlin Principles on Ranking Higher Education Institutions. Limitations, Legitimacy, and Value Conflict, in: *Higher Education* 73 (2/2017), 317-333; Miguel A. Lim, The Building of Weak Expertise. The Work of Global University Rankers, in: *Higher Education* 75 (3/2018), 415-430.

[3] Cf. Martin Kornberger/Chris Carter, Manufacturing Competition: How Accounting Practices Shape Strategy Making in Cities, in: *Accounting, Auditing & Accountability Journal* 23 (3/2010), 325-349.

[4] Cf. Neil Pollock/Luciana D'Adderio, Give me a Two-by-two Matrix and I will Create the Market: Rankings, Graphic visualisations and Sociomateriality, in: *Accounting, Organizations and Society* 37 (8/2012), 565-586.

[5] Cf. Simon Marginson, University Rankings and Social Science, in: European Journal of Education 49 (1/2014), 45-59; Catherine O'Connell, Research Discourses Surrounding Global University Rankings: Exploring the Relationship with Policy and Practice Recommendations, in: *Higher Education* 65 (6/2013), 709-723.

[6] Cf. Wendy Nelson Espeland /Michael Sauder, Rankings and Reactivity. How Public Measures Recreate Social Worlds, in: *American Journal of Sociology* 113 (1/2007), 1-40.

[7] Cf. Judith G. Kelley/Beth A. Simmons, Politics by Number: Indicators as Social Pressure in International Relations, in: *American Journal of Political Science* 59 (1/2015), 55-70.

[8] Cf. Majken Schultz/Jan Mouritsen/Gorm Gabrielsen, Sticky Reputation: Analyzing a Ranking System, in: *Corporate Reputation Review* 4 (1/2001), 24-41.

ing to the often-observed Matthew Effect, advantages accrue disproportionately at the top.[9] Some, however, argue that rankings do not determine organizational behavior but allow for creative forms of "reflexive transformation".[10] Yet others emphasize the distress rankings cause among those who are subject to them, because they threaten to undermine or outright reject organizational identities.[11] (3) Studies on *trajectories of institutionalization* argue that the successful embedding of rankings in fields can be explained by the efforts of powerful actors who use them as a resource of legitimacy.[12] Others apply a sociology-of-knowledge perspective to emphasize the cultural value of rankings, particularly their aura of rationality and modernity.[13] However, statements in public discourses can range from uncritical support to fierce critique, with the latter often evoking counterarguments by supporters, thereby unintentionally contributing to the institutionalization of rankings as a topic of debate and contestation.[14] Comparisons of countries support the claim that discursive processes are fundamental to understanding the varying degrees of institutionalization, showing that public debates in the media play an important part when it comes to defining rankings as more or less convincing and important.[15]

In sum, there is a growing body of literature on rankings that has produced rich insights. However, because this literature has limited its scope predominantly to the last 20-30 years when the modern-day ranking frenzy seems to have started, historical perspectives are still rare. Against this backdrop, we aim to explore rankings by addressing three shortcomings of the existing research: First, the "presentist" focus on recent decades tends to neglect the long-term prerequisites of the

---

9 Cf. Julian Hamann, The Visible Hand of Research Performance Assessment, in: *Higher Education* 72 (6/2016), 761-779; Ellen Hazelkorn, *Rankings and the Reshaping of Higher Education. The Battle for World Class Excellence*, Basingstoke 2011; Richard Münch, *Academic Capitalism. Universities in the Global Struggle for Excellence*, London 2014.

10 Neil Pollock et al., Conforming or Transforming? How Organizations Respond to Multiple Rankings, in: *Accounting, Organizations and Society* 64 (2018), 55-68.

11 Cf. Kimberly D. Elsbach/Roderick M. Kramer, Members' Responses to Organizational Identity Threats. Encountering and Countering the Business Week Rankings, in: *Administrative Science Quarterly* 41 (3/1996), 442-476.

12 Cf. Linda Wedlin, *Ranking Business Schools. Forming Fields, Identities and Boundaries. International Management Education*, Northampton 2006.

13 Cf. Andrea Mennicken, From Inspection to Auditing: Audit and Markets as Linked Ecologies, in: *Accounting, Organizations and Society* 35 (3/2010), 334-359.

14 Cf. Jelena Brankovic/Leopold Ringel/Tobias Werron, How rankings produce competition: The case of global university rankings, in: *Zeitschrift für Soziologie* 47 (4/2018), 270-288.

15 Cf. Ellen Gutterman, The Legitimacy of Transnational NGOs. Lessons from the Experience of Transparency International in Germany and France, in: *Review of International Studies* 40 (2/2014), 391-418; Kerstin Martens/Dennis Niemann, When Do Numbers Count? The Differential Impact of the PISA Rating and Ranking on Education Policy in Germany and the US, in: *German Politics* 22 (3/2013), 314-332.

rise of rankings. We need to study these long-term factors—not only to understand the history of rankings but also to develop a sociological explanation of their recent proliferation that goes beyond vague references to neoliberalism or digitalization. Second, because studies focus mostly on specific cases and fields, particularly universities, they have largely missed the opportunity to learn from comparisons of rankings across fields. And third, the literature has largely failed to determine the distinct characteristics of rankings as specific practices of comparison, particularly in contrast to similar practices such as ratings or benchmarks.

Our chapter aims to address these shortcomings by developing a sociological perspective on the origins and careers of modern rankings. We start by introducing a conceptualization that allows for a more specific characterization of rankings as a modern practice of comparison. Specifically, we define them as social operations combining comparisons of performances, quantification, visualization, and repeated publication, which, by integrating these elements, partake in the social construction of competition. We particularly highlight what we call the *performative dimension* of rankings: the fact that they not only compare and evaluate performances but also visualize the results of these comparisons and publish them on a regular basis. This definition allows us to distinguish rankings from similar practices while also serving as a heuristic tool for historical studies. The theoretical implications for historical studies are discussed in the second section. Here, we argue that our conceptualization draws attention to long-term prerequisites of the institutionalization of rankings, namely to the formation of modern notions of performance, competition, and publicity/transparency as well as to the role of the mass media and different publics. On this basis, the third section explores historical trajectories of rankings in three fields: the arts, competitive sports, and science/universities. Based on this analysis, we argue that the sociocultural prerequisites of today's rankings first came together in the mid-to-late nineteenth to early twentieth century in the Anglo-American world when a new alignment of notions of performance, competition, and publicity/transparency let rankings appear to contemporary observers as a useful, even necessary practice of comparison. We also conclude that the trajectories of rankings in different fields are associated with different discursive manifestations of these notions and with heterogeneous audiences: Whereas in the case of sports, rankings were soon taken for granted and integrated seamlessly into the field, in science and the arts, they became a constant topic of controversy, institutionalizing them as a topic of conversation and object of contention rather than as a part of the field that is simply taken for granted.

What are rankings? Conceptual remarks[16]

We conceptualize rankings as social operations that partake in the construction of public forms of competition: The Human Development Index pushes modern nation states to be constantly striving to improve their GDP, healthcare, and education systems, as a result of which they bolster their reputation at the expense of other nation states; the World University Ranking by Times Higher Education puts universities in the position of seeing other universities, anywhere in the world, as competitors for reputation and students. We argue that modern, fully developed rankings achieve this by combining four analytically distinct operations that, when taken together, contribute to the social construction of competitive fields. These four operations are: (1) comparison of performances, (2) quantification, (3) visualization, and (4) repeated—regular or periodic—publication. We summarize the first two operations as the informative dimension of rankings; but, given the state of research, we particularly emphasize the third and fourth operations, which we define as the performative dimension of rankings.

(1) Sociologically speaking, the *comparison of performances* entails making entities comparable along the same category, defining them as identical or similar, and simultaneously comparing and differentiating them according to some additional criteria.[17] For instance, different social entities are first declared similar by subsuming them under the same category "artist," "university," or "basketball player;" and they are then evaluated and distinguished according to some criteria of performance such as "genius," "excellence," or "points per game." Studies on rankings are often oblivious to the complexities of the social processes undergirding the production of comparisons, because they tend to take categories for granted. They accept the assumption that there is something like "scientific excellence" that only has to be captured by applying "the right instruments." In contrast, seeing rankings as practices of comparison emphasizes that there is nothing natural about the social act of comparing.[18]

---

16 This section is based on Brankovic/Ringel/Werron, How rankings produce competition. Some paragraphs are identical or contain only minor changes (see also Tobias Werron/Leopold Ringel, Rankings in a comparative perspective. Conceptual remarks, in: Stephan Lessenich (ed.), *Geschlossene Gesellschaften* (Verhandlungen des 38. Kongresses der Deutschen Gesellschaft für Soziologie), Essen 2017.

17 Cf. Bettina Heintz, Numerische Differenz. Überlegungen zu einer Soziologie des (quantitativen) Vergleichs, in: *Zeitschrift für Soziologie* 39 (3/2010), 162-181.

18 Cf. Angelika Epple, Doing Comparisons – Ein praxeologischer Zugang zur Geschichte der Globalisierung/en, in: Angelika Epple/Walter Erhart (eds.), *Die Welt beobachten. Praktiken des Vergleichens*, Frankfurt a. M./New York 2015, 161-199; Johannes Grave, Vergleichen als Praxis. Vorüberlegungen zu einer praxistheoretisch orientierten Untersuchung von Vergleichen, in: Angelika Epple/Walter Erhart (eds.), *Die Welt beobachten. Praktiken des Vergleichens*, Frankfurt a. M./New York 2015, 135-159; Willibald Steinmetz, Vergleich. Eine begriffsgeschichtliche

However, we see rankings not merely as comparisons but as *zero-sum comparisons*. With "zero-sum" we wish to highlight that within a ranking, the quality ascribed to one entity is usually not ascribed simultaneously to another entity of the same category. The "sum" of possibilities created by the assumption of comparability is transformed into a dependent relationship between the compared entities. The social production of zero sum is rarely discussed in the literature on rankings—which is surprising given that, after all, many of the qualities measured by rankings such as the genius of an artist, the development of a country, or the excellence of a university do not necessarily come at the expense of other artists, countries, or universities. Rankings, however, seem to be able to create some kind of zero sumness even in these cases. How do they achieve that?

(2) Zero-sum comparisons can be made on qualitative or quantitative grounds. Qualitative comparisons are possible but potentially contentious and limited in scope. By claiming that Juventus F.C. is the greatest football team in the world, we would make a qualitative zero-sum comparison that implies that all other teams are, in some sense, worse and thus cannot claim to be the greatest football team in the world. However, there are certain limitations to such judgments, especially when talking about a large number of entities. If we argue that actually Real Madrid is better than Juventus F.C., the advocate of Juventus might ask us to elaborate on how we came to such a conclusion: Do Real play more efficiently? Do they have a more attractive style? Do they have a particularly rich tradition? The proponent of Real Madrid might have just as many good reasons as does the champion of Juventus F.C. And things would get even more complicated in the case of multiteam comparisons in which you would have to explain not only the hierarchy between Real and Juventus but also the relative greatness of all other teams in the world. In other words, qualitative zero-sum comparisons can easily lead to highly contentious and potentially endless debates.

Against this backdrop, the appeal of *quantification as a rhetorical means of comparison* becomes apparent: By attaching numbers to qualities, rankers can validate their zero-sum statements in seemingly unambiguous terms. After all, a third person might argue that Real Madrid is not just "better" than Juventus F.C. but indeed won the Champions League final in 2017 "four goals to one" against Juventus. From this perspective, Real is of course "better" than Juventus by exactly three goals (at least for the time being). Similarly, the University of Oxford gets a certain "score" on the World University Ranking published by Times Higher Education, which suggests a clear difference between Oxford and lower-scoring universities. At this juncture, it is important to take notice of the communicative quality that quantification adds

---

Skizze, in: Angelika Epple/Walter Erhart (eds.), *Die Welt beobachten. Praktiken des Vergleichens*, Frankfurt a. M./New York 2015, 85-134.

to zero-sum statements: Whereas the literature on rankings often criticizes quantification as a mode of simplification, we argue that it is precisely this "reductive" aspect that makes rankings such a successful tool (combined with their ability to reflect the observations and opinions of others).[19] Thus, neither comparison nor quantification as such, but the combination of both operations, explains the distinct allure of rankings.

(3) *Visualization* allows ranking organizations to present a "picture" of the comparable entities and the differences between them. Visualization does not merely encode information, but fundamentally transforms it.[20] Visualizations are part and parcel of the seductiveness and coerciveness of rankings in that they present a clear overview of differences in performance that are easy to understand. They provide a visual order that affects the very way in which information is received and processed. Visualizations thus should not just be observed with regard to how "accurately" they represent information but also be taken seriously as a performative element of rankings.

The most common device used for this purpose is a table providing an overview of comparable entities in a hierarchical order starting with the best performers on the top. In all of the three fields that we analyze—the arts, sports, and science/universities—tables are the most frequent way of visualizing rankings. They usually contain information about recent performances but can also include references to positions in earlier tables representing the same competitive fields (E.g., Rank 3 in 2017 vs. Rank 7 in 2018), thereby allowing audiences to grasp historical trajectories in a field immediately. Moreover, ranking tables can be made available in digital formats allowing users of websites to create their own individual rankings. To fully account for how rankings suggest competition, analyzing such visual presentations is vital for an adequate understanding of their production, reception, and effects.

(4) As a *social* operation, rankings depend on a fourth element that has not yet been theorized adequately in the literature: the repeated act of *publication*. The continual publication of rankings—annually, monthly, weekly, daily, and even real-time updates—creates a situation in which the ranked entities are constantly observed for and presented to an *audience* or public whose attention and appreciation is imagined as a scarce good for which the compared entities ought to compete. An audience in these terms is not merely a sum of living and breathing people, but a social construction projected in the process of publication. The effective institutionalization of rankings is therefore contingent upon them being published not

---

19   Cf. Elena Esposito/David Stark, What's observed in a Rating? Rankings as Orientation in the Face of Uncertainty, in: *Theory, Culture & Society* 36 (4/2019), Online First.
20   Cf. Hans K. Hansen/Mikkel Flyverbom, The politics of transparency and the calibration of knowledge in the digital age, in: *Organization* 22 (6/2015), 872-889.

just once or twice but continually: This is how they suggest competition for reputation, prestige, or status. Rankings thus combine two performative elements, visualization and repeated publication, that transform quantified comparisons of performances into a powerful publicly available tool. It is this performative dimension that also qualifies them as a particular *social practice* of comparison: a serial practice of comparison with its own visuality, temporality and regularity.

This dimension of rankings is rarely discussed in research on rankings. However, it is on the performative level that modern rankings distinguish themselves from related practices such as ratings or benchmarks. The latter contain some, but not all, of the four elements described above. Ratings are often based on quantifications and invite users to compare performances. However, they do not visually depict all rated actors in repeatedly published tables, and therefore, per se, do not suggest competition between these actors. Benchmarks define a standard based on the top result in a population of organizations, and they test the degree to which these organizations' performance corresponds to the said standard. By identifying a number one, benchmarks aim to motivate all other organizations to catch up. Rankings, on the other hand, produce a hierarchical order of all members of a competitive field; any improvement of some entity is thus imagined as potentially coming at the expense of others. For these reasons, rankings are connected more closely to the idea of competition than are ratings and benchmarks.

Using this definition, we can identify the characteristics of contemporary rankings in order to trace their historical careers in different fields. We can also use it to trace the history of protorankings that share some, but not all, of these characteristics. Taking the performative dimension into account thus helps to define rankings as a particular social practice and to study the social prerequisites of their long-term institutionalization.

On the history of rankings: Theoretical considerations

Based on our conceptualization, we suspect that the historical rise of rankings is contingent on a sociocultural infrastructure rendering the regular public and quantitative comparison of performances plausible or even desirable. This insight draws attention to the formation and content of modern notions of performance/achievement, competition, and publicity/transparency. According to Verheyen,[21] modern notions of *performance/achievement*, which define performance as something that is achieved and can be improved constantly by individual actors, emerged in the late nineteenth century and early twentieth century, forming, among other things, the

---

21   Nina Verheyen, Die Erfindung der Leistung, München/Berlin 2018.

ideal of a "meritocracy." The modern notion of *competition* and its societal advantages emerged in the mid-to-late eighteenth century based on the work of classical political economists on "free competition" (Adam Smith), and it was used to describe and promote market competition. However, since the mid-to-late nineteenth century, it was also used increasingly to discuss and promote competition in other spheres.[22] Both lines of thought are closely intertwined, because competition is often considered to be a product and a driver of performance (creativity, productivity, etc.). Ideas about performance/achievement and competition are also related to modern concepts of *publicity and transparency*: Publicity, that is, the idea that the public has a right to know about political and administrative decisions in order to improve the conduct of those subject to norms of disclosure, became a hot topic in the late eighteenth-century philosophical discourse, spread in the nineteenth and twentieth century, and intensified in the 1980s. Since the 1980s, the discourse commonly refers to "transparency"—now covering all kinds of spheres and not just politics.[23]

At a general level, all three discourses entertain a mutually enhancing relationship with rankings as described above: Rankings compare performances *publicly* on a regular basis, thereby suggesting *competition* to motivate the ranked entities to constantly improve their *performance*. However, field-specific interpretations of these three discourses might also spur criticism of rankings, effectively blocking their diffusion and institutionalization. We therefore suspect that, depending on the different meanings attributed to publicity/transparency, performance, and competition, rankings can be expected to be more or less likely to become institutionalized practices of comparison.

There is a second proposition that we can derive from our conceptualization of rankings: By emphasizing the performative dimension of rankings, particularly their publicity, we suggest that their success, or lack thereof, also depends on the ways in which they address publics, and on the degree to which they succeed in attracting attention and appreciation. The historical background for this assumption is innovations in telecommunication technology during the course of the nineteenth century that provided the material infrastructure for the fast movement of information on a global scale.[24] These changes in the technological infrastructure

---

22   Cf. Tobias Werron, Why do we believe in competition? A historical-sociological view of competition as an institutionalized modern imaginary, in: *Scandinavian Journal of Social Theory* 16 (2015), 186-210.

23   Cf. Leopold Ringel, *Transparenz als Ideal und Organisationsproblem. Eine Studie am Beispiel der Piratenpartei Deutschland*, Wiesbaden 2017.

24   Cf. Roland Wenzlhuemer, Globalization, communication and the concept of space in global history, in: Roland Wenzlhuemer (ed.), *Global communication: Telecommunication and global flows of information in the late 19th and early 20th century* (Special Issue of Historical Social Research, 35), 2010, 19-47.

coincided with the emergence of a global media system that, in the years between 1860 and 1930, was based mainly on a global oligopoly of news agencies.[25] This infrastructure for global communication coupled with the professionalization of journalism, increasing literacy rates, and the establishment of local and national markets for print products helped to erect the modern public sphere as we know it today: a global system for the distribution of "news" differentiated into national publics.[26]

Analyzing the historical implications of mass media communication is crucial for understanding the distinct allure of rankings. Mass media enable intermediaries (journalists, critics, international organizations, etc.) and wider audiences to observe and evaluate performances of primary actors in a field. This opens up new possibilities for the comparison of performances and draws attention to the plurality of expectations of different kinds of publics, particularly because they relate to (assumed) differences in knowledge. High school graduates, for instance, cannot be expected to be able to evaluate the teaching and academic skills of scholars working at their prospective university. University rankings acknowledge this and use it to their advantage by presenting all readers with a (seemingly) clear picture: University A is more excellent than University B, C, or D. The same holds true for connoisseurship in the arts. We can suspect that people who are not dedicated aficionados of the arts are going to have a hard time comparing Monet to Picasso. Thus, when struggling with how to invest their money, they might consult the ranking *Kunstkompass* to identify "good bargains." Rankings can cater to the expectations of those nonprofessional audiences by providing short cuts. However, as soon as they exist, they might retroact on expert discourses as well, thereby creating new connections and relationships between expert and non-expert audiences.

Our suggestion to focus on the performative dimension of rankings draws attention to the fact that addressing and imagining publics is an integral part of how rankings operate.[27] Against this background, it comes as no surprise that rankings often seem to act as a connector between different publics—particularly expert audiences and mass audiences—inviting them to compare performances from their respective vantage points. By doing so, they can also create tensions between both audience perspectives, especially by inspiring experts to criticize the simplicity of

---

25 Cf. Simone M. Müller/Heidi J. S. Tworek, 'The Telegraph and the Bank': On the Interdependence of Global Communications and Capitalism, 1866-1914, in: *Journal of Global History* 10 (2/2015), 259-283, see 283.
26 Cf. John B. Thompson, *The Media and Modernity. A Social Theory of the Media*, Cambridge 1995.
27 Cf. Carlos Spoerhase, Das Maß der Potsdamer Garde. Die ästhetische Vorgeschichte des Rankings in der Europäischen Literatur- und Kunstkritik des 18. Jahrhunderts, in: *Jahrbuch der Deutschen Schillergesellschaft* 58 (2014), 90-126; Carlos Spoerhase, Rankings: A Pre-History, in: *New Left Review* 114 (2018), 114, 99-112; see also Brankovic/Ringel/Werron, How rankings produce competition; Werron/Ringel, Rankings in a comparative perspective.

the rankings and confront them with their own, supposedly more complex views. Taking publics into account is thus crucial to explain the institutionalization of rankings in different societal fields. In the next section, we use this perspective to explore the long-term historical trajectories of rankings in three fields: the arts, professional sports, and science/universities.

On the institutionalization of rankings: Three historical cases

Arts, competitive sports, and science/universities: these three fields share a proclivity to experiment with rankings long before the onset of the frenzy in the 1980s. The historical trajectories of rankings, however, vary considerably from field to field: Whereas in the case of sports, they were incorporated quite quickly and effectively, their career in the arts and science/universities has been more complex and ambivalent. Studying these three fields comparatively thus might help to specify the ways in which, and the conditions under which, rankings are likely to become institutionalized. In all cases, our conceptualization of rankings draws particular attention to (1) discourses of performance, competition, and publicity/transparency; and (2) the roles of, and possible tensions between, expert and non-expert audiences.

From the Balance de Peintres to the Kunstkompass: The artistic field

The field in which some though not all of the characteristics of modern rankings were first assembled may come as a surprise: Instead of athletes, governments, or universities, those subject to table-based public comparisons of performance were artists—painters, writers, composers, and actors.[28] The takeoff point seems to have been the publication of the *Balance des Peintres* by the French critic Roger de Piles in 1708. This is a table that combines some, but not all, of the characteristics of modern rankings. It evaluates European painters from different epochs according to four criteria (composition, design, coloring, and expression) and on a scale from 0-20, and it visualizes the results on a table. However, it neither calculated an overall score nor did it bring the quantitative measurements of performances into a hierarchical order. Instead, the order was alphabetical (see Fig. 1).

The *Balance* apparently struck a chord. Over the course of the eighteenth century, various art critics and commentators from France, German-speaking countries, and Great Britain adopted its basic idea and applied it to other forms, and

---

28 The account of early experiments with art rankings in this section is based on Spoerhase, Das Maß der Potsdamer Garde, to whom we are indebted for the rich variety of empirical examples from which we draw.

Fig. 1: Balance des Peintres (De Piles 1708, in Spoerhase, Rankings: A Pre-History, 96).

NOMS des Peintres les plus connus.	Composition.	Deßein.	Coloris.	Expreßion.
Pouffin.	15	17	6	15
Primatice.	15	14	7	10
R				
Raphaël Santio.	17	18	12	13
Rembrant.	15	6	17	12
Rubens.	18	13	17	17
S				
Fr. Salviati.	13	15	8	8
Le Sueur.	15	15	4	15

this amounted to a vibrant international discourse on the quantitative comparison of artistic *performances*. Among those emulating de Piles were Mark Arkenside's *Balance of Poets* (1746), the anonymously published *Scale to Measure the Merits of Musicians* (1776), as well as the *Kritische Skala der vorzüglichsten deutschen Dichter* (1792) by Christian Friedrich Daniel Schubart.[29] For 100 years, none of these early experiments was followed by the creation of a hierarchical order based on an overall score. It was only at the beginning of the nineteenth century that the copycat process finally resulted in the production of the first table with overall scores *and* a hierarchical order compiled by the French author Jean-Francois Sobry in 1810 (Fig. 2).[30] As it turned out, Raphael, according to Sobry, was the greatest painter of all time.

---

29 Mark Arkenside's *Balance of Poets* (1746), *Scale to Measure the Merits of Musicians* (1776), *Kritische Skala der vorzüglichsten deutschen Dichter* (1792) by Christian Friedrich Daniel Schubart.
30 Jean-Francois Sobry, *Poétique des arts ou cours de peinture et de littérature comparées*, Paris 1810, S. 148–169 (De la balance des peintres).

Fig. 2: Balance des Peintres rectifiée (Sobry 1810, in Spoerhase, Rankings: A Pre-History, 121).

N O M S.	Composition.	Dessin.	Coloris.	Expression.	Résultat.
Raphaël	17	17	12	17	63
Poussin	18	18	9	18	63
Lesueur	18	17	9	18	62
Dominiquin . . , ...	14	17	10	16	57
Michel-Ange	16	18	6	15	55
Léonard-de-Vinci	15	16	10	14	55
Corrège	12	14	17	12	55
Titien	13	16	18	8	55
Rubens	14	14	17	9	54
Lorrain	17	10	17	7	51
Wandick	12	15	17	8	52
Lebrun	15	15	8	14	52

This might have been the first proper art ranking—if it had been continued by similar tables in the following years. However, it seems to have remained the last one of its kind. Indeed, artists and art critics alike had grown deeply skeptical of such types of comparisons early on. Even some of the creators such as Jean-Francois Sobry were among the critics: "'Let us love what is beautiful when we see it, without bothering about weighing it. Let us repay the enthusiasm of talent with the enthusiasm of esteem; and leave the scales to the merchants.'"[31] In this quote, he clearly emphasizes the view, shared by others in the decades to come, that quantitative comparisons resemble economic reasoning and are therefore alien to purist ideals of aesthetic-artistic excellence. We might speculate that rankings and other forms of quantification carry a level of specificity of judgment that is at odds with the somewhat ambiguous understanding of *genius* in the emerging artistic field in the nineteenth century. Furthermore, as Bourdieu (1994) elaborates, the rules of art, institutionalized in the mid-to-late nineteenth century, prescribe the production of artworks for their own sake and not for fame or money.[32] Competition for reputation, as suggested by the rankings, might give rise to "wrong" motives that taint the ideal of *l'art pour l'art*.

---

31 Sobry 1810, in Spoerhase, Rankings: A Pre-History, 111.
32 Cf. Pierre Bourdieu, *The Rules of Art: Genesis and Structure of the Literary Field*, Cambridge, England 1994.

Another distinguishing characteristic of these early experiments can be found in the writings of the aforementioned Christian Friedrich Daniel Schubart: "It is indeed hard to measure spirit and intellect like body height. It still has its value, though: The dwarf sees more clearly that he is indeed a dwarf if he compares himself with the Potsdam guard (our translation)".[33] In applying the metaphor of body height, Schubart rejects the idea of artists striving to improve their performances on the grounds of comparisons with other artists. A dwarf evidently will always be a dwarf because he cannot change his body size. Contemporary rankings, as in the section defined above, build on the opposite idea—that is, the possibility of movement between positions and the notion that everyone can, and should, constantly improve her or his performance. Indeed, most contemporary rankings would not make much sense if scores were final and set in stone. Against this backdrop, it seems as if early experiments with the quantification of artistic performances in the eighteenth to early nineteenth century focused on evaluating the *history of art genres* rather than suggesting the production of competition. According to our conceptualization, they should therefore be designated as protorankings, rather than as rankings in the contemporary sense.

In the decades following the publication of Sobry's ranking, art critics and experts confirmed the critical rejection of any kind of quantitative judgment of artistic performance. In 1866, Carl Justi describes quantitative evaluations as "formulas which attribute numbers to creative minds just like students receive grades"; Clement de Ries, in 1882, calls them "foolish" and "absurd." Others even seemed to fail to get the purpose of creating rank-ordered tables: Richard M. Meyer, referring to Schubart's table, thinks of them as "strange" (1911); Sigmund von Lempicki deems them "odd" (1920).[34] Conspicuously, the demise of these early experiments with the quantitative evaluation of art performances coincided with the professionalization of art criticism, which suggests a successful monopolization of the authority to evaluate artistic performance by a professional group of intellectual "gatekeepers".[35]

Quantitative evaluations of artistic performances remained scarce thereafter. The situation, however, changed in the second half of the 20th century with an influx of new quantified evaluations in the arts.[36] The most visible of those forms did not seem to evaluate artistic performance as such but instead the market value and/or reputation of artists. In other words, in contrast to the protorankings of the eighteenth century, they *do not* claim to be able to quantify *aesthetic comparisons*. The

---

33   Schubart, *Kritische Skala*, in Spoerhase, Rankings: A Pre-History, 123.
34   All quotes are retrieved from Spoerhase, Das Maß der Potsdamer Garde, 93–95, and translated by the authors.
35   Howard S. Becker, *Art Worlds*, Berkeley 2008.
36   Larissa Buchholz, What is a global field? Theorizing fields beyond the nation-state, in: Julian Go/Monika Krause (eds.), *Fielding Transnationalism*, London 2016, 31–60.

best explanation for their emergence and spread since the 1970s might be that the idea of making the market value and reputation of artists *transparent* has become more legitimate[37] without *directly* conflicting with the established view that artistic performance cannot be quantified. Whereas the determination and knowledge of prices had been a matter of private trading networks and/or auctions for centuries, rankings were viewed as instruments with which to unveil the opaque dynamics of the art world—particularly for potential investors who lack the necessary knowledge and expertise to make informed buying decisions.[38] Rankers often make this expansion of scope in terms of audience outreach explicit, for instance in statements such as the following, retrieved from the homepage of the *TOP 100 Artist Ranking*:

> "The Artist Ranking Tool cannot judge the work of a specific artist, it works by ordering artists according to the *professional attention* that is invested in them. It provides the *wider audience with a feeling for the standing of a particular artist in the eyes of the professionals* but is not reflective of the artist's actual economic success. ArtFacts.Net™ acknowledges that there might be a correlation between fame and money but this is not the method of calculation behind the Artist Ranking tool." [emphasis added].[39]

By focusing on indicators such as prices, exhibitions in renowned galleries, or features in magazines, current rankings steer attention to a very specific set of indicators. These indicators relate at best indirectly to artistic performances, but allow for the depiction of movement within a competitive field and thus spark intense discussion between experts as well as in broader audiences. In many cases, those concerned try to delegitimize their opponents often by using vitriolic language.[40] To put it in Bourdieusian terms, market-oriented rankings in the artistic field spark controversy at both the autonomous and the heterogeneous pole of the field. As a result, rankings inspire discussions as to whether such comparisons of perfor-

---

37 Cf. Stefan Wilbers, Grenzarbeit im Kunstbetrieb. Zur Institutionalisierung des Rankings Kunstkompass, in: Leopold Ringel/Tobias Werron (eds.), *Rankings—Soziologische Fallstudien*, Wiesbaden 2019, 57-87.
38 Cf. Paul Buckermann, Back from Business. On Commensuration, Construction, and Communication of a Global Art World in the Ranking Kunstkompass, in: *Kapsula* 1 (3/2016), 12-18.
39 Artfacts, 2018, in: the homepage of the *TOP 100 Artist Ranking*, URL: https://www.artfacts.net/tour/artist-ranking. The quote has been retrieved in 2018 and is not available any more. However, since it sums up very poignantly the ways in which rankings position themselves in the artistic field, we decided to keep it.
40 Cf. Olav Velthuis, ArtRank and the Flippers: Apocalypse now?, in: *Texte zur Kunst* 24 (96/2014), 34-49.

mance are legitimate or not, with participants being engaged in constant and often tense forms of "boundary work".[41]

A prime example is the German *Kunstkompass* (art compass), created by the journalist Willi Bongard and published annually since 1970 (with the exception of 1985, when the ranking took a hiatus) in various magazines such as *Capital*, *Manager Magazin*, and *Weltkunst*.[42] The *Kunstkompass* has used a multiplicity of indicators over the years to measure "Ruhm" (fame, reputation) such as exhibitions in esteemed museums and at major events (e.g., the *documenta* in Kassel or the biennales in Venice) or articles in art magazines. The scores are then published alongside the market prices of the artists, thereby suggesting that audiences should evaluate whether or not an artist is "a good bargain." According to Bongard's original vision, the economic and the artistic sphere can stimulate each other: For progressive art to flourish in Germany and to "catch up" with American artists, the German art scene of the 1960s needed the stimulation of progressive market mechanisms. The need to manufacture market transparency via rankings was thus triggered by the comparison of Germany with the United States. The reactions within the community were fierce, especially because the originator, Willi Bongard, was neither an artist nor an art critic but a journalist who challenged the authority of established gatekeepers (curators and art critics). In contrast to the early experiments in the eighteenth century, the *Kunstkompass* and other contemporary art rankings prevailed, and are regularly produced and published by media organizations to target large (nonexpert) audiences. Some rankings, such as the online platform *ArtRank*, are even more explicit in their emphasis on the market value of art.

To sum up, quantitative comparisons resembling today's rankings emerged initially in the artistic field in the eighteenth to early nineteenth century. We call them protorankings rather than rankings, because in contrast to modern rankings, they did not aim at constructing competition. They quantified the *historical-comparative judgments of critics* about famous dead artists and did not suggest competition between contemporary artists. Even these protorankings were rejected in the artistic field in the nineteenth century, based *not* on resistance against comparison as such but on critique of the economic aura surrounding *quantified* comparisons. The rejection of rankings coincided with the institutionalization of other practices of comparing artistic performances, especially art criticism that tends to see quantified performances as "foolish," "absurd," "odd," or "strange." Rankings based on aesthetic criteria seem to have never fully recovered from this rejection. "Full" rankings and other forms of quantification have emerged only since the 1970s. In contrast to

---

41 Thomas F. Gieryn, Boundary-Work and the Demarcation of Science from Non-Science: Strains and Interests in Professional Ideologies of Scientists, in: *American Sociological Review* 48 (6/1983), 781–795; Wilbers, Grenzarbeit im Kunstbetrieb.

42 Cf. Wilbers, Grenzarbeit im Kunstbetrieb.

the early experiments, they are published regularly and attract considerable attention from both expert and broader audiences. However, they do not contradict the critical view of quantified comparisons in the arts specifically, because they do not claim to measure aesthetic performance directly but rather reputation or market value. Today's art rankings thus seem less concerned with the intricacies of comparing aesthetic performance and more focused on including nonexpert audiences in the field.

Early and eager adopters: Sports

Rankings and statistics have become an inseparable and largely taken-for-granted part of competitive sports.[43] Today, it is hard to imagine one without the other. However, the alignment of sports and rankings is not as natural as it may seem. Whereas both antique and early modern sport cultures knew organized, even professionalized athletic competition, sports rankings have proliferated only since the second half of the nineteenth century, when, based on a combination of standardized rules, new modes of competition, and the regular public comparison of performances, modern sports emerged as a truly autonomous field.[44]

The first sports rankings in the above terms seem to have developed in the context of the invention of a specific mode of competition: the league system. The first leagues were organized in US-American Baseball in the 1870s,[45] soon to be copied by the British *Football League* founded in 1888.[46] Subsequently, the league system and other serial forms of competition spread around the world, arguably turning into the most important modes of modern sports competition.

What made the league system such an important innovation was that it introduced a new kind of temporality into the organization of sports: In contrast to earlier forms of sports competitions such as single contests or knockout tournaments, league systems aim at determining the "champion" over the course of a longer period of time, mostly a year-long "season." Additionally, league systems include a larger number of participants (e.g., clubs), usually between 10 and 30 that compete as members of the league while playing directly against each other only a few times a year. These characteristics of the league system create a competition across spatial distance with a dual relationship to time: It both stretches time (over a season) and compresses time (simultaneity across spatial distance, often comprising a "national" space).

---

43 Cf. Allen Guttmann, *From Ritual to Record*, New York 1978.
44 Cf. Tobias Werron, *Der Weltsport und sein Publikum*, Weilerswist 2010.
45 Cf. Warren Goldstein, *Playing for Keeps. A History of Early Baseball*, Ithaca 1989; George B. Kirsch, *Baseball and Cricket. The Creation of American Team Sports, 1838-1872*, Chicago 1989.
46 Cf. Matthew Taylor, *The Association Game. A History of British Football*, London/New York 2008.

Such forms of competition require modes of comparison that allow the audience (including the participants) to follow the "championship race" from match day to match day over the course of a season. A league table reducing past games to "points" and "overall scores" to determine a league "standing" does exactly that. It can even be argued that it is impossible to understand a league competition without tables. The institutionalization of the league system therefore depended on the publication of tables just as much as the success of rankings depended on the invention of the league system. Put more precisely, the observation of a league competition requires *up-to-date tables* that reflect all the past results of a league competition. This form, which is still in use today, seems to have been available right from the start, including the very term "up to date" (see Fig. 3).

Fig. 3: "The league—Division I" (Nottingham Evening Post, December 3, 1892).

THIS DAY'S FOOTBALL.

THE LEAGUE.—DIVISION I.

The following are the results up to date :—

	Plyd.	Won.	Lost.	Drn.	Goals For.	Agst.	Pts.
Preston North End	15	11	3	1	34	17	23
Sunderland	13	10	2	1	51	14	21
Sheffield Wednesday	15	9	5	1	36	28	19
Aston Villa	17	9	8	0	38	39	18
Bolton Wanderers	16	7	6	3	34	28	17
Stoke	16	7	6	3	32	29	17
West Bromwich Alb.	14	7	5	2	28	34	16
Notts.	14	6	5	3	32	23	15
Whmpton Wanderers	14	6	5	3	28	32	15
Blackburn Rovers	14	3	5	6	25	31	12
Everton	14	4	6	4	29	35	12
Burnley	15	4	8	3	16	25	11
Notts. Forest	17	3	9	5	23	35	11
Derby County	13	3	6	4	24	32	10
Accrington	14	2	7	6	26	40	10
Newton Heath	15	2	8	5	30	38	9

The emergence of league tables was accompanied by an avalanche of statistics on individual players and teams based on categories such as "goals scored" (football) or "batting average" (baseball). Consequently, the meaning of athletic performances changed. Instead of being connected inseparably to particular events (a "match" or "contest"), they could now be understood as a reflection of a larger number of performances over the course of a season or even a career. In American baseball, for instance, such modes of quantitative observation were firmly institutionalized as early as in the 1880s.[47] In the example below (Fig. 4), taken from a baseball yearbook from 1881, the average performance of individual players over the course of a season is used to produce a ranking that includes every single player of the league with a minimum number of games (this particular list included 77 players):

Fig. 4: "The League Averages for 1880", (Beadle's Dime Base-Ball Player, 1881, 41).

THE LEAGUE AVERAGES FOR 1880.

The following are the batting and fielding averages of League players made out by Mr. Steades, of the Boston *Herald*. The table gives the fielding averages regardless of the positions a player may have filled:

Batting rank	PLAYERS.	No. of games.	Batting ave.	Fielding ave.
1	Gore, Chicagos	77	.325	.910
2	Connors, Troys	83	.321	.823
3	Dalrymple, Chicagos	86	.318	.878
	Dignan, Bostons and Worcesters	11	.318	.736
4	Cogswell, Troys	47	.312	.962
5	Anson, Chicagos	85	.302	.960
6	Burns, Chicagos	84	.300	.847
7	Hines, Providence	85	.298	.934
8	Jones, Bostons	66	.294	.845
9	Phillips, Clevelands	85	.293	.964
	Moynahan, Buffalos	27	.293	.852
10	Hornung, Buffalos	85	.291	.899
	Purcell, Cincinnatis	77	.291	.827

As a result of these and similar modes of observation, "performance" or "achievement" in sport have been associated with a sense of consistency. Although both performance and achievement are more demanding, because they focus on excellence over a longer period of time, the fact that they allow even champions to lose occasionally makes them at the same time more forgiving. The affinities between rankings and modern sports thus suggest a preference for consistent and not spectacular performance. In other words, based on the institutionalization of league tables and similar modes of quantification, the notion of athletic achievement assumed a statistical—rather than just a narrative—meaning.[48] The institutionalization of this discourse and these modes of competition combined with the global standardization of rules led to an avalanche of sports statistics starting in the 1870s, which has stayed with us ever since. Sports rankings are not

---

47 Cf. Jules Tygiel, *Past Time. Baseball as History*, Oxford 2000.
48 Cf. Tobias Werron, 'Die Liga': Entstehung, Funktionen und Schwächen eines Konkurrenz-modells, in: Wolfram Pyta (ed.), *Geschichte des Fußballs in Deutschland und Europa seit 1954*, Stuttgart 2013, 51-83.

just a way of observing sports; they are constitutive of the very meaning of modern sports as we know them.

How does this case compare to our account of the artistic field? In contrast, the emergence of sports rankings was tightly connected to the *public interest in consistent performance over longer periods of time* that emerged in the late nineteenth century. By the same token, *competition quickly emerged as the raison d'être of modern sports*. A league system, for instance, is organized competition and does not make much sense without the perception of competition as entertaining and desirable. For these reasons, perhaps, the criticism of modern sports since the nineteenth century, which included controversies surrounding professionalization, "character development," health questions, or audience behavior,[49] never seems to have focused much on rankings and other types of quantified comparisons of performances. Similarly, tensions between the expectations of expert and nonexpert audiences do not seem play an important role in sports. Sports statistics might be complicated, but they are also inclusive, a lingua franca of sorts that you need to speak or at least understand in order to grasp what modern sports are about. Although different segments of the audience are more or less versatile in the statistical language of sports, rankings are largely accepted as a natural element of the sports field. In a sense, then, the sports field turned out to be the ideal environment for the institutionalization of rankings, while rankings, in turn, helped to institutionalize competitive sports.

Adaption and ambivalence: Science and universities

The vast majority of research assumes *America's Best Colleges* (published since 1983 in the *U.S. News & World Report*) to be the natural starting point for examinations of university rankings. A closer historical look, however, reveals an astonishing number of experiments with rankings or related forms of performance measurement in the United States dating back to the late nineteenth century.

The first university rankings originated in the context of the then popular discussions on whether "eminence"—intellectual performance—is due to nature (i.e., hereditary qualities) or nurture (i.e., a person's education).[50] Hence, the field-spe-

---

49 Cf. Melvin. L. Adelman, *A Sporting Time. New York City and the Rise of Modern Athletics, 1820-1870*, Champaign 1986; Gary K. Peatling, Rethinking the History of Criticism of Organized Sport, in: *Cultural and Social History* 2 (3/2005), 353-371.

50 Another possible place of origin of modern university rankings is the emergent field of medical schools in the United States. In the first decades of the twentieth century, the American Medical Association (AMA) produced a list of medical schools bearing some resemblance to modern-day rankings. However, rather than suggesting competition between all medical schools, these tables aimed at denigrating those medical schools that did not follow the ideal of "scientific medicine". When all "non-pure" medical schools eventually disap-

Fig. 5: James McKeen Cattell, Doctorates Conferred by American Universities for Scientific Research, in: Science 8 (190/1898), 197-201, see 198.

Universities.	Humanities.	History and Economics.	Sciences.	Total.
Chicago	12	12	12	36
Yale	19	4	11	34
Johns Hopkins	11	3	19	33
Harvard	12	3	11	26
Pennsylvania	9	7	8	24
Columbia	7	5	10	22
Cornell	7'	1	11	19
Clark			12	12
Michigan	6	1		7
New York	4		1	5
Wisconsin	2	1	2	5
Bryn Mawr	1	1	1	3
Leland Stanford, Jr.			2	2
Nebraska			2	2
Brown			1	1
California.			1	1
Columb'an			1	1
Minnesota	1			1
Total number of Ph.D. degrees conferred	91	38	105	234

cific understanding of performance was itself an object of a scientific debate. In opposition to European scholars, many of whom aligned themselves with Francis Galton's claim that eminence is hereditary (*Hereditary Genius*, 1869), the American psychologist James McKeen Cattell and others were convinced that social factors ("nurture") might be even more important.[51] In 1910, Cattell argued that "eminent

---

peared, the AMA stopped publishing the list. Since our preliminary findings suggest that, in contrast to Cattell and others, the AMA lists had little to no impact on the general ranking discourse within the scientific field, we do not discuss it here in detail (for details cf. Stefan Wilbers/Leopold Ringel/Tobias Werron, Zu den Anfängen der Hochschulrankings: Amerikanische Medical Schools zwischen 1850 und 1930, in: Frank Meier/Thorsten Peetz (eds.), *Organisation und Bewertung*, Wiesbaden (forthcoming)).

51 David S. Webster, *Academic Quality Rankings of American Colleges and Universities*, Springfield 1986.

men are lacking; and this we must attribute to changes in the social environment rather than to deterioration of the stock."[52] To emphasize the importance of such factors, he created several tabular representations of the "scientific strength" of American institutions of higher education which he used to claim that evidently the place of study has an impact on an individual's "eminence".[53] In his first ranking, published in the journal *Science*, which he also edited, Cattell used the number of PhDs conferred by universities as an indicator of their scientific strength (see Fig. 5). In so doing, he explicitly drew attention to *organizations* as facilitators of individual performance.

Cattell experimented with a variety of indicators. He is best known for sending questionnaires to esteemed American scientists whom he asked to evaluate the "eminence" of their colleagues.[54] He used the responses to attribute weighted scores to individuals that he then aggregated to organizational scores. Curiously, his rankings compared a variety of organizations such as universities, government agencies, and museums, as Figure 6 demonstrates. This ranking is remarkable in that it compares performance not only synchronically but also diachronically (movement over time) as indicated by the column on the right entitled "Gain or Loss" (a couple of years earlier, Cattell had already collected data based on questionnaires). *The scientific strength of the leading institutions* is, in other words, the first attempt to create a competitive scientific field by reflecting and visualizing changes in performance over time. There was no follow up, however, making this ranking for a longer time the last of its kind in the scientific field.

In contrast to Cattell's dedication to universities, which he saw as the main determinant of whether a significant number of individuals are able to develop "eminence," those arguing for hereditary factors tried to downplay the role of organizations because they were convinced that education cannot change what has already been determined by hereditary factors. The following quote of Francis Galton makes precisely this point:

> "One-third of those who sent replies have been educated at Oxford or Cambridge, one-third at Scotch, Irish or London universities, and the remaining third at no university at all. *I am totally unable to decide which of the three groups occupies the highest scientific position: they seem to me very much alike in this respect*" [emphasis added].[55]

Cattell and his successors saw rankings primarily as a means to the end of discovering environmental factors that have a positive impact on the performance of

---

52 James McKeen Cattell, *A statistical study of American men of science*, New York 1910, 577.
53 Björn Hammarfelt/Sarah De Rijcke/Paul Wouters, From Eminent Men to Excellent Universities: University rankings as Calculative Devices, in: *Minerva* 55 (4/2017), 391-411.
54 Hammarfelt/De Rijcke/Wouters, Eminent Men.
55 Francis Galton, *English men of science: Their nature and nurture*, London 1874, 236.

Fig. 6: Cattell: "The scientific strength of the leading institutions" (1910, see 591).

TABLE XI. THE SCIENTIFIC STRENGTH OF THE LEADING INSTITUTIONS

	Weighted Number.	Gain or Loss.
Harvard	146.0	+16.3
Chicago	94.6	+18.0
Columbia	79.3	−13.3
Hopkins	63.4	+ 4.2
Yale	61.7	+12.2
Cornell	57.6	+ 4.6
Wisconsin	49.0	+22.3
Geol. Survey	43.8	−12.2
Dept. Agric.	40.9	− 4.9
Mass. Inst.	37.7	+ 9.5
Michigan	37.1	− 3.5
California	32.4	− 5.0
Carnegie Inst	30.9	+19.4
Stanford	30.0	+ 4.8
Princeton	28.6	+ 7.5
Smithsonian Inst.	26.0	− 7.3
Illinois	25.0	+16.7
Pennsylvania	24.4	− 4.5
Bur. of Standards	18.9	+ 0.1
Clark	16.0	+ 2.0

a population of scientists. In other words, they considered rankings a method of scientific inquiry. Remarkably, Cattell even experimented with comparisons of the scientific "productivity"[56] of nations in order to demonstrate that the United States had to catch up with other nations, particularly Germany, in terms of contributions to psychology (see Fig. 7).

While rankings were clearly compatible with discovering and improving scientific performance, *competition for status or reputation* and *hierarchies* were much less in accordance with the dominant discourse of the time. The scandal revolving around efforts by the United States Federal Government to create a four-tier classification scheme is indicative of scientists' skepticism toward such forms of competition.[57] In 1911, a preliminary report on the classification of higher education institutions was leaked to the American press and spurred adverse reactions by

---

56 James McKeen Cattell, Statistics of American Psychologists, in: *American Journal of Psychology* 14 (3/4/1903), 310-328, see 327.
57 Note that according to our definition, the classification scheme is not a ranking proper because it does not attribute single ranks but clusters organizations.

Fig. 7: "Classification of Contributions to Psychology", James McKeen Cattell, Statistics of American Psychologists, in: American Journal of Psychology 14 (3/4/1903), 310-328, see 328.

TABLE IV.
Classification of Contributions to Psychology.

	Experimental.	Theoretical.	Physiological.	Total.
German,	93	99	290	**482**
French,	102	56	34	**192**
American,	111	31	11	**153**
English,	7	25	31	**63**
Italian,	9	9	39	**57**
Swiss,	8	7	6	**21**
Belgian,	8	5	4	**17**
Spanish,	0	0	8	**8**
Dutch,	2	2	0	**4**
Scandinavian,	1	1	1	**3**
Total,	**344**	**235**	**424**	**1,000**

university leaders.[58] Apparently, the creation of a four-class system, legitimized by the United States Government, created a lot of turmoil and—in consequence—resistance among those concerned. From a sociological perspective, such fierce reaction comes as no surprise, because the scientific field is deeply rooted in the idea of an egalitarian community with its members adhering, in Bourdieusian terms, to the *illusio* of a relentless and communal quest for truth—and for neither status nor reputation.[59] Even though it might very well be the case that, empirically speaking, scientists are often more interested in the accumulation of reputation and status, such motives have only partial legitimacy and thus cannot easily be made explicit. Because rankings suggest competition for individual and organizational reputation, they are likely to be met with skepticism.

There are other examples of similar reactions to hierarchies introduced by rankings. Raymond Hughes published two reports on graduate schools, the first in 1925 and the second in 1934, both based on peer surveys and measuring the reputation of departments (and not entire organizations, as in the case of Cattell). Whereas the first report ranked departments according to their scores, its successor, published nine years later, listed the findings in alphabetical order. The popular *Cartter Report*, published in 1966 and subsequently replicated in 1970, presented rankings of

---

58   Webster, *Academic Quality Rankings*.
59   Cf. Pierre Bourdieu, The Specificity of the Scientific Field and the Social Conditions of the Progress of Reason, in: *Social Science Information* 14 (6/1975), 19-47; Münch, *Academic Capitalism*.

departments in its first edition, while the authors of the replication study claimed that they "tried to de-emphasize the pecking-order relationships".[60]

The Hughes Report and even more so the Cartter Report demonstrate that an important change had taken place over the decades. In their early experiments in the first half of the twentieth century, Cattell and others had the goal of comparing the scientific performances of individuals that they then aggregated to institution-wide scores of "scientific strength." The selection of such "eminent men" was usually made on the grounds of encyclopedias, for example, *American Men of Science* or *Who's Who in America*. Starting in the 1960s, however, reputational rankings of the quality of teaching became more fashionable. Such rankings tended to focus on the performance of departments (which they did not aggregate to institution-wide scores) based on peer evaluations. The emphasis on performance in teaching—and not, or not only, on research—shows that the audience of rankings had become significantly larger: The more recent rankings addressed not only scientists but also prospective students.

An important aspect of this expansion of the comparative scope is the increase in the media infrastructure in the field. For instance, in 1966 the *Chronicle of Higher Education* was founded, an important outlet for bringing discussions on academia and related issues such as rankings to a nonexpert audience. From a macroperspective, the increasing interest in academia and teaching performance does not come as a surprise given the popularization of scientific knowledge and the sanctity attributed to science in the post-World War II era, as documented by research on the "scientization" of the modern world.[61] The producers of rankings, however, were still individual scientists (even renowned sociologists such as Peter M. Blau and Seymour M. Lipset) who published and debated their findings in reports or scientific journals such as *Science*, the *Journal of Higher Education*, and *Change: The Magazine of Higher Learning*. Taking the role of scholars, they were often skeptical of their own findings and reflected them critically. See for instance the study by Blau and Margulies, which contains the following qualification:

"Ideally, one ought to measure the quality of a professional school, of course, by its achievements—the caliber of its alumni and its contributions to the advancement of professional knowledge. But it is difficult to measure professional accomplishments. It is still more difficult to measure how much the training a school gives

---

60 Kenneth D. Roose/Charles J. Andersen, *A Rating of Graduate Programs*, Washington D.C. 1970, 2.
61 Gili S. Drori/John W. Meyer, Scientization. Making a world safe for organizing, in: Marie-Laura Djelic/Kerstin Sahlin-Andersson (eds.), *Transnational governance. Institutional dynamics of regulation*, Cambridge 2006, 32-52.

contributes to the quality of its graduates, because this depends largely on the competence and motivation of its incoming students."[62]

With the advent of rankings produced by media organizations (first in the United States and then in other Western countries), particularly *America's Best Colleges* by *U.S. News & World Report* (USN ranking hereafter), the 1980s were clearly a turning point, both with regard to rankings as such but also in terms of their standing in public discourse. Rankings have become increasingly popular outside academic discussions and, due to their *regular publication*, a newsworthy item.[63] The USN ranking in particular has been discussed intensely by journalists, students, and academics ever since.[64] The 2000s are characterized by yet another expansion from the national to the global level with prime examples being the *World University Ranking* by *Times Higher Education*, the *Academic Ranking of World Universities* by *Shanghai Jiao Tong University*, and the *QS World University Rankings* by *Quacquarelli Symonds*.[65]

The involvement of the mass media in the production and popularization of rankings was accompanied by several remarkable changes in the scientific field. First, rankers started to include nonscientific indicators such as the diversity of the student body, job placement rates, and industry income. As a result, university rankings now often combine the evaluation of the scientific field with broader societal preferences. In terms of the core responsibilities of universities, research, and teaching, national and global rankings set different priorities: Whereas rankings at the national level, broadly speaking, focus on the evaluation of teaching, their global counterparts rely more on indicators for scientific strength such as citations, publications in peer-review journals, or Nobel prizes. Second, whereas national rankings tend to evaluate departments or graduate schools, thus following the trajectory started in the 1960s, global university rankings compare universities as organizations, thus returning to Cattell's approach of interpreting universities to be the main determinant of scientific performance. Third, the academic discourse on quantitative evaluations and especially on rankings underwent a noteworthy intensification, because scientists now voice more praise but also channel, intensify, and organize their criticism.

Those who praise university rankings maintain that such devices help to map the field–that is why they should be *public knowledge* (i.e., made *transparent*), and

---

62 Peter M. Blau/Rebecca Zames Margulies, A Research Replication: The Reputations of American Professional Schools, in: *Change: The Magazine of Higher Learning* 6 (10/1974), 42-47, see 42.
63 Cf. Alex Usher, Short Global History of Rankings, in: Ellen Hazelkorn (ed.), *Global Rankings and the Geopolitics of Higher Education*, London/New York 2017, 23-53.
64 Cf. Espeland/Sauder, Rankings and Reactivity.
65 Cf. Brankovic/Ringel/Werron, How rankings produce competition.

thus have a positive impact on performances. Critical voices, on the other hand, can be divided broadly into two categories: fundamental/normative and methodological:

1. Fundamental critique follows the trajectory of emphasizing the detrimental impacts of competition such as the emergence and perpetuation of hierarchies. Furthermore, such voices criticize the one-sided preference for articles published in peer-reviewed journals to the disadvantage of monographs, edited volumes, or anthologies, symbolizing the specific kind of "academic capitalism" facilitated by rankings.[66] Those lashing out against university rankings increasingly use social media devices to voice their concern; the anonymous Twitter account *University Wankings*, which often posts critical and/or satirical comments, is a prominent example of this kind of critique.

2. The second, methodological type of criticism is much more frequent.[67] Those criticizing rankings on the grounds of methodological concerns do not argue for the abolition of such forms of comparison but consider them "not (yet) good enough." As a result, rankers are often eager to revise and reform their products[68] without losing legitimacy. In fact, we might speculate that it is precisely this type of criticism that plays a crucial role in the institutionalization of rankings in the scientific field because it keeps the conversation going while also supporting the belief that improvement is possible—at least in principle—as an ideal somewhere on the horizon.

To summarize, early university rankings between 1900 and 1980 were quite well received within the academic community as far as their main motive was to *measure performance*. Seeing universities as members of a *dynamic competitive field* was, however, considered detrimental to scientific work and thus contested when evoked. This contestation made rankings an ambivalent topic in the scientific field, earning them both praise and skepticism. With the onset of media interest in the 1980s, when rankings became *published regularly for a much wider audience*, they were met with more praise and criticism, with the latter again emphasizing the detrimental impact of competitive behavior and hierarchies between universities. In other words, rankings have been institutionalized in the university field as a topic of conversation but remain contested, particularly as a mechanism of creating competition.

---

66 Münch, *Academic Capitalism*.
67 Cf. O'Connell, Research Discourses.
68 Cf. Barron, The Berlin Principles; Lim, The Building of Weak Expertise.

Conclusion

Tracing the prehistory of modern-day rankings is crucial to understand the long-term causes of their rise and to answer the question why they are sometimes more and sometimes less successful. We have suggested defining rankings as a modern practice of comparison that, by evaluating performances quantitatively, visually, and publicly on a continual basis, contributes to the social construction of competitive fields. This definition draws particular attention to what we call the performative dimension of rankings: the fact that they are visualized (mostly via tables) and published regularly. We have further pointed to the long-term prerequisites of the rise of rankings, that is, modern notions of performance, competition, and publicity/transparency; and to the role of expert and mass publics in the process of publication and institutionalization. Based on these insights, we have analyzed and compared the historical trajectories of rankings in the arts, competitive sports, and science/universities. What are the main implications of our comparative analysis?

Rankings have become institutionalized in all three fields, though to varying degrees and in different ways. These variations seem to be contingent on (1) the "fit" between rankings and field-specific conceptualizations of competition, performance, and publicity/transparency; and (2) the ways in which rankings address and imagine different audiences. The sports field is the only one that seems to have achieved an almost perfect alignment of dominant ideals of performance, competition, and publicity/transparency with the social practice of ranking. In sports, rankings have become an inseparable part of a particular kind of thinking about athletic performance—favoring long-term consistency and arguing statistically, not just narratively—that emerged in the mid-to-late nineteenth century and is still with us today. Competition, too, is an even more essential feature of the field. Rankings thus have been closely aligned with modern sports since the emergence of the latter in the mid-to-late nineteenth century.

In contrast, the reception of rankings in science and the arts appears to be much more ambivalent. The *scientific field* is rooted in the *illusio* (Bourdieu) of a community pursuing a selfless "quest for truth" that tends to be critical of overt competition for status and reputation. On the other hand, making performances visible via quantified comparisons is a practice that in many ways resembles the logic of modern science: Collect "objective" data, process and interpret it systematically, publish it, and discuss it with colleagues (and perhaps the wider public). To a certain degree, then, rankings look like science and are sometimes discussed like the findings of scientific studies. At the same time, they are often rejected as an antiscientific device that creates competition alien to the field.

Similarly, early experiments with protorankings in the *arts*, between the early eighteenth and early nineteenth century, were rejected as alien to the ideal of *l'art pour l'art* that seems to have become the dominant *illusio* of the field in the course of the nineteenth century. This points to the effective institutionalization of the modern roles of artistic arbiters and gatekeepers such as the critic and the curator, who have successfully claimed the authority to judge artistic talent and quality. From the 1970s onward, however, rankings have become increasingly popular, and are now published regularly despite all criticism levelled against them by artists and art critics. A prominent example is the German *Kunstkompass*, published annually since 1970, that aims to make the dynamics of the art market transparent to a bigger audience. However, even these rankings mostly seem to accept the main point of the critique leveled against quantified aesthetic judgments, because they usually do not claim to directly measure aesthetic performance but rather focus on the artists' reputation or the market prices of art works.

Our analysis indicates that the institutionalization of rankings in the scientific and artistic field differs from that in competitive sports. Both fields are similar in that there is a deeply rooted skepticism regarding the competition for reputation suggested by rankings. And in both cases, the continual production of new rankings since the 1970s and 1980s is part of an attempt to address and attract audiences beyond expert circles. Rankings in the scientific and artistic field are thus not taken for granted, but have become institutionalized as *topics*, that is, as constant objects of debate and controversy attracting the attention of supporters and critics alike. In other words, a growing choir of both disapproving and affirmative voices together in both fields has effectively institutionalized rankings as an ambivalent topic of debate that is unlikely to disappear anytime soon. However, there are also important differences between the two: In the arts, even the quantification of aesthetic judgments is considered alien to the inner workings of the field; whereas in science, there is no shortage of affirmative methodological contributions that believe in the quantification of scientific performances and aim to improve rather than criticize rankings.

On a more general note, our findings suggest that the origins of rankings can be located in the mid-nineteenth to early twentieth century *Anglo-American realm*. Whereas the protorankings of the early eighteenth to early nineteenth century were part of a European arts discourse, the first rankings in the modern sense—quantified, visualized, and regularly published comparisons of performances aiming at the production of competition—emerged in the context of modern sports in the United States and the United Kingdom, followed by experiments with rankings of universities in the United States. In the case of modern sports, the standardization of rules and the invention of new modes of competition, such as the league system, were closely aligned with the production of rankings in the United States and United Kingdom. Similarly, university rankings reflect a distinctly American situation in the first half of the twentieth century when there was a high demand for mapping the complex and decentralized field of higher education organizations in terms of the quality of science and teaching. We therefore suspect that such practices of comparison embody specific assumptions about performance, competition, and publicity/transparency that originated in the United States and United Kingdom, but have since travelled around the world and become largely universalized concepts. Against this background, it comes as no surprise that with the proliferation of university rankings outside of the United States in the 1980s and the 1990s, a very specific ideal type of university (the research-intensive American university) became the universal model of excellence to be emulated by all other universities in the world.[69]

Based on our analysis, we suspect that the concentration of these developments in the Anglo-American world has to do with the highly developed newspaper industry in the United States and United Kingdom that created demand for entertainment and accelerated the constant observation and comparison of performances. Future studies could trace the origins of rankings in other fields and thereby confirm or readjust our assertion that rankings originated by and large in the Anglo-American world of the mid-nineteenth to early-twentieth century. By implication, our analysis suggests that studies should also investigate the long-term formation of notions of performance, competition, and publicity/transparency along with the process of the universalization of these notions in order to explain the proliferation of rankings—rather than just focus on recent trends such as neoliberalism or digitalization.

References

ADELMAN, Melvin L., *A Sporting Time. New York City and the Rise of Modern Athletics, 1820-1870*, Champaign 1986.

ARKENSIDE, Mark, *Balance of Poets*, 1746.

Artfacts 2018, in: the homepage of the *TOP 100 Artist Ranking*, URL: https://www.artfacts.net/tour/artist-ranking.

BARRON, Garry R., The Berlin Principles on Ranking Higher Education Institutions. Limitations, Legitimacy, and Value Conflict, in: *Higher Education* 73 (2/2017), 317-333.

BECKER, Howard S., Art Worlds, Berkeley 2008.

BLAU, Peter M./MARGULIES, Rebecca Zames, A Research Replication: The Reputations of American Professional Schools, in: *Change: The Magazine of Higher Learning* 6 (10/1974), 42-47.

BOURDIEU, Pierre, *The Rules of Art: Genesis and Structure of the Literary Field*, Cambridge 1994.

---

69 Brankovic/Ringel/Werron, How rankings produce competition.

BOURDIEU, Pierre, The Specificity of the Scientific Field and the Social Conditions of the Progress of Reason, in: *Social Science Information* 14 (6/1975), 19-47.

BRANKOVIC, Jelena/RINGEL, Leopold/WERRON, Tobias, How rankings produce competition: The case of global university rankings, in: *Zeitschrift für Soziologie* 47 (4/2018), 270-288.

BUCHHOLZ, Larissa, What is a global field? Theorizing fields beyond the nation-state, in: Julian Go/Monika Krause (eds.), *Fielding Transnationalism*, London 2016, 31-60.

BUCKERMANN, Paul, Back from Business. On Commensuration, Construction, and Communication of a Global Art World in the Ranking Kunstkompass, in: *Kapsula* 1 (3/2016), 12-18.

CATTELL, James McKeen, *A statistical study of American men of science*, New York 1910.

CATTELL, James McKeen, Statistics of American Psychologists, in: *American Journal of Psychology* 14 (3/4/1903), 310-328.

CATTELL, James McKeen, Doctorates Conferred by American Universities for Scientific Research, in: *Science* 8 (190/1898), 197-201.

DE RIJCKE, Sarah et al., Comparing Comparisons. On Rankings and Accounting in Hospitals, in: Joe Deville/Michael Guggenheim/Zuzana Hrdlickova (eds.), *Practising Comparison. Logics, Relations, Collaborations*, Manchester 2016, 251-280.

DRORI, Gili/MEYER, John W., Scientization. Making a world safe for organizing, in: Marie-Laura Djelic/Kerstin Sahlin-Andersson (eds.), *Transnational governance. Institutional dynamics of regulation*, Cambridge 2006, 32-52.

ELSBACH, Kimberly D./KRAMER, Roderick M., Members' Responses to Organizational Identity Threats. Encountering and Countering the Business Week Rankings, in: *Administrative Science Quarterly* 41 (3/1996), 442-476.

EPPLE, Angelika, Doing Comparisons – Ein praxeologischer Zugang zur Geschichte der Globalisierung/en, in: Angelika Epple/Walter Erhart (eds.), *Die Welt beobachten. Praktiken des Vergleichens*, Frankfurt a. M./New York 2015, 161-199.

ESPELAND, Wendy Nelson/SAUDER, Michael, Rankings and Reactivity. How Public Measures Recreate Social Worlds, in: *American Journal of Sociology* 113 (1/2007), 1-40.

ESPOSITO, Elena/STARK, David, What's observed in a Rating? Rankings as Orientation in the Face of Uncertainty, in: *Theory, Culture & Society* 36 (4/2019), Online First.

GALTON, Francis, *English men of science: Their nature and nurture*, London 1874.

GIERYN, Thomas F., Boundary-Work and the Demarcation of Science from Non-Science: Strains and Interests in Professional Ideologies of Scientists, in: *American Sociological Review* 48 (6/1983), 781-795.

GOLDSTEIN, Warren, *Playing for Keeps. A History of Early Baseball*, Ithaca 1989.

GRAVE, Johannes, Vergleichen als Praxis. Vorüberlegungen zu einer praxistheoretisch orientierten Untersuchung von Vergleichen, in: Angelika Epple/Walter Erhart (eds.), *Die Welt beobachten. Praktiken des Vergleichens*, Frankfurt a. M./New York 2015, 135-159.

GUTTERMAN, Ellen, The Legitimacy of Transnational NGOs. Lessons from the Experience of Transparency International in Germany and France, in: *Review of International Studies* 40 (2/2014), 391-418.

GUTTMANN, Allen, *From Ritual to Record*, New York 1978.

HAMANN, Julian, The Visible Hand of Research Performance Assessment, in: *Higher Education* 72 (6/2016), 761-779.

HAMMARFELT, Björn/DE RIJCKE, Sarah/WOUTERS, Paul, From Eminent Men to Excellent Universities: University rankings as Calculative Devices, in: *Minerva* 55 (4/2017), 391-411.

HANSEN, Hans K./FLYVERBOM, Mikkel, The politics of transparency and the calibration of knowledge in the digital age, in: *Organization* 22 (6/2015), 872-889.

HAZELKORN, Ellen, *Rankings and the Reshaping of Higher Education. The Battle for World Class Excellence*, Basingstoke 2011.

HEINTZ, Bettina, Numerische Differenz. Überlegungen zu einer Soziologie des (quantitativen) Vergleichs, in: *Zeitschrift für Soziologie* 39 (3/2010), 162-181.

JEACLE, Ingrid/CARTER, Chris, In TripAdvisor we trust: Rankings, Calculative Regimes and Abstract Systems, in: *Accounting, Organizations and Society* 36 (4/2011), 293-309.

KELLEY, Judith G./SIMMONS, Beth A., Politics by Number: Indicators as Social Pressure in International Relations, in: *American Journal of Political Science* 59(1/2015), 55-70.

KIRSCH, George B., *Baseball and Cricket. The Creation of American Team Sports, 1838-1872*, Chicago 1989.

KORNBERGER, Martin/CARTER, Chris, Manufacturing Competition: How Accounting Practices Shape Strategy Making in Cities, in: *Accounting, Auditing & Accountability Journal* 23 (3/2010), 325-349.

LIM, Miguel A., The Building of Weak Expertise. The Work of Global University Rankers, in: *Higher Education* 75 (3/2018), 415-430.

MARGINSON, Simon, University Rankings and Social Science, in: *European Journal of Education* 49 (1/2014), 45-59.

MARTENS, Kerstin/NIEMANN, Dennis, When Do Numbers Count? The Differential Impact of the PISA Rating and Ranking on Education Policy in Germany and the US, in: *German Politics* 22 (3/2013), 314-332.

MEHRPOUYA, Afshin/SAMIOLO, Rita, Performance Measurement in Global Governance: Ranking and the Politics of Variability, in: *Accounting, organizations and society* 55 (2016), 12-31.

MENNICKEN, Andrea, From Inspection to Auditing: Audit and Markets as Linked Ecologies, in: *Accounting, Organizations and Society* 35 (3/2010), 334-359.

MÜLLER, Simone M./TWOREK, Heidi J. S., 'The Telegraph and the Bank': On the Interdependence of Global Communications and Capitalism, 1866-1914, in: *Journal of Global History* 10 (2/2015), 283.

MÜNCH, Richard, *Academic Capitalism. Universities in the Global Struggle for Excellence*, London 2014.

O'CONNELL, Catherine, Research Discourses Surrounding Global University Rankings: Exploring the Relationship with Policy and Practice Recommendations, in: *Higher Education* 65 (6/2013), 709-723.

PEATLING, Gary K., Rethinking the History of Criticism of Organized Sport, in: *Cultural and Social History* 2 (3/2005), 353-371.

POLLOCK, Neil et al., Conforming or Transforming? How Organizations Respond to Multiple Rankings, in: *Accounting, Organizations and Society* 64 (2018), 55-68.

POLLOCK, Neil/D'ADDERIO, Luciana, Give me a Two-by-two Matrix and I will Create the Market: Rankings, Graphic visualisations and Sociomateriality, in: *Accounting, Organizations and Society* 37 (8/2012), 565-586.

RINGEL, Leopold, *Transparenz als Ideal und Organisationsproblem. Eine Studie am Beispiel der Piratenpartei Deutschland*, Wiesbaden 2017.

ROOSE, Kenneth D./ANDERSEN, Charles J., *A Rating of Graduate Programs*, Washington D.C. 1970.

SCHUBART, Christian Friedrich Daniel, *Kritische Skala der vorzüglichsten deutschen Dichter*, 1792.

SCHULTZ, Majken/MOURITSEN, Jan/GABRIELSEN, Gorm, Sticky Reputation: Analyzing a Ranking System, in: *Corporate Reputation Review* 4 (1/2001), 24-41.

SOBRY, Jean-Francois, *Poétique des arts ou cours de peinture et de littérature comparées*, Paris 1810.

SPOERHASE, Carlos, Rankings: A Pre-History, in: *New Left Review* 114 (2018), 99-112.

SPOERHASE, Carlos, Das Maß der Potsdamer Garde. Die ästhetische Vorgeschichte des Rankings in der Europäischen Literatur- und Kunstkritik des 18. Jahrhunderts, in: *Jahrbuch der Deutschen Schillergesellschaft* 58 (2014), 90-126.

STEINMETZ, Willibald, Vergleich. Eine begriffsgeschichtliche Skizze, in: Angelika Epple/Walter Erhart (eds.), *Die Welt beobachten. Praktiken des Vergleichens*, Frankfurt a. M./New York 2015, 85-134.

TAYLOR, Matthew, *The Association Game. A History of British Football*, London/New York 2008.

THOMPSON, John B., *The Media and Modernity. A Social Theory of the Media*, Cambridge 1995.

TUCHMAN, G., Wannabe U: *Inside the Corporate University*, Chicago 2009.

TYGIEL, Jules, *Past Time. Baseball as History*, Oxford 2000.

USHER, Alex, Short Global History of Rankings, in: Ellen Hazelkorn (ed.), *Global Rankings and the Geopolitics of Higher Education*, London/New York 2017, 23-53.

VELTHUIS, Olav, ArtRank and the Flippers: Apocalypse now?, in: *Texte zur Kunst* 24 (96/2014), 34-49.

VERHEYEN, Nina, *Die Erfindung der Leistung*, München/Berlin 2018.

WEBSTER, David S., *Academic Quality Rankings of American Colleges and Universities*, Springfield 1986.

WEDLIN, Linda, *Ranking Business Schools. Forming Fields, Identities and Boundaries. International Management Education*, Northampton 2006.

WENZLHUEMER, Roland. Globalization, communication and the concept of space in global history, in: Roland Wenzlhuemer (ed.), *Global communication: Telecommunication and global flows of information in the late 19th and early 20th century* (Special Issue of Historical Social Research, 35), 2010, 19-47.

WERRON, Tobias, Why do we believe in competition? A historical-sociological view of competition as an institutionalized modern imaginary, in: *Scandinavian Journal of Social Theory* 16 (2015), 186-210.

WERRON, Tobias, ‚Die Liga': Entstehung, Funktionen und Schwächen eines Konkurrenz-modells, in: Wolfram Pyta (ed.), *Geschichte des Fußballs in Deutschland und Europa seit 1954*, Stuttgart 2013, 51-83.

WERRON, Tobias, *Der Weltsport und sein Publikum*, Weilerswist 2010.

WERRON, Tobias/RINGEL, Leopold, Rankings in a comparative perspective. Conceptual remarks, in: Stephan Lessenich (ed.), *Geschlossene Gesellschaften* (Verhandlungen des 38. Kongresses der Deutschen Gesellschaft für Soziologie), Essen 2017.

WILBERS, Stefan, Grenzarbeit im Kunstbetrieb. Zur Institutionalisierung des Rankings Kunstkompass, in: Leopold Ringel/Tobias Werron (eds.), *Rankings – Soziologische Fallstudien*, Wiesbaden 2019, 57-87.

WILBERS, Stefan/RINGEL, Leopold/WERRON, Tobias, Zu den Anfängen der Hochschulrankings: Amerikanische Medical Schools zwischen 1850 und 1930, in: Frank Meier/Thorsten Peetz (eds.), *Organisation und Bewertung*, Wiesbaden (forthcoming).

Histories

The Weight of Comparing in Medieval England

David Gary Shaw

Abstract[1]

How important and common were the practices of comparing in medieval England (1150-1500)? Focusing on activities that tended to have a pragmatic rather than purely logical intention, this chapter first considers medieval comparing on technical matters such as weighing and measuring for the market and for agricultural efficiency. Then, however, we consider as well the more controversial comparing of humans by examining its place in taxing and ranking people; in assessing religious diversity; and even discerning the moralizing uses of comparing in literature and art. As it turns out, comparing could be perilous when humans were the subjects.

Introduction

It is possible that comparison might be everywhere in history, but we might also suppose that comparing might matter less in some moments and places than others. Especially given the sense that there is something distinctive and powerful about comparison in contemporary life, it is important to try to get a sense for the range, variety, and importance of modes of comparison in other times and places. In this chapter, I inquire into the place and weight of comparative thinking in England in the later medieval period.

It is not an easy task, because the definition of the comparative and of comparative practices is hardly settled. There is probably some amount of comparative activity in all European societies and moments, but we can expect that the composition of the comparative practices will vary and maybe vary significantly; and that will raise problems for making any longer-term narratives. Comparing comparisons might be the hardest task of all. In a specific context, the particular character

---

1 Research on this article has been supported by a Mercator fellowship which was granted by the Collaborative Research Center SFB 1288 "Practices of Comparing. Changing and Ordering the World", Bielefeld University, Germany, funded by the German Research Foundation (DFG). Research was also funded by The Colonel Return Jonathan Meigs First (1740-1823) Fund, created with the funds left by Dorothy Mix Meigs and Fielding Pope Meigs, Jr.

of the comparative will also be affected by the degree to which comparing is self-conscious. The benefit of thinking in terms of comparative practices is, in part, that they can be found even where they operated quietly with less overt self-reflection. It is even possible to imagine comparison unmediated by language. The challenge, of course, is that it can be too easy to assume comparative practices *were* acting rather than being able to demonstrate it.

On this point, however, it still seems wise to have an open-minded approach and only a tentative commitment to the particular quality of comparison that we might find in the Middle Ages. After all, things that are on their way to being the most robust sort of comparison might have emerged from earlier, related forms in the medieval period. In the area of imaginative literature, we are sure to find a vast array of comparative techniques: the world of metaphor and allegory. As elusive as the comparative elements might sometimes be, the tertium of the comparison—the thing by which two others things are compared—is often clear enough in literary and imaginative texts.[2] Much in mathematical reasoning also has a comparative structure to it in terms of the logics of proportion. And geometry was a crucial part of medieval mathematical thinking.

On the other hand, the medieval propensity for lists and hierarchies is more challenging, and a list of ranked items might not be framed or understood with comparative intent at all. Red, blue, and yellow are the primary colors, but saying so and itemizing them is not necessarily to compare them. The use of categories and concepts and subsumption was a vast and powerful mode of medieval thought. Did it hide the comparative thinking they were using or block them from comparing? Causing comparison in a later and unknown viewer or reader is not to compare at the moment of creation. Then, more simply, there is juxtaposition, whether on purpose or by accident, that might be too easily seen as evidence of comparison. What this all suggests is that the form of evidence of comparison will often come without certainty about comparative intent and this will properly be problematic.

By contrast, in this chapter, I look at literatures and practices that had at least a more clearly social or pragmatic intention. To understand comparison or its close relations probably benefits from trying to understand a wide variety of these possible practices in proximity to each other. In a more comprehensive work on medieval or any other regime of comparison, one would very much want to know how much, how often, and how easily comparative forms jumped from their home domain to work elsewhere—from poetry or mathematics to social commentary or legislative agendas. While I do not have space to touch on all types of nonimaginative uses

---

2   Cf. Clive Staples Lewis, *The Allegory of Love. A Study in Medieval Tradition*, Oxford 1936; Ann R. Meyer, *Medieval Allegory and the Building of the New Jerusalem*, Rochester 2003; and Maureen Quilligan, *The Languages of Allegory. Defining a Genre*, Ithaca 1979; Conrad Rudolph, *The Mystic Ark: Hugh of Saint Victor, Art, and Thought in the Twelfth Century*, Cambridge 2014.

of comparison in England, even if I was assiduous enough to have tracked them all down, I would rather like to focus on some that bent toward the social, ethical, and political. So, working within the kingdom of England after the Norman Conquest, I want to look for comparative thinking in such diverse activities as: weighing and measuring, baking, taxing and ranking, philosophizing, plowing, moralizing, burying, and educating.

In other words, I would like to find the comparative wherever it lies and not assume that the most explicit, political, or challenging sorts of comparison are necessarily the most important. Looking even at small things, one might end up showing comparison's more general role in medieval England, even if that turns out to be modest. Comparative practices in one period might be significant and shifting with relation to each other, without being more significant in one period than another; they might simply be different. When I think in terms of the weight of comparison, I am thinking of the need to take all the comparisons we can find and try to get a sense for how much they might matter. Like other tricks of language or mind, comparative practices might indeed be more popular in some social quarters or administrative zones than in others. Of course, all of this should contribute to the question of what differences exist between early modern or modern ways of thought and practice and medieval ones.

If one thinks of comparative practices as networks, as mixtures of things and ideas and words as well as people in action, rather than as really inhering in larger structures such as states or peoples, or countries such as England, or periods such as the Middle Ages, one can be prepared for the way in which the comparative might stabilize in one part of the society and then jump, translated, into another by some other circumstance. Maybe the medieval period provides models and matter for later comparing, for jumping. The weight of comparison then is a notion for assessing all these different things in a given world. For later medieval England, comparison was not that heavy, but was in some domains dynamic and pressing forward.

Measuring and weighing

It is with the practice of weighing and measuring itself that I start, because one of the most important and long-term comparative practices involves the creation of measures and literal standards by which to assess, indeed to compare things, all sorts of stuff, the world's goods. From a certain perspective, organizing comparative practices was a centerpiece of medieval kingdom-making and this mainly meant establishing regimes of comparing weights and measures and money via standards. Practices such as the comparative pricing of bread, the relation of weight to money, and the ideas of length and their regimes continued in some form from the twelfth and thirteenth centuries until the nineteenth and twentieth.[3] While the extent of universalization of standards in the country was often to be doubted in practice, the universal recourse to measuring to a standard, often regional or local, was achieved.

"Standard of comparison" needs to be recognized as a fairly robust and precise idea. I mean the official stipulation of measures; but, unlike the more abstract forms used today, I focus here on the tangible objects used to control other objects. Measuring to a standard is not just a sort of comparative metaphor but more like a whole reiterative network of comparison.[4] Something is stipulated as the thing against which other things are compared directly. Its reusability and stability means that separate acts of measuring work transitively with all the comparata. In other words, a standard allows things to have a common denominator. Where successful, however, the creation of standards of comparison promises an ongoing, reproducible, comparative process.

The germ of English weights and measures seems to derive from the pre-Norman, Anglo-Saxon kingdoms. In the tenth century already, there was an edict of King Edgar (959–75) on "mynetum and gemetum—money and measures" that orders that there be only one sort of money and one sort of measure of weight in the kingdom.[5] What matters is that ideas of length and weight became a standard, a pattern, and these were typically fashioned into a real object kept in the treasury from which precise pragmatic copies were made. What is more, specific, purpose-built standards were constructed as needed: So, for instance, in 1197, Richard II issued an assize at the request of his bishops and barons to control the size of woolen cloths. It was regulated to be two ells width, the royal ordinance stressing that "the ell shall be the same in the whole realm and of the same length and the ells shall be of iron."[6]

---

3   On the use of standard weights and measures in England, see Ronald E. Zupko, *British Weights and Measures. A History from Antiquity to the Seventeenth Century*, Madison 1977; for practices, see James Davis, *Medieval Market Morality: Life, Law and Ethics in the English Marketplace*, Cambridge 2012, see 189–95, 331–34; see also Ronald E. Zupko, Medieval English Weights and Measures: Variation and Standardization, in: *Studies in Medieval Culture* 4 (1974), 238–243, see 238.

4   The standard of comparison operates as one of two comparata, the other being the object assessed. The tertium is actually the length or weight or capacity. It seems now that the term and concept might also have a late medieval origin, see Lei Zhu, On the Origin of the Term Tertium Comparationis, in: *Language and History* 60 (2017), 35–52.

5   Agnes J. Robertson (ed.), *Laws of Kings of England from Edmund to Henry I*, Cambridge 1926, 28–9. For a sense of the diversity that grew up or existed, see, for instance, Sir John Miller, *Speeches in the House of Commons upon the Equalization of the Weights and Measures of Great Britain*, London 1790.

6   See William Stubbs (ed.), Roger de Hoveden, *Chronica Magistri Rogeri De Houedene* (Rerum britannicarum medii aevi scriptores or chronicles and memorials of Great Britain and Ireland

A document that dates from some time in the thirteenth century, the *Tractatus de Ponderibus et Mensuris*, was used within government and became one of a group of official templates for a series of standard measurements. Here, the focus on the penny should not be lost, because the currency anchored much in the system and was most vigorously defended by law.[7] Weights were effectively controlled by the pennyweight and these could then denominate all other objects. The start is most straightforward: "Per Ordinance of the whole realm of England the measure of the King is composed namely of a penny, which is called a sterling, round & without clipping, weighs thirty-two grains of wheat in the middle of the Ear. And an ounce weight twenty pence. And twelve ounces make a pound of London. And twelve & a half pounds make a stone of London. And eight pounds of wheat make a gallon. A pound contains twenty shillings." [8]

Here one can see the intricate order of things. Weight starts with wheat—as did length—the precious food, and the penny of silver is linked to wheat. There is a sort of mediated comparison within this, but it is certainly the basis of a comparative order and a family of comparative practices. The regulation of the sale of bread, ale, and wine, of cloth and wool, and many other common commodities could be regulated, calibrated, and tested by comparable schemes.

Assize of bread comparisons

The policy on bread was the most comprehensive, and it was meant to apply to all retail baking in the kingdom. Certainly, with many local variations, the Assize of Ale and Bread was used across the kingdom throughout the Middle Ages. It also encouraged the incorporation of a schedule of breads that was perhaps comparative

---

    during the Middle Ages, 51/4), London 1868, 33–34, for a reiteration of the general need for standards. The *Compositio Ulnarum et Perticarum*, which apparently dates sometime prior to Edward II and possibly as early as Henry III, provides a simple statement that an inch is three grains of wheat and then explains feet, yards, or ells and perches as well as multiplying and squaring these to describe the acre. My point, in part, is that there is something in arithmetic and proportion that is itself a comparative structure or invitation. See Danby Pickering (ed.) *Statutes at Large from Magna Charta to the end of the Eleventh Parliament of Great Britain, anno 1761*, volume 1, Cambridge 1762, 400. Davis, *Medieval Market Morality*, 192, 421. It is, as ever, difficult to decide if accusations of evasion of the standard prove the norm or prove the law's failure to standardize.

7   On the money, see Martin Allen, *Mints and Money in Medieval England*, Cambridge 2012, see 41–72 on the twelfth and thirteenth century centralization of supply and management, and 134–70 on the physical standards.

8   John Raithby (ed.), *Statutes of the Realm. Printed by command of his majesty King George the Third, in pursuance of an address of the House of Commons of Great Britain. From original records and manuscripts*, 1, London 1810, 204.

in and of itself, price being the common measure, keyed to the varying sizes of the different qualities of loaf. These regulations exist in various versions.[9] An ordinance of the reign of Henry III made clear that a baker whose bread weights varied too much—low or high, as it turns out—would be fined and might even be punished in the pillory.[10]

To take the example of Southampton, the local expectation around 1300 was that nine kinds of bread might be offered for sale. If the cost of grain were 2s. for a quarter, then the relative weights were as shown in parentheses, meaning the size of loaf is proportional to the money value indicated. These details are keyed to a farthing (quarter penny) loaf:

1. Wastel (£3 10 6)
2. Cocket, greater (£3 12 6)
3. Cocket, lesser (£3 15 6)
4. Simmel (£3 8 6)
5. French (£3 8 6)
6. Ranger (£5 5 9)
7. Whole wheat (£5 13 0)
8. Treet (£6 0 0) est.
9. Common Wheat (£7 11 0)

It would seem that this became a routine and repeated structure, reset occasionally as prices or seasons changed. It constituted a kind of comparison among the sorts of bread.

Whether or not it was involved in the calculations by bakers, weavers, and consumers, comparison was built into the work of the officers who inspected the markets by whom those standard weights and measures would be deployed. So inspection by officers using official national and local criteria actively compared objects to impose regimes of accountability and economy and power. The normal work of the king's market clerk or the local authorities who took this power was to check upon the assize of bread, wine, and ale; bushels, gallons, and els; and other weights.[11] There are very rich records of local courts in medieval England, and given any manorial or urban monthly court record, one sees evidence of these practices of

---

9   See, for instance, *Statutes of the Realm*, 199–200. Generally, see Alan S. C. Ross, The Assize of Bread, in: *Economic History Review*, N.S. 9 (1956), 332–342; but especially James Davis, Baking for the Common Good: A Reassessment of the Assize of Bread in Medieval England, in: *The Economic History Review* 57 (2004), 465-502.

10 Cf. Pickering, *Statutes at Large*, I, 28–29, 1266 also covers pillory construction.

11 See for instance, Francis Hill, *Medieval Lincoln*, Cambridge 1948, 125, 242. Most sizeable boroughs and many others, acquired the franchise for themselves and were expected to change the personnel not the standards.

comparison at work.¹² The key is that set standards of comparison were on hand to enable later and complex comparative practices. They might be modeled for different sorts of occasions or materials. One can then conclude that a sort of administrative comparison existed in medieval England, anchored in governmental goals and enabled by the development of standards of money, weight, and measures.

Rating and ranking people: consumption and taxation

Comparison was certainly not a large element within the workings of English law and legislation in the medieval period. While the Common Law's famous reliance on precedential reasoning might be a special form of comparing, its certain and characteristic development awaited the later sixteenth and seventeenth centuries.[13] An influential fourteenth-century judge favorably quoted in court an earlier judge saying "Non exemplis sed rationibus adiudicandem est." "Our judgements are founded not on examples {precedents} but on reason."[14] However, an interesting possible exception occurred in some legislation of the post-plague period. These laws touch on consumption and taxation, and each works rather radically with distinctions in the body politic. They have a certain structural similarity to the assize of bread in the way that a variety of types is graded and related in terms of an economic commonality.

Sumptuary legislation and concern for spending excessively were quite common in the later Middle Ages across Europe. Especially after the population shock of the Black Death, significant anxiety and economic pressure built up; and so, in 1363, members of the House of Commons petitioned for an intervention to restrain excessive consumption. Here is the gist of the petition:

> "the commons declare: that whereas the prices of various victuals within the realm are greatly increased because various people of various conditions wear various apparel not appropriate to their estate; that is to say, grooms wear the apparel of craftsman, and craftsmen wear the apparel of gentlemen, and gentlemen wear

---

12   For instance, Canterbury Cathedral Archives (CCA), CC J/Q/264; and see James Davis, Market Regulation in Fifteenth-Century England, in: Ben Dodds/Christian D. Liddy (eds.), *Commercial Activity, Markets and Entrepreneurs in the Middle Ages: Essays in Honour of Richard Britnell*, Woodbridge 2011, 81–106; and Judith Bennett, *Ale, Beer, and Brewsters in England: Women's Work in a Changing World*, 1300–1600, Oxford 1996, 98–121 and 158–187.
13   Cf. John Baker, Case Law in Medieval England, in: John H. Baker, *Collected Papers on English Legal History*, Cambridge 2014, 547–578; and John Baker, Case Law in England and Continental Europe, in: John H. Baker, *Collected Papers on English Legal History*, Cambridge 2014, 612–620; T. Ellis Lewis, The History of Judicial Precedent, in: *Law Quarterly Review* 46 (1930), 207–224, and 48 (1932), 230–247.
14   Lewis, Judicial Precedent, vol. 46, 220.

the apparel of esquires, and esquires wear the apparel of knights, the one and the other wear fur which only properly belongs to lords and knights, poor and other women wear the dress of ladies, and poor clerks wear clothes like those of the king and other lords. Thus the aforesaid merchandises are at a much greater price than they should be, and the treasure of the land is destroyed, to the great damage of the lords and the commonalty. Wherefore they pray remedy [...]."[15]

The bill that was accepted as a result was very detailed. On the one hand, the late medieval society of ranks and degrees remains fundamental. On their own, one might not call a listing of the different ranks a comparison, because it might be thought to be more like descriptive social anatomy. In this case, things go further: These are hierarchically presented, and certain sorts of consumption are reserved only to people of sufficient status. So, to take one clause from the second lowest rank:

"that craftsmen and people called yeomen shall not take or wear cloth for their clothing or shoes of a higher price than 40s. for the whole cloth, by way of purchase or otherwise; nor precious stones, cloth of silk or silver, or a belt, knife, brooch, ring, garter, or clasps, ribbons, chains, bracelets, seals or other things of gold or silver, or any manner of apparel embroidered, enamelled or of silk, in any way. And that their wives, daughters and children shall be of the same condition in their clothing and apparel; and that they shall not wear any veil of silk, but only of yarn made within the realm, and or any manner of fur [...] except only that of lamb, rabbit, cat and fox."[16]

Thus, it proceeds in a similar vein for seven different ranks or statuses.

In some sense, this seems an act of comparing, for the additions of the permitted clothing to relate explicitly to different sorts of people, but it most certainly inscribes the degrees by which the society at the moment saw itself. Just such a comparing move becomes more explicit, however, when it comes to the more elite ranks. Here, something rather novel appears. After detailing the limitations on "esquires and gentlemen of all sorts" who did not have land and rents of £100 a year, the text moves on to merchants, citizens, and burgesses, artisans and craftsmen who clearly have goods and chattels to the value of £500, and says that they "*may*

---

15   Edward III, October 1363, Item 25, in: Chris Given-Wilson et al. (eds.), *Parliament Rolls of Medieval England*, Woodbridge 2005, British History Online, URL: http://www.british-history.ac.uk/no-series/parliament-rolls-medieval/october-1363 [last accessed June 10, 2018]. There are many shrewd studies of sumptuary legislation: classic in England is Frances E. Baldwin, *Sumptuary Legislation and Personal Regulation in England*, Baltimore 1926; Catherine Killerby, *Sumptuary Law in Italy. 1200–1500*, Oxford 2002; Martha C. Howell, *Commerce Before Capitalism in Europe. 1300–1600*, Cambridge 2010, 208–260.

16   Edward III, October 1363, Item 25.

take and wear in the same manner as the esquires and gentlemen who have land and rent to the value of £100 a year" (my emphasis.)

The specific common denominator can be discerned, and it is one across which there can be changes. In this case, a system of graduated wealth is linked to social degrees, and variance on that level allows for differential assessment. The invocation of the logic of equivalence—that an urban character of a certain sort should be treated as a country character—renders the whole thing particularly interesting and clearly comparative.

One means by which a comparative practice might develop further and become entrenched as a mode is by further appropriation in neighboring areas. There was some sign of this being possible in the socially volatile period after the Black Death. Following this comparative approach to sumptuary legislation, one comes to the somewhat notorious poll taxes of the late 1370s and 1380s. The one that is most intriguing for the present purposes is the tax of 1379, a levy that one of the shrewdest contemporary chroniclers called *unprecedented*; and that it might well be because of its new relational and comparative form.[17] As the law put it, "a sum of silver shall be levied from various persons of the kingdom, in the manner which follows, both within royal franchises as well as outside them; namely"; and then it proceeds to list the kingdom's people by rank-specific names in a few instances, but mainly by type; and from each, it lists an amount of tax due.[18] So, the Duke of Lancaster and the Duke of Brittany each had to pay 10 marks. After this, a graduated scale follows for men with equivalences for widows. So, it says, "also every widowed countess of England, *as much as earls*—£4." Then, however, as with the sumptuary legislation one gets, somewhat unnecessarily now, urban equivalents: "Also, the mayor of London is to pay as much as an earl—£4." And so on. Money valuations provide the basis of comparison along with the named description of status.

It seems indeed that one can posit a moment of more comprehensive comparative thinking at work within the government, connecting to some extent with a mood or understanding among the members of parliament, and probably especially the members of the House of Commons. Comparison, it should be stressed, is not a method of demonstration here, but a sort of organizing principle, incorporated into a project with a different goal—namely, raising money. However, the logic involved did not become popular even within government, and there are few comparable instances in the subsequent period. This was due in part to the poll tax being a political disaster. The 1379 tax did not raise as much money as expected,

---

17 Wendy R. Childs/John Taylor (eds.), *Anonimalle Chronicle 1333–1381* (York: Yorkshire Archaeological Society Record Series 147), 127.
18 Richard II, April 1379, Paragraphs 13-16, in: Chris Given-Wilson et al. (eds.), *Parliament Rolls of Medieval England*, Woodbridge 2005, *British History Online*, URL: http://www.british-history.ac.uk/no-series/parliament-rolls-medieval/april-1379. Membrane 6 [last accessed June 10, 2018].

was evaded, and the 1381 levy led to the Peasants' Rebellion in which the radical leader John Ball said, apropos of status, "When Adam delved [dug] and Eve span [wool], who was then the gentleman?"[19] Comparison lost a bit of fashion as a political technique. Later sumptuary legislation was also much more simply worded, and the explicit logic of equivalence was removed and a more traditional sense of status preserved.[20]

Roger Bacon's comparative religion

Someone who would probably have experienced the fruits and consequences of the assize of bread and ale was Roger Bacon. It is perhaps one of the clearest signs of the supposed limited practices of comparison that one can sometimes identify a first use of some recognizable or contemporary practice within medieval life. From this point of view, the quite extraordinary English Franciscan thinker Bacon is the first to attempt a comparative account of religion. I do not claim he was inspired by bread schedules or vice versa. He undertook his comparative analysis toward the end of perhaps his greatest general work, the *Opus Majus*, written around 1267, at the behest of Pope Clement IV.[21] Bacon is perhaps most often seriously known as an avatar of modern science or as a practitioner of medieval magic and astrology; he was known to some medieval people as the *Doctor Mirabilis*, the wonderful doctor. The *Opus Majus* is an extraordinary and engaging work, wide-ranging, and sometimes surprising. In his section on moral philosophy, Bacon does not opt merely to explain the superiority of Christianity in however much detail; he chooses first to work from the facts as it were of the known world. This leads him to want to understand Christianity's superiority against the backdrop of other religions. Perhaps as interesting are the six religions he knows. I quote him: "I shall now state the principal nations in which the various sects are found that are now existing

---

19   Thomas Walsingham, *The St Albans Chronicle: The Chronica Maiora of Thomas Walsingham, Volume I: 1376-1394*, ed. by John Taylor/Wendy Childs/Leslie Watkiss, Oxford 2003, 547.

20   For later English sumptuary legislation, which is frequent till 1610, see, Baldwin, *Sumptuary Legislation*, 144-247; and, for instance, John Raithby (ed.), *Statutes of the Realm. Printed by command of his majesty King George the Third, in pursuance of an address of the House of Commons of Great Britain. From original records and manuscripts*, 2, 399 (1463); Statutes of the Realm 2, 468 (1483) and John Raithby (ed.), *Statutes of the Realm, Printed by command of his majesty King George the Third, in pursuance of an address of the House of Commons of Great Britain. From original records and manuscripts*, 2, 8-9 (1510); and *Statutes of the Realm*, 3, ch. 6, 179-82 (1515); *Statutes of the Realm*, 3, 430 (1533). There were many notable changes.

21   The best place to start in understanding Bacon overall is Amanda Power, *Roger Bacon and the Defence of Christendom*, Cambridge 2012, see 84-125 on the *Opus Majus*.

throughout the world, namely, Saracens, Tartars, Pagans, Idolaters [Buddhists], Jews, Christians."[22]

Bacon moves through the several religions in various ways before going on to use philosophy to show why Christianity is in fact the best one and "the only one that should be spread throughout the world."[23] He is certainly engaged in quite clear comparison as a mode and practice of analysis. In other words, he is not merely listing and juxtaposing—important intellectual and artistic activities that can encourage comparison—he is comparing.

Here's the comparative key in this case: Invoking Al-Farabi and Aristotle, Bacon says that religions have aims and these provide a basis for considering them together. The aims provide the tertium comparationis, so to speak, the things by which they might all be assessed and considered. While he mentions several, he goes on to stress that all religions seek "the felicity of the other life, which is sought and striven after in different ways."[24] Again to be explicit: there is a listing of sects and we have **x**, their performance, which will be determined along the access of their "pursuit of happiness," as one might rightly call it.

Bacon argues that some religions seek future happiness in the delights of the body, some the delights of the soul, and others a combination of both. Tartars are focused on a "lust for domination" and use their model of religion, a belief in one dominant god, to guide their passion for worldwide domination. The "real Pagans," whom he takes the Prussians to exemplify, focus on the material delights of this life and "they believe the life to come similar in every way to this. Hence at death they have themselves burned publicly, together with their precious stones, gold, silver, equipment, family, friends, and all their wealth and goods, hoping to enjoy all these things after death." As for the Idolaters, they have priests who deny themselves worldly pleasures personally but their people are fully focused on material life and its benefits and all are expected to share in the good afterlife regardless of their activities in this life. [25]

Bacon then sees a second grouping, and here he first discusses the Jews who "hoped for blessings both temporal and eternal in a different way, however, since with spiritual discernment by virtue of their law they aspired after blessings not only of the body, but also of the soul."[26] Even their pursuit of temporal goods is shaped by the law and God's guidance thereby.

---

22   Translations are from *Opus Majus*, trans. Robert Belle Burke, Pennsylvania 1928, 789. The translation is based on the edition of J. H. Bridges (ed.), Roger Bacon, *Opus maius*, (3 vols. Oxford 1897–1900).
23   *Opus Majus*, 788.
24   *Opus Majus*, 788.
25   *Opus Majus*, 789
26   *Opus Majus*, 789.

Finally, Christianity is discussed, and here there is the pursuit of "spiritual blessings by spiritual means." Christians are allowed material benefits from their weakness and to enable them to work on the spiritual benefits that are alone salvific. But in the afterlife, the material things are no longer relevant, for as Bacon seems fond of stressing, "For the animal body will become spiritual, and the whole [person] will be glorified, and will be with God and the angels."[27] So, the comparison moves on the axis of the pursuit of happiness, further modulated by the split between the spiritual and the temporal or material. Each religion is discussed in this respect.

Bacon proceeds to a very pithy comparative divinity. The question of gods provides the comparative axis in this section, and the six sects provide the details conforming to this comparative category. Among the pagans, each "fashions a god to his own liking and worships whatever he pleases and sacrifices at will"; the Idolaters "maintain that there are many gods but none of them is omnipotent"; the Tartars "adore and worship one God as omnipotent, but they nevertheless venerate fire" and so on, although Muslims are skipped in this section.[28]

Bacon's thought is clearly more analytically comparative than the administrative materials discussed so far in this chapter, and three elements of context help to explain his comparative turn. First, there is his knowledge of new information about some of these peoples and religions, most of which he had from reading first-hand accounts fresh from emissaries and missionaries in the thirteenth century and those who were involved in the Crusades against the Prussians and in the Levant. He knew some of the sources personally.[29]

Second and related, Bacon had earlier in his treatise and at surprising length, extolled the virtues of learning foreign languages. The question of getting texts accurate so that profitable interpretation and translation could be achieved was large in his mind as a related issue. Connected to this was the growing interest in editorial collation: Language moved Bacon to think about the related business of editing manuscripts, the recognition that one is right, one wrong; one does not have a certain section of Aristotle's ethics, the other does—what to do and how to do it best? There is a clear if implicit practice of comparison involved in such work, and it might have set him up to consider comparing further.[30]

Last, Bacon lived in the century when the pursuit of heresy had become advanced. It was normal in manuals discussing such heretics to spend some time

---

27 *Opus Majus*, 790.
28 *Opus Majus*, 790.
29 See Power, *Bacon and the Defence of Christendom*, 213-15. A fellow Franciscan William of Rubruck travelled through the Mongol empire and wrote on this before discussing it with Roger.
30 *Opus Majus*, 811: "We must assume as a fundamental principle in this consideration that the histories of all nations are to be accepted on an equal footing when we take up the form in which the disputation is to proceed."

anatomizing them and detailing their errors. There is a sort of formal similarity to Bacon's approach, although such books were much less likely to show true comparison. They seem more to be giving descriptions of species within a genus, or merely listing things like a mere juxtaposition. It is not at all easy to explain why Bacon moved to compare; he was in many ways a bold and independent thinker. But formally, the combination of strongly knowing which of the compared was right and having a complex group of others formed through a strong pre-existent category such as faiths might open doors for a robust and to some extent safe mode of comparative reflection.

Agricultural improvement: Walter of Henley

Let me now turn to a second example, the product of a nearly exact English contemporary of Roger, a man called Walter of Henley, probably a minor estate-holding landlord, in other words a knight, who wrote a book *On Husbandry*, completed by the mid-1280s. Walter shows how money and even processes such as rendering a financial account might enable a turn from juxtaposition to comparison. Notably, he makes some distinct economic comparisons. The most striking engages a debate underway over the utility of horses for plowing in lieu of the traditional oxen. He was skeptical of the all-equine plow.[31]

> "With a team of oxen with two horses you draw quicker than with a team of all horses [...] Why? I will tell you: the horse costs more than the ox. Besides, a plough of oxen will go as far in the year as a plough of horses [...] Further, in very hard ground where the plough of horses will stop, the plough of oxen will pass."

Here Walter makes several quick points on comparative efficiency, and seems to opt for a mixed team's advantage, but the middle point is of course shrewd. Given a whole year, the oxen can cover as much ground. But the sharpest comparative consideration follows:

> "And will you see how the horse costs more than the ox? I will tell you. It is usual that [the horse] should have every night at the least the sixth part of a bushel of oats, price one halfpenny, and at the least twelve pennyworth of grass in summer. And each week more or less a penny in shoeing, if he must be shod on all four feet. The sum is twelve shillings and five pence in the year, without fodder and chaff.

---

31 Cf. Dorothea Oschinsky (ed.), *Walter of Henley and other treatises on estate management and accounting*, Oxford 1971; Michael T. Clanchy, *From Memory to Written Record: England 1066-1307*, Oxford/Malden, 49-50, 99-100. Elizabeth Lamond (ed.), *Walter of Henley, On Husbandry, together with an anonymous Husbandry, Seneschaucie, and Robert Grosseteste's Rules*, London et al. 1890, 18.

And if the ox is to be in a condition to do his work, then it is necessary that he should have at least three sheaves and a half of oats in the week, price one penny, and ten sheaves of oats should yield a bushel of oats in measure; and in summer twelve pennyworth of grass: the sum three shillings, one penny, without fodder or chaff. And when the horse is old and worn out then there is nothing but the skin, and when the ox is old then with 10d worth of grass, he shall be fit for the larder."[32]

The use of money operates with time as a comparative framework. It gives precision to the comparative problem of working out horses and oxen as plow animals. Variables are resolved into money and then tallied one against the other. There are few treatises or even comments about the horse plowing revolution. There are, however, many estate financial accounts that show decisions made on this very issue, and many of these must have emerged from some comparable reasoning. This highlights of course the difficulty of the sources when it comes to recognizing where the practices of comparing actually were most important.[33] By the same token, Walter has many other reasoning moves in his arsenal.

Here is a case in Walter on rearing calves effectively that seems more like a juxtaposition than strong comparing. "And let your cows have enough food, that the milk may not be lessened. And when the male calf is calved, let it have all the milk for a month; at the end of the month take away a teat, and from week to week a teat, and then it will have suckled eight weeks, and put food before it that it may learn to eat. And the female calf shall have all the milk for three weeks, and take from it the teats as with the male."[34] There is none of the narrative or explanation of benefit or doubt. This one seems less like a comparison then a juxtaposition, possibly based on generic differences, indeed gender differences. This would not mean that there would be no reasons to explain the differential treatment, but one might expect them to go back to the core character or balance of the type: the bovine version female, version male.

A third instance from Walter seems intermediary, closer to comparison especially given his clear ability to reason comparatively. Here he is juxtaposing cows and sheep, but is also probably comparing the quality of a location, namely either salt marsh or forest as pasture:

"If your cows were sorted out, so that the bad were taken away, and your cows fed in pasture of salt marsh, then ought two cows to yield a wey [measure] of cheese and half a gallon of butter a week. And if they were fed in pasture of wood, or in meadows after mowing, or in stubble, then three cows ought to yield a wey of

---

32 Lamond, *On Husbandry*, 18.
33 See John Langdon, The Economics of Horses and Oxen in Medieval England, in: *Agricultural History Review* 30 (1982), 31–40.
34 Lamond, *On Husbandry*, 25.

cheese and half a gallon of butter a week between Easter and Michaelmas [...] And twenty ewes which are fed in pasture of salt marsh ought to and can yield cheese and butter as the two cows before named. And if your sheep were fed with fresh pasture or fallow, then ought thirty ewes to yield butter and cheese as the three cows before named."[35]

The quote manifests the fine-grained character of his thought and the narrow way in which comparative rationalities are at play. It is worth stressing how this is again facilitated by the mathematical and monetary that I previously showed connected to measures and weights. Walter turns his thinking into money, and one might then associate it quite rightly with the notable growth of monetization across Europe in this period. Money is a convenient method of account and facilitates comparison. This is especially so because in the transactions described, very little money as object would in fact move. Workers were not paid, oxen not rented, manure not bought. Money facilitates comparing, and hidden within the usually quiet work of large-scale estate management, comparison probably was a significant element in thinking and practice. Walter is probably a tip of a comparative iceberg.

Comparisons are odious

The author John Lydgate (1370–1451) has to hold pride of place in reflections on later medieval English comparison. He after all provides us with one of the most pregnant and quoted remarks on comparison of any age: "Comparisons are odious." Lydgate's is a sort of legal account, so law or adjudication is one of the elements within which the comparative works. In this case, we have the account of a trial before two judges, "the hardy lyon" and the "emperial egle"—these were, Lydgate says, "the dredful royal judges." The issue they faced was complex but not "too deep," as Lydgate put it. The judges needed to listen to the arguments of the horse, the goose, and the sheep and to decide, and I quote, "whyche of them was to man most profitable (v. 25):"[36] To be brief, they make their cases. The horse and goose rather confidently; the sheep sheepishly, but he makes some good points too, playing the bashful passive soul who only inadvertently has managed to provide the vellum for books and the wool to fend off winter.

As an aside, it is interesting to note that within this poem, in stanza 9, there is a section on the relation of the word horse to concepts, as in cheval leads to chevalier, or that "in Duch a rider called is knight."[37] One can point out here what might

---

35   Lamond, *On Husbandry*, 27
36   John Lydgate/Max Degenhardt (eds.), *The Hors, Goos, and the Sheepe*, Erlangen/Leipzig 1900, 49.
37   Lydgate/Degenhardt, *Hors, Goos, and the Sheepe*, 51.

seem obvious: Language and translation or travel can be—but are not inevitably—a great invitation to comparative thinking. Lydgate's move is a small one, but among Bacon's most characteristic sections of the *Opus Majus* was that on the importance and utility of learning languages.[38] Forms of translation, like forms of discovery, lurk, and their relationship to comparing is interesting because they might entice the practice out of the woodwork, so to speak.

In the end, the judges reject all three animals' claims of superiority, even as the horse has challenged them as to whether, "to put it simply, whether a goose or a sheep in any way can be likened or compared to a horse"[39] (150–154). Can they indeed? The poem proves yes, but should they be? From stanza 72, one gets the judgment of the Lion and Eagle. They argue for calm and complacency in one's lot; they tell:

> "The horse, be kynde to live in travaille,
> Goose, with her goselynges to swymme in the lake,
> The sheepe, whos wollis doth so moche availe,
> In her pasture grasen and mery make.
> {Their} comparisouns of one assent forsake
> Allwey remembryng, howe Gode and nature
> To a goode ende made evry creature."[40]

The conclusion is quite pointed, bringing both moral and social concerns to the fore:

> "Odious of olde is all comparisouns
> And of comparisouns engendered is hattrede,
> Al folk be not of lyke condicions
> Nor lyke disposid of thought, word or deed."[41]

Here we find for the first time this aphorism of considerable durability in English: Comparisons are odious. First, the poem would seem to make a literary comparison to comment on the practice of social comparison and social circumstances. One sort of context affects another. The practice of literary comparison might have an interesting relation to the social, and while this chapter has not tried to assess the literary comparative tropes, here one becomes aware that there might have been an interesting crossover. However, the key is probably Lydgate's desire to bring social or ethical commentary to the fore just because there were new challenges, even anxieties about the business of comparing.

---

38   *Opus Majus*, part three, 75-115 in Burke translation.
39   Lydgate/Degenhardt, *The Hors, Goos, and the Sheepe*, 55.
40   Lydgate/Degenhardt, *The Hors, Goos, and the Sheepe*, 73-74.
41   Lydgate/Degenhardt, *The Hors, Goos, and the Sheepe*, 74.

Looking back on the tensions around the legislation on consumption and taxation and the resentments these both revealed and engendered, it is hard not to see Lydgate's work as a response. What is more, other later medieval social expression of considerable popularity would seem to be grappling with the relation between the diversity of statuses and lives. The different sorts of people with whom later medieval England was plainly fascinated is so clear from *The Canterbury Tales* (1387–1400). Here Chaucer describes the 24 pilgrims "to telle yow al the condicioun of ech of hem, so as it semed me,//And whiche they weren and of what degree" and puts juxtaposition if not comparison to the test as to whether they are different.[42]

However, there is no large moralizing frame in Chaucer—this is not Dante. Such moralizing work, however, was taking place in other areas of art at the same time, and Lydgate knew it. There seems to be a comparing impulse at work in the theme of the Danse Macabre or Dance of Death, for instance. This image, created apparently in Paris in the 1420s, depicts all the sorts of people, each finding that, in the end, notwithstanding their differences, death would unite them and find them the same, except for their state of grace. It is not surprising to find that our same John Lydgate provided his own English version of the Dance of Death.[43] As a comparison, the diversity of social types and the sameness of their attitude to death are set at play.

The fifteenth century also saw, contemporary with Lydgate, the arrival of the remarkable cadaver tombs.[44] They seem to be in close connection with the Danse Macabre. The tombs feature verisimilar carvings of the subject in his or her worldly splendor on the top. Underneath, however, as it were in the ground, we find instead the effects of time and corruption, the carving below the cadaver, sometimes just a skeleton, sometimes wasted flesh, maybe with the odd worm. It would be hard not to see here again a sort of visual comparing of before and after, very much in line with the important point that the body's splendor, the person's wealth, did not matter. The differences are underlined by the act of comparison. Chaucer's granddaughter Alice, Duchess of Suffolk, was a rare woman who opted for this

---

42   Geoffrey Chaucer/Jill Mann (ed.), *The Canterbury Tales*, Harmondsworth UK, General Prologue, lines 38-41.

43   See Lydgate's in Florence Warren (ed.), *The Dance of Death*, Early English Text Society, OS 181, London 1931. See Sophie Oosterwijk, Of Corpses, Constables and Kings: The Danse Macabre in Late Medieval and Renaissance Culture, in: *Journal of the British Archaeological Association* 157 (2004): 61-90; and Amy Appleford, The Dance of Death in London: John Carpenter, John Lydgate, and the Daunce of Poulys, in: *Journal of Medieval and Early Modern Studies* (2008) 38, 285-314.

44   See Kathleen Cohen, *Metamorphosis of a Death Symbol: The Transi Tomb in the Late Middle Ages and the Renaissance*, Berkeley/London 1973; Pamela M. King, The Iconography of the Wakeman Cenotaph in Tewkesbury Abbey, in: *Transactions of the Bristol and Gloucestershire Archaeological Society* 103 (1985), 141-48; and Paul Binski, *Medieval Death: Ritual and Representation*, Ithaca 1996, 139-52.

Fig. 1: Cadaver Tomb of Henry Chichele, Archbishop of Canterbury, Canterbury Cathedral, Kent, built circa 1443.

Fig. 2: Cadaver Tomb of Alice Chaucer, Duchess of Suffolk, Ewelme Church, Oxforshire, built circa 1475.

tomb style. She was the tertium comparationis, her body in the middle casket, the depiction of her social person on top, the image of her cadaver below, each brought into relation with her true person: body for the resurrection and immortal soul.

While Lydgate's thinking probably grew alongside these wider concerns with a new sort of comparative or juxtaposing social vision, his statements remain virtually the first English commentary on the practice of comparisons itself. Comparison is criticized as tending to the unethical and the un-Christian, but it plays the role here of supporting social norms as well. There is still a sense that people cannot, compared to each other, improve themselves, and it is a crossover sort of performance; medieval social complacency and religious charity pushing back against something perhaps a bit too egotistical or simply too this-worldly.

Lydgate's final four lines quoted above deserve attention and might be profound. It is possible, on the framework that he provides, to see that comparison is especially odious because it is futile, an operation akin to what philosophers call a category mistake. There are places, we might imagine, where one can usefully evaluate and compare, but there are others in which the operation is both idle and conducive to unhappiness. It is not, on this account, possible for comparison to be a useful practice in such human cases.

The laws

Aside from Roger Bacon, the most comprehensive use of comparison for analysis is certainly that of Sir John Fortescue (1395–1477), one of the most notable English jurists and political theorists of the latter parts of the Middle Ages. In his mid-40s, he attained the position of chief justice of the King's Bench. In the 1460s, while in exile with the defeated Lancastrian king, Fortescue wrote a dialogue—*In Praise of the Laws of England*—to educate the Lancastrian crown prince of England, who had been raised and lived in a foreign realm and who needed some education about his own country—just like the fictive prince and chancellor in the dialogue.

Clearly stimulated by the experience of exile and the prospects of return, Fortescue opened up the logics of comparison much more than had his contemporaries. There is certainly an argument to be made that war, the Hundred Years war, helped to make political and national comparison more meaningful or apt. The particular facts of the book sharpen this: The Prince who planned to recover his kingdom has focused on martial skills and the arts of war; but his interlocutor, the Chancellor, wants to intervene and tell him that knowledge of and respect for the laws is essential to successful rule.

Fortescue's book sets out to argue for the worthy character of the laws of England and its commitment to a certain sort of what we might call constitutional regime, namely, a *dominium politicum et regale, a political and royal realm*.[45] The burden of this sort of state is that the laws exist by consent of the people *and* the king,

---

45   Found in John Fortescue/Shelley Lockwood (eds. and trans.), *On the Laws and Governance of England*, Cambridge 1997. For discussion of Fortescue additionally to Lockwood, see S. B. Chrimes, Sir John Fortescue and His Theory of Dominion, in: *Transactions of the Royal Historical Society* 17

and the king is bound to the laws. For the purposes of seeking out practices of comparison, it is clear that the two species of monarchy are being set up in parallel. In the event, one is represented typically by France, one by England. However, this is only part of the comparative story: The second framing comparison is the contrast between the Civil Law and the English or Common Law. In Chapter 19, the chancellor moves to answer the Prince's question as to whether the "laws of England deserve to be adjudged as fitting, effective, and convenient for this kingdom of England as the civil laws are for the Empire." Then he says an interesting thing:

> "Comparisons, indeed, Prince, as I remember you said at one time, are reputed odious, and so I am not fond of making them but you will be able to gather more effectively whether one more richly deserves praise than the other, not from my opinion, but from those points wherein they differ, the superiorities of the more excellent law will appear after due reflection. Let us, therefore, bring forward some cases of this sort, so that you can weigh in a fair balance which of the laws shows its superiorities better and more justly".[46]

First, this maxim reveals a self-conscious reference to John Lydgate's conclusion about the pernicious character of comparing, but one also learns from Fortescue the reasons why comparison is deemed valuable. He makes clear that comparison is a form of demonstration. Certainly, on that basis, one can imagine both the illustrations of the cadaver tombs and the discussions of Walter of Henley coming to mind. In taking this mode, Sir John turns to the things themselves in conjunction with each other rather than to his own "opinions." The idea is that comparative thinking forces a sort of discipline onto those making the judgement.

The method of observation via comparison would seem to be a strong tendency of Fortescue's thought. "In order that these things may appear more clearly to you, consult your experience of both governments; begin with the results of only royal government, such as that with which the king of France rules his subjects; then examine the practical effect of the royal and political government, such as that with which the king of England rules over his subject people."[47] His injunction here to "consult your experience of both governments" really lays the stress on reflection as investigation. This move has the effect of bringing things together in tandem in order to draw out further concrete reflection. This is the cognitive and logical core of comparison as a mode of thought.

In substance, Fortescue moves through a series of targeted examples and compares the facts—as he sometimes fancifully sees them—and opens out the argu-

---

(4th series, 1934): 117–147 and Felix Gilbert, Sir John Fortescue's *'dominium regale et politicum'*, in: *Medievalia et Humanistica*, II (1944), 88–97.
46 Fortescue/Lockwood, *On the Laws and Governance of England*, 29.
47 Fortescue/Lockwood, *On the Laws and Governance of England*, 49.

ments and logics that allow one law to be assessed in this limited respect against the other. The examples are the use of juries rather than mere witnesses; the use of torture; the different definitions of a bastard; or the question of maternal versus paternal importance in the legal status of children. His conclusion is perhaps unsurprising, because he finds that the civil law is deficient in justice. More important for the dynamics of comparing, Fortescue can properly be cited as the origin for a cluster of comparative attitudes between France and England with considerable resonance in English national reflection.

The discussion of legal comparison can widen out to social and ethnic comparison, and it did so naturally within Fortescue—in part, because his analysis of the difference between France and England is based partly on a perception that two very wealthy countries had, in part because of their legal constitutions, produced very different results for their people. According to him, the French people suffered arbitrary billeting of the king's armies, they had to pay tax if they wanted an essential such as salt, and they were so impoverished that they had to drink water; whereas to quote him, in England, "They do not drink water, except those who sometimes abstain from other drinks by way of devotional or penitential zeal."[48]

This needs a lot more reflection and investigation, but the emergence of the popular national kingdom especially in the context of warfare might well have provided an impetus for comparative political thinking. In that realm, as often as not, comparison's otiose quality was easier to overlook than within the realm of personal and moral reflection. Certain sorts of comparison tended to social disharmony, as Lydgate argued. But comparison across national lines not only helped to inscribe those national lines, but to give national or ethnic units their own content, and this included validating pride or superiority. Here we can compare Bacon's thinking on religion and Fortescue's on laws to see how comparison enabled sharper, more objective reflection, even as it might work to strengthen the prejudice built into the framework.[49] When it came to nations, comparison was less important, because the odium was perhaps more acceptable.

If in personal religious or ethical life, comparison was apparently frowned upon, its methodological powers of demonstration, with a hint of the objective, could brush off such incivility in other quarters. War and the needs of the kingdom wanted the truth that comparison might deliver. Other sorts of comparative

---

48 Fortescue/Lockwood, On the Laws and Governance of England, 52.
49 This was by no means a natural path. A work of nationalist vigour, such as George Warner (ed.), *The Libelle of Englyshe Polycye: A Poem on the Use of Sea-Power 1436*, Oxford 1926, shows relatively little clearly comparative thought. There is arguably even less in John Gough Nichols (ed.), *William Worcestre's Boke of Noblesse*, London 1860: for Worcestre the French might be dishonourable but they and the English are not really compared. Indeed, if there is a comparative turn it comes in the guise of learning lessons from history, a potentially interesting avenue for further reflection.

practices, however, such as whether money was weighed correctly so that bread could be sold honestly, became routinized practices or networks. They remained comparisons but methodological ones. This does not mean that they might not gather political importance later when the poor were urged to eat cake or when the use of the metric system might have meant selling beer or milk in some size that was not an old-fashioned pint.

Tracing the differences between one sort of comparison and another, seeing how they worked together and worked against each other, will be the big job in understanding the dynamics of comparison in medieval England or anywhere else. It would not be right from this selective survey to say that comparison was a common mode of reflection in medieval England. One might argue that it was an embedded form in terms of market operations and money transactions. However, in social and ethical life, it developed a complicated and limited place. Its disruptive character in some social contexts was at least suspected. The religious element here was important too. The suspicion that Lydgate brought was not isolated. One should trust that Fortescue saw his point in earnest, even if he was willing to push carefully forward. It is an interesting moral turn, attempting, in the very moments that comparison was rearing its social head, to push back against it. A sermon of around 1400 stressed that looking at each other's religious performance when we hoped to be saved was pernicious. The preacher feared the logic of competition, making people act as if it were a race to heaven; and for him, that idea was part of what was wrong with much contemporary religion, "We shulden reste in this hope that we shal come to hevene, and leve ich veyne comparisouns."[50] These lines come from work associated with that proto-Protestant heresy, native to England, known as Lollardy, initiated by the Oxford philosopher John Wyclif. Here one finds comparison dangerous to the soul. Vain comparisons indeed. In the end, one finds that the tentative medieval use of comparison examined here has turned up some rather revolutionary comparers of law and religion, but also some strong and perhaps forgotten warnings about the perils of using comparison at all. Medieval ambivalence toward comparison set limits to its use.

---

50   Thomas Arnold (ed.), *Select English Works of John Wyclif, volume 1: Sermons on the Gospels*, Oxford 1869. Sermon XVII for the "the seventeenth sondai aftir trinite", 42. These are not now taken to be by Wyclif but by his followers.

References

ALLEN, Martin, *Mints and Money in Medieval England*, Cambridge 2012.

APPLEFORD, Amy, The Dance of Death in London: John Carpenter, John Lydgate, and the Daunce of Poulys, in: *Journal of Medieval and Early Modern Studies* (2008), 285-314.

ARNOLD, Thomas (ed.), *Select English Works of John Wyclif, volume 1: Sermons on the Gospels*, Oxford 1869.

BACON, Roger, *Opus Majus*, ca. 1267, translated by Robert Belle Burke, Pennsylvania 1928, based on J. H. Bridges (ed.), Opus Maius 1-3, Oxford 1897-1900.

BAKER, John, Case Law in England and Continental Europe, in: John H. Baker, Collected Papers on English Legal History, Cambridge 2014, 612–620.

BAKER, John, Case Law in Medieval England, in: John H. Baker, Collected Papers on English Legal History, Cambridge 2014, 547–578.

BALDWIN, Frances E., *Sumptuary Legislation and Personal Regulation in England*, Baltimore 1926.

BENNETT, Judith, *Ale, Beer, and Brewsters in England: Women's Work in a Changing World, 1300–1600*, Oxford 1996.

BINSKI, Paul, *Medieval Death: Ritual and Representation*, Ithaca 1996.

Canterbury Cathedral Archives (CCA), CC J/Q/264.

CHAUCER, Geoffrey/MANN, Jill (ed.), *The Canterbury Tales*, Harmondsworth.

CHILDS, Wendy R./TAYLOR, John (eds.), *Anonimalle Chronicle 1333–1381* (York: Yorkshire Archaeological Society Record Series 147).

CHRIMES, S. B., Sir John Fortescue and His Theory of Dominion, in: *Transactions of the Royal Historical Society* 17 (4th series, 1934), 117–147.

COHEN, Kathleen, *Metamorphosis of a Death Symbol: The Transi Tomb in the Late Middle Ages and the Renaissance*, Berkeley/London 1973.

DAVIS, James, *Medieval Market Morality: Life, Law and Ethics in the English Marketplace*, Cambridge 2012.

DAVIS, James, Market Regulation in Fifteenth-Century England, in: Ben Dodds/Christian D. Liddy (eds.), *Commercial Activity, Markets and Entrepreneurs in the Middle Ages: Essays in Honour of Richard Britnell*, Woodbridge 2011, 81–106.

DAVIS, James, Baking for the Common Good: A Reassessment of the Assize of Bread in Medieval England, in: *The Economic History Review* 57 (2004), 465-502.

EDWARD III, October 1363, Item 25, in: Chris Given-Wilson et al. (eds.), *Parliament Rolls of Medieval England*, Woodbridge 2005, British History Online, URL: http://www.british-history.ac.uk/no-series/parliament-rolls-medieval/october-1363 [last accessed June 10, 2018].

FORTESCUE, John/LOCKWOOD, Shelley (eds. and trans.), *On the Laws and Governance of England*, Cambridge 1997.

GILBERT, Felix, Sir John Fortescue's 'dominium regale et politicum', in: *Medievalia et Humanistica*, II (1944), 88–97.

HILL, Francis, *Medieval Lincoln*, Cambridge 1948.

HOWELL, Martha C., *Commerce Before Capitalism in Europe. 1300–1600*, Cambridge 2010.

KILLERBY, Catherine, *Sumptuary Law in Italy. 1200–1500*, Oxford 2002.

KING, Pamela M., The Iconography of the Wakeman Cenotaph in Tewkesbury Abbey, in: *Transactions of the Bristol and Gloucestershire Archaeological Society* 103 (1985).

LANGDON, John, The Economics of Horses and Oxen in Medieval England, in: *Agricultural History Review* 30 (1982).

LAMOND, Elizabeth (ed.), *Walter of Henley, On Husbandry, together with an anonymous Husbandry, Seneschaucie, and Robert Grosseteste's Rules*, London et al. 1890.

LEWIS, Clive Staples., *The Allegory of Love. A Study in Medieval Tradition*, Oxford 1936.

LEWIS, T. Ellis, The History of Judicial Precedent, in: *Law Quarterly Review* 48 (1932), 230–247, and 46 (1930), 207–224.

LYDGATE, John/DEGENHARDT, Max (eds.), *The Hors, Goos, and the Sheepe*, Erlangen/Leipzig 1900.

MEYER, Ann R., *Medieval Allegory and the Building of the New Jerusalem*, Rochester 2003.

MILLER, John Riggs, Sir, *Speeches in the House of Commons upon the Equalization of the Weights and Measures of Great Britain*, London 1790.

NICHOLS, John Gough, *William Worcestre's Boke of Noblesse*, London 1860.

OOSTERWIJK, Sophie, Of Corpses, Constables and Kings: The Danse Macabre in Late Medieval and Renaissance Culture, in: *Journal of the British Archaeological Association* 157 (2004), 61-90.

OSCHINSKY, Dorothea (ed.), *Walter of Henley and other treatises on estate management and accounting*, Oxford 1971.

PICKERING, Danby (ed.), *Statutes at Large from Magna Charta to the end of the Eleventh Parliament of Great Britain, anno 1761*, volume 1, Cambridge 1762.

POWER, Amanda, *Roger Bacon and the Defence of Christendom*, Cambridge 2012.

QUILLIGAN, Maureen, *The Languages of Allegory. Defining a Genre*, Ithaca 1979.

RAITHBY, John (ed.), *Statutes of the Realm. Printed by command of his majesty King George the Third, in pursuance of an address of the House of Commons of Great Britain. From original records and manuscripts*, 3, London 1817.

RAITHBY, John (ed.), *Statutes of the Realm. Printed by command of his majesty King George the Third, in pursuance of an address of the House of Commons of Great Britain. From original records and manuscripts*, 1, London 1810.

RICHARD II, April 1379, Paragraphs 13-16, in: Chris Given-Wilson et al. (eds.), *Parliament Rolls of Medieval England*, Woodbridge 2005, British History Online, URL: http://www.british-history.ac.uk/no-series/parliament-rolls-medieval/april-1379. Membrane 6 [last accessed June 10, 2018].

ROBERTSON, Agnes J. (ed.), *Laws of Kings of England from Edmund to Henry I*, Cambridge 1926.

ROSS, Alan S. C., The Assize of Bread, in: *Economic History Review*, N.S. 9 (1956), 332–342.

RUDOLPH, Conrad, *The Mystic Ark: Hugh of Saint Victor, Art, and Thought in the Twelfth Century*, Cambridge 2014.

STUBBS, William (ed.), *Roger de Hoveden, Chronica Magistri Rogeri De Houedene* (Rerum britannicarum medii aevi scriptores or chronicles and memorials of Great Britain and Ireland during the Middle Ages, 51/4), London 1868.

WALSINGHAM, Thomas, *The St Albans Chronicle: The Chronica Maiora of Thomas Walsingham*, Volume I: 1376-1394, ed. by John Taylor/Wendy Childs/Leslie Watkiss, Oxford 2003.

WARNER, George (ed.), *The Libelle of Englyshe Polycye: A Poem on the Use of Sea-Power 1436*, Oxford 1926.

WARREN, Florence (ed.), *The Dance of Death, Early English Text Society*, OS 181, London 1931.

ZHU, Lei, On the Origin of the Term Tertium Comparationis, in: *Language and History* 60 (2017), 35-52.

ZUPKO, Ronald E., *British Weights and Measures. A History from Antiquity to the Seventeenth Century*, Madison 1977.

ZUPKO, Ronald E., Medieval English Weights and Measures: Variation and Standardization, in: *Studies in Medieval Culture* 4 (1974), 238-243.

The Shifting Grounds of Comparison in the French Renaissance
The Case of Louis Le Roy

Andrea Frisch

Abstract[1]

Comparison between the present and what was perceived as a lost past was the bedrock of Renaissance intellectual life. However, rather than come ever nearer, the horizon of universal—and even simply shared—values supposedly located in Greco-Roman Antiquity receded as the past began to appear both irredeemably contingent and deeply foreign in the intense light cast on it by the philological labor originally undertaken to restore it. Louis Le Roy's 1575 treatise De la vicissitude ou variété des choses en l'univers *offers a compact illustration of the ways in which the Renaissance Humanist practice of comparison ultimately revealed profound differences between past and present, thereby undermining its own motivating assumptions.*

As is well known, one of the primary foundations of the cultural ideology of the European Renaissance was the imitation of ancient examples, a practice that involved comparing the Greco-Roman past to the European present. There are countless statements about the utility of Ancient history for the Renaissance reader in Humanist historiography of the fifteenth and sixteenth centuries.[2] In the preface to

---

1   Research on this article has been supported by a Mercator fellowship which was granted by the Collaborative Research Center SFB 1288 "Practices of Comparing. Changing and Ordering the World," Bielefeld University, Germany, funded by the German Research Foundation (DFG).
2   The locus classicus for this desire for communion with the ancient past is Petrarch, who in his unfinished "Letter to Posterity" wrote "Among the many subjects which interested me, I dwelt especially upon antiquity, for our own age has always repelled me, so that, had it not been for the love of those dear to me, I should have preferred to have been born in any other period than our own. In order to forget my own time, I have constantly striven to place myself in spirit in other ages, and consequently I delighted in history" (I cite from Mark Musa's English translation in *The Italian Renaissance Reader*, New York 1987, 6. Of course, Petrarch's status as the "first" Humanist has been vigorously debated and his relationship to Antiquity nuanced in specialized scholarship on the question; see, e.g., Ronald G. Witt, *In the Footsteps*

his widely-circulated French translation of Plutarch's *Lives* (itself a suite of comparisons, also known as the Parallel Lives, that juxtaposes famous figures from Greek and Roman Antiquity), Jacques Amyot declares that History *"est une règle et instruction certaine, qui par exemples du passé nous enseigne à juger du present, & à prévoir l'avenir"* (is a certaine rule and instruction, which by examples past, teacheth us to judge of things present, and to foresee things to come).[3] The historian's claim to revivify the values and practices of a distant time was, moreover, hardly limited to secular arts and letters; it was also at the core of the Protestant Reformation. In fact, one of the few places in which the term "renaissance" is used in France during the period itself is in Protestant Church history, such as Théodore de Bèze's 1580 *Histoire ecclésiastique* or in Simon Goulart's account of the French Wars of Religion, which recounts the *"laborieuse renaissance de l'Eglise Françoise."*[4] One could therefore say that comparison, in this case between the present and what was perceived as a lost past, was the bedrock of Renaissance intellectual life, insofar as it was framed in terms of Renaissance and Reformation.

Amyot explicitly stipulates that the kind of instruction he has in mind is not based upon abstract moral precepts, which he sees as the domain of philosophy rather than history, but rather on the record of specific actions. Examples are more apt to teach effectively than mere precepts, he maintains, because examples are particular, and include an account of circumstances. Implicit here, of course, is the belief that the "circumstances" of the past and those of the present (as well as those of the future) are comparable in all of the ways relevant to the concerns of moral philosophy that the Humanists sought to address by turning to Greco-Roman history. The implicit assumption of a common ground of comparison is evident when Amyot imagines an objection to his method of teaching prudence via history: He does not worry that past conditions might be too different from present ones to license imitation of the Ancients as a pedagogical program, but rather anticipates the charge that direct experience is more effective than is reading for this purpose. To this Amyot replies that experience is certainly a good teacher,

---

of the Ancients: The Origins of Humanism from Lovato to Bruni, Leiden 2000. For an overview of the status of Antiquity in the Renaissance, see Georg Voigt, *Die Wiederbelebung des classischen Alterthums: Oder, das erste Jahrhundert des Humanismus*, Berlin 1960.

3 Amyot's French translation of Plutarch was first published in 1559 in Paris. This French version was republished several times throughout the sixteenth and seventeenth centuries, and served as the basis of Thomas North's *Lives of the Noble Grecians and Romanes*, published in London in 1579. I cite North's English versions here.

4 The extended title of Bèze's History is *Histoire Ecclesiastique Des Eglises Reformées Au Royaume de France: en laquelle est descrite au vray la renaissance & accroissement d'icelles depuis l'an MDXXI iusques en l'annee MDLXIII, leur reiglement ou discipline*, Anvers 1580. Goulart uses this expression in his *Memoires de l'estat de France, sous Charles IX* ("Meidelbourg" [Geneva]: "Henry Wolf" [Eustache Vignon] 1578, 430v).

but it carries great risks; reading history, on the other hand, allows one to acquire prudence from the comfort of one's study. Thus, in Amyot's widely read text, the past conveyed in history books is tacitly situated alongside the present (and indeed, the future) upon a common ground of moral and political action.

In order to grasp the character of Renaissance comparison, and ultimately to trace the *effects* of this particular gesture of comparison (which shall be my primary concern here), one point is crucial: In the case of both secular Humanism and Christian reform, the comparison between past and present proceeded in terms that were at once figural *and* empirical. For the Humanists, Greco-Roman Antiquity was both a quasimythical Golden Age and a set of historical phenomena that could become the object of philological research. For the Reformers (particularly the Calvinists in France and Switzerland), Christian doctrine was both God-given and manifested in the practices of the early church. In other words, the past against which the present was to be measured functioned *both* as a site of universal values *and* as a set of contingent historical conditions that could be researched and thereby restored.

Obviously, the assumption in both secular and religious "recovery" of the past was that the historical moments under scrutiny were privileged manifestations of universal values that were the ultimate *telos* of the undertaking. However, rather than come ever nearer, the horizon of universal—and even simply shared—values receded as the past began to appear both irredeemably contingent and profoundly foreign in the intense light cast on it by the philological labor originally undertaken to restore it.

This is a case—I say "a case," but we are talking about a broad cultural shift—in which the act of comparing had truly transformative effects, precisely because those effects were completely unforeseen by those who undertook the comparison. In many contemporary critiques of the practice of comparison, there is either an implicit assumption or an explicit critique that the agent of comparison holds all the power.[5] Yet here, at what can be seen as a crucial turning point in the intellectual history of comparison, the practice of comparison itself destabilized the hierarchy that it was meant to subtend. I shall sketch this process of destabilization in broad strokes before I turn to the writings of the sixteenth-century French Humanist Louis Le Roy for a more detailed examination of its consequences.

---

5 See the essays in Rita Felski/Susan Stanford Friedman (eds.), *Comparison: Theories, Approaches, Uses*, Baltimore 2013, esp. Rajagopalan Radhakrishnan's opening essay, "Why Compare?" and the essays in Part Two, "Comparison in the World: Uses and Abuses"; Natalie Melas, *All the Difference in the World: Postcoloniality and the Ends of Comparison*, Stanford 2007; Aram A. Yengoyan (ed.), *Modes of Comparison: Theory and Practice*, Ann Arbor 2006. For methodological reflections on the problem of ethnocentric comparison in the legal context, see Günter Frankenberg, *Comparative Law as Critique*, Cheltenham/Northampton 2016, esp. Chapter 8, "Thick comparison?".

As North American scholars in comparative literature have convincingly argued, Renaissance techniques developed to recover a lost historical past, and the technologies that supported and disseminated the abundant and controversial fruits of Renaissance historical research, eventually upset rather than consolidated the hierarchy between an idealized past, and a degenerate present postulated by the original comparison.[6] The evidence that was assembled with the goal of restoring Roman law, to take one of the most far-reaching examples, ended up being read as undeniable proof of the inapplicability of Roman law to the sixteenth-century monarchies that had sought to claim Roman heritage.[7] The more that Humanist researchers learned about Antiquity, the more difficult it seemed to articulate the relevance of the Antique past to the antiquarian's present. In other words, the *a priori* assumption of a common ground, of a fundamental resemblance, which implicitly legitimated the broad comparison between past and present in the first place, did not survive the local acts of comparison that were intended to build upon that very ground.

Michel de Montaigne was famously skeptical about the postulate of resemblance that implicitly motivated so much Humanist scholarship in the fifteenth and sixteenth centuries. In the third volume of his *Essais* (published in 1588), he observed that

> "La consequence que nous voulons tirer de la ressemblance des evenemens est mal seure, d'autant qu'ils sont tousjours dissemblables: il n'est aucune qualité si universelle en cette image des choses que la diversité et varieté"

—which Montaigne's first English translator John Florio rendered as "The consequence we seeke to draw from the conference of events is unsure, because they are ever dissemblable. No quality is so universall in this surface of things as variety and diversity."[8]

---

6   The paradoxical, self-undermining quality of the project of imitating Antiquity in the Renaissance is highlighted in work in comparative literature by Thomas Greene, *The Light in Troy. Imitation and Discovery in Renaissance Poetry*, New Haven/London 1982; David Quint, *Origin and Originality in Renaissance Literature: Versions of the Source*, New Haven/London 1983; and Timothy Hampton, *Writing from History. The Rhetoric of Exemplarity in Renaissance Literature*, Ithaca/London 1990.

7   For an account of this phenomenon in sixteenth-century France, see Donald Kelley, *Foundations of Modern Historical Scholarship: Language, Law, and History in the French Renaissance*, New York/London 1970.

8   The first two books of Michel de Montaigne's *Essais* were published in 1580 (Bordeaux: Simon Millanges); the essay cited here, "De l'expérience," first appeared in the three-volume 1588 edition (Paris: Abel L'Angelier). The modern edition of reference, which I cite, is that of Pierre Villey and V.L. Saulnier (Paris: PUF, several printings beginning in 1965, with identical pagination; available online at https://www.lib.uchicago.edu/efts/ARTFL/projects/montaigne/). The quoted passage is on page 1065. Florio's English translation first appeared in 1603. I cite

In Richard Popkin's magisterial *History of Scepticism*, Montaigne's overall posture of doubt is seen as a manifestation of a loss of faith in religious authority that spread throughout Europe in the wake of the Reformation.[9] The essayist's doubts about resemblance, however, suggest rather a loss of faith in the quintessentially Humanist habit of comparing the Ancient past to the present. If events are ultimately steeped in contingency, we cannot simply assume that history "is a certaine rule and instruction, which by examples past, teacheth us to judge of things present, and to foresee things to come." In questioning the legitimacy of the assumption of a common ground for the comparison of past to present, Montaigne crystallizes the fundamental tension within the Renaissance Humanist practice of comparison: Whereas the impetus for comparison was an assumed resemblance, the effect of comparison was a heightened sense of difference.

Montaigne articulated as a philosophical principle a perspective that had become increasingly apparent in French Renaissance historiography, where the Humanist practice of comparison endorsed by Amyot was applied to an ever greater variety of material. Over a decade before Montaigne published the third volume of his essays, the Humanist Louis Le Roy had attempted to come to terms with the cultural variety and diversity that Renaissance philology (and European expansion) had revealed. Le Roy's treatise *De la vicissitude ou variété des choses en l'univers* (1575), a wide-ranging survey of human activity across time and space encompassing all the known regions of the globe from the beginning of recorded time, was reprinted six times at Paris between 1575 and 1584, was translated into Italian in 1585 (this was reprinted in 1592), and translated into English in 1594.[10] Le Roy wrote a good generation after the advent of Humanist education and the rise of Reformation polemics in France under François I. His career was largely concerned with the reception of Greek and Latin texts, and especially with configuring the relation of Greek political thought to contemporary France (he translated into French, among others, works by Xenophon, Aristotle, and Plato, all with extensive prefaces and copious glosses that struggle to articulate the relationship between Greek wisdom and current French affairs). Le Roy's book on vicissitude is in many ways a compact

---

from the 1613 edition (*Essays written in French by Michael Lord of Montaigne, Knight of the Order of S. Michael, gentleman of the French Kings chamber: done into English, according to the last French edition, by John Florio reader of the Italian tongue*, London 1613, 600).

9 *The History of Scepticism from Savonarola to Bayle* (third edition, Oxford University Press, 2003). Earlier editions published as *The History of Scepticism From Erasmus to Descartes* (Assen: Van Gorcum, 1960) and *The History of Scepticism from Erasmus to Spinoza* (University of California Press, 1979).

10 Loys Le Roy, *De la Vicissitude ou Varieté des choses en l'univers et concurrence des armes et des lettres par les premieres et plus illustres du monde, depuis le temps où à commencé la civilité, & memoire humaine jusques à present*, Paris 1575. French citations are to this edition. For longer passages, I give the 1594 English translation by Robert Ashley (London, 1594).

illustration of the way in which the Renaissance Humanist practice of comparison ultimately undermined its own motivating assumptions.

In the summary titles of the *Vicissitude*'s twelve "books" or chapters, one can see that Le Roy's treatise is made up of comparisons between various aspects of the civilizations of what he calls "les plus célèbres peuples du monde." As we might expect, the Ancient Greeks emerge as a privileged term of comparison, as one can see in the full title of Book V: *Of the Learning, Poesie, Eloquence, Power, and other Excellencie of the Greekes. A Comparison of them with the Egiptians, Assyrians, Persians, Indians. The Empire of Greece. A Comparison of Alexander the great, with Cyrus, Agesilaus, Themistocles, Pericles, Achilles, Vlysses, Diomedes, Bacchus, Hercules, and others. A Comparison of the Grecian Philosophers, with the Chaldees of Babylon, and the Priestes of Egipt. The Nobilitie of aunciant Greece. The Artisans and workes of the Grecians.* The Ancient Romans take over this role from the Greeks in Books VI and VII (in which "militie" or warfare is added to the list of Rome's qualities along with those that had been attributed to Greece). One can already get a sense of how Humanist research into the ancient world has expanded the field of play to include, among others, the Assyrians, the Egyptians, and the Chaldeans as candidates for comparison with Greece and Rome and thereby with the European present. However, it is essential to recall here that Le Roy's sources of information about these civilizations were Ancient Greek and Roman historians, so we have not yet got to the point where Greco-Roman Antiquity has lost its privilege as that which delineates the very ground of Renaissance comparison. Indeed, this chapter ends with comparisons "of the Latin Authors with the Greek; namely of Cicero with Demosthenes" and "a Comparison of the Latin tongue with the Greek."

Book IX, by contrast, is one place where we might locate a real shift in the framework of Le Roy's enterprise of comparison. The civilization under consideration in this chapter is that of what Le Roy calls the Arabs or Sarrasins, about whom there are obviously no ancient sources. Now at first, in Book VIII, the Arabs are compared, perhaps inevitably, to the Greeks and the Romans, as well as to the other ancient civilizations that had already appeared in the previous book (the summary of this book ends with "A Comparison of the Arabian learning with the Greek, Egiptian, Chaldean, Persian, Romain, or Latin: Of the Arabian tongue, with the Greek, Latin, and Hebrew"). But in its companion Book IX, we get a chapter devoted exclusively to what we could here call a "post-Ancient" civilization, one that does not (indeed, cannot) depend on Ancient Greco-Roman sources. And it turns out that Le Roy does not frame this chapter in terms of comparison at all: It is an account of the spread of Islam. Le Roy effectively abandons comparison in his narrative of Islamic expansion, which thereby serves as a turning point, a hinge between an account of history in which "the most celebrated peoples in the world" supply both the grounds and the privileged term of comparison, on the one hand, and an account of history structured by a chronological narrative whose ground repeatedly shifts, on the other.

In the latter part of Le Roy's treatise, in the absence of a common ground, people and events are not so much compared as they are juxtaposed. This change in approach is not immediately apparent: Having arrived at the present in his account of global history, Le Roy trumpets in the summary title to his Book X the technological advances of his own age that were unknown to Greco-Roman Antiquity, namely, printing, the nautical compass, and gunpowder.[11] We may note that Montaigne made fun of European self-congratulation on that score:

> "Nous escriïons du miracle de l'invention de nostre artillerie, de nostre impression; d'autres hommes, un autre bout du monde à la Chine, en jouyssoit mille ans auparavant" (908)— "We make a mighty business of the invention of artillery and printing, which other men at the other end of the world, in China, had a thousand years ago" (510).

Next to Montaigne's cosmopolitan skepticism, Le Roy's European claim on these inventions initially appears merely to invert the past-over-present hierarchy of Renaissance comparison while retaining its implicit grounding in Greco-Roman Antiquity. But the rest of Le Roy's tenth book suggests that like Montaigne, he has, in fact, broken with the Renaissance practice of comparison.

Le Roy is frequently invoked as an early exponent of the rhetoric of progress that would be taken up and turned into a research program by the likes of Bacon and Descartes.[12] Yet it becomes clear that this chapter of the treatise on vicissi-

---

11   Robert Ashley's 1594 English translation of the full title, nearly as long as the chapter itself, and to whose highlighted passages I shall refer in my main text, is "How that **in this age haue bin restored the tongues, and knowledges, after they had surceased about almost twelue hundred yeres, hauing newly receaued great light, and increase**; where are considered, **the meruailes of this present age**, thorough Europe, Asia, Africke, The new-found lands, in the East, West, North, and South: **beginning at the great, & inuincible Tamberlan**, whose power, valiancy, and felicity is briefly represented. **During whose raign began the restitution of Learning & of Arts**: By what persons & means it hath bin continued in diuers nations: The Princes that most haue fauoured it. Moreouer **how that many goodly things vnknowen to antiquity haue bin newly found out**, especially **Printing, The direction to sayle by the needle** of steele rubbed on the Lode-stone, carying alwaies the point answerable to the place where we imagine the pole Artique, by means whereof the whole Sea hath bin sayled ouer, and the whole world knowne thorough out. **Then the skill of Ordinance, and Artillery, which hath made all other auncient military instruments to cease, which by this one are all surpassed in impetuosity, swiftnes, and violence. Also how amongst the meruailes of this age haue risen new and strange Diseases vnknowen heretofore, and diuers Sects haue sprong vp in all countries, which haue much altered the common quiet, and weakned the mutual charitie of men**."
12   A recent intervention in this direction (which includes a survey of previous arguments by Hans Baron, Anthony Grafton, and Marc Fumaroli for Le Roy's modernity), is Emma Claussen, A Sixteenth-Century Modern? Ancients and Moderns in Loys Le Roy's De la vicissitude, in:

tude is not at all a simple hierarchical inversion according to which the European present is seen as superior to the Ancient past, and the future as potentially better than the present. Rather than situate the beginning of the "restitution of learning and the arts"—that is, the Renaissance—in Europe, Le Roy locates this moment in the reign of Tamerlane, the fourteenth-century Turko-Mongol military leader who conquered most of the Muslim world, central Asia, and parts of India.[13]

After an extended account of Tamerlane's conquests, Le Roy explains that

> "During the raigne of TAMBERLAN, began the restitution of the tongues; and of all sciences. The first that applyed himselfe to this worke was Franciscus Petrarcha, opening the Libraries which til then were shut vp; and beating away the dust and filth, from the good bookes of aunciut authours" (108–9).

The third term of comparison represented by the narrative of Islamic history here disrupts a practice of comparison between (Greco-Roman) past and (European) present, creating a genealogy for the Renaissance that abandons the implicit postulate of resemblance that subtended the more static comparisons between Greco-Roman excellence and the rest of the world. The narrative of Islamic expansion has not merely shaken the ground upon which Renaissance Humanist comparisons were made; it has effected a qualitative shift in the terrain upon which civilizations are compared.

Early Modern French Studies 37 (2/2015), 76-92. Such readings privilege the work's final chapter, in which Le Roy more or less throws up his hands in the face of the contradictions his analysis has revealed, and retreats to an invocation of Divine Providence as the only stable point of reference in human history. And because God's will is unknowable, Le Roy suggests that we might consider believing that perhaps things will get better after all. I tend to agree with the assessment of John B. Bury, who notes that "having conducted us to this pessimistic conclusion Le Roy finds it repugnant, and is unwilling to acquiesce in it. Like an embarrassed dramatist he escapes from the knot which he has tied by introducing the deus ex machina. Philosophically, Le Roy's conclusion is lame enough. We are asked to set aside the data of experience and act on an off-chance" (*The Idea of Progress: An Enquiry Into its Origin and Growth*, New York 1932, 34). Bury, however, ultimately finds in this gesture "the determination of the optimist to escape from the logic of his own argument" (ibid.). I find more desperation than optimism in Le Roy's conclusion.

13 This aspect of Le Roy's account of history was highlighted by Eric Voegelin in "Political Theory and the Pattern of General History", in: *American Political Science Review* 38 (1944); repr. in *The Collected Works of Eric Voegelin vol. 10*, Columbia, Missouri 2000, 157-167. It has also received attention from scholars of the English Renaissance working with the 1594 English translation of Le Roy's treatise, such as Mary Floyd-Wilson, *English Ethnicity and Race in Early Modern Drama*, New York 2003. For a more detailed account of Tamerlane's fortunes in Humanist letters as they informed Le Roy's portrait here, see Maria Elena Severini, Tamerlan vs. Bajazet: L'origine de la modernité chez Loys Le Roy lecteur de Machiavel, in: *Bibliothèque d'Humanisme et Renaissance* 76 (1/2014), 55-72.

This shift profoundly changes the complexion of the remark about printing and the compass, because it completely explodes the binary terms of the dominant comparison between Greco-Roman Antiquity and Renaissance Europe with which Le Roy's treatise begins. Not surprisingly, then, the thesis of a simple hierarchical inversion on the old grounds of comparison runs into further obstacles in Book X. It is indeed remarkable how quickly the celebratory tone of the opening lines of the chapter summary, announcing the "marvels of the present time," turns gloomy. Le Roy is clearly not a fan of the third great "modern" invention, heavy artillery, which he characterizes as more impetuous, swifter, and more violent than ancient weapons. It is unambiguous here that Le Roy sees these "improvements" in a negative light. This pessimistic tone is amplified by the implicit irony of the concluding lines of the title, which state that one of the "marvels" of the present age is the appearance of new and strange diseases (the chapter itself suggests he is talking about syphilis), and which further report that there has been an increase in religious strife, which has, as the English translation puts it, "weakened the mutual charity of men."

I want to take a closer look at how Le Roy characterizes the era of religious strife in Book X because this is where one can most easily grasp the complex relationship between "variety" and "vicissitude," and understand their power to destabilize the postulates of Renaissance Humanist practices of comparison. In the very same chapter in which he celebrates a widespread revival of devotion to learning and the arts, listing such quintessential "Renaissance" figures as Petrarch, Ficino, Budé, Erasmus, Sleidan, and More, Le Roy deplores the utter depravity of his age in every corner of the globe:

> "Every where the publike estates have bin afflicted, changed, or destroied; and every where the Religion troubled with heresies. Not only all Europe, but also the farthest regions of Asia, and Africk; the inhabitants of the new found lands, and of the East and West Indies being innumerable in multitude, and dispersed into infinite places, have bin troubled with foreine and civile warres, long continued: wherence hath followed the excessive price of all things, with often famines and pestilences. We must think that God being angrie with men, sendeth such calamities generally, and particularly, to correct our vices; and to bring us to a greater knowledge, and reverence of him: For there was never in the world more wickednes, more impietie, or more disloialtie; Devocion is quenched; simplicitie and innocencie mocked at; and there remayneth but a shadow of Iustice. All is turned upside downe, nothing goeth as it ought."[14]

---

14   The quote is on an unnumbered page between pages 112 and 113 in Ashley's 1594 English translation.

Le Roy's apocalyptic rhetoric enlists recognized *topoi* in the literature of the French Wars of Religion, and it is clear that the experience of those conflicts is coloring his view here.[15] The larger point, however, is that Le Roy's postulate of "variety," originally enunciated to account for the increasingly complex and multifaceted view of the past that emerged from Humanist research in Greco-Roman sources, leads him to paint an equally complex picture of the present, one in which it is hard to identify any dominant characteristic. Yes, we have compasses and gunpowder, but we are also spreading disease with the help of our compasses and blasting each other to bits with our new artillery. The postulate of variety, not just among different entities, but within them, ultimately makes it impossible to create any sort of hierarchy among the civilizations Le Roy considers in this volume; it also makes variety (cultural difference) increasingly difficult to distinguish from vicissitude (changes over time within a single culture). Both the terms and the criteria of comparison are continually shifting, and as we see in the remarks on war and disease, individual comparanda are portrayed as multifaceted and thus impossible to characterize in any definitive way. In a universe of vicissitude, every possible term of comparison is a moving target.

Throughout the work, Le Roy has chronicled how the "ordre & perfection" of Antiquity had fallen into confusion. Looking back at Le Roy's Book VI, one sees that the account of Rome's excellence has to share the same space with the account of Rome's decadence. Here, the complexity of the comparandum is less a function of the level of detail in the portrait than it is due to the factoring in of time understood as an agent of inevitable change. Once "perfection" is conceived of as a historical process rather than as a state of affairs, the "perfection" of Antiquity no longer figures as a still point of comparison, but rather becomes simply one point in time among others. It may still be "supérieure" to the present in some ways and "inférieure" in others, depending on the terms of comparison, but now its outstanding feature is simply its historical difference, another cog in the wheel of variety and vicissitude. The Ancient past as term of comparison goes from being a putatively stable, self-situating object of nostalgia and a perfect model to be imitated, to an imperfect object of imperfect knowledge that must continually be *resituated*.

Thus, in Le Roy's eleventh chapter (of twelve), in which he attempts an overall comparison between Greco-Roman Antiquity and his present day, the results are mixed. Whereas at the outset of his treatise, Le Roy assumed Greek and Roman excellence as the ground upon which civilizations could be compared, here, he performs an analysis that posits excellence (and a series of other terms) as the *tertium*

---

15 I discuss in more detail the relationship between Le Roy's writings on the French Wars of Religion and his view of history in "Le Dissensus et l'exception française: Louis Le Roy, les guerres de religion, et la politique internationale", in: Paul-Alexis Mellet/Laurent Gerbier (eds.), *Dissensus: Pratiques et représentations de la diversité des opinions 1500–1650*, Paris 2016, 127–140.

comparationis according to which civilizations, including Ancient Greece and Rome, can be evaluated. Moreover, rather than presume or establish a hierarchy between the past and the present *en bloc*, Le Roy uses the principle of variety—a principle originally articulated to manage the surfeit of information Humanist research into the Greco-Roman past had yielded—to undertake a series of subcomparisons between different aspects of each civilization. Under this new framework, we are no longer limited to contests whose finish line has been set *a priori* in Greco-Roman Antiquity. Compared with a standard exterior to Antiquity, the best philosophers still turn out to be those who lived in Ancient Greece; Demosthenes and Cicero are still considered the best orators; the best historians are Herodotus, Thucydides, Tacitus, and Livy. Yet Renaissance mathematicians are approaching the heights of Euclid and Archimedes, and astrology and cosmography are undeniably more advanced than they were in Ptolemy's time: "Cosmographie, and Astrologie, are so beautified [*illustrées*], that if Ptolomey the father of them both were alive againe, he would scarce know them [il les *mecognoistroit*], being increased [*augmentées*] in such sort by the late observations, and navigations" (126).

The (quite hazy) criteria of excellence, eminence, illustriousness, and so forth ground acts of comparison whose results do not tally with those obtained via the practice of comparison that assimilates excellence to the Antique past. Nor, as we have just seen, does Le Roy's penultimate chapter simply establish a new hierarchy on the same ground by relocating excellence in the present (or the future). We have already seen Le Roy's ambivalence in the face of the technological advances of his day; with this ambivalence in mind, we can better grasp the import of Le Roy's use of the verb "méconnaître" to describe what he imagines would be Ptolemy's reaction to Renaissance astrology and cosmography. Rather than see them as advanced forms of the sciences he fathered, Le Roy suggests that he would simply not recognize them as versions of the "same thing." This is evidence of the difficulty Le Roy has in making a theoretical distinction between progress and difference: At what point does change within a single entity (vicissitude) produce something that is not a subsequent development (whether seen as progress or degeneration), but rather a different entity entirely (variety)? If Ptolemy, the father of cosmography, does not recognize something as cosmography, can we still speak in terms of a common ground of genealogical affiliation? If we cannot, on what grounds can we compare them?

If Le Roy does in fact judge that progress has been made in astrology and cosmography—papering over the hint of incommensurability contained in his image of a Ptolemy who does not recognize what is supposed to be his own intellectual progeny—he privileges the lack of common ground between the European present and the Ancient past in a remarkable passage in his final chapter. Here, he catalogs that which distinguishes Antiquity from "our" present without reference to any hierarchy between them:

"Many things invented by the Ancients, are lost. The wisdome of the Egiptians, Persians, Indians, and Bactrians, hath not come unto us; many good Greek and Latine Authours are not found; And amongst those that remayne, there are few agreable to the present maners, and affaires. We do not build now adaies after the fashion of Vitruuius; neither tyl the ground, nor plant, according to Varro, or Columella; nor take foode or physick after the ordinance of Hippocrates, and Galen: We iudge not according to the Ciuil Law of the Romaines; neither plead we as did Demosthenes, and Cicero; or gouerne our common wealthes, by the Lawes of Solon, and Lycurgus; or following the politicke precepts of Plato, and Aristotle. We sing not as did the Auncients."(128)

This is neither a nostalgic lament nor a pitch for the latest fashion; it is simply a recognition of difference. There is no "increase"; nothing has been "beautified" (or disfigured). By virtue of having been "lost," the Ancients have gone from being "excellent" to being simply "not agreable to the present maners, and affaires." "We sing not as did the Auncients": neither better nor worse. The intersection of variety and vicissitude in Le Roy's treatise configures "cultures" and "civilizations" as polyvalent and unstable, like Heraclitus's river. His work suggests that a truly comparative history would be infinite, ranging over time and space, and enlisting varying criteria on ever-shifting grounds.

References

Ashley, Robert (ed.), *Of the interchangeable course, or variety of things in the whole world: and the concurrence of armes and learning, thorough the first and famousest nations: from the beginning of ciuility, and memory of man, to this present. Moreouer, whether it be true or no, that there can be nothing sayd, which hath not bin said heretofore: and that we ought by our owne inuentions to augment the doctrine of the auncients; not contenting our selues with translations, expositions, corrections, and abridgments of their writings. Written in French by Loys le Roy called Regius: and translated into English by R.A.*, London, 1594.

Bèze, Théodore de, *Histoire Ecclesiastique Des Eglises Reformées Au Royaume de France: en laquelle est descrite au vray la renaissance & accroissement d'icelles depuis l'an MDXXI iusques en l'annee MDLXIII, leur reiglement ou discipline*, Anvers 1580.

Bury, John B., *The Idea of Progress: An Enquiry Into its Origin and Growth*, New York 1932.

Claussen, Emma, A Sixteenth-Century Modern? Ancients and Moderns in Loys Le Roy's De la vicissitude, in: *Early Modern French Studies* 37 (2/2015), 76-92.

Felski, Rita/Friedman, Susan Stanford (eds.), *Comparison: Theories, Approaches, Uses*, Baltimore 2013.

FLORIO, John (ed.), *Essays written in French by Michael Lord of Montaigne, Knight of the Order of S. Michael, gentleman of the French Kings chamber: done into English, according to the last French edition, by John Florio reader of the Italian tongue*, London 1613.
FLOYD-WILSON, Mary, *English Ethnicity and Race in Early Modern Drama*, New York 2003.
FRANKENBERG, Günter, *Comparative Law as Critique*, Cheltenham/Northampton 2016.
FRISCH, Andrea, Le Dissensus et l'exception française: Louis Le Roy, les guerres de religion, et la politique internationale, in: Paul-Alexis Mellet/Laurent Gerbier (eds.), *Dissensus: Pratiques et représentations de la diversité des opinions 1500–1650*, Paris 2016, 127-140.
GOULART, Simon, *Memoires de l'estat de France, sous Charles IX*, "Meidelbourg" [Geneva] 1578.
GREENE, Thomas, *The Light in Troy. Imitation and Discovery in Renaissance Poetry*, New Haven/London 1982.
HAMPTON, Timothy, *Writing from History. The Rhetoric of Exemplarity in Renaissance Literature*, Ithaca/London 1990.
KELLEY, Donald, *Foundations of Modern Historical Scholarship: Language, Law, and History in the French Renaissance*, New York/London 1970.
LE ROY, Loys, *De la Vicissitude ou Varieté des choses en l'univers et concurrence des armes et des lettres par les premieres et plus illustres du monde, depuis le temps où à commencé la civilité, & memoire humaine jusques à present*, Paris 1575.
MELAS, Natalie, *All the Difference in the World: Postcoloniality and the Ends of Comparison*, Stanford 2007.
MUSA, Mark/BONDANELLA, Julia Conaway, *The Italian Renaissance Reader*, New York 1987.
NORTH, Thomas, *Lives of the Noble Grecians and Romanes*, London 1579.
POPKIN, Richard, *History of Scepticism from Savonarola to Bayle*, Oxford 2003.
QUINT, David, *Origin and Originality in Renaissance Literature: Versions of the Source*, New Haven/London 1983.
RHADAKRISHNAN, Rajagopalan, Why Compare?, in: Rita Felski/Susan Stanford Friedman (eds.), *Comparison: Theories, Approaches, Uses*, Baltimore 2013, 15-33.
SEVERINI, Maria Elena, Tamerlan vs. Bajazet: L'origine de la modernité chez Loys Le Roy lecteur de Machiavel, in: *Bibliothèque d'Humanisme et Renaissance* 76 (1/2014), 55-72.
VILLEY, Pierre/SAULNIER, Verdun L., *Les essais de Michel de Montaigne*, Paris 1965, URL: https://www.lib.uchicago.edu/efts/ARTFL/projects/montaigne/ [last accessed April 9, 2020].
VOEGELIN, Eric, Political Theory and the Pattern of General History, in: *American Political Science Review* 38 (1944); repr. in *The Collected Works of Eric Voegelin* vol. 10, Columbia, Missouri 2000, 157-167.

VOIGT, Georg, *Die Wiederbelebung des classischen Alterthums: Oder, das erste Jahrhundert des Humanismus*, Berlin 1960.

WITT, Ronald G., *In the Footsteps of the Ancients: The Origins of Humanism from Lovato to Bruni*, Leiden 2000.

YENGOYAN, Aram A. (ed.), *Modes of Comparison: Theory and Practice*, Ann Arbor 2006.

Comparison and East-West Encounter
The Seventeenth and the Eighteenth Centuries

Zhang Longxi

Abstract

East and West, as cultures and traditions, become possible to conceptualize only in comparison and in the encounters of trade, travel, and other kinds of interactions. If Marco Polo in the thirteenth century represented an early stage of the East-West encounter in trade and the expansion of geographical knowledge in Europe, the seventeenth and the eighteenth centuries became the important time of intellectual contact in East-West encounters through the mediation of Jesuit missionaries and because of the internal development of European culture and society during the time of the Enlightenment. Not only did the trend of chinoiserie changed European taste and aesthetics in material life, but philosophers like Leibniz and Voltaire found in China what they were seeking for a state and society, built on reason rather than religious belief. To revisit the East-West encounters of that time may help us attain a better understanding of comparison and difference in cross-cultural interrelations, which remains an issue of particular relevance and importance for our time today.

As Benedict de Spinoza famously put it: "determination is negation."[1] Things are defined not in and of themselves, but they become definite and recognizable always in comparison and differentiation, and it is by negating or differentiating from something else that we may determine what it is that we are contemplating. Comparison, in other words, is ontologically and epistemologically necessary and methodologically useful in our understanding and interpretation. "To compare or not to compare, unlike to be or not to be: that is *not* the question," as I have argued elsewhere. "On a most basic level, ontologically speaking, we cannot but compare, and we compare all the time in order to differentiate, recognize, understand, make judgments or decisions, and act upon our decisions. All our actions in cognitive and physical terms depend on making comparisons, and we have no other alternative but to compare."[2] The one and the many, unity and diversity, the *yin* and the *yang*

---

1 Benedict de Spinoza, Correspondence, in: Benedict de Spinoza, *The Chief Works of Benedict de Spinoza*, trans. by R. A. M. Elwes, 2 vols., New York 1951, 2:370.
2 Zhang Longxi, *From Comparison to World Literature*, Albany 2015, see 11.

or the feminine and the masculine, such basic ideas are all clearly articulated in the wisdom of both the East and the West. "All under heaven knows beauty and how it is beautiful, and ugliness is generated; and they all know good and how it is good, and the no-good is generated," says the ancient Chinese philosopher Laozi in the famous *Tao te ching* or the *Classic of the Dao*. Everything is differentiated from its opposite and also gives rise to its counterpart. "Having and not-having generate one another; difficulty and easiness complement one another," Laozi continues; "long and short are formed in comparison; high and low are mutually defined; different sounds come together to harmonize; before and after follow one another."[3] Like all such fundamental concepts and terms in binary opposition, "east" and "west" also form a pair of basic notions to orientate ourselves in comparison to acquire a sense of direction. When we speak of the East and the West as geographical regions and cultural systems on a global scale, however, that sense of direction is extraordinarily enlarged to refer roughly to the continents of Asia and Europe, and their different cultures, histories, and traditions. East and West in this sense first became possible to conceptualize only when routes of travel and trade, like the ancient Silk Road, brought peoples together from the world's far ends, and comparison of the East and the West naturally arose to give articulation to both their differences and affinities. The Silk Road was, however, so remote in time that we can hardly relate it to a particular name, a living person with a story that may reveal what life was like in its vividness and credibility.

That was the significance of Marco Polo (1254—1324), the first European well-known for his travel to the East, which came to us in a narrative with some degree of details that may give us the feel of a lived experience. Marco Polo, a Venetian, was able to travel to China when the invincible Mongol army led by Genghis Khan conquered large areas by sheer military force and opened up routes across the huge landmass of Eurasia from Siberia all the way to Eastern Europe, cutting through Central and Western Asia that used to form a barrier between East Asia and Christian Europe. Through adventurous roads and long voyages, Marco Polo went to China with his father and uncle when Kublai Khan, a grandson of Genghis Khan, ascended the imperial throne and started the Mongolian dynasty of Yuan in Chinese history. As John Larner argues, the important contribution of Marco Polo is the expansion of geographical knowledge in Europe. "The truth is that in the geographical culture of the Middle Ages from Solinus, to Isidore, to Gossuin, there is to be found nothing like the Book of Marco Polo," says Larner.[4] "Never before or since has one man given such an immense body of new geographical knowledge to the

---

3   *Laozi dao de jing* (*Laozi's Classic of the Dao with Annotations*), annotated by Wang Bi, Beijing 1985, chap. 2, 2.
4   John Larner, *Marco Polo and the Discovery of the World*, New Haven 2001, 77.

West."⁵ An indication of this new knowledge in Europe is the fact that many place names in Asia in the Catalan Atlas, which gave Europe one of the earliest glances at the vast world outside, were evidently taken from the descriptions in Marco Polo's *Travels*.

Marco Polo was not an intellectual type, however, and he went to China at the time when Kublai Khan set up the Mongol dynasty of Yuan in Chinese history, which did not provide him with much opportunity to get in touch with the Han Chinese majority and to observe traditional Chinese culture. That is part of the reason why the veracity of Marco Polo's travel to China has been questioned from time to time.⁶ In my view, however, it was the high praise of the Mongol emperor in Marco's book, more than anything else, that had made his fellow Europeans uncomfortable and doubtful. In speaking of wealth, power and prosperity, Marco compared Asia and Europe and presented a picture of Cathay or China in a very different light from what most Europeans could have imagined. For example, in commenting on Kublai Khan, he claimed that "all the emperors of the world and all the kings of Christians and of Saracens combined would not possess such power or be able to accomplish so much as this same Kubilai, the Great Khan."⁷ Statements like this sounded incredible to European readers at the time and even long after, but Marco's narrative nonetheless left a deep impression on the European mind and stimulated the imagination of a fabulously rich East. The fact that so many illuminated manuscripts of Marco Polo's *Travels* in various European languages still exist today in various libraries and museums testifies to his "considerable contemporary fame," which, as Larner remarks, was "an unparalleled record in the Middle Ages for translations effected during the life of the author."⁸ From a historical perspective, particularly looking back today with a postcolonial sensibility, we may see the importance of Marco Polo as a predecessor of East-West encounter, and we may appreciate the significance of his travels and adventures to the East as offering a way of conceptualizing East-West encounter entirely different from what has become quite dominant in the discourse on the East as Orientalism. Very different from the influential theoretical models of Orientalism and postcolonialism, Marco Polo's medieval travelogue before European colonial expansion in the nineteenth century offers a different model of East-West encounter based, as I have argued elsewhere, not on the desire "to conquer or to take possession," but "to know and

---

5   Larner, *Marco Polo and the Discovery of the World*, 97.
6   There are quite a few debunkers of Marco Polo's travels, among whom perhaps Frances Wood is most well-known for her book with a rhetorical title: *Did Marco Polo Go to China?*, London 1995.
7   Marco Polo, *The Travels of Marco Polo*, trans. by Ronald Latham, London 1968, 78.
8   Larner, *Marco Polo and the Discovery of the World*, 44.

to understand," an alternative model of East-West encounter that is especially valuable for our world today.⁹

During the Renaissance of the fifteenth and the sixteenth centuries, Marco's *Travels* became more popular and was, together with Dante's *Comedia* and Thomas Aquinas's *Summa theologica*, one of the most important books widely read by the humanists. Its fame went beyond the scholarly circles, however, and when Columbus sailed out to reach Asia, he carried a copy of Marco's *Travels*, which, says Larner, served as "a useful textbook."¹⁰ Modern historians see China as an inspiring goal for not only Columbus, but many other aspiring adventurers and explorers at the time. Because of Marco's book, Timothy Brook argues, "China held a powerful place in the popular imagination. Europeans thought of it as a place of power and wealth beyond any known scale," and the quest to get to China became "a relentless force that did much to shape the history of the seventeenth century, not just within Europe and China, but in most of the places in between."¹¹ Chinese porcelain, silk, tea, wall paper, and other material goods stimulated European artists in the seventeenth and the eighteenth centuries to create innovative and decorative works of the *chinoiserie* and the Rococo styles, while blue and white Chinese porcelain and other oriental motifs were frequently featured in Dutch still life paintings and Vermeer's interiors. Great French painters like Antoine Watteau and François Boucher all painted imaginary Chinese figures and contributed to the popularity of the *chinoiserie*. "What appears in Boucher's paintings, drawings and tapestries is the life of the Chinese as he imagined it," as I have argued in discussing the image of China in the Western mind, "joyful, peaceful, harmonious, and strange at the same time, a happy land of bright colors and fascinating details depicted with a typical gaiety and suave that are the signature of Boucher's art."¹² The image of China in the seventeenth and the eighteenth centuries in Europe was very different from that in the more recent history of the last two hundred years.

The seventeenth century was the time when images of China, fantastic and imaginary, started to emerge in poetry as well as in popular imagination. John Milton, the most learned English poet of his time, mentioned

---

9   Zhang Longxi, Marco Polo, Chinese Cultural Identity, and an Alternative Model of East-West Encounter, in: Suzanne Conklin Akbari/Amilcare A. Lannucci (eds.), *Marco Polo and the Encounter of East and West*, Toronto 2008, 295.
10 Larner, *Marco Polo and the Discovery of the World*, 140.
11 Timothy Brook, *Vermeer's Hat: The Seventeenth Century and the Dawn of the Global World*, London 2008, 19.
12 Zhang Longxi, The Myth of the Other, in: Zhang Longxi, *Mighty Opposites: From Dichotomies to Differences in the Comparative Study of China*, Stanford 1998, 32.

"the barren plains
Of Sericana, where Chinese drive
With sails and wind their cany wagons light."[13]

Such images of Chinese wagons with sails can still be found in some European *mappa mundi*, and China became associated with the change of aesthetic sensibilities in the seventeenth and the eighteenth centuries. The "cany wagons light" with sails driven by wind suit perfectly the image of things Chinese as light, delicate, dexterous, and also fragile. In Alexander Pope's mock-heroic poem, *The Rape of the Lock*, for example, the breaking of a "fragile China jar" marks an ominous moment foreboding the comic and melodramatic main action.[14] A hauntingly beautiful poem by Samuel Taylor Coleridge, in which he dreamed of Kublai Khan and his "stately pleasure-dome," shows how powerfully Marco's description of the Mongol emperor could still evoke the imagination of a romantic poet in the nineteenth century.[15] And Italo Calvino's novel, *Invisible Cities*, first published in 1972 in Italian and became widely known in numerous translations ever since, in which Kublai Khan and Marco Polo converse on Marco's journey and the many cities he had visited, provides a wonderful example of twentieth-century relevance of Marco Polo's travels in imagining the world in a time of global connectedness of peoples and cities.

For the European imagination of China or the East in the seventeenth and the eighteenth centuries, however, it was not Marco Polo, but more importantly the Jesuit missionaries, who played a central role. If Marco Polo in the thirteenth century represented an early stage of East-West encounters mainly in trade and the expansion of European geographical knowledge, for significant cultural encounters and interactions we had to wait for several more hundred years till Christian missionaries in the late sixteenth and the early seventeenth centuries—Alessandro Vilignano (1539—1606), Michele Ruggieri (1543—1607), and Matteo Ricci (1552—1610), just to mention three famous Italian Jesuits—came to the East and made the first substantive intellectual and cultural contact with China and the whole of East Asia. It was this wave of cultural and religious encounters between the East and the West that brought intercultural comparison to the fore. When Matteo Ricci arrived in Beijing of the Ming dynasty in 1601 with Emperor Wanli's (reigned 1572—1620) special permission, the China he found was a society and a culture very different from that of Europe, but affluent and well organized with a history dating back long before

---

13   John Milton, Paradise Lost, III, 437-39, in: Scott Elledge (ed.), *John Milton: Paradise Lost: an authoritative text; backgrounds and sources; criticism*, 2nd ed., New York 1993, 76.

14   Alexander Pope, The Rape of the Lock, in: Alexander Pope, *Selected Poetry and Prose*, ed. William K. Wimsatt, 2nd ed., New York 1972, 110.

15   Samuel Taylor Coleridge, Kubla Khan: Or, A Vision in a Dream, a Fragment, in: Samuel Taylor Coleridge, *The Complete Poems*, ed. William Keach, London 1997, 250.

Christ. China at that time made a deep impression on Ricci and the other Christian missionaries. Taking the Jesuit accommodation approach, Ricci learned the Chinese language and wrote his treatise on Christian doctrine in Chinese, published as *Tian zhu shi yi* [The True Meaning of the Lord of Heaven] in 1604. The Jesuits thought that the Chinese had developed such a sophisticated civilization that it was desirable to find similarities between Chinese and Christian traditions so as to achieve the ultimate purpose of converting the Chinese to Christianity.

Missionaries are compulsory comparatists. Comparing Chinese with European cultures, Ricci argued that there were "traces of Christianity" in Chinese culture and customs, including "evidences of the cross among the Chinese."[16] He also made use of his reading of Chinese classics and found in ancient Chinese texts the ideas and terms of *tian* (Heaven), *zhu* (Lord), and *shangdi* (Lord on High) as appropriate words for translating God and the other Christian concepts into Chinese. Of the Chinse word *tianzhu* (Lord of Heaven) to translate God, Ricci wrote in his diary that the missionaries "could hardly have chosen a more appropriate expression."[17] For him, Chinese and European civilizations were perfectly comparable and compatible despite obvious differences in language, culture, and history. He discussed Christian doctrine by using ancient Chinese concepts and terms and writing in the Chinese language as a fully appropriate medium. His book *Tian zhu shi yi* [The True Meaning of the Lord of Heaven] "consisted entirely of arguments drawn from the natural light of reason, rather than such as are based upon the authority of Holy Scripture," says Ricci, and it "contained citations serving its purpose and taken from the ancient Chinese writers; passages which were not merely ornamental, but served to promote the acceptance of this work by the inquiring readers of other Chinese books."[18] In the seventeenth and the eighteenth centuries, what Ricci and the other Jesuits described as the "natural light of reason" in China had a remarkable resonance with the intellectual ambience in Europe when many of the Enlightenment philosophers were seeking to establish reason as the way to organize social life out of the shadow of the Catholic Church. With confidence in the efficacy of comparison as a way to understand different cultures and traditions, Ricci was another pioneer in East-West cross-cultural understanding, who greatly contributed to the intercultural relations of Asia and Europe.

Ricci and the other Jesuit missionaries were remarkably successful in the China mission, because they had some of the high-ranking officials and even members of the royal family converted to Christianity. One prominent example was Xu Guangqi (1562—1633), an important official baptized as Paul, with whom Ricci collaborated

---

16 Matteo Ricci, *China in the Sixteenth Century: the Journal of Matthew Ricci: 1583-1610*, trans. by Louis J. Gallagher, New York 1953, 110, 111.
17 Ricci, *China in the Sixteenth Century*, 154.
18 Ricci, *China in the Sixteenth Century*, 448.

in translating the first six books of Euclid's *Elements*. Two other eminent figures were Li Zhizao (1565—1630) and Yang Tingyun (1557—1627), together with Xu, they were known as the three pillars of Chinese Catholicism, who made their home region of Shanghai and Hangzhou a center of missionary activities in late Ming China. That was already at the end of the Ming dynasty, and soon there was a tumultuous dynastic change from the Ming to the Qing in the late seventeenth century, but the new Manchu Emperors of the Qing dynasty, Shunzhi (reigned 1643—1661) and Kangxi (reigned 1662—1722), continued to befriend the Jesuit missionaries and were keenly interested in the European knowledge they brought to China. With his interest in mathematics and geometry and his friendly relations with some Jesuit fathers at the time, Emperor Kangxi in particular encouraged a hopeful vision among some Christian missionaries and their correspondents in Europe for the conversion of China into a Christian country, seeing Kangxi as potentially another Constantine the Great.

Gottfried Wilhelm Leibniz (1646—1716), for example, wrote with enthusiasm about Kangxi. "Who indeed does not marvel at the monarch of such an empire?" says Leibniz. "Yet he is educated according to custom in virtue and wisdom and rules his subjects with an extraordinary respect for the laws and with a reverence for the advice of wise men. Endowed with such eminence he seems fit indeed to judge."[19] Leibniz's follower Christian Wolff (1679—1754) was even more enthusiastic, and he considered Emperor Kangxi and Chinese rulers in general as exemplary sovereigns who had realized Plato's ideal of "philosopher-kings." To rule with the natural light of reason, the monarch should have a philosophical mind, Wolff argues. "This is the case of the Chinese, among whom kings were philosophers and philosophers kings."[20] This idea came from earlier influential works by European travelers and Jesuit missionaries, such as Juan González de Mendoza (1545—1618), Louis Daniel Le Comte (1655—1728), and Jean-Baptiste Du Halde (1674—1743), which were instrumental in presenting China as a kind of ideal polity for European scholars of the seventeenth and the eighteenth centuries. "China was the realization of Plato's dream—a state ruled by 'philosophers'," says Arthur Lovejoy in a learned and important essay, and he quoted Athanasius Kircher's *China illustrate* (1670) as an example, in which Kircher described the Chinese emperor as *"un Roy qui peut philosopher ou qui souffre du moins qu'un philosophe le gouverne et le conduit* [a king who can philosophize or at least allow a philosopher to teach and guide

---

19 Gottfried Wilhelm Leibniz, Preface to the *Novissima Sinica* (1697 /1699), in: Gottfried Wilhelm Leibniz, *Writings on China*, trans. by Daniel J. Cook/Henry Rosemond, Jr., Chicago 1994, 48.
20 Christian Wolff, On the Philosopher King and the Ruling Philosopher (1730), in: Julia Ching/Willard G. Oxtoby (eds. and trans.), *Moral Enlightenment: Leibniz and Wolff on China*, Nettetal 1992, 193.

him]."²¹ An important factor in creating this positive image of Chinese ruler as philosopher-king came from Jesuit reports about the traditional Chinese examination system, which recruited ruling elites from scholars on the basis of their knowledge as testified in the scores of their civil examinations. Without considerations of family background, wealth, or social status, the Chinese examination system, which had started in the Sui dynasty in the seventh century and was normalized in the Tang dynasty in the ninth century, did provide scholars opportunities to change their lives and use their knowledge to serve in the imperial bureaucratic system. The imperial civil examination system thus gave rise to two important concepts for European modernity, namely, meritocracy and social mobility.

Leibniz compared Europe with China and saw them as complementary to one another. In his letter to the superior of the Jesuit mission in China, Father Claude Philip Grimaldi, he proposed that "a new exchange of knowledge should take place between distant peoples"; while the Jesuits brought to the Chinese "a compendium of European knowledge," he would like to see that "the secret knowledge of the Chinese concerning the physical [world], which has been preserved and augmented through the tradition of a people who have prospered so many centuries, should also be made known to us." Leibniz thus calls for a mutual enlightenment: "let us exchange gifts and enkindle light from light!"²² In the preface to the *Novissima Sinica* (1697/1699), he rearticulated the same idea: "Certainly the condition of our affairs, slipping as we are into ever greater corruption, seems to be such that we need missionaries from the Chinese who might teach us the use and practice of natural religion, just as we have sent them teachers of revealed theology."²³ Seventeenth-century Europe, as Timothy Brook argues, was looking toward China with respect and aspiration, and this can be seen clearly in many aspects of European life. "Thus, by the beginning of the seventeenth century, the Chinese already figured in European eyes as, above all, masters in the great practical art of government," says Arthur Lovejoy. "And as such they continued to figure for nearly two hundred years."²⁴ Soon the Chinese were also praised for their perfection of morality. "By the end of the century, then," Lovejoy continues to say, "it had come to be widely accepted that the Chinese—by the light of nature alone—had surpassed Christian Europe both in the art of government and in ethics."²⁵ And that, as we shall see, was the main idea about China in Europe during the seventeenth and the eighteenth centuries.

---

21   Arthur O. Lovejoy, The Chinese Origin of a Romanticism, in: Arthur O. Lovejoy, *Essays in the History of Ideas*, Baltimore 1948, 104; quoting from a French translation of Kircher's work.
22   Gottfried Wilhelm Leibniz, Letter to Father Grimaldi (1692), in: Julia Ching/Willard G. Oxtoby (eds. and trans.), *Moral Enlightenment: Leibniz and Wolff on China*, Nettetal 1992, 64.
23   Leibniz, Preface to the *Novissima Sinica* (1697/1699), *Writings on China*, 51.
24   Lovejoy, The Chinese Origin of a Romanticism, 103-04.
25   Lovejoy, The Chinese Origin of a Romanticism, 105.

Lovejoy's main point, however, is to examine the Chinese influence on European aesthetic sensibilities and artistic practice in the late seventeenth and the eighteenth centuries, when an incipient romanticism emerged with several phenomena, including "the admiration for the Chinese garden and, in a less degree, for the architecture and other artistic achievements of the Chinese."[26] He commented on Sir William Temple as "the earliest, and certainly the most zealous enthusiast for the Chinese" in England, who thought the Chinese in political theory and practice excelled "all those imaginary schemes of the *European* wits, the Institutions of *Xenophon*, the Republic of *Plato*, the Utopias and Oceanas of our modern writers."[27] When Temple in his essay *Upon the Gardens of Epicurus* (1685) praised the Chinese idea of beauty as a natural one without the imposition of artificial order and regularity, he did not know he was, says Lovejoy, "laying down the principles of the future *jardin anglais*."[28] Through eighteenth-century English writers and poets such as William Mason, Joseph Addison, Alexander Pope and many others, the idea of natural beauty, and in particular that of the "picturesque," constituted "a prelude to Romanticism."[29] The strange word Temple used, *sharawadgi*, supposedly from the Chinese, was understood as a term conveying the Chinese idea of beauty, a kind of "natural wildness," to borrow Addison's phrase. In writing to a friend in 1750, Horace Walpole said that he was "almost as fond of the Sharawadgi, or Chinese want of symmetry, in buildings as in grounds and gardens."[30] Lovejoy cited many other writers, including Sir William Chambers, "the chief enthusiast and propagandist for Chinese gardens in the second half of the eighteenth century."[31] In all these we can see a change of taste, a rebellion against the aesthetic standards of neoclassicism, and therefore a prelude to romanticism in the late eighteenth and the nineteenth centuries. "A turning point in the history of modern taste was reached when the ideals of regularity, simplicity, uniformity, and easy logical intelligibility, were first openly impugned, when the assumption that true beauty is 'geometrical' ceased to be one to which 'all consented, as to a Law of Nature,'" says Lovejoy. "And in England, at all events, the rejection of this assumption seems, throughout most of the eighteenth century, to have been commonly recognized as initially due to the influence and the example of Chinese art."[32] Even though the idealization of the Chinese gardening eventually turned sour in England towards the latter half of

---

26 Lovejoy, The Chinese Origin of a Romanticism, 101.
27 Lovejoy, The Chinese Origin of a Romanticism, 110, quoting William Temple, *Upon Heroick Virtue* (1683).
28 Lovejoy, The Chinese Origin of a Romanticism, 111.
29 Lovejoy, The Chinese Origin of a Romanticism, 114.
30 Quoted Lovejoy, The Chinese Origin of a Romanticism, 120.
31 Lovejoy, The Chinese Origin of a Romanticism, 122.
32 Lovejoy, The Chinese Origin of a Romanticism, 135.

the eighteenth century, as an important episode in the history of ideas, the "Chinese origin" of a romanticism, as Lovejoy emphasizes, may still be valuable for us to recognize and appreciate in our own time.

In France, Voltaire's admiration of Confucius and of Chinese culture is well-known. He not only wrote a dramatic work *L'Orphelin de la Chine* (1753), based on a thirteenth-century Chinese play, but also wrote the famous *Essai sur les moeurs* (1760), in which he praised China as *"le plus sage empire de l'univers."*[33] The Chinese might not be as advanced as the Europeans of his time in mechanics or physical sciences, but, says Voltaire, "they have perfected morality, which is the first of the sciences."[34] He greatly admired Confucius for teaching virtue in absolute clarity, in "pure maxims in which you find nothing trivial and no ridiculous allegory."[35] For Voltaire and the Encyclopedists, China was not only a model of wealth as in Marco Polo's description, but a model of political state built on the foundation of rational thinking. "With Voltaire's *Essai sure les moeurs* of the year 1760 admiration of China reached its zenith," argues Adolf Reichwein in his seminal study of the intellectual and artistic encounters of China and Europe.[36] Reichwein even considered Confucius as "the patron saint of eighteenth-century Enlightenment. Only through him could it find a connection link with China."[37]

China and Confucius thus had a very positive image and influence in Enlightenment European moral and political philosophy. In material life, China was already known for such imported goods as silk, porcelain, wall paper, lacquer and many other merchandise that influenced the European taste and created the fashion of *chinoiserie*, which, as Hugh Honour argues, "may be defined as the expression of the European vison of Cathay."[38] "Sublimated in the delicate tints of fragile porcelain, in the vaporous hues of shimmering Chinese silks," as Reichwein also remarks, "there revealed itself to the minds of that gracious eighteenth-century society in Europe a vision of happy living such as their own optimism had already dreamed of."[39] The positive images of China and Confucius in Voltaire and the other Enlightenment philosophers were constructed partly on Jesuit reports sent back from China, and partly on the basis of their own social imagination. Without a predominant church and with an examination system that recruited officials and ruling

---

33 François Marie Arouet de Voltaire, *Essai sur les moeurs et l'esprit des nations et sur les principaux faits de l'histoire depuis Charlemagne jusqu'à Louis XIII*, ed. René Pomeau, vol. 1, Paris 1963, 224.
34 Voltaire, *Essai sur les moeurs*, 68.
35 Voltaire, *Essai sur les moeurs*, 70.
36 Adolf Reichwein, *China and Europe: Intellectual and Artistic Contacts in the Eighteenth Century*, trans. by J. C. Powell, New York 1925, 79.
37 Reichwein, *China and Europe*, 77.
38 Hugh Honour, *Chinoiserie: The Vision of Cathay*, New York 1961, 7-8.
39 Reichwein, *China and Europe*, 25-26.

elites from learned scholars regardless of their family backgrounds or social status, China seemed to offer a model of secular and rational life and of social mobility based on learning and knowledge, just the kind of life the Enlightenment philosophers envisioned for Europe at a time when European society was still heavily influenced by the Church and socially stratified as ruled over by a rigid hereditary system of aristocracy. As a methodology, then, comparison with China in the works of many seventeenth- and eighteenth-century writers seemed to be used more for the social critique of European life than for the understanding of a different and distant culture and society. Very much in the same way Michel de Montaigne used Brazilian cannibals to criticize the corruption of seemingly civilized Europeans, or Montesquieu's commentaries on French society through the mouthpiece of two Persian noblemen, Oliver Goldsmith in *The Citizen of the World* also satirized the British by writing from the outsider's perspective of an imagined Chinese philosopher.

The use of China as a tool for self-critique had a most curious manifestation in *An Historical Essay Endeavoring a Probability That the Language Of the Empire of China is the Primitive Language*, written by John Webb and published in 1669. As Umberto Eco observes, many European theologians, philosophers, writers and scholars were all obsessed with "the story of the confusion of tongues, and of the attempt to redeem its loss through the rediscovery or invention of a language common to all humanity."[40] The search for the perfect language had as its background the biblical story of the confusion of tongues at Babel, which put all European languages out of the pool of candidacy as they were all cursed by God to be mutually incomprehensible, and the search was motivated by the idea that humanity might find a way back to innocence and paradise if men could rediscover the primitive (in the sense of the first, primary or *première*) language created by God and spoken by Adam in the Garden of Eden before the fall. In the seventeen century, Jesuit missionaries' reports about China and its ancient history dating back far beyond biblical chronology made it possible to think of the Adamic language outside Hebrew, Egyptian, and Greek. In his dedicatory epistle to Charles II, dated 29 May 1668, Webb presented his essay as an effort to "advance the DISCOVERY of that GOLDEN-MINE of Learning, which from all ANTIQUITY hath lain concealed in the PRIMITIVE TONGUE" or "the First Speech."[41] With his syllogistic argument firmly grounded on the authority of the Holy Scripture and "credible History," Webb's argument must have impressed his contemporaries as logically simple and forceful when he says:

"Scripture teacheth, that the whole Earth was of one Language until the Conspiracy at BABEL; History informs that CHINA was peopled, whilst the Earth was so

---

40   Umberto Eco, *The Search for the Perfect Language*, trans. by James Fentress, Oxford 1994, 1.
41   John Webb, *An Historical Essay Endeavoring a Probability That the Language Of the Empire of China is the Primitive Language*, London 1669, ii, iii.

of one Language, and before that Conspiracy. Scripture teacheth that the Judgment of Confusion of Tongues, fell upon those only that were at BABEL; History informs, that the CHINOIS being fully setled before, were not there; And moreover that the same LANGUAGE and CHARACTERS which long preceding that Confusion they used, are in use with them at this very DAY; whether the Hebrew, or Greek Chronology be consulted."[42]

Webb did not know any Chinese, but drawing on Jesuit missionaries' reports and other materials available at the time and relying on the authority of the Bible, he was able to argue that "*China* was after the Flood first planted either by *Noah* himself, or some of the sons of Sem, before they remove to Shinaar," and that "it may with much probability be asserted, *That the Language of the Empire of CHINA, is, the PRIMITIVE Tongue, which was common to the whole World before the Flood.*"[43] Like Wolff and other writers at the time, Webb also declares that the Chinese are "*de civitate Dei*, of the City of God," and "their Kings may be said to be Philosophers, and their Philosophers, Kings."[44] In the modern time, all these claims may sound strange and absurd, little more than the fantasies of an uninformed Sinophile, but as Rachel Ramsey points out, Webb was a royalist and architect bitterly disappointed for failing to secure the position of the Surveyor he was hoping for and thought himself well deserved after the Restoration, and therefore, put in the context of the political reality of Restoration England and Webb's personal history, his strange argument becomes understandable as a disguised critique of the English society and the patronage system of his time as well as an expression of his personal grudges. Moreover, as an interesting episode in the seventeenth-century history of ideas, Webb's *Essay* "demonstrates how China served as an effective means for political conservatives wishing to launch a mediated critique in the erosion of their hopes for the restored monarchy," as Ramsey argues. "Perhaps more importantly, a seemingly offbeat treatise such as *An Historical Essay* suggests that China's influence on European conceptions of history, government, and patronage in the seventeenth century is more complex and nuanced than even most sinologists have recognized."[45] Indeed, the general perception of China in the West today, which tends to be negative, has been so much shaped and influenced by the more recent and very different history of the era of European colonialism and imperialism that it would take a sort of historical archeology to rediscover the image of China and the East as conceptualized in the European mind in the seventeenth and the eighteenth centuries.

---

42 Webb, *An Historical Essay*, iii-iv.
43 Webb, *An Historical Essay*, 31-32, 44.
44 Webb, *An Historical Essay*, 32, 93.
45 Rachel Ramsey, China and the Ideal of Order, in: *Journal of the History of Ideas* 62 (3/2001), 483-503, see 503.

Of course, like any complex phenomenon, interactions of peoples and cultures, and the encounter between the East and the West have always been multifaceted, and there has never been a moment in European history when the image of China is a single and unified one. In the seventeenth and the eighteenth centuries, while Leibniz and Voltaire may represent a more positive and enthusiastic view of China and Confucianism, there are other philosophers, including Jean-Jacques Rousseau, Montesquieu, and François Fénelon, who remained skeptical and critical of the Chinese political system and cultural influence. In the eighteenth century, English writers like Daniel Defoe already started to disparage the Chinese from the point of view of a militant imperialist. Generally speaking, however, we may conclude that China in the seventeenth and the eighteenth centuries stood as a foil to Europe by and large in a rather positive light, offering a model of social imaginary in ethical and political terms that fit well with what the Enlightenment philosophers were looking for—a society built on the basis of reason rather than religious faith, with social mobility for scholars who participated in governance through knowledge and learning rather than by right of inheritance of an aristocratic lineage. In comparison with Europe, China appeared attractive because of its difference, and when that different image, either authentic or distorted in idealization, suited the social and political imagination of the Enlightenment, it produced a very positive effect.

In today's world, China is emerging as an old civilization on the rise again after a long slumber and spiritual torpor in the past two hundred years. Particularly in the last forty years since the end of the disastrous ten-year-long Cultural Revolution (1966—1976), China has completely changed itself, and the rapid economic growth and quick raise of living conditions of a very large population in a big country prove to be one of the most remarkable events in world affairs that astonishes all, including the Chinese themselves. At the same time, as a country still ruled by one communist party with tight ideological control, China's rise is perceived by most Europeans and the Americans to be a challenge and even a threat to Western democracies. How to understand China as a country and a nation both old and new seems to become an intriguing and important question today. Therefore, it is far more than just to satisfy an antiquarian interest for us to look back at earlier periods of East-West encounters, and at the image of China in Europe before the age of imperialism and colonialism, an image very different from that of a weak and benighted people in decline and lethargy. Isn't history a mirror for the purpose of looking at the present? Isn't it a helpful way to make sense of our world today to revisit the world of a very different time in the spirit of equality and sympathetic understanding, the spirit of an open-minded cosmopolitanism? The future of our world will in very large ways depend on such cross-cultural understanding and better relationships between the East and the West, and for that reason comparison, particularly in terms of East-West comparative studies, has a social and political relevance to our world today as it does to its future.

References

BROOK, Timothy, *Vermeer's Hat: The Seventeenth Century and the Dawn of the Global World*, London 2008.

COLERIDGE, Samuel Taylor, Kubla Khan: Or, A Vision in a Dream, a Fragment, in: *Samuel Taylor Coleridge, The Complete Poems*, ed. by William Keach, London 1997.

ECO, Umberto, *The Search for the Perfect Language*, trans. James Fentress, Oxford 1994

HONOUR, Hugh, *Chinoiserie: The Vision of Cathay*, New York 1961.

Laozi dao de jing (Laozi's Classic of the Dao with Annotations), annotated by Wang Bi, Beijing 1985.

LARNER, John, *Marco Polo and the Discovery of the World*, New Haven 2001.

LEIBNIZ, Gottfried Wilhelm, Preface to the Novissima Sinica (1697/1699), in: Gottfried Wilhelm Leibniz, *Writings on China*, trans. by Daniel J. Cook/Henry Rosemond, Jr., Chicago 1994, 48.

LEIBNIZ, Gottfried Wilhelm, Letter to Father Grimaldi (1692), in: Julia Ching/Willard G. Oxtoby (eds. and trans.), *Moral Enlightenment: Leibniz and Wolff on China*, Nettetal 1992, 64.

LOVEJOY, Arthur O., The Chinese Origin of a Romanticism, in: Arthur O. Lovejoy, *Essays in the History of Ideas*, Baltimore 1948, 104.

MILTON, John, Paradise Lost, III, 437-39, in: Scott Elledge (ed.), *John Milton: Paradise lost: an authoritative text; backgrounds and sources; criticism*, 2nd ed., New York 1993.

POLO, Marco, *The Travels of Marco Polo*, trans. by Ronald Latham, London 1968.

POPE, Alexander, The Rape of the Lock, in: Alexander Pope, *Selected Poetry and Prose*, ed. William K. Wimsatt, 2nd ed., New York 1972.

RAMSEY, Rachel, China and the Ideal of Order, in: *Journal of the History of Ideas* 62 (3/2001), 483-503.

REICHWEIN, Adolf, *China and Europe: Intellectual and Artistic Contacts in the Eighteenth Century*, trans. by J. C. Powell, New York 1925.

RICCI, Matteo, *China in the Sixteenth Century: the Journal of Matthew Ricci: 1583-1610*, trans. by Louis J. Gallagher, New York 1953.

SPINOZA, Benedict de, Correspondence, in: Benedict de Spinoza, *The Chief Works of Benedict de Spinoza*, trans. by R. A. M. Elwes, 2 vols., New York 1951, 2:370.

VOLTAIRE, François M. A. de, *Essai sur les moeurs et l'esprit des nations et sur les principaux faits de l'histoire depuis Charlemagne jusqu'à Louis XIII*, ed. René Pomeau, vol. 1, Paris 1963.

WEBB, John, *An Historical Essay Endeavoring a Probability That the Language Of the Empire of China is the Primitive Language*, London 1669.

WOLFF, Christian, On the Philosopher King and the Ruling Philosopher (1730), in: Julia Ching/Willard G. Oxtoby (eds. and trans.), *Moral Enlightenment: Leibniz and Wolff on China*, Nettetal 1992, 193.

WOOD, Frances, *Did Marco Polo Go to China?*, London 1995.

ZHANG, Longxi, *From Comparison to World Literature*, Albany 2015.

ZHANG, Longxi, Marco Polo, Chinese Cultural Identity, and an Alternative Model of East-West Encounter, in: Suzanne Conklin Akbari/Amilcare A. Lannucci (eds.), *Marco Polo and the Encounter of East and West*, Toronto 2008, 280-296.

ZHANG, Longxi, The Myth of the Other, in: Zhang Longxi, *Mighty Opposites: From Dichotomies to Differences in the Comparative Study of China*, Stanford 1998.

Japan as the Absolute 'Other'
Genealogy and Variations of a Topos

Emmanuel Lozerand

Abstract

Japan has been the subject of a comparative discourse since the Portuguese first broached it in the sixteenth century. One of the most constant motifs of this comparative discourse is the notion of Japan as the "absolute other", an extremely alien culture, a perfect antithesis. This motive emerged early in a text written in 1585 by Jesuit Luis Frois. It has undergone several variations, like that of the "topsy-turvydom", and has recently resurfaced among several contemporary thinkers who never tire of brooding on this apparently inexhaustible topos.

If, to "compare comparisons"[1], we analyze the words that mean "compare" or "comparison" in Chinese or Japanese, we immediately notice the following: As we try to connect the Western (?) notion of the word "comparison" with its Chinese or Japanese equivalents, we do find translations quite easily; by doing so, we are creating what I would like to call a "space of translatability", between Chinese and Japanese on the one hand, and between each of these languages and our European languages on the other. So there is the notion of "comparison" both in China and Japan as well as in Europe.

As we examine the way comparisons are made in these languages, we realize the importance of its concrete dimensions, whether we compare side-by-side or cross-reference; as well as of location in space; reducing the distance between distant objects. We immediately begin to ask for the possible purposes of the comparison, whether they are cognitive (identify differences and similarities, highlight one aspect or another) or practical (identify merits and defects, make elements compete to find out which one is better, but also simply to have a relationship with and appreciate one another).

Especially in moments of historical transformation, when a given world order is disrupted by a new development, comparison can thus be a particularly effective

---

1   Emmanuel Lozerand, Comparer les comparaisons. Parcours buissonnier, in: *Socio-anthropologie* 36 (2017), 43-58 (26.11.2017), URL: http://socio-anthropologie.revues.org/3095, DOI: 10.4000/socio-anthropologie.3095.

method to face this change, diminish differences, tame strangeness, or welcome something alien; but it can also be a formidable weapon to keep the 'other' firmly at bay by pinning it down in a position from which it can not easily escape. To the actors of the day, comparison always seems to be an instrument to get a grip on the world and to organize their activities. In this respect, Japan is a remarkable case in point since it has been the subject of a comparative discourse since the Portuguese first broached it in the sixteenth century. It is a discourse led by Westerners who use interpretations of the Japanese archipelago as a benchmark for their own actions. One of the most constant motifs of this comparative discourse is the notion of Japan as the "absolute other", an extremely alien culture, a perfect antithesis. This motive emerged early on in the phrase "our moral antipodes" (*"nos antipodes en morale"*), which has undergone several variations, like that of the *"topsy-turvydom"*, and has recently resurfaced among several contemporary thinkers who never tire of brooding on this apparently inexhaustible topos.

Comparison as a tool of proselytism: Luis Frois's "Contradictions and differences of customs"

One sixteenth century text plays a fundamental and emblematic role in the history of Western representations of Japan. It was first published by a German and accompanied by a German translation in the mid-twentieth century, yet I don't know if it is even known in Germany today. Written in Portuguese in 1585 by Jesuit Luis Frois, the text is entitled *Tratado em que se contem muito susinta e abreviadamente algumas contradições e diferenças de custumes antre a gente de Europa e esta provincia de Japão*, which means "A very succinct and abridged treatise on some contradictions and differences in customs between Europeans and the inhabitants of the province of Japan". This manuscript remained unpublished and unknown for a long time, until Jesuit Josef Franz Schütte discovered it in a Madrid library in 1946. In 1955, Schütte published an annotated edition of the Portuguese text in Japan with the title *Kulturgegensätze Europa-Japan (1585)*, accompanied by a translation into his mother tongue[2]. A Japanese translation appeared in 1965 with the title *Nichiô bunka hikaku*, which means "A comparison of Japanese and European cultures"[3]. A French translation appeared in 1993, entitled *Traité de Luís Fróis, S.J. (1585) sur les contradictions de mœurs*

---

2   Luís Fróis,*Kulturgegensätze Europa-Japan [1585]. Tratado em que se contem muito susinta e abreviadamente algumas contradições e diferenças de custumes antre a gente de Europa e esta provincia de Japão*, ed. by Josef Franz Schütte, Tokyo 1955.

3   Akio Okada, *Nichiô bunka hikaku* (Daikôkai jidai sôsho [Great Voyage Series] 11), Tokyo 1965, 495-636. Republished as a paperback version (Iwanami bunko) in 1991 entitled *Yôroppa bunka to Nihon bunka* [The cultures of Europe and Japan]. There is another translation by Matsuda Kiichi and Engelbert Jorissen entitled *Furoisu no Nihon oboegaki: Nihon to Yôroppa no fûshû no*

entre Européens et Japonais (republished as a paperback in 1998 with a preface by Claude Lévi-Strauss[4]); a new Portuguese edition in 2001 under the title *Tratado das Contradições e Diferenças de Costumes entre a Europa e o Japão*, a Spanish one in 2003, *Tratado sobre las contradicciones y diferencias de costumbres entre los europeos y japoneses* (1585), an English one in 2004 entitled *Topsy-turvy 1585*, by Robin D. Gill (reissued in 2014 under the title *The First European Description of Japan*), an Italian one in 2017: *Il "Trattato" di Luís Fróis: Europa e Giappone. Due culture a confronto nel secolo XVI*. I haven't found any trace of a current edition in German since Schütte's first edition in Japan in 1955, which might be an error on my part.

As we know, since the end of the thirteenth century, Marco Polo's reports have fueled the Western notion of the existence of land called "Cipango" (or Zipangu, or Zipangri; spellings vary according to manuscripts and editions), brimming with gold, located in eastern China. "Cipango" is a distortion of the Chinese *rìbĕnguó*, which literally means "the land where the day begins", "the land of the rising sun" (*Land der aufgehenden Sonne*), which was the Chinese name for Japan, but today, is the country's official Japanese name (*Nihonkoku*). It is this imaginary region of Cipango—as represented, for example, on Paolo Toscanelli's fantastical map of 1463—that drove Christopher Columbus and his successors to take to the seas. Upon his return to Lisbon in March 1493, Columbus is purported to have said that he had just returned "from discovering the islands of Cipango"[5]. But it was not until 1542 or 1543, half a century later, that the Portuguese actually landed on what they called "Japão" (after a Malaysian name "Japang" found in Malacca), a land they then identified as Marco Polo's "Cipango". The missionaries followed the adventurers on the heels. François Xavier arrived in Kagoshima on August 15, 1549. The Jesuits were highly successful in their efforts to convert nonbelievers, and Japan seemed a particularly fertile ground for Christianization.

One of the great figures of this astounding missionary endeavor was Luis Frois[6], author of the *Tratado* that is the subject of our study, alongside Alessandro

---

chigai [Notes by Fróis on Japan: Differences in customs between Japan and Europe], Tôkyô, Chûô kôron-sha, 1983.

4 A French translation appeared in 1993, entitled *Traité de Luís Fróis, S.J. (1585) sur les contradictions de mœurs entre Européens et Japonais*, republished as a paperback in 1998 entitled *Européens et Japonais – traité sur les contradictions et différences de mœurs*, with a preface by Claude Lévi-Strauss. All our quotations of the *Traité* come from the first french edition. Cf. Luís Fróis, *Traité de Luís Fróis, S.J. [1585] sur les contradictions de mœurs entre Européens et Japonais*, ed. by Xavier de Castro/Robert Schrimpf/José Manuel Garcia, Paris 1993; Luis Fróis, *Européens et Japonais – traité sur les contradictions et différences de mœurs*, ed. by Xavier de Castro/Claude Levi-Strauss, Paris 1998.

5 Cf. José Manuel Garcia, Préface, in: Luís Fróis, *Traité de Luís Fróis, S.J. [1585] sur les contradictions de mœurs entre Européens et Japonais*, ed. by Xavier de Castro/Robert Schrimpf/José Manuel Garcia, Paris 1993, 7-39, see 7.

6 Cf. Garcia, Préface, 19-21.

Valignano (1539-1606) and João Rodrigues (1562-1633), and after François Xavier, who died in 1552. Born in Lisbon in 1532, he was raised at the court of King John III. In February 1548, he joined the Jesuit Order, and a few weeks later, at the age of only 16, embarked on a voyage to India. Arriving in Goa in October 1548, he met François Xavier. As soon as he was ordained for priesthood in 1561, he was sent to Japan where he landed on July 6, 1563. Except for a three-year stint in Macau, he spent the rest of his life in Japan and never returned to Europe. During this long period spanning more than three decades, he was immersed in the country and became an accomplished expert on Japanese language and culture, which made him indispensable to all his superiors, who, in 1579, asked him to write a "Commentary on the progress of the Faith in Japan, the composition of this land, its rulers, its inhabitants, and the wars that hindered the spread of the Gospel, as well as other details about its history"[7]. This task was the origin of his *History of Japan*—which has to be read as a history of the Christianization of Japan by the Jesuits; "the Japanese matter", as François Xavier called it. A first volume was completed in 1586, a second one in 1594. Frois arrived in Japan at a time when Christianity had its first remarkable successes in the country with the 1563 conversion of the lord (daimyo) of Omura, who came to be known as Bartholomew and died in Nagasaki in 1597, a few months after twenty-six Japanese and European clergy members were crucified in that city[8]. The event marked the beginning of a period of persecution that is echoed in Martin Scorcese's 2016 movie *Silence*. While Frois's letters were widely distributed in handwritten or printed form in the West "where they found an eager readership"[9], two other works of his met a more complicated fate.

Although his monumental *History of Japan* informed the writings of other Jesuits, such as those of Valignano, it never evolved beyond the state of a mere manuscript. It was only in 1894 that a copy was found; the first full edition was not completed until 1984.

The *Tratado* is even more mysterious, because the exact purpose of this singular, likely unfinished text of 40 sheets of 16 x 22 cm Japanese paper, dated June 14, 1585, remains unclear.

The treatise consists of 611 comparisons formulated in a few lines following a simple model—"we" (*nos*) or "people of Europe" (*gente* or *homens de Europa*) do it this way; "they" (*elles*), the Japanese (*Os Japões*) do it differently. For example: VI.15. We smell the melon at its head; the Japanese smell it at its tail. *Our cheiramos o melão pola cabeça; elles polo pé.*

---

7   Cf. Garcia, Préface, 29.
8   Cf. Fróis, *Traité de Luís Fróis*, 129.
9   Cf. Garcia, Préface, 23-29.

These comparisons are grouped by topics, because, as the author explains, "so as not to confuse certain things with others, we have ordered all this in chapters with the grace of Our Lord[10]". The *Tratado* is thus composed of thirteen thematic chapters, plus a complementary one, each containing 19 to 68 comparisons:

Chapter I. Men, their personality & their clothes.
Chapter II. Women, their personality & their customs (the longest with 68)
Chapter III. Children & their customs.
Chapter IV. Monks & their customs.
Chapter V. Temples, icons, and matters relating to the exercise of their religion.
Chapter VI. The way Japanese people drink & eat.
Chapter VII. Offensive & defensive weapons of the Japanese & warcraft.
Chapter VIII. Horses.
Chapter IX. Diseases, doctors & medicines. (the shortest chapter with 19)
Chapter X. Japanese writing, their books, paper, ink & letters.
Chapter XI. Houses, workshops, gardens & fruits
Chapter XII. Boats, their uses & "dogus" [ship equipment]
Chapter XIII. Plays, farces, dances, songs & musical instruments of Japan.
Chapter XIV. Some miscellaneous items & extraordinary things that would not fit in any of the previous chapters.

Comparisons were very popular in the Renaissance, in particular comparisons between Antiquity and the Modern Age, as is evident, from works such as Nicolas Machiavel's 1531 *Discourses upon the First Decade of Titus Livius*; but also, thanks to the expansion of their world, between indigenous peoples and Europeans, as in Jean de Léry's 1578 *History of a Voyage to the Land of Brazil*. The Jesuits in Japan were just as prolific, such as Valignano who, immediately upon his 1579 arrival on the archipelago, drew up an inventory of the differences between the Chinese and the Japanese[11].

It should be noted, however, that it was not at all a foregone conclusion that such a text would have to be a survey of differences, since the very first descriptions of Japan in Western languages focused more on similarities than on differences. This is the case for José Alvares's *Information on Matters of Japan*[12]. The navigator was in Japan in 1547 and wrote this text upon his return to Malacca at the request of François Xavier; it is also true for a letter from Father Nicolas Lanzillotto, written in Goa in 1548, probably based on a report by Anjirô, a Japanese man who fled his

---

10 Fróis, *Traité de Luís Fróis*, 41.
11 Cf. Robert Schrimpf, Commentaire, in: Luís Fróis, *Traité de Luís Fróis, S.J.* [1585] *sur les contradictions de mœurs entre Européens et Japonais*, ed. by Xavier de Castro/Robert Schrimpf/José Manuel Garcia, Paris 1993, 119-180, see 136.
12 Cf. Schrimpf, Commentaire, 163-172.

country aboard Alvares's ship[13]. But what is the logic behind Frois's comparisons, given that never expressly stated the purpose of his comparative endeavor? First of all, let's point out that there is something paradoxical about it. While the pattern of comparison might seem simplistic, even primordial, in its plain binarism, all commentators nevertheless agree on the high quality of its observations, to the point that historians of sixteenth century Japan consider the work as quality source of the utmost importance. Admittedly, some of his observations are stunningly accurate:

> XIV, 48: We clean our nostrils with our thumb or index finger; they, whose nostrils are very narrow, do it with their little finger.

Or:

> I, 10. Because of our buttons and laces, we cannot easily lay our hands on our bodies; Japanese men and women do not have this problem: in every season, and especially in winter, they wear wide, hanging sleeves, holding their hands right up against their bodies.

As for his approach per se, the very title of his manuscript already suggests that Frois was aware that not all of his comparisons are of the same nature, since he speaks of *"contradictions and differences"* (*contradições e diferenças*). He takes obvious pleasure in spotting genuine opposites or symmetries—is that what he means by "contradictions" (*contradições*)?

For example:

> I.11. We wear the best clothing on top and the poorest underneath; they wear their best clothes underneath and the poorest on top.
> III.1 In Europe, we regularly cut our children's hair; in Japan, they let it grow until the age of fifteen.
> III.9. Our children learn to read first and then write; children in Japan start writing first, and then learn to read.
> VI.41. We are reluctant to eat dog meat, but we do eat beef; they are reluctant to eat beef, but quite like to eat dog meat for medical purposes.
> VI.26. In Europe, we cool the wine; in Japan, they heat it before they drink it in almost every season.
> VI.55. In Europe, we eat wild boar cooked; the Japanese eat it in thin, uncooked slices.
> XI.22. In Europe, horse manure is spread in the gardens and human excrements are thrown on the streets. In Japan, horse manure is thrown on the street, and human excrements are used in the gardens.

---

13   Cf. Schrimpf, Commentaire, 173-180.

Not to mention two other peculiarities to which we have become accustomed in the age of mangas and futons:

> X.4. Where the last pages of our books end, theirs begin.
>
> XI.14. Our mattresses always stay in place on our beds; Japanese mattresses are rolled up and stored away, hidden from view.

But often, the comparisons seem to be mere "differences" (the *diferenças* mentioned in the title?). The boundary between the two categories *contradições* and *diferenças* is not always very clear:

> I.30. For us, black is the color of mourning; for the Japanese, it is white.
>
> I.49. We wash our clothes by rubbing them with our hands; they do it by treading them with their feet.

The following examples, however, can hardly be called "contradictions". They are simple "differences":

> I.6. The honor and elegance that Europeans put in their beards, the Japanese put in their hair, which they wear tied in the neck.
>
> VI.2 Our everyday food is wheat bread; the Japanese staple is boiled unsalted rice.
>
> VI.24. Europeans enjoy chickens, partridges, pâtés and white meats; the Japanese love to eat jackals, cranes, monkeys, cats, and raw seaweed.
>
> VI.27. Our wine is made of grapes; theirs is made of rice.
>
> IX.15. We pull out teeth with forceps, pincers, parrot beaks [a kind of shoe stripper], etc.; the Japanese do it with a chisel and a mallet, or a bow and arrow attached to the tooth, or even forge hooks.
>
> XIV.21. We emphasize nouns; the Japanese verbs.

Another type of opposite that Frois highlights is that of presence and absence. What one people does, the other just doesn't do:

> VI.21. We wash our hands before and after meals; the Japanese, who do not eat with their fingers, have no need to wash their hands.
>
> II.22. Women in Europe wear rings with gems and other jewels; Japanese women do not use ornaments, neither gold nor silver jewelry.

Japanese customs can sometimes seem really strange (from a Western point of view):

> VI.14. We count the hours from 1, 2, 3 to 12, the Japanese count them this way: 6, 5, 4, 4, 9, 8, 7, 6, etc.
>
> XIV.3 In our country, when a fire breaks out, everyone comes running with water and demolishes the neighboring houses, the Japanese get on the other roofs, waving straw fans and shouting at the wind to go away.

II.47. In our country, female first names are inspired by saints; Japanese women are named after pots, cranes, water turtles, sandals, tea, reeds, etc.

But the most striking aspects are variances judgments of decorum or tact:

I.45. In Europe, it is inappropriate to get undressed, even to bare just the bottom of one's feet, to warm oneself at the hearth; in Japan, someone standing by the fire is not ashamed to get naked for the same purpose.
VI.60. In our country, burping at the table in front of guests is very rude; in Japan, it is very common and no one takes offence.

To be more precise, when the Japanese act differently from "us" Europeans in a way that may seem shocking to us, they too have their own point of view, and therefore their own sense of what is right or wrong, good or bad:

I.29. We find it discourteous if a servant does not stand while the master is seated; in their case, it is wrong not to have the servant sit down.
VI.39. We like dishes made with milk, cheese, butter or bone marrow; the Japanese abhor all that and it smells very bad to them.

When it comes to value judgments, they also interpret things their own way:

I.27. We consider walking to be pleasant, healthy and recreational; the Japanese never go for walks and are very surprised to see us do something they consider a chore or a penance.

A modern reader will also be surprised by the fact that Frois does not express any clear hierarchy in his listing of differences between Europeans and the Japanese. In general, Frois does not seem to have any sense of superiority or feel any contempt for the Japanese.

Certainly, Japan does not seem perfect to him in all respects. For instance, he seems to find it hard to appreciate Japanese theater and music:

XIII.9. In our country, masks go down all the way to the tip of the beard; Japanese masks are so small that you can see the beard of the actors who play women.
XIII.15. In our country, choral music is resonant and soft; that of Japan, where they all blare out with one voice, is the most horrible music you'll ever hear.

It also seems to him that European men are generally better built than Japanese men, and he considers European horses to be far better.

I.1 Most Europeans are of tall stature and well built; the Japanese are usually smaller in body and stature than we are.
I.5. Most Europeans have a thick beard; most Japanese have sparse and very untidy beards.
I.11. In our country, it is considered a blemish to have scars on your face; the

> Japanese pride themselves on them, and as the scars are poorly cared for, they are even more unsightly.
> VIII.1 Our horses are very beautiful, those of Japan are much inferior to them.
> VIII.2 Ours stop immediately while in full stride, their horses are less docile.

But the domain where he loses all equanimity and becomes outright hostile and unilateral is the subject of religion, or more precisely that of the Japanese Buddhist clergy, the monks, of whom he paints a ferocious picture, particularly in chapters IV and V of his *Tratado*:

> IV.1 In our country, men enter the clergy to do penance and find salvation; Japanese monks do so to escape work and live a life of idle pleasures.
> IV.25. In all things, we hate and abhor the demon; Japanese monks worship and adore him, build temples and make great sacrifices to him.
> III. 10 Our teachers teach the children doctrine and holy and virtuous manners; Japanese monks teach them music, singing, games, fencing, and do their abominable things with them.
> V.8. [Our religious imagery] is beautiful and inspires devotion; theirs is horrible and terrifying with devilish figures raging in the flames.

Frois also makes several observations to highlight a particular cruelty of the Japanese:

> I.24. We practice sword fighting on poles or animals; the Japanese do it on human corpses.
> IV.41. In Europe, upon the death of their master, his servants escort the deceased to the tomb and mourn him; in Japan, some open their own bellies and others slice off their fingertips and throw them into pyre where the body is burned.
> VII. 41. It is a grave sin for us to kill; when the Japanese are at war and can no longer go on, they open their bellies, which is considered a sign of great valor.
> XIV. 6. In our country, killing a man is shocking, while killing cattle, chickens, or dogs is not shocking at all; the Japanese are shocked to see us kill animals, but in their country killing people is commonplace.
> XIV.9. We do not have crucifixion; in Japan, it is a very common punishment.
> XIV.10. In our country, servants are punished and slaves are whipped; in Japan, punishment and chastisement is beheading.

And even:

> XIV.24. In our country, killing flies with one's hand is considered dirty, in Japan princes and lords do it, tearing off the wings before throwing them away.

Another very interesting chapter is the one on women, which begins as follows:

II.1 In Europe, the honor and greatest asset of a young woman is her modesty and the unviolated sanctuary of her purity; the women of Japan do not care about virgin purity at all; and losing it does not dishonor them or prevent them from marrying.

In this vein, some of their behaviors seem downright criminal to him:

II.38. In Europe, abortion, as far as it even exists, is not frequent; in Japan, it is so common that some women have up to twenty abortions.

II.39. In Europe, killing a newborn is a rare occurrence that almost never happens; Japanese women smother their babies by stepping on their necks, killing almost everyone they think they can't feed.

Generally, Japanese women seem very indecent to him:

II.54. In Europe, it is very inappropriate for a woman to drink wine; in Japan it is very common; on holidays, they sometimes drink until they are rolling on the ground.

He doesn't, however, seem sensitive to their charm:

II.16. European women find ways and means to whiten their teeth; Japanese women use iron and vinegar to make their mouths and teeth as black as coal.

II. 4 European women scent their hair with pleasant essences; Japanese women always smell bad from the oil they grease themselves with.

However, he is able to see the positive aspects of what he encounters:

II.13. Europeans very quickly get white hair; Japanese women can reach sixty years of age without a single white hair, because they grease it with oil.

Beyond that, however, Frois paints a portrait of the women's situation in Japan that might perhaps even have appealed to European women of his time (even if he himself did not necessarily think well of what he described):

II.32. In our country, according to their corrupt nature, it is men who reject their wives; in Japan, it is often women who reject the men.

II.34. In Europe, young girls and maidens are confined constantly and very rigorously; in Japan, girls go wherever they want by themselves, for one or more days, without having to account to their parents for it.

II.35. Women in Europe do not leave the home without their husbands' consent; Japanese women have the freedom to go anywhere they want, without their husbands knowing anything about it.

II.45. In our country, women rarely know how to write; an honorable woman in Japan would be held in low esteem if she did not know how to do so.

II.51. In Europe, it is usually women who prepare food; in Japan, men and even gentlemen take pride in cooking.

One area where Frois seems to consider the Japanese to be clearly superior is that of childrearing.

> III. 6 In our country, a four-year-old child does not yet know how to eat with his hands, while in Japan, children from the age of three eat on their own using *faxis* [chopsticks].
>
> III.11. Children in Europe reach adolescence before they even know how to write a note; in Japan, children seem to have written fifty of them by the age of ten, judging by the intelligence and judgment they exhibit.
>
> III.12. In our country, a young man barely knows how to handle the sword before he reaches twenty years of age; Japanese boys from twelve or thirteen years of age carry *catanas* and *vaqizaxis*.
>
> III.13. Our children show little judgment and refinement in their manners; those in Japan do it so early that one must admire them.
>
> III.14. Our children are mostly shy and reserved when they go to the theater, Japanese children are uninhibited, free, graceful, and lively in their roleplay.

Each comparison gives the advantage to Japanese children. Sometimes it is unclear why, because while Frois notes:

> III.7. We whip and punish our boys; in Japan, they rarely do that or even just reprimand them.he also adds:
>
> III.15. Europeans are raised with lots of hugs and sweetness, good food and good clothes; Japanese children are half naked and almost deprived of tenderness and attention.

There are other areas in which he considers Japan to be superior:

> I.33. We spit all the time and anywhere; the Japanese usually swallow their saliva.
>
> VI.1 We eat everything with our fingers; Japanese men and women use two chopsticks from childhood.
>
> IX.8. The flesh of the Europeans, which is delicate, heals very slowly; that of the Japanese, which is very robust, heals much better and faster from serious wounds, lacerations, pustules [abscesses], or accidents.

So what are we to make of this, what are the intentions or effects of this remarkable comparative system set up by Frois? Of course, his careful, almost obsessive alignment of a very large number of precise and varied observations (more than 600, let's recall) must, at least at first sight, give the impression of strong otherness, even bizarreness. The mechanical repetition of the binary difference "us *versus* them" – never relieved by the slightest statement of even the smallest similarity – seems to create a spectacular, impassable cultural gap. As Valignano said in his *Summario*, "everything is so different and contrary that they are almost nothing like us"[14].

While this sentiment is undeniable, the effects of Frois's system are more complex and subtle than it seems. Another effect of this enumeration of differences is to put a crack into European ethnocentrism, to limit its universalist claims, to introduce a form of relativism: Overall, by their sheer number and variety, Frois's observations prove that one can live quite well with a lifestyle that is starkly different from the European way of life.

Even more importantly, the systematic nature of the differences rouses a notion that the apparent oddness of the Japanese is perhaps more reasonable than it seems, that their behaviors, however amazing and confusing they may be, have their own inherent logic.

On January 14, 1549, even before he landed in Japan, François Xavier wrote to Ignatius of Loyola:

> "I'm sending you the Japanese alphabet. Japanese writing differs greatly from others because the Japanese start from the top and go down. I asked Paul, the Japanese man, why they don't write our way. He answered me: Why don't you write our way?... And he gave me the reason that, just as a man has his head up in the air and his feet down on the ground, he must write from top to bottom, as well. "[15]

What can one reply to that? What Xavier implies here was expressed bluntly in 1588 by another Jesuit, Maffei, just three years after Frois's *Tratado*:

They have their reasons to act the way they do [...] Europeans can only seem ridiculous to them, for the same reason that they seem ridiculous to Europeans.[16]

Not only does Frois often mention that the Japanese find us as different from them as we find them different from ourselves, but reading his text, one gets the notion that the Japanese are in a way symmetrical or inverted European figures, and thus resembling them. All of a sudden, the apparent differences no longer seem so fundamental. In many areas, in fact, the Japanese share the same fundamental values and principles as we do, but they apply them differently. To return to the first example we mentioned, it does not matter that they smell a melon at its tail and we at the top; ultimately, we both just want to pick a good melon by its smell. How exactly we achieve that does not really matter. As Lévi-Strauss pointed out in his 1998 preface, Frois really just repeated an argument by Herodotus from the 5th century BC according to which the Egyptians "in all things behave the opposite way from other peoples". As Lévi-Strauss explains, "the symmetry we recognize

---

14 Cf. Schrimpf, Commentaire, 157.
15 Cf. Frédéric Tinguely, Le monde multipolaire des missionnaires Jésuites, in: Frédéric Tinguely (ed.), *La Renaissance décentrée. Actes du colloque de Genève*, Genève 2008, 67.
16 Cf. Frédéric Tinguely, *La Lecture complice. Culture libertine et geste critique*, Genève 2016, 49-63.

between two cultures unites them by their very contrast". As Plato says in Lysis, "it is the most opposite that is the closest friend of its opposite". In his search for symmetry, the traveler equips himself with "the means to tame strangeness, to make it familiar"[17].

Thus, we can hypothesize that one of the purposes of Frois's comparative system was to describe a people ideally suited to be converted to Christianity, because, despite its apparent otherness, it seems to be much closer to European Christians than one first imagined. Their shortcomings, the immorality of monks and women, are presented as mere obstacles to be overcome, and compensated by the qualities of Japanese children that are assets, if not a great promise. This analysis is, of course, consistent with the assumption that the *Tratado* may have served as an introduction to *History of Japan*. This assumption finds further support in this remark in Frois's preface:

And many of their customs are so foreign & distant from ours that it seems almost incredible that there can be so many opposites in a people of such great policy, alertness of mind, and natural wisdom as they possess[18].

Valignano developed a similar analysis two years earlier in his *Sumario* of 1583:

"And what I admire is that in everything, they govern themselves as a prudent and policed nation, while it would not be surprising if they behaved like barbarians. But to see that everything is the reverse from the way it is in Europe (*todo van al revés de Europa*) and that they have been able to organize their rites and customs in such a regulated and reasonable way (*tan políticas y puestas en razón*) for those who understand them well (*para quien bien las entiende*), is cause for great admiration (*es cosa que puede causar no pequeña admiració*)."[19]

We can thus understand François Xavier's enthusiasm, which resonates in the comments later reported by Frois: All the way from Rome to Japan, there is no people more predisposed to embrace Christianity than the Japanese (letter dated October 25, 1564).[20]

One can easily guess the exaltation that this promise immediately aroused in Europe. For example, in *Marvels of the world and mainly about admirable things about India and the New World*, published in 1553, Guillaume Postel, based on the very first letters of Francis Xavier, described "Giapan" as the "sovereign point of the East", and the "Giapangians" as "the most perfect humans in the world": "Thus it pleased God[to] to make them long ago."[21]

---

17 Lévi-Strauss, Claude, Préface, in: Luís Fróis, *Européens et Japonais – traité sur les contradictions et différences de mœurs*, ed. by Xavier de Castro/Claude Levi-Strauss, Paris 1998, see 7-11.
18 Fróis, *Traité de Luís Fróis*, 41.
19 Cf. Tinguely, *La Lecture complice*, 49-63.
20 Cf. Schrimpf, Commentaire, 123.
21 Cf. Bernard Frank, *Dieux et bouddhas au Japon*, Paris 2000, 36.

Other classical comparisons: our "moral antipodes"?

In certain ways, Frois's comparative work has remained unparalleled. Even though the text as such was not published or widely distributed before the second half of the twentieth century, the mindset it represents has doubtlessly been exerting a strong subliminal influence on Western representations of Japan. In order to better grasp the impact of this inspiration and understand which types of variations have emanated from it, we must compare it to other takes on Japan. As we will see, they also addressed the question of Japan's *alterity*, or otherness, albeit in a distinctly different way. We find a first interesting variation in Frois's own environment, for example in a letter by Valignano dated 25 July 1579:

> "When it comes to attire and food, and in almost all their demeanor, they are so different from European or other races that one almost thinks they are making a deliberate effort to act the opposite way from everyone else, in particular from the Chinese, to whom they trace back their origins. In every way, they are trying to do just the opposite. [...] Japan is a world apart and the people there behave in a thousand original ways that are novel to the rest of humanity."[22]

In his *Summario* of 1583, he writes: "One might say that they have done all they can in order not to resemble any other nation."[23]

This notion, a fleeting idea amongst the missionaries, that Japan was not merely different, but that there was a distinct intention and *will to be different*, was eloquently expressed by major seventeenth century Jesuit priest François Garasse. In his *Curious doctrine of the beaux esprits of our times, or those who pretend to be*, written between 1623 and 1624, he harnesses the Japanese argument to attack libertines. When he calls the Japanese "true idiots", "extravagant in their actions [...] and consequently quite foolish", it is precisely because they "purposefully" seek to be different, just like the libertines. The same desire to stand out, to distinguish oneself by being the opposite of the ordinary, he argues, is the basis of the moral affinity between these strong-minded *esprits forts*[24]. As Garasse puts it, "Thank God that we in Paris have Japanese folks who wallow in fanciful extravagance in order to be taken for more artful people and join the ranks of the Beaux Esprits".

Garasse was, in fact, influenced by the *History of Navigation* by Jan Huygen van Linschoten (1563-1611), which was published in Dutch in 1596 and in French in 1610, resuming the Jesuit practice of contrasting the Japanese with other peoples, yet putting them in a conceptual framework taken from Juan Gonzalez de Mendoza's 1585 *History of the Great Kingdom of China*. This work elaborates on the theme of

---

22 Cf. Schrimpf, Commentaire, 136-137.
23 Cf. Schrimpf, Commentaire, 157.
24 Cf. Tinguely, *La Lecture complice*, 49-63.

the Japanese people's "extreme resentment" towards the Chinese, thus making the Japanese cultural difference, in the words of Frédéric Tinguely, a "vindictive commemoration, by their very customs, of a break with the legitimate powers[25]". The philosophers of the Age of Enlightenment were to engage in a different type of instrumentalization. For example, in his 1748 work *The Spirit of the Laws*, in chapter 13 of book 6, entitled "The Powerlessness of Japanese Laws", Montesquieu cites the case of Japan to illustrate his notion of despotism (and, in doing so, reactivating Aristotle's ancient theme of "oriental despotism").

> "Extravagant penalties can corrupt despotism itself. Let us look at Japan. In Japan, almost all crimes are punished by death because disobedience to so such a great emperor as Japan's is an enormous crime. It is not a question of correcting the guilty man, but of avenging the prince. These ideas are drawn from servitude and derive chiefly from the fact that the emperor is the owner of all the goods and so almost all crimes are committed directly against his interests. [...] It is true that the astonishing character of these opinionated, capricious, determined eccentric people who brave every peril and every misfortune seems at first sight to absolve their legislators for their atrocious laws."[26]

Here, the bizarre nature of the Japanese people serves to explain the severity of their laws. In contrast, Voltaire highlighting only similarities in chapter CXLII of his 1756 work "About Japan" in his *Essay on the Manners and Spirit of Nations*, assuming the view that "at its core, human nature is the same everywhere":

> "Of all the countries of India, Japan is not the one that deserves the least attention from a philosopher. [...] This kingdom borders on our continent, as we delimit it on the opposite side. I don't know why the Japanese have been called our moral antipodes, there are no such antipodes amongst peoples who cultivate reason. The dominating religion in Japan allows for rewards and penalties beyond death. Their principal commandments, which they call divine, are exactly like ours. Lies, impudence, theft, murder, are also forbidden, it is natural law condensed into concrete principles. [...] Their customs may be different from ours, but so are those of all the oriental nations, from the Dardanelles all the way to Korea."[27]

Let's briefly turn our attention to the expression he cites: "our moral antipodes". Even though it seems to echo Frois's *contradictions and differences in customs*, its exact origin is difficult to determine. In his *Curious doctrine*, Garasse attributed it to Mafffei, who supposedly spoke of "*antipodas morum*" in his 1588 *Historiarum Indicarum*. Garasse paraphrases the expression by saying "they are so extravagant that

---

25 Tinguely, *La Lecture complice*, 49-63.
26 Montesquieu, *L'Esprit des lois*, Paris 1817, 73.
27 Voltaire, *Essai sur les mœurs* (Œuvres complètes de Voltaire, 18), Paris 1784, 277.

they are antipodes in manners and customs", but researcher Frédéric Tinguely reports not having found the expression in the cited source[28].

Whatever the exact origin of the expression, it was quite popular. In a description of Japan from 1600, Joao de Lucena, whose observations follow Frois's narrative about starkly different manners, points out that Japanese customs "are remarkable only because of the great difference from our own", adding: "It is safe to say that the Japanese are our antipodes even more by their manners than by their location."[29]

In 1626, François Solier proposed explanations that resemble those of Luis Frois. He, too, uses the formula:

"Because in all their ways, they do things so differently from us that it seems as if they purposefully want to do everything reversely from Europe. This is what caused a very erudite and eloquent figure of our time to describe them as our antipodes, both in temperament and in a location and country. It would take too long to note all the particularities. I will list only a few here."[30]

While this discourse on the Japanese as "antipodes" echoed throughout the seventeenth century, the notion was refuted by several eighteenth century authors, from Father Charlevoix in his *History of Japan*, first published in 1715, to Voltaire in 1756, as we have seen, but also Simon-Nicolas-Henri Linguet in his 1768 *Impartial History of the Jesuits*. Charlevoix wrote:

"It may not be a bad idea for me to now elaborate a little on this parallel, certainly much more suitable to get to know the Japanese than to point out some contrasts between their customs and ours, which have been eagerly collected, and that led us to the conclusion that they should be called our moral antipodes. To quote some examples, they use white as their color of mourning, and black as an expression of joy [...]; they wear ceremonial clothes inside the house, and take them off when they go out; in Japan, they greet with their feet instead of their hands or heads. These things have nothing to do with one's way of thinking, let alone one's feelings of the heart, which truly constitute the character of the mind; they are pure customs, which may have been born from a simple whim, or something even less significant."[31]

Linguet wrote:

---

28   Tinguely, *La Lecture complice*, 49-63.
29   Cf. Garcia, Préface, 39.
30   François Solier, *Histoire ecclésiastique des isles et royaumes du Japon (Ecclesiastical History of the Islands and Kingdoms of Japan). Collected by Father F. Solier, monk of the Jesuit Order, Paris*, ed. by Sébastien Cramoisy, 1627-1629, 2 volumes, Bordeaux 1628, 66.
31   Père Charlevoix, *Histoire et description du Japon*, Tours 1842, 20.

"The Japanese have customs that many of our Europeans have found extraordinary. They mourn in white; they greet each other by wiggling their shoes. This led travelers with little common sense to call them our moral antipodes, as if it were morality that governs the color of our clothes and our forms of salutation. Rather, we should have admired the similarity between so many of our own practices and those of these islanders, whom nature placed at the bottom of Asia."[32]

While Charlevoix minimizes the differences in Japanese customs by attributing them to the simple effect of their long isolation, Linguet, in a Voltairean tradition, laments that we have not been more sensitive to the similarities between them and us. As we can see, there are varying motives for the "difference and contrast of customs". Garasse leverages these differences to vilify both Libertines and Japanese in one fell swoop by insinuating malicious intentions. Montesquieu uses the Japanese otherness as the very picture of despotism. While Garasse considers the notion of "moral antipodes" a sign of reprehensible extravagance, those who believe in religious conversion, like Charlevoix, contest it, as do those who insist on the proximity between the Japanese and the Europeans, like Voltaire.

Modern variations: Japan as the *topsy-turvydom*

In the nineteenth century, the discourse on Japanese otherness took a sharp turn, influenced by several factors, including the rise of a racial discourse. Without dwelling on a subject that would take us too far, let's just point out that from the 10th edition of Linné's *Systema Naturae* in 1758, then in Blumenbach's *De Generis Humani Varietate Nativa* in 1775, or in Gobineau's *Essay on the Inequality of Human Races* from 1853 onwards, these discourses profoundly changed descriptions of human diversity.

While Frois, in the tradition of Marco Polo, considered the skin of the Japanese as white:

I.8 In our country, there are many men and women with freckles on their skin; there are very few in Japan, although they are white.

Nineteenth century writings placed the Japanese in the category of the "yellow race", as is the case with Gobineau: "Japan therefore seems to have tend in the direction of Chinese civilization as a result of many yellow immigrants." The yellow race is defined as follows:

"In terms of their customs, none of these strange excesses that are so common among dark-skinned people. Weak desires, a will that is rather obstinate than ex-

---

32 Simon Linguet, *Histoire impartiale des Jésuites*, Paris 1768, 360.

treme, a perpetual but quiet taste for material pleasures; gluttony is rare, more variety than the negroes have in the dishes tended to satisfy it. In all things, tendencies towards mediocrity; fairly good comprehension of all matters that are neither too sublime nor too profound; love for what is useful, respect for rules, awareness of the advantages of a certain measure of freedom. The yellows are practical people in the narrow sense of the word. They do not dream, do not appreciate theories, they invent little, but are able to appreciate and adopt what is useful. Their desires are limited to living as gently and comfortably as possible. It is obvious that they are superior to the negroes. They are a population and petty bourgeoisie that any civilizer would love to choose as the basis of his society: there is not, however, anything to create this society or to give it spirit, beauty and action."[33]

We have left the realm of concrete, reasonable, and localized observations, of differences in customs. Instead, we are seeing a globalizing, abstract, and general discourse on a psychological and moral disposition.

In particular, the new opening of Japan in the mid-nineteenth century following the expedition of Commodore Perry in 1853 revived the discourse on Japanese particularities, now gradually giving rise to the English adjective *topsy-turvy*.

Rutherford Alcock, the first diplomat deployed to in Japan in 1858, explains in his 1863 *The Capital of the Tycoon*:

"Japan is essentially *a country of paradoxes and anomalies*, where all—even familiar things—put on new faces and are curiously reversed. Except that they do not walk on their heads instead on their feet, there are few things in which they do not by some occult law, to have been impelled in a perfectly opposite manner and a reversed order. [...] The course of all sublunary things appears reversed. Their day is for the most part our night, and this principle of antagonism crops out in the most unexpected an bizarre way in all their moral being, customs and habits."[34]

The word *topsy-turvy* appears in his book, but in a concrete sense, to describe inverted furniture.

Topsy-turvy was first used in 1888 to characterize Japan in Percival Lowell's influential work *The Soul of The Far East*. For Lowell, Japan's *"antipodal situation"* causes the Japanese to "see everything topsy-turvy". This work has never been translated into French (it was translated into German in 1911 under the title *Die Seele des Fernen Ostens*), but it has nevertheless had a significant influence in France, since it is at the root of an inexhaustible theme, namely the absence of personality, individuality, or subject in Japan. It can be found in the works of Alexandre Kojève, Jacques

---

33   Joseph Arthur Gobineau (Comte de), *Essai sur l'inégalité des races humaines*, vol. I, Paris 1853, 215.

34   Robin D. Gill, *Topsy-turvy 1585*, Key Biscayne 2004, 38-39.

Lacan, and Roland Barthes[35], and it is also, as we will see, at the root of Augustin Berque's theses on the Japanese milieu[36]. Lowell writes:

> "If we take, through the earth's temperate zone, a belt of country whose northern and southern edges are determined by certain limiting isotherms, not more than half the width of the zone apart, we shall find that we have included in a relatively small extent of surface almost all the nations of note in the world, past or present. Now if we examine this belt, and compare the different parts of it with one another, we shall be struck by a remarkable fact. The peoples inhabiting it grow steadily more personal as we go west. So unmistakable is this gradation of spirit, that one is tempted to ascribe it to cosmic rather than to human causes. It is as marked as the change in color of the human complexion observable along any meridian, which ranges from black at the equator to blonde toward the pole. In like manner, the sense of self grows more intense as we follow in the wake of the setting sun, and fades steadily as we advance into the dawn. America, Europe, the Levant, India, Japan, each is less personal than the one before. We stand at the nearer end of the scale, the Far Orientals at the other. If with us the I seems to be of the very essence of the soul, then the soul of the Far East may be said to be Impersonality."[37]

Without relying on racial considerations, Lowell searches different "cultural" domains—family, the Japanese language, art, relationship to nature, religion—for certain psychological features, or a specifically Japanese mindset".

It was the great British Japanologist Basil H. Chamberlain who coined the term "Topsy-turvydom" for Japan by using it as a section title in *Things Japanese*, which appeared in six editions between 1890 and 1936. Taking up several of Frois's arguments (although they had not been published at the time), it goes like this:

> "It has often been remarked that the Japanese do many things in a way that runs directly counter to European ideas of what is natural and proper. To the Japanese themselves our ways appear equally unaccountable. It was only the other day that a Tōkyō lady asked the present writer why foreigners did so many things topsy-turvy, instead of doing them naturally, after the manner of her country-people. Here are a few instances of this contrariety:—
> Japanese books begin at what we should call the end, the word finis (終) coming

---

35 Cf. Emmanuel Lozerand, La dilution du sujet japonais chez les intellectuels français au tournant des années 1970. Avatars d'un stéréotype, in: Fabien Arribert-Narce/Kôhei Kuwada/Lucy O'Meara (eds.), *Réceptions de la culture japonaise en France depuis 1945. Paris-Tôkyô-Paris: détours par le Japon*, Paris 2016, 51-70.

36 Cf. Augustin Berque, *Poétique de la Terre: histoire naturelle et histoire humaine: essai de mésologie*, Paris 2014, 29-58.

37 Percival Lowell, *The Soul of The Far East*, Boston/New York 1888, 15.

where we put the title-page. The foot-notes are printed at the top of the page, and the reader inserts his marker at the bottom. In newspaper paragraphs, a large full stop is put at the beginning of each.

Men make themselves merry with wine, not after dinner, but before. Sweets also come before the *pièces de résistance*. The whole method of treating horses is the opposite of ours. A Japanese (of the old school) mounts his horse on the right side, all parts of the harness are fastened on the right side, the mane is made to hang on the left side; and when the horse is brought home, its head is placed where its tail ought to be, and the animal is fed from a tub at the stable door.

Boats are hauled up on the beach stern first.

On leaving an inn, you fee not the waiter, but the proprietor.

The Japanese do not say "north-east," "south-west," but "east-north," "west-south." They carry babies, not in their arms, but on their backs. Many tools and implements are used in a way which is contrary to ours. For example, Japanese keys turn in instead of out, and Japanese carpenters saw and plane towards, instead of away from, themselves. The best rooms in a house are at the back; the garden, too, is at the back. When building a house, the Japanese construct the roof first; then, having numbered the pieces, they break it up again, and keep it until the substructure is finished. In making up accounts, they write down the figures first, the corresponding items next. Politeness prompts them to remove, not their head-gear, but their foot-gear. Their needle-work sometimes curiously reverses European methods. Belonging as he does to the inferior sex, the present writer can only speak hesitatingly on such a point. But a lady of his acquaintance informs him that Japanese women needle their thread instead of threading their needle, and that instead of running the needle through the cloth, they hold it still and run the cloth upon it. Another lady, long resident in Tōkyō, says that the impulse of her Japanese maids is always to sew on cuffs, frills, and other similar things, topsy-turvy and inside out. If that is not the *nec plus ultra* of contrariety, what is? Men in Japan are most emphatically not the inferior sex. When (which does not often happen) a husband condescends to take his wife out with him, it is my lord's jinrikisha that bowls off first. The woman gets into hers as best she can, and trundles along behind. Still, women have some few consolations. In Europe, gay bachelors are apt to be captivated by the charms of actresses. In Japan, where there are no actresses to speak of, it is the women who fall in love with fashionable actors. Strangest of all, after a bath the Japanese dry themselves with a damp towel!"[38]

It is difficult to discern the deeper logic of Chamberlain's remarks, but it seems to me that he is simply highlighting a curious, picturesque aspect of Japan (the word

---

38   Basil H. Chamberlain, *Things Japanese*, London 1905, 480-482.

"picturesque" is frequently associated with Japan in the late nineteenth and early twentieth centuries).

While the theme, even the form, of radical Japanese otherness represented in Chamberlain's *topsy-turvydom* seems to go back to Frois, albeit via rather complex, meandering paths, including the notion of the "moral antipodes"[39], the two authors do, however, pursue different objectives. Chamberlain, who, by the way, also acquired scientific expertise about Japan, no longer uses the logic of topsy-turvy as a means of taming strangeness, but on the contrary, to lock the Japanese in a persistent state of weirdness, of turning them into "curiosities". Let's not forget that what became the "West" in the nineteenth century, especially according to Hegel (*das Abendland*) was a concept that went beyond Europe and probably cultivated a stronger sense of superiority over non-Western peoples, a stronger feeling of being at the forefront of civilization, than what sixteenth-century missionaries would have felt, who were, of course, buttressed by their Christian faith, but at the same time very fragile and isolated, thousands of miles from their native land.

The theme of Japan as the opposite of the West is also found in two books from 1896. The first one, *Feudal and Modern Japan* was written by Arthur May Knapp, a Unitarian pastor from Massachusetts who led a mission to Japan in 1889. In the book, he develops his idea of a *"principle of inversion"* that governs Japanese customs:

> "Inversion is the confirmed habit of the far Oriental. It characterizes, not only the general mode as well as every detail of his outward life, but also his intellectual and moral being. It is not simply that his ways and thoughts differ from ours. They are the total reversal of ours. In our childhood we were accustomed to picture the inhabitants of the antipodes as standing upron their heads. We were so far right in our imaginings that that is really the oly thing the oriental does not to do in the inversion of our ways."[40]

In the same year, 1896, Englishwoman Emily Patton published a very nice work entitled *Japanese Topsyturvy-Dom* in Japan, this time, however, with the intent to fight, as she wrote, against narrow-minded anti-Japanese prejudice.

After World War II, Martin Heidegger saw in Japan the possibility of a completely different "House of Being"[41], and Alexandre Kojève viewed it as an alternative to the triumph of the "American Way of Life"[42]. However, it was undoubtedly Roland Barthes who, in his 1970 *Empire of Signs*, most clearly put Japan in this role of

---

39   Chamberlain states: "Japanese logic is the very antipodes of European logic". Quoted by Gill, *Topsy-turvy 1585*, 43.
40   Gill, *Topsy-turvy 1585*, 47-48.
41   Martin Heidegger, Aus einem Gespräch von der Sprache. Zwischen einem Japaner und einem Fragenden, in: Friedrich Wilhelm von Herrmann (ed.), *Unterwegs zur Sprache (1950-1959)*, Gesamtausgabe, vol. 12, Frankfurt a. M. 1985.
42   Cf. Lozerand, La dilution du sujet japonais.

the great "Other" of the West, a fascinating "empire of empty signs" to oppose to the horrible "Western Semiocracy", fantasizing about finding a language abounding in "irreducible differences" that would "make the entire West crumble".[43]

In his lectures held in Japan during his travels to the country in the late 1980s, Claude Lévi-Strauss revived this theme once again, but in a more subtle way and making a better case. In his 1986 "A Recognition of Cultural Diversity: What Japanese Culture Can Teach Us", he lists some oppositions lifted from, or in the vein of, Frois and Chamberlain:

> "One certainly does not have to be an anthropologist to notice that a Japanese carpenter uses the saw and the plane the opposite way his Western colleagues do: He saws and planes towards himself, not by pushing the tool away from himself. At the end of the 19th century, this observation had already been made by Basil Hall Chamberlain, professor at the University of Tokyo, an astute observer of Japanese life and culture and an eminent philologist. In his famous book "Things Japanese", under the heading Topsy-turvidom, he records this and other facts as oddities of no particular significance. In short, he goes no further than Herodotus more than twenty-four centuries ago, who noticed that the ancient Egyptians did everything the opposite way from his Greek compatriots. On the other hand, experts in Japanese linguistics have noted the curiosity that a Japanese person who needs go to away for a moment (to post a letter, or buy a newspaper or a pack of cigarettes) will often say something like "Itte mairimásu"; to which the other will reply "Itte irasshai". The emphasis is thus not placed on the decision to leave, as a Westerner would put it, but on the intention of coming right back. Similarly, a specialist in ancient Japanese literature will point out that a journey is experienced as painful, uprooting, and haunted by an obsession to return home. Finally, on a more prosaic level, a Japanese cook doesn't throw food into the fryer, but rather lifts it out (ageru)..."[44]

He goes on:

> "An anthropologist will refuse to consider these petty facts as independent variables, as isolated particularities. On the contrary, he will be struck by what they have in common. Across a variety of fields and under different modalities, there is always this theme of bringing back to oneself, or of returning to oneself inwardly. Instead of departing from the "self" as an autonomous and already constituted entity, everything happens as if the Japanese were constructing their "self" from the outside. The Japanese "self" thus appears, not as a primitive predetermined

---

43   Cf. Lozerand, La dilution du sujet japonais.
44   Claude Lévi-Strauss, Reconnaissance de la diversité culturelle: ce que nous apprend la civilisation japonaise, in: Claude Lévi-Strauss, L'Anthropologie face aux problèmes du monde moderne, Paris 2011, 101-142.

parameter, but as a result towards which one strives without any certainty to ever reach it. I am not surprised when people tell me that Descartes's famous adage: "I think, therefore I am" is absolutely untranslatable into Japanese! In fields as varied as spoken language, craftsmanship, culinary arts, history of ideas [...], a very profound difference, or more precisely, a system of invariable differences, manifests itself between what I would simply call the Western soul and the Japanese soul. This difference can be summarized as the opposition between a centripetal movement and a centrifugal movement. An anthropologist can use this dichotomy as a working hypothesis to try to better understand the relationship between the two civilizations."[45]

Lévi-Strauss developed his point even more clearly in his 1988 "The place of Japanese culture in the world", showing how Japan, differently from the rest of the East, is a sort of an inverted symmetrical image of the West that shows us our own reflection like a mirror. "Protected from the metaphysical resignation of Eastern religions" as well as from the "static sociology of Confucianism", Japan has "inverted" its rejection of the centrifugal Western subject "the way you invert a glove", creating a centripetal subject. The rhetoric of inversion allows Lévi-Strauss to elegantly navigate around a thorny dilemma. By making Japan a pure symmetry of the West, it retains its particularity, but at the same time he places the two extremes of the Eurasian continent in the same category, completely distinct from that of the continental empires.[46]

It is therefore not surprising that Lévi-Strauss clearly expressed his admiration for Frois and Chamberlain, whose method and observations he adopts, even mentioning them on the same breath in a laudatory preface to the 1998 pocket edition of Frois's *Tratado*[47].

Frois does not seem to have had any major emulators since Lévi-Strauss, but it must be said that bestsellers on this topic continue to flourish. The latest one by a certain Elena Janvier was published in France in 2011 under the title *In Japan, lovers don't say 'I love you'*. It goes like this:

"This book is an attempt to draw a lighthearted inventory of the thousand and one differences between our civilizations. From small details of everyday life to the more intimate universe of emotions, it offers its readers an unexpected and humorous key to deciphering Japanese mysteries and to understand the ways we live and love."[48]

---

45   Claude Lévi-Strauss, Reconnaissance de la diversité culturelle.
46   Cf. Claude Lévi-Strauss, Place de la culture japonaise dans le monde, in: Claude Lévi-Strauss, *L'Autre face de la lune*, Paris 2011, 49-55.
47   Cf. Lévi-Strauss, Préface.
48   Elena Janvier, *Au Japon ceux qui s'aiment ne disent pas je t'aime*, Paris 2012.

It aptly illustrates one of the latest avatars of how the French view Japan: As a gently exotic country, a great change of scenery, and... a new tourist destination.

But when it comes to instrumentalizing Japan to construct fake "mirrors", philosophers are not to be outdone. In *Cosmos* in 2015, where he presented a "philosophy of nature" as part of his "Brief Encyclopedia of the World", Michel Onfray took his turn to sing the tune of a "West formatted by Judeo-Christianity, which implies the separation between a Creator and his creature, a subject before everything else, and objects after this subject". This he contrasts with the charms of a Japanese haiku:The thought that exists before a haiku is written does not suffer from this damaging separation: no "I" or "me" that pre-exists in the world, no dualism that would oppose a celestial world and an earthly world, no separation between self and nature.[49]

Onfray is not afraid to summarize his analysis with a stone-cold: "Christianity has damaged humankind, Shintoism has upheld it", before he goes on, still on the subject of the haiku:

> "There is no exposed 'I', no exhibited 'me', no lyrical expansion, no schizophrenic dualism, no self that is separate from the world, no consciousness that is distinct from nature, no creator opposed to creation, no verbal religion, no concept of temptation, no literary formalism, no obscuration of the world. On the contrary, there is a body that feels, looks, tastes, enjoys the world, experiences reality, grasps both the detail and the universality of nature, of the cosmos, the word at the service of empirical life, a minimal phenomenology for maximal poetry, a tiny stylistic proposal capable of producing the sensation of the sublime, a clarification of what truly is."[50]

Augustin Berque's analyses are hardly any different. One year prior, in his 2014 *Poetry of the Land*, he invites his readers to Touraine to meet a person who says: "My name is René Descartes". Then he goes on to pursue the tracks of Percival Lowell, towards Levant, and after a long walk through the Hercynian forest he ends up in a country, Japan, where there is "no I", where the "subject" gives way to an "ambient", where a philosophy emerges "antipodally" that is "diametrically opposed" to that of the West and its "modern ontological topos"[51].

While raciological discourses have obstinately provided a baseline for the discourse on Japan since the nineteenth century, they are often supplemented, or replaced, by the equally insistent motif of the "country where everything is turned upside down" (*topsy-turvydom*), or by that of the "Great Other" of the West, from Marin Heidegger or Alexandre Kojève to Michel Onfray, and Augustin Berque via

---

49 Cf. Michel Onfray, *Cosmos*, Paris 2015, 560.
50 Onfray, *Cosmos*, 569.
51 Berque, *Poétique de la Terre*, 29-58.

Roland Barthes, Jacques Lacan, or Claude Lévi-Strauss. This discourse never ceases to nourish "anti-modern" discourses that are critical of what the contemporary West has become, especially after World War II.

Conclusions

The theme and rhetoric of Japan's absolute otherness therefore have had a long history. Born from a Jesuit worldview, which leveraged the method of comparison to diminish the strangeness of the Japanese without denying it, while at the same time making them targets of their missionary enterprise, this discourse has produced a long series of avatars spanning four centuries until today. Since Marco Polo, Japan tends to be a fantastical and inaccessible country, an embodiment of a utopia. Yet since Luis Frois in the sixteenth century, and since the revival of Herodotus's approach towards the Egyptians, it also tends to occupy the spot of the "ideal opposite".

Despite the profound inertia of this veritable wrinkle in European and then Western thought, it has nevertheless undergone some variations. The phraseology of the "contradiction of customs" has thus been transformed into that of "antipodes", then of *"topsy-turvydom"*, to mention only the most striking catchphrases.

There even seems to have been some sort of alternation between periods that liked to inventory differences—the sixteenth and seventeenth centuries, then the nineteenth and twentieth centuries—and those periods that sought to diminish their importance in order to better highlight similarities (the eighteenth century). It should be noted, however, that the meaning and function of a model can change, even if its form suggests a sense of continuity. The pattern of the "contradiction of customs" does not serve the same purpose when Frois uses it in the sixteenth century as when the Anglo-Saxons propagated the *topsy-turvydom* in the late nineteenth and early twentieth centuries; the vision of Japan as "extremely foreign" does not have the same meaning for French (and German?) intellectuals in the second half of the twentieth century as it does for French philosophers who dabble in Japanology in the early twentyfirst century. Let's admit for our part that, with all due respect for the work of Claude Lévi-Strauss, we find it deeply regrettable that he has chosen to follow in the footsteps of Frois and Chamberlain, because—does it have to be pointed out?—Japan *is not* the absolute Other of the West, but just another world among the many that inhabit our planet, without any exceptional glory nor indignity, with many similarities to other cultures, and of course, with certain singularities. There is no case to portray Japan as an inverted mirror of a vilified West. So how do we escape this discourse of absolute otherness in the twentyfirst century, which is now well underway? Probably by continuing to compare, but in a more flexible, agile way, from varying the angles and using multiple levels of comparison. Because a critical moment in any comparative endeavor that does not want to be comparatistical is the moment we leave the details to see the big picture, rise beyond the treetops to see the woods. It is the moment when observation becomes systematic and tends to thicken, or concentrate, those differences into a sort of essence. The issue here is not to refuse systematization, because then we would refuse to think and go back to wandering amongst the trees; it is to use multiple systematizations to make sure no single system becomes dominant, to avoid that the merry-go-round of comparisons, of "strangeness" and/or "familiarization" grinds to a stop. This might be the key to a proper use of comparisons in our age, a time torn between universalism and relativism, to ensure that the comparisons themselves are also objects of comparison, or, to put it another way, that they contain a meta-comparative dimension. This is an essential condition for them to stay agile, subtle, and open, to maintain "the humor and alacrity" that constitute their real merit.

In "Killing a Chinese Mandarin", Carlo Ginzburg reflects on the "moral implications of distance" which, in various contexts, tends to numb our sense of humanity.[52] The question of what is near or far goes beyond that of mere geographical proximity, and perhaps the true purpose of comparison is to keep us from killing "Chinese mandarins", because, to put it another way, our moral imagination is not disconnected from our intellectual imagination.

References

BERQUE, Augustin, *Poétique de la Terre: histoire naturelle et histoire humaine: essai de mésologie*, Paris 2014.
CHAMBERLAIN, Basil H., *Things Japanese*, London 1905.
CHARLEVOIX, Père, *Histoire et description du Japon*, Tours 1842.
FRANK, Bernard, *Dieux et bouddhas au Japon*, Paris 2000.
FRÓIS, Luís, *Européens et Japonais – traité sur les contradictions et différences de mœurs*, ed. by Xavier de Castro/Claude Levi-Strauss, Paris 1998.
FRÓIS, Luís, *Traité de Luís Fróis, S.J. [1585] sur les contradictions de mœurs entre Européens et Japonais*, ed. by Xavier de Castro/Robert Schrimpf/José Manuel Garcia, Paris 1993.
FRÓIS, Luís, *Kulturgegensätze Europa-Japan [1585]. Tratado em que se contem muito susinta e abreviadamente algumas contradições e diferenças de custumes antre a gente de Europa e esta provincia de Japão*, ed. by Josef Franz Schütte, Tokyo 1955.

---

52   Carlo Ginzburg, Tuer un mandarin chinois. Des conséquences morales de la distance, in: Carlo Ginzburg, *À distance. Neuf essais sur le point de vue en histoire*, traduit de l'italien, Paris 2001, 174.

GARCIA, José Manuel, Préface, in: Luís Fróis, *Traité de Luís Fróis, S.J. [1585] sur les contradictions de mœurs entre Européens et Japonais*, ed. by Xavier de Castro/Robert Schrimpf/José Manuel Garcia, Paris 1993, 7-39.

GILL, Robin D., *Topsy-turvy 1585*, Key Biscayne 2004.

GINZBURG, Carlo, Tuer un mandarin chinois. Des conséquences morales de la distance, in: Carlo Ginzburg, *À distance. Neuf essais sur le point de vue en histoire*, traduit de l'italien, Paris 2001, 165-180.

GOBINEAU (COMTE DE), Joseph Arthur, *Essai sur l'inégalité des races humaines*, vol. I, Paris 1853.

HEIDEGGER, Martin, Aus einem Gespräch von der Sprache. Zwischen einem Japaner und einem Fragenden, in: Friedrich Wilhelm von Herrmann (ed.), *Unterwegs zur Sprache (1950-1959)*, Gesamtausgabe, vol. 12, Frankfurt a. M. 1985, 79-146.

JANVIER, Elena, *Au Japon ceux qui s'aiment ne disent pas je t'aime*, Paris 2012.

LÉVI-STRAUSS, Claude, Reconnaissance de la diversité culturelle: ce que nous apprend la civilisation japonaise, in: Claude Lévi-Strauss, *L'Anthropologie face aux problèmes du monde moderne*, Paris 2011, 101-142.

LÉVI-STRAUSS, Claude, Place de la culture japonaise dans le monde, in: Claude Lévi-Strauss, *L'Autre face de la lune*, Paris 2011, 13-55.

LÉVI-STRAUSS, Claude, Préface, in: Luís Fróis, *Européens et Japonais – traité sur les contradictions et différences de mœurs*, ed. by Xavier de Castro/Claude Levi-Strauss, Paris 1998, 7-11.

LINGUET, Simon, *Histoire impartiale des Jésuites*, Paris 1768.

LOWELL, Percival, *The Soul of The Far East*, Boston/New York 1888.

LOZERAND, Emmanuel, Comparer les comparaisons. Parcours buissonnier, in: *Socio-anthropologie* 36 (2017), 43-58 (26.11.2017), URL: http://socio-anthropologie.revues.org/3095, DOI: 10.4000/socio-anthropologie.3095.

LOZERAND, Emmanuel, La dilution du sujet japonais chez les intellectuels français au tournant des années 1970. Avatars d'un stéréotype, in: Fabien Arribert-Narce/Kôhei Kuwada/Lucy O'Meara (eds.), *Réceptions de la culture japonaise en France depuis 1945. Paris-Tôkyô-Paris: détours par le Japon*, Paris 2016, 51-70.

MONTESQUIEU, *L'Esprit des lois*, Paris 1817.

OKADA, Akio, *Nichiô bunka hikaku* (Daikôkai jidai sôsho XI), Tokyo 1965.

ONFRAY, Michel, *Cosmos*, Paris 2015.

SCHRIMPF, Robert, Commentaire, in: Luís Fróis, *Traité de Luís Fróis, S.J. [1585] sur les contradictions de mœurs entre Européens et Japonais*, ed. by Xavier de Castro/Robert Schrimpf/José Manuel Garcia, Paris 1993, 119-180.

SOLIER, François, *Histoire ecclésiastique des isles et royaumes du Japon* (Ecclesiastical History of the Islands and Kingdoms of Japan). Collected by Father F. Solier, monk of the Jesuit Order, Paris, ed. by Sébastien Cramoisy, 1627-1629, 2 volumes, Bordeaux 1628.

TINGUELY, Frédéric, *La Lecture complice. Culture libertine et geste critique*, Genève 2016.

TINGUELY, Frédéric, Le monde multipolaire des missionnaires Jésuites, in: Frédéric Tinguely (ed.), *La Renaissance décentrée*. Actes du colloque de Genève, Genève 2008.

VOLTAIRE, *Essai sur les mœurs* (Œuvres complètes de Voltaire, 18), Paris 1784.

"Goût de Comparaison"
Practices of Comparative Viewing in Eighteenth-Century Connoisseurship

Joris Corin Heyder

Abstract

In 1719, Jean-Baptiste Dubos described the connoisseurial judgement as a veritable "goût de comparaison," literally, a taste of comparison. This early reflection on the importance of practices of comparing is surprising, and can serve as the starting point for investigating its fundamental role in art connoisseurship. What kind of preconditions, merits, implications, and limits can be connected to comparative arrangements in the late seventeenth and eighteenth centuries? Is it even possible to ascertain a change of comparative practices within the history of connoisseurship? Connoisseurs—so the argument—expanded specific skills by means of increasingly efficient comparisons that enabled them to systematize and categorize the vast heritage of artistic artifacts.

Introduction

> "Connoisseurship can [...] be presented quite differently in terms of a range of visual skills that are cultivated with a high level of self-awareness. Frequently these are put to commercial ends, which does not render the skills themselves any less valuable. Because connoisseurship is fundamentally comparative, it provides a possible model for historians who seek to develop their ability to make precise discriminations based on close visual inspection."[1]

---

1   Ludmilla J. Jordanova, *The Look of the Past: Visual and Material Evidence in Historical Practice*, Cambridge 2012, 212.

By linking practices of connoisseurship[2] to both reflective visual skills and a necessarily comparative approach, Ludmilla Jordanova has accentuated two aspects whose relationship has so far remained largely unconsidered. Certainly, in accordance with the powerful modernism narrative, many studies have been written on a new organization of the visual in the nineteenth century.[3] This applies equally for the importance of the comparative stimulus in art history at the latest when the double slide projection[4] gained significant importance in academic lecture halls.[5] However, the shift to an entirely new visuality as well as its interrelation with doing comparisons did not come out of nowhere. On the contrary, already in the late seventeenth and early eighteenth centuries, in a time when objectivity was emerging more and more as a scientific ideal and practice,[6] the connoisseurs' discourses and evolving working routines indicated an increasing sensitivity toward visual phenomena in general, and toward the treatment of a growing number of images in particular. "Seeing as a way of knowing," to borrow the words of Lorraine Daston in her explanation of the "epistemic image," is a skill required explicitly in scientific circles from the mid-sixteenth century onward.[7] Whereas the use of images in scientific illustrations often obeys the premise of offering the reader/observer an idealized "stand-in for the too plentiful and too various objects,"[8] art connois-

---

2   In this contribution, "practices" are principally understood from the perspective of recent practice theories as "a routinized way in which bodies are moved, objects are handled, subjects are treated, things are described and the world is understood." See Andreas Reckwitz, Toward a Theory of Social Practices. A Development in Culturalist Theorizing, in: *European Journal of Social Theory* 5 (2/2002), 243–263, see 250, URL: https://doi.org/10.1177/13684310222225432 [last accessed: August 12, 2018]. A concise and recent summary on the use of practice theory in art historical research subjects can be found in Johannes Grave et. al. (eds.), The Agency of Display. Objects, Framings and Parerga—Introductory Thoughts, in: *The Agency of Display. Objects, Framings and Parerga, Parerga and Paratexts. How Things Enter Language. Practices and Forms of Representation in Goethe's Collections*, Dresden 2018, 7–19, see 10–11.

3   A brief and succinct criticism of this master narrative has been formulated in, for instance: Jonathan Crary, *Techniques of the Observer: On Vision and Modernity in the Nineteenth Century* (An October Book), Cambridge 1991, 3–4.

4   For a short insight into the conditions and problems of art historical slide lectures, see Robert S. Nelson, The Slide Lecture, or the Work of Art 'History' in the Age of Mechanical Reproduction, in: *Critical Inquiry* 26 (3/2000), 414–434.

5   It is only very recently that art history and cultural studies have rediscovered their familiar interest in phenomena of comparison, see Matthias Bruhn/Gerhard Scholtz (eds.), *Der vergleichende Blick: Formalanalyse in Natur- und Kulturwissenschaften*, Berlin 2017; Jaś Elsner (ed.), *Comparativism in Art History*, London 2017.

6   On objectivity in the history of science, see Lorraine Daston/Peter Galison, *Objectivity*, New York 2010.

7   Lorraine Daston, Epistemic Images, in: Alina A. Payne (ed.), *Vision and Its Instruments: Art, Science, and Technology in Early Modern Europe*, University Park, Penn. 2015, 13–35, see 17.

8   Daston, Epistemic Images, 18.

seurship, in contrast, had to circle around every single image and could not simply merge results in an idealized illustration.[9] Consequently, other strategies were indispensable for achieving knowledge on art objects, and comparative viewing occurred as one of the most important, but hitherto neglected approaches. This is all the more astonishing when looking at the three central domains of connoisseurship formulated by Roger de Piles (1635–1709) as early as 1677 in his *Conversations sur la Connoissance*,[10] that have been regarded as valid ever since. These domains are, first, the judgment of quality; second, the attribution of the art work; and, third, the differentiation between original and copy.[11] All three domains are undoubtedly based on doing comparisons.

The main objective of this chapter is, first, to show that comparative viewing became a significant characteristic in the judgment of art long before the institutionalization of academic art history; second, to exemplify different levels of practices of the "comparative imperative" in connoisseurship; and, third, to ask whether those practices themselves were distinct from earlier habits of comparative viewing. De Piles' three domains serve here as a point of departure for structuring the following considerations.

1. The judgment of quality or the "Taste of comparison"

Eighteenth-century scholarship on art and literature circled to a great extent around the question of taste.[12] Treatises on aesthetic phenomena had already been

---

9 It is doubtful whether the manipulation of an art object ranges on the same level as idealizing an illustration as proposed by Kristel Smentek with reference to practices of mounting and changing drawings known from the connoisseur Pierre-Jean Mariette (1694–1774). See Kristel Smentek, *Mariette and the Science of the Connoisseur in the Eighteenth-Century Europe*, Farnham et al. 2014, 9.

10 Roger de Piles, *Conversations sur la connoissance de la peinture, et sur le jugement qu'on doit faire des tableaux. Où par occasion il est parlé de la vie de Rubens, & de quelques-uns de ses plus beaux ouvrages*, Paris 1677.

11 De Piles, *Conversations*, 3–4, 7.

12 The literature on the "era of taste"—"*Zeitalter des Geschmacks*"—is so vast that I shall mention only those titles that are useful for the following reasoning: Raymond Keller, 'à la mode française': Geschmack und ästhetische Urteile als Grundlage für Kennerschaft, in: Stephan Brakensiek/Anne-Katrin Sors (eds.), *Copy.Right Adam von Bartsch. Kunst, Kommerz, Kennerschaft*, Petersberg 2016, 20–29; Susan Bracken, Collectors in England: Evolutions in Taste 1580–1630, in: Tarnya Cooper/Aviva Burnstock/Maurice Howard (eds.), *Painting in Britain*, Oxford 2015, 384–391; Aaron Meskin/Jon Robson, Taste and Acquaintance, in: *The Journal of Aesthetics and Art Criticism* (2015), 127–139; Johannes Grave, Das Jahrhundert des Geschmacks. Zur Kultur des Sinnlichen im Zeitalter der Aufklärung, in: Monika Bachtler (ed.), *Wie es uns gefällt. Kostbarkeiten aus der Sammlung Rudolf-August Oetker*, München 2014, 15–29; Charlotte Guichard, Taste Communities: The Rise of the Amateur in Eighteenth-Century Paris, in:

grappling with this central philosophical concept decades before Alexander Gottlieb Baumgarten's (1714–1762) *Aesthetica*[13] was published in 1750/58; and in Immanuel Kant's (1724–1804) *Critique of Judgment* from 1790,[14] taste still played a central role as the *"sensus communis"*[15] for the conceptualization of two subjective universal judgments: the beautiful and the sublime. Almost seventy years earlier, in 1719, the Abbé Jean-Bapiste Dubos (1670–1742) had put forward a popular eighteenth-century treatise on art called *Réflexions critiques sur la poésie et sur la peinture*.[16] In this programmatic work, Dubos is particularly interested in two main concepts: the sentiment (*"sentiment"*) and the taste (*"goût"*). Human intellectual formation should always pursue good taste, and even though sentiment is explicitly subjective, the author argues for the possibility of an agreement on a common taste. This raises the question of how such common taste can be acquired. Following Dubos's ideal-typical program, circles of "curieux" or amateurs—the public—are able to value and judge a poem or a picture 'correctly' in terms of its quality, if those circles are:

"limited to persons that read, and have a knowledge of theatrical entertainments, who see or hear people talk of pictures, and who have acquired by some means or other, that discernment which is called the *Taste of Comparison* [...]".[17]

Dubos's "public" is what Charlotte Guichard has characterized as a taste community, as "small societies, structured by interpersonal relationships, civility,

---

Eighteenth-Century Studies (2012), 519–547; Patrick Michel, *Peinture et plaisir: les goûts picturaux des collectionneurs parisiens au XVIIIe siècle*, Rennes 2010; Maurice Rheims, *Les collectionneurs: de la curiosité, de la beauté, du goût, de la mode et de la spéculation*, Paris 2002; Hans-Joachim Pieper, *Geschmacksurteil und ästhetische Einstellung: eine Untersuchung zur Grundlegung transzendentalphilosophischer Ästhetik bei Kant und ein Entwurf zur Phänomenologie der ästhetischen Erfahrung*, Würzburg 2001; Fabienne Brugère, *Le goût: art, passions et société*, (Philosophies, 130), Paris 2000; Yves Michaud, *Critères esthétiques et jugement de goût*, Nîmes 1999; Luc Ferry, *Homo aestheticus: l'invention du goût à l'âge démocratique* (Le collège de philosophie), Paris 1990; Rémy G. Saisselin, *Taste in Eighteenth Century France: Critical Reflections on the Origins of Aesthetics or an Apology for Amateurs*, Syracuse 1965; Samuel-Élie Rocheblave, *L'art et le goût en France de 1600 à 1900* (Nouvelle édition), Paris 1923.

13   Alexander Gottlieb Baumgarten, *Ästhetik. Übersetzt, mit einer Einführung, Anmerkungen und Registern von der Herausgeberin*, ed. by Dagmar Mirbach, Hamburg 2007.

14   Immanuel Kant, *Critique of Judgement*, ed. by Nicholas Walker, trans. by James Creed Meredith, Oxford 1989 [1952]. See also the rich commentary by Manfred Frank and Véronique Zanetti: Immanuel Kant, *Schriften zur Ästhetik und Naturphilosophie, Text und Kommentar*, ed. by Manfred Frank/Véronique Zanetti, 2 vols., Frankfurt a. M. 2001.

15   Kant, *Critique of Judgement*, part 1, §20, 92–93 and part 1, §40, 169–173.

16   Jean-Baptiste Dubos, *Réflexions critiques sur la poésie et sur la peinture*, 2 vols., Paris 1719. All following text passages are cited according to the translation by Thomas Nugent: Jean-Baptiste Dubos, *Critical reflections on poetry, painting, and music*, trans. by Thomas Nugent, 3 vols., London 1748.

17   Dubos, *Critical reflections*, vol. 2, chap. XXII, 245 [my italics].

and forms of sociability, within which artistic and erudite judgments could be exchanged and discussed."[18] A few chapters after first mentioning the "taste of comparison," Dubos at last explains both the meaning of this utterance as well as how taste communities achieve good taste:

> "but to acquire this comparative taste, which inables [sic] us to judge of a present by an absent picture, a person must have been in the very center of painting. He must have frequent opportunities, especially in his younger days, of beholding several excellent pictures in perfect ease and tranquility. Liberty of mind is as necessary, in order to be sensible of the intire beauty of a work, as to compose it. To be a good spectator, one must have that peace of soul, which rises not from the exhausting, but from the serenity of the imagination."[19]

On the one hand, these passages are valuable because they describe contemporary practices or at least instructions for such practices that should enable the reader to acquire a good taste, too. On the other hand, we can learn from them that, in Dubos' explanation, at least two steps are necessary to arrive at the "comparative taste" that is required for every judgment: first, the repeated contemplation of excellent pictures; second, a certain degree of knowledge as well as a performative participation in discussions about and in the physical presence of art. Those who shaped public opinion the most were the "connoisseurs" who, according to Dubos: "have studied painting as much as the artists themselves."[20] In a drawing (Fig. 1)[21] by Gabriel Jacques de Saint-Aubin (1724–1780)[22]—an obsessive observer and draftsman in the times of Louis XV who seismographically sketched public life—two connoisseurs are immersed in conversation in front of a wall full of paintings and sculptures.

The subjects of the sketched pictures are executed only in part, but we can say with some certainty that the bulk of them represent history paintings, regarded as

---

18   Guichard, Taste Communities, 532.
19   Dubos, *Critical reflections*, vol. 2, chap. XXIX, 293.
20   Dubos, *Critical reflections*, vol. 2, chap. XXII, 249.
21   Gabriel de Saint-Aubin, Carnet Groult, Sketch page for the Salon of 1765, Paris, Musée du Louvre, département des arts graphiques, fol. 43v.
22   Cf. Xavier Salmon, *Gabriel de Saint-Aubin. Le Livre de croquis de Gabriel Saint-Aubin* (Carnets et albums), Paris 2017; Kim de Beaumont, Les Salons de Gabriel de Saint-Aubin (1724–1780), in: *Le Salon de l'Académie royale de peinture et de sculpture*, ed. by Isabelle Pichet, Paris 2014, 9–32. Pierre Rosenberg/Sue Welsh Reed/François Basan (eds.), *La vente Mariette: le catalogue illustré par Gabriel de Saint-Aubin. Catalogue raisonné des différens objets de curiosités dans les sciences et arts, qui composoient le cabinet de feu Mr Mariette, controleur général de la Grande Chancellerie de France, honoraire amateur de l'Académie Rle. de Peinture, et de celle de Florence*, Milan 2011; Pierre Rosenberg, Quelques bien modestes observations sur les estampes de la collection Mariette et sur leurs catalogues de vente illustrés par Gabriel de Saint-Aubin, in: *Nouvelles de l'estampe*, 230 (2010), 8–15. Pierre Rosenberg/Colin B. Bailey (eds.), *Gabriel de Saint-Aubin 1724–1780*, Paris 2007.

Fig. 1: Sketch page for the Salon of 1765, Gabriel de Saint-Aubin, Carnet Groult, Paris, Musée du Louvre, département des arts graphiques, fol. 43v

the highest form of painting since Leon Battista Alberti (1404–1472)[23] and hanging closely next to each other, as was fashionable at the time.[24] It is not without

---

23   See Anthony Blunt, *Artistic Theory in Italy, 1450–1660*, Oxford 1985, 11–12.
24   In the German-speaking context, this form of gallery presentation is known as the '*Petersburger Hängung*' or the 'pendant principle.' In our subproject C 01, "Comparative Viewing. Forms, Functions and Limits of Comparing Images", Robert Eberhardt works on a doctoral thesis that focuses particularly on practices of comparing image pairs. See also: Ganz, David/Thürlemann, Felix (eds.), *Das Bild im Plural. Mehrteilige Bildformen zwischen Mittelalter*

irony that de Saint-Aubin shows us both men absorbed by the conversation without paying any attention to the paintings, although one of them even points in their direction. However, the sketch demonstrates a culture of discussion in the presence of artworks that was propagated by Dubos and others; and the venue for this practice is a room full of art that invites the spectator to at least compare those pictures that are hanging in close proximity to each other.[25]

Why could this kind of presentation be important for an understanding of the connoisseurs' work, and what does the tiny sketch tell us about their habits? The draftsman is certainly referring to a complex system of images of different sizes and various degrees of legibility, and even different genres; he is presenting not only a fashionable eighteenth-century salon situation, but also two people entangled in a plurality of images. The contrast between clearly distinct pictures and those that have been reduced to their mere outlines could be regarded as an imitation of the blurring effect that results from the searching of the eyes in such a setting. The beholder's eyes cannot focus on the entire wall at once, but only on individual pictures one at a time; and, moreover, not even the entire picture, but actually only certain parts of these pictures. Just how much the drawing is evidence of a veritable "taste of comparison" becomes clearer when we remember de Piles's three central domains of connoisseurship: the judgment of quality, the attribution of the art work, and the distinction between original and copy.[26] The two connoisseurs are immersed in a discussion; they are judging or maybe even attributing the picture(s) to which they are pointing. It is one characteristic way to represent connoisseurs; the other would have been to show them—as many caricatures did—with magnifiers standing closely in front of a painting or a print while studying details.[27]

---

    und Gegenwart, Berlin 2010; Gerd Blum et al. (eds.), *Pendant plus. Praktiken der Bildkombinatorik*, Berlin 2012.

25   Since the growing interest in phenomena of reception aesthetics, the 'public' has constantly attracted the attention of the scholarly debate. Two positions with a particular interest in the eighteenth-century connoisseurial 'public' have been submitted by: Eva Kernbauer, *Der Platz des Publikums: Modelle für Kunstöffentlichkeit im 18. Jahrhundert* (Studien zur Kunst, 19), Köln 2011; Anja-Isabelle Weisenseel, *Bildbetrachtung in Bewegung: der Rezipient in Texten und Bildern zur Pariser Salonausstellung des 18. Jahrhunderts* (Ars et Scientia, 14), Berlin 2017. See also the reviews on Weisenseel's book by: Britta Hochkirchen, Rev. of: Bildbetrachtung in Bewegung. Der Rezipient in Texten und Bildern zur Pariser Salonausstellung des 18. Jahrhunderts (Ars et Scientia, 14), by Anja Weisenseel, in: *Zeitschrift für Kunstgeschichte* 82 (2019), 138–143; Valérie Kobi, Rev. of: Bildbetrachtung in Bewegung. Der Rezipient in Texten und Bildern zur Pariser Salonausstellung des 18. Jahrhunderts, by Anja Weisenseel, in: *Regards croisés. Deutsch-französisches Rezensionsjournal zur Kunstgeschichte und Ästhetik* 8 (2019), 150–152.

26   De Piles, *Conversations*, 3–4, 7.

27   Some rough caricatures have been published in an article by: Nina Christine Dusartz de Vigneulle, Das Sehende Auge. Die Kunstkennerschaft seit dem 18. Jahrhundert, in: Stephan Brakensiek/Anne-Katrin Sors (eds.), *Copy.Right Adam von Bartsch. Kunst, Kommerz, Kennerschaft*, Petersberg 2016, 305–319.

Obviously, there are different kinds of looking at a picture. Every reader will confirm that it makes a difference to see a painting on a wall or to study it from a close distance. De Saint-Aubin's drawing seems to invite the beholder to reflect on the viewing experience of the two connoisseurs. How does it differ from our own way of approaching an art work? How meaningful is it to believe that connoisseurs had a particular way of looking at a painting? Anja Weisenseel seeks to describe the act of seeing in the eighteenth century as a perceptive movement between near and far. Pursuant to that, it is particularly the performative quality of the *visus* that appears to be characteristic for an eighteenth-century approach. Additionally, the author underlines the fact that *visus* also had a connotation of *tactus*.[28] As a matter of fact, from Roger de Piles's time onward, the reception process between artwork and beholder has been described and conceptualized repeatedly as an act of penetration (*"pénétration"*).[29] Studying auction catalogues from that time shows that it was common to outline seeing as a visual touch ("toucher").[30] Therefore, the question stands whether the work of the connoisseur has to be understood as being much more corporal than the work of an art historian today. Not much is known about the relevance of involving the artwork's material quality in processes of judging. In a time when a living presence was attributed to sculptures, and, as Caroline van Eck could demonstrate,[31] the practice of touching objects was quite common. It cannot be ruled out that connoisseurs would have touched, for instance, the painting's surfaces not only with their eyes, but also with their hands to compare qualities. At least, it is known that such tactile-based comparisons played a crucial role in the judgment of prints in order, for example, to be able to differentiate between various paper qualities.

Weisenseel's description of a movement between near and far also becomes another facet with regard to the working routines of connoisseurs. It could be said that the 'connoisseurial vista' should be understood not only corporally but also, figuratively speaking, as a movement between 'completeness' (the far) and 'fragmentation' (the near).[32] The epistemological impact of such a description is twofold: By collecting and ordering artifacts, connoisseurs aim at a certain completeness. This process of assembling a high number of artifacts is accompanied by practices such as comparing, classifying, or judging. Close observations, on the other hand, were

---

28   Weisenseel, *Bildbetrachtung*, 93–212.
29   Weisenseel, *Bildbetrachtung*, 253–258.
30   Jérôme Delaplanche, *Un tableau n'est pas qu'une image* (Collection "Art & société"), Rennes 2016, 154–158.
31   Caroline Van Eck (ed.), Introduction, in: *Art, Agency and Living Presence: From the Animated Image to the Excessive Object* (Studien aus dem Warburg-Haus), Boston 2015, 11–28.
32   I first conceptualized this auxiliary dichotomy in the context of the conference "Vistas" organized by the Nineteenth Century Studies Association (NCSA), Philadelphia, in March 2018.

as important as gaining an overview over a broad stock of art objects. By analyzing the details of single art works, the connoisseur was pretending to make their inner structure 'legible.' The 'secret science' of 'reading' the fragment claims to decipher meaning by pure sight penetration of the painting's surface. This sorcery might have provoked representations of connoisseurs as donkeys or apes armed with magnifiers in the first place. But how did they actually 'read' single artworks? They were thrown back upon appearances such as hatches, light, the structure of a brush stroke, the material quality of the surface, and so forth. De Piles had already emphasized that 'reading' meant 'comparing' the findings with those in other art in 1708: "All objects that enter a painting, all lines, & all colors, all lights & all the shadows are not big or small, strong or faint, other than by *comparison*."[33] Such routinely implemented, unuttered comparative practices, however, usually remain in a prediscursive midpoint. The connoisseur[34] is studying details, and, for instance, is looking for a treatment that is characteristic for a particular painter. But to be able to judge about certain characteristics and qualities, he is forced to know enough other relevant comparative material in which these specific features are present as well. Therefore, I would argue that connoisseurial practices cannot escape a 'comparative imperative,' given that these practices typically also comprise operations such as balancing and/or subsuming.

The question stands whether or not a 'comparative imperative' in de Piles's sense of the perception of a picture as set out above is what Dubos had in mind by introducing the *"goût de comparaison."* At least, de Piles's and Dubos's utterances seem to reflect an awareness of the fact that practices of comparing on different levels determine the work of a connoisseur in manifold ways. That, in the age of enlightenment, comparisons generally could enfold a dynamizing potential in the emerging sciences—including natural sciences as well as the humanities—becomes a more and more probable assumption; corresponding arguments can be found in different disciplines such as the history of science or in historiographical approaches in history, literature, and philosophy.[35] It is astonishing to realize that in the eighteenth century, sometimes one person was involved in both natural history

---

33 [My translation and emphasis]. Original quote: *"Tous les objets qui entrent dans le Tableau, toutes les lignes & toutes les couleurs, toutes les lumieres & toutes les ombres ne sont grandes ou petites, fortes ou foibles que par* comparaison." See Roger De Piles, *Cours de peinture par principes*, Paris 1708, 105.

34 The masculine form used in this text for *'connoisseur'* reflects the fact that hardly any female connoisseurs are known. However, the masculine form is meant to include all possible gender and sexual identities.

35 I refer only to the most recent positions: Michael Eggers, *Vergleichendes Erkennen: zur Wissenschaftsgeschichte und Epistemologie des Vergleichs und zur Genealogie der Komparatistik* (Germanisch-romanische Monatsschrift), Heidelberg 2016; Epple, Angelika/Walter Erhard, Die Welt beobachten. Praktiken des Vergleichens, in: Angelika Epple/Walter Erhard (eds.), *Die Welt beobachten. Praktiken des Vergleichens*, Frankfurt a. M./New York 2015, 7–31; Andreas

and art connoisseurship at the same time.[36] In both fields, scholars proceeded in a very similar manner, namely, by collecting objects and/or artifacts and by trying to categorize these items taxonomically. However, what distinguished both worlds, the natural science and art connoisseurship, is beyond others the 'aesthetic surplus' of art works. Whereas it was a relevant category in the judgment of art, it soon lost its significance for the natural sciences. The judgment of art cannot be limited to the morphological formalism alone present in taxonomic methods; it goes far beyond such practices.[37] I shall come back to the question of the 'aesthetic surplus' in the final part of this chapter.

Other practices of comparing within art connoisseurship were perhaps as important as the comparative viewing itself, but they concerned different types of comparisons. Early art connoisseurship was not limited to methodological instruments such as classification and/or visual juxtaposition alone: In 1708, de Piles, who so precisely defined the connoisseur's endeavors, invented one of the first known ratings. This special type of comparison was quickly assimilated and evolved in, for example, the fields of sports and economics.[38] A closer look at the phenomenon

---

Mauz/Hartmut von Sass (eds.), *Hermeneutik des Vergleichs: Strukturen, Anwendungen und Grenzen komparativer Verfahren* (Interpretation interdisziplinär), Würzburg 2011.

36 It would be worth also examining the juxtapositions to morphological approaches in the history of art. Starting from the collection and the illustrious life of the erudite Antoine-Joseph Dezallier d'Argenville (1680–1765), Daniela Bleichmar argues toward an inextricable entanglement of natural science and connoisseurship in art in early and mid-eighteenth-century France, including the level of the actors as well as the level of collecting and exhibiting objects. In her argument, the connoisseur's eyes even become a "taxonomical instrument" (p. 89). See Daniela Bleichmar, Learning to Look: Visual Expertise across Art and Science in Eighteenth-Century France, in: *Eighteenth-Century Studies* 46 (1/2012), 85–111, https://doi.org/10.1353/ecs.2012.0084 [last accessed April 19, 2018]. In a historical overview, Karin Leonhard demonstrates the interfaces between art production, social networks, and collecting shells: Karin Leonhard, Shell Collecting: On 17th-Century Conchology, Curiosity Cabinets and Still Life Painting, in: Karl A. E. Enkell/Paul J. Smith (eds.), *Early Modern Zoology* (Intersections, 7), Leiden 2007, 177–214. It is also remarkable to note the common disinterest in the reasons why the once shared way went on to develop in distinct directions.

37 Insight into the relationship between a taxonomic natural history and practices of comparing can be found in, for instance: Thomas Stach, Anmerkungen zur Rolle des Vergleichs in der Morphologie, in: Matthias Bruhn/Gerhard Scholtz (eds.), *Der vergleichende Blick. Formanalyse in Natur- und Kulturwissenschaft*, Berlin 2017, 41–53.

38 De Piles's contribution has been emphasized as one of the first Western rankings/ratings by: Victor Ginsburgh/Sheila Weyers, On the contemporaneity of Roger de Piles' *Balance des peintres*, in: Jack Amariglio (ed.), *Sublime economy: on the intersection of art and economics*, London, 2009, 112–123; Kathryn Graddy, Taste Endures! The Rankings of Roger de Piles (†1709) and Three Centuries of Art Prices, in: *The Journal of Economic History* 73 (3/2013), 766–791, https://doi.org/10.1017/S0022050713000600 [last accessed May 23, 2018]; Carlos Spoerhase, Das Maß der Potsdamer Garde: die ästhetische Vorgeschichte des Rankings in der europäischen Literatur- und Kunstkritik des 18. Jahrhunderts, in: Deutsche Schillergesellschaft (ed.),

of art criticism, however, reveals that it was perhaps particularly the difficult-to-describe stubbornness of art that predestinated the aesthetic field to be the birthplace of systematic ratings/rankings. With the help of ratings, authors such as de Piles were able to clarify their judgments in terms of an ideal-typical system of values. De Piles analyzed art by referring to the categories composition ("*composition*"), drawing ("*dessein*"), coloring ("*coloris*") and expression ("*expression*").[39] These categories were extracted from earlier art theory treatises and had to persist in a field in which normative rules tended every now and then to be thrown overboard. The invention of the "balance of painters" is a new way to offer not only complex comparisons but also concrete visualizations of the author's 'taste of comparing.' Of course, the complexity is accessible only to those who are familiar with the kind of values, ideas, preliminary decisions, and—most important for this context—chains of comparisons hidden behind certain numeral values. De Piles uses numbers between zero and twenty to evaluate the performance of the artists in each category. Sometimes, he even turns entire scholarly disputes into good or bad notes, as in for instance, the famous "*querelle du coloris*."[40] This becomes obvious by considering names such as "Rubens" and "Poussin" (Fig. 2).[41]

The painters indicate opposite poles of the famous "*querelle*": Whereas Rubens stood for a preference for 'color,' Poussin, on the other hand, exemplified a preference for 'drawing.' De Piles's leading role in the debate and his positioning for the colorists has been made available in a painstakingly rich volume by Bernard Teyssèdre,[42] so that it comes as no surprise to find again the author's predilection for the colorists in his table. With the exception of the category drawing (13), Peter Paul Rubens (1577–1640) reaches high numbers only in composition (18), coloring (17), and expression (17), whereas de Piles conceded Nicholas Poussin (1594–1665)

Jahrbuch der Deutschen Schillergesellschaft, internationales Organ für neuere deutsche Literatur 58 (2014), 90–126.

39   See De Piles, *Cours de peinture*, 489–498. Instead of the "balance of painters," the English translation offers at the end of the volume a brief summary of the then famous British artists, see Roger de Piles, *The art of painting, with the lives and characters of above 300 of the most eminent painters: containing a complete treatise of painting, designing, and the use of prints […]*. London 1754.

40   On the "*Querelle de coloris*," see Daniel Dauvois, Les armes de la philosophie dans la Querelle du coloris, in: Frédéric Cousinié (ed.), *L' artiste et le philosophe* (Aesthetica), Rennes 2011, 303–320; Emmanuelle Delapierre, *Rubens contre Poussin: la querelle du coloris dans la peinture française à la fin du XVIIe siècle; Musée des Beaux-Arts d'Arras, 6 mars au 14 juin 2004*, Amsterdam 2004; Jacqueline Lichtenstein, *La Couleur éloquente: rhétorique et peinture à l'âge classique*, Paris 1989; Thomas Puttfarken, *Roger de Piles' Theory of Art*, New Haven 1985; Bernard Teyssèdre, *Roger de Piles et les débats sur le coloris au siècle de Louis XIV* (Bibliothèque des Arts, 13), Paris 1965.

41   Page from Roger de Piles's "Balance of painters" in: De Piles, *Cours de peinture*, without page number.

42   Teyssèdre, *Roger de Piles*.

Fig. 2: Page from Roger de Piles's "Balance of painters", in: Cours de peinture par principes. Paris 1708, without page number.

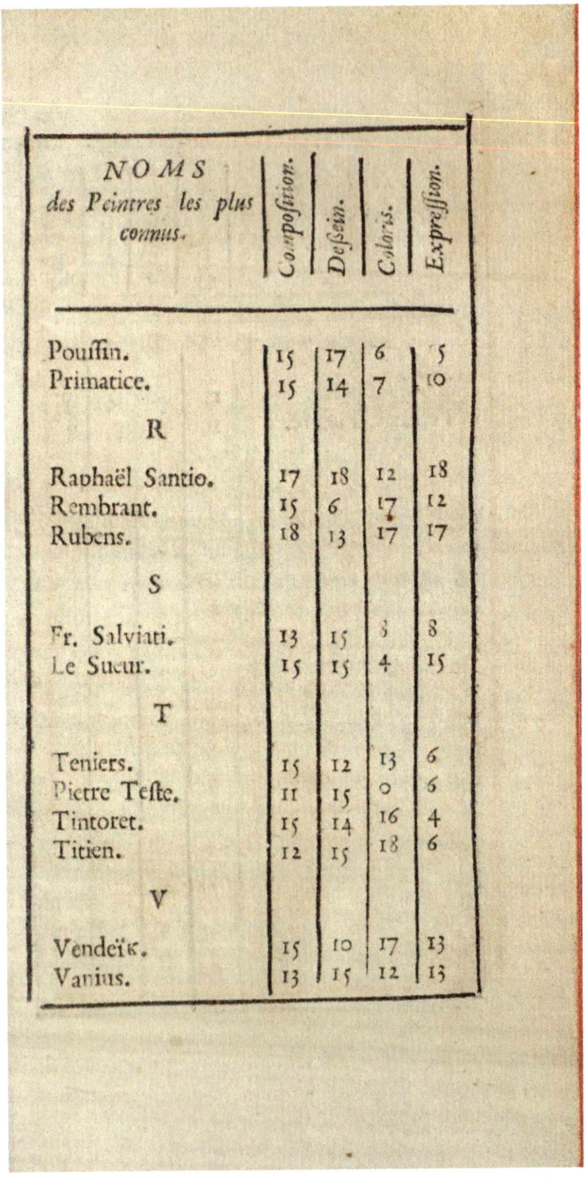

NOMS des Peintres les plus connus.	Composition.	Dessein.	Coloris.	Expression.
Poussin.	15	17	6	15
Primatice.	15	14	7	10
R				
Raphaël Santio.	17	18	12	18
Rembrant.	15	6	17	12
Rubens.	18	13	17	17
S				
Fr. Salviati.	13	15	8	8
Le Sueur.	15	15	4	15
T				
Teniers.	15	12	13	6
Pietre Teste.	11	15	0	6
Tintoret.	15	14	16	4
Titien.	12	15	18	6
V				
Vendeïk.	15	10	17	13
Vanius.	13	15	12	13

certainly high numbers in the first two categories composition (15) and drawing (17), but gave him poor marks for color (6) and expression (5). De Piles's evaluation diverges enormously from the high esteem that Poussin enjoyed at that time in the vicinity of the French royal academy that was still influenced by the classicist position of Charles Le Brun (1619–1690), André Félibien (1619–1695), and others. However, as Victor Ginsburg and Sheila Weyers have pointed out, de Piles was careful enough to not define the weight of each category so that it remains unclear if one has to compute all scores equally or if certain categories are, for example, three times as important as others.[43] This can lead to concurring readings and it may well explain why de Piles thought about the *"balance of painters"* rather as a game than as a helpful working tool.[44] However, in the most obvious calculation that sums up all four categories with a similar value of twenty—which means eighty all together—de Piles's most important artists would have been Raphael and Rubens (65), the Carraci (58), as well as Domenichino and Le Brun (56), whereas Michelangelo (37), for example, ranks toward the bottom of the field.[45]

2. The Attribution of the art work or practices of connoisseurial comparative viewing

Numbers are one way of comparing things with each other, but as de Piles's evaluations have shown, they are already the result of prior comparative operations. Analytically speaking, they represent complex forms of clustered comparisons that were used quantitatively in the evaluation of art. However, as results of previous qualitative judgments, it could be said that they can always be traced back to de Piles's second domain, the attribution of art works that was itself the result of practices of comparative vision. In fact, neither collecting art nor the practice of arranging images next to each other were eighteenth-century innovations. We can find, for instance, countless examples of juxtaposed images in the typological arrangements of medieval altarpieces or reliquary caskets.[46] What, then, makes comparative viewing in art connoisseurship most remarkable? Put in a nutshell, connoisseurs developed a particular interest in a plurality of images neither because

---

43 Ginsburgh/Weyers, On the contemporaneity, 116.
44 *"J'ay fait cet essai plutôt pour me divertir que pour attirer les autres dans mon sentiment"*, see De Piles, *Cours de peinture*, 489 [my italics].
45 See Nikolaus Pevsner, *Die Geschichte der Kunstakademien*, München 1986, 103, 336, note 111.
46 For the biblical 'typology' as a visual system founded in comparisons, see, for instance: Arwed Arnulf, Studien zum Klosterneuburger Ambo und den theologischen Quellen bildlicher Typologien von der Spätantike bis 1200, in: *Wiener Jahrbuch für Kunstgeschichte*, vol. 48, 1995, 19–23; Marek T. Kretschmer, *La typologie biblique comme forme de pensée dans l'historiographie médiévale* (Textes et études du Moyen Âge), Turnhout 2014.

of certain religious, political, or aesthetical functions, nor because of an artistic interest in specific techniques, motifs, and so forth. Rather, it allowed them to systematize artifacts taxonomically, and, as a consequence, to (re-)construct their position within an art historical narrative of whatsoever nature. Even if many of the first art connoisseurs were artists themselves,[47] their interests shifted little by little toward the relevance, the history, and the intellectual contexts of the art works, their provenance, and their artistic origin. In the beginning, such a curiosity may have been driven by the wish to formulate a normative canon in art schools providing an orientation for younger art students. But later, the intellectualization and assimilation of connoisseurial knowledge would become a main strategy within an institutionalizing academic art history. At the moment, it can be nothing other than a hypothesis that refunctionalized comparative viewing made a major contribution in the process of this 'scientification' process. While comparative viewing always formed part of the reception of artifacts, it first became an explicit methodical analyzing tool in the eighteenth century.

Such an analyzing way of comparative viewing in connoisseurship could profit from different impulses. Those worth mentioning are circles of early experts such as the one around Pierre Crozat (1661/1665–1740),[48] in which knowledge was accumulated and discussed starting from a magnificent private collection. Another, but overlapping field in which comparative viewing played a crucial role was the blossoming art market. Particularly the market for prints offered connoisseurs such as Michel de Marolles (1600–1681), Pierre-Jean Mariette (1694–1774), or Edme-François Gersaint (1694–1750) opportunities to try out and establish different practices of comparative viewing. Personal overlaps to the French *Académie* existed, where comparative approaches to images, as well, played a predominant role. In lectures, better known as the *conférences*,[49] the members of the *Académie* sought to theorize and systemize artistic and aesthetic rules.[50] When analyzing those lectures, it is not

---

47   Johannes Rößler has emphasized that until the 1870s, key positions in German museums remained in the hands of trained artists, see Johannes Rößler, Das Notizbuch als Werkzeug des Kunsthistorikers: Schrift und Zeichnung in den Forschungen von Wilhelm Bode und Carl Justi, in: Christoph Hoffmann (ed.), *Daten sichern. Schreiben und Zeichnen als Verfahren der Aufzeichnung*, Zürich 2008, 73–102, see 75, note 10.

48   See for instance: Cordélia Hattori, The Drawings Collection of Pierre Crozat (1665–1740), in: *Collecting Prints and Drawings in Europe, c. 1500–1750*, Farnham et al. 2003, 173–181.

49   For the edited volumes of the conferences of the Royal Academy of Painting and Sculpture held between 1648–1793, see https://www.perspectivia.net/publikationen/conference [last accessed May 16, 2018].

50   A good example for the rule-and-canon-oriented approach has been brought together by the secretary of the Royal Academy in a volume demonstrating all contemporary academic rules in texts and tables, see Henri Testelin, *Sentimens des plus habiles peintres du tems, sur la pratique de la peinture et sculpture: recueillis & mis en tables de preceptes, avec six discours academiques, extraits des conferences tenuës en l'Academie Royale desdits arts … par Henry Testelin, peintre du roi,*

difficult to see that many of them cannot be imagined without prior practices of comparisons. It is, moreover, important to emphasize that judging the quality between two artworks/artists, attributing the responsible masters, or distinguishing between the original work and the copies were also crucial for the academical discourse. The everyday connoisseurial practices entered the academic efforts from its very beginnings.

To become more concrete and to distinguish between the different practices of comparing, connoisseurs, first and foremost, experimented with different systems of ordering art in albums. They arranged prints and drawings according to a relative subject (e.g., jesters), a certain narrative (e.g., a passion sequence), the alphabetic order of the artist's names, the artist's reputation, the affiliation to an artistic profession (e.g., painters, engravers, etc.), according to chronological or topographical aspects, or even artistic techniques (e.g., engravings, colored woodcuts).[51] Those and other criteria are present in the structure of all broader eighteenth-century collections of engravings. It is important to emphasize that different principles of ordering were sometimes used synchronically by one and the same connoisseur. It would, therefore, be reductive to imagine a straightforward development of certain ordering principles in a connoisseur's collection. The famous art collector Michel de Marolles[52] offers a good example for someone who is analogously realizing different structures in his collection(s). Not only did he hold the largest collection of prints in France at the time of Louis XIV (1638–1715), but he also sold it to the king in 1667, and—in a very short span of time—was able to bring together a second print collection of fairly the same extent of circa one hundred and twenty thousand leaves.[53] His methods of collecting exemplify an early degree of professionalized connoisseurship that found its successors with a particular interest in those albums that were arranged according to artists, schools, regions, and fame. Two-

---

professeur & secretaire en ladite Academie, ed. by Académie royale de peinture et de sculpture, La Hague 1680.

51 A meticulous analysis of the different order structures of Michel de Marolles's albums has been presented by Brakensiek, Stephan, *Vom 'Theatrum mundi' zum 'Cabinet des Estampes': das Sammeln von Druckgraphik in Deutschland 1565–1821* (Studien zur Kunstgeschichte, 150), Hildesheim 2003, 17–39.

52 Cf. Jean Jouberton, Une relecture du *Livre des peintres et graveurs* de Michel de Marolles, in: *Nouvelles de l'estampe* 249 (2014), 4–15; Véronique Meyer, Marolles illustré: Chauveau, Mellan, Nanteuil et les autres, in: Peter Fuhring/Barbara Brejon de Lavergnée/Marianne Grivel (eds.), *L'estampe au grand siècle*, Paris 2010, 277–291; Stephan Brakensiek, Sammeln, Ordnen und Erkennen: frühneuzeitliche Druckgraphiksammlungen und ihre Funktion als Studien- und Erkenntnisorte; das Beispiel der Sammlung Michel de Marolles' (1600–1681), in: Robert Felfe/Angelika Lozar (eds.), *Frühneuzeitliche Sammlungspraxis und Literatur*, Berlin 2006, 130–162.

53 Brakensiek, *Theatrum mundi*, 18, 22–23.

Fig. 3: Album double page from the Michel de Marolles print collection, Paris, Bibliothèque nationale de France, Estampes et photographie, Reserve EC-37-Boite Fol 1, fol. 82v–83.

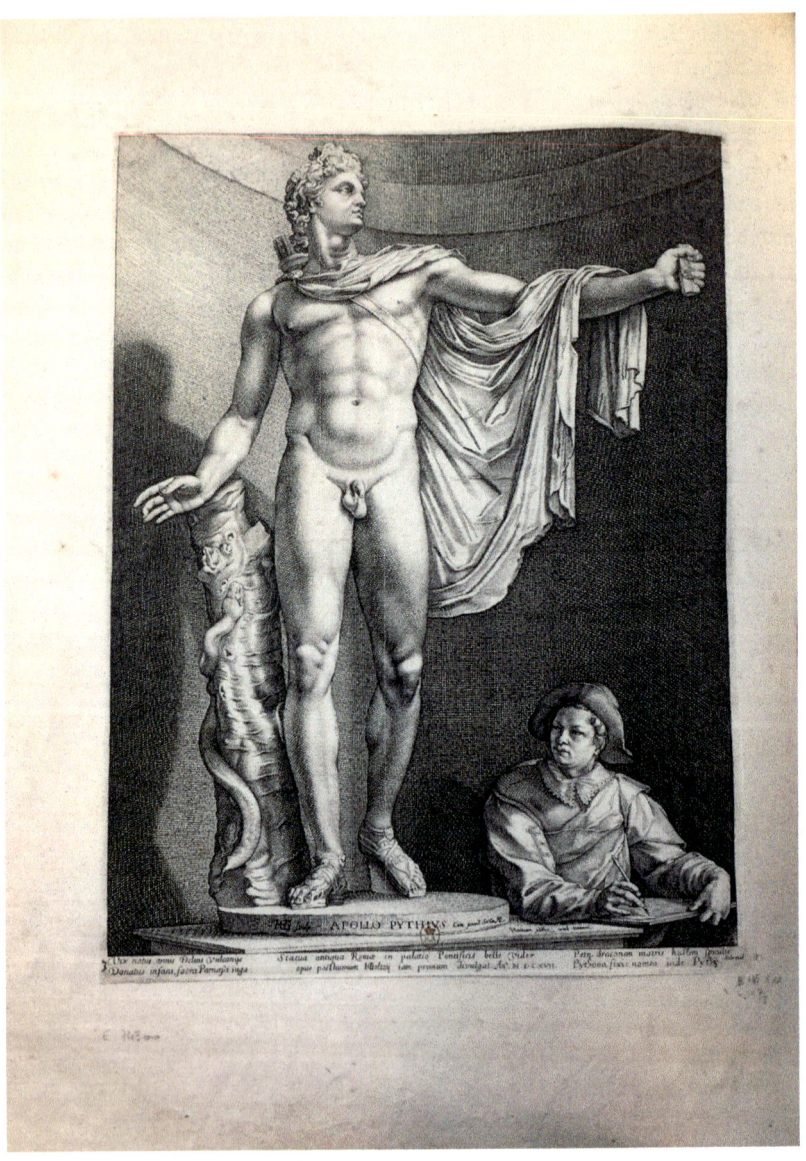

thirds of his collection, however, were systematized according to an older principle that is reminiscent of Samuel Quicchelberg's (1529–1567) universal approach

of gathering all phenomena known to humankind.[54] In altogether seventy cate-

---

54   Cf. Brakensiek, Sammeln, Ordnen und Erkennen, 136. This claim is already present in Quicchelberg's title "rerum universitatis singulas materias et imagines": Samuel Quicchelberg, *Inscriptiones vel tituli Theatri amplissimi, complectentis rerum universitatis singulas ma-*

gories, Marolles organized prints with respect to the *Artes liberales*,[55] conceding that one of the main objectives of his albums was educational.[56] However, the question arises how well Marolles's albums satisfy the demand to acquire universal knowledge from the gathered engravings, given that not only the different order structures within his collection but also the side-by-side confrontations of engravings point to very different levels of comparisons. Stephan Brakensiek has underlined how difficult it sometimes is to ascertain the underlying order principle of an album double page. In Brakensiek's opinion, Marolles sticks with the principles of *curiositas* and *varietas*[57] that were central epistemic strategies in early modern curiosity cabinets. Yet, the different levels of comparison also result, amongst others, from particular conditions of visual comparisons themselves—that is, for instance, the almost endless possibilities of identifying *tertia comparationis* and assumptions of comparability ("*Gleichartigkeitsannahmen*"). What is meant by that? Analytically speaking, by doing comparisons, one is juxtaposing at least two *comparata* and is relating both to one or more *tertia comparationis*. It is useful to understand comparisons as practices that are performed by at least one actor and are always situated in a particular context. Moreover, one could say that every comparison is based on an implicit or explicit assumption of comparability.

How crucial is it to know more about the 'intended' *tertium comperationis*, if any? It seems to be worth raising this question with regard to a characteristic relict of Marolles's connoisseurial activities: By applying the definition to the arrangement of a double page (Fig. 3)[58] from one of Marolles's albums with prints by Hendrick Goltzius (1558–1617), it rapidly comes to the point at which it is difficult to precisely specify the historical intention of the presented comparison of prints.

It is vital to note that the following considerations are not intended to describe a historical practice of comparing, but, first of all, the difficulties that generally accompany practices of comparing images. The two Goltzius albums form part of

---

terias et imagines eximias etc, München 1565, URL: http://www.europeana.eu/portal/record-ABO/%2BZ178696704.html [last accessed July 16, 2018].

55 Cf. Brakensiek, Sammeln, Ordnen und Erkennen, 135; Michel de Marolles, *Catalogue de livres d'estampes et de figures en taille douce: avec un dénombrement des pieces qui y sont contenuës; fait à Paris en l'anneé 1666*, Paris 1666, 9–14.

56 Cf. Brakensiek, Sammeln, Ordnen und Erkennen, 144; Marolles, *Catalogue*, 9: "Cependant s'il faut parler de leur [i.e., prints] utilité pour l'instruction de ceux qui les aiment, ou pour former l'esprit d'un jeune Prince, il est certain que les Estampes bien choisies & bien disposées donnent agreablement la connoissance, non seulement de toutes les Sciences, & de tous les beaux Arts, mais encore de toutes les choses imaginables."

57 Cf. Brakensiek, Sammeln, Ordnen und Erkennen, 139.

58 Album double page from the Michel de Marolles print collection, Paris, Bibliothèques nationale de France, Estampes et photographie, Reserve EC-37-Boite Fol 1, fol. 82v–83, URL: http://catalogue.bnf.fr/ark:/12148/cb43601416n [last accessed July 18, 2018].

a comprehensive collection that was sold to King Louis XIV and rearranged completely by Marolles before it entered the royal collection.[59] Hence, in all probability, the two albums represent a structure that had been set carefully. The double page[60] shows on the left side the second state of the famous *Apollo Belevedere* executed by Goltzius,[61] whereas on the right side, four leaves are placed next to each other, that is, first, the *Unequal couple* by Claes Jansz. Visscher (1587–1652), on which both Goltzius's family armor and the monogram "HG" imply his authorship;[62] second, the *Hercules Boarium* executed by an anonymous artist and signed on the pedestal with *"HGoltzius fecit"*;[63] third, the engraving *Death surprising a young man* by Jan Saenredam (1565–1607) after a design by Goltzius;[64] and fourth, *Judith with the head of Holofernes* by Goltzius after a design by Bartholomeus Spranger (1546–1611).[65] This complex combination of engravings demonstrates the general ambiguity of images in accounting for a certain *tertium comparationis*; this is aggravated by the fact that the *comparata* as well as the assumption of comparability are not defined either. It is, thus, not perfectly clear whether the combination of engravings bears a deeper significance or not, because, thematically, they vary widely. The *Apollo Belvedere* is one of the most famous Roman sculptures that became a prototype for 'perfect antiquity' in neoclassical times. The engraving represents not only the Palatine sculpture but also the moment when young artist takes a sketch of it in chalk. Also, the *Hercules Boarium* represents a Roman sculpture, now, however, a sculpture that has been made in bronze and not in marble. Just like the *Apollo Belvedere*, the Roman demigod is executed in a sharp view from below. Therefore, the perspective on the sculpture could be the requested *tertium* that sets the comparison between the two prints. Another of the prints, *Judith with the head of Holofernes*, is also composed from a worm's eye perspective that increases its dramatic effect. However,

---

59 Album double page from the Michel de Marolles print collection, Paris, Bibliothèques nationale de France, Estampes et photographie, Reserve EC-37-Boite Fol 1, fol. 82v–83.
60 Album double page from the Michel de Marolles print collection, Paris, Bibliothèques nationale de France, Estampes et photographie, Reserve EC-37-Boite Fol 1, fol. 82v–83.
61 Marjolein Leesberg/Huigen Leeflang (eds.), *The New Hollstein Dutch & Flemish Etchings, Engravings and Woodcuts 1450-1700 – Hendrick Goltzius*, part ii, Amsterdam 2012, NH 380/II, 370.
62 Leesberg/Leeflang, *New Hollstein Hendrick Goltzius*, part iv, NH D9, 253. The inscription is: "Decrepitus juvenem lepidamque movere Puellam /Conatur, turpi victus amore senex /Cascus ait, cascam: corpucula digna patula /Quaero: conjugii spes tibi nulla mei." (Translation: "Taken by shameful love the decrepit old man tries to persuade the jolly girl. But she says: Old goes with old, I look for a lid that fits my jug. I think you do not match me").
63 Leesberg/Leeflang, *New Hollstein Hendrick Goltzius*, part iv, NH D9, 253.
64 Leesberg/Leeflang, *New Hollstein Hendrick Goltzius*, part iii, NH 530, 222. The inscription is: "*FVI, NON SVM. ES, NON ERIS*" (Translation: "What I was, I am not; what you are, you will not be").
65 Leesberg/Leeflang, *New Hollstein Hendrick Goltzius*, part ii, NH 336/I, 298. The inscription is: "*Nemo suis nimium confidat viribus, ausis Nemo suis temerè; Docet hoc Holophernis amarus Exitus [...]*." A translation is given in the text.

different kinds of heroism could also be the subject of the juxtaposition that link the three prints. Neither the one nor the other *tertium* appear to be addressed in the two prints hitherto not mentioned. Whereas the first one takes into consideration the inappropriate desire of an old man and a young woman's refusal, the second shows a young man strolling through a graveyard with an Egyptian pyramid in the background. He bumps into a skeleton that reminds him of his own mortal condition. Apparently, in this case, the experience of time or an idea of vanitas may have been the *tertium*, and one could ask whether or not this is also true for the other three prints. Given the inscription present in the Judith print that clearly points to the transience of forceful men ("No one should trust its own forces too much, nor its reckless boldness; this teaches the bitter end of Holofernes [...]"), the other two effigies of god and demigod are also no more than a distant echo of a time in which the histories and legends connected with the two protagonists were still commonly known. Finally, it is also conceivable that Marolles had just one detail in mind that serves him as *comparatum*, for example, the figures' hands. Consequently, the perspective changes once again because the *tertium* may now be a particular gesture of the hand.

What becomes obvious from a brief analysis of the double page is that the historical practice of connoisseurial comparative viewing is far from being one that discloses its secrets unequivocally. On the contrary, more than in the polysemy of texts, images withdraw themselves from an unequivocal 'readability.' If, furthermore, a paratext on the image always creates a new visibility that stands against the visible as such—as can be argued with Michel Foucault (1926–1984)—then the ambiguity of the dispositive will increase even further.[66] Connoisseurial practices of arranging images in albums are pre-textual, but they nevertheless might aim toward a certain goal. Insofar we have to assume that they are intentional to a certain degree. They create—so the hypothesis—a hiatus comparable to the one between the visible and the sayable. The medial and material quality of 'the things visible' are obvious focal points for this underestimated effect. For instance, by arranging prints with different paper qualities, by juxtaposing an original with a copy—both distinguishable only through minor differences between lines, hatches, shadows, and so forth—the connoisseur nails down a particular but unuttered relationship between the chosen prints. This parapractice that comprises, for instance, the selection process, the differentiation between material qualities, or the alignment of prints in the portfolio might enfold the same impact as a paratext.

---

66 Falk Wolf describes the gap between the visible and the sayable as one that has determined art historical writing from the beginning, see Falk Wolf, *Kunstgeschichte als Bild. Medien- und Wissenschaftstheoretische Positionen der Kunstgeschichte im 19. Jahrhundert*, Doctoral dissertation, University of Basel, Switzerland, 2017, 4–7.

It is important to emphasize that the connoisseurial arrangements must not always have pursued a specific meaning or goal. On the contrary, it appears probable that, for example, formalistic reasons could likewise have been decisive elements that dominated the everyday experience of the connoisseur. Certain aspects can be recognized in the blink of an eye or a 'coup d'œil.'[67] Marolles might have chosen the five prints on the double page (Fig. 3) because all of them show freestanding figures. This formalistic similarity[68] is perhaps trivial, but it brings to the fore a general phenomenon present in images: On the one hand, it is much easier to perceive the content of one or more images—as opposed to that of a text—in a very short span of time. In the case of the double page, this might be the topic 'freestanding figure.' In that sense, as some forms of comparisons—metaphors for instance—can be understood as a shorthand method, image arrangements could also present certain aspects instantly. On the other hand, a detailed picture analysis might require much more time and prerequisites than every thorough textual analysis, as has been shown by the arduous search for a *tertium* or the assumption of comparability on only one double page of Marolles' Goltzius album. Of course, comparing images can be a particularly effective way to grasp a certain topic, but it does not guarantee a mutual understanding of the intention of the comparative arrangement. Such arrangements may allow us to make an argument beyond any textual dimension, but that provides both clearly highlighted *tertia* and assumptions of comparability. For the moment, we have to assume that for Marolles, the initiator of the comparative arrangement, the latent openness of his 'composition' with respect to the *tertia* and the assumption of comparability poses no problem at all. The context—a portfolio with works by Goltzius—clarifies the most important task of such juxtapositions, namely the attribution to a particular artist. In the eyes of the author of the comparative arrangement, the decision for a topic such as 'freestanding figure' might have facilitated statements on how Goltzius solved certain artistic tasks. This raises, however, the question whether or not practices of comparing in the eighteenth century are in any way new or distinct from those already common two or more centuries earlier.

---

67 The term '*coup d'œil*' is connected to the request of eighteenth-century theorists that a 'tableau' has to be apprehensible in a single glance of an eye, see Smentek, *Mariette and the Science of the Connoisseur*, 149–151. How complex the interplay between contemplative and cursory sight can be has been discussed vividly by Norman Bryson who differentiates between the concepts "gaze" ("regard") and "glance" ("*coup d'œil*"), see Norman Bryson, *Vision and painting: the logic of the gaze* (Language, discourse, society), London 1988, 87–133.

68 Dorothee Kimmich has emphasized the relationship between similarity as a theoretical paradigm and comparison in a lecture within the framework of the Collaborative Research Center SFB 1288 "Practices of Comparing. Changing and Ordering the World", Bielefeld University, in July 2018. She stressed that—as with comparisons—similarities are always context-related. See also: Anil Bhatti/Dorothee Kimmich (eds.), *Similarities*, Tulika 2018.

3. Differentiating between original and copy or distinct practices of comparing in connoisseurship

An early example of connoisseurship and art expertise is Giorgio Vasari's private collection of drawings. Parallel to his famous *Lives of the most eminent painters, sculptors and architects*,[69] first published in 1550 and then in an expanded version in 1568, the painter-author, sometimes called the 'father of art history', assembled a vast collection of original drawings on approximately five hundred to seven hundred sheets that he referred to as his *"libro de' disegni"*—his book of drawings.[70] Unfortunately, none of the ten to twelve original volumes has been preserved. However, single sheets survived and their discovery, such as that of the one kept in the National Gallery in Washington attracted the attention of art historians (Fig. 4).[71]

The album page represents a composition of four single metal point drawings on the recto from which—in reference to the large size of the album page of 56.7 x 45.7 cm—every drawing could have stood alone for itself. However, Vasari apparently invested much effort in pasting them together in one arrangement. He not only ordered them symmetrically, but also invented an architectural framework.[72] The viewer is invited to perceive them as parts of a sixteenth-century palazzo wall decoration.[73] One of the purposes of such an arrangement might have been the creation of a visual argument by comparing drawing styles with each other and establishing an artistic identity. This can be deduced from the two cartouches at the bottom of the two central drawings with the head of a young boy above and different body studies below. Whereas the sepia rendered drawing below has been attributed by Vasari to the artist Filippo Lippi (1406–1469), the cartouche of the head study remained empty. Today, both drawings have been reattributed, the different body studies to Filippo Lippi's son Filippino (1457–1504), the young man's head to Sandro Botticelli (1445–1510), but it is not clear whether or not Vasari knew that the head is not from Filippo Lippi's hand. Whatever the reason, the author of the

---

69 Giorgio Vasari, *Le vite de' piv eccellenti pittori, scvltori, et architettori*, 3 vols., 2nd & expanded ed., Fiorenza 1568.
70 Cf. Anna Forlani Tempesti, Giorgio Vasari and the 'Libro de' Disegni': A Paper Museum or Portable Gallery, in: Maia Wellington Gahtan (ed.), *Giorgo Vasari and the Birth of the Museum*, Farnham et al. 2014, 31–52; Kimberly Schenck, A Page from Giorgio Vasari's 'Libro de' Disegni' as Composite Object, in: *Facture. National Gallery of Art* 1 (2013), 2–31.
71 Album page from *Libro de' Disegni*; sheets probably 1480–1504; mounting and framework by Giorgio Vasari, after 1524; 56,7 x 45,7 cm, Washington, National Gallery of Art, Woodner Collection, Patrons' Permanent Fund 1991.190.1.
72 As far as we can say, Giorgio Vasari was the first to introduce such architectural frames, see Catherine Monbeig-Goguel, Le dessin encadré, in: *Revue de l'art* 76 (1987), 25–31.
73 Kimberly Schenck has further specified that the "wall" resembles the "frescoes in the Chamber of Fortune (1548) at his [Vasari's] home (Casa Vasari) in Arrezo [...]", see Schenck, A Page from Giorgio Vasari's 'Libro de' Disegni', 11.

Fig. 4: Album page from "Libro de' Disegni"; sheets probably 1480–1504; mounting and framework by Giorgio Vasari, after 1524; Washington, National Gallery of Art, Woodner Collection, Patrons' Permanent Fund 1991.190.1.

album collage has worked toward a stylistic correspondence and interrelationship. He thereby involved himself artistically by creating an architectural frame. Such a supplementary structure should not be underestimated given that *"parerga* [...] can have a decisive impact on the question of which agency may be produced in a given situation,"[74] and that *"parerga* may be understood as a hinge or a threshold between object und subject."[75] Moreover, in this example, the parerga perform an obvious function because they bring together more than one ergon and, therefore, aim to represent an aesthetic unity. The empty cartouche under the study of a young man's head might epitomize Vasari's doubts about the attribution of this

---

74 Grave et al., Agency of Display, 11 [italics in original].
75 Grave et al., Agency of Display, 14 [italics in original].

very drawing, but the entire page enshrines Filippo Lippi's authorship or at least it insinuates the execution in the same workshop. Likewise, the verso of the album leaf with altogether six mounted drawings in different techniques appears to prove Vasari's intention to establish the full range of Filippo's drawing style: a rare colored drawing with *Saint Roch between Saints Anthony Abbot and Catherine of Alexandria* today attributed to Raffaellino del Garbo (1466–1527) is—once again—(erroneously) identified in the cartouche as a work by Filippo Lippi.[76] As early as 1930, Erwin Panofsky stressed the didactic impact of Vasari's framings that provided initial evidence for the practice of evaluating objects from an indisputable art historical perspective.[77] As Vasari understood the *"arte del disegno"* as the *"Urkunst"*[78] (original art) for all three spatial arts (architecture, sculpture, painting), the comparative arrangement of his *libro di disegni* might have had the aim to extract a certain *summa* of every master present in his collection. However, his treatment prevents beholders from reformulating any attribution. On the contrary, they are fixed in individual but normative solutions in which the drawings are often enough even trimmed to fit into a certain composition.

One of the principal connoisseurs of the eighteenth century, Pierre-Jean Mariette,[79] knew Vasari's individualizing approach because he could buy not just some sheets but a complete volume of Vasari's *libro de' disegni* on the French art market.[80] This chance discovery prompted him to discuss the function of Vasari's collection of drawings for the conception of his *Vite*. Thus, in his posthumously published *Abcedario*, Mariette assumes that: "one would have no doubt that this discussion cannot be done but through *comparison*. Vasari's album would have been a perpetual and unquestionable school of critique."[81] Mariette's remarkable historicizing

---

76   Colored illustrations of the Washington recto and verso as well as many details are reproduced in Schenck, A Page from Giorgio Vasari's 'Libro de' Disegni', 2–31.

77   Cf. Erwin Panofsky, Das erste Blatt aus dem 'Libro' Giorgio Vasaris: eine Studie über die Beurteilung der Gotik in der italienischen Renaissance; mit einem Exkurs über zwei Fassadenprojekte Domenico Beccafumis, in: *Städel-Jahrbuch* 6, Frankfurt a. M. 1930, 25–72, see 63; see also Monbeig-Goguel, Le dessin encadré, 26.

78   Panofsky, Das erste Blatt, 58.

79   For the most recent monographic volumes on Pierre-Jean Mariette and his drawing collection, see Valérie Kobi, *Dans l'œil du connaisseur. Pierre-Jean Mariette (1694–1774) et la construction des savoirs en histoire de l'art* (Collection "Art & société"), Rennes 2017; Smentek, *Mariette and the Science of the Connoisseur*; Pierre Rosenberg/Laure Barthélemy-Labeeuw, *Les dessins de la collection Mariette: école française*, vol. 1 A–E, vol. 2 F–W, Milan 2011.

80   The information is given in: Pierre-Jean Mariette, *Abecedario de P. J. Mariette et autres notes inédites de cet amateur sur les arts et les artists. Ouvrage publié d'après les manuscrits autographes conservés au cabinet des estampes de la Bibliothèque impériale*, vol. 3, Paris 1851–1860, 160–161, note 1.

81   [My translation and emphasis]. Original quote: "[...] *on n'auroit eu aucun doute; cette discussion ne se pouvant bien faire que par* comparaison, *le recueil du Vasari auroit été une perpétuelle et une sûre école de critique.*", see Mariette, Abecedario, vol. 3, 160, note 1.

classification should, however, be treated with some caution, because what he suggests for Vasari's practice describes rather his own *"goût de comparaison."* Without question, Mariette imitated some of Vasari's most obvious idiosyncrasies: A good example is Vasari's effort to painstakingly repair Botticelli's drawing with the head of a young man in the lower right corner by carefully using a wash of almost the same color. Mariette, too, executed innumerable repairs and also followed Vasari by integrating his drawings into illusionistic arrangements such as frames or reticent architectures as can be seen in the example with the drawing of a putto bending down that is now attributed to Giorgione (1477/78–1510) (Fig. 5).

Fig. 5: Giorgione (attributed), Putto bending down, *mounting and framing by Pierre-Jean Mariette: New York, Metropolitan Museum, Rogers Fund, 1911, acc. no. 11.66.5.*

However, while Vasari took an artistic approach with individual solutions for his arrangements, Mariette established a rather systematic way to frame his drawings—and what is even more important—he preferred mats for every single drawing as far as they were medium sized. One could argue that Mariette was fully aware of the fact that "material and performative interventions of isolation, focusing, framing and staging make the object addressable as a single object."[82] Indeed, they underline the visual integrity of the drawing and force the viewer to examine it with the same attention as a framed painting. Appropriately, Mariette characterized his framings as a way of bringing drawings "back to life,"[83] giving his framing practice a "museum effect."[84] It is true that the decision for more or less unified (characteristic blue) mats of medium size as well as the adoption of Vasari's system of cartouches for the artists' names are strategies still used today in drawing collections.[85] With regard to conservation and presentation, the connoisseur anticipates museum principles that expose the particular quality of every single drawing.[86] Consequently, in most cases, Mariette avoided doing precisely what this chapter is primarily about, namely a comparative arrangement of drawings. It would be premature to conclude that Mariette—similarly to the romantic tendency present, for example, in the writings of Wilhelm Heinrich Wackenroder (1773–1798) and Ludwig Tieck (1773–1853)—thought that "comparison is a serious impediment to any appreciation."[87] On the contrary, as indicated in his writings, the advantage of his

---

82   Grave et al., Agency of Display, 13.
83   Smentek, *Mariette and the Science of the Connoisseur*, 145. French original: "les avois fait revivre les tira du rebut", see Pierre-Jean Mariette, Lettre sur Léonard de Vinci, Peintre Florentin. A Monsieur le C: de C., in: *Recueil de testes de caractère & de charges dessinées par Léonard de Vinci Florentin & gravées par M. le C de C*, Paris 1730, 19.
84   However, he was not the first to use blue mats for framing his drawing collection: "Que penser en fin de compte de l'appellation 'Bleu Mariette'? Il faut observer que Mariette n'en fut pas l'inventeur et qu'il semble s'être inspure de ses prédécesseurs immédiats. On sait, par exemple. qu'un Antoine Coypel rhabilla de bandes bleues les dessins issus de la collection Jabach achetés par Louis XIV", see Dominique Le Marois, Les montages de dessins au XVIIIe siècle: l' exemple de Mariette, in: *Bulletin de la Société de l'Histoire de l'Art Français*, 1982, 87–96, see 90.
85   Interestingly, Le Marois has differentiated between three categories of blue "Mariette mats" from which not all had a cartouche with the artist's name beneath the drawing; consequently, the author categorizes these mats as "Montages de 'recherche'", see Le Marois, Les montages, 94.
86   Smentek, *Mariette and the Science of the Connoisseur*, 149; see Svetlana Alpers, The Museum as a Way of Seeing, in: Ivan Karp/Steven D. Lavine, *Exhibiting cultures: the poetics and politics of museum display*, Washington D.C. 1991, 25–32, see 27.
87   Romantic reasoning calls for an emotional rather than a rational approach, and in the case of Wackenroder and Tieck, it comes with a reevaluation of northern art and architecture. The full quote is: "But now I will turn my attention exclusively to you, my dear Albrecht [Dürer]. *Comparison* is a serious impediment to any appreciation, and even the most sublime beauty in art makes its full and proper impact on us only when our gaze is not distracted by other

system lies in its high degree of flexibility: "je ne suis pas étonné que celui qui est parvenu au point de connoissance dont je parle, se voïe le plus souvent obligé de quitter ses premiers sentimens, ou du moins de rectifier les idées qu'il avoit prises de certains Maistres."[88] Mounting the greater part of his collected drawings independently was the only way to ensure that all could be compared to each other at any given moment, and that attributions could be changed if necessary.[89] As has been shown by Kristel Smentek, Mariette himself, of course, also experimented with concrete juxtapositions in which the comparative quality is even reflected in captions such as *"Achetypon [...] Apographum"* or *"juxta methodum."*[90] Another *modus operandi* is present in an album without any mats that is preserved in the Metropolitan Museum, New York.[91] Here, different stages and variants of prints were glued only selectively onto the support, so that Mariette and probably also his father Jean Mariette (1660–1742) would have the opportunity to rearrange the entire page if new findings were to require any corrections.[92] It is no coincidence that the arrangement of the Metropolitan Mariette album is reminiscent of Marolles's album pages discussed in the second section of this chapter. The Metropolitan album continues a systematic approach established between 1717 and 1719 by Mariette and his father Jean Mariette for the print collection of Prince Eugene of Savoy (1663–1736).[93]

---

beauties. Heaven has so distributed its gifts among the great artists of the world that we must pause before each one and pay to each his fair share of our respect. Genuine art may flourish not only under Italian skies or under majestic domes and Corinthian columns, but under pointed arches, fantastically ornamented buildings, and Gothic spires.", see Wilhelm Heinrich Wackenroder/Ludwig Tieck, *Outpourings of an Art-Loving Friar*, New York 1975, 58 [my italics].

88 Mariette, Lettre sur Léonard de Vinci, 2; see also: Smentek, *Mariette and the Science of the Connoisseur*, 157.

89 This practice has been mentioned by De Piles already in 1699: "Ils en *jugeront* promptement par la facilité de feüilleter quelques papiers, & de *comparer* ainsi les Productions d'un Maître avec celles d'un autre [...]", see Roger de Piles, *Abregé de la vie des peintres, avec des reflexions sur leurs ouvrages, et un Traité du peintre parfait, de la connoissance des desseins, & de l'utilité des estampes*, Paris 1699, 83 [my italics], URL: http://gallica.bnf.fr/ark:/12148/bpt6k6568782t [last accessed August 27, 2018].

90 Smentek, *Mariette and the Science of the Connoisseur*, 156–157.

91 Album Mariette, New York, The Metropolitan Museum of Art, Harris Brisbane Dick Fund, 1927, 27.78.2, URL: https://www.metmuseum.org/art/collection/search/361938 [last accessed August 27, 2018].

92 To my knowledge, Michel de Marolles has first underlined that it is useful to fix prints and drawings only on the four, reinforced corners, see Marolles, Catalogue, 9: *"Il n'est pourtant pas necessaire de les y coller à plat, & sur tout, les pieces rares & precieuses des grands Maistres, qui se trouvent quelquefois si malaisément, À quoy peu de colle de farine ou d'amidon, peut suffire aux quatre coins sur de beau papier, dont la dépence aussi bien que de la Reliure des Livres est assez considerable."*

93 Chiara Gauna has highlighted the comparability of the Metropolitan Mariette album and the project executed for Prince Eugene, see Chiara Gauna, Pierre-Jean Mariette e le 'connoissances multipliées': classificazioni, gerarchie, valori, in: Chiara Gauna (ed.), *La sfida delle*

Of course, the value and uniqueness of prints is different from that of drawings, and here may lie a convincing explanation for the distinct organization of an album page with multiple prints on the one hand and the preference for single drawings under blue mats on the other. However, in both cases, it can be said that Mariette did not just continue Vasari's practice of creating intentionally normative collages, but instead incorporated a skepticism into his system of attribution. Comparisons are crucial for every aesthetic judgment, but they are rather unable to yield normative results. Accordingly, the comparative quality in Vasari's *libro de' disegni* is not very pronounced—on the contrary, lots of his attributions could not withstand a refined connoisseurial practice. One could think of Charles Coypel's critic of the *"pêle-mêle dans de vieux portefeuilles,"*[94] where still at the beginning of the eighteenth century, a differentiation between original and copy existed only very rarely. But the differentiation between original and copy became the most important task of all for the decades to come.

A productive misreading of Coypel's phrase "est sans nule comparaison" as "useless comparison"[95] in Esther Bell's article points to a remarkable question:[96] Is the change of connoisseurial practices possibly present in the increasing efficiency of comparative doing itself? Mariette's practice-oriented work stands as an example for the connoisseur's specific skills that, besides the development of a particular vocabulary in the sense of the *"sciences des mots,"*[97] enabled them to systematize and categorize the vast heritage of artistic artifacts. This also implied the exclusion of once admired art pieces and a strict culture of separating and dismissing even helpful copies. It "was inseparable from a massive reorganization of knowledge and social practices that modified in myriad ways the productive, cognitive, and desiring capacities of the human subject."[98] The reorganization of knowledge again, as has already been recognized critically by Antoine Quatremère de Quincy

---

      stampe. Parigi Torino 1650–1906, Torino 2017, 7–31, see 10. Consistent with this observation, Valérie Kobi enfolds the crucial formative impact of the Viennese project for the young Pierre-Jean Mariette, see Kobi, *Dans l'œil du connaisseur*, 61–94.

94 "*Les desseins du Roi sont aujourd'hui dans un ordre très different de celui où ils étoient lorsque ce depôt fut reunis a la garde des mon Père ... Les desseins originaux et les copies étoient pêle-mêle dans de vieux portefeuilles et malheureusement le nombre des copies est sans nule comparaison plus considerable que celui des originaux.*", Paris, Institut Custodia, inv. no. 9555, see Esther Bell, A Curator at the Louvre: Charles Coypel and the Royal Collections, in: *Journal18: a journal of eighteenth-century art and culture* 2 (2016), 1–16 [13–14], URL: https://doi.org/10.30610/2.2016.6 [last accessed August 27, 2018].

95 A more precise translation reads as following: "[...] the number of copies is without any comparison more considerable than [...]".

96 Bell, Curator at the Louvre, 5.

97 Marc-Antoine Laugier, *Maniere de bien juger des ouvrages de peinture*, Paris 1771, 8.

98 Jonathan Crary, *Techniques of the Observer: On Vision and Modernity in the Nineteenth Century*, Cambridge 1991, 3.

(1755–1849), is accompanied by some sort of manipulation: "You know that in every part of human knowledge there exists a sort of manipulation that makes every scientific department resemble a workshop *["espèce d'attélier"]* in which every worker has his part and deals only with his part."[99] And, truly, the new *"Übersichtlichkeit' des Zuhandenseins,"*[100] the clarity of the present-to-hand, not only often upholds a surprising lack of systematization as Hans Christian Hönes has pointed out, but it is won at the price of an artificial, manipulating specialism. The connoisseur's visual experiences gained in life-long comparative practices are gained in the *"espèce d'attélier,"* and, generally, they almost never find their way 'out' into the art discourse.

A first outlook

Connoisseurial knowledge results more from the doing than from the application of contemporary theories. This is why a practice-theoretical approach is able to enfold in a particular way those types of questions that are focusing on, for example, the routinization of practices, the treatment of artifacts, and the interrelating of social networks. That the "taste of comparison," first described by Dubos, played a crucial role in the wide range of connoisseurial practices but also in further strategies of a developing academic art history becomes obvious in many of the examples discussed above. Two last cases may illustrate on very different levels why the 'aesthetic surplus'—namely the artwork's infinite and unclosed potential to create meaning[101]—is maybe the reason for comparative connoisseurial practices being discredited increasingly in the nineteenth to twenty-first centuries. In one plate from Jean Baptiste Seroux d'Agincourt's (1730–1814) *Histoire de l'art par monumens*[102] (Fig. 6), the observer is invited to compare drawings by Raphael (1483–1520) with antique fragments of sarcophagi in order to understand in a glance the principles of the 'Re-naissance' of the Antique in sixteenth-century art.

---

99 [My translation]. Original quote: "Vous savez qu'il existe, dans chaque partie des connoissances humaines, une sorte de manipulation qui fait ressembler chaque département de la science, à une espèce d'attélier, dans lequel chaque ouvrier a sa partie, et ne s'occupe qu'elle.", see Antoine Chrysostôme Quatremère de Quincy, *Lettres sur le préjudice qu'occasionneroit aux arts et à la science, le déplacement des monuments de lart de l'Italie*, Paris 1796, 27. See also: Pascal Griener, *La République de l'oeil: l'expérience de l'art au siècle des Lumières* (Collection du Collège de France), Paris 2010, 12.
100 Hans C. Hönes, *Kunst am Ursprung: das Nachleben der Bilder und die Souveränität des Antiquars* (Image, 69), Bielefeld 2014, 236.
101 This concept forms a crucial part of Gottfried Boehm's conceptualization of the 'iconic difference', see Gottfried Boehm, Die Wiederkehr der Bilder, in: Gottfried Boehm (ed.), *Was ist ein Bild?* (Bild und Text), München 1994, 11–38.
102 Jean Baptiste Seroux D'Agincourt, *Histoire de l'art par les monumens, depuis sa décadence au IVe siècle jusqu'à son renouvellement au XVIe: ouvrage enrichi de 325 pl.*, 6 vols., Paris 1823.

Fig. 6: Jean Baptiste Louis Georges Seroux d'Agincourt, Histoire de l'art par les monumens, depuis sa décadence au IVe siècle jusqu'à son renouvellement au XVIe: Planches. Peinture; deuxième et troisième parties. Tables générales des matières, vol. 6, Paris 1823, plate 183.

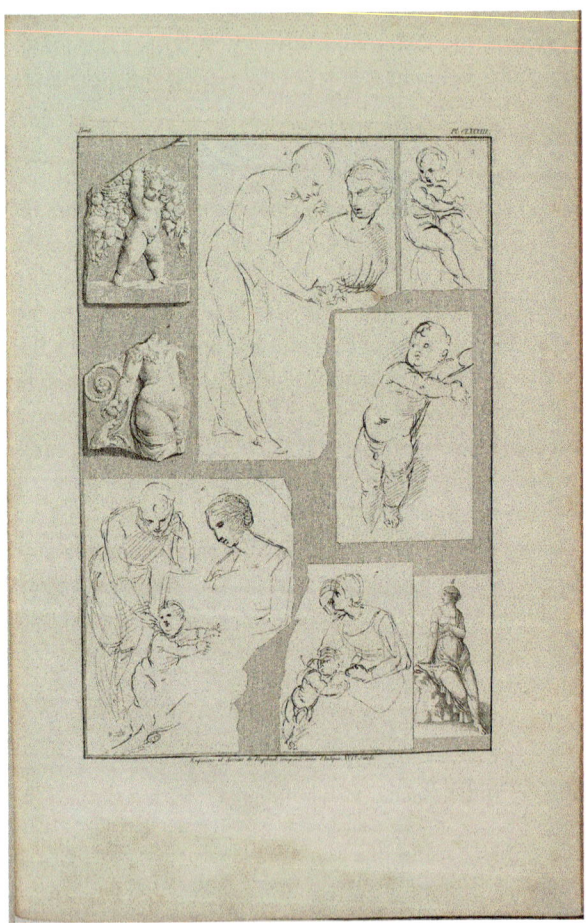

The book project concentrates on the illustrative power of hundreds of plates, but this example is particularly astonishing, because it nonverbally encapsules a complex argument: Raphael's putti are oriented toward the representational mode of antique art (here: sculptural design), as can be said for Renaissance art in general. Not coincidentally, it seems to me, Seroux d'Agincourt chose drawings for this evocative comparison, because they can stand for the concept of Vasari's disegno

Fig. 7: Adam Bartsch, Catalogue raisonne de toutes les estampes qui forment l'oeuvre de Rembrandt, Vienna 1797, plate 1.

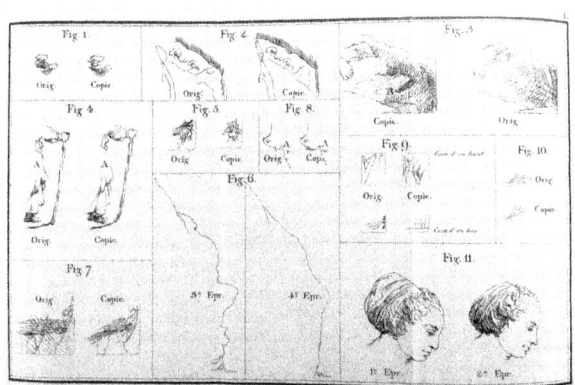

that marks a genuine shift in sixteenth-century art theory to something entirely new. However, as convincing as the visual juxtaposition might be, if it is to become comprehensible, it not only needs the contextualizing caption "*Esquisses et dessins de Raphael comparés avec l'Antique. XVIe. Siécle*", but also presumes the Vasarian narrative of the decline of arts in the Middle Ages. Without text, the visual argument is at risk of ending up in a direction that is altogether different. This is also because of the 'aesthetic surplus' that offers more than one loose end to interpret the illustration's meaning. The visual argument together with its paratext, therefore, exposes itself to being highly manipulative and still allows enough room for just another 'reading.' In order to escape such an interpretative scope, connoisseurs such as Adam von Bartsch (1757–1821) started to fragment their examples in comparisons up to single lines (Fig. 7).

The aim of these 'micro-comparisons' was to differentiate very precisely between original and copy or first and second state of a print and so forth. However, von Bartsch's plate is far from being instantaneously legible. It remains abstract without textual description and without the background knowledge on what the prints in the comparison look like entirely. Long before Giovanni Morelli's (1816–1891) famous method of a quasimedical examination of art, von Bartsch's attempt fails to make things more objective. By reducing the artwork to pure formalistic details, he artificially ignores the 'aesthetic surplus' and initiates a tendency for the "taste of comparison," whose protagonists were later denigrated as '*Faltenzähler*,' that is, counters of pleats or nitpickers. Both Seroux d'Agincourt and von Bartsch started to fix their comparative practice into illustrative juxtapositions, the one by propagating an epochal development, the other by pointing to minimal morphological differences. These examples demonstrate the continuous actualization of methods of comparing. They underline the different interests that can be brought together from diverse visual types of juxtapositions. Most and foremost, they mark a switch from an atelier practice of the visual "taste of comparison" to a practice that more and more exhibits its institutionalized research results.

References

Album Mariette, New York, The Metropolitan Museum of Art, Harris Brisbane Dick Fund, 1927, 27.78.2, URL: https://www.metmuseum.org/art/collection/search/361938 [last accessed August 27, 2018].
ALPERS, Svetlana, The Museum as a Way of Seeing, in: Ivan Karp/Steven D. Lavine, *Exhibiting cultures: the poetics and politics of museum display*, Washington D.C. 1991, 25–32.
ARNULF, Arwed, Studien zum Klosterneuburger Ambo und den theologischen Quellen bildlicher Typologien von der Spätantike bis 1200, in: *Wiener Jahrbuch für Kunstgeschichte*, vol. 48, 1995, 19–23.
BAUMGARTEN, Alexander Gottlieb, *Ästhetik. Übersetzt, mit einer Einführung, Anmerkungen und Registern von der Herausgeberin*, ed. by Dagmar Mirbach, Hamburg 2007.
BEAUMONT, Kim de, Les Salons de Gabriel de Saint-Aubin: (1724–1780), in: *Le Salon de l'Académie royale de peinture et de sculpture*, ed. by Isabelle Pichet, Paris 2014, 9–32.
BELL, Esther, A Curator at the Louvre: Charles Coypel and the Royal Collections, in: *Journal18: a journal of eighteenth-century art and culture* 2 (2016), 1–16, URL: https://doi.org/10.30610/2.2016.6 [last accessed August 27, 2018].
BHATTI, Anil/KIMMICH, Dorothee (eds.), *Similarities*, Tulika 2018.
BLEICHMAR, Daniela, Learning to Look: Visual Expertise across Art and Science in Eighteenth-Century France, in: *Eighteenth-Century Studies* 46 (1/2012), 85–111, URL: https://doi.org/10.1353/ecs.2012.0084 [last accessed April 19, 2018].
BLUM, Gerd et al. (eds.), *Pendant plus. Praktiken der Bildkombinatorik*, Berlin 2012.
BLUNT, Anthony, *Artistic Theory in Italy, 1450–1660*, Oxford 1985.
BOEHM, Gottfried, Die Wiederkehr der Bilder, in: Gottfried Boehm (ed.), *Was ist ein Bild?* (Bild und Text), München 1994, 11–38.
BRACKEN, Susan, Collectors in England: Evolutions in Taste 1580–1630, in: Tarnya Cooper/Aviva Burnstock/Maurice Howard (eds.), *Painting in Britain*, Oxford 2015, 384–391.
BRAKENSIEK, Stephan, Sammeln, Ordnen und Erkennen: frühneuzeitliche Druckgraphiksammlungen und ihre Funktion als Studien- und Erkenntnisorte; das Beispiel der Sammlung Michel de Marolles' (1600–1681), in: Robert Felfe/An-

gelika Lozar (eds.), *Frühneuzeitliche Sammlungspraxis und Literatur*, Berlin 2006, 130–162.

BRAKENSIEK, Stephan, *Vom 'Theatrum mundi' zum 'Cabinet des Estampes': das Sammeln von Druckgraphik in Deutschland 1565–1821* (Studien zur Kunstgeschichte, 150), Hildesheim 2003, 17–39.

BRUGÈRE, Fabienne, *Le goût: art, passions et société* (Philosophies, 130), Paris 2000.

BRUHN, Matthias/SCHOLTZ, Gerhard (eds.), *Der vergleichende Blick: Formanalyse in Natur- und Kulturwissenschaften*, Berlin 2017.

BRYSON, Norman, *Vision and painting: the logic of the gaze* (Language, discourse, society), London 1988, 87–133.

CRARY, Jonathan, *Techniques of the Observer: On Vision and Modernity in the Nineteenth Century* (An October Book), Cambridge 1991.

DASTON, Lorraine, Epistemic Images, in: Alina A. Payne (ed.), *Vision and Its Instruments: Art, Science, and Technology in Early Modern Europe*, University Park, Penn. 2015, 13–35.

DASTON, Lorraine/GALISON, Peter, *Objectivity*, New York 2010.

DAUVOIS, Daniel, Les armes de la philosophie dans la Querelle du coloris, in: Frédéric Cousinié (ed.), *L' artiste et le philosophe* (Aesthetica), Rennes 2011, 303–320.

DE PILES, Roger, *The art of painting, with the lives and characters of above 300 of the most eminent painters: containing a complete treatise of painting, designing, and the use of prints. [...]*, London 1754.

DE PILES, Roger, *Cours de peinture par principes*, Paris 1708.

DE PILES, Roger, *Abregé de la vie des peintres , avec des reflexions sur leurs ouvrages, et un Traité du peintre parfait, de la connoissance des desseins, & de l'utilité des estampes*, Paris 1699, 83, URL: http://gallica.bnf.fr/ark:/12148/bpt6k6568782t [last accessed August 27, 2018].

DE PILES, Roger, *Conversations sur la connoissance de la peinture, et sur le jugement qu'on doit faire des tableaux. Où par occasion il est parlé de la vie de Rubens, & de quelques-uns de ses plus beaux ouvrages*, Paris 1677.

DELAPIERRE, Emmanuelle, *Rubens contre Poussin: la querelle du coloris dans la peinture française à la fin du XVIIe siècle; Musée des Beaux-Arts d'Arras, 6 mars au 14 juin 2004*, Amsterdam 2004.

DELAPLANCHE, Jérôme, *Un tableau n'est pas qu'une image* (Collection "Art & société"), Rennes 2016.

DUBOS, Jean-Baptiste, *Critical reflections on poetry, painting, and music*, trans. by Thomas Nugent, 3 vols., London 1748.

DUBOS, Jean-Baptiste, *Réflexions critiques sur la poésie et sur la peinture*, 2 vols., Paris 1719.

DUSARTZ DE VIGNEULLE, Nina C., Das Sehende Auge. Die Kunstkennerschaft seit dem 18. Jahrhundert, in: Stephan Brakensiek/Anne-Katrin Sors (eds.),

Copy.Right Adam von Bartsch. Kunst, Kommerz, Kennerschaft, Petersberg 2016, 305–319.

Edited volumes of the conferences of the Royal Academy of Painting and Sculpture held between 1648–1793, URL: https://www.perspectivia.net/publikationen/conference [last accessed May 16, 2018].

EGGERS, Michael, *Vergleichendes Erkennen: zur Wissenschaftsgeschichte und Epistemologie des Vergleichs und zur Genealogie der Komparatistik* (Germanisch-romanische Monatsschrift), Heidelberg 2016.

ELSNER, Jaś (ed.), *Comparativism in Art History*, London 2017.

EPPLE, Angelika/ERHARD, Walter, Die Welt beobachten. Praktiken des Vergleichens, in: Angelika Epple/Walter Erhard (eds.), *Die Welt beobachten. Praktiken des Vergleichens*, Frankfurt a. M./New York 2015, 7–31.

FERRY, Luc, *Homo aestheticus: l'invention du goût à l'âge démocratique* (Le collège de philosophie), Paris 1990.

FORLANI TEMPESTI, Anna, Giorgio Vasari and the 'Libro de' Disegni': A Paper Museum or Portable Gallery, in: Maia Wellington Gahtan (ed.), *Giorgo Vasari and the Birth of the Museum*, Farnham et al. 2014, 31–52.

GANZ, David/THÜRLEMANN, Felix (eds.), *Das Bild im Plural. Mehrteilige Bildformen zwischen Mittelalter und Gegenwart*, Berlin 2010.

GAUNA, Chiara, Pierre-Jean Mariette e le 'connoissances multipliées': classificazioni, gerarchie, valori, in: Chiara Gauna (ed.), *La sfida delle stampe. Parigi Torino 1650–1906*, Torino 2017, 7–31.

GINSBURGH, Victor/WEYERS, Sheila, On the contemporaneity of Roger de Piles' Balance des peintres, in: Jack Amariglio (ed.), *Sublime economy: on the intersection of art and economics*, London, 2009.

GRADDY, Kathryn, Taste Endures! The Rankings of Roger de Piles (†1709) and Three Centuries of Art Prices, in: *The Journal of Economic History* 73 (3/2013), 766–791, https://doi.org/10.1017/S0022050713000600 [last accessed May 23, 2018].

GRAVE, Johannes et al. (eds.), The Agency of Display. Objects, Framings and Parerga—Introductory Thoughts, in: *The Agency of Display. Objects, Framings and Parerga, Parerga and Paratexts. How Things Enter Language. Practices and Forms of Representation in Goethe's Collections*, Dresden 2018, 7–19.

GRAVE, Johannes, Das Jahrhundert des Geschmacks. Zur Kultur des Sinnlichen im Zeitalter der Aufklärung, in: Monika Bachtler (ed.), *Wie es uns gefällt. Kostbarkeiten aus der Sammlung Rudolf-August Oetker*, München 2014, 15–29.

GRIENER, Pascal, *La République de l'oeil: l'expérience de l'art au siècle des Lumières* (Collection du Collège de France), Paris 2010.

GUICHARD, Charlotte, Taste Communities: The Rise of the Amateur in Eighteenth-Century Paris, in: *Eighteenth-Century Studies* (2012), 519–547.

HATTORI, Cordélia, The Drawings Collection of Pierre Crozat (1665–1740), in: *Collecting Prints and Drawings in Europe, c. 1500–1750*, Farnham et al. 2003, 173–181.

HOCHKIRCHEN, Britta, Rev. of: Bildbetrachtung in Bewegung. Der Rezipient in Texten und Bildern zur Pariser Salonausstellung des 18. Jahrhunderts (Ars et Scientia, 14), by Anja Weisenseel, in: *Zeitschrift für Kunstgeschichte* 82 (2019), 138–143.

HÖNES, Hans C., *Kunst am Ursprung: das Nachleben der Bilder und die Souveränität des Antiquars* (Image, 69), Bielefeld 2014.

JORDANOVA, Ludmilla J., *The Look of the Past: Visual and Material Evidence in Historical Practice*, Cambridge 2012.

JOUBERTON, Jean, Une relecture du *Livre des peintres et graveurs* de Michel de Marolles, in: *Nouvelles de l'estampe* 249 (2014), 4–15.

KANT, Immanuel, *Schriften zur Ästhetik und Naturphilosophie, Text und Kommentar*, ed. by Manfred Frank/Véronique Zanetti, 2 vols., Frankfurt a. M. 2001.

KANT, Immanuel, *Critique of Judgement*, ed. by Nicholas Walker, trans. by James Creed Meredith, Oxford 1989 [1952].

KELLER, Raymond, 'à la mode française': Geschmack und ästhetische Urteile als Grundlage für Kennerschaft, in: Stephan Brakensiek/Anne-Katrin Sors (eds.), *Copy.Right Adam von Bartsch. Kunst, Kommerz, Kennerschaft*, Petersberg 2016, 20–29.

KERNBAUER, Eva, *Der Platz des Publikums: Modelle für Kunstöffentlichkeit im 18. Jahrhundert* (Studien zur Kunst, 19), Köln 2011.

KOBI, Valérie, Rev. of: Bildbetrachtung in Bewegung. Der Rezipient in Texten und Bildern zur Pariser Salonausstellung des 18. Jahrhunderts, by Anja Weisenseel, in: *Regards croisés. Deutsch-französisches Rezensionsjournal zur Kunstgeschichte und Ästhetik* 8 (2019), 150–152.

KOBI, Valérie, *Dans l'œil du connaisseur. Pierre-Jean Mariette (1694–1774) et la construction des savoirs en histoire de l'art* (Collection "Art & société"), Rennes 2017.

KRETSCHMER, Marek T., *La typologie biblique comme forme de pensée dans l'historiographie médiévale* (Textes et études du Moyen Âge), Turnhout 2014.

LAUGIER, Marc-Antoine, *Maniere de bien juger des ouvrages de peinture*, Paris 1771.

LEESBERG, Marjolein/LEEFLANG, Huigen (eds.), *The New Hollstein Dutch & Flemish Etchings, Engravings and Woodcuts 1450–1700 – Hendrick Goltzius*, 4 vols., Amsterdam 2012.

LE MAROIS, Dominique, Les montages de dessins au XVIIIe siècle: l'exemple de Mariette, in: *Bulletin de la Société de l'Histoire de l'Art Français*, 1982, 87–96.

LEONHARD, Karin, Shell Collecting: On 17th-Century Conchology, Curiosity Cabinets and Still Life Painting, in: Karl A. E. Enenkel/Paul J. Smith (eds.), *Early Modern Zoology* (Intersections, 7), Leiden 2007, 177–214.

LICHTENSTEIN, Jacqueline, *La Couleur éloquente: rhétorique et peinture à l'âge classique*, Paris 1989.

MARIETTE, Pierre-Jean, *Abecedario de P. J. Mariette et autres notes inédites de cet amateur sur les arts et les artists. Ouvrage publié d'apès les manuscrits autographes conservés au cabinet des estampes de la Bibliothèque impériale*, 6 vols., Paris 1851–1860.

MARIETTE, Pierre-Jean, Lettre sur Léonard de Vinci, Peintre Florentin. A Monsieur le C: de C., in: *Recueil de testes de caractère & de charges dessinées par Léonard de Vinci Florentin & gravées par M. le C de C*, Paris 1730, 19.

MAROLLES, Michel de, *Catalogue de livres d'estampes et de figures en taille douce: avec un dénombrement des pieces qui y sont contenuës; fait à Paris en l'anneé 1666*, Paris 1666.

MAUZ, Andreas/SASS, Hartmut von (eds.), *Hermeneutik des Vergleichs: Strukturen, Anwendungen und Grenzen komparativer Verfahren* (Interpretation interdisziplinär), Würzburg 2011.

MESKIN, Aaron/ROBSON, Jon, Taste and Acquaintance, in: *The Journal of Aesthetics and Art Criticism* (2015), 127–139.

MEYER, Véronique, Marolles illustré: Chauveau, Mellan, Nanteuil et les autres, in: Peter Fuhring/Barbara Brejon de Lavergnée/Marianne Grivel (eds.), *L'estampe au grand siècle*, Paris 2010, 277–291.

MICHAUD, Yves, *Critères esthétiques et jugement de goût*, Nîmes 1999.

MICHEL, Patrick, *Peinture et plaisir: les goûts picturaux des collectionneurs parisiens au XVIIIe siècle*, Rennes 2010.

MONBEIG-GOGUEL, Catherine, Le dessin encadré, in: *Revue de l'art* 76 (1987), 25–31.

NELSON, Robert S., The Slide Lecture, or the Work of Art 'History' in the Age of Mechanical Reproduction, in: *Critical Inquiry* 26 (3/2000), 414–434.

PANOFSKY, Erwin, Das erste Blatt aus dem 'Libro' Giorgio Vasaris: eine Studie über die Beurteilung der Gotik in der italienischen Renaissance; mit einem Exkurs über zwei Fassadenprojekte Domenico Beccafumis, in: *Städel-Jahrbuch* 6, Frankfurt a. M. 1930, 25-72.

PEVSNER, Nikolaus, *Die Geschichte der Kunstakademien*, München 1986.

PIEPER, Hans-Joachim, *Geschmacksurteil und ästhetische Einstellung: eine Untersuchung zur Grundlegung transzendentalphilosophischer Ästhetik bei Kant und ein Entwurf zur Phänomenologie der ästhetischen Erfahrung*, Würzburg 2001.

PUTTFARKEN, Thomas, *Roger de Piles' Theory of Art*, New Haven 1985.

QUATREMÈRE DE QUINCY, Antoine Chrysostôme, *Lettres sur le préjudice qu'occasionnerait aux arts et à la science, le déplacement des monuments de l'art de l'Italie*, Paris 1796.

QUICCHELBERG, Samuel, *Inscriptiones vel tituli Theatri amplissimi, complectentis rerum universitatis singulas materias et imagines eximias etc*, München 1565, URL: http://www.europeana.eu/portal/recordABO/%2BZ178696704.html [last accessed July 16, 2018].

RECKWITZ, Andreas, Toward a Theory of Social Practices. A Development in Culturalist Theorizing, in: *European Journal of Social Theory* 5 (2/2002), 243–263, URL: https://doi.org/10.1177/13684310222225432 [last accessed August 12, 2018].

RHEIMS, Maurice, *Les collectionneurs: de la curiosité, de la beauté, du goût, de la mode et de la spéculation*, Paris 2002.

Rocheblave, Samuel-Élie, *L'art et le goût en France de 1600 à 1900* (Nouvelle édition), Paris 1923.

Rosenberg, Pierre/Barthélemy-Labeeuw, Laure, *Les dessins de la collection Mariette: école française*, vol. 1 A–E, vol. 2 F–W, Milan 2011.

Rosenberg, Pierre, Quelques bien modestes observations sur les estampes de la collection Mariette et sur leurs catalogues de vente illustrés par Gabriel de Saint-Aubin, in: *Nouvelles de l'estampe*, 230 (2010), 8–15.

Rosenberg, Pierre/Bailey, Colin B. (eds.), *Gabriel de Saint-Aubin: 1724–1780*, Paris 2007.

Rosenberg, Pierre/Reed, Sue Welsh/Basan, François (eds.), *La vente Mariette: le catalogue illustré par Gabriel de Saint-Aubin. Catalogue raisonné des différens objets de curiosités dans les sciences et arts, qui composoient le cabinet de feu Mr Mariette, controleur général de la Grande Chancellerie de France, honoraire amateur de l'Académie Rle. de Peinture, et de celle de Florence*, Milan 2011.

Rössler, Johannes, Das Notizbuch als Werkzeug des Kunsthistorikers: Schrift und Zeichnung in den Forschungen von Wilhelm Bode und Carl Justi, in: Christoph Hoffmann (ed.), *Daten sichern. Schreiben und Zeichnen als Verfahren der Aufzeichnung*, Zürich 2008, 73–102.

Saisselin, Rémy G., *Taste in Eighteenth Century France: Critical Reflections on the Origins of Aesthetics or an Apology for Amateurs*, Syracuse 1965.

Salmon, Xavier, *Gabriel de Saint-Aubin. Le Livre de croquis de Gabriel Saint-Aubin* (Carnets et albums), Paris 2017.

Schenck, Kimberly, A Page from Giorgio Vasari's 'Libro de' Disegni' as Composite Object, in: *Facture. National Gallery of Art* 1 (2013), 2–31.

Seroux d'Agincourt, Jean Baptiste, *Histoire de l'art par les monumens, depuis sa décadence au IVe siècle jusqu'à son renouvellement au XVIe: ouvrage enrichi de 325 pl.*, 6 vols., Paris 1823.

Smentek, Kristel, *Mariette and the Science of the Connoisseur in the Eighteenth-Century Europe*, Farnham et al. 2014.

Spoerhase, Carlos, Das Maß der Potsdamer Garde: die ästhetische Vorgeschichte des Rankings in der europäischen Literatur- und Kunstkritik des 18. Jahrhunderts, in: Deutsche Schillergesellschaft (ed.), *Jahrbuch der Deutschen Schillergesellschaft, internationales Organ für neuere deutsche Literatur* 58 (2014), 90–126.

Stach, Thomas, Anmerkungen zur Rolle des Vergleichs in der Morphologie, in: Matthias Bruhn/Gerhard Scholtz, *Der vergleichende Blick. Formanalyse in Natur- und Kulturwissenschaft*, Berlin 2017, 41–53.

Testelin, Henri, *Sentimens des plus habiles peintres du tems, sur la pratique de la peinture et sculpture: recueillis & mis en tables de preceptes, avec six discours academiques, extraits des conferences tenuës en l'Academie Royale desdits arts ... par Henry Testelin, peintre du roi, professeur & secretaire en ladite Academie*, ed. by Académie royale de peinture et de sculpture, La Hague 1680.

TEYSSÈDRE, Bernard, *Roger de Piles et les débats sur le coloris au siècle de Louis XIV* (Bibliothèque des Arts, 13), Paris 1965.

VAN ECK, Caroline (ed.), Introduction, in: *Art, Agency and Living Presence: From the Animated Image to the Excessive Object* (Studien aus dem Warburg-Haus), Boston 2015, 11–28.

VASARI, Giorgio, *Le vite de' piv eccellenti pittori, scvltori, et architettori*, 3 vols., 2nd & expanded ed., Fiorenza 1568.

WACKENRODER, Wilhelm Heinrich/TIECK, Ludwig, *Outpourings of an Art-Loving Friar*, New York 1975.

WEISENSEEL, Anja-Isabelle, *Bildbetrachtung in Bewegung: der Rezipient in Texten und Bildern zur Pariser Salonausstellung des 18. Jahrhunderts* (Ars et Scientia, 14), Berlin 2017.

WOLF, Falk, *Kunstgeschichte als Bild. Medien- und Wissenschaftstheoretische Positionen der Kunstgeschichte im 19. Jahrhundert*, Doctoral dissertation, University of Basel, Switzerland, 2017.

Photo Credits

Fig. 1: Xavier Salmon. *Gabriel de Saint-Aubin. Le "livre de croquis de Gabriel Saint-Aubin"*. Carnets et albums. Paris 2017.

Fig. 2: Roger de Piles *Cours de peinture par principes [...]* without page number.

Fig. 3: Author's photograph.

Fig. 4: National Gallery of Art.

Fig. 5: Kristel Smentek. The Collector's Cut: Why Pierre-Jean Mariette Tore up His Drawings and Put Them Back Together Again, in: *Master Drawings*, Vol. 46, No. 1, Seventeenth- and Eighteenth-Century Draftsmen and Collectors (Spring, 2008), 36–60, see 46.

Fig. 6: Jean Baptiste Louis Georges Seroux d'Agincourt, *Histoire de l'art par les monumens [...]*, plate 183.

Fig. 7: Adam Bartsch, *Catalogue raisonne [...]*, plate 1.

Inventing White Beauty and Fighting Black Slavery
How Blumenbach, Humboldt, and Arango y Parreño Contributed to Cuban Race Comparisons in the Long Nineteenth Century

Angelika Epple

Abstract

Humboldt's essay on Cuba is famous for his realistic description of the atrocities of the Cuban slave regime. A convinced abolitionist, Humboldt denied the comparability of slavery with feudal serfdom, because these comparisons would only play down the inhumanity of slavery. At the same time, Humboldt compared different slave regimes arguing that there are better and worse types of slavery. He concluded that slavery should only be overcome step by step. The contribution shows that these two standpoints can be traced back to two different sources: first, the Göttingen comparative anatomist and abolitionist Johann Friedrich Blumenbach, and second the Cuban economist and defender of slavery Francisco de Arango y Parreño. Even though, until today, Blumenbach might be known for the invention of the beauty of the so-called "Caucasian race," his main aim was to prove that all people belonged to just one species and that consequently, all forms of slavery were inhuman. Arango y Parreño, in contrast, was of the opinion that a lesson learned from the Haitian revolution was that white supremacy was in danger when either slavery was too cruel or when black slaves outnumbered the white population. He—in his eyes!—helped to establish a slavery regime that made Cuban slaves "the happiest in the world." The contribution shows how these two standpoints differently negotiate racial equality and racial differences and how Blumenbach, Humboldt, and Arango y Parreño shaped race comparisons in Cuba until the end of the long 19th century. However important the idea of human equality, the invention of the Caucasian race and the paternalistic approach to ending slavery also opened the door for a long-lasting tradition of racist comparisons.

In the last chapter of his famous *"Essai politique sur l'île de Cuba"* (1826),[1] Alexander von Humboldt recalls an answer given by a slave trader during an investigation by the British parliament in 1789. Asked about the treatment of African slaves on board (during the terrifying "middle passage"), the slave trader justified whipping slaves to make them dance and force them to sing, because it showed that living among Whites was fun. His explanation was simple: "This only proves the care we show for their health."[2] This short quotation contains the meaning of the slave trade in a nutshell: transforming human beings into a trading product—not only to exploit their labor but also to dominate and eventually destroy their bodies and minds. "Slaving," the very process of dehumanizing, follows a specific schema that can be observed historically in all parts of the world.[3] However, every slave regime works along different lines. In contrast to Haiti where the slave revolution 1791–1804 led to a republic, the neighboring island of Cuba experienced an epoch of ever-growing slave trade in the nineteenth century. Thanks to the exploitation of an increasing number of enslaved Africans within sugar, coffee, and tobacco production, Cuba became Spain's wealthiest colony between 1780 and 1840.[4] Michael Zeuske con-

---

1   Alexander von Humboldt, *Essai politique sur l'île de Cuba* (T. 1), Paris 1826, 310. The first complete French edition of Humboldt's sociopolitical essay on Cuba containing all appendices is entitled: "Essai politique sur l'île de Cuba, in: Relation Historique du voyage aux regions équinoxiales du Nouveau Continent fait en 1799, 1800, 1801, 1802, 1803 et 1804 par Al[exandre]. de Humboldt et A[imé]. Bonpland. Rédigé par Alexandre de Humboldt. Band III (J. Smith et Gide Fils), Paris 1825." However, in reality, it appeared only in 1831, see: commentary to the German edition by Hanno Beck, in: Alexander von Humboldt/Hanno Beck (ed.), *Cuba-Werk, Darmstädter Ausgabe Vol. 3.*, Darmstadt 2008, 231).

2   [My translation]. Original quote: "*Si l'on fouette les esclaves [...] cela ne prouve que les soins que nous prenons pour la santé des hommes.*" Humboldt, *Essai politique*, 310; Alexander von Humboldt, Political Essay on the Island Cuba: A Critical Edition, Alexander von Humboldt in English, Vol. 2, Chicago 2011, 144.

3   The term was coined by Joseph C. Miller. See for instance, Joseph Miller, Slaving as historical process: Examples from the ancient Mediterranean and the modern Atlantic, in: Enrico Dal Lago/Constantina Katsari (eds.), *Slave Systems: Ancient and Modern*, 70–102, Cambridge 2008; as to different world regions, see the impressive recent books by Michael Zeuske, *Handbuch Geschichte der Sklaverei. Eine Globalgeschichte von den Anfängen bis zur Gegenwart*, Berlin/Boston 2013; Michael Zeuske, *Sklaverei. Eine Menschheitsgeschichte von der Steinzeit bis heute*, Stuttgart 2018.

4   Cf. Aline Helg, *Slave but not Citizen. Free people of color and blood purity in Colonial Spanish American Legislation*, URL: http://http//dx.doi.org/10.6035/Millars.2017.42.4, 2017, 76–99, see 92 [last accessed May 25, 2019]. Helg also has the numbers on Cuban slave trade (Helg, *Slave but not Citizen*, 96): "Between 1791 and 1866, the total number of Africans deported to Cuba reached 752,000—and additional slaves were imported from the Caribbean and continental America. Out of these, 620,000 were illegally imported after 1817, when Spain signed with Great Britain a first treaty prohibiting the slave trade". VOYAGES Database (2010), *Voyages: The Trans-Atlantic Slave Trade Database*, URL: http://www.slavevoyages.org, [last accessed May 25, 2019].

vincingly divides Cuban slave history into four phases, each with its own specific features when it came to bodily treatments such as branding.[5] Slavery eventually came to an end in Cuba in 1886.

The justification given by the perpetrator before the British parliament also harbors another interesting point: Without any self-criticism, the slave trader assumes that living among (what he calls) Whites must be something appealing. It goes without saying that for him, slaves as such were non-Whites. Humboldt, while telling this justification story to his readers at the time, profiled his own position: Slavery for him was a most cruel and disgusting sign of barbarism, a disaster for humankind. Even though his paternalistic standpoint runs throughout his descriptions and does not allow for the inside perspective of a slave, he characterized the Cuban slave regime more realistically and as being more violent than any German scholar had done before. The above-mentioned last chapter even went beyond this. The empirical sociopolitical part of the *"essai"* had already shown Humboldt as a convinced abolitionist; the last chapter, which deals mainly with slavery, however, had a different tone. It was basically a manifesto against any kind of slavery—slavery for him being something even more inhumane than other unjust societal orders. He even criticizes all comparisons between slavery and other forms of violent labor force oppression such as *Leibeigene* (literally body ownership) or serfs in European feudalism for downplaying the cruelty of slavery.[6] For him, slavery was incomparable in this sense. However, what was important to him, in contrast, was comparing different slave regimes. The first French version of the *"essai"* came out already in 1826—however, without the appendices. This version became seminal not only in Europe but also in Cuba and other American countries.[7]

Ramón de la Sagra, for instance, born in Spain, immigrated to Cuba and married a Cuban. He was professor of natural history in Havana, Venezuelan consul in Paris, and later anarchist. His history of Cuba published in 1831 included references to Humboldt's 1826 version of the *"essai."*[8] He self-confidentially located himself in

---

5 Cf. Michael Zeuske, Die Nicht-Geschichte von Versklavten als Archiv-Geschichte von "Stimmen" und Körpern, in: *Jahrbuch für Europäische Überseegeschichte* 16, Wiesbaden 2016, 65–114.
6 Cf. Humboldt, *Political Essay*, 143. Humboldt, *Essai politique*, 308: "des serfs moyen âge [sic!]."
7 Despite the Spanish translation being banned in Cuba immediately after its appearance in 1827, the "essai" became a point of reference in official Cuban documents (see: Humboldt, appendix II., German edition, 178) but also in other books such as Anastasio Carrillo y Arango, *Elógico histórico del excelentísmo Sr. D. Francisco de Arango y Parreño*, first published in 1837, reprinted in: Francisco de Arango y Parreño, *Obras del Excmo. Señor D. Francisco de Arango y Parreño* vol. I, Habana 1888, XLVIII.
8 Cf. Ramón de la Sagra, *Historia económico-politica y estadística de la isla de Cuba ó sea de sus progresos en la población, la agricultura, el comercio y las rentas*, La Habana 1831, 8. It seems probable that de la Sagra did not know the complete Humboldt edition that also appeared in 1831. On page 8 of his "Historia," de la Sagra refers to an edition of Humboldt's work of Cuba that had appeared in 1826 without considering the censuses of 1817 and 1827. De la Sagra gives only

the tradition of "*Sr. Baron de Humboldt*" and his "highly appreciated and well-known work" on Cuba.[9] De la Sagra first lamented that Humboldt, unfortunately, not had enough time to study the Cuban population in more depth, before adding modestly that he himself has sorted out new documents, arranging them as "this wise man" would have done, so that his findings could be considered as complementing those of Humboldt.[10] In his opinion, the careful study of data is even more important "in a century in which everything is subject to calculation and observation."[11] According to de la Sagra, Humboldt's chapter on the Cuban population is based on official investigations and comparisons between "the classes White, free of Color, slave and general of Color."[12] And indeed, at first sight, these are the categories employed in the official Cuban censuses since 1774. However, it is part of "census policy," so to say, that the categories applied in the respective census could be traced back to older censuses in order to make temporal comparisons possible.[13] I shall show that the categories also changed slightly, but significantly over time.

When it came to comparisons of population by numbers, Humboldt obviously relied on official documents. This should not hide the fact that he, at the time, helped to establish racial categories that evolved alongside the growing unease among White Cuban elites caused by growing numbers of free born or freed people of Color. Humboldt himself did not make this connection. Instead, he seems to have been proud of his influence on demographic government. In his Appendix II, for instance, he underlines that the introduction to the official Cuban census carried out in 1827 had used and also praised the first edition of his "*essai*" (Paris 1826).[14]

the Spanish title without mentioning whether this was a Spanish edition or his own translation. There is much to suggest that he might have been referring to the French two-volume publication by J. Smith et Gide Fils in Paris that actually appeared in 1826—five years earlier than the complete Humboldtian original edition including all appendices and also five years earlier than de la Sagra's own history of Cuba.

9   Sagra, *Historia*, IV/VI. He erroneously also thanks the translator into French named "Sr. Huber": "El Sr. Baron de Humboldt en su apreciabilísima y bien conocida obra" /"y á su traduccion francesa por el Sr. Huber."
10 Sagra, *Historia*, 8: "*Refiriéndome al trabajo de este sábio.*"
11 Sagra, *Historia*, V: "*Por otra parte, en un siglo en que todo se somete al cálculo y á la observacion.*"
12 [My translation]. Original quote: "*Las clases blanca, libre de color, esclava y general de color.*" Sagra, *Historia*, 8.
13 It is not just de la Sagra who mentions and uses the census of 1774 (Sagra, *Historia*, 2); the 1774 census became a topos. The official census of 1907, for instance, traces the augmentation of the population back to the first census in 1774 without any criticism of the numbers (301). This is interesting, because in the first pages, the director of the census gives information about their own difficulties in getting the numbers right and how to instruct the supervisors to ask the right questions (9–19). Censo de la República de Cuba bajo de la administración provisional de los Estados Unidos 1907, Washington 1908.
14 Cf. Alexander von Humboldt, *Tableau Statistique de l'île de Cuba pour les années 1825–1829*, Paris 1831, 6. According to Humboldt, the official census appeared with the title "*Cuatro estatístico*

In addition to official statistical documents, Humboldt also had other informative sources for population comparisons. One of the most important was Francisco de Arango y Parreño, a Cuban economist, Criollo bourgeois, slave trader, slaveholder, and an eloquent though also enlightened defender of the slave system. In 1795, only four years after the Haitian revolution had begun, Arango wrote about the importance of "census figures in hand" when importing slaves. For him a lesson learned was that Blacks should never outnumber the Whites in the population.[15]

I shall come back to this argument later. Arango did not just help Humboldt with additional information, he also helped him judge the reliability of existing official statistics such as the census of 1791—in Arango's words, the first and, until 1810, the only reliable one.[16] Arango did not just have close contacts with Humboldt during his stay in Cuba; the two men also had a lively correspondence over several years after Humboldt left the island.[17] Arango's close reading and his thoughtful comments on Humboldt's "*essai*" were published in his *obras completas* in 1837.[18] Up to now, the subtle but fundamental influence of Arango y Parreños on Humboldt's ambivalent perspective on Cuban slavery has been underestimated.[19]

What de la Sagra also did not mention (and probably did not know) was that Humboldt's racial comparisons were also influenced by a completely different

---

de la siempre fiel Isla de Cuba, correspondiente al año 1827, formado por una Comisión de jefes y officiales de orden y bajo la dirección de Escelentisimo Señor Capitán General Don Francisco Dionisio Vivés, precedido de una descripción histórica, física, geográfica, y acompañada de quantas notas son conducentes para la ilustración del cuadro, Havanna 1829."

15 Helg, *Slave but not Citizen*, 76–99, see 93. Arango y Parreño points repeatedly to the fact that the relation of slaves and free people of Color to Whites is crucial for preventing rebellions. See, for example, Arango y Parreño, *Obras*, Vol. 2, 339.

16 In this context, Humboldt quotes Don Francisco de Arango y Parreño, "one of the most progressive and best-informed statesmen" who had told him that the census of 1791 was the first (and until 1810 the last) reliable census. Following de Arango y Parreño, it was carried out under the administration of Don Luis de las Casas. See Humboldt, *Political Essay*, 73, Humboldt, *Essai politique*, 133: "*un des hommes d'état les plus éclairés et les plus profondément instruit de la position de sa patrie.*"

17 Humboldt also mentions Arango y Parreño in his diaries. See, for more details, the informative commentary on Humboldt's Havanna diary: Michael Zeuske, Alexander von Humboldt, die Sklavereien in den Amerikas und das "Tagebuch von Havanna 1804". Zur Edition von "Isle de Cube", in: Ottmar Ette (ed.), *edition humboldt digital*, Berlin-Brandenburgische Akademie der Wissenschaften, Berlin. Version 1 from May 10, 2017. For further information, see the helpful online series by Vera M. Kutzinsky and Ottmar Ette, *Alexander von Humboldt in English*, see: Francisco de Arango y Parreño, in: press.uchicago.edu, [last accessed April 26, 2019].

18 Arango y Parreño, Francisco de, Observaciónes al "Ensayo politico sobre la isla de Cuba", escritas en 1827, in: Francisco de Arango y Parreño, *Obras completas*, vol. I, 1837, 533–546 (as it reads in the second footnote, he commented on the French edition of 1826).

19 There is one exception: Michael Zeuske points to the fundamental importance of Arango for Humboldt. See the excellent comment on Humboldt's diaries in Zeuske, Sklavereien in den Amerikas.

source: Before starting his journey to Latin America, Humboldt had studied, among other subjects, comparative anatomy with the German professor of anthropology Johann Friedrich Blumenbach at the University of Göttingen. Until today, Blumenbach, above all in US-American literature, counts as the founder of anthropology and as an important promoter of racial hierarchies.[20] Even though this judgment might not be completely accurate, his writings are one of the most prominent sources suggesting that the "Caucasian race" is the most beautiful, especially in its female version. The proverbial beauty of Caucasian women had also been disseminated by Christoph Meiners, a self-confessing anti-Semite, misogynist, racist, and colleague of Johann Friedrich Blumenbach at Göttingen. "Caucasian" became a synonym in the United States (and some other countries) for White people. In contrast to Meiners, who's main endeavor was illustrating White supremacy over the course of history, Blumenbach's intention was to show race equality through the similarities between all human variations. Drawing on countless comparisons in his huge skull collection, he tried to prove scientifically that behind all varieties, there was but one human species tracing back to Adam and Eve. Even though Blumenbach might have taken the term "Caucasian" from Meiners, he did not argue along the same lines.[21] Things were more complicated. Like his famous pupil Alexander von Humboldt, Blumenbach was a highly committed abolitionist. Fighting slavery was an important issue in his comparative anatomy. Inventing White beauty and fighting Black slavery were but two sides of a single coin.

In the following, I shall show that analyses of comparative practices can give us new insights into how scholars such as Blumenbach and Humboldt, but also de la Sagra or Cuban historians such as the historians Villanova and Morales in the 1880s and 1890s or the sociologist Ortíz in the early twentieth century, negotiated race equality and racial differences. However important the idea of human equality, the invention of the "Caucasian race" also opened the door for a long-lasting tradition of racist comparisons. A close reading of Humboldt's comparisons including an analysis of his teacher's comparing practices reveals that his plea for abolition and his humanitarian approach in the Cuban context were accompanied by racial discrimination of people of Color. Whereas Blumenbach inserted an aesthetic difference between Whites and non-Whites, Humboldt transferred the aesthetic difference into what could be called a "paternalistic difference." Francisco de Arango y Parreño seems to have played a major role in this.

Of course, there were also other voices in Cuba. In the 1880s, the Cuban politician and poet, José Martí, dreamt of overcoming races in the future: Mixed

---

20   See, for instance, Stephen J. Gould, *The Mismeasure of Man*, New York/London 1981.
21   Keel exaggerates the influence of Meiners on Blumenbach, see, Terence Keel, *Divine Variations. How Christian Thought became Racial Science*, Stanford 2018, 23.

races would eventually blur all race differences. Historical reality was different: The Cuban *"guerra de razas"* in 1912 became a massacre of approximately 5,000 to 6,000 non-White Cubans.[22] The legitimation was that the leaders and also the objectives of the rebellion were themselves racist.[23] White supremacy and a language of race equality were not contradictory.

Race and *limpieza de sangre*: Fluid concepts that shaped history

The history of White and Black people has a long tradition. In her seminal book on the history of Whites, Nell Painter writes that White people did not exist in Greek Antiquity.[24] The assumed "nonexistence" of White people points to the fact that in Greek Antiquity, membership of human groups was marked differently. Although ethnographic thinking dates back to Ancient history,[25] the term "race" was not used to distinguish different human groups before the end of the Middle Ages. It was only in the era of the Spanish *reconquista* that the term *"raza"* began to distinguish not only different species of horses but also human groups. In contrast to the social hierarchy within a stratified order, the term *raza* introduced a criterion allowing a horizontal classification that ran through different social estates.[26] The term showed up together with a new classification along the line of genealogy: *"limpieza de sangre."*[27] It translates literarily into "cleanliness of the blood" and asks for confirmation of so-called "blood purity" for Christian officials. Christians could demonstrate their "blood purity" within the metropole by proving that they

---

22 Cf. Aline Helg, Race in Argentina and Cuba, in: Richard Graham (ed.), The Idea of Race in Latin America, 1870-1940, Austin 1990, 55. Aline Helg, Our Rightful Share, The Afro-Cuban Struggle for Equality, 1886–1912, Chapel Hill 1995, 225. The Cuban government puts the figure at 2,000 killed, whereas American figures go up to 5,000 to 6,000.
23 The Cuban race war has a very complex background, and further investigation is needed to sort out all the conflict lines. However, the tensions between racial segregation practices influenced by the United States and the Cuban myth of racial integration have been discussed broadly. Here are just some basic recommendations for further reading: The excellent analysis of Alejandro de la Fuente starts with the decade before the race war, see Alejandro de la Fuente, *Una Nación para todos. Raza, desigualdad y política en Cuba 1900–2000*, La Habana 2014; Ada Ferrer was one of the first to give a detailed insight into the last third of the nineteenth century, see Ada Ferrer, *Insurgent Cuba, Race, Nation, and Revolution in Cuba 1868–1898*, Chapel Hill 1999; and, of course, the seminal book by Aline Helg, *Our rightful share*.
24 Cf. Nell Irvin Painter, *The History of White People*, New York/London 2010, 1.
25 See subproject of the SFB 1288 on "Practices of Comparing" at Bielefeld University headed by Raimund Schulz (https://www.uni-bielefeld.de/(en)/sfb1288/projekte/b04.html).
26 Cf. Christian Geulen, *Geschichte des Rassismus*, München 2007, 14.
27 Helg, *Slave but not Citizen*; Stefan Rinke/Andrea Riedemann, Chile, in: Wolfgang Benz (ed.), *Handbuch des Antisemitismus. Judenfeindschaft in Geschichte und Gegenwart* Vol. 1, München 2008, 71.

had no Muslim or Jewish ancestry. The proof of "blood purity" became compulsory for access to nonmanual professions as well as to positions within the militia, the church, or state administration. Within the Spanish colonies, "blood purity" was adopted and modified. This changed by 1570, when eventually after a long discussion including the famous *controversy of Valladolid* (1550/1), the *conquista* was declared to not fit into the legal concept of a "just war" against heretics. That the *conquista* was not classified a just war was most important for the few native Americans who had survived not only slavery but also the new diseases imported by the Spaniards. The classification implied that Amerindians had the chance to become Christians and prove "blood purity," because they were not thought to be contaminated by the Muslim or Jewish religions or by heresy. Even though native Americans could no longer be enslaved legally, their fate did not change for many years to come. The situation changed only toward the end of colonialism when the White elites realized that they needed soldiers for their wars of independence.

For Afro-Americans the negative classification of the *conquista* had severe implications. As Aline Helg puts it, "Blacks ended up being the only legal slaves, because they were implicitly captured in just wars against Muslims in Africa."[28] *Limpieza de sangre* helped order the world both at home in Spain and in the colonies. At first glance, it might seem as if the *limpieza de sangre* and also race provided a clear classification system that, once implemented, would make all comparisons either obsolete or very easy. Reality was different. Spaniards, Indians, and Africans mixed, often as a result of rape by Spaniards.[29] As a result, the distinction between different people of Color such as Blacks, Mestizos (Indian–White), Mulattos (Black–White), Zumbas (Indian–Black), Castizo (Mestizo–White), Cuarterón (Mulatto–White), Quinterón (Cuarterón–White), and different kinds of Whites (Europeans, Spaniards, and Criollos) led to ever new contestations of respective privileges and prohibitions. Not to mention Asian migrants and all possible combinations. All legitimizations and all contestations relied on comparisons. As Fernando Ortíz stated correctly in 1911 shortly before the race war began, race is such a fluid category that it can be used for any kind of argument that always ends up in severe conflicts.[30] In Latin America, the Christian background of *limpieza of sangre* faded out over the centuries and the racial component with its bodily characteristics (such as skin color) and social implication (such as manual work and slave history) became most prominent.

---

28 Helg, *Slave but not Citizen*, 80.
29 Cf. Helg, *Slave but not Citizen*, 82.
30 Cf. Fernando Ortíz, Los dos racismos, in: Ortíz, Fernando, *La reconquista de America. Reflexiones sobre el panhispanismo*, Paris 1911, 42–48.

European discussions on race and slavery: The Göttingen setting around 1800

In Europe, in contrast, the Christian background of race concepts became even more important, when during the Enlightenment, race concepts were combined with theories of human development. Already before George-Louis Leclerc, Comte de Buffon brought out his theory of monogenesis embedded in his environmental explanation of human development in 1749,[31] European scholars had struggled with the question of how the sameness and difference of human people came about over time, given that they all had a common origin in Adam and Eve. The French author L'Abbé Prévost, for instance, evaluated human groups in general and Africans in particular in terms of "the possibility of moral progress or regression" ending with the speculation that Africans, these *"machines animales* were perhaps 'a different species.'"[32] Polygenity, the idea that different species had different origins, was of course a heretic position at the time. Many intellectuals such as Prévost only "played" ambivalently with the idea. The polygenity–monogenity question came up again in the ardent *dispute of the New World*, a discussion that fascinated scholars, explorers, intellectuals, writers, philosophers such as Voltaire and de Pauw, the German historian Christoph Meiners, Alexander von Humboldt, or the German poet Johann Wolfgang von Goethe.[33]

In the meantime, American voices from Thomas Jefferson to the Jesuit Clavier, who had lived in Mexico for years, were setting other priorities. For European scholars, what was most important was whether or not different human races "really" existed. This question was far from being sophisticated. It had an everyday impact: If all humans are of equal origin, does that imply that all humans are also equal when it comes to, for instance, human rights? If so, how then could varieties and existing hierarchies in humankind be explained? Christoph Meiners is a good example showing that "race" comparisons not only helped to hierarchize people of the globe when he put White people on the top of all humankind, but that "race"

---

31   Cf. George-Louis (Comte de) Leclerc, Histoire naturelle de l'Homme, in: *Histoire naturelle, générale et particulière* Tome II, Paris 1749–1788, 157–228.
32   Andrew S. Curran, *The Anatomy of Blackness. Science and Slavery in an Age of Enlightenment*, Baltimore 2011, 80–81. Curran in the following points out how Abbé Prévost retracted the idea of polygenesis, and mused instead about the degeneration of Africans as compared to Europeans.
33   Cf. Angelika Epple, Comparing Europe and the Americas: The Dispute of the New World between the Sixteenth and Nineteenth Centuries, in: Willibald Steinmetz (ed.), *The Force of Comparison*, Oxford/ New York 2019, 137-163. For an enlightening insight into the debate at the end of the eighteenth century, see Ottmar Ette, 'Die ‚Berliner Debatte' um die Neue Welt. Globalisierung aus der Perspektive der europäischen Aufklärung', in: Vicente Bernaschino et al. (eds.), *Globalisierung in Zeiten der Aufklärung. Texte und Kontexte zur ‚Berliner Debatte' um die Neue Welt (17./18. Jh.)*, vol. 1, Frankfurt a. M. 2015, 27–55.

comparisons also helped to hierarchize local societies. In an article on the nature of the Africans that appeared in 1790, he parallelized Jews and Africans, saying that as long as they stayed Jews and Africans, they just could not have the same rights and the same freedom as Christians and Whites. Even a shared origin, he continues, would never legitimize equality in respect to human rights.[34]

Christoph Meiners was not just contradicting Buffon or Blumenbach in an academic dispute. It has to be borne in mind that even in Europe, criticism of slavery was becoming more forceful at the time. The Haitian revolution (1791–1804) also scared other slaveholder states as well as slavery profiteers all over the world. Hence, the Haitian revolution made the circum-Caribbean an iconic region in which all conflict lines met: from the quest for universal human rights to the questioning of colonial dominance and rule, to global economic and political entanglements.

The European bourgeois public observed these events with great attention. Narrations, novels, dramas, newspaper articles, the slave issue, and the abolition movement were discussed broadly.[35] The conflict lines were difficult to spot both locally (in the Caribbean multiethnic societies or in the rural East-Prussian region with its *Leibeigene*) and globally (in the interplay of universal and particular interests as well as in the development of humanitarian discourse).

Interestingly enough, within these discussions, the term "race" became one of the most influential categories for sorting things out. But what did "race" mean? Race categories in enlightenment discourse were far from fixed or clear-cut. They were subject to dispute and these disputes were carried out more often than not on the ground of comparisons. Race comparisons at the time came within a semantic net of a bundle of categories such as skin color, other bodily characteristics, sexuality, gender, religion, social status, or class. In addition, climatic conditions seemed to influence all categories in particular and their interplay in general.

Johann Friedrich Blumenbach: Forerunner of later racism or enlightened abolitionist?

This was the setting in which Johann Friedrich Blumenbach started his research. Until today, he is seen as a forerunner for so-called "modern" racism that claims to

---

34   Cf. Christoph Meiners, *Über die Natur der afrikanischen Neger, und die davon abhangende Befreyung, oder Einschränkung der Schwarzen*, Hannover 1790, 6, 17.

35   Sibylle Fischler already showed in 2004 it is only in the twentieth century that the Haitian revolution has been neglected. The events in the Caribe were present and also discussed broadly in Europe among intellectuals but also in popular forms throughout the nineteenth century right from the beginning. See Sibylle Fischler, *Modernity Disavowed. Haiti and the Cultures of Slavery*, Durham 2004.

rely on scientific, mere secular findings and rational, objective arguments.[36] This is right in one sense, but, at the time, misleading. Blumenbach was indeed one of the most prominent points of reference for later racists. He was a highly influential and controversial anatomist in Göttingen from the 1770s onward until his death in 1840. His main research interests were evolution theory, epigenesis, and the varieties of humankind—research questions that also drove the aforementioned *dispute of the New World*.

On the other hand, Blumenbach fought slavery. When the debate on polygenesis versus monogenesis came up again, he ardently argued for the latter. As a supporter of monogenesis theory, he considered that all humans were equal in respect of most human qualities and especially in terms of mental capacities. In contrast to scholars such as Samuel Thomas Soemmerring or Christoph Meiners, he argued that the cultural and intellectual talents of Africans could be seen everywhere.[37] Blumenbach collected books written by Black authors to illustrate their intellectual talent.[38] Nevertheless, he was intrigued by the idea of substantiating varieties within the single species of human beings; and, what is more, in the end, he also found an "evident" hierarchy. In his seminal book on "The Anatomy of Blackness," Andrew S. Curran underlined convincingly the ambivalence of Blumenbach's endeavor. In the first place, Blumenbach used his comparative studies to refute substantial differences between different human groups while simultaneously introducing the means to measure difference.[39] It is this ambivalence that is at the very center of the practices of comparing.

Let me take a closer look at Blumenbach's arguments. In the preface of his doctoral thesis, first published in Latin in 1775, Blumenbach underlined that Linné's classification system has two disadvantages: First, it is artificial and does not grasp the underlying natural order; and second, it is not appropriate, because too many mammals do not fit into it.[40] With all the new species discovered recently, the

---

36 Already in the early 1980s when Stephen J. Gould published his classical if controversial book "The Mismeasure of Man," the origin of modern racism was traced back to Johann Friedrich Blumenbach. See Gould, *Mismeasure of Man*, 32; also Painter, *History of White People*, 86; Curran, *Anatomy of Blackness* 75, 173; Keel, *Divine Variations*, 23; Terence Keel, Blumenbach's race science in the light of Christian supersessionism, in: Nicolaas Rupke/Gerhard Lauer (eds.), *Johann Friedrich Blumenbach. Race and Natural History, 1750–1850*, London 2018, 123–141, see 123.
37 Blumenbach also explained his conviction in letters to Soemmerring. See for an excerpt from their correspondence: Samuel Thomas Soemmerring Anthropologie. Über die körperliche Verschiedenheit des Negers vom Europäer (1785), rev. and ed. by Sigrid Oehler-Klein, Vol. 15, Stuttgart et al. 1998, 263 (footnote 4, 15); Curran, *Anatomy of Blackness*, 172–173.
38 Cf. Gould, *Mismeasure of Man*, 36.
39 Cf. Curran, *Anatomy of Blackness*, 171–173.
40 Cf. Johann Friedrich Blumenbach, On the Natural Variety of Mankind, sec. I, Of the difference of man from other animals, in: The Anthropological Society (ed.), *The Anthropological*

classification would have to accept too many exceptions to maintain an added explanatory value.

Apart from Linné's classification system, Buffon's theory of development was also on offer. Blumenbach prefers, however, to ascribe central thoughts not to Buffon, but to John Ray, a naturalist in seventeenth century England. John Ray was among the first to define a species—"long before Buffon"[41] as Blumenbach pointedly remarks—in the following way: "One species never springs from the seed of another nor vice versa".[42] This means, in other words, that animals belong to the same species when they can mate. Even though Blumenbach sticks to this definition, he finds it difficult to prove. He asks doubtfully: "How void is the hope to motivate wild animals to prove such a unification? [...] especially if their native countries are widely apart?"[43] With an ironic undertone, Blumenbach muses about the chimpanzees of Angola and the orangutans of Borneo. If empirical proofs are difficult, what can science offer, though? His conclusion is the following: "So that I almost despair of being able to deduce any notion of species in the study of zoology, except from *analogy* and resemblance."[44]

For Blumenbach, analogy, a term that at the time was not yet completely fixed in its meaning,[45] signified the comparison between two relations. Analogy, and with it also comparing, became the very center of his scientific methodology. For him, comparing was the very basis of all anatomic investigations. Comparing had a productive effect: It made ordering his findings possible. Comparisons helped to finally find the distinctive features for humans as an own species: distinctive features were among others, their upright position, relative defenselessness, and

---

Treatises of Blumenbach and Hunter, London 1865, 163, URL: http://www.blumenbach-online.de/Einzelseiten/HTML-Texte/Texte/000010/000010.html?q=on%20the%20natural#pbtitlePage_0003 [last accessed April 9, 2020].

41 Blumenbach, On the Natural Variety of Mankind, sec. II, § 23 What is species?, in: The Anthropological Society of London (ed.), *The Anthropological Treatises of Blumenbach and Hunter*, London 1865, 188, URL: http://www.blumenbach-online.de/Einzelseiten/HTML Texte/Texte/000010/000010.html?q=on%20the%20natural#pbtitlePage_0003 [last accessed April 9, 2020] ; Blumenbach, *De Generis Humani varietate nativa*, 3rd ed., Göttingen 1795, 67, "Raius quidem, vir immortalis praeterito seculo, adeoque diu ante Buffonium ea animantia ad eandem speciem referenda esse censuit, quae invicem coëant et foecundam prolem gignant, [...]"

42 John Ray, *Historia plantarum generalis*, London 1686, "neque haec ab illius semine oritur, aut vice versa," 40, (Translation: Edmund Silk, cited by: Barbara G. Beddall, Historical Notes on Avian Classification, in: *Systematic Biology* 6 (1957), 134).

43 Blumenbach, *Natural Variety*, 189; Blumenbach, *De Generis humani*, 69, "praesertim si longe diversa ipsis patria fuerit."

44 Blumenbach, *Natural Variety*, 190; Blumenbach, *De Generis humani*, 70, "Adeo ut fere desperem posse aliunde quam ex analogia et verisimilitudine notionem speciei in zoologiae studio depromi."

45 Cf. Willibald Steinmetz, 'Vergleich' – eine begriffsgeschichtliche Skizze, in: Angelika Epple/Walter Erhart (eds.), *Die Welt beobachten. Praktiken des Vergleichens*, Frankfurt a. M./New York 2015, 85–134, see 100–103.

the hymen of women.⁴⁶ Taking the hypothesis that all humans belong to just one species as a starting point, Blumenbach looked at the differences between mammals in respect to five categories: color, hair, physical size, shape of the body, and, most importantly, skulls.

Blumenbach's skull collection

Blumenbach's interest in comparing different skulls is not singular. It is no exaggeration that from the Enlightenment until the mid-twentieth century, collecting, measuring, and comparing skulls was a widespread obsession. Comparing also became part of what could been called a collecting mania of the time.⁴⁷ Blumenbach's main sources were not just descriptions of skulls in travelogues but mainly real skulls. The common interest in skulls was impressive, and had a lot to do with anthropological appropriation within the colonial project.⁴⁸ Georg Gliddon, for instance, an English-born American Consul in Cairo and trained Egyptologist, sent more than 100 skulls he had taken out of Ancient Egyptian tombs back to Philadelphia.⁴⁹

Whatever Blumenbach tried to prove, however high his (or his pupils') respect for cultural diversity was, the collection of human bodies, bones, and skulls cannot be seen outside the system of coloniality⁵⁰ and more concretely, outside the Royal Navy. Blumenbach's network was impressive. He used his connections to scholars

---

46   See, for instance, Blumenbach, *Natural Variety*, 107.
47   See, on the fascination with collecting things, Anne Mariss, Globalisierung der Naturgeschichte im 18. Jahrhundert. Die Mobilität der Dinge und ihr materieller Eigensinn, in: Debora Gerstenberger/Joël Glasman (eds.), *Techniken der Globalisierung. Globalgeschichte meets Akteur-Netzwerk-Theorie* (Histoire Band 78), Bielefeld 2016, 67–93, see 92.
48   Cf. Malin Wilckens, *Aus aller Welt – Die Schädel-Korrespondenz des Johann Friedrich Blumenbach*. Unpublished MA-Thesis, Bielefeld 2018; Bettina Brockmeyer, Menschliche Gebeine als Glaubensobjekte. Koloniale Kriegsbeutenahme, Vergleichspraktiken und Erinnerung seit dem späten 19. Jahrhundert, in: WERKSTATT *Geschichte* 77 (2017), 47–64. For a profound analysis of the influence of German science and comparable practices, see Moritz von Brescius, *German Science in the Age of Empire: Enterprise, Opportunity and the Schlagintweit Brothers*, Cambridge 2018.
49   Gould, *Mismeasure of Man*, 61.
50   Even though Walter Mignolo's understanding of power structures and their persistence based on what he calls the "colonial matrix" is not completely convincing, the term "coloniality" is very useful. It points to the fact that people such as Blumenbach, Humboldt, or many others could not have collected seemingly neutral information about other world regions without the asymmetrical relations between colonizers and colonized. Alexander von Humboldt also relied heavily on recommendations by slave trade promoters or even slaveholders to get permission from Spanish officials to travel through the Americas, see: Zeuske, Sklavereien in den Amerikas.

all over the world to gain possession of more than 200 skulls. Sir Joseph Banks, for instance, a British naturalist who had already accompanied James Cook on his first voyage, was not only the director of the African Association in London, but also sent Blumenbach many skulls, old and new, male and female, of children and adults from all over the world. Craniology was not only an innocent scientific affair. It was a colonial practice and still has its aftermath today in the institutes or museums of anatomy.[51]

Blumenbach's practice of comparing: The making of white beauty

What Blumenbach actually did after the skulls came into his possession can be surmised roughly via another genre of sources. Famous students of Blumenbach such as Arthur Schopenhauer wrote vividly about his lectures to which he attracted young men such as the Humboldt brothers from many German-speaking states. Following Schopenhauer, Blumenbach was not only a good entertainer, he also performed autopsies on animals and vivisections in front of his students. He reported on curiosa from natural history and commented on the works of other scholars with decisive opinions. The title of Schopenhauer scripts is telling: "... *die Kunst zu sehen*"—the art of seeing.[52] Blumenbach's "art of seeing" influenced not only scholars such as Schopenhauer but also many explorers such as zu Wied or Humboldt.

From Schopenhauer's script of the lectures in comparative anatomy, we can deduce that Blumenbach's main activity was describing. After describing, he measured the skulls or bones in question, and then he started comparing. The measurement obviously predefined the subsequently applied *tertia* and vice versa. In his doctoral thesis on "the natural varieties of mankind," he had written how difficult it was to find adequate *tertia*. Of course, he did not use the term. When he complained, however, about the difficulty in translating a "sensible impression" into a linguistic expression, it was nothing else than naming the difficulty in finding an adequate *tertium*:

> that it is much easier to distinguish any species from its congeners at the first glance by a sort of divination of the senses, than to give an account of, or express in words those distinctive characters themselves.[53]

---

51 Cf. Wilckens, *Aus aller Welt*.
52 See Jochen Stollberg/Wolfgang Böker (eds.), "... die Kunst zu sehn." Arthur Schopenhauers Mitschriften der Vorlesungen Johann Friedrich Blumenbachs (1809–1811), Schriften zur Göttinger Universitätsgeschichte 3, Göttingen 2013.
53 Blumenbach, *Natural Variety*, 163; Blumenbach, *De Generis Humani*, 2, "ubi subinde longe facilius aliquam speciem a congeneribus primo intuitu et sensuali quadam perceptione distinguere, quam ipsos istos characteres disctinctivos enarrare et verbis exprimere valemus."

In contrast to a mere subsumption, the quote shows that Blumenbach was in search of the criteria for the commonalty of humans as a single species.[54] Hence, he was searching for adequate *tertia*. Only by finding the *tertia*, could he find words to describe the specificity of the respective comparata and then decide whether they belonged to the same species (*genus proximum*). The "art of seeing" in Blumenbach's world is nothing other than explaining how to be able to "see" *tertia* and the *differences* between at least two entities. It is, in other words, comparing. One can, at a glance, understand why the making of a classification system is based on comparisons and how, at the time, the *tertia* and the *comparata* shape themselves respectively.

With his suggestions, Blumenbach argued against two contemporary positions that worked with different classification systems: On the one hand, there was Linné who understood apes and humans as just one species, because he never found a *diferentia specifica*. In contrast to Linné, Blumenbach was of the opinion that there were specific differences between apes and human beings (upright position, defenselessness, hymen) and that they did not belong to just one species.

On the other hand, there were those who were in favor of the plurality of human species (e.g., Voltaire) or, like Meiners, were reluctant to accept the common origin of all humans. Blumenbach, in contrast, argued that there is no specific difference between human races. What he found instead was "an almost insensible and indefinable transition from the pure white skin of the German lady through the yellow, the red, and the dark nations, to the Ethiopian of the very deepest black."[55]

The "insensible transition" between human varieties is Blumenbach's answer to the Black-and-White discourse of his time. Even though he overcomes the binary system, his take remains ambivalent. Humans belong to just one species (assumption of similarity), they share commonalities, but they are different; and between both difference and similarity, there are many transitions.

This conviction did not prevent him from continuing his comparing of skulls. Today, Blumenbach is less well known for his proof of a unique species of humans in contrast to apes, but for the varieties of human "races" within that single species. The most famous finding is the one you can see in figure 1.

Where his scientifically based arguments came to an end, his presumably aesthetic considerations began. If no *diferentia specifica* in the strict sense could be detected between the variants of human beings, for him one difference remained: the

---

54 Blumenbach refers here to the classical Aristotelian distinction of genus proximum and diferentia specifica. In practice, the Aristotelian distinction does not necessarily involve comparing. The *diferentia specifica* is mainly about subsumption. Put simply, if "quadruped" is defined as a species and I want to know if an animal belongs to this very species, I just have to count its feet. Comparing does not have to be involved. In Blumenbach's case, things were different. The *genus proximum* was not given; instead, it was in question.

55 Blumenbach, *Natural Variety*, 107.

Fig. 1: On the Natural Variety of Mankind

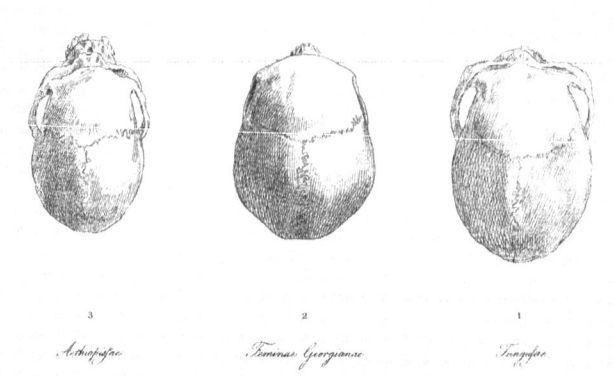

The picture reads: Plate III., which represents, by way of specimen, three skulls disposed in the order mentioned. The middle one (fig. 2) is a very symmetrical and beautiful one of a Georgian female; on either side are two skulls differing from it in the most opposite way. The one (fig. 3) elongated in front, and as it were keeled, is that of an Ethiopian female of Guinea; the other (fig. 4) dilated outwardly toward the sides, and as it were flattened, is that of a Reindeer Tungus. (Blumenbach, On the Natural Variety of Mankind, 1795, 237)

beauty of the Georgian female. One has to know that Georgian females belong to the Caucasian people.

With this observation, Blumenbach again underlined his systematic approach: With his concentration on identifying different types of skulls, he did not bother about their age. He compared skulls from Ancient Egypt with skulls of only recently deceased Indians. Via comparisons, he hoped to refute the popular arguments of his time, one of which was Buffon's, de Pauw's, and Meiners' ideas on the climatic degeneration of non-White people. Neither Blumenbach's intervention against clear-cut differences between human varieties nor his term "insensible transition" prevented him from stereotyping the varieties of humankind into initially four (1775) and later five (1781) different types. Comparison-based, this typing was not innocent from its beginning. Caucasian women, such as the Georgians, were already famous for their beauty in Antiquity. Ironically, it is these very same people, says Nell Painter, especially their women, who have also been enslaved since Antiquity.[56] It is interesting to note that Blumenbach's intention was to argue against the assumption of a negative development provoked by environmental

---

56   Cf. Painter, *History of White People*, 36, 84.

conditions such as a humid and hot climate. He contrasted degeneration with a typology based on comparisons.

Blumenbach and his talented pupil Alexander von Humboldt

Alexander von Humboldt visited Blumenbach's lectures in Göttingen for only two terms, in winter and summer (April 1789–March 1790).[57] However, correspondence between the two intensified after Humboldt left Göttingen.[58] They stayed in contact even when Humboldt accompanied by Bonpland took off for his great journey to the Americas. Changing plans on the spot, they decided to first travel through the Venezuelan region before exploring Cuba (and thus by accident escaped the yellow fever epidemic on Cuba at the time).[59]

An entry in Humboldt's diary shows how effectively Blumenbach's skull network was:

"We searched for particularly characteristic skulls for [Johann Friedrich] Blumenbach and to this end opened many mapire [baskets]. Poor wretches! Even in your graves your peace and quiet is disturbed! The Indians observed this operation with great reluctance, especially a few Indians from Guaicia who had known White people for hardly four months. We collected skulls, a child´s skeleton and two skeletons of adults. [...] Night fell while we were rummaging about among the bones. The expressions of our Indian guides told us that we had desecrated the burial ground enough and should at last bring the sacrilege to an end. [...].
[...] We dragged our skeletons by water to Angostura and from there by land to [Nueva] Barcelona through the Caribbean missions. Nothing escapes the Indian sensitivity. The bones were in double mapire and seemed completely invisible to us. But as soon as we arrived in a Caribbean village, and as soon as the Indians gathered to see our animals (capuchin and tiger monkeys), the bones were discovered immediately. They refused to give us mulas [mules] because the carcass would kill them."[60]

---

57 Cf. Fernando Ortíz, Introducción, in: Alejandro de Humboldt: *Ensayo político sobre la isla de Cuba por Alejandro de Humboldt, con un mapa de Cuba. Introducción por Fernando Ortíz y correcciones, notas y appendices por Francisco de Arango y Parreño*, Tomo I, La Habana 1930, XVI; Norbert Klatt, *Kleine Beiträge zur Blumenbach-Forschung*, vol. 1, Göttingen 2008, 12.
58 Klatt, *Kleine Beiträge*, 17.
59 Cf. Ortíz, Introducción.
60 [My translation]. Original quote: "*Wir suchten recht charakteristische Schädel für* [Johann Friedrich] *Blumenbach und öffneten daher viele Mapire* [Körbe]. *Armes Volk, selbst in den Gräbern stört man deine Ruhe! Die Indianer sahen diese Operation mit großem Unwillen an, besonders ein paar Indianer von Guaicia, welche kaum vier Monate lang weiße Menschen kannten. Wir sammelten Schädel, ein Kinderskelett und zwei Skelette erwachsener Personen.* [...] *Die Nacht brach ein, indem*

I have quoted this entry at some length, because it is telling in different respects. First, Humboldt names only one skin color: "white." This is astonishing because the description as "Whites" for Europeans usually emerges only when someone underlines the civilizing mission. A good example is the justification of the slave trader mentioned at the beginning of this contribution. One could even ask whether Humboldt's quote is a random change of perspective: A European explorer looks at his European peer group through the eyes of the American (in this case: Venezuelan) inhabitants. This change of perspective is not taken up in the "*essai*" and it is also, second, framed within that very quote in a way that undermines it. Humboldt feels pity for the locals ("poor wretches") and he knows that he is disturbing their peace. "Poor wretches" ("*Armes Volk*") frames the change of perspective insofar as it shows the narrator as a person standing above the observed scene, because he is from a higher social level. It is the tone of an aristocrat. Third, Humboldt's commitment to skull collecting is so strong that he continues digging until late, despite realizing that the surrounding "Indians" did not feel comfortable about it. He probably was aware of the fact that back home in Europe, this activity would count as desecration of a grave, an activity he presumably would never have carried out in Berlin.[61]

Humboldt's "*essai*," its translations, and the Thrasher controversy in 1856

Humboldt stayed in Cuba twice (19.12.1800–15.3.1801 and 19.3.–29.4.1804). During his stays, he resided in the house of a Mr. Cuesta, who owned one of the biggest trading houses in America, and in the house of Duke O'Reilly, both belonging to the ruling classes.[62] What is more, he was also familiar with the aforementioned Fran-

---

wir noch unter den Knochen wühlten. Die Mienen unserer indianischen Führer sagten uns, dass wir diese Grabstätte genug entheiligt hätten und den Frevel endlich endigen sollten. [...] Wir schleppten unsere Skelette zu Wasser bis Angostura und von da zu Lande bis [Nueva] Barcelona durch die Missionen der Cariben. Dem Spurgeist der Indianer entgeht nichts. Die Knochen waren in doppelten Mapire und schienen uns völlig unsichtbar. Kaum aber kamen wir in einem Caribischen Dorfe an, und kaum versammelten sich die Indianer, um unsere Tiere (Kapuziner- und Tigeraffen) zu sehen, so waren sogleich die Knochen ausgespürt. Man weigerte sich, uns mulas [Maultiere] zu geben, weil der Kadaver sie töte." Margot Faak, (ed.), *Alexander von Humboldt: Reise durch Venezuela. Auswahl aus den amerikanischen Reisetagebüchern*, Berlin 2000, 324–325.

61   Of course, the prohibition of opening graves did not prevent all researchers in Europe from doing so, but Humboldt would still have preferred not to be such an extreme researcher in Prussia.

62   Humboldt, *Essai politique*, 36, "*Nous trouvâmes, dans la famille de M. Cuesta, qui formoit alors avec M. Santa Maria une des plus grandes maisons de commerce de l'Amérique.*"

cisco de Arango y Parreño, who lived close by[63] and took him to see his *"ingenios"* (sugar plantations): *La Ninfa, Río Blanco*, and *La Holanda*.[64] As Humboldt points out in his *"essai,"* Arango seemed to him to have the utmost experience when it came to economic questions, statistical data, and understanding the specificity of the slavery regime in Cuba.

Comparisons run through the whole essay including general observations, egoistic considerations, and respective chapters on climate, population, agriculture (mainly sugar, coffee, tobacco, and wax), trading, and slavery.[65] In the following, I shall focus only on Humboldt's comparisons concerning the population and his considerations on races or slavery.[66]

More than 20 years had passed between Humboldt's last visit of the island and the appearance of his study. Unfortunately, he did not use the time to turn it into a systematic study. The *"essai"* is full of interesting insights and good observations, but it is also redundant, and a leitmotiv is sometimes difficult to spot. During this period, Humboldt corresponded with Cuban officials and scholars, one of whom was Francisco de Arango y Parreño. Humboldt continuously added to his extensive data collection on flora, fauna, natural resources, and, most importantly, the Cuban population. As already mentioned, the compendium of the *"essai"* with its ardent plea for abolition was rounded off by an appendix with statistics.

After the seminal work on Cuba had appeared in French, it was soon translated into other European languages. Humboldt had been a presence in the French- and Spanish-speaking world since the late 1820s. The *"essai"* was omnipresent in Cuban statistical works as well as in the official census, reports, and publications,[67] even

---

63 In today's Havanna, the so-called "casa de Humboldt" is a small museum, and the casa de Arango y Parreño is a medical institution. A small information board fixed outside the house does not mention that Francisco de Arango y Parreño was one of the most important slave traders and slavery defenders of the time. This can be read only between the lines: The information reads *"Doctor en leyes, humanista, economista, orador y hacendado azucarero,"* private photo April 24, 2019.

64 Ortíz mentions that Arango showed Humboldt and Bonpland his *"ingenios."* Ortíz, Introducción, XXXIII.

65 This does not just hold for the essay. See on the importance of comparing in Humboldt's travelogues, Christine Peters, Reisen und Vergleichen. Praktiken des Vergleichens in Alexander von Humboldts Reise in die Äquinoktial-Gegenden des Neuen Kontinents und Adam Johann von Krusensterns Reise um die Welt, in: *Internationales Archiv für die Sozialgeschichte der Literatur (IASL)* 42 (2/2017), 441–465.

66 Oliver Lubrich is completely right when he says Humboldt should be read as a literary author. He convincingly shows the double-coded discourse on slavery and also the construction of Cuba as an in-between space. See the inspiring analysis of Humboldt's *"essai"*: Oliver Lubrich, In the Realm of Ambivalence: Alexander von Humboldt's Discourse on Cuba, in: *German Studies Review* 26 (1/2003), 63–80.

67 It was probably the French version of 1826 that gained most attention in France. Francisco de Arango y Parreño even commented on it in 1827. See Francisco Arango y Parreño, Observa-

though the Spanish edition of the *"ensayo"* had been banned by the local government in Havana in its session on 27 November in 1827 due to its "observations in respect to slavery."[68]

The German translation by Theresa Huber-Forster and her son Victor Aimé did not get as much attention.[69] The English translation by John Sidney Thrasher, American Consul in Cuba and supporter of an annexation of the Cuban island, even became part of a controversy during the 1856 US presidential election. Thrasher's intention was certainly to back the Democrat's candidate and later president James Buchanan (a supporter of Cuban annexation as well as of slavery) with a publication by the renowned German scholar. Voters with a German background were decisive in the election. However, Thrasher left out Humboldt's criticism of slavery while nonetheless suggesting that he had made a complete translation.[70]

Underestimating how Humboldt would react, Thrasher sent him a letter saying "I have taken the liberty to differ with you on some of the general principles of social economy in this continent, but I have endeavored to do so with a proper diffidence to your great attainments and eminent powers."[71] Humboldt, though already very old, was furious and did not just answer personally. In July 1856, he published an article in a German newspaper in which he attacked Thrasher severely for having omitted the chapter on slavery: "I assign far greater importance to this part of my text than to the arduous work on determining astronomic positions, exploring magnetic intensity, or [compiling] statistical data."[72] This article was taken up by several newspapers in the United States such as the *New York Herald*, and the

---

ciones al "Ensayo politico sobre la isla de Cuba", escritas en 1827, in: Francisco de Arango y Parreño, *Obras completas*, vol. II, 1889, 533–546, see 533.

68 José L. Franco, Prólogo, in: *Cuadernos de Historia Haberna* 69 (1960), 20. Franco assumes that even some Afro-Cubans felt insulted by Humboldt's *"ensayo."* To the best of my knowledge, Franco is the only source that mentions this assumption.

69 Therese Heyne-Forster-Huber (1754–1829), whose first marriage had been to Georg Forster, together with her son Victor Aimé, translated Humboldt's *"essai"* including the appendices into German in 1829–1832, cf. Beck, commentary to the German edition, 240–241.

70 Cf. John S. Thrasher, preface, in: Alexander von Humboldt, *The Island of Cuba* [1827], New York 1856.

71 Quoted in German by Beck, commentary to the German edition, 254. It is uncertain whether Thrasher knew about the English translation (without the appendices) by Helen Maria Williams published in London in 1829.

72 [My translation]. Original quote: *"Auf diesen Teil meiner Schrift lege ich eine weit größere Wichtigkeit als auf die mühevollen Arbeiten astronomischer Ortsbestimmungen, magnetischer Intensitätsversuche oder statistischer Angaben"*. The German quote is cited in Beck, commentary on the German edition, 256–257.The article appeared in the *Berlinische Nachrichten von Staats- und gelehrten Sachen* on July 25, 1856. For more details, see Beck, commentary to the German edition, 252–260.

New York Daily Times in mid-August 1856.[73] Thrasher felt obliged to respond to the editors and justify his approach. His reply was published twice on August 13 and 17, 1856.[74] He defended himself by assuming that the chapter on slavery was an addition to the *"essai"* and not really part of it—an interpretation that contradicts the first sentences of Humboldt's chapter. This controversy was first taken up at the end of the 1880s in the Cuban journal *La Semana* by the Cuban journalist and historian Manuel Villanova.[75] This led to Humboldt's chapter on slavery experiencing a second phase of reception in Cuba.[76]

At the time, the *New York Tribune*, the leading journal of the young Republican party, did not intervene in this controversy directly, but also tried to win voters through Humboldt's authority. They supported their candidate, John C. Frémont by publishing another letter by Humboldt from the early 1850s in which he had praised the merits of Frémont. Despite all efforts, the convinced abolitionist Frémont lost the election. Only in 1930 when Fernando Ortíz edited Humboldt's *"essai"* in Spanish again and when he wrote a laudatory introduction of roughly 80 pages did the controversy over Humboldt and Thrasher gain some international attention.[77]

---

73 See the very informative and helpful online series by Vera M. Kutzinsky and Ottmar Ette: *Alexander von Humboldt in English*, see: Humboldt-Thrasher-controversy, in: press.uchicago.edu [last accessed April 26, 2019].

74 The *New York Daily Times* referred to the article as published in *Spenersche Zeitung*. See *New York Daily Times*, August 17, 1856. Thrasher's article also appeared in *The New York Herald* on August 13, 1856.

75 In September 1887, the Cuban journalist Manuel Villanova published a series of articles on Humboldt and Thrasher in the Cuban weekly journal *La Semana*. It started on September 5, 1887 with a publication of Humboldt's article and Thrasher's answer together with a critical commentary on Thrasher. In the following weeks, Villanova commented on it broadly. Villanova read Humboldt with a lot of admiration, and also discussed the passages in which Humboldt compared Cuban domestic slaves to Jamaican domestic slaves. In the following, he criticized the Cuban slave regime in far more detail than Humboldt. The whole series including the translation of Humboldt's article and Thrasher's response were reproduced in 1960. See for the letters, Manuel Villanova, Humboldt y Trasher, in: *Cuadernos de Historia Haberna* 69 (1960), 32–34; for the criticism of the Cuban slave regime, 46–52.

76 A decade later, the historian Vidal Morales y Morales also wrote an article in three parts that appeared in the journal *El Figaro* under the title "El Barón de Humboldt an las Isla de Cuba: 1800–1801–1804" (*El Figaro* 1897, June n. 21, 23, 24). See Kutzinsky/Ette, *Humboldt in English*, "Brief Timeline: The *Political Essay* in Cuba", press.uchicago.edu [last accessed April 26, 2019].

77 Cf. Alejandro de Humboldt, *Ensayo político sobre la isla de Cuba por Alejandro de Humboldt, con un mapa de Cuba. Introducción por Fernando Ortíz y correcciones, notas y appendices por Francisco de Arango y Parreño, J.S. Thrasher y otros*, Tomo I, La Habana 1930.

The objectivity of the numbers: Censuses in Cuba

But it was not just Humboldt's elaborations on slavery that became influential. Until today, Humboldt is more famous for his comparative methodology than for his criticism of slavery. Even if Blumenbach is not mentioned in the *"essai,"* and even if Humboldt does not carry out anatomic comparisons, Blumenbach's approach and his understanding of both scientific objectivity and neutrality are omnipresent. When Humboldt reflected on his methodology, he was of the opinion that he only clarified facts: "As a historian of America, I wanted to clarify facts and specify ideas by means of comparisons and statistical data."[78] This is something he might have learned from Blumenbach: observing, describing, translating into numbers (measuring), and comparing. In his view, his meticulously detailed investigation into the facts seemed necessary to fight both benevolent gullibility and hateful passions. Both feelings, so his conviction, had led to the most erratic and erroneous data. Criticizing earlier narrations and descriptions of the island was simply an effective tool for framing his study as scientific, objective, and politically neutral.

Already in the introduction to his *"essai,"* Humboldt cites the official censuses of 1791, 1810, and other statistical data until 1824. In the specific chapter on population, he elaborates on this in more detail. What are his population comparisons about? Different types of comparisons are involved: The statistical data are comparisons between people from the countryside and those living in Havana, comparisons between people living in different Cuban provinces, and comparisons between Cuban inhabitants and those living in Jamaica, the Antilles, the United States, Brazil, or even other Latin-American countries. He usually distinguishes different "classes" in the graphs: "White," "free Colored" (including Mulatto and African), and "slaves"; and he then compares these with the same group of people in, for instance, different regions. In the text, he is more precise and also distinguishes between Mulattos and Negros, both free and enslaved, or, what is more unusual at the time, between different Whites: White inhabitants and strangers from different European countries. The strangers never make it into the graphs, whereas the "Mulattos" are included. In the text, he prefers the term *"Pardos"* for people of mixed White–African origin. However, the term "Pardo" never shows up in the graphs.

Reading the graphs and the text is a challenging task, because different lines of argumentation run through the chapter. On the surface, he gives only the numbers of people in each group as if they could speak for themselves. Usually, Humboldt

---

[78] Humboldt, *Political Essay*, 142. Humboldt, *Essai politique*, 305–306, "Historien de l'Amérique, j'ai voulu éclaircir les faits et préciser les idées, à l'aide de comparaisons et de tableaux statistiques."

repeats in the text only what can also be seen at first glance in the graphs. Sometimes he adds calculations about the different groups and their respective mortality rate, how they are increasing or diminishing. Meanwhile, the graphs are an alleged proof of high scientific standards. In the text, he puts their reliability into perspective. To express this frankly: The graphs hide the fact that they are not objective. With reference to Arango y Parreño, he concludes that they are more often than not the result of only estimated calculations.[79]

The interplay of text and graphs is interesting, especially when he accumulates the outcomes of the graphs, for instance, when explaining: "The relationship of the different classes of inhabitants grouped according to their origin and their state of civil liberty offers the most striking contrasts in those countries in which slavery has established very deep roots."[80] The graph shows Whites and free people of Color in different columns. Only in the main text can one find a reduced graph that sums up Whites and free people so that they appear as a single group of free people (of Color and White). On the same page, he concludes that free people make up 64% of the whole population of Cuba but only 19% in the British Antilles. Already in the next phrase, he returns to his usual practice of assembling instead all people of Color into one group, be they free or slaves: "In the whole archipelago of the Antilles, the people of Color (Negros and Mulattos, free and slave) make a mass of 2,360,000 or 83/100 of the whole population."[81]

That for a moment, Humboldt had assembled all free people (White and of Color) in just one group suits his humanitarian endeavor of abolition. Sharing the results of Blumenbach's investigation, he believed that all people were of the same kind. A closer reading shows that this endeavor, as serious as he might have been about pursuing it, was contaminated by a second line of argumentation, a line that is not so obvious at first glance. In contrast to Blumenbach who implemented an aesthetic argument for making a difference between "Caucasian" White people and all other people, Humboldt implements what could be called the "paternalistic difference." This line of argumentation is certainly also based on comparing "classes" of people in different settings, but it goes beyond this: It is, as I will show, also based on a comparison of slave regimes, some of which are better than others. The

---

79 According to Humboldt, the numbers from the censuses of 1791 and 1811, for instance, draw only on incomplete data. See Humboldt, *Political Essay*, 73. Humboldt, *Essai politique*, 133, "Les résultats, publiées en 1811, ne se fondent donc que sur ces données incomplètes et sur les évaluations approximatives de l'augmentation de 1791 à 1811."
80 [My translation]. Original quote: "Le rapport des diverses classes d'habitants groupés d'après leur origine et l'état de leur liberté civile, offre les contrastes les plus frappants dans les pays dans lesquels l'esclavage a jeté des racines très-profondes." Humboldt, *Essai politique*, 115.
81 [My translation]. Original quote: "Dans tout l'archipel des Antilles, les hommes de couleur (nègres et mulâtres, libres et esclaves) forment une masse de 2,360,000 ou de 83/100 de la population totale." Humboldt, *Essai politique*, 118.

existence of "better" slave regimes than others opens the door for his "paternalistic difference": The baseline of this argumentation is that White people who do not fight the cruel system of slavery do not acknowledge enlightenment's humanitarian mission. They are the cause of all evil. People of Color who fight the cruel system of slavery for understandable reasons tend to rebel. Rebellion, however, is never a solution for humanitarian challenges. It only provokes violence. The *"essai,"* though, is written for enlightened elites, to make them aware of the fact that their task is to find a way out. These are imagined to be White. If White elites do not find a solution, a rebellion of people of Color cannot be prevented. Humankind depends on White enlightened elites fighting Black slavery.

Comparing slave regimes:
The manipulating influence of Arango y Parreños

It comes as no surprise that Humboldt was not in favor of the Haitian revolution. Preventing a rebellion of people of Color was an objective he shared with many others, one of whom was Francisco de Arango y Parreño. However, regarding what that prevention could mean, they all had different things in mind: Humboldt's interest was humanitarian with a European background. Arango was primarily a businessman with a Cuban background. He had travelled through Europe to collect information on industrialization processes such as refining sugar. He became a leading figure in transforming Cuba's sugar plantations into sugar factories that refined the sugar on the spot before exporting it. In other words, he was one of the engineers of "slaving modernity."[82] Whenever Humboldt quotes Arango, he praises him as an expert in economics, as an impressive statesman, and also as an enlightened intellectual. What he does not mention in his *"essai"* is that they jointly visited Arango's *ingenios* that had become factories thanks to the labor of slaves.[83]

Arango was indeed a highly talented economist, politician and, I would like to add, an extremely successful manipulative lobbyist. Reading his *obras completas*, one quickly understands that his main goal was to combine personal with Cuban interests. The key to doing this was to make a profit with Cuba's main agricultural products such as sugar, cocoa, and tobacco. Three examples might suffice to underline this: In 1791 and again in 1803 when he travelled to St. Domingue as a

---

[82] See Michael Zeuske, Die Nicht-Geschichte von Versklavten als Archiv-Geschichte von "Stimmen" und Körpern, in: *Jahrbuch für Europäische Überseegeschichte* 16, Wiesbaden 2016, 2; Dale W. Tomich/Michael Zeuske, The Second Slavery. Mass Slavery, World-Economy, and Comparative Microhistories, in: *Review: Fernand Braudel Center* XXXI, (2/2008) 91-100; Michael Zeuske, Out of the Americas. Slave traders and the Hidden Atlantic in the nineteenth century, in: *Atlantic Studies* 15, (1/2018), 103-135.

[83] Cf. Ortíz, Introducción, XXXIII.

member of a royal commission, he stated very openly that Cuba should take advantage of the unfortunate Haitian situation. Cuba depended on the labor of slaves and Spain took advantage of a prospering Cuban economy. To secure the slave regime in Cuba, he recommended not to "import" too many Africans, because they should never outnumber the Whites in the population. In his analysis of the Haitian catastrophe, he mentions three reasons why a similar upheaval in Cuba would be rather improbable: the fierce loyalty of the elites to the King of Spain, more soldiers than the French had in Haiti, and most important, better legislation on the treatment of slaves. Slaves in Cuba, he was convinced, "are the happiest of the world."[84] The already mentioned phrase that Cubans should import slaves only with "census figures in hand" reveals his pragmatic approach. For him, humanitarian reasons did not matter in 1791. From his perspective, the censuses seemed to be a helpful tool for controlling the number of slaves and thus preventing rebellions.

Arango's influence became even more important when he became a member of the *Consejo de India* roughly twenty years later. Cuban delegates had already prevented abolition from also being implemented in the Americas (as it was in Spain) in the Cádiz constitution of 1812[85]—a step recommended by Arango.[86] As a member of the *Consejo de India*, he also convinced the respective commission to not help the "race in chains" because it would do injustice to Cuban White elites. In the introductory "Historical Elegy" to Arango's *obras completas* in 1837, Arango is honored for having at the last moment prevented "African blood" from being preferred to "European blood."[87] His basic theorems that he was still repeating in his publications in the 1820s are as follows: Production should meet the growing demand. To achieve this, Cuban agriculture would need, first, to industrialize its sugar industry and, second, to also strengthen its labor force. Only free trade in general including slaves in particular guaranteed the prosperity of Cuban welfare. Welfare could be guaranteed only if a rebellion could be prevented. Preventing rebellion is easy to achieve by first treating slaves well and second getting the numbers right and not importing more people of African descent than there are White people living in the country. Censuses are an important tool for guaranteeing the right mix of the population.

In 1832, he seems, at first glance, to have changed his mind and to now favor abolition. However, he is simply arguing more subtly. He no longer doubts that abolition would be a good thing. For him, the remaining question is how to achieve

---

84 Francisco de Arango y Parreño, Representación hecha á S.M. con motivo do la sublevación de esclavos en los dominios franceses de la isla de Santo Domingo (1791), in: *Obras completas*, vol. I, 1888, 49.
85 Helg, *Slave but not Citizen*, 94.
86 Arango y Parreño, *Obras completas*, vol. II.
87 Anastasio Carillo y Arango, Elogio histórico, in: Francisco de Arango y Parreño, *Obras del Excmo. Señor D. Francisco de Arango y Parreño* vol. I, La Habana 1888, XLII.

it. His arguments are still based on a comparative history of slave regimes that shows why the French system, in contrast to the Spanish, became so cruel in the eighteenth century. He repeats that not much needed to be done for slaves in Cuban towns, because "in general, they are happy with their status."[88]

Nonetheless, the categories change slightly in his later publications. He now distinguishes members of the free elite (including people of Color and White people) from less privileged free people of Color and from slaves. This is a group formation found previously only in Humboldt's *"essai."* Now, Arango is also arguing that it is quite "natural" for people to mix. He even quotes Humboldt's *"essai,"* saying that no one should envy another person for being "whiter." Surprisingly enough, it is not only the skin color he is referring to. In his view, *"blancura"* (whitening), which means nothing other than gaining *limpieza de sangre*, should not be most important, because what should be most important is becoming a free person.[89] For him, it seems impertinent to force persons to prove that they "have not a drop of Black blood."

It is important to note that his main arguments in favor of slavery remain untouched by this. He still believes that Cuba's agriculture needs the labor of slaves.[90] He still believes that if slaves are well treated, they are better off than freed nonelite people of Color. The bright businessmen Arango had realized in the 1820s that it might be a good idea to have Pardo and Mulatto elites as allies and not as enemies. This is an interesting move, because even if it might not alter his arguments in favor of slavery completely, it does, so to say, change their color. If he accepts people of Color as fellow elites, then slavery no longer appears racist in a narrower sense.

The writings of Arango are worth studying for their own sake. It is fascinating to see how Arango manages to adapt his enthusiasm for slavery from the 1790s to the 1820s in an ever-changing discursive environment, and, what is more, in a period of historical transition on a global level. In 1832, even an Arango finds it better to hide his economic arguments and clothe them in a humanitarian sounding paternalistic discourse. Even though still polemicizing against "filantropic positions," he underlines that all he wants is societal progress. According to Arango in 1791, slaves in Cuba were already the happiest in the world; and forty years later, he was still doing everything to ensure that this situation would never change.

88　Arango, Representación al Rey sobre la exstinción de tráfico de negros y medios de mojorar la suerte do los esclavos coloniales (28.5.1832), in: *Obras completas*, vol. II, 649–659, see 657.

89　Arango, Carta al Secretario del Supremo Consejo de Indias en que el autor avisa estar traduciendo una "Memoria sobre la Abolición de la Esclavidud en las Colonias europeas" (24.8.1831), in: *Obras completas*, vol. II, 659–741, see 722.

90　Maybe even more so, because one of his own *ingenio*, la Ninfa, which he had also shown to Humboldt and had always served as "best practice," had failed in 1819. Zeuske, Sklavereien in den Amerikas.

One could ask why Humboldt was so fascinated by him. The texts of both men influenced each other in subtle but profound ways. When comparing the Spanish with the French, British, or American slave regime, Humboldt concludes that the "terrifying catastrophe of Santo Domingo" was the outcome of an ignorant ruling dynasty. Humboldt was convinced that legislation in the Antilles and the civil status of the people of Color had to change for the better—otherwise a "bloody catastrophe"[91] would be unavoidable. Maybe not as empathically, but these arguments can also be found in Arango's writings. When expressing his disgust at slavery, Humboldt's quotes refer more often than not to slave regimes outside Cuba. Actually, he could be seen as a forerunner of the "Tannenbaum thesis". In 1946, the sociologist Frank Tannenbaum published a book on the comparative history of slavery saying that Anglo- and Latin-American slave regimes differed insofar as they either impeded or facilitated the transition from bondage to citizenship. In Latin America, Tannenbaum argued, the slave could, once freed from bondage, even purchase whiteness; in the United States, in contrast, a Black could never do this. The thesis has provoked heated discussions until today.[92]

Humboldt's sympathy for the Cuban situation becomes most evident when he speaks about Arango's concept of the *"cuatro consuelos"* (four consents) of 1796 in which Arango explains in detail that four rights should be guaranteed for slaves ("choice of a less severe master, the right to marry whom he pleases, and the possibility of working to purchase his freedom, [...] the right to own property and to pay for his wife and children's freedom").[93] Compared to Arango's suggestions of 1832, his arguments over slavery have hardly changed as such. What has changed instead is the call for an alliance with free people of Color among the elites. Arango's rational argumentation, his (verbal) engagement for the rights of slaves, his good education, his worldliness, and noble background—all of this might have impressed Humboldt and it might have also fostered his belief that slavery should be transformed only gradually and slowly under the careful guidance of enlightened and also noble intellectuals.

---

91 Humboldt, *Political Essay*, 68. Humboldt, *Essai politique*, 118, "cette catastrophe sanglante."
92 Cf. Frank Tannenbaum, *Slave and Citizen*, New York 1947; Ann Twinam, *Purchasing Whiteness*, Stanford 2015, 9; Helg, *Slave but not Citizen*, 2017, 76. This discussion about "whitening" as a process of manumission and overcoming *limpieza de sangre* (*"gracias al sacar"* as Tannenbaum and Twinam would call it) should not be confused with the practice of "whitening" in the sense of attracting White European immigrants to make Cuba "whiter." Arango and Humboldt use the terms in both contexts. Humboldt explicitly refers to official whitenings in his "essai" (Humboldt, *Essai politique*, 144, *"blanchîment officiel"*). Arango's and Humboldt's argument that people of Color should not outnumber the White population had a long aftermath.
93 Humboldt, *Political Essay*, 150. Humboldt, *Essai politique*, 326, "M. d'Arango [...] accorde à l'esclave quatre droits (quatro consuelos)."

Main findings

Blumenbach played an important role in introducing comparisons as a key methodology in academia. One of his most famous investigations was his comparisons of skulls in search of commonalties. He could do this only in a negative mode: He had to deny the existence of a *diferentia specifica*. Only then could he argue that all human beings belong to just one species.

Blumenbach did not leave it at that. After having identified the species, he used species as a category and as a starting point for further comparisons. As a result, he determined that female Caucasian skulls, in respect to their symmetry, were the most beautiful. I have called this the *"aesthetic difference."* He can be labeled the inventor of White beauty.

Humboldt, of course, was not just influenced by Blumenbach when it comes to comparisons.[94] But he definitely shared his approach in many respects. For both scholars, the activity of comparing began with thick descriptions of the respective *comparata*. Like Blumenbach, Humboldt was also often searching for a *tertium comparationis*, and this provoked endless descriptions. This makes Humboldt's writings on Cuba such heavy reading. Once he has identified *comparata* and *tertia*, comparisons seem to be the best way to prove scientific objectivity and personal neutrality in contrast to the irrational, invented, speculative findings of earlier scholars. This is most evident in Humboldt's considerations on flora, fauna, climate, and geological questions, but it is also true for his investigation of population numbers.

When it comes to comparing with numbers, all uncertainties about their reliability were hidden. Although Humboldt (and also official censuses such as the 1909 census) is often skeptical about numbers, graphs represent comparisons as objective and thus help to naturalize the categories (people of Color, Blacks, Whites) employed.

Like Blumenbach, Humboldt is also generally interested in finding commonalties within all differences. This is closely connected to their shared humanitarian endeavor. Both argue against slavery and racial hierarchies. At the same time, both also introduce evaluative differences between races. Humboldt does not do this as explicitly as Blumenbach does. Humboldt does not investigate the making of race categories himself (in contrast to his investigations of different slave regimes). He just takes the race categories from the official censuses and from Arango's data collections. However, a close reading reveals that Humboldt prefers a transformation

---

94 It has been shown only recently that Humboldt employed global comparisons throughout his work as powerful epistemological devices that more often than not fall back upon "Eurocentric ideas of art, politics, society, and beauty." Blumenbach was just one of many other Eurocentric influences on Humboldt. See, Peters' chapter on travels and comparisons in this book.

of Cuban society under the guidance of careful elites. In a society in which *limpieza de sangre* still reserves higher societal positions for White people alone, this attitude has a racial undertone, even if Humboldt might not have thought about it. I have called this the "paternalistic difference." Fighting black slavery, though, in this world view, was the task of only White people. Roughly fifty years later, Kipling spoke of the "White man's burden."

Comparing—and this cannot be underlined often enough—is an ambivalent activity. Comparing simultaneously creates similarities and differences in respect to a *tertium* (such as race). Overcoming racial discrimination in everyday life would mean overcoming discourses on racial comparisons.

Humboldt's comparisons of slave regimes place his general disgust of slavery in perspective. His arguments tie in with the so-called "Tannenbaum thesis" of the mid-twentieth century. The controversy centers on the question whether or not former slaves could become the equals of Whites (in other words, could they overcome *limpieza de sangre*). Interestingly enough, it is the slaveholder Arango who in his writings of 1832 refers to the impertinence of blood purity (mainly because Whites also had to prove it when applying for certain higher positions) and suggests that elites of African descent should gain the same rights as all Whites have. This shift in his argument can help him save his defense of the slave regime as not being based on racial categories.

The passion with censuses for proving how many people of Color live in a region is not as innocent, neutral, or objective as Humboldt implies. For Arango, the main objective of official censuses is to control people of Color so that they do not outnumber Whites. For him, this is essential to prevent rebellions. Having Arango in mind, it becomes even clearer that Humboldt also believes that there should never be too many people of Color, either free or slave.

Humboldt's and Arango's comparisons are most telling when it comes to different slave regimes. Humboldt adopts Arango's vision of a "good" slave regime that he had explained already in 1796 in his *cuatro consuelos* (four consents). Within this context of slave regime comparisons, Humboldt is looking only for differences. This is in contrast to his comparisons in other contexts in which the objective is finding commonalties. Until his writings in 1832, Arango remained a defender of (paternalistic) slave regimes, arguing that Cuban slaves have always been "the happiest of the world." Arango's influence on Humboldt was fundamental. His analyses, his visions, his evaluations of numbers, and probably also their personal discussions as well as their joint trips to the countryside and the *ingenios* (sugar plantations) led Humboldt to believe that there could be such a thing as an acceptable slave system.

Blumenbach, Humboldt, Arango, and other scholars of the time established discourses on both humanitarian progress and White supremacy. Comparing was a way of combining both. We can also find the aftermath of their comparisons in the works of scholars during the long nineteenth century until Fernando Ortíz and his writings on Cuban racism in 1911 or even on Humboldt in 1930.

When it comes to the practices of comparing, one finding is most telling: Humboldt underlines that slavery should not be compared to other systems of violence. What follows, however, are comparisons—comparisons of different slave regimes. These comparisons have the effect of undermining his main argument that slavery was *always* and with *no exception* a threat to humanity.

Blumenbach, Humboldt, Arango together with others shaped how slavery history was written for many years to come. They obviously excluded the voices of slaves, freed slaves, and other people with an Afro-Cuban background. Instead, they dealt with what they believed to be bigger questions: Humboldt contributed to the humanitarian discourse on slavery and abolition; Arango to the economic discourse on free trade—including the commodity "human beings from Africa." However, discourses and practices have different velocities of change. Maybe Humboldt and Arango would have been more controversial if they had talked about whether or not Arango should free his own slaves. For the sake of the equality of all humans, Carlos Manuel de Céspedes did this in 1868. This was the beginning of the thirty-year-long war of Cuban independence.

References

ARANGO Y PARREÑO, Francisco de, Carta al Secretario del Supremo Consejo de Indias en que el autor avisa estar traduciendo una "Memoria sobre la Abolición de la Esclavidud en las Colonias europeas" (24.8.1831), in: *Obras completas*, vol. II, 1889, 659–741.

ARANGO Y PARREÑO, Francisco de, *Obras completas*, vol. II, 1889.

ARANGO Y PARREÑO, Francisco de, Observaciones al "Ensayo politico sobre la isla de Cuba", escritas en 1827, in: Francisco de Arango y Parreño, *Obras completas*, vol. II, 1889, 533–546.

ARANGO Y PARREÑO, Francisco de, Representación al Rey sobre la exstinción de tráfico de negros y medios de mojorar la suerte do los esclavos coloniales (28.5.1832), in: *Obras completas*, vol. II, 1889, 649–659.

ARANGO Y PARREÑO, Francisco de, Representación hecha á S.M. con motivo do la sublevación de esclavos en los dominios franceses de la isla de Santo Domingo (1791), in: *Obras completas*, vol. I, 1888, 49.

Blumenbach, On the Natural Variety of Mankind, sec. I, Of the difference of man from other animals, in: The Anthropological Society (ed.), *The Anthropological Treatises of Blumenbach and Hunter*, London 1865, URL: http://www.blumenbach-online.de/Einzelseiten/HTML-Texte/Texte/000010/000010.html?q=on%20-the%20natural#pbtitlePage_0003 [last accessed April 9, 2020].

BLUMENBACH, On the Natural Variety of Mankind, sec. II, § 23 What is species?, in: The Anthropological Society (ed.), *The Anthropological Treatises of Blumenbach and Hunter*, London 1865, URL: http://www.blumenbach-online.de/Einzelseiten/HTML-Texte/Texte/000010/000010.html?q=on%20the%20natural#pbtitlePage_0003 [last accessed April 9, 2020]

BLUMENBACH, *De Generis Humani varietate nativa*, 3rd ed., 1795.

BRESCIUS, Moritz von, *German Science in the Age of Empire: Enterprise, Opportunity and the Schlagintweit Brothers*, Cambridge 2018.

BROCKMEYER, Bettina, Menschliche Gebeine als Glaubensobjekte. Koloniale Kriegsbeutenahme, Vergleichspraktiken und Erinnerung seit dem späten 19. Jahrhundert, in: *WERKSTATT Geschichte* 77 (2017), 47–64.

CARRILLO Y ARANGO, Anastasio Elógico histórico del excelentísmo Sr. D. Francisco de Arango y Parreño, first published in 1837, reprinted in: Francisco de Arango y Parreño, *Obras del Excmo. Señor D. Francisco de Arango y Parreño*, vol. I, Habana 1888.

Censo de la República de Cuba bajo de la administración provisional de los Estados Unidos 1907, Washington 1908.

CURRAN, Andrew S., *The Anatomy of Blackness. Science and Slavery in an Age of Enlightenment*, Baltimore 2011.

DE LA FUENTE, Alejandro, *Una Nación para todos. Raza, desigualdad y política en Cuba 1900–2000*, La Habana 2014.

EPPLE, Angelika, Comparing Europe and the Americas: The Dispute of the New World between the Sixteenth and Nineteenth Centuries, in: Willibald Steinmetz (ed.), *The Force of Comparison*, New York/Oxford 2019, 137-163.

ETTE, Ottmar, 'Die ,Berliner Debatte' um die Neue Welt. Globalisierung aus der Perspektive der europäischen Aufklärung', in: Vicente Bernaschino et al. (eds.), *Globalisierung in Zeiten der Aufklärung. Texte und Kontexte zur ,Berliner Debatte' um die Neue Welt (17./18. Jh.)*, vol. 1, Frankfurt a. M. 2015, 27-55.

FAAK, Margot (ed.), *Alexander von Humboldt: Reise durch Venezuela. Auswahl aus den amerikanischen Reisetagebüchern*, Berlin 2000.

FERRER, Ada, *Insurgent Cuba, Race, Nation, and Revolution in Cuba 1868–1898*, Chapel Hill 1999.

FISCHLER, Sibylle, *Modernity Disavowed. Haiti and the Cultures of Slavery*, Durham 2004.

FRANCO, José L., Prólogo, in: *Cuadernos de Historia Haberna* 69 (1960), 7-28.

GEULEN, Christian, *Geschichte des Rassismus*, München 2007.

GOULD, Stephen J., *The Mismeasure of Man*, New York/London 1981.

HELG, Aline, *Slave but not Citizen. Free people of color and blood purity in Colonial Spanish American Legislation*, URL: http://http//dx.doi.org/10.6035/Millars.2017.42.4, 2017.

HELG, Aline, *Our rightful share. The Afro-Cuban Struggle for Equality, 1886–1912*, Chapel Hill 1995.

HELG, Aline, Race in Argentina and Cuba, in: Richard Graham (ed.), *The Idea of Race in Latin America, 1870-1940*, Austin 1990, 37-69.

HUMBOLDT, Alexander von, *Political Essay on the Island Cuba: A Critical Edition, Alexander Von Humboldt in English. Vol. 2*, Chicago 2011.

HUMBOLDT, Alexander von/BECK, Hanno (ed.), *Cuba-Werk, Darmstädter Ausgabe Vol. 3.*, Darmstadt 2008.

HUMBOLDT, Alejandro de: *Ensayo político sobre la isla de Cuba por Alejandro de Humboldt, con un mapa de Cuba. Introducción por Fernando Ortíz y correcciones, notas y appendices por Francisco de Arango y Parreño, J.S. Thrasher y otros*, Tomo I, La Habana 1930.

HUMBOLDT, Alexander von, *Essai politique sur l'île de Cuba* (T. 1), Paris 1826.

HUMBOLDT, Alexander von, *Tableau Statistique de l'île de Cuba pour les années 1825–1829*, Paris 1831.

KEEL, Terence, Blumenbach's race science in the light of Christian supersessionism, in: Nicolaas Rupke/Gerhard Lauer (eds.), *Johann Friedrich Blumenbach. Race and Natural History, 1750–1850*, Milton 2018.

KEEL, Terence, *Divine Variations. How Christian Thought became Racial Science*, Stanford 2018.

KLATT, Norbert, *Kleine Beiträge zur Blumenbach-Forschung*, vol. 1, Göttingen 2008.

KUTZINSKY, Vera M./ETTE, Ottmar, *Alexander von Humboldt in English*, in: press.uchicago.edu [last accessed April 26, 2019].

LECLERC, George-Louis (Comte de), Histoire naturelle de l'Homme, in: *Histoire naturelle, générale et particulière* Tome II, Paris 1749–1788.

LUBRICH, Oliver, In the Realm of Ambivalence: Alexander von Humboldt's Discourse on Cuba, in: *German Studies Review* 26 (1/2003).

MARISS, Anne, Globalisierung der Naturgeschichte im 18. Jahrhundert. Die Mobilität der Dinge und ihr materieller Eigensinn, in: Debora Gerstenberger/Joël Glasman (eds.), *Techniken der Globalisierung. Globalgeschichte meets Akteur-Netzwerk-Theorie* (Histoire Band 78), Bielefeld 2016, 67–93.

MEINERS, Christoph, *Über die Natur der afrikanischen Neger, und die davon abhangende Befreyung, oder Einschränkung der Schwarzen*, Hannover 1790.

MILLER, Joseph, Slaving as historical process: Examples from the ancient Mediterranean and the modern Atlantic, in: Enrico Dal Lago/Constantina Katsari (eds.), *Slave Systems: Ancient and Modern*, 70–102, Cambridge 2008.

ORTÍZ, Fernando, Introducción biobibliográfica, in: Alejandro de Humboldt, *Ensayo político sobre la isla de Cuba por Alejandro de Humboldt, con un mapa de Cuba. Introducción por Fernando Ortíz y correcciones, notas y appendices por Francisco de Arango y Parreño*, Tomo I, La Habana 1930, V-CXXXVIII.

ORTÍZ, Los dos racismos, in: Ortíz, Fernando, *La reconquista de America. Reflexiones sobre el panhispanismo*, Paris 1911, 42–48.

PAINTER, Nell Irvin, *The History of White People*, New York/London 2010.

PETERS, Christine, Reisen und Vergleichen. Praktiken des Vergleichens in Alexander von Humboldts Reise in die Äquinoktial-Gegenden des Neuen Kontinents und Adam Johann von Krusensterns Reise um die Welt, in: *Internationales Archiv für die Sozialgeschichte der Literatur (IASL)* 42 (2/2017).

RAY, John, *historia plantarum generalis*, London 1686 (Translation: Edmund Silk, cited by: Barbara G. Beddall, Historical Notes on Avian Classification, in: *Systematic Biology* 6 (1957), 134).

RINKE, Stefan/Riedemann, Andrea, Chile, in: Wolfgang Benz (ed.), *Handbuch des Antisemitismus. Judenfeindschaft in Geschichte und Gegenwart* Vol. 1, München 2008.

SAGRA, Ramón de la, *Historia económico-politica y estadística de la isla de Cuba ó sea de sus progresos en la población, la agricultura, el comercio y las rentas*, La Habana 1831.

SOEMMERRING, Samuel Thomas, *Anthropologie. Über die körperliche Verschiedenheit des Negers vom Europäer (1785)*, rev. and ed. by Sigrid Oehler-Klein, Vol. 15, Stuttgart et al. 1998.

STEINMETZ, Willibald, 'Vergleich' – eine begriffsgeschichtliche Skizze, in: Angelika Epple/Walter Erhart (eds.), *Die Welt beobachten. Praktiken des Vergleichens*, Frankfurt a. M./New York 2015.

STOLLBERG, Jochen/BÖKER, Wolfgang (eds.), *"... die Kunst zu sehn." Arthur Schopenhauers Mitschriften der Vorlesungen Johann Friedrich Blumenbachs (1809–1811)*, Schriften zur Göttinger Universitätsgeschichte 3, Göttingen 2013.

TANNENBAUM, Frank, *Slave and Citizen*, New York 1947.

THRASHER, John S., preface, in: Alexander von Humboldt, *The Island of Cuba* [1827], New York 1856.

TOMICH, Dale W./ZEUSKE, Michael, The Second Slavery. Mass Slavery, World-Economy, and Comparative Microhistories, in: *Review: Fernand Braudel Center* XXXI, (2/2008), 91-100.

TWINAM, Ann, *Purchasing Whiteness*, Stanford, 2015.

VILLANOVA, Manuel, Humboldt y Trasher, in: *Cuadernos de Historia Haberna* 69 (1960), 29–52.

VOYAGES Database (2010), *Voyages: The Trans-Atlantic Slave Trade Database*, URL: http://www.slavevoyages.org, [last accessed May 25, 2012].

WILCKENS, Malin, *Aus aller Welt – Die Schädel-Korrespondenz des Johann Friedrich Blumenbach*. Unpublished MA-Thesis, Bielefeld University 2018.

ZEUSKE, Michael, Out of the Americas. Slave traders and the Hidden Atlantic in the nineteenth century, in: *Atlantic Studies* 15, (1/2018), 103-135.

ZEUSKE, Michael, *Sklaverei. Eine Menschheitsgeschichte von der Steinzeit bis heute*, Stuttgart 2018.

ZEUSKE, Michael, Alexander von Humboldt, die Sklavereien in den Amerikas und das "Tagebuch von Havanna 1804". Zur Edition von "Isle de Cube", in: Ottmar Ette (ed.), *edition humboldt digital*, Berlin-Brandenburgische Akademie der Wissenschaften, Berlin, Version 1 from May 10, 2017.

ZEUSKE, Michael, Die Nicht-Geschichte von Versklavten als Archiv-Geschichte von "Stimmen" und Körpern, in: *Jahrbuch für Europäische Überseegeschichte* 16, Wiesbaden 2016, 65–114.

ZEUSKE, Michael, *Handbuch Geschichte der Sklaverei. Eine Globalgeschichte von den Anfängen bis zur Gegenwart*, Berlin/Boston 2013.

The Politicisation of Comparisons
The East-West Dispute over Military Force Comparisons in the Cold War

Thomas Müller

Abstract

In the wake of NATO's Double-Track Decision in 1979, East and West engaged in a propaganda battle over the assessment of the conventional and nuclear balances in Europe. Both sides published special booklets that substantiated the respective balance assessments through detailed comparisons of the military forces of NATO and the Warsaw Pact. The chapter reconstructs this propaganda battle as an exploratory case study of how comparisons are politicized—that is, become matters of political and public disputes—in situations of competition and conflict such as the Cold War. It shows that the arms control negotiations between East and West were not only key factors driving the politicization of military force comparisons but also crucial forums for the development of a shared comparative framework, and thus the depoliticization of these comparisons.

1. Introduction[1]

One central characteristic as well as driver of the Cold War was the military competition and arms race between the two superpowers and their respective military alliances. Comparisons were integral to how the superpowers and their alliances assessed the distribution of military capabilities, publicly legitimised their own armament efforts and sought to curb and de-escalate the military competition and arms race through arms control negotiations. This chapter analyses the political disputes over military force comparisons between NATO and the Warsaw Pact in the 1980s as an exploratory case study of the politicisation of comparisons that,

---

[1] I would like to thank Mathias Albert and Kerrin Langer for the productive discussions in our SFB project on military force comparisons. This chapter benefited greatly from these discussions. I am also grateful to Angelika Epple and the audience at the SFB conference for their valuable feedback on my presentation and draft chapter.

under certain conditions, arises from and shapes situations of competition and conflict such as the Cold War.

Existing research shows that East and West perceived the balance of power differently during the Cold War.[2] This research, however, focuses mostly on national debates over the state of the balance of power and has not yet systematically analysed the international disputes that took place between East and West over their diverging interpretations of the balance of power.[3] Moreover, research on power comparisons is generally more interested in whether the power comparisons were accurate[4] than in the 'power politics of power analysis' through which various actors seek to establish their preferred comparisons as 'social facts'.[5] By focusing on the politicisation of comparisons in the interaction between East and West, this chapter aims to contribute to a better understanding of international disputes over the distribution of power.

In particular, this chapter makes two contributions: First, it develops a framework for analysing the politicisation and depoliticisation of comparisons. This (de)politicisation of comparisons constitutes a special case of the 'politics of comparison'.[6] The chapter conceptualises the politics of comparison more broadly than Ann Stoler, who views it as the attempts of various actors to make their preferred comparisons socially and politically relevant. Comparisons become politicised when these attempts clash—the result being public disputes and political struggles over which forms of comparisons are to be used and which not.

Second, the chapter explores how the (de)politicisation is shaped by, and shapes, situations of competition and conflict. It shows that the politicisation of military force comparisons was closely related to attempts to regulate the military competition via conventional and nuclear arms control negotiations between East and West. Whereas the politicisation of force comparisons already began with conventional arms control negotiations in the 1970s, it reached a new level in the

---

2 See William C. Wohlforth, *The Elusive Balance: Power and Perceptions during the Cold War*, Ithaca 1993.

3 Debates within the Soviet elite have been reconstructed by Wohlforth, *The Elusive Balance*. The political debates in the USA have been analysed by, for instance, David M. Walsh, *The Military Balance in the Cold War: US Perceptions and Policy, 1976–85*, London 2008. For a partial exception, see Timothy Barney, *Mapping the Cold War: Cartography and the Framing of America's International Power*, Chapel Hill 2015, 183–192 who covers the use of geographical representations in the East–West dispute of the 1980s.

4 For an overview, see Charles Glaser, *Rational Theory of International Politics: The Logic of Competition and Cooperation*, Princeton 2010, 194–200.

5 Stefano Guzzini, *On the Measure of Power and the Power of Measure in International Relations* (DIIS Working Paper, 28), Copenhagen 2009, 10, 15.

6 Ann Laura Stoler, Tense and Tender Ties: The Politics of Comparison in North American History and (Post) Colonial Studies, in: *The Journal of American History* 88 (2001), 829–865, see 861–864.

early 1980s when both sides started to publish special booklets to legitimise their respective balance interpretations in the context of the public disputes over the deployment and control of intermediate-range nuclear forces in Europe. Moreover, the disputes over military force comparisons were resolved through the development of joint comparative frameworks at the end of the eventually successful arms control negotiations that, in turn, helped to stabilise and de-escalate the Cold War conflict.

The chapter is structured in the following way: The second section discusses the politicisation of comparisons—and, in particular, military force comparisons—in situations of competition and conflict. The third section reconstructs how the booklets restaged for a broader public the disputes over comparisons that hampered the arms control negotiations. The fourth section analyses how the balance disputes were gradually depoliticised and resolved in the second half of the 1980s. The fifth section then shows that shared repertoires are not only the result of negotiations that depoliticise comparisons but may also be fostered through dynamics related to the politicisation of comparisons. The conclusion finally reflects on how peculiar the described patterns and dynamics are to situations of competition and conflict.

2. The politicisation and depoliticisation of comparisons

The Cold War can be described as a multi-layered situation of competition and conflict between East and West.[7] Situations of competition and conflict are characterised by the *contest ensuing from two or more actors striving for superior shares of some socially valued goods of which only a limited afmount exists*.[8] In the Cold War, these socially valued goods included both 'hard' goods such as economic wealth and military capabilities as well as 'soft' goods such as status and political legitimacy. The contest amounts to a conflict when the actors conceive their respective aims as opposing or incompatible and accordingly engage in moves and countermoves through which they seek to prevail over the other(s). The Cold War, notably, was fuelled by an ideological conflict between capitalism and communism. In the military dimension of the Cold War, some phases of the competition were more conflictive than others. After a phase of détente, the military competition between NATO and the Warsaw Pact entered a new phase of conflict in the late 1970s driven by a renewed conventional and nuclear arms race.[9]

---

7   For histories of the Cold War, see John Lewis Gaddis, *The Cold War*, London 2005, and Odd Arne Westad, *The Cold War: A World History*, New York 2017.
8   For a discussion of the competition for 'hard' and 'soft' goods in international politics, see Tobias Werron, Worum konkurrieren Nationalstaaten? Zu Begriff und Geschichte der Konkurrenz um 'weiche' globale Güter, in: *Zeitschrift für Soziologie*, 41 (2012), 338–355.
9   For a general account of this last phase of the Cold War, see Westad, *The Cold War*, 475–616.

Military force comparisons can be defined as the *set of practices through which actors assemble, assess, and disseminate information about differentials between two or more armed forces—for example regarding their expenditures, capabilities, performances, or power.*[10] It is possible to compare the military capabilities of states that are not in competition or conflict with one another. However, power is context-dependent: states—or, more precisely, the institutions states task with monitoring and assessing differentials in military capabilities and power—therefore usually make force comparisons not in the abstract.[11] Rather, their comparative assessments are informed by assumptions and background knowledge about given or expected situations that they deem to affect their security and in which they anticipate having to (potentially having to) use their armed forces.

During the Cold War, states shared a certain repertoire of semantics and modes of comparing military power and power more broadly. This shared repertoire notably included classificatory concepts such as 'great powers' or 'superpowers' and the assessment and representation of the distribution of (military) power in terms of a 'balance of power'. Yet, the fact that states share a certain repertoire of semantics and modes of comparison does not mean that they apply this repertoire in the same way or arrive at the same conclusions about the differentials in military capabilities and power. A shared repertoire often 'remains inherently ambiguous', even in communities of practice, and subject to constant renegotiation.[12] Indeed, as studies on power perceptions emphasise, the balance of power was somehow 'elusive' in the Cold War, and East and West differed in how they interpreted it.[13]

Not all of these interpretational differences lead to, or are signs of, the politicisation of comparisons. The *politicisation of comparisons* can be conceptualised as the *emergence (or intensification) of political disputes and struggles over which comparisons are to be used as base for the interpretation and/or regulation of a given situation*. The literature highlights several indicators of processes of politicisation: disagreements over an issue became more salient, the prevalent opinions on this issue become more polarised, and the group of actors involved in the debate on the issue widens.[14] For

---

10   For useful discussions of the practice — and limits — of force comparisons, see John M. Collins/Anthony H. Cordesman, *Imbalance of Power: An Analysis of Shifting U.S.–Soviet Military Strength*, San Rafael 1978; Dieter S. Lutz, *Towards a Methodology of Military Force Comparison*, Baden-Baden 1986; and Simon Lunn, The East–West Military Balance: Assessing Change, in: *Adelphi Papers* 236 (1989), 49–71.

11   See David Baldwin, *Power and International Relations: A Conceptual Approach*, Princeton 2016, 114–122.

12   Cf. Etienne Wenger, *Communities of Practice: Learning, Meaning, and Identity*, Cambridge 1998, 82–85 (see 82 for the quote).

13   Cf. Wohlforth, *The Elusive Balance*. See also William C. Wohlforth, The Perception of Power: Russia in the Pre-1914 Balance, in: *World Politics* 39 (1987), 353–381.

14   Cf. Michael Zürn, *A Theory of Global Governance: Authority, Legitimacy and Contestation*, Oxford 2018, 139–142; Edgar Grande/Swen Hutter, Beyond Authority Transfer: Explaining the Politi-

instance, the publication of the booklets was part of a broader process in which force comparisons became a matter of public dispute rather than simply a matter of dispute among a small circle of military analysts and diplomats.

The likelihood of the politicisation of power comparisons increases when two conditions are met: The first condition is that the interpretational differences stem from the use and promotion of different comparisons that result in diverging assessments of the given situation. The second condition is that the interpretational differences have to be perceived to matter in terms of how the competition and/or conflict play(s) out. When different comparisons imply different distributional effects, then actors are likely to prefer and promote those comparisons that maximise their shares of the socially valued good(s) for which they are competing.

The question of distributional effects often arises in the context of governance practices that seek to organise, regulate, and order a social domain. Arms control negotiations and treaties are an example for such practices, because they serve to impose rules and limits on the military competition among states. Whereas the characteristics of certain types of comparisons can facilitate the politicisation of comparisons,[15] it is, in this sense, the mobilisation and contestation of comparisons in the context of governance practices that causes the respective comparisons to become politicised—that is, to become a matter of political and public dispute.[16] This politicisation is particularly likely to occur if the underlying issue is already contested, which is often the case in situations of competition and conflict that are per definition characterised by competing preferences (though not necessarily always competing political preferences).

The politicisation of comparisons overlays and intertwines the existing situation of competition/conflict with an additional layer of competition/conflict. To take the example of military force comparisons in the Cold War, the first layer consists in the competition between West and East over superior military capabilities and power. The additional layer created by the politicisation of comparisons, in turn, is a conflict about whose measures of military capabilities and power are to be used to interpret the distribution of military capabilities and power. Whereas the first layer is thus about a competition over hard goods, namely superior mil-

---

cisation of Europe, in: *West European Politics* 39 (2016), 23–43, see 25–26; and Stephane J. Baele/Thierry Balzacq/Philippe Bourbeau, Numbers in Global Security Governance, in: *European Journal of International Security*, 3 (2018), 22–44, see 25, 34–37.

15 For instance, the 'mobility' and 'combinality' of numbers implies that the mobilisation of numbers for political purposes can be countered by 'producing rival numbers', as Baele et al., Numbers, 35 highlight.

16 The literature on politicisation in world politics often focuses on a special type of regulatory practices, namely authority-based modes of governance of international organisations. See Zürn, *Global Governance*; and Grande/Hutter, Beyond Authority Transfer.

itary capabilities, the second layer is about a soft good: the social power to shape and determine how the situation is (to be) assessed.

Comparisons can become *depoliticised—that is, cease to be matters of public and political disputes and struggles*—in several ways. First, the differences over the comparisons could persist, but the political significance ascribed to them could decrease, so that these differences cease to be matters of public political disputes and struggles. Second, the actors could fail to agree on a common set of comparisons, but, in parallel, one of the actors could succeed in convincing the relevant audience that its comparisons are the best and most pertinent for assessing the issue or situation in question, thus effectively deciding the public contest over the comparisons. Third, the actors could agree, through persuasion and negotiations, on a common set of comparisons, thus resolving their contest over the comparisons. These ways are not mutually exclusive and may also influence each other. For instance, if one of the actors wins the support of the relevant audience for its comparisons and interpretations, then this support will probably also strengthen its position in the negotiations.

3. A new level of politicisation in the first half of the 1980s

The politicisation of force comparisons happened in two interrelated arenas: First, the conventional and nuclear *arms control negotiations* between East and West made the interpretational differences over the state of the East–West military balance diplomatically and politically salient. Second, the politicisation reached a new level with a novel form of public *propaganda battle* in the early 1980s. The increased public contestation of NATO's Double-Track decision in Western societies, especially in Europe, led to a 'War of Facts' (as the US chief negotiator termed it[17]) in which both the West and the East published special booklets to promote their interpretations of the arms race, the military balance, and the most appropriate forms of arms control vis-à-vis Western publics.[18]

The two arenas were intertwined through disputes over the conventional and the intermediate nuclear balance. Chronologically, the conventional arms control negotiations had started well before the propaganda battle, whereas the intermediate nuclear arms control negotiations started concurrently. The conventional arms control negotiations were conducted in the form of the Mutual and Balanced Force Reduction (MBFR) talks from 1973 to 1989 and then in the form of the negotiations

---

17 Cf. Maynard W. Glitman, *The Last Battle of the Cold War: An Inside Account of Negotiating the Intermediate Range Nuclear Forces Treaty*, Houndmills 2006, 133–134.
18 On the public debates, see Leopoldo Nuti et al. (eds.), *The Euromissile Crisis and the End of the Cold War*, Washington D.C. 2015.

on the Conventional Forces in Europe (CFE) Treaty from 1989 to 1990.[19] The MBFR talks were hampered by the dispute over whether the conventional balance in Europe was, as the East maintained, characterised by a rough equality between NATO and the Warsaw Pact; or whether, as the West insisted, the Warsaw Pact enjoyed a conventional superiority over NATO. The dispute over the intermediate nuclear balance, in turn, complicated the negotiations on the Intermediate Nuclear Forces (INF) Treaty that took place formally from 1981 to 1983 and from 1985 to 1987.[20] NATO argued that the Soviet deployment of new intermediate nuclear missiles (SS-20) created an imbalance. NATO sought to remedy this with its Double-Track decision of 1979, which stipulated the US deployment of intermediate nuclear missiles to Europe should intermediate nuclear arms control negotiations between the US and the Soviet Union fail. The Soviet Union, on the contrary, maintained that, all things considered, a rough balance existed and accused NATO of upsetting this balance.

These balance disputes involved high stakes for the outcomes of the arms control negotiations, because they were tied to divergent preferences regarding the arms control measures and formats. In the case of conventional arms control, the West argued for asymmetrical reductions that would transform the existing imbalance into a balance by removing the Soviet superiority, whereas the East insisted on symmetrical reductions based on its interpretation of an already existing conventional balance. In the case of INF, the Soviet Union criticised the US position of including only Soviet and US intermediate land-based missiles. For the Soviet Union, the calculation of the intermediate nuclear balance also had to include other nuclear delivery systems (e.g. nuclear-delivery-capable aircraft) as well as the nuclear forces of the two other European nuclear powers (i.e. Great Britain and France) and consequently demanded that these nuclear delivery systems and nuclear powers be likewise considered in the intermediate nuclear arms control negotiations.

The propaganda battle consisted in a sequence of official publications in which both sides substantiated their respective balance interpretations. It revolved around three main series of publications: 'Soviet Military Power', published by the USA in ten editions between 1981 and 1991; 'Whence the Threat to Peace', published by the Soviet Union in four editions between 1982 and 1987; and NATO's 'Force Comparisons' booklets, published in 1982 and 1984. The booklets were widely dis-

---

19   For overviews over these two conventional arms control negotiations, see Christoph Bluth, Arms Control as a Part of Strategy: The Warsaw Pact in MBFR Negotiations, in: *Cold War History* 12 (2012), 245–268 and Rüdiger Hartmann/Wolfgang Heydrich/Nikolaus Meyer-Landrut, *Der Vertrag über konventionelle Streitkräfte in Europa: Vertragswerk, Verhandlungsgeschichte, Kommentar, Dokumentation*, Baden-Baden 1994.

20   For a discussion of the INF negotiations, see Thomas Risse-Kappen, Did 'Peace Through Strength' End the Cold War? Lessons from INF, in: *International Security*, 16 (1991), 162–188.

tributed and addressed not only the respective domestic public but also a broader transnational public and were for that purpose translated in several languages.

Whereas the balance disputes had been publicly addressed before, the propaganda battle marked a new, unprecedented stage in the politicisation of military force comparisons in the relations between West and East. The booklets were a reaction to the growing public protests in Europe against the planned deployment of US intermediate range nuclear missiles to Europe. The beginning of the propaganda battle, though, was also closely linked to the start of the INF negotiations. Each side had concluded that 'a successful conclusion to the INF issue would require the support' of Western publics.[21] The INF negotiations formally started in November 1981 and the first editions of the three mentioned booklet series appeared around the same time: 'Soviet Military Power' in September 1981, 'Whence the Threat to Peace' in February 1982, and NATO's 'Force Comparisons' in May 1982.

In order to substantiate the balance interpretations, the booklets employed both qualitative and quantitative comparisons of the military forces and capabilities of the two alliances. However, whereas the NATO booklets were—as their title suggests—purposively designed as comparative assessments of the military balance, 'Soviet Military Power' and 'Whence the Threat to Peace' contained not only sections comparing the two alliances but also sections depicting only the military forces of the respectively other side. That said, comparisons played a prominent role in the argumentation of both the West and the East, and each side foregrounded the comparisons that best suited its balance arguments.

The differences between the comparisons stemmed partly from disparate data and partly from incongruent measures of relative capabilities. The conventional balance in Europe, for instance, was presented in different numbers by both sides. Among the most controversial figures was the number of tanks: in the respective 1982 editions, 'Whence the Threat to Peace' spoke about a rough parity of 24,000 NATO tanks versus 25,000 Warsaw Pact tanks in Europe, whereas NATO's 'Force Comparisons' counted 13,000 NATO tanks versus 42,500 Warsaw Pact tanks.[22] Two years later, NATO revised its figures for the conventional balance between NATO and the Warsaw Pact and now differentiated between forces already in place (13,470 vs 26,900 tanks) and 'fully reinforced forces' (17,730 vs 46,230 tanks).[23] 'Whence the Threat to Peace' more or less repeated its previous account, this time counting about 25,000 tanks on each side.[24]

---

21 Glitman, *Last Battle*, 142.
22 Cf. Soviet Union, *Whence the Threat to Peace*, 1st edition, Moscow 1982, 69 and NATO, *Force Comparisons*, 1982, 11.
23 Cf. NATO, *NATO and the Warsaw Pact: Force Comparisons*, Brussels 1984, 8.
24 Cf. Soviet Union, *Whence the Threat to Peace* 1984, 78. Of the 25,000 NATO tanks, 17,000 were described as being in active service and 8,000 as being in storage.

The non-strategic nuclear balance in Europe was assessed by East and West with different measures. In accordance with the Soviet INF position, 'Whence the Threat to Peace' framed it as a balance of 'medium-range nuclear weapon systems in Europe'; that is, the medium-range missiles and bombers of the Soviet Union on the one side and those of the USA, Great Britain, and France on the other side. It claimed that their number had 'for years remained at roughly the same level—some 1,000 units on either side'.[25] Moreover, even with the SS-20 deployment factored in, NATO was said to 'enjoy an advantage of some 50 percent' in the total 'number of warheads on medium-range missiles and aircrafts'.[26] The Western booklets acknowledged that the balance of 'intermediate- and short-range nuclear forces' comprised missiles, aircraft, and tube artillery; but argued that, on the whole, 'the Warsaw Pact has a substantial numerical advantage'.[27] The booklets pointed particularly to the imbalance in land-based missiles. Shortly after the US deployment of its Pershing II and GLCM missiles to Europe began in late 1983, 'Soviet Military Power' contrasted the then 25 deployed Pershing II and GLCM missiles on NATO's side with the 602 deployed SS-4, SS-5, and SS-20 on the Soviet side.[28] NATO's second booklet, moreover, argued in a graph that even after the full deployment of all 108 Pershing II and 464 GLCM missiles, NATO would have fewer than 600 nuclear warheads on longer-range INF missiles, whereas the Soviet missiles were said to already have about 1,400 warheads on their launchers in late 1983.[29]

Each side accused the other of seeking superiority instead of balance and of being the driving force behind the arms race. Both sides produced graphs that compared the evolution of weapon systems in order to substantiate these claims. Notably, the very first comparative graph in 'Whence the Threat to Peace' was an overview showing that the USA was consistently the first mover in the development of the following six weapon systems: nuclear weapons, intercontinental strategic bombers, nuclear-powered submarines, nuclear-powered aircraft carriers, multiple independently targetable re-entry vehicles (MIRV), and the neutron bomb.[30] Two years later, the second NATO booklet responded with two graphs comparing the nuclear modernisation programmes of both sides for strategic nuclear forces as well as short- and middle-range delivery systems. The two graphs stressed that

---

25 Soviet Union, *Whence the Threat to Peace*, 1984, 71.
26 Soviet Union, *Whence the Threat to Peace*, 1984, 72.
27 NATO, *Force Comparisons*, 1984, 30. The INF balance is discussed on pp. 30–43.
28 US Department of State, *Soviet Military Power*, 1984, p. 51. NATO's 'Force Comparisons' booklet of the same year spoke of 224 SS-4 and 378 SS-20 on the Soviet side and 9 Pershing II as well as 32 GLCM missiles on NATO's side. See NATO, *Force Comparisons*, 1984, 34.
29 Cf. NATO, *Force Comparisons*, 1984, 35.
30 Cf. Soviet Union, *Whence the Threat to Peace*, 1982 (1st edition), 7.

the Soviet Union had developed and deployed a considerably larger number of new nuclear weapon systems than the West in the 1970s.[31]

On the whole, the propaganda battle broadened the balance dispute. As discussed above, the arms control negotiations politicised two balances: the conventional balance in Europe as well as the intermediate nuclear balance in Europe. Although these two balances featured prominently in the propaganda battle, the balance discussions in the booklets were not limited to them. In fact, two of the booklet series—'Whence the Threat to Peace' and the NATO booklets—advanced systematic assessments of the state of the balance that discussed all relevant (sub-)balances step by step.[32] This broader approach also brought other balances into play. For instance, whereas the Soviet booklets insisted that a rough parity still existed in the strategic balance, the Western booklets argued that key indicators showed a shift in the strategic balance in the second half of the 1970s that gave the Warsaw Pact 'relative advantages'.[33]

At the same time, the propaganda battle continued a trend that had emerged in the conventional arms control negotiations in the 1970s: the politicisation of force comparisons played out to a considerable degree as a dispute over numbers (as the examples above illustrate). This trend was driven by two features of the dispute: On the one hand, the debate about the balance(s) was dominated by a relatively small set of numerical indicators.[34] This set notably included manpower and tank numbers for the conventional balance and missile, bomber, and warhead numbers for the intermediate nuclear balance. What was probably the most important factor for this salience was that the arms control negotiations—that is, the relevant governance practice to which the politicisation was related—essentially defined the balance(s) in terms of numerical parity. The visualisation strategy underpinning the booklets added a second factor. Whereas the booklets contained both qualitative and quantitative assessments of the various balances, these assessments were usually summarised and visualised through tables and graphs that were based on static, quantitative comparisons.

---

31   Cf. NATO, *Force Comparisons*, 1984, 27, 32.
32   The 'Whence the Threat to Peace' editions discussed all sub-balances in a special chapter on the East–West balance, whereas the NATO booklets discussed the conventional and nuclear balances in separate chapters. 'Soviet Military Power' did not feature a special chapter on the balance until 1988.
33   See for example Soviet Union, *Whence the Threat to Peace*, 1984, 69–71 and NATO, *Force Comparisons*, 1984, 29.
34   This feature fits with Aaron Friedberg's observation that the late nineteenth-century British debates on its changing international standing were characterised by the 'widespread use of a handful of simple, compact indicators'. See Aaron Friedberg, *The Weary Titan: Britain and the Experience of Relative Decline, 1895-1905*, Princeton 1988, 283.

On the other hand, the West and the East pursued different data strategies in the propaganda battle. Whereas the Western booklets were revised versions of Western intelligence assessments that were declassified for the publication, the East remained—as in the arms control negotiations—reluctant to fully divulge its own data. The Western booklets—and especially the two NATO booklets—consequently featured more detailed and more comprehensive quantitative data on the balance(s) than the 'Whence the Threat to Peace' series.[35] In particular, whereas the NATO booklets presented data on the number of divisions and several major weapon systems in their assessment of the conventional balance, the respective sections of 'Whence the Threat to Peace' included only select comparative numbers (notably for divisions and tanks) and additionally sometimes posited ratios for some weapon systems without backing them up with concrete numbers.[36] The comparison of Western and Eastern booklets thus strengthened NATO's argument that is was more transparent about its military forces than the Warsaw Pact, which, in turn, supported NATO's broader arms control strategy of engaging the Warsaw Pact to disclose and share more quantitative data on its military forces.

4. Gradual depoliticisation in the second half of the 1980s

In the second half of the 1980s, the politicisation of force comparisons gradually eased off and gave way to a joint agreement on rules and limits for the arms race based on a shared comparative framework. These rules and limits were enshrined in two arms control agreements: first the Treaty on Intermediate-Range Nuclear Forces (INF) signed by the USA and the Soviet Union in December 1987[37] and then the Treaty on Conventional Forces in Europe (CFE) signed by 22 members of NATO and the Warsaw Pact in November 1990.[38]

This section analyses how the politics of comparison shifted from the confrontational style of the propaganda battle to a more constructive style that resulted in the two arms control agreements. The first sub-section highlights that the INF treaty marked a watershed after which two of the three booklet series were no longer published; and the new round of booklets issued by the two alliances was characterised by a different, more constructive style. The second sub-section then

---

35 See Richard J. Herzog/John K. Wildgen, Tactics in Military Propaganda Documents: A Content Analysis of Illustrations, in: *Defense Analysis*, 2 (1/1986), 35–46.
36 See for example NATO, *Force Comparisons*, 1982, 11 and 1984, 8 as well as Soviet Union, *Whence the Threat to Peace*, 1984, 76–69 and 1987, 74–76.
37 For the text of the treaty, see https://www.state.gov/t/avc/trty/102360.htm [last accessed May 19, 2019].
38 For the text of the treaty, see https://www.state.gov/t/avc/trty/108185.htm [last accessed May 19, 2019].

identifies the arms control negotiations as the decisive arena in which the balance disputes were overcome and discusses how this depoliticisation of force comparisons was related to the broader de-escalation and end of the Cold War conflict.

The new character of the booklets

The booklets represent an example for a practice that emerges in reaction to a conflict and then disappears again once the conflict ends. As highlighted above, the booklets were first published in 1981/82 as new propaganda tools for the contest over transnational public opinion with regard to the INF missiles crisis in particular and the renewed West–East arms race more generally. Their publication ended when the arms race abated. The last edition of NATO's 'Force Comparisons' appeared in 1984; the last edition of 'Whence the Threat to Peace', in 1987. Two of the three booklet series were, in other words, no longer published once the INF treaty had been concluded. Only 'Soviet Military Power' continued to be published until 1991 when the dissolution of the Soviet Union signified the end of the Cold War competition between the two superpowers.

The two alliances issued a last round of force comparisons in November 1988 (NATO) and January 1989 (Warsaw Pact).[39] These two booklets, though, differed strikingly from the booklets published before. They assessed only one balance—namely, the balance of conventional forces between the two alliances in Europe. Moreover, they were designed as compilations of quantitative data that assembled the relevant figures for the categories of forces and weapon systems under consideration in the conventional arms control negotiations. Apart from the forewords, the two booklets accordingly contained only quantitative tables and graphs with some explanatory notes, but, in contrast to the previous booklets, neither qualitative balance assessments nor pictures of the weapon systems.

The two booklets symbolised a new, less polarised, and more constructive character of the politics of comparison. At the time of their publication, the two alliances were in the final stage of their negotiations for a follow-up format to the failed MBFR talks, and the new format, the CFE negotiations, was soon to be formally opened (in March 1989). As a mutual gesture of military transparency, each alliance issued a booklet that assembled and displayed the figures on those conventional forces of both alliances that it considered to be pertinent for the upcoming CFE negotiations. The Warsaw Pact's booklet for the first time presented substantial Eastern data on the conventional balance, thus departing from the East's pre-

---

39   Cf. NATO, *Conventional Forces in Europe: The Facts*, Brussels 1988 and Soviet Union, *Warschauer Pakt – NATO: Kräfteverhältnis in Europa*, Moskau 1989.

vious restrictive data strategy.[40] Although differences in the data and definitions still persisted, the Warsaw Pact furthermore contributed to a convergence of the arms control positions of the two alliances. Its booklet acknowledged that the conventional balance was characterised by certain imbalances and asymmetries, and pointed to the Warsaw Pact's already initiated unilateral reduction of troops and weapon systems as a signal that the Warsaw Pact members were willing to address and remedy these imbalances.[41]

The continuing publication of 'Soviet Military Power' stood in some contrast to the changing character of the other booklets. The new editions of 'Soviet Military Power' acknowledged that profound changes were happening, but argued that these changes had so far related to Soviet intentions rather than Soviet capabilities—which were still deemed a 'threat' in September 1990[42]—and that it was consequently still uncertain how the military competition would evolve in the future.[43] Interestingly, 'Soviet Military Power' became more comparative once the politics of comparison between West and East were depoliticised. In fact, the 1988 edition was the first to feature special chapters dedicated to the assessment of the military balance and competition.[44] The analysis of the 'technological competition', moreover, moved partially beyond East–West comparisons and started to compare US technologies not only with those of the Warsaw Pact but also with those of 'Non-US NATO', Japan and—depending on the technology—select additional countries,[45] thus implying a changing competitive environment.

Arms control and the end of the Cold War conflict

The changes in the character of the booklets indicate a gradual depoliticisation of force comparisons in the second half of the 1980s. How was this depoliticisation related to the end of the underlying Cold War conflict? Or, to put it differently, was the depoliticisation of force comparisons just a function of the more general de-escalation of the Cold War conflict or did it, at least to some degree, also contribute to the de-escalation of the Cold War conflict?

Three aspects are relevant for answering these questions: First, regarding the interplay between the two arenas of the politicisation of force comparisons, the

---

40 Cf. Anton Krakau/Ole Diehl, *1989: 'Annähernde Parität' der Streitkräfte in Europa? Eine kritische Analyse des östlichen Streitkräftevergleichs* (Berichte des Bundesinstituts für ostwissenschaftliche und internationale Studien), Köln 1989, 1, 32.
41 See Soviet Union, *Warschauer Pakt – NATO*, 4–5.
42 US Department of Defense, *Soviet Military Power*, 1990, 4.
43 Soviet intentions were said to be both 'debatable' and 'changeable'. US Department of Defense, *Soviet Military Power*, 1989, 9.
44 Cf. US Department of Defense, *Soviet Military Power*, 1988, chap. 6 and 7.
45 See, in particular, US Department of Defense, *Soviet Military Power*, 1989, 137.

evolution of the propaganda battle seems to have largely followed the evolution of the arms control negotiations. As highlighted above, two of the three booklet series were published only during the time of the INF negotiations between 1981 and 1987. The negotiated resolution of one of the two balance disputes—the dispute over the intermediate nuclear balance—through an arms control agreement (the INF treaty) thus eased off the propaganda battle. Moreover, the new impulses and progress in the conventional arms control negotiations—that is, the shift from the MBFR to the CFE format—were mirrored by a more constructive and technical style of the last round of NATO and Warsaw Pact booklets in late 1988 and early 1989. Furthermore, the arms control negotiations were the sites at which the balance disputes were overcome through a jointly agreed framework for the assessment and regulation of the two balances—and in this sense, the more important of the two arenas for ending the politicisation of comparisons.

Second, the breakthroughs in the arms control negotiations, in turn, were initiated and made possible through the parallel reorientation of the foreign policy of the two superpowers. Both the US government under President Ronald Reagan and the new Soviet government led by Mikhail Gorbachev now more actively sought to curb the nuclear arms race through arms control measures.[46] In the resumed INF negotiations, the Soviet Union abandoned its earlier demand to include the British and French nuclear forces, and eventually agreed with the USA to eliminate all their intermediate-range and shorter-range nuclear missiles with a range between 500 and 5,500 km. As a result, the INF treaty of December 1987 essentially reflected the comparative approach promoted by the West: a bilateral regulation of the intermediate nuclear balance that covered only ground-based missiles.

The de-escalation of the superpower relations also ameliorated relations between NATO and the Warsaw Pact. In parallel to the INF negotiations, the two alliances worked on a follow-up format for the MBFR talks after 1986. Similar to the dispute over the intermediate nuclear balance, the Soviet Union then made an important step towards overcoming the politicisation of force comparisons. As noted above, it acknowledged in late 1988 and early 1989 that the conventional balance featured certain imbalances that had to be addressed through asymmetric reductions, thus converging on the Western position in the dispute over the conventional balance.[47]

Third, whether and to what extent the shift from the politicisation of force comparisons to a joint comparative framework contributed to the end of the Cold War depends on the interpretation of the Cold War conflict. If the Cold War is

---

46   For the decisive role of Gorbachev's new policies, see Risse-Kappen, Lessons from INF, 182–185.
47   See also Hartmann/Heydrich/Meyer-Landrut, Vertrag, 25–26.

conceived foremost as an ideological conflict between two opposing social, economic, and political systems, then Gorbachev's domestic reforms and the series of revolutions in Eastern Europe were arguably more consequential factors.[48] Most interpretations, nevertheless, treat the military confrontation and arms race between the two superpowers and their alliances as a key characteristic of the Cold War. The two arms control agreements were the tools chosen by the two alliances to stop the arms race and to stabilise and even reduce military competition. The governance practices made possible by the negotiated resolution of the disputes over force comparisons were thus central to de-escalating the *military dimension* of the Cold War conflict. However, as hinted at, the de-escalation of the military dimension was but one factor among others that shaped how the Cold War ended. The depoliticisation of force comparisons was therefore one element, though arguably not the decisive element, that contributed to the end of the underlying situation of competition and conflict.

5. Disputed and shared repertoires of comparisons

The arms control negotiations thus eventually produced a shared comparative framework for the intermediate nuclear balance and the conventional balance in Europe. The development of this framework was a means to an end. The arms control agreements would arguably not have been possible without overcoming the balance disputes. The purpose of the arms control agreements—the fixation and implementation of equal limits on the number of certain weapon systems—required a common set of definitions that subsumed the actual weapons of both sides under common abstract categories of weapon systems so that the arsenals of both sides could be counted and regulated within a common framework. The CFE Treaty, for instance, defined five categories of weapon systems for which it set aggregate arsenal limits for West and East: each side was allowed no more than 20,000 battle tanks, 30,000 armoured combat vehicles, 20,000 pieces of artillery, 6,800 combat aircraft, and 2,000 attack helicopters (see articles II and IV). Both in the case of the INF Treaty and the CFE Treaty, the joint comparative framework served not only to set normative limits for the military competition but was also backed up by provisions for the ongoing verification—through information exchanges and inspections—of whether the military competition would in the future stay within the agreed normative limits.

It would however be to too superficial to associate shared repertoires of comparisons solely with situations after—or without—disputes over comparisons. It would, relatedly, also be too superficial to equate the effects of the politicisation

---

48 See for instance Westad, *The Cold War*, 579–616 and Gaddis, *The Cold War*, 237–259.

of comparisons solely with the intensification of differences and disputes. In fact, political disputes over comparisons usually draw on a common repertoire; and, moreover, politicisation can generate dynamics that foster shared repertoires.

On the one hand, the politics of comparison usually involve a certain degree of shared comparative practices. As the present case study illustrates, both the East and the West assessed the distribution of military power in terms of several functional and regional 'balances' (e.g. the intermediate nuclear balance, the conventional balance in Europe, and the strategic nuclear balance) and thus used the same comparative template and standard. What is more, this comparative standard was shared in a twofold way: first, as a standard for measuring the distribution of military power existing prior to the arms control agreements; and second, as a normative standard—interpreted as numerical parity of weapon systems—that guided the ordering and modification of the distribution of military power through the arms control treaties.

On the other hand, the shared repertoire may be deepened through the very dynamics that drive the politicisation of comparisons. The arms control negotiations and the propaganda battle point to two mechanisms that generate such effects: the first mechanism relates to the synchronisation of the comparative practices within the two alliances. As the arms control negotiations were essentially conducted not between individual states but between the two alliances, each alliance had to internally develop and maintain a coherent group position on the comparisons and balance interpretations it sought to promote. This internal synchronisation was all the more important because differences and inconsistencies in the statements of different members of the same alliance could potentially be exploited by the other alliance in the public contest over the most appropriate comparisons and balance interpretations. For example, because France and Spain refused to be included in NATO's 'Force Comparisons', the East could accuse NATO of downplaying its numerical strength—and thus of deliberately distorting its balance interpretation—by not including all the armed forces that were likely to fight on the Western side in case of a war.[49] The politicisation of force comparisons therefore increased the pressure on each alliance to use a shared and coherent set of comparisons.

The second mechanism stems from the nature of the struggles over comparisons as a contest in which each side reacts to the arguments and moves of the other side. The shared repertoire, for instance, grows if these action–reaction dynamics lead to the mirroring of the argumentative style of the respective other side. Notably, the depiction of US and NATO armed forces in 'Whence the Threat to Peace' imitated to a considerable degree the depiction of Soviet and Warsaw Pact forces in 'Soviet Military Power'. Moreover, as already highlighted, the politics of comparison were dominated by a relatively small set of key comparative

---

49   See e.g. Soviet Union, *Whence the Threat to Peace*, 1984, 78–79.

indicators. The disputes over comparisons in this sense condensed the field of relevant comparisons and generated a common discourse and repertoire of arguments and counter-arguments over some select comparisons. Two characteristics of the balance disputes fostered this effect: the long-time stagnation of the balance disputes, especially in the case of MBFR, gave rise to a repetitive pattern of arguments and counter-arguments. And the arms control negotiations functioned as reference points that foregrounded those numerical comparative indicators that formed part of the proposed arms control frameworks.

6. Conclusion

This chapter started with the question how the politicisation of comparisons shapes, and is shaped by, situations of competition and conflict. Although situations of competition and conflict do not lead automatically to the politicisation of comparisons, such situations are, nevertheless, particularly conducive to public disputes over comparisons when they have certain characteristics. The empirical case study underscored that competing political preferences over governance practices—in the present case study: the conventional and intermediate nuclear arms control negotiations—trigger such disputes when the choice for a particular comparison or a particular set of comparisons is deemed by the relevant actors to be relevant and decisive for the form and outcome of the governance practices.

The next research step is to examine how typical the politicisation of comparisons is for situations of competition and conflict. How frequent is the politicisation of comparisons in such situations, and which characteristics of situations of competition and conflict increase the likelihood for the politicisation of comparisons and the ensuring public disputes over comparisons? Moreover, whether or not the politicisation of comparisons is typical for situations of competition and conflict is a question of the variance of patterns and dynamics of practices of comparing across different types of situations. Is the politicisation of comparisons more likely to arise and to be more frequent in situations characterised by competition and conflict than in situations that are not (or are less) defined and shaped by competition and conflict?

Whereas these questions focus on the effects of the situational characteristics on the politicisation of comparisons, the present chapter showed that the politicisation of comparisons also reshapes the situations in which it arises. In fact, the politicisation of comparisons—which, after all, creates and/or intensifies a particular type of contest, namely, a contest over the uses of comparisons—adds a (further) layer of competition/conflict to the underlying situation. In other words, even if the underlying situation does not (yet) amount to a situation of competition and conflict, the politicisation of comparisons nonetheless transforms this situation into a situation of competition and conflict.

References

BAELE, Stephane J./BALZACQ, Thierry/BOURBEAU, Philippe, Numbers in Global Security Governance, in: *European Journal of International Security*, 3 (2018), 22–44.

BALDWIN, David, *Power and International Relations: A Conceptual Approach*, Princeton 2016.

BARNEY, Timothy, *Mapping the Cold War: Cartography and the Framing of America's International Power*, Chapel Hill 2015.

BLUTH, Christoph, Arms Control as a Part of Strategy: The Warsaw Pact in MBFR Negotiations, in: *Cold War History* 12 (2012), 245–268.

COLLINS, John M./CORDESMAN, Anthony H., *Imbalance of Power: An Analysis of Shifting U.S.-Soviet Military Strength*, San Rafael 1978.

FRIEDBERG, Aaron, *The Weary Titan: Britain and the Experience of Relative Decline, 1895-1905*, Princeton 1988.

GADDIS, John Lewis, *The Cold War*, London 2005.

GLASER, Charles, *Rational Theory of International Politics: The Logic of Competition and Cooperation*, Princeton 2010.

GLITMAN, Maynard W., *The Last Battle of the Cold War: An Inside Account of Negotiating the Intermediate Range Nuclear Forces Treaty*, Houndmills 2006.

GRANDE, Edgar/HUTTER, Swen, Beyond Authority Transfer: Explaining the Politicisation of Europe, in: *West European Politics* 39 (2016), 23–43.

GUZZINI, Stefano, *On the Measure of Power and the Power of Measure in International Relations* (DIIS Working Paper, 28), Copenhagen 2009.

HARTMANN, Rüdiger/HEYDRICH, Wolfgang/MEYER-LANDRUT, Nikolaus, *Der Vertrag über konventionelle Streitkräfte in Europa: Vertragswerk, Verhandlungsgeschichte, Kommentar, Dokumentation*, Baden-Baden 1994.

HERZOG, Richard J./WILDGEN, John K., Tactics in Military Propaganda Documents: A Content Analysis of Illustrations, in: *Defense Analysis*, 2 (1986), 35–46.

KRAKAU, Anton/DIEHL, Ole, *'Annähernde Parität' der Streitkräfte in Europa? Eine kritische Analyse des östlichen Streitkräftevergleichs* (Berichte des Bundesinstituts für ostwissenschaftliche und internationale Studien), Köln 1989.

LUNN, Simon, The East–West Military Balance: Assessing Change, in: *Adelphi Papers* 236 (1989), 49–71.

LUTZ, Dieter S., *Towards a Methodology of Military Force Comparison*, Baden-Baden 1986.

NATO, *NATO and the Warsaw Pact: Force Comparisons*, 2 Editions, Brussels 1982–1984.

NATO, *Conventional Forces in Europe: The Facts*, Brussels 1988.

NUTI, Leopoldo et al. (eds.), *The Euromissile Crisis and the End of the Cold War*, Washington D.C. 2015.

RISSE-KAPPEN, Thomas, Did 'Peace Through Strength' End the Cold War? Lessons from INF, in: *International Security*, 16 (1991), 162–188.

SOVIET UNION, *Whence the Threat to Peace*, 4 Editions, Moskow 1982–1987.

SOVIET UNION, *Warschauer Pakt – NATO: Kräfteverhältnis in Europa*, Moskau 1989.

STOLER, Ann Laura, Tense and Tender Ties: The Politics of Comparison in North American History and (Post) Colonial Studies, in: *The Journal of American History* 88 (2001), 829–865.

US DEPARTMENT OF DEFENSE, *Soviet Military Power*, 10 Editions, Washington D.C. 1981–1991.

WALSH, David M., *The Military Balance in the Cold War: US Perceptions and Policy, 1976–85*, London 2008.

WENGER, Etienne, *Communities of Practice: Learning, Meaning, and Identity*, Cambridge 1998.

WERRON, Tobias, Worum konkurrieren Nationalstaaten? Zu Begriff und Geschichte der Konkurrenz um 'weiche' globale Güter, in: *Zeitschrift für Soziologie*, 41 (2012), 338–355.

WESTAD, Odd Arne, *The Cold War: A World History*, New York 2017.

WOHLFORTH, William C., The Perception of Power: Russia in the Pre-1914 Balance, in: *World Politics* 39 (1987), 353–381.

WOHLFORTH, William C., *The Elusive Balance: Power and Perceptions during the Cold War*, Ithaca 1993.

ZÜRN, Michael, *A Theory of Global Governance: Authority, Legitimacy and Contestation*, Oxford 2018.

Genealogies of Modernism
Curatorial Practices of Comparing in the Exhibitions *Cubism and Abstract Art* and *documenta I*

Britta Hochkirchen

Abstract

The article examines how exhibitions come up with their own diverging definitions of the genealogies of modern art through curatorial practices of temporal comparing. The focus will be on the exhibitions Cubism and Abstract Art *that took place 1936 in the Museum of Modern Art in New York and on* documenta I *in Kassel in 1955. Both exhibitions deal with the concept of abstraction, which is proposed to be the teleological quality of modernism. While both exhibitions are widely recognized as examples of a formalistic view on the artworks and the development in the history of art, we will see that they use completely different practices of comparing to point out these formal issues.*

I. Preliminaries

"Learning from Athens"—this was the guiding notion behind the *documenta 14* in Kassel in summer 2017.[1] This seemed to be a striking title for an exhibition dedicated to contemporary art, or more precisely, one that should show the current state of the art. Is this a return to classicism and its strict norms? On the contrary, Adam Szymczyk, the artistic director of the fourteenth volume of *documenta*, altered the plans for this venerable major exhibition of contemporary art that has been held in Kassel, Germany, since 1955. In contrast to all the former volumes of this exhibition, *documenta 14* was held in two locations at nearly the same time: Athens and Kassel. Artworks were exhibited in both places where they were supposed to take issue with each city. According to Szymczyk, the idea was to drop the auctorial perspective—the hegemonial authority over meaning assumed by northern and western Europe—in favor of presenting *different nonhierarchical points of view and ways of thinking at the same time*. The curator's emphasis on contemporaneity

---

1 The *documenta 14* was held in Kassel from 10 June to 17 September 2017 and in Athens from 8 April to 17 July, 2017.

is striking, because it alludes to the perpetual defining question at any *documenta*: "What is contemporary art?"

Documenta 14 offered the possibility of a relation between two perspectives, but they could be perceived, and *compared*, only through a bodily and temporal shift: Visitors had to travel from one city to the other and therefore still perceived the works successively. They compared a "beforehand" with an "afterward"—at least in their own perception and experience. But even the separate exhibition venues in Kassel and Athens created, by juxtapositions, a condition that prompted comparative viewing: Marta Minujín's *Parthenon of Books*, a work of contemporary art alluding to the temple for Pallas Athena in Athens as a democratic symbol[2] decked with censored books, was installed next to the Fridericianum, the first public museum building on the European Continent from the eighteenth century, and one that is oriented architectonically toward Greek antiquity. Standing next to each other stimulated the visitor's comparative view. The architectonic pillars-and-pediment structure is the *tertium comparationis* of these two buildings, which in this constellation, both turn out to be imitations of an antique ideal—but imitations originating in different times: the eighteenth century and our contemporary time. The act of comparing, executed with the viewer's body presence together with both the *comparata*, produces by this means new relations between past, present, and future.

These temporal dimensions are the topic of this chapter. Let me make a few brief preliminary remarks about what it means to examine practices of comparing with respect to curatorial practices at exhibitions. The phenomenon of changing temporary exhibitions demonstrates what the art historian Felix Thürlemann contended about pictures in general: "they are more than one image."[3] This statement

---

2   Marta Minujín, *The Parthenon of Books*, 2017, Installation. Kassel, Friedrichsplatz, *documenta* 14. The Parthenon of censored books was placed at the Friedrichsplatz where the National Socialists burned books on May 19, 1933.

3   Felix Thürlemann, *Mehr als ein Bild. Für eine Kunstgeschichte des hyperimage*, München 2013. Thürlemann brings up the concept of the hyperimage that is also useful for research on exhibitions: "Mit hyperimage *wird eine kalkulierte Zusammenstellung von ausgewählten Bildobjekten – Gemälden, Zeichnungen, Fotografien und Skulpturen – zu einer neuen, übergreifenden Einheit bezeichnet. Der Begriff verweist auf verschiedene Arten des Zusammenspiels von Bildern, wie sie bei der Präsentation von Kunstwerken in Museen und Ausstellungen, bei der Projektion im Unterricht, aber auch im Layout von Bildbänden beobachtet werden können*" (7). As an amplification to Thürlemann's concept of the hyperimage, practices of comparing open up the possibility of also looking at those aspects that are cropped and cut down through combining or linking two or more pictures. Furthermore, practices of comparing do not just concentrate on the intended meaning by the acteur–curator but are also sensitive for the meanings that occur coincidentally in a specific context. For the hyperimage, see also: Felix Thürlemann, Vom Einzelbild zum hyperimage. Eine neue Herausforderung für die kunsthistorische Hermeneutik, in: Gerd Blum et al. (eds.), *Pendant Plus*, Berlin 2012, 23–46; David Ganz/Felix Thürlemann (eds.), *Das Bild im Plural. Mehrteilige Bildformen zwischen Mittelalter und Gegenwart*, Berlin 2010.

is surprising if one considers how much the definition of modern art is based on the idea of autonomy, that is, on the independence and self-referentiality of the individual work. However, every exhibition is, in fact, per se a site of comparing of multiple works of art. It is therefore a contradictory act when modern art is deeply connected with the temporal exhibition that is, in itself, a modern medium.[4] The characteristic quality of exhibitions of art is the interaction of different times in a performative mode.[5] On the level of the artworks, there is a clash between the different times of their origins, but also of the times they depict, and, not least, the multiple times of their reception.[6] But the exhibition transforms these different kinds of temporalities into a new logic of time: First, there is the overall quality of presence through which the exhibition brings all these different times toward a contemporaneity of presence for the experience of the beholder. The presence is emphasized even more through the ephemeral character of the so-called *temporal exhibition*. But, furthermore, the exhibition forms and produces the temporality of the presented artworks: The pieces of art are not shown separated on their own, but in special constellations and displays to initiate a comparative viewing by the

---

4   One of the many "births" of the temporary exhibition is the so-called "Salon" in Paris, the exhibition of the Académie royale de peinture et de sculpture held regularly every year or every second year from 1737 onward. The "Salon" was open to the public and showed the contemporary art of the members of the academy. See Anja Weisenseel, *Bildbetrachtung in Bewegung. Der Rezipient in Texten und Bildern zur Pariser Salonausstellung des 18. Jahrhunderts* (Ars et Scientia. Schriften zur Kunstwissenschaft, vol. 14), Berlin/Boston 2017, 10.

5   Cf. Beatrice von Bismarck, Der Teufel trägt Geschichtlichkeit oder Im Look der Provokation: When Attitudes become Form, Bern 1969/Venice 2013, in: Eva Kernbauer (ed.), *Kunstgeschichtlichkeit. Historizität und Anachronie in der Gegenwartskunst*, Paderborn 2015, 233–248, see 234; Beatrice von Bismarck, The Exhibition as Collective, in: Kai-Uwe Hemken (ed.), *Kritische Szenografie. Die Kunstausstellung im 21. Jahrhundert*, Bielefeld 2015, 185–199, see 186. See for the question of the special quality of time in exhibitions: Beatrice von Bismarck et al. (eds.), *Timing. On the Temporal Dimension of Exhibiting* (Cultures of the Curatorial, vol. 2), Berlin 2014. See further: Krzysztof Pomian, *L'Ordre du temps*, Paris 1984.

6   See for the differentiation between the multiple temporalities of pictures, especially between the time of the depiction and the depicted time: Heinrich Theissing, *Die Zeit im Bild*, Darmstadt 1987; Gottfried Boehm, Bild und Zeit, in: Hannelore Paflik (ed.): *Das Phänomen Zeit in Kunst und Wissenschaft*, Weinheim 1987, 1–24; Götz Pochat, *Bild – Zeit. Zeitgestalt und Erzählstruktur in der bildenden Kunst von den Anfängen bis zur frühen Neuzeit*, Wien 1996. For the reception-esthetic temporality of pictures, see Johannes Grave, Der Akt des Bildbetrachtens. Überlegungen zur rezeptionsästhetischen Temporalität des Bildes, in: Michael Gamper/Helmut Hühn (eds.), *Zeit der Darstellung. Ästhetische Eigenzeiten in Kunst, Literatur und Wissenschaft*, Hannover 2014, 51–72; Johannes Grave, Form, Struktur und Zeit. Bildliche Formkonstellationen und ihre rezeptionsästhetische Temporalität, in: Michael Gamper/Eva Geulen/Johannes Grave et al. (eds.), *Zeit der Form – Formen der Zeit* (Ästhetische Eigenzeiten, vol. 2), Hannover 2016, 139–162.

beholder.[7] This transforms the specific temporality of a work of art and superimposes a new temporality produced through curatorial practices of comparing.[8] Hanging one piece of art next to another (or more) leads the beholder to compare between them. The comparison between two (or more) *comparata* produces one or more *tertium comparationis*: If there is one landscape hanging next to another, the genre landscape will be the aspect of similarity. On the basis of this similarity, the *tertium comparationis* highlighted by the comparison could be, for example, the color scheme, the brushwork, or a compositional element. If one of these landscapes is hung next to a completely different painting, the aspect being emphasized will also change. To bring it to the point, curatorial practices of comparing within exhibitions shift those features and qualities of a piece of art that are highlighted. To put it even more strongly, the highlighted qualities are not essential parts of the pieces of art, but are produced through the act of comparing.[9] Here, the performative modus of the exhibition becomes connected with the performative modus of comparing.

Curatorial practices, such as the selection of works of art and the form of their presentation, create microsituations of comparing between different pieces of art in individual exhibition rooms.[10] Every exhibition accordingly initiates spaces of potential comparative viewing. The curatorial practices of comparing emphasize particular characteristics of the *comparata*; others recede into the background. Therefore, the qualities of a work of art can shift depending on which artwork it is being compared to in which situational context. Curatorial practices that stimulate the viewer to look comparatively are a strategy with which to generate visual evidence.[11] Exemplary research studies have shown that every exhibition draws out a specific interpretation of, for example, an artist's oeuvre, an art movement, or a

---

7   Beatrice von Bismarck therefore emphasizes the need to look at an exhibition as a "collective" that consists of a continuous change of relations between the constellations of the works of art and the beholders. Von Bismarck, The Exhibition as a Collective, 186.

8   For the shifting temporal effect with regard to the practices of comparing pictures, see Johannes Grave, Vergleichen als Praxis. Vorüberlegungen zu einer praxistheoretisch orientierten Untersuchung von Vergleichen, in: Angelika Epple/Walter Erhart (eds.), *Die Welt beobachten. Praktiken des Vergleichens*, Frankfurt a. M./New York 2015, 135–159, esp. 150.

9   For the manipulating quality of practices of comparing, see Angelika Epple/Walter Erhart, Die Welt beobachten – Praktiken des Vergleichens, in: Angelika Epple/Walter Erhart (eds.): *Die Welt beobachten. Praktiken des Vergleichens*, Frankfurt a. M./New York 2015, 7–34, esp. 15.

10 These microsituations are examined exemplarily to determine the way the exhibition bears its meaning: through not only curatorial intention but also situational and material performative coincidences.

11 See Grave, Vergleichen als Praxis, 138.

style; and, of course, of a historical epoch such as modernism.[12] Curatorial practices of comparing produce specific significations and hierarchizations by *showing* a particular narration of history or art history—namely, by means of a chosen relationship between past, present, and future. Thus, practices of comparing suggest attributes such as "before" and "after," even though everything that we see at an exhibition is present to the same degree. These temporal comparisons play an important role in exhibitions dealing with a genealogy of a special time such as modernism.[13] They help to mediate the underlying historiographic concept of the exhibition. Values are attached to these categories of "before" and "after" that may cater to specific political ideologies.[14] However, as practices of comparing at exhibitions, most of the time these power-laden values remain unspoken and suggestive.

My intent throughout, though, is to see how exhibitions come up with their own diverging definitions of modern art and their own definitions of the genealogies of modern art through curatorial practices of temporal comparing. I shall focus on the exhibition *Cubism and Abstract Art* held in the Museum of Modern Art in New York in 1936. I shall also return to *documenta*, but then to the first one in 1955. Both exhibitions deal with the concept of abstraction that is proposed to be the teleological quality of modernism. To argue for the development of abstraction as a modernist indicator, the artworks have to be compared to pieces of art that follow a figurative, respectively mimetic mode of depiction. Whereas both exhibitions are widely recognized as examples for a formalistic view on artworks and developments in art history, I shall show that they use completely different practices of comparing to point out these formal issues.

The dichotomy between abstraction and figuration or, respectively, a mimetic mode of depiction is often connected with twentieth-century visual art.[15] Most of the time, these representational conventions are assigned very unidimensionally to

---

12 See Hubert Locher, Die Kunst des Ausstellens. Anmerkungen zu einem unübersichtlichen Diskurs, in: Hans D. Huber/Hubert Locher/Karin Schulte (eds.), *Kunst des Ausstellens. Beiträge, Statements, Diskussionen*, Ostfildern-Ruit 2002, 15–30, see 18-19.
13 In this chapter, the concept of modernism is taken as an ever-changing construction driven by, for example, practices of comparing within exhibitions. For a similar definition of modernism, see Katja Hoffmann, *Ausstellungen als Wissensordnungen. Zur Transformation des Kunstbegriffs auf der Documenta 11*, Bielefeld 2013, 71.
14 For an understanding of the exhibition as a "political ritual" in modern democratic societies, see Dorothea von Hantelmann/Carolin Meister, Einleitung, in: Dorothea von Hantelmann/Carolin Meister (eds.), *Die Ausstellung. Politik eines Rituals*, Zürich/Berlin 2010, 7–18, see 8-9.
15 See Serge Guilbeut, *Wie New York die Idee der Modernen Kunst gestohlen hat. Abstrakter Expressionismus, Freiheit und Kalter Krieg* [1983], Dresden 1997; Christine Lindlay, *Art in the Cold War. From Vladivostok to Kalamazoo, 1945–1962*, London 1990. The concept of abstraction is interpreted in many different ways with regard to its pictorial relation to the world and its historical classification. See Gottfried Boehm, Abstraktion und Realität. Zum Verhältnis von Kunst

political systems or ideologies: abstraction to the West, which flirts with aesthetical and political autonomy; figuration to the East, which uses art for explicit political purposes. But there are also some temporal references that can be assigned to the mode of the mimetic and the nonmimetic depiction. In image theory, the temporal characteristics of abstraction and figuration are based primarily on what Sebastian Egenhofer has set forth as "an artwork's relationship with the world,"[16] which is assumed to have changed during modernism. According to him, the model of the representational image—an image that depicts something according to the principle of resemblance and follows a mimetic modus—always refers to a past world, to an original image (an *Urbild*) that is conceived as *anteceding* it, even when that image is a product of the imagination.[17] This concept is based on resemblance, on referentiality, and it is therefore connected with a temporality of the past, because the image shows something that was "before itself." Egenhofer argues that because of their nonmimetic mode, works of abstraction do not refer to some *antecedent*. Instead, they are situated solely within the context of the world beyond the image. They participate only within the context of a continually changing "outside" that makes the abstract work of art always refer to the *future*.[18] Egenhofer's argument with regard to the theory of images is that the representational, referential work of figuration stays linked to the past, whereas the abstract work, at any point, makes reference to the future. Following on from these theoretical assumptions with regard to the temporal structure of the image, this chapter will show that abstraction and figuration can be seen as indicators of the temporal qualities of the construction of (art-)historiographical models of modernism. Abstraction and figuration are relational qualities, as is the concept of modernism on the whole, that are constructed through practices of comparing. Hence, this chapter links an examination of comparative practices with questions of temporality, assuming that exhibitions always relate different times to each other in a complex way. In the development and realization of these (potential) time references, practices of comparing are of particular importance. The chapter asks about the importance of comparative curatorial practices for the accentuation of temporal references by examining the emergence of modernism concepts in two exemplary exhibitions.

Within the Collaborative Research Center "Practices of Comparing", we are examining different but connected lines of change in practices of comparing: alterations to which these practices are subjected, as well as alterations that trigger them. We ask, on the one hand, how practices of comparing change; and on the

---

und Kunstphilosophie in der Moderne [1990], in: Gottfried Boehm, *Die Sichtbarkeit der Zeit. Studien zum Bild in der Moderne*, ed. by Ralph Ubl, Paderborn 2017, 173–185.

16 Sebastian Egenhofer, *Abstraktion, Kapitalismus, Subjektivität. Die Wahrheitsfunktion des Werks in der Moderne*, München 2008, 13 ("Weltverhältnis des Werks").

17 Cf. Egenhofer, *Abstraktion*, 13.

18 Egenhofer, *Abstraktion*, 11–12.

other hand, how alterations in these practices of comparing bring about historical change. Transferred to exhibitions, this means, to inquire into how comparing in the form of curatorial practices changes over the course of history, more specifically, what different kinds of comparisons are produced. With regard to the twentieth century, I shall compare curatorial comparisons by isolating and analyzing some exemplary microsituations of comparing from exhibitions. Thus, I can demonstrate that, historically, differing comparison aspects were employed to negotiate a forced distinction between abstraction and figuration in order to declare a concept of modernism.[19] Thereby, in the following, I shall show that figuration and abstraction are not fixed and are not essential qualities of works of art, but are produced through practices of comparing within exhibitions.

Comparing is a practice that has to be performed.[20] In the following, I shall therefore show that curatorial practices of comparing are not fully controllable, despite their great interest in highlighting a particular reading of abstraction and modernism.[21] The specific narration that curators intend for their exhibition is frequently underscored in the exhibition's paratexts.[22] I denote as paratexts all statements published before or during the exhibition, but foremost, also all exhibition texts or didactical signs within the exhibition. These paratexts also introduce verbal and visual comparisons—for example, by placing two reproduced pictures side by side. All the visual comparisons are framed verbally within these paratexts. If those comparisons are then transferred to the exhibition—often on the basis of the same compared pieces of art—those comparisons frequently seem to contradict the prescribed reading: The comparison does not work out in the same way as it did in the medium of language. With the materiality and size of the work of art as well as with real space, resistances emerge. In "real space," two juxtaposed works of art suddenly suggest different aspects of comparison. When the viewer performs the comparative view at the exhibition, her or his bodily participation, the very physical presence of the works, and their presentation produce within their spatial situation something new and unintended that may even run counter to the original idea. Then the exhibition becomes not only an indicator but also a factor of historical change—and practices of comparing, as I shall show, are fundamental in this.

---

19 For practices of comparing as a mode of constructing a genealogy of modernism, see also Epple/Erhart, Die Welt beobachten, 27–28.
20 Cf. Epple/Erhart, Die Welt beobachten, 19; Grave, Vergleichen als Praxis, 152.
21 For the aspect of performance of exhibitions, see von Bismarck, The Exhibition as Collective, 198.
22 For the concept of the paratext, see Gérard Genette, *Paratexte. Das Buch vom Beiwerk des Buches* [French Original 1987], Frankfurt a. M. 1989.

II. Abstraction by comparing motifs: *Cubism and Abstract Art*

In 1936, the founding director of the Museum of Modern Art, Alfred H. Barr, organized the exhibition *Cubism and Abstract Art* displaying 400 works from the visual arts including painting and sculpture but also graphic design, architecture, film, and design.[23] As Barr explained in the catalogue, the exhibition considered itself to be a retrospective on "an important movement in modern art,"[24] by which he primarily meant a retrospective on abstraction, especially on abstract art in Europe descending from Cubism.[25] Barr is widely known and criticized for having laid down the formalist narration for western modernism:[26] on the one side, in the exhibition catalogue; on the other side, within the exhibition. I want to show that there are some differences in the way this narration is told and presented. Barr describes the historical derivation of abstraction in the catalogue as follows:

"Sometimes in the history of art it is possible to describe a period or a generation of artists as having been obsessed by a particular problem. The artists of the early fifteenth century for instance were moved by a passion for imitating nature".[27]

That which is depictable, the dictum of similitude, which Barr pointed out here for Renaissance art, is therewith based on the modus of referentiality. The image is, when recalling Egenhofer's remarks on temporality and image theory, related back to a preceding *Urbild*, if not to nature itself. This means that the depicting image is

---

23   The exhibition was held from March 2 to April 19, 1936 and was shown afterward in San Francisco, Cincinnati, Minneapolis, Cleveland, Baltimore, Providence, and Grand Rapids, Michigan. See the exhibition catalogue: Alfred H. Barr (ed.), *Cubism and Abstract Art. Painting, Sculpture, Constructions, Photography, Architecture, Industrial Art, Theatre, Films, Posters, Typography*, New York 1936. For Barr's curatorial work, see Sybil Gordon Kantor, *Alfred H. Barr, Jr. and the Intellectual Origins of the Museum of Modern Art*, Massachusetts 2002. The display of the exhibition *Cubism and Abstract Art* is examined in Mary Anne Staniszewski, *The Power of Display. A History of Exhibition Installations at the Museum of Modern Art*, London 1998, 60–83.

24   Alfred H. Barr, *Cubism and Abstract Art*, 9.

25   For this indication, see Susan Noyes Platt, Modernism, Formalism, and Politics: The "Cubism and Abstract Art" Exhibition of 1936 at The Museum of Modern Art, in: *Art Journal* 47 (4/1988), 284–295, see 284: "*Cubism and Abstract Art* [...] established Cubism as the central issue of early modernism, abstraction as the goal." In 1927, Barr also organized an exhibition entitled *Progressive Modern Painting from Daumier and Corot to Post Cubism* at Wellesley that highlighted the development of Cubism out of nineteenth-century art. See Platt, Modernism, Formalism, and Politics, 287. See also Leah Dickerman, Abstraction in 1936: Cubism and Abstract Art at the Museum of Modern Art, in: Leah Dickerman (ed.), *Inventing Abstraction 1910–1925: how a radical idea changed modern art*, London 2012, 364–369, here 364.

26   See, e.g., William J. T. Mitchell, *Picture Theory. Essays on Verbal and Visual Representations*, Chicago/London 1994, 231–236; Benjamin H. D. Buchloh, From Faktura to Factography, in: Annette Michelson et al. (eds.), *October: The First Decade, 1976–1986*, Cambridge 1987, 77–113.

27   Barr, *Cubism and Abstract Art*, 11.

implicitly conveyed as being connected to the *past*. The art of modernism operates entirely differently, according to Barr's implicit argumentative comparison:

> "In the early twentieth century the dominant interest was almost exactly the opposite. The pictorial conquest of the external visual world had been completed and refined many times and in different ways during the previous half millennium. The more adventurous and original artists had grown bored with painting facts. By a common and powerful impulse they were driven to abandon the imitation of natural appearance".[28]

For Barr, modern art, consequently, negated the generation of likeness, and definitely did not refer to something antecedent to itself: It is claimed to be non-mimetic. Hence an immanent vector in the direction of the future enters into modern art, which Barr equates with abstraction. He therefore also proposes a definition of abstraction that emphasizes the nonreferentiality and concreteness of the picture: "For an 'abstract' painting is really a most positively concrete painting since it confines the attention to its immediate, sensuous, physical surface far more than does the canvas of a sunset or a portrait."[29] These statements are the reason why Barr has been recognized as a formalist: He proposed modernism in a "proto-Greenbergian language"[30] only by reference to formal issues. But, as I shall show, Barr's formalism was thus constructed through practices of comparing based on the aspect of similarity as the mimetic motif. Only through the comparison of several mimetic motifs could he point to the abstraction he wanted to assume on the formal level.

Barr's idea of the development of modern art in the form of a teleological history of progress is translated specifically into a diagram that he designed and used to adorn the catalogue's front cover (Fig. 1).[31] This chart shows, from top to bottom, the network and genesis of the individual "isms" of western modernism over the last 45 years—namely, from 1890 to 1935, therefore, almost up to the present time of the exhibition. Following the chart in the vertical direction, one gets to know, for instance, that Neoimpressionism influences Cubism, which in turn, exerts an influence on Constructivism, which ultimately ends in Geometrical Abstract Art. The transitions are marked by arrows; non-Western influences are mentioned in

---

28 Barr, *Cubism and Abstract Art*, 11.
29 Barr, *Cubism and Abstract Art*, 11.
30 Kantor, *Alfred H. Barr, Jr.*, 318.
31 See Astrit Schmidt-Burkhardt, *Stammbäume der Kunst. Zur Genealogie der Avantgarde*, Berlin 2005, 114–187. See also Hal Foster, Museum Tales of Twentieth-Century Art, in: *Studies of Art* 74 (2009), 253–375.

Fig. 1: Alfred H. Barr, Cover of the exhibition catalogue ›Cubism and Abstract Art‹, MoMA 1936. New York, Museum of Modern Art (MoMA).

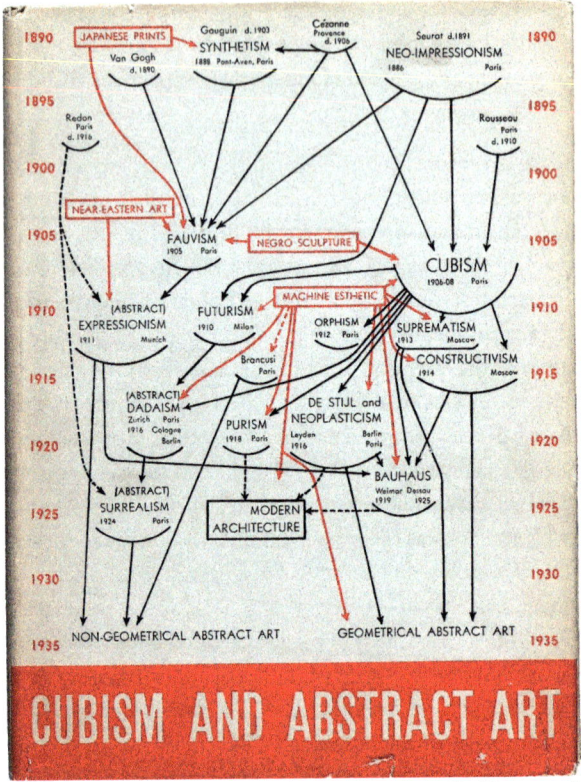

Offset, printed in color, 7 3/4 x 10 1/4' (19.7 x 26 cm). The Museum of Modern Art Library, New York. MA143.

red and framed in boxes, for instance, "Japanese prints" or "Negro sculpture."[32] Along the horizontal, these "isms" branch out into the division between "non-geometrical abstract art" and "geometrical abstract art." The illustration ends with this distinction at its lower edge for 1935; both these branches are the "main traditions of abstract art,"[33] as Barr explains in the catalogue. According to him, both

---

32 There were also comparisons to non-European art within the exhibition when Barr juxtaposed Picasso's *Dancer* with an African sculpture. See Platt, Modernism, Formalism, and Politics, 284.
33 Barr, *Cubism and Abstract Art*, 19.

traditions find their origin in Impressionism. Nevertheless, one essential disparity separates them that Barr emphasizes very strongly in the catalogue: Nongeometric abstract art works with organic forms, is emotional, decorative, and irrational, whereas geometric abstract art is intellectual and structural. This distinction becomes very apparent in Barr's diagram with the division of both parts occurring at the latest in 1935. It is only in the foregoing years that some "isms" still seem to be changing allegiances. The art historian Julia Voss has pointed out that Barr's model for an evolving history of modern art resembles the evolution diagram of *On the Origin of Species* from 1859 by the natural scientist Charles Darwin.[34] She emphasizes that there is one important difference, though: In Barr's diagram, the "losers" and those influences external to art would remain invisible. According to Voss, his model presents art history as an autonomous process of development.[35] Furthermore all the arrows point in only one direction: into the future, and the future is abstraction.[36] Voss argues that coincidence and environment, two factors that were of great importance to Darwin, are not indicated by Barr—they simply do not figure at all.[37]

Right at the beginning of the catalogue and in Barr's introductory text, there is an invitation to perform comparative viewing (Fig. 2).[38] There is a juxtaposition of two reproductions of posters for the World Press Exhibition (*Weltpresseausstellung*) held in Cologne in 1928. The figures in this case are not equally large. These illustrations are literally "trimmed" for the purpose of the comparison and are reproduced in the catalogue's uniform black-and-white print at the same horizontal level. Their placement side by side makes common aspects stand out: In both instances, they are posters from the exhibition in Cologne in 1928; so, a contemporaneity does

---

34 See Julia Voss, Wer schreibt Kunstgeschichte? Kritik, Kunstwissenschaft, Markt und Museum, in: *Zeitschrift für Kunstgeschichte* 78 (2015), 16–31, see 18. For a discussion of Barr's diagram, see also Charlotte Klonk, *Spaces of Experience. Art Gallery Interiors from 1800 to 2000*, New Haven/London 2009, 135–141; Glenn D. Lowry, Abstraction in 1936: Barr's Diagrams, in: Leah Dickerman (ed.), *Inventing Abstraction 1910–1925: how a radical idea changed modern art*, London 2012, 359–363, see 361; Hoffmann, *Ausstellungen als Wissensordnungen*, 95; Marcia Brennan, *Curating Consciousness. Mysticism and the Modern Museum*, London 2010, 30–57; Mitchell, *Picture Theory*, 231–235. For the development of Barr's diagram and its relation to other art historiographical models, see Astrit Schmidt-Burkhardt, Shaping Modernism. Alfred Barr's genealogy of art, in: *Word & Image* 16 (4/2000), 387–400.
35 Cf. Voss, Wer schreibt Kunstgeschichte?, 19.
36 For the naturalizing modus of Barr's diagram, see also Katja Hoffmann, *Ausstellungen als Wissensordnungen*, 101; Eward R. Tufte, *Beautiful Evidence*, Ceshire 2006, 67.
37 Cf. Voss, Wer schreibt Kunstgeschichte?, 19–21. See also the critique of the complete separation of figuration and abstraction by the art historian Meyer Schapiro in his article The Nature of Abstract Art, in: *Marxist Quarterly* 1 (1/1937), 78–97. See also Platt, Modernism, Formalism, and Politics, 292.
38 Barr, *Cubism and Abstract Art*, 10, figs. 1 and 2.

Fig. 2: Illustration in ›Cubism and Abstract Art. Painting, Sculpture, Constructions, Photography, Architecture, Industrial Art, Theatre, Films, Posters, Typography‹, ed. by Alfred H. Barr, New York 1936, 10.

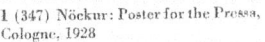

1 (347) Nöckur: Poster for the Pressa, Cologne, 1928   2 (334) Ehmcke: Poster for the Pressa, Cologne, 1928

exist. In both instances, we see the Cologne Cathedral, the River Rhine, the Hohenzollern Bridge, and the tower on the exhibition grounds. However, in one case, the cathedral is visible on the left-hand side; and in the other, on the right-hand side; the poster on the right is a plan view. The *tertium* produced here by the juxtapositioning of the pictures is a motif, in this case, Cologne Cathedral. It is only on the basis of this common theme, the motif, that the difference in the formalistic manners of depiction becomes obvious. Furthermore, the arrangement provokes a before-and-after sequence, that is, a temporal order: On the left-hand side of the page, there is figuration; on the right-hand side, abstraction. Barr's text on this page then points out the underlying ideologies and their modification in changing times:[39]

> "Why were two posters published and why do they differ in style? Because one was designed for the Anglo-American public, the other for the German public. In 1928 it was thought that Americans, accustomed to an over-crowded and banally realistic style, would not appreciate the simplicity and abstraction of the right hand poster.

---

39   For Barr's shifting opinion toward abstraction in connection with the empowerment of the totalitarian politics through Stalinism and the National Socialists that he experienced through his visit to Germany in 1932–1933, see Platt, Modernism, Formalism, and Politics, 289.

> The German public, on the contrary, through the activity of its museums and progressive commercial artists was quite used to an abstract style. Today times have changed. The style of the abstract poster, which is just beginning to interest our American advertisers, is now discouraged in Germany."[40]

The emphasis on the *manner* of depiction, Barrs's formalistic argument for abstraction, succeeds in this comparison only because of the presence of a common mimetic motif. Thus, ultimately, it works on the basis of the recognitional gaze and a correlation back to an *antecedent* in nature. The referentiality of the depiction is at the very forefront. Thus, it is the comparing aspect of mimetic figuration that creates a basis of similarity for a notion of abstraction that is so meaningful for Barr's formalist narration of the genealogy of modernism.

It is interesting now to look at how this aspect of comparison is applied in curatorial practices within the exhibition space in the Museum of Modern Art. Barr hung paintings together with architectural models, furniture, and graphic prints in uniformly whitewashed exhibition rooms. Brian O'Doherty coined the term "white cube" for this form of white and "clean" exhibition room that emerged in the 1920s and prevailed throughout the 20th century.[41] The white cube plays a decisive role in the inquiry into the practices of comparing and their temporal dimension.

> "Unshadowed, white, clean, artificial—the space is devoted to the technology of aesthetics. Works of art are mounted, hung, scattered for study. Their ungrubby surfaces are untouched by time and its vicissitudes. Art exists in a kind of eternity of display, and though there is lots of "period" (late modern), there is no time. This eternity gives the gallery a limbolike status; one has to have died already to be there."[42]

According to O'Doherty, the white, closed gallery space is so neutralizing that even the changing times are shut out. But precisely this neutrality makes the act of comparing much more effective, and the same applies to the difference between the "before" and "after."

However, the arrangements on the walls do not illustrate the development that Barr delineates in his diagram. Barr placed the "isms" into their own separate exhibition rooms: There is, for example, one room with "De Stijl and Neo-Plasticism" (Fig.3) and a room displaying analytical "Cubism" (Fig. 4). This practice of separating the "isms" prevents a direct comparative viewing of the difference between mimetic and nonmimetic pictures from the physical standpoint of the visitor inside

---

40 Barr, *Cubism and Abstract* Art, 10.
41 Brian O'Doherty, *Inside the White Cube* [Original in *Artforum* 1976], introd. by Thomas McEvilley, Santa Monica/San Francisco 1999. See also Jérome Glicenstein, *L'Art: une histoire d'expositions*, Paris 2009, 29–37.
42 O'Doherty, *Inside the White Cube*, 15.

Fig. 3: Installation view of the exhibition ›Cubism and Abstract Art‹. MoMA, NY, March 2, 1936 – April 19, 1936. New York, Museum of Modern Art (MoMA).

Photographic Archive. The Museum of Modern Art Archives, New York. Acc. n.: IN46.11B.

one room. Because the "isms" are presented in separate rooms from one another, the disparity between nongeometrical and geometric abstract art does not motivate their critical comparison. Instead, the aspect of comparison relates *either* to a motif *or* to the manner of depiction. Furthermore, the separation suggests a comparison between nearly synchronic works of art: The development of abstraction is recognizable only through a comparison between the different rooms and "isms." As I shall show, this partitioning of comparative aspects carries its own message. Those spaces working with geometrical forms are represented as nonmimetic and therefore nonreferential (Fig. 3). The room displaying works by Theo van Doesburg, Georges Vantongerloo, and others prompts the comparative gaze to see what is common among their formalistic *manners of depiction*. As a result, the comparative view emphasizes the abstract manner of all shown paintings here on a formalistic level. There is no referentiality to a precedent natural form: Thus, remembering Egenhofer's image-theoretical arguments, there is no longer any connection to the past. By means of this comparison, Barr promotes geometrical abstraction as the pictorial modus of the present and, what is more, of the future.

This alludes to the differentiation between "pure-abstraction" and "near-abstractions" Barr explained within the catalogue. "Pure-abstraction," as in the paintings in this room, "has absolutely no dependence upon natural forms. It is purely

Fig. 4: Installation view of the exhibition ›Cubism and Abstract Art‹. MoMA, NY, March 2, 1936 – April 19, 1936.

Gelatin silver print, 5 x 7" (12.7 x 17.7 cm). Photographer: Beaumont Newhall (copyright: The Museum of Modern Art, NY) Photographic Archive. The Museum of Modern Art Archives, New York. Object Number: IN46.2. New York, Museum of Modern Art (MoMA).

abstract in its genesis as well as in its final form."[43] In a comment from 1925, Barr emphasizes the impossibility of comparing motifs within artworks of the modern era: "If all artists painted or drew Madonnas as they once did, how conveniently we could compare them—but they don't."[44] On the contrary, this is the case in a room containing works by Georges Braque and Pablo Picasso in which the human face, if not the whole body, becomes the basis of similarity that enables the act of comparing (Fig. 4). This means that, here again, the comparison is drawing to the forefront a motif and a reference external to the image. Barr refers to this effect in his catalogue text with the concept of "near-abstractions" that he defines as "compositions in which the artist, starting with natural forms, transforms them into abstract or nearly abstract forms. He approaches an abstract goal but does not quite reach it."[45] To conclude, there is, in Barr's opinion, a qualitatively hierarchized development in abstraction in itself: from the "near-abstractions" up to the "pure abstraction." Barr emphasizes these hierarchized values of abstraction within the

---

43 Barr, *Cubism and Abstract Art*, 12.
44 Cited by Platt, Modernism, Formalism, and Politics, 286. She gives the following reference (293): "The Museum of Modern Art Archives: Alfred Hamilton Barr, Jr., Papers, unlabeled lecture notes for seminar report (dated on internal evidence to Spring 1925)."
45 Barr, *Cubism and Abstract Art*, 12–13.

exhibition by practices of comparing, thereby separating these two modes of depiction. The result is mimetic and nonmimetic pictures in one exhibition dealing with the development of abstraction. There would have been an entirely different effect if a work by Picasso were to have been hung next to a composition by van Doesburg: Then the attention would not have been attracted to a still depictive motif via the *tertium*. Considered from the perspective of image theory, Barr's hanging arrangement and the comparative aspects produced by it summoned the past by reference to antecedent nature for the "near-abstractions" so that they are understood as a step toward the final "pure-abstraction."

Looking at the exhibition display, it is striking that although Barr placed abstraction on the highest rung of his teleological history of progress, the actual display largely denied it. His use of curatorial practices of comparing emphasized the figurative motif very strongly as the aspect of similarity that provoked the comparison. This contradicts the proposition made in the exhibition catalogue that modern art is no longer about imitation and therefore no longer connected to antecedent past. This contradiction was exacerbated by the situational context of the exhibition space. The material presence of the artworks and the real space operate as factors in the act of comparing that can counteract the intended meaning. When, in the act of comparing, the material or "real space" resists the intended aim, the extent to which modernism is constructed becomes apparent. The comparisons afforded by the exhibition space literally outbid the imitation theory, respectively the mimetic quality, of the picture by presenting a comparison motif in "real space." Marcel Duchamp's *Nude Descending a Staircase* (1912) was, in fact, hung next to a real stairway, again guiding a viewer's attention to the motif of the steps as a *tertium* (Fig. 5).[46] Here again, the formalistic manner is not emphasized through the act of comparing.

A similarly motif-weighted aspect of figurative comparison was produced with an artwork by Malevich that was Barr's example for "pure-abstraction" that "confines the attention to its immediate, sensuous, physical surface" and not to the representation of a motif. "Pure-abstraction" is, in Barr's opinion, nonreferential and therefore connected with the future, not with the past. But a different understanding occurs within the exhibition room because of the practices of comparing: Malevich's *Suprematist Composition: white on white* (1918) was presented between two blinded windows covered in white cardboard (Fig. 6).[47]

---

46 For this display, see also Brennan, Curating Consciousness, 33–40.
47 Kazimir Malevich, *Suprematist Composition: white on white*, 1918, oil on canvas, 80 x 80 cm. Lent anonymously. Platt also refers to the striking display of Malevich's artwork describing that this juxtaposition "underscored its inherent elegance." Platt, Modernism, Formalism, and Politics, 285.

Genealogies of Modernism 365

Fig. 5: Installation view of the exhibition ›Cubism and Abstract Art‹. MoMA, NY, March 2, 1936 – April 19, 1936.

Gelatin silver print, 4 1/2 × 6 1/2" (11.4 × 16.5 cm). Photographer: Beaumont Newhall (copyright: The Museum of Modern Art, NY). Photographic Archive. The Museum of Modern Art Archives, New York. Object Number: IN46.22A. New York, Museum of Modern Art (MoMA).

Comparative viewing highlights the aspect of the motif of the window. Again, it is the aspect of figuration that brings up the idea of abstraction that is, therefore, bound back to the past. In the history of art since Leon Battista Alberti's treatise on painting, the window is a theme that opens the eye to illusionistic spatial depth and therefore exemplarily stands for the model of likeness.[48] In this situation, it was assigned double significance: not only as a motif but also semantically. It underscored one more time that the comparisons prompted by the exhibition placed the motif of the window and therefore the referentiality at the focus of attention.[49] The formalistic manner of depiction, in contrast—which, of course, constitutes the decisive criterion for abstraction and its specific temporality—was less prominent.

This also becomes evident in a central juxtapositioning of two works by Picasso at opposite ends of an exhibition room (Fig. 7 and Fig. 8).

---

48 Leon Battista Alberti, *Della Pittura – Über die Malkunst*, ed. by Oskar Bätschmann/Sandra Gianfreda, Darmstadt 2007, 93.
49 Nonetheless, it is striking that the image of the opaque window corresponds with the norms of formalism because it does not present anything else but itself.

Fig. 6: Installation view of the exhibition ›Cubism and Abstract Art‹. MoMA, NY, March 2, 1936 – April 19, 1936.

Gelatin silver print, 4 1/2 x 6" (11.4 x 15.2 cm). Photographer: Beaumont Newhall (copyright: The Museum of Modern Art, New York). Photographic Archive. The Museum of Modern Art Archives, New York. Object Number: IN46.36B. New York, Museum of Modern Art (MoMA).

Both paintings depict the scene of a painter and his model.[50] The choice of the topic on its own, "painter and model," already elicits the reference to an antecedent likeness. Here, too, the figuratively recognizable motif is the *tertium* uniting the two *comparata*. However, in this case, the viewer is notably compelled to stand in the space between the pictures and thus to occupy the external space personally. The thesis advanced in the catalogue that modern art is gradually detaching itself from any mimetic referentiality to preexisting nature is contradicted by the situations of comparison set in the exhibition by the arrangements of the works of art and the spatial interplay with the visitor's body. By separating the "isms," Barr also splits the *tertia*—on one side, the motif; on the other side, the formalistic manner—to provoke the temporal experience of the development of art up to "pure-abstract" geometric art. The temporal comparison that results in the understanding of an evolution does not take place within one display or room, but between the separated "isms" and their highlighted mimetic or nonmimetic manner. "Stylistic

---

50 See Platt, Modernism, Formalism, and Politics, 285. Pablo Picasso, *The Studio*, 1928, oil on canvas, 59 cm x 84 cm. New York, Museum of Modern Art, Gift of Walter P. Chrysler Jr.; Pablo Picasso, *The Painter and His Model*, 1928, oil on canvas, 130.2 x 97.2 cm. New York, Collection Sidney Janis.

Figs. 7 and 8: Installation view of the exhibition ›Cubism and Abstract Art‹. MoMA, NY, March 2, 1936 – April 19, 1936.

(Fig. 7) Gelatin silver print,4 4 1/2 x 6 1/2" (11.4 x 16.5 cm). Photographer: Beaumont Newhall (copyright: The Museum of Modern Art, NY). Photographic Archive. The Museum of Modern Art Archives, New York. Object Number: IN46.23. New York, Museum of Modern Art (MoMA). (Fig. 8) Gelatin silver print,4 4 1/2 x 6 1/2" (11.4 x 16.5 cm). Photographer: Beaumont Newhall (copyright: The Museum of Modern Art, NY). Photographic Archive. The Museum of Modern Art Archives, New York. Object Number: IN46.24A. New York, Museum of Modern Art (MoMA).

developments"[51] connected to modernism are thus presented on the back of the *tertium* of a mimetic motif.

III. Abstraction by comparing formalistic issues: *documenta I*

Turning now to the practices of comparing at the first *documenta*, I shall show that almost the same narration of modernism—a formalistic promotion of abstraction as the art of the present day and, most of all, the future[52]—was fulfilled by a completely different manner of comparing. The *documenta I* bearing the title "Art of the 20th Century" was organized by Arnold Bode and Werner Haftmann in 1955 to be presented in the heavily war-damaged Fridericianum in Kassel.[53] Bode's aim was to

---

51   Platt, Modernism, Formalism, and Politics, 286.
52   Hoffmann therefore describes the concept of art underlying the *documenta I* as connected closely to the discourse of modernism within the USA: "Zugleich positionierten sich die Kasseler Kunstereignisse mit ihrer exklusiven Ausrichtung auf die Abstraktion als Antipode zum Sozialistischen Realismus und flankierten damit eine insbesondere von der USA forcierte Kulturpolitik." Hoffmann, *Ausstellungen als Wissensordnungen*, 72.
53   The exhibition took place from July 15 to September 18, 1955. For the first *documenta*, see Harald Kimpel, *Documenta. Mythos und Wirklichkeit*, Köln 1997; Walter Grasskamp, documenta – Die Kunst des XX. Jahrhunderts. Internationale Ausstellung im Museum Fridericianum in Kassel. 15. Juli bis 18. September 1955, in: Bernd Klüser/Katharina Hegewisch (eds.), *Die Kunst*

reconnect with the European modern art that the National Socialists had banned as "degenerate"—and even to show its continuity within contemporary German art.[54] Thus in 1955, the intention was also to take stock of contemporary art and to record its development; but again, with regard to abstraction as the teleological quality of modernist painting. Therefore, in his publication *Painting in the Twentieth Century*, which was published in 1954, the art historian Werner Haftmann promoted the notion that there had been a historical change within painting from mimetic painting up to abstract painting:

> "Modern painting is indeed the most striking expression of the universal process by which one cultural epoch with a long history yields its place to another. It bears witness to the decline of an old conception of reality and the emergence of a new one. The view of the world that is being superseded today is that which was first shaped by the early Florentine masters with their naïve enthusiasm for the concrete reality of the visible world, which they set out to define."[55]

Here again, we remember Barr's introductory text about the change from the mimetic to the abstract picture of modernism. Haftmann also goes back to Renaissance art to explain this shift. Haftmann, who was mainly in charge of the selection of artworks in *documenta I*, was, like Barr, driven by a formalist understanding of a teleological development in art history that aims toward abstraction.[56] The exhibition accordingly presented works of art from the most important trends in twentieth-century European art such as Fauvism, Cubism, and Expressionism.[57] However, non-European art, socially engaged art, and figurative art such as, for instance, the "Social Realism" prescribed by the East German state (GDR), were left out.[58] Against this backdrop, Werner Haftmann, who had

---

    der Ausstellung. Eine Dokumentation dreißig exemplarischer Kunstausstellungen dieses Jahrhunderts, Frankfurt a. M./Leipzig 1991, 116–125.

54 This is the main thesis of the chapter "Coming to terms with the past" in: Harald Kimpel, *documenta. Die Überschau. Fünf Jahrzehnte Weltkunstausstellung in Stichwörtern*, Köln 2002, 11–26. Walter Grasskamp also emphasizes the "comparison" (101, 113) as a main practice in this exhibition with regard to narration of an ongoing modernism and narration of "German discontinuity" (98). Walter Grasskamp, *Die unbewältigte Moderne. Kunst und Öffentlichkeit*, München 1989. See also Walter Grasskamp, documenta I 1955, in: Bernd Klüser/Katharina Hegewisch (eds.), *Die Kunst der Ausstellung. Eine Dokumentation dreißig exemplarischer Kunstausstellungen dieses Jahrhunderts*, Frankfurt a. M./Leipzig 1991, 116–125, see 117. Kurt Winkler, II. documenta 59 – Kunst nach 1945, in: Uwe M. Schneede (ed.), *Stationen der Moderne. Die bedeutenden Kunstausstellungen des 20. Jahrhunderts in Deutschland*, Berlin 1988, 426–473, see 427.

55 Werner Haftmann, *Painting in the Twentieth Century* [German Original 1954], London 1960, 10.

56 See Hoffmann, *Ausstellungen als Wissensordnungen*, 76.

57 Cf. Charlotte Klonk, Die phantasmagorische Welt der ersten documenta und ihr Erbe, in: Dorothea von Hantelmann/Carolin Meister (eds.), *Die Ausstellung. Politik eines Rituals*, Zürich/Berlin 2010, 131–160, see 142.

58 Cf. Klonk, Die phantasmagorische Welt der ersten documenta und ihr Erbe, 142.

assisted Bode in preparing the exhibition, wrote emphatically: "Now, for the first time, we can compare how European countries are reacting to each other by their present artistic expressions."[59] To show this, Haftmann and also Bode wanted to focus on the manner of depiction, not on the motif.

For this formalist purpose, Bode set one artwork by an internationally renowned artist next to one by a contemporary German artist in the central space on the first floor of the Fridericianum: On the one forefront, he hung Picasso's work *Girl before a Mirror*; on the other, he installed Fritz Winter's remittance work *Komposition vor Blau und Gelb* at the opposite ends of the exhibition hall (Fig. 9 and Fig. 10).[60]

Figs. 9 and 10 (following page): Installation view of the large painting hall, Museum Fridericianum, documenta I (1955).

59 Werner Haftmann, Einleitung, in: Arnold Bode (ed.), *documenta – Kunst des XX. Jahrhunderts. Internationale Ausstellung im Museum Fridericianum in Kassel*, München 1955, 15–25, see 25.
60 Pablo Picasso, *Girl before a Mirror*, 1932, oil on canvas, 162.3 x 130.2 cm. New York, Museum of Modern Art, Gift of Mrs. Simon Guggenheim. Fritz Winter, *Komposition vor Blau und Gelb* (title today: *Durchbrechendes Rot*), 1955, 381 x 615 cm, oil on canvas. Wadersloh-Liesborn, Museum Abtei Liesborn des Kreises Warendorf, Leihgabe Fritz-Winter-Haus, Ahlen. See for Winter's painting, Anna Rühl, Ausgewählt. Der neue Kernbestand der Fritz-Winter-Stiftung, in: *Fritz Winter. Ausgewählt. Kernbestand der Fritz-Winter-Stiftung*, München 2018, 55–95, esp. 71–72. For the confrontation of these two paintings, see Klonk, Die phantasmagorische Welt der ersten documenta und ihr Erbe, 143; Klonk, *Spaces of Experience*, 179; Christian Spies, Fritz Winter. Kontinuität und Experiment, in: Wilfried Utermann (ed.), *Fritz Winter. Vom Bauhaus zur Documenta*, Dortmund 2018, 34–47, see 34.

As had been the case with Picasso's paintings at the exhibition on *Cubism and Abstract Art*, the viewer stood between the two artworks, and this required an alternating turn of the head and gaze. Moreover, the viewer was also placed between twenty years of art history, the twenty years of fascism:[61] Picasso's work is from 1932 and Fritz Winter's piece of art from 1954/55. Hence, Haftmann and Bode installed a temporal comparison that functions on the basis of diachronism[62] in contrast to Barr's temporal comparison that was based on what was nearly a synchronism of the artworks. But to make this comparison possible within the Fridericianum, something actually had to be *done*: The size of Winter's painting had to be trimmed 20 cm on all four sides to realize the confrontation with Picasso at the front ends of the great hall.[63] Nevertheless, there was a huge difference within the size and dimensions of these two confronted paintings: whereas Winter's painting takes the size of the whole wall, Picasso's *Girl before a Mirror* is surrounded by much painted wall space. But also the *tertium* of the comparison in Kassel is completely different to the *tertium* of the motif in the exhibition *Cubism and Abstract Art*. Whereas Picasso's piece presents a girl in front of a mirror reflecting a completely blurry image that is impossible to discern (Fig. 9); we see in Fritz Winter's composition

---

61   Cf. Hoffmann, *Ausstellungen als Wissensordnungen*, 79.
62   Cf. Hoffmann, *Ausstellungen als Wissensordnungen*, 78.
63   Cf. Iris Herpers, Fritz Winter, "Durchbrechendes Rot". Restaurierung und Transport eines großformatigen documenta I-Gemäldes, in: *VDR-Beiträge zur Erhaltung von Kunst- und Kulturgut*, Bonn 2011, 61–67, see 63. I thank Peter Gaida for the suggestion regarding these circumstances.

a play of forms and colors that presents no likeness and thus subverts any referentiality (Fig. 10). This comparison offers no *similarity* and no *tertium* on the level of a motif. Instead, the *tertium* is on the level of formal issues such as colors and linear forms. This comparison constructs the thesis of an augmenting rejection of referentiality: The development of art aims teleologically toward abstraction. The juxtapositioning with Picasso's *Girl before a Mirror* detaches Winter's composition from any reference to antecedent nature, and hence presents it as pointing into the future (a process ongoing since the early Avant-gardes of the twentieth century, a progress that was destroyed by the Nazi regime).[64] The comparative gaze prompted by Bode in this microsituation does not aim at the motif but at the manner of depiction, and is, in this case, even more formalistic than most of the comparisons we can find in Barr's *Cubism and Abstract Art*.

Looking at these two exhibitions, one can consider that they both follow the idea of a teleological development of art that finds its aim in the abstract mode characterizing modernism. Both exhibitions promote a linear development of art based on the change in the formalistic manner. But a close look at the microsituations of comparing within these two exhibitions reveals differences in the relational construction of abstraction. Most of the comparative views initiated in Barr's exhibition *Cubism and Abstract Art* are based on the figurative, still mimetic, motif. Beyond that, most of the comparisons staged in this exhibition are synchronistic, because they deal with comparata of more or less the same time. This is in direct contrast to Bode's and Haftmann's use of the comparative view: They arrange diachronic comparata that bear formalistic *tertia*. Both exhibitions promote the western discourse of modernism, but the narration of the development of art is shown via different manners of temporal comparisons: In *Cubism and Abstract Art*, abstraction is bound back to the past, whereas the first *documenta* evolves abstraction only around formalistic issues on the level of the present and the future. In both exhibitions, the analyses of the practices of comparing disclose the construction of modernism and abstraction as relational qualities.

But this relational quality often becomes naturalized through the practices of comparing that are provoked within exhibitions: At the end of *documenta 14*, the state of the art embodied by the *Parthenon of Books* has been revealed to be nothing more than a scaffolding and a construction next to the Fridericianum. Again, the *tertium* of the comparative view is a mimetic motif: the antique Parthenon as a sign for democracy but also for the idealism of classicism. Perhaps, therefore, this new occasion for comparing has also evidenced that "learning from Athens" may well sound intriguing in current-day politics; but in art history, it just leads to classical frames of reference and genealogies.

---

64 See Grasskamp, *Die unbewältigte Moderne*, 113.

References

ALBERTI, Leon Battista, *Della Pittura – Über die Malkunst*, ed. by Oskar Bätschmann/Sandra Gianfreda, Darmstadt 2007.

BARR, Alfred H. (ed.), *Cubism and Abstract Art. Painting, Sculpture, Constructions, Photography, Architecture, Industrial Art, Theatre, Films, Posters, Typography*, New York 1936.

BODE, Arnold (ed.), *documenta – Kunst des XX. Jahrhunderts. Internationale Ausstellung im Museum Fridericianum in Kassel*, München 1955.

BOEHM, Gottfried, Abstraktion und Realität. Zum Verhältnis von Kunst und Kunstphilosophie in der Moderne [1990], in: Gottfried Boehm, *Die Sichtbarkeit der Zeit. Studien zum Bild in der Moderne*, ed. by Ralph Ubl, Paderborn 2017, 173–185.

BOEHM, Gottfried, Bild und Zeit, in: Hannelore Paflik (Ed.): *Das Phänomen Zeit in Kunst und Wissenschaft*, Weinheim 1987, 1–24.

BISMARCK, Beatrice von, Der Teufel trägt Geschichtlichkeit oder Im Look der Provokation: When Attitudes become Form, Bern 1969/Venice 2013, in: Eva Kernbauer (ed.), *Kunstgeschichtlichkeit. Historizität und Anachronie in der Gegenwartskunst*, Paderborn 2015, 233–248.

BISMARCK, Beatrice von, The Exhibition as Collective, in: Kai-Uwe Hemken (ed.), *Kritische Szenografie. Die Kunstausstellung im 21. Jahrhundert*, Bielefeld 2015, 185–199.

BISMARCK, Beatrice von et al. (eds.), *Timing. On the Temporal Dimension of Exhibiting*, (Cultures of the Curatorial, vol. 2), Berlin 2014.

BRENNAN, Marcia, *Curating Consciousness. Mysticism and the Modern Museum*, London 2010.

BUCHLOH, Benjamin H. D., From Faktura to Factography, in: Annette Michelson et al. (eds.), *October: The First Decade, 1976–1986*, Cambridge 1987, 77–113.

DICKERMAN, Leah, Abstraction in 1936: Cubism and Abstract Art at the Museum of Modern Art, in: Leah Dickerman (ed.), *Inventing Abstraction 1910–1925: how a radical idea changed modern art*, London 2012, 364–369.

EGENHOFER, Sebastian, *Abstraktion, Kapitalismus, Subjektivität. Die Wahrheitsfunktion des Werks in der Moderne*, München 2008

EPPLE, Angelika/ERHART, Walter, Die Welt beobachten. Praktiken des Vergleichens, in: Angelika Epple/Walter Erhart (eds.), *Die Welt beobachten. Praktiken des Vergleichens*, Frankfurt a. M./New York 2015, 7–34.

FOSTER, Hal, Museum Tales of Twentieth-Century Art, in: *Studies of Art* 74 (2009), 253–375

GENETTE, Gérard, *Paratexte. Das Buch vom Beiwerk des Buches* [French Original 1987], Frankfurt a. M. 1989.

GLICENSTEIN, Jérome, *L'Art: une histoire d'expositions*, Paris 2009.

GRASSKAMP, Walter, documenta – Die Kunst des XX. Jahrhunderts. Internationale Ausstellung im Museum Fridericianum in Kassel. 15. Juli bis 18. September 1955, in: Bernd Klüser/Katharina Hegewisch (eds.), *Die Kunst der Ausstellung. Eine Dokumentation dreißig exemplarischer Kunstausstellungen dieses Jahrhunderts*, Frankfurt a. M./Leipzig 1991.

GRASSKAMP, Walter, documenta I 1955, in: Bernd Klüser/Katharina Hegewisch (eds.), *Die Kunst der Ausstellung. Eine Dokumentation dreißig exemplarischer Kunstausstellungen dieses Jahrhunderts*, Frankfurt a. M./Leipzig 1991, 116–125.

GRASSKAMP, Walter, *Die unbewältigte Moderne. Kunst und Öffentlichkeit*, München 1989.

GRAVE, Johannes, Form, Struktur und Zeit. Bildliche Formkonstellationen und ihre rezeptionsästhetische Temporalität, in: Michael Gamper et al. (eds.), *Zeit der Form – Formen der Zeit* (Ästhetische Eigenzeiten, vol. 2), Hannover 2016, 139–162.

GRAVE, Johannes, Vergleichen als Praxis. Vorüberlegungen zu einer praxistheoretisch orientierten Untersuchung von Vergleichen, in: Angelika Epple/Walter Erhart (eds.), *Die Welt beobachten. Praktiken des Vergleichens*, Frankfurt a. M./New York 2015, 135–159.

GRAVE, Johannes, Der Akt des Bildbetrachtens. Überlegungen zur rezeptionsästhetischen Temporalität des Bildes, in: Michael Gamper/Helmut Hühn (eds.), *Zeit der Darstellung. Ästhetische Eigenzeiten in Kunst, Literatur und Wissenschaft*, Hannover 2014, 51-72.

GUILBEUT, Serge, *Wie New York die Idee der Modernen Kunst gestohlen hat. Abstrakter Expressionismus, Freiheit und Kalter Krieg* [1983], Dresden 1997.

HAFTMANN, Werner, *Painting in the Twentieth Century* [German Original 1954], London 1960.

HAFTMANN, Werner, Einleitung, in: Arnold Bode (ed.), *documenta – Kunst des XX. Jahrhunderts. Internationale Ausstellung im Museum Fridericianum in Kassel*, München 1955, 15–25.

HANTELMANN, Dorothea von/MEISTER, Carolin, Einleitung, in: Dorothea von Hantelman/Carolin Meister (eds.), *Die Ausstellung. Politik eines Rituals*, Zürich/Berlin 2010, 7–18.

HERPERS, Iris, Fritz Winter, "Durchbrechendes Rot". Restaurierung und Transport eines großformatigen documenta I-Gemäldes, in: *VDR-Beiträge zur Erhaltung von Kunst- und Kulturgut*, Bonn 2011, 61–67.

HOFFMANN, Katja, *Ausstellungen als Wissensordnungen. Zur Transformation des Kunstbegriffs auf der Documenta 11*, Bielefeld 2013.

KANTOR, Sybil Gordon, *Alfred H. Barr, Jr. and the intellectual origins of the Museum of Modern Art*, Massachusetts 2002.

KIMPEL, Harald, *documenta. Die Überschau. Fünf Jahrzehnte Weltkunstausstellung in Stichwörtern*, Köln 2002.

KIMPEL, Harald, *Documenta. Mythos und Wirklichkeit*, Köln 1997.

KLONK, Charlotte, Die phantasmagorische Welt der ersten documenta und ihr Erbe, in: Dorothea von Hantelmann/Carolin Meister (eds.), *Die Ausstellung. Politik eines Rituals*, Zürich/Berlin 2010, 131–160.

KLONK, Charlotte, *Spaces of Experience. Art Gallery Interiors from 1800 to 2000*, New Haven/London 2009.

LINDLAY, Christine, *Art in the Cold War. From Vladivostok to Kalamazoo, 1945–1962*, London 1990.

LOCHER, Hubert, Die Kunst des Ausstellens. Anmerkungen zu einem unübersichtlichen Diskurs, in: Hans D. Huber/Hubert Locher/Karin Schulte (eds.), *Kunst des Ausstellens. Beiträge, Statements, Diskussionen*, Ostfildern-Ruit 2002, 15–30.

LOWRY, Glenn D., Abstraction in 1936: Barr's Diagrams, in: Leah Dickerman (ed.), *Inventing Abstraction 1910–1925: how a radical idea changed modern art*, London 2012, 359–363.

MITCHELL, William J. T., *Picture Theory. Essays on Verbal and Visual Representations*, Chicago/London 1994, 231–236.

O'DOHERTY, Brian, *Inside the White Cube* [Original in *Artforum* 1976], introd. by Thomas McEvilley, Santa Monica/San Francisco 1999.

PLATT, Susan Noyes, Modernism, Formalism, and Politics: The "Cubism and Abstract Art" Exhibition of 1936 at The Museum of Modern Art, in: *Art Journal* 47 (4/1988), 284–295.

POCHAT, Götz, *Bild – Zeit. Zeitgestalt und Erzählstruktur in der bildenden Kunst von den Anfängen bis zur frühen Neuzeit*, Wien 1996.

POMIAN, Krzysztof, *L'Ordre du temps*, Paris 1984.

RÜHL, Anna, Ausgewählt. Der neue Kernbestand der Fritz-Winter-Stiftung, in: *Fritz Winter. Ausgewählt. Kernbestand der Fritz-Winter-Stiftung*, München 2018, 55–95.

SCHAPIRO, Meyer, The Nature of Abstract Art, in: *Marxist Quarterly* 1 (1/1937), 78–97.

SCHMIDT-BURKHARDT, Astrit, *Stammbäume der Kunst. Zur Genealogie der Avantgarde*, Berlin 2005.

SCHMIDT BURKHARDT, Astrit, Shaping Modernism. Alfred Barr's genealogy of art, in: *Word & Image* 16 (4/2000), 387–400.

SPIES, Christian, Fritz Winter. Kontinuität und Experiment, in: Wilfried Utermann (ed.), *Fritz Winter. Vom Bauhaus zur Documenta*, Dortmund 2018, 34–47.

STANISZEWSKI, Mary Anne, *The Power of Display. A History of Exhibition Installations at the Museum of Modern Art*, London 1998.

THEISSING, Heinrich, *Die Zeit im Bild*, Darmstadt 1987.

THÜRLEMANN, Felix, *Mehr als ein Bild. Für eine Kunstgeschichte des hyperimage*, München 2013.

THÜRLEMANN, Felix, Vom Einzelbild zum hyperimage. Eine neue Herausforderung für die kunsthistorische Hermeneutik, in: Gerd Blum et al., (eds.), *Pendant Plus*, Berlin 2012, 23–46.

TUFTE, Eward R., *Beautiful Evidence*, Ceshire 2006.

Voss, Julia, Wer schreibt Kunstgeschichte? Kritik, Kunstwissenschaft, Markt und Museum, in: *Zeitschrift für Kunstgeschichte* 78 (2015), 16–31.

Weisenseel, Anja, *Bildbetrachtung in Bewegung. Der Rezipient in Texten und Bildern zur Pariser Salonausstellung des 18. Jahrhunderts* (Ars et Scientia. Schriften zur Kunstwissenschaft, vol. 14), Berlin/Boston 2017.

Winkler, Kurt, II. documenta 59 – Kunst nach 1945, in: Uwe M. Schneede (ed.), *Stationen der Moderne. Die bedeutenden Kunstausstellungen des 20. Jahrhunderts in Deutschland*, Berlin 1988, 426–473.

Photo Credits

Fig. 1 and 3–8: © 2020. Digital image, The Museum of Modern Art, New York/Scala, Firenze.

Fig. 2: *Cubism and Abstract Art. Painting, Sculpture, Constructions, Photography, Architecture, Industrial Art, Theatre, Films, Posters, Typography*, ed. by Alfred H. Barr, New York 1936, 10.

Fig. 9–10: © documenta Archiv (Dauerleihgabe der Stadt Kassel)/Foto: Günther Becker.

Comparing in the Digital Age
The Transformation of Practices

Anna Neubert/Silke Schwandt

Abstract

What do we do when we compare? This central question of the Research Center at Bielefeld University does not only apply to historical actors but to us and our contemporary practices as well. This article focuses on these contemporary practices, questioning the transformation of practices that accompany the ongoing digitization of all fields of society. The lens through which we observe these transformations are digital practices of comparing in the academic field. The article discusses these practices as a change in scholarly practices and methods but also as a change on the larger scale of how digitization needs to be analyzed as a motor of cultural transformation.

Introduction

Comparing would seem to be a ubiquitous operation in our everyday lives. We constantly compare ourselves to others, we compare prices at the supermarket, or we use comparative platforms on the Web to do such comparisons for us. Applying for jobs or schools, moving to another city, and choosing a suitable neighborhood to raise our children—all these activities are accompanied by practices of comparing. Using Internet platforms and digital devices for these comparisons leads us straight to the question presented in this chapter: What does it mean to compare in the digital age? At first glance, comparing in the digital age connotes comparing things to each other digitally, or comparing digital or digitized objects. However, it is also about comparing lots of data. Going back to the impressions from comparing in everyday life, large amounts of data seem to enhance the reliability of comparisons. But is that true? Or do we merely rely on the sense that having lots of information will naturally improve its reliability?

Likewise, in academia, comparing is one of the most important and most well-known scholarly practices. And, as with our everyday examples, comparing in the digital age poses quite a few challenges to this practice and requires innovations. Dealing with digital data and digital objects changes the way in which comparing is being done across all the sciences. It furthers the development of tools and algorithms that help us deal with lots of information at one and the same time. But when algorithms compare, are they actually doing the same thing as researchers did before?[1]

The *computational turn* has long since arrived in the humanities and "is fundamentally changing the way in which we engage in the research process [...] affecting both the epistemologies and ontologies that underlie a research programme."[2] Furthermore, libraries, archives, and other memory institutions have engaged in many digitization projects, making their material available in ways accessible to everyone. But what does that imply? In which ways are research questions linked to the digitization of historical or literary sources?

For as many as nearly 70 years now, researchers from across various fields of the humanities have been developing tools[3] and standardized formats[4] that help to create and analyze digital objects. Most of these projects can be placed in the field of digital humanities—"a genuinely intellectual endeavor with its own professional practices, rigorous standards, and exciting theoretical explorations."[5] One of its main lines of research addresses the question how research practices—ranging from digitization to the development of new methodologies with their own questions and perspectives—is changing in the digital age.

Therefore, this chapter will follow a twofold perspective: On the one hand, it will analyze the transformation of the scholarly practice of comparing in the digital age; on the other hand, it will look at historical practices and their digital representation. After taking a closer look at selected examples, it introduces a research approach implemented within the Collaborative Research Center 1288 for working on a "*Begriffsgeschichte*" of the "Practices of Comparing." It will close by thinking about the various challenges and opportunities the digital holds for exploring the past.

---

1   Cf. Elena Esposito, *Reading With Algorithms: Interpretation and Information in Digital Text Processing*, 2018 (unpublished manuscript).
2   David M. Berry, The Computational Turn: Thinking About the Digital Humanities, in: *Culture Machine* 12 (2011), 1–12, see 1.
3   For a first overview, see TAPor at http://tapor.ca/home or DiRT – Digital Research Tools at http://dirtdirectory.org/ [both links last accessed June 8, 2018].
4   For instance, the Text Enocding Initiative (TEI) at http://www.tei-c.org/index.xml or CIDOC-CRM at http://www.cidoc-crm.org/ [both links last accessed June 8, 2018].
5   N. Katherine Hayles, *How We Think: Digital Media and Contemporary Technogenesis*, Chicago 2012, 24.

Comparing as a scholarly practice

In a talk back in 2000, the professor of English and university librarian John Unsworth proposed a model for translating scholarly practices into the digital age that has served as a basis for many discussions on modeling scholarly workflows until today. He deliberated the question: "which methods have humanities researchers in common, and how might our tools reflect this?"[6] This question is central to the whole enterprise of digital humanities and all related disciplines. Digitization provides us with a lot of material that can be viewed online and stored in corpora and repositories. But it is the documentation and advancement of scholarly practices that enable the further development of digital methods.

Unsworth identified seven scholarly practices that he described as having "some basic functions common to scholarly activity across disciplines, over time, and independent of theoretical orientation."[7] These operations thus consist of "discovering, annotating, comparing, referring, sampling, illustrating, and representing."[8] The intention in collecting these as basic research functions is to make them transferable into the field of computing. It is only by modeling these practices in a machine-readable way that we can start to translate them properly into algorithms and other forms of technologically enhanced methods.

Comparing, according to Unsworth, is

> "one of the most basic scholarly operations—a functional primitive of humanities research, as it were. Scholars in many different disciplines, working with many different kinds of materials, want to compare several (sometimes many) objects of analysis, whether those objects are texts, images, films, or any other species of human production".[9]

Researchers compare in order to make sense of data—data being understood as a general term encompassing all kinds of research material. Following Unsworth, several factors are involved in comparing:

- Comparing relates to space. Researchers can only compare things that share the same space—be it, for example, objects in a museum or printed books on a table. The same thing might be true for concepts or ideas shared in the space

---

6   John Unsworth, Scholarly primitives: What methods do humanities researchers have in common, and how might our tools reflect this? in: *University of Virginia*, May 13, 2000, URL: http://www.people.virginia.edu/~jmu2m/Kings.5-00/primitives.html [last accessed June 8, 2018].
7   Unsworth, Scholarly primitives.
8   Unsworth, Scholarly primitives.
9   Unsworth, Scholarly primitives.

- of a common imagination. Virtual space changes our spatial perception. It lets us put things together in one space that normally do not appear together.
- Using a computer program or a comparative website to compare allows more operations in less time. The relations of thousands of tokens can be compared to each other in seconds.
- Comparing in the digital age, according to Unsworth, is free from hierarchies. We can compare anything we want, and we shall still generate a statistically or mathematically valid result. Also, comparing can overcome existing categorizations and generate new ones. Seeing things in relation that we did not see before can provoke new interpretations. This is one way in which practices of comparing can initialize, change, or stabilize order.
- Comparing in the digital age enables us to see new relations between objects and preserve them by way of creating linked data. Through linking, or annotating, the researcher can preserve all logical or structural relations in the material.

The range of transformations in the practices of comparing through the digital can be illustrated very well in different areas of humanities research. Many digital research projects known in the scientific community emphasize important aspects of developments in the digital practices of comparing and demonstrate a high standard of data models, visualizations, aggregations, and analyses of their respective research material. To understand the change in these practices, the selected examples listed below showcase the altered parameters. They shape a new approach to the future of processes of scholarly research and may also modify the scholarly primitives themselves.

Premises and requirements for digital research in the humanities are manifold[10] and rely on various basic conditions such as the digital representation of research objects and several layers of data that allow the research process to be performed. Digital tasks that are carried out on this basis then include "statistical processing [...] linking [...] modelling [...] the creation of structured data [...] and iterative editing and version control."[11] These practices are shaping the research process profoundly, and they pave the path for new ways of making analogue comparisons in digital space as well as enabling new practices of comparing that were not yet possible without data processing in the background.

The following selection of projects will grant a first insight into the scope and limits of comparing in the digital age for humanities researchers.[12] The examples

---

10   Cf. Jeffrey Schnapp, A short guide to the digital humanities, in: Anne Burdick et al. (eds.), *Digital_Humanities*, Cambridge 2012, SG2—SG15.
11   Schnapp, A short guide, SG3.
12   Needless to mention that the chosen examples represent a small scale of possible DH projects that showcase new possibilities of the practices of comparing in the digital age. The

highlight two modes of how the digital is transforming researchers' practices. Examined are, first, the ways in which the digital is changing general research practices, methods, and theories; and, second, the ways in which research material and findings are being published and made available. The wide range of humanities data in all cases is not to be dismissed and is thus always the key component of the modeling process. The high heterogeneity of data and the different approaches to theories and methods provide many opportunities for digital endeavors to create new ways of understanding research materials.

Distant Reading

Our first example is a chart generated with Google Ngram Viewer.[13] It shows two separate lines: one representing the use of the word *comparison*; the other, the use of the word *comparing*. The y-axis shows the frequency of the respective term; the timeline on the x-axis represents the years ranging from 1600 to 2000.

Fig. 1: Chart for "comparison" and "comparing" in the English corpus from 1600 to 2000.

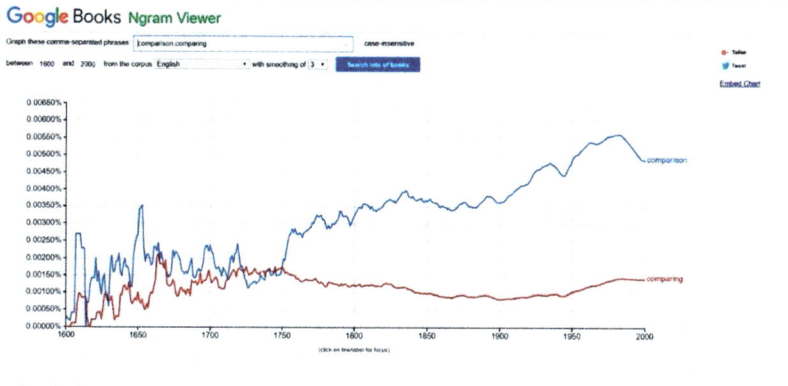

There are two levels of comparison linked to this figure: One level concerns the chart itself and what it suggests to the eyes of the researcher. We immediately start to relate the lines to each other, noticing the way they rise, sink and cross. The other

---

selection derives from the personal background of the two authors who have years of experience in the field of digital humanities and decided that these were the projects that best emphasized their argument on the transformation of practices.

13 Cf. Google Ngram Viewer, URL: https://books.google.com/ngrams [last accessed June 8, 2018].

level concerns the data represented by the graphs. Linking the data points in the form of a line compares them to each other in relation to their respective values on the axes. And although the operation seems natural and facilitated by the way of visualization, there are questions to be asked considering the way the data has been compiled.

- Although the chart shows percentages for the frequency of the words at a certain point in time, it does not tell us the amount of books providing the basis for this calculation. It is rather improbable that there are as many publications in Google books for the seventeenth century as there are for the twentieth century.
- The chart also does not give any information on the kind of data that it represents. The observer does not know which books or genres she or he is looking at. However, for humanities researchers, the provision of corpus data is important for the scientific value and the interpretation of findings.
- Reliable information that can be taken from the graph is that the two lines cross around 1750, and whereas the red line for "comparing" remains relatively stable, the blue line for "comparison" rises. Without further information, however, this observation remains superficial.

For digital comparing as a scholarly practice, this carries several insights: Graphs guide the practice of comparing by specifying the way in which we compare. They do so by ways of visualization. Therefore, the reflection on practices of comparison needs to comprise the reflection on visualization practices. Such practices determine practices of interpretation because they decide which data is represented and therefore have to be part of the analysis.[14]

With their work on digital literary sources, Franco Moretti and his colleagues at the Stanford Literary Lab[15] serve as our second example. Moretti has coined the paradigm of "distant reading."[16] In his article on "Conjectures in World Literature," first published in 2000, he motivates this concept by referring to the work of Immanuel Wallerstein, who, like almost any other researcher, bases his synthesis on the analyses carried out by others before him. In order to write about world literature, Moretti argues, one has to do the same and keep one's distance from the texts themselves to see the system. "But in that case, literary history will become [...] second hand: a patchwork of other people's research, without a single direct textual reading."[17] In a way, Moretti makes the argument for Google Ngrams when

---

14 Cf. Silke Schwandt, Digitale Methoden für die Historische Semantik. Auf den Spuren von Begriffen in digitalen Korpora, in: *Geschichte und Gesellschaft* 44 (2018), 107–134.
15 Stanford Literary Lab, URL: https://litlab.stanford.edu/ [last accessed June 8, 2018].
16 Cf. Franco Moretti, *Distant Reading*, Konstanz 2016.
17 Moretti, *Distant Reading*, 44.

he says "we know how to read texts, now let's learn how not to read them" and offers a definition for what he means by "distant reading":

> "distance [...] is a condition of knowledge: it allows you to focus on units that are much smaller or much larger than the text: devices, themes, tropes—or genres and systems. And if, between the very small and the very large, the text itself disappears, well, it is one of those cases when one can justifiably say, less is more. If we want to understand the system in its entirety, we must accept losing something."[18]

Following this train of thought, that which we move aside for a new practice is the single text and the practice of "close reading."

This is not the place to trace Moretti's arguments and those of his opponents in their entirety, but what is important for the transformation of scholarly practices is that there is a controversy about how we should read, if we should read, and what we should read. Joseph North in his book "*Literary Criticism*," published in 2017, argues that Moretti's method "is not really reading at all: rather, it is a method that, when it appears elsewhere as the uncontroversial stock-in-trade of many scientific or social-scientific disciplines, is unproblematically labeled things like 'data analysis,' 'data mining' (if using specialized search engines), or similar."[19] Here, it seems, the argument is not about the fact that practices change and develop once the material they deal with changes. Rather, it is about the labeling that Moretti chose for his new perspective on how to write a history of world literature. North continues:

> "The phrase [distant reading] seems to be offered as a kind of antonym to "close reading," but [...] the two terms are not opposites at all, because they do not refer to the same order of things: the real opposition here is that between data analysis and reading per se. Our question then becomes as to what is gained by framing an argument against reading-in-general as an argument against "close reading" in particular".[20]

Another tool that illustrates a different approach to the dichotomy of close and distant reading is the tool "DiaCollo"[21] available from the German Text Archive. This provides scholars with the possibility to look up typical collocations of a keyword over a particular period of time. By "visualizing global features,"[22] it shows fre-

---

18 Moretti, *Distant Reading*, 48.
19 Joseph North, *Literary Criticism. A Concise Political History*, Cambridge/London 2017, 110.
20 North, *Literary Criticism*, 112; Cf. Esposito, *Reading with Algorithms*.
21 Cf. DiaCollo, URL: http://kaskade.dwds.de/dstar/dta/diacollo/ [last accessed April 17, 2018].
22 Stefan Jänicke et al., On Close and Distant Reading in Digital Humanities: A Survey and Future Challenges, in: Rita Borgo/Fabio Ganovelli/Ivan Viola (eds.), *Europgraphics Conference on Vizualization (EuroVis)—STARs*, The Eurographics Association, 2015, 2.

quently used words and changes in the meaning of those words.[23] Figure 2 shows the beginning of a timeline that presents all words related to the term *"Vergleich*"* from 1850 to 1940 running on the corpus of the German Text Archive.

Fig. 2: Screenshot—DiaCollo with the term "Vergleich*" from 1850- 1940.

Within the tool, there are various scenarios of comparing that allow the user to interact with the research material: the first one being a keyword and its collocations; the second option being the comparison of two similar keywords by differences in their collocations in different time periods; and the third option being the comparison of several similar keywords with regard to their frequency of use in certain time periods. These presentations benefit from close reading by implication and enable new ways of interacting with the textual features.[24]

It can be argued that we have to bridge the divide between close and distant reading and take the changes in scholarly practices brought by the digital age seriously. Looking at big data and comparing quantitative data offers new perspectives that might lead to new interpretations.[25] However, we have to acknowledge the methods and traditions of our respective disciplines and try to integrate the new methods into the old. It is always necessary to go back to the text after looking at the big picture in order to come up with a solid interpretation of the material. It is important to zoom in and zoom out, to move from distant back to close. It is imperative for the fruitful implementation of digital methods in the humanities to carefully design these methods.

Another field of research within the digital humanities is concerned with editing texts. Our following examples thus provide an insight into how comparing in the field of scholarly editing is transformed through the digital.

---

23   See https://clarin-d.de/de/kollokationsanalyse-in-diachroner-perspektive [last accessed April 17, 2018].
24   Cf. Schwandt, Digitale Methoden.
25   Cf. Schwandt, Digitale Methoden, 131.

Digital music edition

Like any other scholarly editor, music editors produced and still produce their critical editions by traveling from archive to archive around the globe, scanning through different sources, and taking notes. In order to publish a critical edition of a musical piece, editors need to compare over space and time and therefore have to rely solely on their notes and their memories of similarities and differences in their sources. Furthermore, money and access restrictions to important sources complicate progress and sometimes make the management of the formation process distressing.[26] Published versions of the music edition—in most cases[27] —consist of two printed parts: the edited text in one part and the critical apparatus with results of the transacted comparisons in another part.[28] Music editions are sold at a high price, so that it is almost always only libraries that can afford to buy and provide access to this field of research. Because access to and dealing with these special research materials in and after the research process is not always an easy task, the digital provides new opportunities to deal with various obstacles and initiates new possibilities for research in this field.

The research project Edirom[29] at the University of Paderborn and the School of Music in Detmold was established in 2006 to develop "tools for digital forms of critical music editions".[30] As pioneers in this field of research, the project implemented a research software that changed the formation and publication process of music editions altogether.[31] By aligning images of various sources and the underlying data in an XML format in the standard of the Music Encoding Initiative (MEI),[32] the music editor is now able to compare sources on the basis of measures—so-called aligned concordances.

---

26 Cf. Joachim Veit, Musikwissenschaft und Computerphilologie—eine schwierige Liaison? in: *Jahrbuch für Computerphilologie* 7 (2005), 67–92. See http://computerphilologie.tu-darmstadt.de/jg05/veit.html [last accessed June 8, 2018].
27 Most music editions are published in print, but funding bodies and publishing houses increasingly expect digital components (cf., e.g., music editions funded by the Akademie der Wissenschaften und der Literatur, Mainz; see http://www.adwmainz.de/projekte/musikwissenschaftliche-editionen.html [last accessed April 17, 2018]).
28 Cf. Johannes Kepper, *Musikedition im Zeichen neuer Medien: Historische Entwicklung und gegenwärtige Perspektiven musikalischer Gesamtausgaben*, Norderstedt 2011, 5–19.
29 Cf. Edirom, archived project page, URL: http://www.edirom.de/edirom-projekt/das-forschungsprojekt/ [last accessed April 17, 2018].
30 Cf. Edirom, archived project page.
31 The software is still maintained and further developed at https://github.com/Edirom/Edirom-Online [last accessed April 17, 2018].
32 Music Encoding Initiative (MEI), URL: http://music-encoding.org/ [last accessed April 17, 2018].
33 See the Digital edition of the opera "Der Freischütz" by Carl Maria von Weber at http://freischuetz-digital.de/edition/ [last accessed April 17, 2018].

Fig. 3: Screenshot—Concordances of the digital edition of "Der Freischütz."[33]

Figure 3 shows ten different sources for the opera "Der Freischütz," an opera by the German composer Carl Maria von Weber and one of the first digital music editions ever published. The whole publication consists of fifteen musical sources, sixteen sources of the libretto, twelve associated texts, and six recordings of the opera. Technically, it is possible to align all sources simultaneously and compare these sources all at once on a computer screen without being limited to the materials that are physically and immediately at hand. By browsing from measure to measure, editors are given various possibilities of interacting with their sources, and they can perform comparisons right on the spot.[34] The edition created in this way can be published online—thus users are able to comprehend and pursue each step of the decisions the scholar made—but also in the usual print media.

Another option customized by these tools is the display of variants and the results of comparing in one place. Figure 4 illustrates the view of a commentary in the digital critical apparatus of "Der Freischütz" that contains the comment on the left upper side along with all sources affected by the results of the comparison. In print, the critical apparatus consists of only textual descriptions that detail the findings of the editor; in digital, each variance is visible on screen.

In Edirom, editors—and users—are also able to compare transcribed librettos, other textual sources dealing with topics related to the opera, and recordings. These add another layer of understanding and facilitate new interpretations of the musical work of the composer—a feature that is only possible through the digital. As demonstrated, the digital medium provides a broader and more comprehensive view of the music edition and allows access to digital objects involved in the research process.

---

34 For more information on technical features of Edirom tools, visit http://www.edirom.de/edirom-projekt/software/ [last accessed April 17, 2018].

Fig. 4: Screenshot—Display of variants in all affected sources in the digital edition of "Der Freischütz".

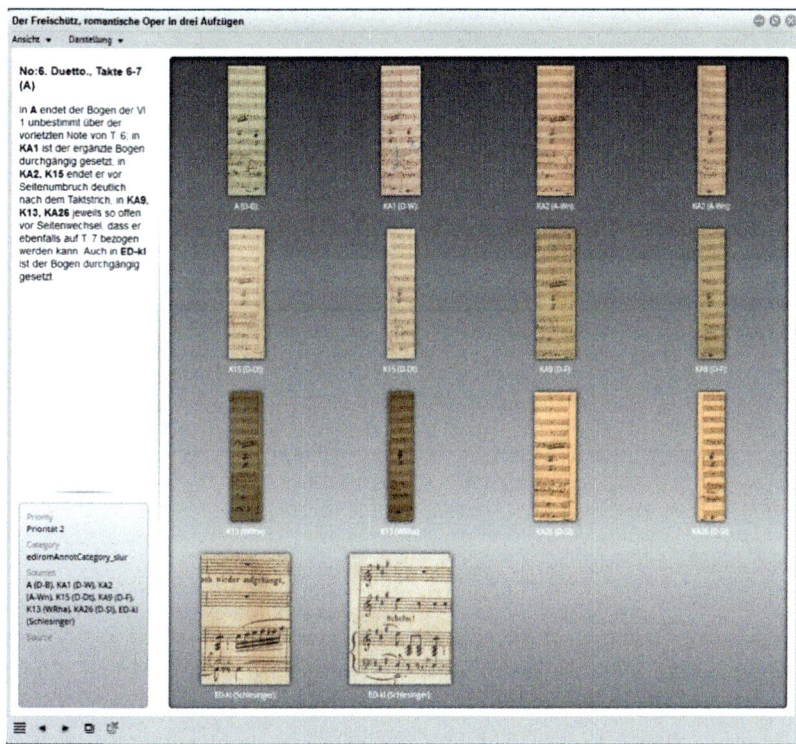

Digital text edition

Digitality in text editions clusters new demands and "envisage[s] fresh conceptualizations for the future"[35] of critical editing.[36] These conceptualizations appear in different models and formats, as demonstrated by the two following examples. The projects highlight different approaches to the modes of access and representation of their materials and findings in the digital age.

The "Vincent van Gogh—The Letters" digital edition, "a product of 15 years of research at the Van Gogh Museum and Huygens ING," contains digitized versions

---

35 Cf. Hans W. Gabler, Foreword, in: Matthew J. Driscoll/Elena Pierazzo (eds.), *Digital Scholarly Editing: Theories and Practices*, Cambridge 2016, xiii.
36 For more information on digital scholarly editing, cf. Matthew James Driscoll/Elena Pierazzo, *Digital Scholarly Editing—Theories and Practices*, Cambridge 2016.

and authorized English translations of all of Van Gogh's letters, "richly annotated and illustrated," as well as supplementary material such as sketches and paintings.[37]

Fig. 5: Screenshot—Alignment of different versions of a text in the "Vincent van Gogh—The Letters" digital edition.

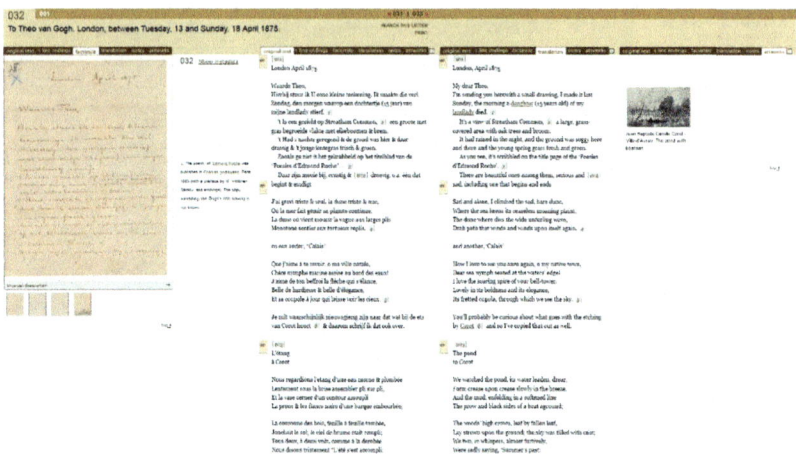

Figure 5 illustrates another approach that is enabled through the deployment of digital tools. The alignment of facsimile, commentary, transcription, and translation of the original text with the respective artwork shows various layers of information on one screen and opens up wide possibilities for the editor and the user to search, browse, and interact with the texts—practices that enrich comparisons in the digital realm. Within the digital edition, the search for letters according to criteria such as "sketch" and "person" and the possibility of combining criteria in many sophisticated ways establishes new ways of understanding and interpreting texts.[38]

Another approach for displaying and making results on the scholarly practice of comparing available is implemented by the "Internet Shakespeare Edition,"[39] an endeavor that has been running at the University of Victoria since 1996. It is also possible to review facsimiles of all sources and browse through any content—as in

---

37 See http://vangoghletters.org/vg/ [last accessed April 17, 2018].
38 This feature is supported by paradigmatic regression in graphical user interfaces that delivers new dynamics of methodological interaction with text as it is (cf. Joris van Zundert, Barely Beyond the Book?, in: Matthew J. Driscoll/Elena Pierazzo (eds.), *Digital Scholarly Editing: Theories and Practices*, Cambridge 2016, 86.).
39 See http://internetshakespeare.uvic.ca/ [last accessed April 17, 2018].

the "Vincent van Gogh—The Letters" digital edition. One additional feature of this edition is the possibility of displaying all variants inline. This facilitates a feeling for the change of words over time and through different sources.

Fig. 6: Screenshot—Display of different word variants in the "Internet Shakespeare Edition".

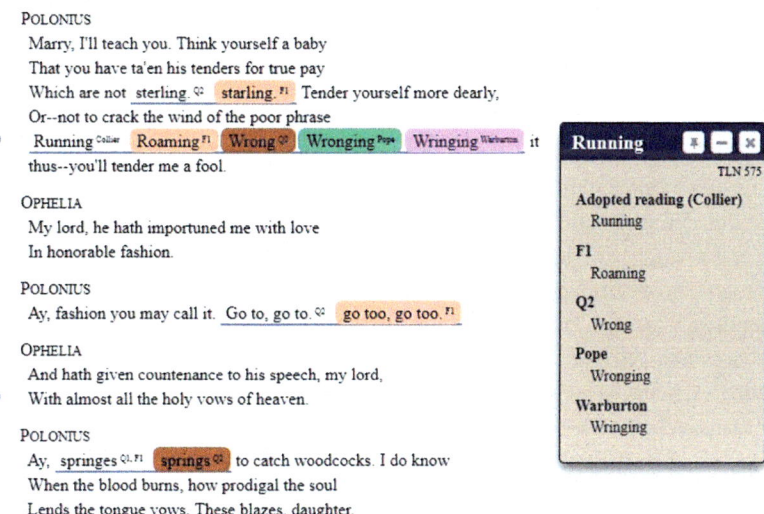

As shown in Figure 6, the word "Running" was transcribed quite differently in various sources (e.g., "Roaming," "Wrong," "Wronging," and "Wringing") that all have different meanings and each change the context of the sentence. This practice of making comparisons visible right on the spot introduces a whole new way of interacting with the research material itself and provides a perspective for communicating and disseminating scholarly research on a different level.

The interoperability and integration of the works at hand and their presentations change the way in which humanities scholars interact with their material and open up new prospects on research material and respective questions as well as on the practices of comparing. All these practices and the resulting computational tools contribute to a reformulation of questions and "have the potential to transform the content, scope, methodologies, and audience of humanistic inquiry."[40]

---

40   Cf. Schnapp, A short guide, SG3.

Historical practices of comparing and their digital analysis

The lines of inquiry presented in the different contributions to this volume all circle around two central questions: What do we do when we compare? And what do or did (historical) actors do when they compare(d)? The focus in answering these questions lies in the analysis of practices—not just scholarly practices, but also historical practices. It lies with the paradigm of "doing comparisons."[41] But what are these practices and how do we find them? Comparisons can be defined as operations that relate at least two objects to each other. The specificity of a relation that constitutes a comparison is that this relation is constructed with a comparative intention of relating the objects to each other in a specific regard.[42] For example, comparing apples to oranges can be done with regard to them being fruits, with regard to their color, or with regard to their taste. In this way, the result of the comparison highlights either commonalities, similarities, or differences. Following this definition and dealing mostly with textual evidence, comparisons should be easy enough to address. But this is only true on a superficial level. Comparisons as cognitive operations seem to follow a specific logic that can be linked to a specific linguistic structure. Practices of comparing are more than that. They comprise obvious comparisons in which the compared objects and the comparative regard are stated explicitly as well as statements or practices that state them only implicitly or that describe practices that represent comparisons. Examples for these different levels could be statements like these:

Fig. 7: Some examples for speech acts performing comparisons.

(1) I am older than Anna.

(2) Like Anna, I am wearing glasses.

(3) Anna and I are both women.

(4) Women in digital humanities research are still an exception.

(5) ...

Applying digital methods to the analysis of practices of comparison makes it necessary to look for the common structure in these sentences. In a way, we need to compare that which we believe to be a comparison. And we do that through modeling. Modeling is "a process by which researchers make and manipulate external

---

41   Cf. Angelika Epple/Walter Erhart, Die Welt beobachten. Praktiken des Vergleichens, in: Angelika Epple/Walter Erhart (eds.), *Die Welt beobachten. Praktiken des Vergleichens*, Frankfurt a. M./New York 2015, 7–31, see 17.
42   Epple/Erhart, Die Welt beobachten, 7–31.

representations [...] to make sense of the conceptual objects and phenomena they study."[43] It is a scholarly practice in itself. And although it seems more common to researchers in the field of the natural sciences than in the humanities, it is also quite common in digital humanities. Computer-enhanced methods for humanities research work mostly with patterns and models. In order to develop digital methods and tools, our workflows need to be modeled in a way that can be adapted by a computer program. It is this abstract view on research methods and practices that makes digital humanities not only a convenient toolbox but a theoretical framework of its own.

Modeling the ways in which we as researchers compare helps us to understand practices on an abstract level. It enables us to comprehend structures and modes of comparing that can be translated into a machine-readable model leading us to new tools for research. Taking the researcher's practices of comparing as a research object will provide insight into the history of the humanities or the history of scholarship. On a theoretical level, this helps us to understand how changing practices might change our view of the world.

Observing practices and applying digital methods

Focusing on historical actors and their practices of comparing works in a similar way. We want to observe and model historical practices of comparing. How did artists and curators integrate practices of comparison in their work? How did travelers implement them into their travelogues, using practices of comparing to bring new discoveries into the existing view of the world? How did legal frameworks have to change through practices of comparing the colonists' law to the legal practices of indigenous peoples?[44] Willibald Steinmetz and his 7

colleagues focus on the conceptual history of (practices of) comparisons.[45] This historical discipline is one of the most productive fields for the implementation of digital methods.[46] This is partly because the methods of *"Begriffsgeschichte"* can be translated easily into digital methods, as shown in the example of text mining

---

43 Arianna Ciula/Øyvind Eide, Modelling in digital humanities: Signs in context, in: *Digital Scholavrship in the Humanities* 32 (2017), i33–i46, see i33.
44 Cf. the research program of the SFB 1288: https://www.uni-bielefeld.de/sfb1288/ [last accessed May 3, 2018].
45 Cf. https://www.uni-bielefeld.de/(en)/sfb1288/projekte/c03.html [last accessed May 3, 2018] and Willibald Steinmetz, 'Vergleich' – eine begriffsgeschichtliche Skizze, in: Angelika Epple/Walter Erhart (eds.), *Die Welt beobachten. Praktiken des Vergleichens*, Frankfurt a. M./New York 2015, 85–134.
46 Cf. Schwandt, Digitale Methoden, 109.

with DiaCollo. The practice of collecting all instances in a corpus in which a certain keyword is being used and then analyzing the results statistically can be done with almost any form of digital corpus.[47] Some of the research questions regarding practices of comparison can be addressed in this way. A simple keyword in a context search will find any instances that use any word form of *comparison* or *compare*, or their German equivalents *Vergleich/vergleichen/vergleichbar*. The following graphs (Figures 7 and 8) show the frequency of the German terms *Vergleichung* and *Vergleich* in the corpus of the Digital Dictionary of the German Language.[48] Both graphs plot the frequency on a timeline dating from 1600 to 1990.

Fig. 8: Total frequency of the German term "Vergleichung" in the digital corpus of the DTA.[49]

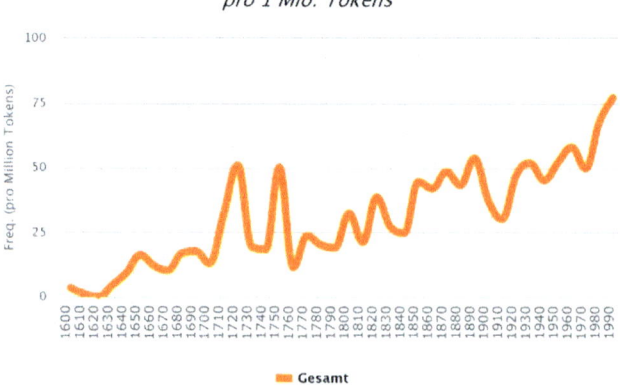

Looking at these graphs, researchers immediately start comparing. Again, two levels of practices can be observed: One is the researcher comparing single data points to each other by drawing a graph or comparing two graphs to each other; the other is the data set itself representing the historical evidence for the use of the terms *Vergleichung* and *Vergleich*.

But practices of comparison do not only happen in speech acts containing words from the word family of *comparison/compare/comparative*. Willibald Steinmetz

---

47   Cf. as a further example, Silke Schwandt, Virtus as a Political Concept in the Middle Ages, in: *Contributions to the History of Concepts* 10 (2/2015), 71–90.
48   Cf. https://www.dwds.de/ [last accessed May 3, 2018]. "*Vergleichung*" can also be translated as "comparison" or "collation."
49   Graph taken from Steinmetz, 'Vergleich', 97.
50   Graph taken from Steinmetz, 'Vergleich', 98.

Fig. 9: Total frequency of the German term "Vergleich" in the digital corpus of the DTA.[50]

has argued that a conceptual history of comparison should encompass not only analyses of the use of the vocabulary itself, but also analyses of speech acts that can themselves be understood as practices of comparing. He suggests that these sentences would adhere to any of the following patterns:

- Simple as well as complex statements of similarity or difference: a is like b; seen from perspective x, a is like b; a is to b as x is to y; a is not like b; and so forth
- Comparative comparisons: a is better than b; a is best among n
- Ordering or classificatory comparisons: Regarding x, a is like or similar to b, but differs from b regarding y (and therefore belongs to another category)
- Comparisons stating equivalence despite dissimilarity: Although a is completely different from b, it is worth as much as b, or as suitable as b to achieve goal y
- Statements of incomparability: a is incomparable to b (sentences like these seem to be paradox, because they suggest that a comparison—mostly from a third party—has already been made)[51]

Categorizations or models like these take us away from the keyword in context and pose a new challenge: How do we model these patterns in order to make them understandable to an algorithm?

---

51 Cf. Steinmetz, 'Vergleich', 88–89. [Translations by Silke Schwandt].

Going back to the examples in Figure 6, the mapping of the suggested sentences to Steinmetz's models could look like this:

Fig. 10: Mapping sentences to models.

(1) I am older than Anna.   (1) Comparative comparison

(2) Like Anna, I am wearing glasses.   (2) Simple statement of similarity

(3) Anna and I are both women.   (3) Simple statement of similarity

(4) Women in digital humanities   (4) Complex statement of similarity
    research are still an exception.

Applying a model like this shows how similar the apparently different sentences are. In this way, the model serves as a strategy for making sense. "Contextualizing modeling within a semiotic framework means indeed to consider it as a strategy to make sense (signification) via practical thinking (creating and manipulating models)."[52] Formalizing this kind of categorization for our example could look like this:

Fig. 11: Interface of a Filemaker Database collecting Data Sets of Speech Acts Performing Comparisons.[53]

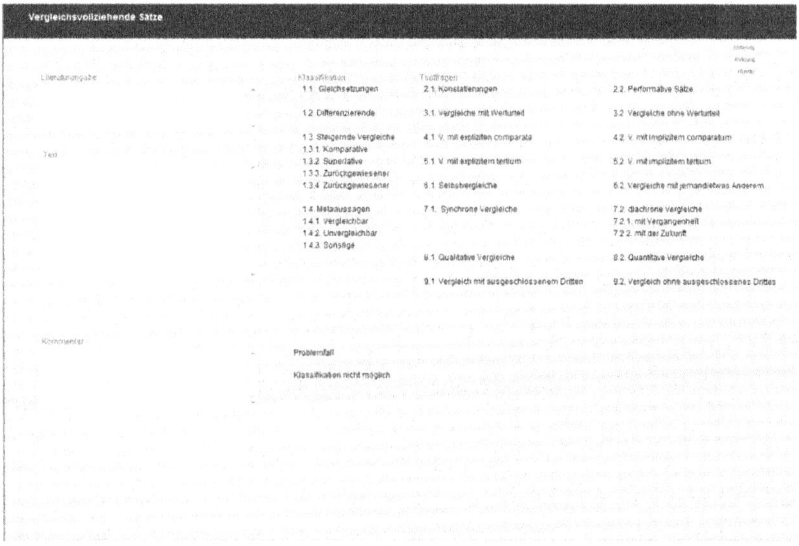

---

52   Ciula/Eide, Modelling in digital humanities, i34.

By way of a database interface, researchers can mark sentences as comparisons and apply different categories representing certain types of comparisons. This practice of categorization can be understood as what John Unsworth called "annotating."[54] Through categorization, we arrive at what can be called linked data—data sets that are related to each other and can be visualized, for example, as networks. A category such as "statements of incomparability" can then be a node in the network linking different speech acts to each other. Researchers arrive at such categories by observing their own practices: Which criteria lead us to identify a specific speech act as a "statement of incomparability?" Following this observation, the researcher creates a semantic annotation. Unfortunately, semantic knowledge is still a form of knowledge specific to human interpretation, and it is difficult to teach to a computer program.

But even if our examples in Figure 9 seem to belong to the same or similar categories semantically, they remain different linguistically. A model that looks more at such formalities might be helpful in order to find a way of identifying speech acts performing comparisons automatically. One possible set of formalities to describe language is provided in linguistic models. The example below shows the application of a model with part of speech tags.[55] [56]

Fig. 12: Part of speech tags for sentences performing practices of comparing.

(1) I am older than Anna.

(2) Like Anna, I am wearing glasses.

(3) Anna and I are both women.

(4) Women in digital humanities research are still an exception.

(1) I/**PRP** am/**VBP** older/**JJR** than/**IN** Anna/**NNP** ./.

(2) Like/**IN** Anna/**NNP** ,/, I/**PRP** am/**VBP** wearing/**VBG** glasses/**NNS** ./.

(3) Anna/**NNP** and/**CC** I/**PRP** are/**VBP** both/**DT** women/**NNS** ./.

(4) Women/**NNP** in/**IN** digital/**JJ** humanities/**NNS** research/**NN** are/**VBP** still/**RB** an/**DT** exception/**NN**./.

There are several part of speech tags that seem to hint at comparisons. The most obvious is JJR (= adjective, comparative) in the first example. Looking for this morphological characteristic in a (historical) text corpus might generate a subcorpus

---

53   This database is part of the research process within SFB 1288. It represents an early stage of the system of categories used in Subproject C03 by Willibald Steinmetz and his team.
54   John Unsworth, Scholarly Primitives.
55   Brill tagger: https://cst.dk/online/pos_tagger/uk/index.html [last accessed 08 May 2018]. First published in "A Simple Rule-Based Part of Speech Tagger" by Eric Brill, 1992.
56   Cf. tag set used in the Penn Treebank Project for English. See https://www.ling.upenn.edu/courses/Fall_2003/ling001/penn_treebank_pos.html [last accessed May 8, 2018].

of comparative comparisons. Applying a part of speech tagger to such a subcorpus will then provide the researcher with more information on the morphological structure of comparative comparisons. Examples (2) and (3) suggest that simple statements of similarity can be identified through the combination of IN (= preposition or subordinating conjunction) and NNP (= proper noun singular), while the use of DT (= determiner) alone is not enough to denote a comparison. Here, again, it would be more promising to look for combinations with NNP or NNS (= noun, plural).

Although the morphological annotation with part of speech tags does supply the researcher with a more formalistic model, the potential for the automatic identification is still improvable. The sole annotation with morphological information is too unspecific. Part of speech tags annotating adverbs or determiners can denote a large number of words that may or may not be part of a comparison. It seems to be necessary to expand the levels of annotation to syntactic and/or semantic annotations. Hence, it becomes clear that the automatization of research practices is a complex task.

Conclusions: Digital research practices and practices of comparing

The computational turn has brought about quite a few transformations of practices and makes even more of them necessary. In our article, we have shown that by using digital techniques and methods, scholars can add new meaning to old research questions and pose new questions that arise by taking on innovative approaches and challenges. The accessibility of a vast array of resources in a digital form and their alleged synchronicity change our view of research material and provide a new perspective, thus fundamentally changing viewing patterns and breaking with long-established practices and habits.

For using various tools to perform comparisons, scholars require knowledge of digital standards, tools, and methods in order to be able to read, compare, and edit sources in different formats. These new modes of practices and (re)presentations alter the interaction with research material. Collecting data from digital material as well as producing digital material in the process of doing research will enable us to compare the modeled practices. From there it will be easier to arrive at a typology of practices of comparing—both digital and historical.

Hence, considering various practices of comparing in the digital age leads us in two directions:

- It helps us to reflect on our own practices of comparing, evaluating, and historicizing them. It also makes us aware of the necessity to look at the impact

of digitization on scientific practices—the impact that can already be observed as well as the impact that is yet to be expected.
• Modeling research practices enables us to find new perspectives on historical practices of comparing. Observing and modeling increase the level of abstraction and further the conjected concept of a typology of practices.

Resulting from these reflections, work on the presented topics within the field of digital humanities is not only about developing research with digital methods but also about contributing to research on digital methods and digitization.

References

AKADEMIE DER WISSENSCHAFTEN UND DER LITERATUR, Mainz, music editions, URL: http://www.adwmainz.de/projekte/musikwissenschaftliche-editionen.html [last accessed April 17, 2018].
BERRY, David M., The Computational Turn: Thinking About the Digital Humanities, in: *Culture Machine* 12 (2011), 1–12.
BRILL, Eric, A Simple Rule-Based Part of Speech Tagger, in: *Third Conference on Applied Natural Language Processing*, Trento 1992, Brill tagger, URL: https://cst.dk/online/pos_tagger/uk/index.html [last accessed 08 May 2018].
CIDOC-CRM, URL: http://www.cidoc-crm.org/ [last accessed June 8, 2018].
CIULA, Arianna/EIDE, Øyvind Modelling in digital humanities: Signs in context, in: *Digital Scholarship in the Humanities* 32 (2017), 133–146.
DIACOLLO, URL: http://kaskade.dwds.de/dstar/dta/diacollo/ [last accessed April 17, 2018].
DIGITAL DICTIONARY OF THE GERMAN LANGUAGE, URL: https://www.dwds.de/ [last accessed May 3, 2018].
DiRT—Digital Research Tools, URL: http://dirtdirectory.org/ [last accessed June 8, 2018].
DRISCOLL, Matthew James/PIERAZZO, Elena, *Digital Scholarly Editing—Theories and Practices*, Cambridge 2016.
EDIROM, archived project page, URL: http://www.edirom.de/edirom-projekt/das-forschungsprojekt/ [last accessed April 17, 2018].
EDIROM, technical features of Edirom tools, URL: http://www.edirom.de/edirom-projekt/software/ [last accessed April 17, 2018].
EDIROM, URL: https://github.com/Edirom/Edirom-Online [last accessed April 17, 2018].
EPPLE, Angelika/ERHART, Walter, Die Welt beobachten. Praktiken des Vergleichens, in: Angelika Epple/Walter Erhart (eds.), *Die Welt beobachten. Praktiken des Vergleichens*, Frankfurt a. M./New York 2015, 7–31.

ESPOSITO, Elena, *Reading With Algorithms: Interpretation and Information in Digital Text Processing*, 2018 (unpublished manuscript).

GABLER, Hans W., Foreword, in: Matthew J. Driscoll/Elena Pierazzo (eds.), *Digital Scholarly Editing: Theories and Practices*, Cambridge 2016, xiii.

GOOGLE NGRAM VIEWER, URL: https://books.google.com/ngrams [last accessed June 8, 2018].

HAYLES, N. Katherine, *How We Think: Digital Media and Contemporary Technogenesis*, Chicago 2012.

JÄNICKE, Stefan/FRANZINI, Greta/CHEEMAM, Muhammad F./SCHEUERMANN, Gerik, On Close and Distant Reading in Digital Humanities: A Survey and Future Challenges, in: Rita Borgo/Fabio Ganovelli/Ivan Viola (eds.), *Europgraphics Conference on Vizualization (EuroVis)—STARs*, The Eurographics Association, 2015.

KEPPER, Johannes, *Musikedition im Zeichen neuer Medien: Historische Entwicklung und gegenwärtige Perspektiven musikalischer Gesamtausgaben*, Norderstedt 2011.

MORETTI, Franco, *Distant Reading*, Konstanz 2016.

MUSIC ENCODING INITIATIVE (MEI), URL: http://music-encoding.org/ [last accessed April 17, 2018].

NORTH, Joseph, *Literary Criticism. A Concise Political History*, Cambridge/London 2017.

PENN TREEBANK PROJECT FOR ENGLISH, URL: https://www.ling.upenn.edu/courses/Fall_2003/ling001/penn_treebank_pos.html [last accessed May 8, 2018].

SCHNAPP, Jeffrey, A short guide to the digital humanities, in: Anne Burdick et al. (eds.), *Digital_Humanities*, Cambridge 2012.

SCHWANDT, Silke, Digitale Methoden für die Historische Semantik. Auf den Spuren von Begriffen in digitalen Korpora, in: *Geschichte und Gesellschaft* 44 (2018), 107–134.

SCHWANDT, Silke, Virtus as a Political Concept in the Middle Ages, in: *Contributions to the History of Concepts* 10 (2/2015), 71–90.

STANFORD LITERARY LAB, URL: https://litlab.stanford.edu/ [last accessed June 8, 2018].

STEINMETZ, Willibald, 'Vergleich' – eine begriffsgeschichtliche Skizze, in: Angelika Epple/Walter Erhart (eds.), *Die Welt beobachten. Praktiken des Vergleichens*, Frankfurt a. M./New York 2015, 85–134.

TAPor, URL: http://tapor.ca/home [last accessed June 8, 2018].

TEXT ENOCDING INITIATIVE (TEI), URL: http://www.tei-c.org/index.xml [last accessed June 8, 2018].

UNIVERSITY OF VICTORIA (ed.), *Internet Shakespeare Edition*, URL: http://internetshakespeare.uvic.ca/ [last accessed April 17, 2018].

UNSWORTH, John, Scholarly primitives: What methods do humanities researchers have in common, and how might our tools reflect this? in: *University of Vir-*

ginia, May 13, 2000, URL: http://www.people.virginia.edu/~jmu2m/Kings.5-00/primitives.html [last accessed June 8, 2018].

VAN GOGH MUSEUM/HUYGENS ING (eds.), *Vincent van Gogh—The Letters, digital edition*, URL: http://vangoghletters.org/vg/ [last accessed April 17, 2018].

VEIT, Joachim, Musikwissenschaft und Computerphilologie—eine schwierige Liaison? in: *Jahrbuch für Computerphilologie 7* (2005), 67–92, URL: http://computerphilologie.tu-darmstadt.de/jg05/veit.html [last accessed June 8, 2018].

WEBER, Carl Maria von, *Der Freischütz*, Digital edition of the opera, URL: http://freischuetz-digital.de/edition/ [last accessed April 17, 2018].

ZUNDERT, Joris van, Barely Beyond the Book?, in: Matthew J. Driscoll/Elena Pierazzo (eds.), *Digital Scholarly Editing: Theories and Practices*, Cambridge 2016, 86.

Authors and Editors

Angelika Epple is vice-rector for International Affairs and Diversity at Bielefeld University and teaches history with a focus on the history of the 19th and 20th century. She is spokesperson of the Collaborative Research Center SFB 1288 "Practices of Comparing".

Walter Erhart is Professor of German Literature at Bielefeld University. He is vice-speaker of the Collaborative Research Center SFB 1288 "Practices of Comparing".

Andrea Frisch is Professor of French at the University of Maryland.

Johannes Grave is Professor of Art History at the Friedrich Schiller University Jena and a Principal Investigator of the Collaborative Research Center SFB 1288 "Practices of Comparing".

Joris Corin Heyder is a Postdoctoral Researcher in Art History at Bielefeld University and in the Collaborative Research Center SFB 1288 "Practices of Comparing".

Britta Hochkirchen is a Research Associate at Bielefeld University and a Principal Investigator in the Collaborative Research Center SFB 1288 "Practices of Comparing".

Emmanuel Lozerand is Professor of Japanese Studies at the Institut national des langues et civilisations orientales (Inalco).

Thomas Müller is a Postdoctoral Researcher in Political Science at Bielefeld University and in the Collaborative Research Center SFB 1288 "Practices of Comparing".

Anna Maria Neubert is a Doctoral Researcher in the Collaborative Research Center SFB 1288 at Bielefeld University.

Kirill Postoutenko is a Research Associate at Bielefeld University and in the Collaborative Research Center SFB 1288 "Practices of Comparing".

Leopold Ringel is a Lecturer in Sociological Theory and General Sociology at Bielefeld University.

David Gary Shaw is Professor of History and Medieval Studies at Wesleyan University.

Silke Schwandt is Professor of Digital Humanities and History oft he Middle Ages at Bielefeld University and a Principal Investigator in the Collaborative Research Center SFB 1288 "Practices of Comparing".

Hartmut von Sass is Professor for Systematic Theology and Philosophy of Religion as well as Heisenberg scholar at Humboldt University in Berlin.

Tobias Werron is Professor of Sociological Theory and General Sociology at Bielefeld University. He is vice-speaker of the Collaborative Research Center SFB 1288 "Practices of Comparing".

Zhang Longxi is Chair Professor of Comparative Literature and Translation at City University of Hong Kong.